Use and Abuse
of
America's Natural Resources

Use and Abuse
of
America's Natural Resources

Advisory Editor

STUART BRUCHEY
Allan Nevins Professor of American
Economic History, Columbia University

Associate Editor

ELEANOR BRUCHEY

CONSERVATION OF OIL & GAS

A Legal History, 1948

EDITED BY

Blakely M. Murphy

ARNO PRESS

A NEW YORK TIMES COMPANY

New York • 1972

Reprint Edition 1972 by Arno Press Inc.

Copyright © 1949 by the Section of Natural
Resources Law (successor to the Section of
Mineral Law) of the American Bar Association
Reprinted by permission of the Section of
Natural Resources Law of the American Bar
Association

Reprinted from a copy in The University of
Illinois Library

Use and Abuse of America's Natural Resources
ISBN for complete set: 0-405-04500-X
See last pages of this volume for titles.

Manufactured in the United States of America

Library of Congress Cataloging in Publication Data

American Bar Association. Section of Mineral Law.
   Committee on Special Publications.
   Conservation of oil & gas, a legal history, 1948.

   (Use and abuse of America's natural resources)
   1. Petroleum law and legislation--United States.
2. Gas, Natural--Law and legislation--United States.
I. Murphy, Blakely McKee, 1914-   ed. II. Title.
III. Series.
KF1852.A95 1972   343'.73'077   72-2858
ISBN 0-405-04522-0

CONSERVATION OF OIL AND GAS

A Legal History, 1948

CONSERVATION OF OIL & GAS

A Legal History, 1948

EDITED BY

Blakely M. Murphy

SECTION OF MINERAL LAW
AMERICAN BAR ASSOCIATION

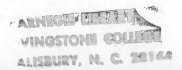

PRINTED IN THE UNITED STATES OF AMERICA

This volume is published under the sponsorship of the Section of Mineral Law, American Bar Association. This does not constitute an official endorsement of its content by the Association or the Section.

Table of Contents

PAGE

Foreword and Acknowledgement   xi

Introduction   xv

Part I

FUNDAMENTALS OF RESERVOIR BEHAVIOR THAT RELATE TO THE CONSERVATION OF OIL AND GAS

CHAPTER

1. The Nature of Petroleum Reservoirs, Reservoir Fluids, and Reservoir Energies   3

Part II

LEGISLATIVE, ADMINISTRATIVE AND JUDICIAL CONCEPTS OF OIL AND GAS CONSERVATION AS APPLIED WITHIN THE JURISDICTIONS OF THE STATES

2. Alabama, 1910–1948   19
3. Arizona, 1912–1948   23
4. Arkansas, 1938–1948   32
5. California, 1931–1948   40
6. Colorado, 1862–1948   56
7. Florida, 1939–1948   64
8. Georgia, 1915–1948   83
9. Idaho, 1931–1948   90
10. Illinois, 1889–1948   92
11. Indiana, 1876–1948   123
12. Iowa, 1939–1948   136
13. Kansas, 1937–1948   138
14. Kentucky, 1819–1948   191
15. Louisiana, 1938–1948   198
16. Michigan, 1938–1948   250
17. Mississippi, 1938–1948   283

CHAPTER | PAGE

18. Missouri, 1948   299
19. Montana, 1913–1948   300
20. Nebraska, 1939–1948   310
21. New Mexico, 1938–1948   312
22. New York, 1864–1948   336
23. North Carolina, 1945–1948   345
24. North Dakota, 1907–1948   347
25. Ohio, 1885–1948   359
26. Oklahoma, 1938–1948   369
27. Oregon, 1923–1948   423
28. Pennsylvania, 1858–1948   425
29. South Dakota, 1881–1948   439
30. Tennessee, 1866–1948   443
31. Texas, 1938–1948   447
32. Utah, 1892–1948   513
33. Virginia, 1939–1948   515
34. Washington, 1933–1948   517
35. West Virginia, 1826–1948   520
36. Wyoming, 1881–1948   529

Part III

THE INTERSTATE COMPACT TO CONSERVE OIL AND GAS AND ITS ADMINISTRATIVE ARM—THE INTERSTATE OIL COMPACT COMMISSION

37. The Oil States Advisory Committee—A Predecessor of the Compact   545
38. The Formation of the Interstate Compact to Conserve Oil and Gas   556
39. The Interstate Compact to Conserve Oil and Gas, The Interstate Oil Compact Commission, 1935–1948   571

Part IV

THE NATIONAL GOVERNMENT AND THE CONSERVATION OF OIL AND GAS

40. The Government in the Capacity of Land Owner   599
41. The Government in the Exercise of the Power Over Interstate Commerce   630

Contents

CHAPTER   PAGE

42. The Government in the Exercise of the Power Over Foreign Commerce   656
43. The Government in the Exercise of the War Power   664
44. The Use of Federal Powers to Supplement Those of the States   681
45. The Contribution of the Federal Judiciary to the Conservation of Oil and Gas   709

APPENDICES

Appendix A. A Table of State Conservation Agencies, Their Personnel and Location   719

Appendix B. A Listing of the Writers of the Monographs and Their Advisers   723

Appendix C. An Interstate Compact to Conserve Oil and Gas, Conservation of the American Oil Supply, and The Interstate Compact to Conserve Oil and Gas   734

Appendix D. The By-Laws of the Interstate Oil Compact Commission   741

Index   747

Foreword and Acknowledgements

Late in 1946 a committee was appointed by the Section of Mineral Law, the American Bar Association, charged with the responsibility of preparing a volume on oil and gas conservation history. The group, composed of Walace Hawkins, chairman, Northcutt Ely, Earl Foster, Robert E. Hardwicke and Blakely M. Murphy, members, during the first months of 1947 explored the possibilities of preparing such a volume, its content, and authorship. Preliminary drafts of possible publications were submitted by various members of the committee, and in April 1947 a meeting was held with Professor W. L. Summers of the University of Illinois College of Law. At the close of this session it was decided that Walace Hawkins would undertake to secure the cooperation of a panel of writers chosen by the committee, and that Blakely M. Murphy, selected as editor, would draft a comprehensive proposal or outline for the guidance of the authors working with the committee. The draft instructions were completed in June 1947 together with a prospectus covering the contents of the book. These proposals envisioned a volume consisting of four sections—the fundamentals of reservoir behavior, the legislative, administrative and judicial concepts of oil and gas conservation within the states, the story of the Interstate Compact to Conserve Oil and Gas and the Compact Commission, and a discussion of the National Government and conservation. A further meeting was held in August 1947 at Great Falls, Montana, where the committee approved the instructions, the content of the book, and the selection of certain writers.

Mr. Hawkins then proceeded with the arduous task of obtaining the consent of writers to their participation in the writing of the state histories, the Interstate Compact, and the National Government. This he did through the fall and winter of 1947 to the time when he finally had writers (and in the opinion of the committee the best men available) to undertake this effort. By letter, by telegram, and by telephone he pursued these individuals. It was no small thing to secure thirty-five state writers. In December 1947 Mr. Hawkins and Mr. Murphy met with those persons advising the committee on the section on reservoir engineering concepts in Oklahoma City, outlined the requirements for that part of the book, and secured promises of assistance. At the time each writer was selected, the committee also chose, with his permission and in some cases assistance, a panel of the people most likely to be conversant with his subject. These were assigned to advise the writer in the preparation of his monograph, and while they did not actually aid in getting the paper in written form, they did supply information, facts, experiences, and above all, functioned as his critics. The writers and their advisers were given the outline prepared by the committee. No attempt was made to dictate what the actual content of the paper might be. In many cases the writers found this schedule of inquiry (really a check list) valuable; others felt it did not fit the particular pattern disclosed in their state and worked on a different basis. Editorial specifications were supplied to direct the footnoting to a uniform style. A deadline for the return of the manuscripts to the chairman was set for June 1, 1948 at which time a majority of them were presented. The committee considered the manuscripts generally, but turned them over to Mr. Murphy for editing and checking. Papers continued to come in during the summer of 1948. Each article was thoroughly edited and returned to the writer for his comment, suggestion, and further instruction. Footnotes were assembled into a pattern of uniformity and checked for accuracy. Finally in August 1948 the committee held a meeting in Oklahoma City to go over the edited materials and make further plans with reference to publishing the volume. At this meeting it was decided to name the as yet untitled volume—*Conservation of Oil and Gas, A Legal History, 1948.* The manuscripts were carefully read by the committee and after undergoing some slight alterations, as the result of criticism by the committee, received its approbation. With the close of August the monographs were directed to the manufacturer for printing. Proofreading was done during September and October again stressing the ultimate in accurate reporting where it was possible to check the contents, and keeping to date with new happenings up to the time when it was no longer possible due to the printing schedule.

The committee has a great sense of appreciation for the voluntary efforts of the writers. Their names are found at the bottom of the chapter title pages together with those of their advisers, and a more complete statement of their competency to write their respective articles is carried in Appendix B of this book. It is impossible to single out any one individual from this group for more generous thanks than another. All did their part without thought of compensation. Many worked long hours at nights after office hours, over weekends and holidays to perform their assignments.

The Section of Mineral Law Chairmen—Arthur M. Gee and Donald C. McCreery—performed their roles admirably, never interfering in the Committee's activity, but always ready with encouragement, assistance, and cooperation in the matters that fell to them.

A great measure of the hoped for success of this book is due to Walace Hawkins, who labored long and hard to bring it to fruition. Without qualification, no one individual contributed so much to the effort. When anything was wanted to carry on the work, Mr. Hawkins got it and at once, whether it was a person, information, a place to work, secretarial assistance, or expert consultants. His enthusiasm for the project, his guidance, and counsel at crucial moments were supreme.

There are other persons to whom the Committee, and through it the Section of Mineral Law, owe an expression of appreciation for their services. Principal among these are: Elisabeth Love Murphy, for her careful attention to editorial·detail in the manuscript; and Dean Albert J. Harno of the College of Law, University of Illinois, for his kindness in supplying office space for the completion of the editorial work and the use of library facilities of his school. The Committee also wishes to acknowledge the courtesy of the Tulane Law Review Association of the Tulane University of Louisiana, New Orleans, for the right to use substantial portions of an article entitled: The Administrative Mechanism of the Interstate

Compact to Conserve Oil and Gas: The Interstate Oil Compact Commission, 1935–1948, 22 Tul. L. Rev. 384–402 (1948), in the preparation of Chapter 39 and its notes.

B. M. M.

Urbana, Ill.
September 1948.

Introduction

The legal history of oil and gas conservation in the United States is in the aggregate confined within the legislation, administrative rules and regulations, and judicial interpretations of each producing state, whose trial and error efforts constitute the events here recorded. This book, together with the first volume published in 1938, presents their conservation records.[1] To make the history complete, a section is included which describes federal conservation activities; still another is devoted to the history, findings and recommendations of the Interstate Oil Compact Commission, a voluntary inter-governmental agency of the oil jurisdictions, whose functions exclusively pertain to the conservation of oil and gas. Since this volume is neither a textbook nor a technical treatise of the regulation of oil and gas production, professional literature has merely been noted.

True conservation—at times hardly identifiable—has emerged in different states at varying rates of speed from a beginning of gross ignorance to an era of known and established principles applied to the discovery, development, and operation of oil and gas reservoirs to prevent waste, protect correlative rights of the producers, and effectuate the public interest. The birth of oil field law is somewhat like that of the gold miners. Experience, characterized by private initiative, free enterprise, and democratic local control, promulgated, administered and adjudicated by the gold miners themselves, produced the miners' code, which, after eighteen years, became the legal system for the regulation of the mining business.

These summaries of the oil producing states record the beginnings and growth of production regulations. Extensions of common law doctrine, principles and extemporized analogies were, at the

[1] Legal History of Conservation of Oil and Gas—A Symposium (1938).

outset, employed to furnish regimen for determining property rights, the privileges and duties of the oil and gas producers, and the public interest.[2] As experience and knowledge of the characteristics and behavior of oil and gas reservoirs increased and developed, new legislative and administrative techniques were designed to control operational practices. These new direct and indirect administrative and legislative rules of conduct had to meet a double test; they had (a) to prove their effectiveness and utility for the future, as well as (b) to meet and overcome established legal and constitutional habits and usages. Legislative, administrative, and judicial literature blueprints these evolving conceptions of property rights and rules of conduct. The doctrines of individual initiative, free enterprise and local regulation, democratically administered and interpreted, weathered the storm of change. The core of resistance to effective mutation centered around surface ownership, rule of capture, offset drilling, competitive production, and freedom to waste. As science and scientific men came on the stage, attention was focused on such conceptions as structure, porous rock, reservoir, irreplaceable resource (oil does not produce itself) water and gas as energy drives, and agencies, reservoir characteristics, waste and ultimate recovery. The final concept spotlighted the reservoir—a distinct mechanism with its own internal energy, the common source of power for all operators, in most cases inadequate without artificial aid to produce all the oil and gas. Physical laws and principles emerged and were stated. Surface owenrship, the legal rights and incidents thereof, conjured up the necessary counterparts of legal duties and obligations to the joint owners of the reservoir and its producing energy source, all meshing into common operational practices designed to prevent waste, protect owners' correlative rights, and serve the public interest.

The first section is devoted to the fundamentals of reservoir behavior. The excuse for an engineering monograph in a legal history of conservation of oil and gas is that it gives definition to the principles and mores of conservation. Conservationists believe that intelligent legislation, administration of rules and regulations, judicial decision and interpretation must, in the last analysis, rest upon the characteristics, habits, and behavior of a particular reservoir as a

[2] Merrill, *Evolution of Oil and Gas Law*, 13 Miss. L. J. 281 (1941).

producing mechanism. The fulcrum of effective regulation in the public interest for the prevention of waste, protection of property rights and free enterprise is the oil and gas reservoir itself and its energy characteristics. These scientific laws and nature's habits apply in times of plenty as well as in times of want. Control of production rate alone confounds disease with its symptoms.

This volume demonstrates (a) that the chief theorem of conservation is valid, namely, that artificial assistance to the preservation and utilization of natural reservoir energy is necessary to secure the greatest ultimate economic recovery of oil and gas—the true focus for the application of man-made regulation; (b) that sound conservation principles and techniques discovered, identified, and established by experience in separate laboratories, now are developed and are available to accomplish purposes accepted by legislators, administrators, the courts, and the informed public; and (c) that local law, administered and interpreted by those acquainted with the problems and in daily contact with regulated operations, supplemented by the Interstate Compact to Conserve Oil and Gas, and supported by the Federal Hot Oil Act, constitutes a system of regulation and administration best designed to prevent waste, to protect correlative rights, and to serve the public interest. Conservation as a method of regulation and its necessary administration may be reaching a maturity requiring only the necessary expansion and elaboration which progress discloses.

W. H.

Dallas, Texas.

Part I

FUNDAMENTALS OF RESERVOIR BEHAVIOR THAT RELATE TO THE CONSERVATION OF OIL AND GAS

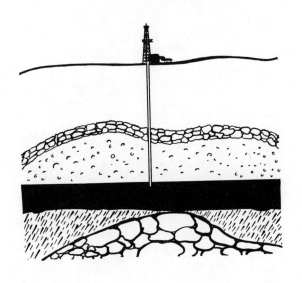

CHAPTER 1

The Nature of Petroleum Reservoirs, Reservoir Fluids, and Reservoir Energies

~/~

THE NATURE OF PETROLEUM RESERVOIRS

Oil and gas are found in underground traps which may occur in any mass of adequately porous and permeable rock. The portion which contains oil or gas is the reservoir. There are three primary characteristics necessary for a rock mass to form a petroleum reservoir: (1) It must be porous to provide storage space. (2) It must have the capacity to permit the passage of fluids. (3) It must be constructed so that it may trap quantities of oil and gas.

The property of the reservoir rock to store fluid is its *porosity*. This may vary from 5 to 35 per cent of the total rock volume. The property which permits the passage of fluids is termed its *permeability*. The requirement that there be porosity and permeability immediately narrows the types of geologic formation which form petroleum reservoirs. Shales and rocks of the granite type do not possess any appreciable internal space within which oil and gas can accumulate. Reservoir rocks usually consist of sand, sandstone, or cavernous and fissured limestone. The nature of pore spaces within a sandstone reservoir might be likened to that which exists within a pile of marbles. Between the marbles there will be open spaces. Although the marbles may be reduced to the size of sand grains, the open spaces remain. Similarly, consider the pore space that would occur if cubical blocks were piled together at random. In a limestone the pore space may be in the form of solution chan-

The Committee on Special Publications, Writer; Dr. John C. Calhoun, Jr. assisted the committee. Advisers to Dr. Calhoun in his advisory capacity were W. H. Carson, H. H. Kaveler, L. E. Elkins, N. Van Wingen, Gorden H. Fisher. (See app. B.)

nels resulting from the continuous trickle of ground-waters dissolving the solid material, or it may be formed by a fracturing action on a massive reservoir bed, resulting in a network of cracks and crevices like those found in a bed of mud as it dries. Permeability depends upon the configuration, connection, and size of the pores. Saying the permeability of a given horizon is greater than that of another is equivalent to stating that one pipe is larger in diameter than another.

To be a trap for oil accumulation a reservoir rock must be overlaid by an impervious layer of shale or other rock, the *cap-rock*, and underlaid by a like impervious material or water. Lateral confinement of oil may be the result of a fault or a blocking of the flow passages due to some change in the property of the formation itself (say a loss in permeability due to excessive cementation), the gradation of the reservoir formation from a sandstone into a shale, or because of a pinching out of the formation entirely.

THE NATURE OF RESERVOIR FLUIDS

A concept which represents one of the most important advances in petroleum technology is a realization that the physical state of oil and gas within the reservoir is not the same as its physical state at the surface. The controlling factors which denote this change in physical status are the pressure and temperature to which the fluids are subjected in the reservoir. Oil and gas produced as separate fluids at the surface of the ground generally exist as but a single composite fluid when under pressure in the reservoir. Everyone is familiar with the solution of carbon dioxide in water to produce soft drinks. Similarly, a natural gas produced along with oil will be dissolved in the oil when a pressure is applied. This is termed *solution gas*. The greater the applied pressure, the more gas goes into solution in the oil. The volume of gas in solution is often as much as 1000 cubic feet to a barrel. There are, however, some crude oils which contain little or no gas in solution.

A reservoir may contain either more or less gas than is capable of being dissolved in the oil. When there is an excess of gas the oil is said to be *saturated* and the excess gas exists as free gas in a gas cap above the oil. When there is less gas in solution than the oil is capable of dissolving, the oil is said to be undersaturated. When oil is saturated, any reduction in pressure causes gas to be released from the solution. When oil is undersaturated, a decrease in reservoir pressure below the saturation pressure must take place before any gas is released.

Gas in solution causes (1) the volume of reservoir liquid to be greater than that of stock tank oil, (2) the density to be less (higher A.P.I. gravity), and (3) the viscosity to be less. When production occurs, pressures are reduced with the result that gas evolves from solution and the reservoir liquid volume is lowered. This loss in volume is the *shrinkage* of oil. It may be as high as 50 per cent of the reservoir oil volume, or as reported in the oil industry, 200 per cent of the stock tank oil volume (2 barrels of reservoir oil equaling one barrel of stock tank oil). The decreased viscosity of the reservoir liquid which accompanies the solution of gas causes it to flow more easily within the reservoir than as stock tank oil. The more gas in solution, the less viscous the liquid.

Gas associated with a reservoir liquid, either as free or solution gas, may contain a fraction of the reservoir liquid in a gaseous phase. There are many commonly encountered parallels. Consider the evaporation of water into air. Air, being a gas, will carry a definite amount of water as water vapor. In a warm room water will continue to evaporate from a pan until the air is completely saturated. Upon cooling water will recondense upon the windows and other surfaces within the room. Another example is that of dew which forms overnight because of the cooling of the earth's surface, but which is re-evaporated by the heat of the morning sun. Similarly, a small amount of oil may be dissolved or evaporated into a natural gas. The amount so carried will vary. The temperature and pressure and the composition of the gas and liquid phases are the determining factors. Upon cooling or compressing such a gas gives up part of its volume as a liquid, called *natural gasoline*. Gas containing a sufficient volume of liquid to be processed is *wet gas*.

Usually liquid is condensed from a gas as pressure is increased. There is, however, within a range of high pressures and temperatures encountered in the deeper reservoirs, an anomalous behavior which gives decrease in the amount of liquid volume as the pressure is increased. Under such conditions of temperatures and pressures the reservoir fluid becomes a single gaseous phase. Upon a release of this pressure, liquid will be released and will be present as a separate liquid phase. The liquid volume will continue to increase with further reductions in pressure, until at a very low pressure a part of this liquid re-evaporates into a gas phase in the normal manner. The reservoir which holds fluids giving this pattern of behavior is a *retrograde reservoir* and the liquid produced is *condensate*, sometimes called *distillate*.

Water found within a producing reservoir is *connate* or *interstitial* water and it is the residual water remaining as a consequence of the deposition of the rock material within ancient seas. Connate waters are usually quite saline, although some relatively soft reservoir waters are known. The amount of salinity in some instances is several times that of present day sea water. The chemical nature of the connate waters depends upon the environment within which the ancient sea existed.

THE DISTRIBUTION OF FLUIDS WITHIN THE RESERVOIR

The relative amounts of water, liquid oil, and free gas present in a reservoir at any time are expressed by the term *saturation*. To say that the water saturation is 20 per cent means that 20 per cent of the pore space which is available to occupancy by fluids is filled with water. Saturations always represent reservoir fluid volumes rather than produced fluid volumes.

If the underground reservoir were an open tank, water would be contained at the bottom, oil in the middle, and any free gas at the top. There is a tendency for this separation to exist within the confines of the reservoir, but it is modified by the retentive power of the reservoir material; such retentive power is termed *capillarity*.

Water is present in some saturation anywhere within the reservoir. The amount of water within the oil zone varies in magnitude from a few per cent to as much as 70 per cent depending upon the pore nature of the reservoir material and the fluid properties. Generally, more connate water will be held in the least permeable portions of the reservoir.

Consider the change in water content that comes with depth

within a reservoir. At a point high in the reservoir the connate water is at a minimum value. At some point of depth as the water table is approached, the water saturation increases until it becomes approximately 100 per cent below the water-oil contact. The change is gradual, and there exists no sharp line of demarcation in passing from the zone of maximum oil saturation to the water table. The zone of change is called the transition zone, and its thickness may vary from a few to as much as 50 feet.

In a similar fashion the retention of oil within the gas zone will be effected. Above the level where there is no free gas, the oil saturation decreases gradually until the region of maximum gas saturation (the gas cap) is reached. Again there is no sharp line separating oil from gas. The transition zone from the oil zone to the gas cap is less gradual than that from water to oil, usually occurring over a few feet.

THE NATURE OF RESERVOIR ENERGIES

Oil itself possesses no inherent energy by which it can be produced from a reservoir. Its production occurs by the action of some energy associated with the reservoir oil or by a secondarily imposed energy. This associative energy may be derived from (1) solution gas under pressure, (2) free gas under pressure, (3) water under pressure, (4) compression of the oil itself, or (5) gravity drainage. Any one or more of these natural occurring energies may be present in any one reservoir. Energy may also be induced into a reservoir by the injection of water or gas under pressure.

It makes no difference whether the energy of displacement comes from that naturally supplied or is injected into the reservoir. Water may be injected to supplement a partially active natural water drive, or to furnish a water drive where no such primary energy is present. Gas may be injected to augment primary gas energy before the pressures are depleted, or it may be injected to supply additional energy when natural pressures are depleted. In any case, and with either fluid, the net effect is to obtain a greater yield of oil by supplying added energy.

To have production of oil it is necessary that the energy naturally associated with or secondarily imposed upon the reservoir oil be operative. This is accomplished by drilling a well and creating a pressure differential between the well bore and the reaches of the reservoir, either by lowering the pressure in the well bore below that in the formation, or by pressuring the formation above that in the well bore.

Reservoirs are ordinarily classified according to the type of energy that predominates. Three distinct groupings are recognized: (1) solution gas drive, (2) gas cap expansion, and (3) water drive reservoirs. (1) Solution gas drive denotes that the oil is propelled to the well bore by an expansion of the gas, which in turn is evolved from solution by a decrease in pressure. The gas separates from the reservoir liquid as movement occurs toward the well bore. This mechanism, therefore, involves the concurrent flow of gas and liquid within common channels. (2) Gas cap expansion is differentiated from solution gas drive by the fact that the oil is displaced, not by gas flowing with it, but by gas pushing it in the manner of a piston. When the gas saturation within the oil zone reaches approximately 10 per cent of the pore space, the piston displacement action breaks down to become concurrent flow. In this respect free gas cap expansion as a separate means of displacement occurs effectively only when conditions are such as to promote gravity drainage. (3) The term water drive denotes that situation in which water is the displacing fluid. The source of the water is not pertinent to the mechanism. In some instances water may be present in a relatively large amount not hydrostatically connected with any outside source, but in a volume large enough to appreciably change the volume upon a release of pressure. The generally considered incompressibility of water is only a relative concept. The order of expansibility of water is such that a million barrels at 3000 pounds would require an additional 10,000 barrels of space if brought to atmospheric pressure. The water which displaces oil may also come by a flow process through the porous and permeable rock in which the oil is found. If the trap is porous and persistent, and outcrops at a level above the reservoir, a continuing supply of water will be furnished for displacement of oil. Water will produce oil by a piston-like action to a much higher percentage recovery than will gas displacement. The dragging action of water following the piston-like displacement is more or less negligible. This is equivalent to saying that after water has been produced from a homogeneous section very little additional oil remains.

TYPES OF RESERVOIR PERFORMANCE

Upon its discovery a reservoir (1) is of a definite physical nature, (2) is under the imposition of a definite pressure and temperature, and (3) its fluids have definite inherent physical characteristics. As a result of these natural circumstances the reservoir might be expected to have a definite performance under any one of the three general energizing classifications. *This is not the case.* The manner in which it will ultimately perform will depend upon the operating principles which are applied. These principles include: (1) the number of wells drilled, (2) their position on the reservoir structure, (3) the manner in which they are completed, (4) the rate at which they produce, (5) the relative amounts of gas, oil, and water withdrawn, and (6) the amount of energy reinjected. It is possible, by varying the manner of operation, to change a reservoir from one type of performance to another.

The following discussion outlines some of the over-all operating characteristics demonstrated by reservoirs in each of the three classifications and the possibility for changing that performance by different operating techniques.

(a) *The Solution Gas Drive Reservoir*

Solution gas drive reservoirs are ordinarily of the stratigraphic type, not permeably connected with a source of water as an available driving agent. They are often lens-like deposits of sand interbedded with shale and may or may not have structure. Energy is derived entirely from the expansion of gas evolved from solution as the pressures are lowered. Withdrawal of fluids from such a reservoir calls for a decrease in pressure with an accompanying evolution of gas, because there is no other naturally occurring energy or displacement agent to counteract withdrawals.

The pressure decline which accompanies the production of oil does not perform according to any simple rule. It is not linear with any particular variable nor does it follow a curve with a definite equation. In general, the pressure decline will be only smooth and generally regular.

As the fluid is produced and the pressure declines, more and more of the reservoir space is occupied by gas. For this reason the gas-oil ratio must increase. The fact that it rises does not necessarily represent an inefficient producing process because the increase is inherent in the mechanics of production. It is only when the ratios in one area of the field increase at very rapid rates and create areas of localized low pressures that inefficient production occurs. The viscosities of the reservoir fluids are important factors in determining the rate of gas-oil ratio increase and the maximum quantity which it will reach. Ordinarily the more viscous the reservoir fluid, the more rapid will be the increase in gas-oil ratio.

Production of a unit of oil from the reservoir will require more gas than was originally in solution within that unit of oil. Therefore, the energy which is possessed inherently by the reservoir fluid will not be sufficient to produce all of the oil. As a general rule of thumb, it is accepted that the gas energy in a solution gas drive reservoir is sufficient to produce only some 10 to 30 per cent of the oil originally within the reservoir.

The ultimate oil recovery which can be expected as a result of solution gas drive depends upon the amount of gas in solution in the oil. The more gas in solution, the more energy available, and consequently it is expected that more oil will be produced; compensating for this increased gas energy will be the additional oil shrinkage usually demanded by a greater volume of gas in solution. The volume of oil produced to the stock tanks from a given volume of reservoir oil is determined from a balance between the effects of the energy of gas in solution and the shrinkage.

Along the same lines one must consider the effect of the viscosity of the reservoir oil. The more viscous this oil, the more energy will be required to move it. Consequently, for a given amount of available gas energy, it will be possible to produce more of a less viscous fluid than of highly viscous fluid.

Thus by the most efficient use of the gas which accompanies oil in solution (provided this is the only source of energy available) a relatively small portion of the reservoir oil can be produced. In addition to this, the possible effects of a non-efficient use of the gas must be considered. Any situation which gives rise to bypassing or to segregation and withdrawal of gas from the top portion of the reservoir represents less than the most efficient amount of oil production.

(b) The Gas Cap Expansion Reservoir

The primary characteristics of a reservoir controlled by gas cap expansion are: (1) it possesses structure, (2) it is homogeneous in character, and (3) it has a rather high permeability. In addition, its reservoir fluid must have a fairly low viscosity, maintained if possible by sustained reservoir pressures. It is not necessary initially that a free gas cap be present; for if conditions are proper for gravity control, a gas cap will be induced.

The energies at work are free gas expansion, solution gas expansion, and gravity drainage. The pressure decline may be rather slow because the gas in the gas cap acts as an expanding cushion. The actual rate of pressure decline accompanying withdrawal depends upon the amount of free gas originally present, the total size of the structure, the compressibility characteristics of the gas, the amount of gas in solution, and the shrinkage of the oil.

The producing gas-oil ratios will be lower than those of a solution gas drive reservoir, because the gas is not produced as it comes from solution but rises to enter the gas cap. Under the most ideal conditions of gravitational segregation, the oil would be produced with no more gas than that which it originally carried within solution. This requires that the oil be withdrawn from the structurally lowest portion of the reservoir, and that the gas within the top portion of the reservoir be entirely conserved.

The ultimate recovery will be much greater than by a solution gas drive process. Should fluid segregation be effected entirely, it is possible to recover as high as 75 per cent of the oil in place. The ultimate recovery in practice will be less depending upon the degree of gas segregation, and how much gas can be retained within the reservoir after segregation. The most efficient segregation will be maintained at the lowest rates of production.

As the cumulative withdrawals from the reservoir increase, the maintenance of a distinct gravity segregation becomes more difficult. In the latter stages of the reservoir's life, continued expansion of the gas cap and thinning of the oil column causes gas from the gas cap to be produced. This results in increasing gas-oil ratios, which again is inherent in the mechanism of displacement.

The action of gravity drainage involves a time factor and in many cases it would be operative if there were sufficient time. A reservoir which inherently should be of the gas cap expansion type can be made to perform essentially as a solution gas drive reservoir, with a resulting lower oil yield, if produced at too rapid rates. The pressure differential from the oil zone to the well bore or to the gas cap may be so great as to overcome the vertical segregation of fluids necessary for gas cap expansion control.

(c) *The Water Drive Reservoir*

A water drive reservoir must be fairly uniform and continuous, and water energy must be available. This is possible only if the oil reservoir is a part of a large, persistent, and highly permeable horizon filled with water. There may or may not be structure present. Water either encroaches from beneath the oil zone as a *bottom water drive*, or laterally through the formation as an *edge water drive*.

The pressure in a reservoir which is controlled by water drive may be sustained near its original value for long periods of time or will decline slowly. In some reservoirs where withdrawals have been too rapid and subsequent shut-ins allow the water drive to catch up, reservoir pressures actually increase. The oil recovery from a water drive reservoir is generally 60 or 70 per cent.

Gas-oil ratios are relatively low. If reservoir pressures can be maintained near their original value, the gas-oil ratio will be substantially equivalent to the solution gas-oil ratio of the reservoir fluid. The gas-oil ratio will increase when withdrawal rates are greater than that at which water can encroach.

The question of bypassing is important in water drive and depends upon the entire structural and stratigraphic conditions of the reservoir. Should the reservoir be rather flat, care must be taken that the water does not bypass the oil as the oil zone becomes thinner, or that water does not cone into the producing well due to excessive withdrawal rates. In a non-homogeneous formation water drive can be active although bypassing may occur through zones of higher permeability if such exist. This effect can be corrected by mechanical changes in the well bore such as squeezing flooded zones and recompleting in unflooded zones.

Similar considerations apply to the reinjection of water energy. In some instances the reservoir pressure has been increased by the injection of water to supplement a natural water drive. This is one means of overcoming the slow rate of advance of a natural drive. It should be noted that so far as the source of water is concerned, whether it be formation or injected water, there is no change in the recovery mechanism. When water is under hydrostatic head, the pressure will be substantially maintained on the reservoir, but when water is expanding to give an active drive, the pressure may decrease depending on the volume of compressed water.

THE ENGINEERING BASIS FOR CONSERVATION

In all reservoirs not one but several of the producing energies may be brought into play. Whatever is accomplished depends upon the operating practices imposed. Rapid rates of withdrawal and excessive water production will nullify the beneficial effects of a water drive. Direct production of the gas from a gas cap will nullify the beneficial effect of a gas cap expansion drive. Either practice changes the producing mechanism from the efficient water drive or gas cap expansion types to the less efficient solution gas expansion type. On the other hand, a reservoir that by natural circumstance would be of the solution gas expansion type may be converted to the more efficient water drive or gas cap drive type by the practice of injecting water or gas into the reservoir for the purpose of supplementing the natural energy of production. Perhaps the most essential conclusion drawn from the technology applying to petroleum reservoirs is a recognition of the fact that operating practices must be such as to utilize efficiently the energy of production, whatever the type be, in order that the greatest and most economic recovery of petroleum be had. This conclusion constitutes the fundamental basis for conservation measures designed to prevent waste.

Those states having conservation laws designed to prevent waste have applied the technical principles by means of, and to the extent that they have, regulations involving: (1) Control of oil production to efficient rates. (2) Limitations of producing gas-oil and water-oil ratios. (3) Control of the volumetric withdrawal as between wells producing from gas, oil, or water bearing areas with the same common source of supply. (4) Control of well spacing and well density. (5) Control of drilling and completion practices. (6) Allocation of production as between separately owned tracts within a common source of supply.

Conservation measures applied in this manner minimize waste in the production of petroleum. A very substantial improvement in increased recovery of crude oil from reservoirs has resulted in those states which have effective conservation laws, over that recovery obtained during the period when petroleum was produced by uncontrolled wide open flow methods of operation. One of the difficulties that stands in the way of a still more effective application of technical principles in accomplishing conservation measures arises from diversity of surface ownership. State regulatory commissions under present circumstances have the problem of not only accomplishing conservation, but also of protecting the correlative rights of separate owners.

The fluids within a reservoir are migratory to the extent that withdrawals from one area will affect all fluids in the common source of supply. The petroleum reservoir is naturally a unit wherein both petroleum and the energy for the production of petroleum are the common property of the owners of the separately owned tracts overlying the reservoir. In instances where the surface ownership of the pool is common, or where such ownership is pooled, the question of correlative rights is removed, and operating practices can be imposed which are designed to conform to the unitary nature of the pool itself. Produced gas or water may then be returned to the reservoir to effect a pressure maintenance or secondary recovery operation whereby the productive energy of the reservoir is maintained. Wells may be located in those parts of the reservoir from which the oil can be most efficiently produced and the daily rate of production of oil can be kept at a high level. This is the method of unit operation. It is only through unit operation that the logical and complete application of present technical knowledge of oil and gas conservation can be accomplished. It is only through unit operation of a common source of supply that individual property rights can be fully protected. It is only through unit operation that the maximum recovery can be achieved and the maximum rate of daily production maintained.

Part II

LEGISLATIVE, ADMINISTRATIVE AND JUDICIAL CONCEPTS OF OIL AND GAS CONSERVATION AS APPLIED WITHIN THE JURISDICTIONS OF THE STATES

CHAPTER 2

Alabama, 1910–1948

Alabama is a newcomer to the roll of states having wells producing commercial quantities of oil and gas. The first commercially productive oil well in Alabama was brought in on February 17, 1944, by H. L. Hunt near Gilbertown in Choctaw County. Today there are 33 producing wells in the state, all located near Gilbertown, although extensive exploratory activity is being carried on in divergent sections. From a conservation standpoint, Alabama was ready when production became a reality, as a comprehensive statute had been adopted by the legislature during its 1945 regular session and approved by the governor May 22, 1945.[1]

THE LEGISLATIVE HISTORY

The history of oil and gas conservation law begins in Alabama with an Act of the 1911 legislature [2] which sought to forbid physical waste of natural gas and to provide penalties for violation. The adoption of this legislation was prompted by the discovery in 1910 of a gas field in Fayette County where flagrant waste of gas took place. In addition to outlawing physical waste of natural gas, the Act required that dry or abandoned wells be properly plugged, that oil and salt water not be allowed to contaminate streams, and that wells be properly encased. No permit or fee for drilling was asked, but the owner or operator of the well was required to furnish well logs to the state authorities. The Act authorized the governor to appoint a suitable person to enforce the law and an appropria-

THOMAS A. JOHNSTON III, WRITER; Walter B. Jones, Zack Rogers, Jr., Douglas Arant, Advisers. (See app. B.)
[1] Ala. Gen. Acts 1945, Act No. 1; ALA. CODE ANN. tit. 26, § 179 (24) *et seq.* (1940).
[2] Ala. Gen. Acts 1911, Act No. 409.

tion was made for that purpose. In the spring of 1912 Governor Emmett O'Neal appointed Dr. Stewart J. Lloyd, the present Assistant State Geologist, to this post with a salary of $25.00 a month and his expenses. According to Dr. Lloyd, the Fayette Field in the meantime had faded out and there was little drilling in other areas, so that the supervisor's duties were light. Visits were made to several counties, including Mobile, De Kalb, and Jackson, where work was taking place but no prosecutions ensued and the chief result of the law was to give the supervisor a chance to study the geophysical features of Alabama. No new gas or oil fields were found, the business slump due to the war in Europe turned all minds to economy in state government, and in 1915 Governor Henderson abolished the office of supervisor. No attempt was made to enforce the law or to write a more comprehensive measure until 1935.

The great East Texas Oil Field had been discovered in 1929, and public interest in oil and gas had been aroused again. A bill was introduced in the 1935 legislature (more complete than that of 1911) calling for the issuance of state permits before drilling so that wells might be checked and watched, and forbidding physical waste of oil and gas. This bill was killed in committee; today the reasons for its defeat are unknown.

The first Mississippi oil field was located in 1939, and exploration was accordingly stimulated in Alabama. Senator Oliver Young of Lamar County introduced a bill forbidding physical waste, calling for proper plugging of dry wells, requiring a permit with fee before drilling, and making mandatory the filing of logs with the supervisor. The enforcement of the law was placed in the hands of the state geologist, who in turn reported to the State Oil and Gas Board. The Board consisted of the governor, the attorney general, and the director of conservation. Power to limit production of any well or pool or field was specifically denied the agency until the total average daily production exceeded 50,000 barrels per day for a period of 90 consecutive days, and no provision was made for unit operations, voluntary or enforced. This bill passed at the 1939 regular session of the Alabama legislature in 1940, and remained in force until succeeded by the present law.[3] While exploration

[3] Ala. Gen. Acts 1939, Act No. 645.

without production prevailed, as it did until 1944, the 1940 measure proved satisfactory.

THE 1945 ACT

The legislature in 1943 established interim committees to investigate various matters and promulgate a program for the 1945 regular session. These committees were called together in January 1945, and Governor Chauncey Sparks recommended to the Interim Committee on Agriculture and Industries that it study the then extant oil and gas law to determine its adequacy in the light of actual commercial production. He had in mind especially the degree of protection afforded with regard to the correlative rights of owners and the growing agitation for federal control of the oil and gas industry based on a purported lack of efficient state control. The committee proceeded to survey the Act of 1940 [4] and to take the testimony of qualified witnesses. It found the law inadequate and appointed a sub-committee, with Thomas A. Johnston III as chairman, to make a complete investigation of the situation and to draft an exhaustive conservation statute for presentation at the next regular session of the legislature. Conferences were held with officials of producing states having a knowledge of the practical administrative problems, and the regulatory laws then in force in all states were studied and compared. Invaluable assistance was rendered by the executive staff of the Interstate Oil Compact Commission. The laws of Arkansas and New Mexico were found particularly good, and the proposed law for Alabama was modeled after them. A final draft of the proposed act was submitted to the full committee, and it was unanimously recommended to the legislature for adoption. The bill, introduced in the House of Representatives by Representatives Thomas A. Johnston III, Mobile, and Moody Redd, Florence, Alabama, on the first day of the 1945 session, was speedily passed and approved by the governor, becoming Act No. 1. There was opposition at first by a small group who maintained that a grant to the Oil and Gas Board of the right to limit production would operate to curtail exploration in Alabama. This argument was, of course, untenable against the logic of con-

[4] *Ibid.*

servation. An act levying a severance tax on petroleum products was adopted,[5] as was a measure requiring cancellation of lapsed or terminated oil, gas and mineral leases by lessees.[6] A resolution was passed ratifying the Interstate Compact to Conserve Oil and Gas.[7]

The conservation act adopted appears to have brought about the orderly development of the oil and gas resources of Alabama, and it has been well received. It embraces practically all features considered essential to a good conservation law and contains a broad definition of waste.[8] It provides for an Oil and Gas Board composed of three members appointed by the governor for staggered terms. The state geologist serves ex-officio as oil and gas supervisor, and the Board has one oil and gas inspector in the field. The regulations adopted by the Board under the act have been sound and it has not in any instance taken an arbitrary stand, but has rather carried out its tasks with discretion and good judgment. There has been no court test of the oil and gas conservation act, the oil and gas severance tax act, nor of any regulation promulgated by the Oil and Gas Board.

[5] Ala. Gen. Acts 1945, Act No. 2; ALA. CODE ANN. tit. 51, § 431 (1) (1940).
[6] Ala. Gen. Acts 1945, Act No. 31; ALA. CODE ANN. tit. 26, § 179 (56) (1940).
[7] Ala. Gen. Acts 1945, HJR 23, p. 89.
[8] Waste, in addition to its ordinary meaning, shall mean physical waste as that term is generally understood in the oil and gas industry. It shall include: (1) the inefficient, excessive, or improper use or dissipation of reservoir energy; and the locating, spacing, drilling, equipping, operating, or producing of any oil or gas well or wells in a manner which results, or tends to result, in reducing the quantity of oil or gas ultimately to be recovered from any pool in this state. (2) The inefficient storing of oil; and the locating, spacing, drilling, equipping, operating, or producing of any oil or gas well or wells in a manner causing, or tending to cause, unnecessary or excessive surface loss or destruction of oil or gas. (3) Abuse of the correlative rights and opportunities of each owner of oil and gas in a common reservoir due to non-uniform, disproportionate, and unratable withdrawals causing undue drainage between tracts of land. (4) Producing oil and gas in such manner as to cause unnecessary water channeling or coning. (5) The operation of any oil well or wells with an inefficient gas-oil ratio. (6) The drowning with water of any stratum or part thereof capable of producing oil or gas. (7) Underground waste however caused and whether or not defined. (8) The creation of unnecessary fire hazards. (9) The escape into the open air, from a well producing both oil and gas, of gas in excess of the amount which is necessary in the efficient drilling or operation of the well. (10) The use of gas, except sour gas, for the manufacture of carbon black. (11) Permitting gas produced from a gas well to escape into the air. (12) Production of oil and gas in excess of reasonable market demand.

CHAPTER 3

Arizona, 1912–1948

~⁓

An ideal conservation statute states basic principles, giving the administrative agency discretion to fill in the details and provide for future contingencies. Points to be considered in evaluating conservation laws are: Does the statute sufficiently define and prohibit waste? Does it confer adequate power on the administrator to make reasonable rules and regulations and to enforce them? Does the statute make provision for ample sanction in case of violation? Does the statute provide adequate safeguards by way of court review?[1]

Immediate causes which led to the passage of the Arizona acts of 1927 and 1939 at the time of their enactment, and the forces of public opinion which supported or opposed their activation cannot now be definitely ascertained. From 1912 to the present there has never been a period when there was not some drilling in the wide acreage available in Arizona.[2] The officers and people of

CHARLES H. WOODS, WRITER; Fred Blair Townsend, J. Early Craig. (See app. B.)

[1] Summers, *The Modern Theory and Practical Application of Statutes for the Conservation of Oil and Gas*, LEGAL HISTORY OF CONSERVATION OF OIL AND GAS— A SYMPOSIUM, (1938). The federal rule in regard to delegation of legislative authority is concisely stated by Reed, J., in U.S. v. Rock Royal Corp., 307 U.S. 533, 574 (1938). The writer has consulted with O. C. Williams, Commissioner of the Land Department, Mulford Winsor, Superintendent of Archives, Eldred D. Wilson, Geologist, Arizona Bureau of Mines, J. E. Busch, Field Engineer, Department of Mineral Resources and Francis J. Owens, Law Librarian.

[2] State land acreage, including school and grant lands, is 10,715,448.62 acres. In 1947 387,217.31 acres were under oil permits. In 1948 500,000 acres are under permit. The United States public land in Arizona available for leasing June 30, 1947 was: outside of grazing districts, 2,411,863 acres and within those districts 8,847,323 acres or a total of 11,259,186 acres. As of the same date leases outstanding on this land under the Mineral Leasing Act, presumably all oil and gas leases, were 76 covering 39,569 acres. Mr. Thomas F. Britt, Acting Manager, Bureau of Land Management, Phoenix, writes May 3, 1948: "We also have possibly 125 oil and gas lease applications which had not been processed to a duly completed lease on June 30,

23

Arizona approach drilling with enthusiasm, energy, and confidence; discouragements temporarily dim their prospects, but do not quench their hopes. At times reported showings of oil and gas have made it appear certain that discovery in paying quantities was imminent.[3] The periods of 1927 and 1938–39 were characterized by this feeling and it is in this general background that the enactments were conceived. That these laws were not vigorously and promptly implemented is due to consequent discovery disappointment. It may be that 1948 will see final realization of these dreams, as there are at least nine wells now drilling.[4]

THE 1927 ACT

The legislature at its regular 1927 session passed S.B. No. 100 "Providing for the conserving of the natural resources of the state, by regulating the drilling and operation of oil and gas wells." [5] At the fourth special session the same year, the Act was

---

1947, totaling possibly 70 to 75,000 acres in Arizona." The Santa Fe Pacific Railroad Company (E. O. Hemenway, Land Commissioner, Albuquerque, New Mexico) has mineral rights on 2,401,944.64 acres of which 6938.65 acres of lands and mineral rights in the state are leased. The total area of Arizona is 113,956 square miles. It has not been possible to secure information with respect to the considerable volume of private land known to be under lease.

[3] For discussion of past happenings and scientific theory see: BUTLER AND TENNEY, UNIV. ARIZ. (Tucson) BUR. MINES, OIL SERIES No. 5, No. 130, (Mar. 1931); WILSON, MINERAL TECHNOLOGY SERIES 41, BULL. No. 152 (Oct. 1944); BUSCH, REGULATIONS GOVERNING MINERAL LOCATIONS IN ARIZONA, DEPT. MINERAL RESOURCES (1946) and HOLM, THE OIL POSSIBILITIES OF ARIZONA, STATE LAND DEPT. (circa 1940). These bulletins contain information regarding past drilling operations and indications of oil and gas there found.

[4] Oil Reporter (Mar. 23, 1948).

[5] Ariz. Laws 1927, c. 59; STRUCKMEYER'S REV. CODE. Ariz. § 2493 ff (1928). The governor in his message to the Eighth Arizona Legislature 30, said: "Drilling operations have been started in several sections of the State in order to find oil. There are no provisions in our statutes to conserve properly this resource if discovered. I recommend enactment of legislation along the following lines: (1) To prevent waste of oil and gas. (2) Regulation for storage tanks and pipe lines. (3) The plugging of abandoned wells and dry holes. (4) For the protection of fresh water in an oil field by casing off fresh and salt water areas so they do not mix. (5) Requiring wells be drilled a sufficient distance back from boundaries so as to prevent what is known as 'offset' drilling. (6) To provide for the violation of such regulations. In this connection I suggest that you give careful consideration to the laws of Wyoming which, as far as I can learn, have been successful in conserving this valuable resource for the people of that State." A comparison of Wyo. Laws 1921, c. 157; WYO. REV. STAT. § 78301–4 (1931) with the Arizona Act indicated the legislature heeded his advice.

amended by H.B. No. 14 becoming Chapter 30 of the Session Laws of Arizona.[6] This is the law that has come down to us, although its language was changed in certain particulars in the 1928 code revision. Section 1 makes it the duty of the State Land Commissioner to prescribe rules and regulations governing the

[6] Ariz. Laws 1927 4th Spec. Sess., c. 30; ARIZ. CODE ANN. § 11–140[1] (1939). The full text of the Act reads:

"AN ACT

TO AMEND CHAPTER 59 OF THE SESSION LAWS OF ARIZONA, 1927, REGULAR SESSION, PROVIDING FOR THE CONSERVING OF THE NATURAL RESOURCES OF THE STATE, BY REGULATING THE DRILLING AND OPERATION OF OIL AND GAS WELLS, AND RE-PEALING ALL ACTS AND PARTS OF ACTS IN CONFLICT HEREWITH.

Be It Enacted by the Legislature of the State of Arizona:

Section 1. That Chapter 59, Session Laws of Arizona, 1927, Regular Session, be and the same is hereby amended to read as follows:

Section 1. For the purpose of conserving the natural resources of the state, and to prevent waste thereof through negligent methods of operations, the State Land Commissioner shall prescribe and enforce rules and regulations governing the drilling, casing and abandonment of oil and/or gas wells and the waste of oil and gas therefrom upon all lands in the State of Arizona, excepting public lands subject to the Act of Congress, approved February 25, 1920 (Public Number 146), being Chapter 85, United States Statutes at large, 66th Congress, Second Session, 1920. The rules and regulations so prescribed shall be those adopted by the Bureau of Mines or by the Secretary of the Interior of the United States or by their successors in the matter of such rules and regulations, pursuant to said Act of Congress governing methods of operators upon lands embraced within permits or leases issued under the provisions of said Act of Congress, and it shall be the duty of all persons, firms, associations and corporations drilling or operating oil and/or gas wells upon patented or state land to comply with the said rules and regulations, to file with the State Land Commissioner all logs of wells and other reports requested thereby, and to case, control, and plug all wells as therein prescribed.

Section 2. The State Land Commissioner is hereby authorized and may from time to time delegate his authority to supervise the abandonment of wells, the shooting of wells, the shutting off of water, the extinguishing of fire, or any other duty which he may deem advisable to an inspector of the bureau of mines or to the field superintendent of any company or operator operating in the same field, who shall receive no compensation; but no such appointment of a special representative shall be made without the written consent of the owner of the well.

Section 3. All well-logs and reports filed with the State Land Commissioner by any operator shall be confidential and shall be disclosed to no person without the written authority of the operator; provided, that said logs and reports may be offered in evidence, if relevant, in any prosecution under this act.

If, from an examination of any well-log, the State Land Commissioner shall determine that oil or gas in commercial quantities may be developed from the well and the lessee has failed or neglected to bring in the well the State Land Commissioner may serve notice upon the lessee to show cause why the well should not be brought in within six months, or the lease forfeited. Appeal may be taken from the State

drilling, casing, and abandonment of oil and gas wells, and the waste of oil and gas upon lands in the state—other than United States public lands covered by the Act of February 25, 1920. The rules and regulations are those adopted in the Bureau of Mines and the Department of the Interior or *by their successors in the matter of such rules and regulations*[7] under the Federal Act governing methods of operators upon lands embraced in permits or leases. All persons are obliged to comply with the rules and regulations, to file with the Commissioner logs of wells and reports requested, and to case, control, and plug all wells according to his demands. Section 2 permits the Commissioner to delegate his authority to supervise abandonment of wells, well shooting, shutting off of waste, extinguishing fire or other duties he deems advisable to an inspector of the Bureau of Mines, or to the field superintendent of any company or operator in the same field. The special representative is not appointed without the written consent of the well owner and receives no compensation. Section 3 states that all well logs and written reports filed with the Commissioner may be disclosed only with the written consent of the operators, though they may be offered in evidence in prosecutions under the Act. Section 3 reads that if the Commissioner, after examination of a well log, determines that oil or gas in commercial quantities may be developed from the well and that the lessee has failed or neglected to bring in the well, he may serve notice on the lessee to show cause why it be not completed within six months, or the lease forfeited. The Commissioner's decision may be appealed in the manner that appeals are taken from his decisions in other causes. Section 4 levies a $1000 fine or imprisonment not to exceed 12 months for

Land Commissioner's decision in the matter as is provided for appeal from his decision in other cases.

Section 4. Any person, firm, association, or corporation violating the provisions of this act or rules and regulations prescribed pursuant hereto or the lawful orders of the State Land Commissioner or his inspector under the rules and regulations shall upon conviction be fined not more than one thousand dollars or imprisoned not more than twelve months.

Section 5. All acts and parts of acts in conflict with the provisions of this act are hereby repealed.

Section 2. All acts and parts of acts in conflict with the provisions of this act are hereby repealed.

Approved November 15, 1927."

[7] Emphasis supplied.

violating the Act, the rules and regulations, or the lawful orders of the Commissioner or his inspector. It is presumed that the Commissioner's inspector referred to is the special representative named in Section 2. All acts and parts of acts in conflict are repealed.

The Act passed at the regular session of 1927 is not specifically repealed, but since the amendatory Act is largely repetitive and supplementary, no serious question arises except as to the penalty section. Section 4 of the amendatory statute makes punishable infractions of lawful orders of the commissioner "or his inspector" making no mention of "subordinates." This statute applies to all Arizona lands except those belonging to the Federal Government covered by the Act of February 25, 1920.

REVISED CODE OF 1928

When the latter Act of 1927 was incorporated in the Revised Code of Arizona of 1928, an important change in wording appeared. Section 1 of the amended enactment stated the rules and regulations to be promulgated are those first issued by the Bureau of Mines, the Secretary of the Interior, "or by their successors in the matter of such regulations pursuant to said Act of Congress." In the revision the words "or by their successors in the matter of such regulations" are omitted. The Supreme Court of Arizona holds [8] the purpose of preparing the 1928 revision was "to reduce in language and avoid redundancy." When a word, phrase, or paragraph is omitted from the 1928 Code, "the intent is rather to simplify the language without changing the meaning, than to make a material alteration in the substance of the law." Is the shift here within this rule of presumption? The code commissioner and his associates [9] must have known of the case of *Scottish Union v. Phoenix Title and Trust Company*,[10] decided by the Supreme

[8] Walker v. Peoples Finance and Thrift Co., 46 Ariz. 224, 49 P. 2d 1005 (1935). See Estate of Sullivan, 38 Ariz. 387, 300 Pac. 193 (1931).

[9] T. C. Struckmeyer, former judge and leading attorney, was Code Commissioner. The Legislative Code Committee consisted of Senators Fred Sutter, T. W. Donnelly and A. H. Favour, Representatives Harry E. Pickett, Nellie T. Bush and B. H. Gibbs, all outstanding Arizona lawyers. The last named was one of the Committee on Public Lands sponsoring the bill for conservation.

[10] 28 Ariz. 22, 235 Pac. 137 (1925).

Court of Arizona while codification was in progress. A statute of Arizona provided no fire insurance policy issue "other than on the form known as the 'New York Standard' as now or hereafter may be constituted," and the court held it an improper delegation of legislative authority, stating that with the elimination of "as now or hereafter may be constituted," the statute would be upheld. If it may be assumed that the code commissioner knew of this deci- sion, what is more natural than that he eliminate from the con- servancy statute of 1927 words of similar import; and thus save the constitutionality of the Act? [11] The conclusion must be reached that the change in the 1928 revision was intentional, leaving the land commissioner no discretion except to adopt the rules of the Bureau or of the Secretary in the form in which they existed December 29, 1928.[12] Whether this is an improper delegation of authority to an administrative officer by requiring the promulgation of rules and regulations is important. Should the question become a practical one, the case of *Wylie v. Phoenix Assurance Ltd.*,[13] will assure trouble, as the Arizona high court on the broad question of delega- tion of authority to an administrative agency, casts its lot with the older and stricter rule of *Dowling v. Lancanshire Ins. Co.*[14] rather than with the recent liberal rule laid down in *State ex. rel. Wiscon- sin Inspection Bureau v. Whitman.*[15] In the *Wylie* case the court had under consideration the same statute as in the *Scottish Union* case modified to read: "No fire insurance company shall issue any

[11] The 1928 REV. CODE was enacted as law under Senate Bill No. 100, December 29, 1928. The Sup. Ct. of Arizona has held that the CODE is a real legislative act, and what appears therein is law, even though the wording is changed from the origi- nal act appearing in the Session Laws. It will not be assumed that the legislature meant to change the meaning as clear legislative intent must appear. City of Tucson v. Tucson Sunshine Climate Club, 64 Ariz. 1, 164 P. 2d 598 (1945); Waara v. Mining Co., 60 Ariz. 252, 135 P. 2d 149 (1945); St. of Ariz. ex. rel. Att'y Gen. v. Glenn, 60 Ariz. 22, 131 P. 2d 363 (1942); St. of Ariz. v. Griffin, 58 Ariz. 162, 112 P. 2d 218 (1941); So. Pac. Co. v. Gila County, 56 Ariz. 499, 109 P. 2d 610 (1941); Peterson v. Cent. Ariz. L. & P. Co., 56 Ariz. 231, 107 P. 2d 205 (1940); Melendes v. Johns, 51 Ariz. 331, 76 P. 2d 1163 (1938); Hunter v. North. Ariz. Util. Co., 51 Ariz. 78, 74 P. 2d 577 (1937) and Moeur v. Chiricahua Ranches Co., 48 Ariz. 226, 61 P. 2d 163 (1936).

[12] The regulations adopted by the Bureau of Mines or the Secretary of the Inte- rior in force at the time of adoption of the revision are those approved by the Secre- tary March 11, 1920 found in 47 Decisions Relating to the Public Lands 437.

[13] 42 Ariz. 133, 22 P. 2d 845 (1933).

[14] 92 Wis. 63, 65 N.W. 738 (1896).

[15] 196 Wis. 472, 220 N.W. 929 (1928).

fire insurance policy . . . other than on the form known as the New York Standard with such changes and endorsements as the Corporation Commission may prescribe," and this delegation of authority was found improper.

THE STATE OIL AND GAS LAND ACT OF 1939

The origin of the state land oil and gas Act goes back to 1915, when the second special session of the legislature enacted Substitute H.B. 1 [16] whose purpose was to provide a code for the systematic administration, care, and protection of the state lands, by vesting necessary powers in a department and creating the office of Commissioner of State Lands.[17] Section 38 authorizes the execution of leases and contracts for leasing state lands containing valuable minerals, shale, slate, petroleum, natural gas and other valuable deposits. Six paragraphs, a to f, supply details. Its framers had gold, silver, and copper in mind, rather than oil or gas. The fourth special session of the 1927 legislature added paragraph g which permitted the department to execute oil and gas prospecting leases for two years, covering not more than 2560 acres. In the event oil or gas be discovered in commercial quantities, the lessee of the prospecting lease is entitled to a five year development and operation lease, and under conditions may secure five year renewals for succeeding terms. Then came the state land oil and gas Act of 1939,[18] providing for the issuance of permits and leases for prospecting, developing and operating state lands for oil and gas repealing paragraph g of the 1927 Act. The Act does not purport to be a conservation measure, but an enabling statute regulating the exploration and development of oil or gas. Its only parts directly or indirectly bearing on conservation are Section 13 relative to unit plans, Section 22 requiring the lessee to keep certain records of drilling, development, and production, and Section 23 which reads: "the department shall issue reasonable rules and regulations governing applications for and form of lease, payment of royalties, drilling and development, casing and plugging wells, and production, trans-

---

[16] Ariz. Laws 2d Spec. Sess. 1915, c. 5.
[17] Commissioner used here means Commissioner of State Lands.
[18] Ariz. Laws 1939, c. 87; Ariz. Code Ann. § 11–1301 *et seq.* (1939).

portation, and storage of oil and gas, and other rules necessary to carry out the provisions of this act." The effective date of the rules and regulations must be specified and not less than 15 days after issue.

RULES AND REGULATIONS OF THE COMMISSIONER

In 1943 the present Commissioner, after a great deal of research and comparison with other states and with the Federal Government, issued a pamphlet bearing this designation: *Oil and Gas Statutes Together with Rules and Regulations Governing Oil and Gas Drilling Permits, Leases and Operations in the State of Arizona, 1943. O. C. Williams, Commissioner.* The introduction to this booklet indicates that Williams faithfully endeavored to comply with the statutes of 1927 and 1939. The Commissioner is now engaged in a complete revision.[19] In the absence of judicial decisions in Arizona bearing upon the subject of conservation, and the lack of any direct experience upon which to base their action, both the legislature and the Commissioner have had to work without guide, except as the experience of other states and the Federal Government might be drawn upon.

SUMMATION

The Act of 1927 was intended as a conservation statute. The purpose of the framers to bestow a measure of discretion upon the Commissioner was so whittled down in the 1928 revision that he has been tied to the rules and regulations of the Bureau of Mines or the Secretary of the Interior in effect December 29th, 1928. There is question whether the statute, even as restricted by the 1928 Code, would be upheld, because in the Arizona judicial view

[19] Letter dated April 30, 1948, from Mr. Melvyn Shelly, special deputy to the Commissioner, states: "At present this office is in the process of redrafting the rules and regulations of 1943, which is being done on the basis of experience gained in the past in giving out oil permits and in preparation for a possible finding of oil in the state which would necessitate the giving out of operating leases. By careful study of the rules and regulations which at present provide for operating leases, we find that they are not sufficiently elastic and broad to meet any and all situations that might arise." The reason for not preparing regulations earlier is indicated "as only the bare fact existed without the details being filled in as provided by law." The

it may improperly delegate legislative authority to an administrative agency. The Act of 1939 is not so certainly a conservation measure, only incidentally does waste prevention enter the picture. Under this statute the Commissioner has considerable power and discretion to adopt and promulgate rules and regulations so long as he remains within the framework of his authority. To sum up— Arizona has a conservation statute of limited scope and doubtful constitutionality, clothing the Commissioner with narrow power to adopt waste regulations prescribed in another jurisdiction years ago. This is the 1927 Act. Arizona has a regulatory statute under which the Commissioner may exercise real judgment and discretion, though how far he can go in waste regulation is uncertain. This is the Act of 1939.

---

new rules and regulations have now been completed and are available to interested persons.

CHAPTER 4

Arkansas,[1] 1938–1948

~*~

Arkansas' oil and gas industry, following unsuccessful attempts in 1937 and 1938 to modify existing laws, anticipated the 1939 meeting of the General Assembly of Arkansas where it was hoped a comprehensive oil and gas conservation act might be adopted. With the passage of a model statute in New Mexico during 1935,[2] and the preparation of a bill for the Illinois legislature in 1937 by W. L. Summers,[3] the groundwork was laid for the Arkansas groups conservation law draft. The Arkansas Board of Conservation authorities, petroleum industry members drawn largely from the Legal Committee (Arkansas-Louisiana Division, the Mid-Conti-

W. HENRY RECTOR, WRITER; O. C. Bailey, Lester F. Danforth, Advisers. (See app. B.)

[1] Crowell, *Conservation of Natural Gas in Arkansas*, I INTERSTATE OIL COMPACT Q. BULL. 53 (1942), CROWELL, A SURVEY OF THE OIL AND GAS INDUSTRY IN ARKANSAS. (1940), Crowell, *Arkansas' Oil and Gas Industry Managed on Engineering Basis*, The Pet. Eng. 55 (Ann. 1942), Crowell, *Controlled Oil Production by Arkansas' New Regulation*, Oil Weekly 35 (Feb. 20, 1939), Crowell, *Latest Engineering Practices Embodied in Arkansas' Conservation Act*, Oil and Gas Jour. 35 (Feb. 15, 1940). Rector, *Legal History of the Conservation of Oil and Gas in Arkansas*, LEGAL HISTORY OF THE CONSERVATION OF OIL AND GAS, A SYMPOSIUM 21 (1938). Nicholson, *Arkansas Contributes Much to Sound Conservation Methods*, Oil Weekly 15 (May 11, 1942). Weber, *Production and Development Controlled at Magnolia*, Oil and Gas Jour. 44 (July 20, 1939). U.S. Temporary National Economic Committee. *Investigation of Concentration of Economic Power*, pt. 15, 81–87 (1940). Cook, *Statutes Pertaining to Oil and Gas Conservation in the State of Arkansas and Orders Having Special Reference to Magnolia Field*. U.S. Bur. Mines Rep. of Investigation, No. 3720, 99–115 (1943), McKay and Danforth, *Oil and Gas Development in Arkansas in 1947*, STATISTICS OF OIL AND GAS DEVELOPMENT (1947).

[2] N.M. Laws 1935, c. 72; N.M. STAT. ANN. § 69–202 (1941).

[3] HB No. 84, An Act to Create an Oil and Gas Commission, Journal of the House of Representatives of Illinois, 1st Spec. Sess. 112, 161 (1938). Summers, *The Modern Theory and Practical Application of Statutes for the Conservation of Oil and Gas*, LEGAL HISTORY OF CONSERVATION OF OIL AND GAS, A SYMPOSIUM, 13, 15 (1938).

nent Oil and Gas Association), and members of the Arkansas Bar met and prepared a conservation law prior to the assemblage. The fruit of their efforts was Act 105, the Session of 1939.[4]

ACT 105 OF 1939

This statute created the Arkansas Oil and Gas Commission to assume responsibility for administering the conservation and production control sections the Act contains. In short, its duties under the law are to prevent waste and protect correlative rights of persons owning underground oil and gas deposits.[5] All common sources of crude oil and natural gas located after January 1, 1937 have their production controlled and regulated. Waste of oil and gas—including underground waste—is expressly condemned by the new statutory definitions.[6] For the first time in the laws of Arkansas appear sanctions against illegal oil,[7] illegal gas,[8] and illegal product.[9] Selling, purchasing, acquiring, transporting, refining, processing, or handling of such unlawful substances is prohibited and their

[4] Ark. Acts 1939, Act 105; ARK. DIG. STAT. § 1–27 (Cum. Supp. 1944).

[5] In the protection of correlative rights Arkansas did not have as far to go as her sister state—Texas. See HAWKINS, EL SAL DEL REY (1947). The Spanish idea as to the ownership of minerals recognized no correlative rights.

[6] (a) The inefficient, excessive or improper use or dissipation of reservoir energy; and the locating, spacing, drilling, equipping, operating or producing of any oil or gas well or wells in a manner which results, or tends to result, in reducing the quantity of any oil or gas ultimately to be recovered from any pool in this state. (b) The inefficient storing of oil; and the locating, spacing, drilling, equipping, operating or producing of any oil or gas well or wells in a manner causing, or tending to cause, unnecessary or excessive surface waste. (c) Abuse of the correlative rights and opportunities of each owner of oil and gas in a common reservoir due to non-uniform, disproportionate, and unratable withdrawals causing undue drainage between tracts of land. (d) Producing oil or gas in such a manner as to cause unnecessary water channeling or coning. (e) The operation of any oil well or wells with an inefficient gas-oil ratio. (f) The drowning with water of any stratum or part thereof capable of producing oil or gas. (g) Underground waste however caused and whether or not defined. (h) The creation of unnecessary fire hazards. (i) The use of gas for the manufacture of carbon black. (k) Permitting gas produced from a gas well to escape into the air.

[7] Illegal oil is that oil produced within the state from any well during any time the well has produced in excess of the amount allowed by rule, regulation or order of the Commission.

[8] Illegal gas is that gas produced within the state from any well during any time the well has produced in excess of the amount allowed by rule, regulation or order of the Commission.

[9] Illegal product is that product of oil or gas, any part of which was produced or derived in whole or in part from illegal oil or gas.

seizure and sale as contraband permitted by the state government. After disposal in accord with the laws of the state with relation to ordinary sales of attached property, the sold oil, gas, or product is cleansed of its illegal characteristics. With the passage of Act 105 it became unlawful to negligently permit wells to "run wild." Owners of these wells must within 24 hours after losing control make reasonable efforts to assume dominion over the well. Should the operator make no attempt to harness the well, the task is assigned to Commission employees or hired contractors whose expenses are a lien upon the property.

LEGISLATION AFTER 1939

Entrance of Arkansas into the Interstate Compact to Conserve Oil and Gas came at the extra-ordinary session of 1941.[10] During this same term an act was adopted permitting the execution of cooperative joint study agreements of reservoir control between the Bureau of Mines, the Department of the Interior, and the Arkansas Oil and Gas Commission.[11] Other action by the Arkansas General Assembly at this session was the adoption of an amendment to Section 14 of Act 105.[12] Secondary recovery in oil and gas condensate fields is the subject of statutory enactment in the 1943 assembly; Act 302 [13] defines primary and secondary recovery, water and gas drive, water and gas injection, water flooding, repressuring and pressure maintenance, cycling, recycling, and gas condensate. Secondary recovery studies, the Act states, must be made by the Commission to ascertain their desirability.[14] Agreements between cooperating operators in the use of secondary methods are taken from within the area of monopoly control forbidden in Arkansas.[15]

[10] Ark. Acts Ex. Sess. 1941, Act 86; ARK. DIG. STAT. § 2–4 (Cum. Supp. 1944).
[11] Ark. Acts Ex. Sess. 1941, Act 353; ARK. DIG. STAT. § 1–2 (Cum. Supp. 1944).
[12] Ark. Acts Ex. Sess. 1941, Act 305; ARK. DIG. STAT. § 14 (Cum. Supp. 1944).
[13] Ark. Acts 1943, Act 302; ARK. DIG. STAT. § 1–6 (Cum. Supp. 1944). See report of the Research and Coordinating Committee, Interstate Oil Compact Commission, *Secondary Recovery Methods in Arkansas*, I INTERSTATE OIL COMPACT Q. BULL. 51 (1942).

[14] ARK. OIL & GAS COMM., SECONDARY RECOVERY OF PETROLEUM IN ARKANSAS— A SURVEY (1947), a report based on a complete and scholarly four year survey of secondary recovery in Arkansas prepared by George H. Fancher and Donald K. McKay.

[15] Monopolies or Conspiracies to Control Prices, c. 113 ARK. DIG. STAT. (1937).

THE ADMINISTRATIVE FUNCTION

The Arkansas Oil and Gas Commission created by Act 105 is the regulatory and administrative agency governing production of oil and gas. Composed of seven members chosen by the Governor of Arkansas, it is the largest commission provided by the legislators to control conservation. The original enactment had two Commissioners appointed for two years, two for four years and three for six years; on expiration of these terms appointments were made for a full six year period.[16] Members of the Commission are required to be citizens and residents of the state, at least 30 years of age, and a majority of them experienced in the development, production, or transport of petroleum. Remuneration is provided by statute only to reimburse members for attendance at hearings and traveling expenses.[17] The Commission is charged with the administration of Arkansas law, the holding of hearings, and the preparation and adoption of rules, regulations, and decisions growing from these hearings. The Commission employs a director of production and conservation, together with needed personnel.[18] The director is ex-officio secretary of the Commission charged with keeping records and minutes. His duties center in the administration of state laws and rules and regulations emanating from the agency. Under his direction are the two major establishments of the body—engineering and fiscal. The engineering department is composed of two subordinate sections, field and office engineering, under the management of a chief engineer. The field group is responsible for supervision of drilling, production practices, pressure surveys, gas-oil ratio tests, spacing, and pollution work. Mapping, drafting of charts, assembling factual data, and making reports are assigned the office staff. The chief accountant's work is divided into oil and gas accounting which encompasses the preparation of transportation, production, tender operations, bookkeeping, and oil

[16] Each incoming governor—whose term is for two years—thus has a chance to fill at least two posts.

[17] Expenses of the Commission are low, averaging about one-fifth cent per barrel of production. See Jordan, *A Survey of the Administration of Oil and Gas Conservation Laws—Arkansas*, II INTERSTATE OIL COMPACT Q. BULL. 37 (1943).

[18] Employees are selected on the basis of qualification. They are not permitted to indulge in political activity. Employment status is not affected by changes in government.

and gas reports; the fiscal section handles routine financial procedure for the Commission. Enforcement of agency rules and regulations is assigned under Act 105 to the Attorney General of Arkansas, although in emergencies district prosecuting attorneys act. Special counsel may be employed for legal work.

Commission powers extend to persons and property essential to the administration of the Act and to all conservation measures. In the exercise of its authority the agency determines the existence or imminence of waste through gathering data, examining oil properties, checking refinery books and modes of petroleum transport. After giving of notice and a hearing under the direction of the Act, the agency adopts rules and regulations which: (a) require proper drilling, casing and plugging of wells to prevent escape, intrusion or pollution by oil, gas, water and salt water; (b) prevent drowning by water of producing strata and irregular encroachment of water reducing ultimate recoveries; (c) require gas-oil ratios; (d) prevent blowouts, caving, seepage and fires; (e) identify ownership of all field and transportation properties; (f) regulate shooting, chemical treatment and secondary recovery methods; (g) limit production of oil or gas to prevent waste; (h) require certificates of clearance; (i) regulate well spacing and drilling units; (j) prevent reasonably avoidable drainage not equalized by counter drainage.

Absent an emergency the Commission makes rules and regulations only after seven days notice and a public hearing. Notice is by personal service, or in a manner ordered by the agency. Where personal service is given, the applicable Arkansas rules of law prevail. Faced with an emergency the Commission dispenses with notice and hearing prior to issuance of its rule or regulation. This finding remains in force ten days. In the main, Commission rules are implementations of the conservation laws. It is customary for the board to issue general state-wide rules in printed form.[19] It issues field rules for each new field discovered. Under its rule making authority the board has established a system of minimal basic re-

---

[19] Ark. Oil & Gas Comm., General Rules and Regulations, 1944. Under the title definition there are 4 rules; drilling and production, 37 rules; oil control, 9 rules; gas control, 14 rules; transportation and processing, 2 rules each. The agency also issues specific rules to cover special cases as they may arise.

porting forms required at regular intervals.[20] Normally a producer files only one report. A gas-oil ratio statement comes from the engineering section. Drilling records are made by filing eight reports, the majority of which do not recur.

The Arkansas Commission is empowered to create drilling units and compel producers to pool their lands within a unit for the prevention of waste and excessive drilling.[21] A drilling unit, according to Act 105, is the maximum area efficiently and economically drained by one well. In an oil field no unit greater than 40 acres in extent is allowed.[22] A well must be centered geographically unless this requirement is demonstrated to be unreasonable. The agency must prepare its unitizing orders in terms that will not require drilling of additional wells to recover the fair equitable share of petroleum under the pooled area, or which would permit unequalized drainage from the unit. Production from each unit is confined to its fair proportion of oil and gas in the pool. Voluntary pooling agreements are permitted; however, where such contracts are not negotiated the agency orders compulsory pooling. While a drilling unit can be created against the wishes of some of those persons owning land within its boundaries, Act 105 confers no such power as to the unitization of a field or a portion of a field. Such field unit operations as exist in Arkansas are the result of voluntary agreements. After notice and hearing the Commission enters its integration order which must be fair, reasonable, and allow each owner to recover his share of the oil and gas in the pool. Costs are assessed in the orders against producers in ratio to their interest in the unit.

[20] Organization Report, Notice of Intention to Drill, Well Record, Application to Plug, Plugging Record, Shooting, Perforating or Treating Report, Producer's Certificate of Compliance and Authorization to Transport Oil from Lease, Forecast Tender Gathering, Crude Oil Delivery Tender, Well Completion, Monthly Producers Report, Well Status Report and Gas-Oil Ratio, Combined Monthly Report on Gas Wells and Gas Pipe Lines, Gasoline Plant Report, Monthly Transportation, Storage and Tender Operation Report, Refinery Receipts and Tender Statement and Refinery Operating Statement.

[21] For a demonstration of the integration technique and the method used in avoiding drilling of unnecessary wells see Crowell, *Practical Application of Planned Optimum Rate Proration*, The Pet. Eng. 37 (Dec. 1940) 54 (Jan. 1941). By January 1948 35 orders of integration had been written by the Commission while at the same time that body had granted 1249 drilling permits.

[22] In a gas field there is no acreage limitation.

THE JUDICIAL FUNCTION

Conservation statutes in Arkansas amply provide for the protection of interest of persons "adversely affected by a statute with respect to the conservation of oil or gas or both or by any rule, regulation or order made by the Commission . . . or any act done or threatened . . . ," if administrative remedies have been exhausted. The judicial test is by injunctive proceedings maintained in the chancery court of the county where the property is situated. In determining the legality of the statute or of agency activity the court is not bound by the record made at the hearing, but "all pertinent evidence with respect to the validity and reasonableness of the order . . . shall be admissible." Review is broad. Trial is *de novo* and while agency findings are entitled to great respect and prevail in the absence of proof of their invalidity or unreasonableness, any proper evidence is received upon the question of legality or reasonableness. Temporary restraining orders may be granted after three days notice with the proviso that the Commission have a final hearing within ten days. All proceedings which affect the validity of an order, rule, or regulation take precedence over previously docketed cases. Appeals are allowed as in suits in equity. Appellate hearings are *de novo*. Appeals in suits contesting the validity of the Act, or of the rules, regulations or orders of the agency take precedence on the calendar of the Supreme Court of Arkansas, being advanced over other causes for hearing. There has been but one reported decision in Arkansas dealing with the validity of an order of the conservation authority. In that case the Commission made an emergency order closing in the controlled Arkansas fields.[23]

A GOOD LAW ADMIRABLY ADMINISTERED

The best law in the world fails in the attainment of its purposes without a sane, sensible, and conscientious administration. Arkansas is fortunate because it has had and now has an oil and gas agency

[23] Lion Oil Ref. Co. v. Bailey, 200 Ark. 436, 139 SW 2d 683 (1940) which held § 12 C, Ark. Acts 1939, Act 105, providing for emergency orders valid; that whether an emergency existed or not was for the Commission and not the Court to determine; that the Commission order showed on its face that it was made in the interest of conservation and that an emergency existed even though the word "emergency" did not appear in the order.

composed of men imbued with the idea of conserving natural resources. There have been no halfway measures of enforcement. Very little waste of oil and gas takes place due to the effective manner in which the agency administers the state statutes. The Commission's record is enviable.[24] Both the law and its administration are recognized outside Arkansas as notable.[25] However, an amendment to the Arkansas statutes giving the Commission authority to unitize fields for secondary recovery purposes would strengthen the conservation of oil and gas; studies have been made by the board and its experts looking to the adoption in future state legislative sessions of amendments to Act 105 patterned after the enactments of Louisiana [26] and Oklahoma.[27] The present law in its administration benefits the citizens of Arkansas, those who hold title to the oil and gas, and their lessees. A small royalty owner is protected no less than a producer even though the latter be one of the great integrated companies. No trend conducive to monopolistic control can be discerned by those working with the Commission in its tasks. We—in Arkansas—think it the best oil and gas agency in the United States.

[24] The Legal Committee of the Interstate Oil Compact Commission accorded Act 105 the compliment of adopting in their model enactment many of its basic terms. Chairman William P. Cole of the Petroleum Investigating Committee, Sub-Committee of the Interstate Commerce Committee, House of Representatives, United States Congress, said ". . . if all of the oil producing states of this country had statutes as well drawn as the law of Arkansas and were administering them . . . [as] in the major fields of your state, I do not think we would have much reason to be here." See Crowell, *Arkansas' Oil Conservation Program Attracts Wide Commendation,* Oil and Gas Jour. 56 (Feb. 3, 1940) and Bailey, *Highlights of Progress in Oil and Gas Conservation in Arkansas,* Oil, 17 (May, 1941).

[25] Murphy, *The Legislative and Administrative Concept of Oil and Gas Conservation in Arkansas, 1917–1947,* 1 Ark. L. Rev. 236, 248 (1947): "The Arkansas program, both from a legal standpoint and from its demonstrated efficiency in achieving actual conservation of the state's natural resources, creates considerable envy among the other states." *Ibid.,* page 247: "A consistent policy to promote the greatest ultimate recovery in both oil and gas fields is firmly established in the Arkansas Oil and Gas Commission. Concern is appropriately displayed for the 'maintenance of stability of reservoir conditions by maintenance of reservoir pressures' and the 'restriction and ratable production of the reservoir contents of each pool in order to obtain the ultimate in recovery.' At all times since the adoption of the optimum rate formula the market demand for Arkansas oil has exceeded normal efficient production." The writer is indebted to Professor Murphy for his assistance and with his permission he has drawn extensively upon this article from which the quotations are taken.

[26] La. Acts 1940, Act 157; La. Gen. Stat. Ann. § 4741.11–4741.31 (1939).

[27] Okla. Laws 1945, tit. 52, c. 3b; Okla. Stat. tit. 52 § 286.1–286.17 (Cum. Supp. 1945).

CHAPTER 5

California, 1931–1948

The past ten years have seen little change in the legal history of conservation of oil and gas in California. The absence of statutory proration of oil production remains either an anachronism or a monument of the far west's resistance to an ever expanding bureaucracy.[1] Prior to 1941 many would have doubted that statement, citing it as proof of the overwhelming efficacy of a well financed minority using practically every mode of propaganda to convince a people who desire "two cars in every garage" that proration of oil production means monopoly and high priced gasoline —a shortage in a land of plenty.[2] In the years before World War II California produced oil and more oil—from 25,000 to 50,000 barrels a day in excess of market demand, with attendant off-shore shipments of distress storage to the Orient. Before 1938 discoveries occurred with surprising regularity, lending color to the belief that the supply was inexhaustible.[3] Voluntary proration continued to be practiced by the vast majority of the producers[4] and the industry muddled through without the intolerable conditions of East Texas.[5] Prices remained fairly constant with but intermittent gasoline price wars. In 1938 and 1939 who could foresee a second world war, much less an increase in population on the Pacific

WILLIAM L. HOLLOWAY, WRITER; J. Howard Marshall, T. C. Monroney, William Scully, Mortimer Kline, Advisers. (See app. B.)

[1] Marshall, *Legal History of Conservation of Oil and Gas, California,* LEGAL HISTORY OF CONSERVATION OF OIL AND GAS—A SYMPOSIUM 28 (1938).

[2] *Hearings before a Subcommittee of the Committee on Interstate and Foreign Commerce on H. Res. 290 and H.R. 7372,* 76th Cong. 621 et seq. (1940).

[3] Collom, *Production and Supply of Natural Gas from Oil and Gas Fields in California,* Petroleum World, 33 (Sept. 1947).

[4] Marshall *supra* note 1, 28, 29.

[5] Hardwicke, *Legal History of Conservation of Oil and Gas, Texas,* LEGAL HISTORY OF CONSERVATION OF OIL AND GAS—A SYMPOSIUM 214–232 (1938).

coast? In those seven years following 1940 some 3,900,000 people with automobiles came to California.[6] And who could then tell that the discovery of the Wilmington Field in 1937 and the Coalinga Nose Field in 1938 would ring down the curtain on major new discoveries in California for an indefinite period, and that in ten years time California fields would have to produce at rates in excess of those compatible with conservation principles to meet the state's market demand?

LEGISLATIVE HISTORY IN CALIFORNIA.

The defeat of the Sharkey bill[7] by referendum in May 1931 did not end the efforts of the conservationists.[8] In 1938 it became known that the governor would call a special session of the California State Legislature during the summer and that he would include an oil conservation act in his call. A comprehensive act was prepared, modeled on the Mississippi law then considered the last word in conservation legislation.[9] Meetings of producers were held and every effort made to satisfy not only the stripper well operators, but particularly the small group who led the fight against the Sharkey bill. For some unexplained reason, the governor at the last moment refused to include the conservation act within his call. Nevertheless, when the state legislature met in January 1939 the proponents of conservation were ready with a new and more comprehensive bill, introduced by Maurice E. Atkinson, Assemblyman from Long Beach, and a representative of labor with alleged CIO influence.[10] After the usual rough and tumble of controversial legislation, the bill passed and was signed by Governor Olson July 2, 1939.[11] It would have become law November 2, 1939. Immediately referendum petitions were circulated by substantially the same

[6] See Rep. Metropolitan Life Ins. Co. Statisticians, San Francisco Chronicle, Feb. 22, 1948, p. 5, col. 4.

[7] Cal. Stat. 1931, c. 585. See: Full Text of Sharkey Bills, Oil Bull. (June 1931), Why the Sharkey Bill, Oil Bull. (May 1932), What Do You Know About the Sharkey Bill?, Oil. Bull, (Feb. 1932), 19. An interesting discussion on both sides of the bill is found in The Sharkey Oil Bill, 8 The Commonwealth 39 (Apr. 26, 1932).

[8] Marshall supra note 1, 28.

[9] Laws Miss. 1932, c. 117 § 40; Miss. Code Ann. c. 166b (Supp. 1938).

[10] See note 2 supra.

[11] Cal. Stat. 1939, c. 811.

group that had opposed the Sharkey bill, with the usual 10 to 20 cents per name paid the procurators. Sufficient signatures were obtained, the petitions filed with the Secretary of State and the effective date of the Act postponed until after the November 1939 general election. Preceding the election came a vigorous campaign with charges, counter charges, pleas and public addresses by President F. D. Roosevelt, ex-President Hoover, Governor Olson, Secretary Ickes and the United States War and Navy Departments. The unfortunate popular name of the 1931 Act—the Sharkey bill —came into play, with the major oil companies pictured as sharks eating the independent producers and the consuming public. The Atkinson bill was to these propagandists the Sharkey bill with a less picturesque title. Again the people of California took the law into their hands and by a vote of 1,755,625 to 1,110,316 decided that California could do without regulation of its oil production.[12] The fight against the Atkinson bill was led by the Independent Petroleum and Consumers Association; a group never heard of before or since, but which expended $392,454 to defeat the measure.[13] In hearings before the Cole Committee, held in Los Angeles in the spring of 1940, the secretary of that association had considerable difficulty in explaining its membership—particularly in naming the consumers who were protecting their interests by defeating the Act.[14]

THE CONSERVATION COMMITTEE OF CALIFORNIA OIL PRODUCERS

Before the war, potentials were the basis of the voluntary proration system. The Conservation Committee of California Oil Producers (the voluntary administrative agency set up by the producers) recommended a total production of some 3,400,000 barrels a day, but there was no recommendation that any flush field produce at capacity. It was generally conceded that the potentials were the result of up-grading by the operators to hold their respective

[12] Telegram to writer from Hon. Frank M. Jordan, Sec. of St., California, May 4, 1948.

[13] *Hearings, supra* note 2, 655, 656.

[14] *Ibid* at 631 *et seq.*

positions in the recommended allowables.[15] From 1938 until the president's declaration of a national emergency May 27, 1941 [16] voluntary proration continued much in the manner described by Marshall.[17] When war came no thought was given to curtailing production; the question was could California fulfill the requirements of an army, navy, and air force preparing for all out war? The Pacific Theatre looked largely to California for vital fuel. As the war progressed, Congress and the United States Navy were prevailed upon to develop and produce Naval Petroleum Reserve No. 1 (Elk Hills) to supplement the state's current production.[18] From May 27, 1941 until the termination of the war, production was controlled, first by the Petroleum Coordinator for National Defense, and within a year by the Petroleum Administrator for War. Consideration must be given the war period because the functions of the PAW [19] left lasting impressions on the industry in California and brought change in the method of allocating production under the voluntary proration system. During this time ". . . it is probable that the oil and gas fields of California were never more efficiently operated." [20] California, with Washington, Oregon, Arizona, Nevada, and the Territories of Hawaii and Alaska comprised District Five. California was the only producing jurisdiction in the area, and the production problems of District Five were those of California. The over all thesis of ". . . insuring that the supply of petroleum and its products will be accommodated to the needs of the Nation and the National Defense Program . . ." [21] was vested in a general advisory committee appointed by the Petroleum Coordinator for National Defense. This committee functioned in part through operating committees; one of which, the Produc-

[15] The application of engineering principles to establish maximum efficient rates of production by the Coordinator in 1942 was the first realistic approach and produced startling results—the MERs of daily production for all pools of California could not exceed 900,500 barrels, or one-fourth the potential allocation.

[16] Presidential Proclamation Declaring an Unlimited National Emergency, May 27, 1941, 6 Fed. Reg. 2617 (1941).

[17] Marshall *supra* note 1.

[18] 58 STAT. 280 (1944), 34 U.S.C. § 524 (Supp. 1947).

[19] SCOTT, PETROLEUM INDUSTRY COMMITTEES IN WORLD WAR II, DISTRICT V (1947).

[20] Collom *supra* note 3.

[21] Letter President F. D. Roosevelt May 28, 1941, appointing Harold L. Ickes Petroleum Coordinator for National Defense, 6 Fed. Reg. 2760 (1941).

tion Committee, was charged with the duty of advising the Coordinator or his district representative on matters relating to ". . . the development and utilization with maximum efficiency of our petroleum resources and our facilities, present and future, for making petroleum and petroleum products available, adequately and continuously . . . to meet military and civilian needs. . . ." [22]

The plan for the control of production in District Five, Recommendation 19, was approved by the Coordinator December 11, 1941 and placed in effect. It was superseded by Petroleum Directive 19 on July 19, 1944. Recommendation 19 and Petroleum Directive 19 had the following purposes: the proper development, production, and utilization of the reserves of petroleum and natural gas, making petroleum and products available at the proper places to meet military and civilian needs, the effective use of critical materials, transportation, storage and refining facilities, the elimination of unnecessary drilling, the prevention of above and below ground physical waste, and the use of natural gas produced in conjunction with petroleum primarily for the efficient recovery of oil. [23] The Committee as a basis for recommendations had the duty of determining the ". . . maximum rate at which petroleum can be produced from the several fields, pools and wells in compliance with recognized engineering practices and principles of conservation, . . ." and . . . to distribute the state's production demand, as [fixed and] certified by the Coordinator, among the various fields, pools and wells ". . . without unreasonable discrimination in favor of any field, pool or well as against any other field, pool or well . . . ," giving consideration to various factors such as gas-oil ratios, water production, regularity of water encroachment, maintenance of reservoir pressures, regularity of reservoir pressure patterns, efficient rates of maximum production for large wells and minimum production for small wells, and other factors. [24] The Coordinator after making such revision as he thought advisable determined the production for the state and its distribution among fields and operators. Petroleum Directive 19 made practically no

[22] *Ibid.*
[23] 6 Fed. Reg. 6617 (1941); 7 Fed. Reg. 2278 (1942); 9 Fed. Reg. 7525 (1944).
[24] SCOTT, *op. cit. supra* note 19, at 73 *et seq.*

change in these principles of distribution and allocation.[25] After the Petroleum Administration for War became the controlling agency, the Production Committee made its recommendations for distribution and allocation in collaboration with the district director of production, and when approved by the Petroleum Administrator or his deputy, its schedule became effective for production.[26]

The Production Committee operated largely through sub-committees in recommending production quotas. In this field the Conservation Committee of California Oil Producers, handling voluntary proration since 1929, continued to function during the war.[27] The Conservation Committee consisted of 25 members and 25 alternates, one member and one alternate being elected by the producers from the 25 districts into which California was divided for administration. This going organization (headed by a general manager in lieu of an oil umpire as previously had been the case) had a staff of engineers, draftsmen and analysts, and a wealth of information in its files with respect to production and productive potentials of the fields and pools in California. The Production Committee moved into the office of the Conservation Committee and used its funds to defray all Production Committee expenses. The conservation group was financed, as it had been and is, by voluntary assessments on producers based on a per barrel basis.

Working largely through sub-committees,[28] the Production Committee classified the state pools as restricted and unrestricted, and determined the maximum efficient rates at which the restricted pools could be produced. In 1943 the Production Committee formulated general rules for establishing maximum efficient rates of production (MERs), taking into account the permeability of formation, size and shape of reservoir, production behavior, pressure, and other factors; these rules are largely followed today by the

[25] *Cf.* Recommendation 19, 6 Fed. Reg. 6617 (1941), as amended, 7 Fed. Reg. 2278 (1942) with Petroleum Directive 19, 9 Fed. Reg. 7525 (1944).

[26] 9 Fed. Reg. 7525 (1944).

[27] For description of functions of Conservation Committee of California Oil Producers, see *Marshall, supra* note 1, 28 *et seq,* also I Oil Cons. News, published by Cons. Committee, California Oil Producers (1948).

[28] These were the engineering subcommittee, the MERs subcommittee, the pool classification subcommittee, the allocation subcommittee and others. See Scott, *supra* note 19.

Conservation Committee in its findings as to production rates.

Prior to the war the Conservation Committee used a formula in making recommendations for intra-pool allocations, which took into account minimum well allotments and variable percentages of well potential. This was applied in all fields and pools.[29] War-time controls radically changed this formula. The Production Committee adopted what became known as the *General Formula*, which discarded potentials and applied a 139 barrel well producible limit and set a depth gravity minimum. Though this formula was used throughout the war, it was changed to meet economic conditions and rapidly increasing production. By the end of 1943 the depth gravity minimum was replaced by a depth minimum. A volumetric formula was introduced which met with widely diverse views among producers and was not fully used except where agreed by all pool operators. In some instances a compromise was adopted, which distributed one-half the pool quota on a well basis and the other half volumetrically; in pools having unit operation and pressure control programs, special considerations were needed. These formulae are largely followed today by the committee in its intra-pool allocations.

During the war the Production Committee in recommending quotas for production of various pools had to consider normal peace time factors as well as war demands. The quality of crude, whether adaptable for aviation gasoline or fuel oil, required constant change in allocation schedules. Abnormal production of light oil fields to augment natural gas gasoline production in the early phases of the war resulted in a surplus of light oil stocks, but corrective factors came into play by late 1942. Then a second phase—the need for fuel oil—again threatened the balance of production. Demand increased repeatedly until the fall of 1944 when it exceeded the MERs of all pools in California. Pools were permitted to produce over their MERs when certified by the Petroleum Administrator as necessary in the war effort. The excess production was distributed between the pools best able to absorb it with the least harm to conservation principles.

The sporadic abnormal production of various kinds and qualities of crudes to supply wartime demand naturally brought some blow

[29] Collom, *supra* note 3.

of gas into the air; through the cooperation of the industry and the Production Committee gas blow was reduced in 1943 to a minimum by the installation and operation of gas storage projects, rearrangement of transportation facilities and extensive development of dry gas fields.[30] One of these projects was started under PAW with funds contributed by the RFC accompanied by an action to condemn the reservoir for storage. The demands for gas by the utilities, both to supply war industries and the war swollen population, conflicted with the expressed Committee policy that it would not ". . . recommend for approval of PAW the production of crude oil in excess of the MERs to secure additional oil well gas unless and until all available dry gas was first utilized, and unless and until a request was made by the PAW to the Production Committee to so produce fields in excess of their MERs." [31]

With the arrival of VJ Day many in the industry believed the old problem of overproduction would return, that market demand would approximate 750,000 barrels a day, requiring the shutting in of some 125,000 barrels of current war production. They failed to appreciate that the several million people who had come to California and its wartime factories would remain, and still others continue to come.

CALIFORNIA JUDICIAL REVIEW

In the years since the *Bandini* and *Associated* cases [32] the oil producers in California have become more and more conscious of the value of oil field gas as an aid to oil production. The usefulness of the California Gas Conservation Act [33] ". . . runs to implementing secondary recovery projects or repressuring of oil fields rather than for legal action using the blow of gas as prima facie evidence of waste." [34] In the last ten years the state has had recourse to the courts but twice to enjoin unreasonable waste of gas.

In May 1939 suit was brought by California against several of

[30] Scott, *op. cit. supra* note 19 at 85.
[31] *Ibid* at 84.
[32] Bandini Pet. Co. v. Sup. Court, 110 Cal. App. 123 (1930), 284 U.S. 8 (1931). People v. Assoc. Oil Co., 211 Cal. 93 (1930).
[33] Cal. Stat. 1929, c. 535; Cal. Pub. Res. Code § 3300–13, 3500–03 (1944).
[34] Collom, *supra* note 3.

the operators in the West Montebello Oil Field.[35] A substantial portion of this field was in the city limits of Montebello on town lots. Production increased rapidly due to competitive drilling; by May 1939 approximately 50,000 MCF (thousand cubic feet) of gas was produced daily, 30,000 MCF of which was blown into the air. A temporary injunction was obtained by the state, which originally provided for ". . . the reduction in gas production from each well to such amount of gas as may be necessary to efficiently produce 250 barrels of oil per day pending trial or further hearing upon this order. . . ." The effect of the injunction was to cut waste by about 25 per cent. Under its terms operators were required to file weekly statements of oil and gas production by days for each well, and of the disposition made of the gas. It was recognized that this injunction was vulnerable to attack as directly regulating oil production. On an order to show cause, a new and further preliminary injunction issued, which fixed a gas allowable for the field at 23,000 MCF daily and ordered the production distributed between the wells in the field. The court indicated that it would not close in any well beyond a gas allowance which would produce a living wage of oil. A number of operators, taking advantage of the living wage theory, subsequently asked the court to increase the gas allowable in certain wells; in October 1939 the preliminary injunction was again modified, providing that any well which could not produce 100 barrels of oil with the gas allotment provided was permitted to produce such amount of gas as would enable it to meet this production, provided that this amount did not exceed 1500 MCF. This injunction, with some additional amendments, remained in effect until October 1941 when it was dismissed by mutual agreement between the operators and the state, because by that time the blow was negligible.[36] As an interesting sidelight, two of the defendants refused to obey the modified June preliminary injunction and were cited for contempt and found guilty. They then attacked the injunction's validity by application for writs of habeas corpus. The court held that since the trial court had jurisdiction to issue the injunction, the correctness of the daily allotment of gas

[35] People v. Wood-Callahan et al., Los Angeles Superior Court Action No. 441402. See *Summary of Operations California Oil Fields*, vol. 31, no. 1, 16 (1945).
[36] *Ibid.* at 18.

could not be reviewed on habeas corpus and denied the writs.[37]

The second case was brought at the request of the PAW against Alliance Petroleum Corporation November 30, 1942 to enjoin the unreasonable waste of gas in the Ventura Oil Field.[38] This company was blowing to the air some 1300 MCF of wet gas containing approximately 2000 gallons of gasoline. At the hearing the defendant argued that the gas was not being wasted, as its wells were produced at reasonable gas-oil ratios and the gas blown into the air had been put to a beneficial use in the production of oil. The court refused the injunction but before an appeal was taken, defendant's most prolific well died and remained idle until 1944, when satisfactory arrangements were made for treating the gas and selling the dry gas for commercial use.[39]

UNIT OPERATIONS

The Legislature of California in 1929 expressly authorized agreements for unit operations whenever the State Oil and Gas Supervisor should find "it is in the interest of the protection of oil or gas from unreasonable waste." [40] From the enactment's date until 1942, 18 unit agreements had been made, largely as a result of the benefits obtainable under the Federal Mineral Leasing Act respecting lands of the United States.[41] The growing realization of the value of gas for injection in secondary recovery, pressure maintenance, and pressure control [42] has overcome the practical difficulties

[37] In re Wood, 34 Cal. App. 546 (1939).
[38] People v. Alliance Pet. Corp. et al., Ventura County Superior Court Action No. 25650.
[39] See *Summary of Operations in California Oil Fields*, vol. 31, no. 1, 18 (1945).
[40] See note 33 *supra*.
[41] 41 STAT. 437 (1920), 30 U.S.C. § 226 (1942).
[42] For all practical purpose today there is little unconserved gas that could be gathered and adapted to useful purposes. December, 1946, unconserved gas amounted to approximately two per cent of production. Collom, *supra* note 3. Oil field gas is being used primarily to recover crude oil and its liquefied petroleum products by injection, secondary recovery, artificial gas drive, cycling and recycling, pressure maintenance and repressuring. There were active December, 1946, fifteen injection plants at pools producing 457,000 MCF of formation gas, 327,000 MCF of which was being injected. The Commonwealth Club of California, San Francisco, through its Section on Public Utilities undertook a survey of the California fuel outlook which began in the winter of 1946. In Feb. 1948 the Section presented its official report. This report which is found in 24 The Commonwealth 45 (June 21, 1948)

of unitization to some extent and in the last six years, seven outstanding agreements for unitization of oil pools, with attendant gas injection programs, have been approved by the state and placed in operation.[43] With one or two exceptions, these unit plans have not included lands of the United States. At present a number of pressure maintenance and pressure control programs are under negotiation, and unquestionably in the next year or two many of these will be implemented as plans for unit operation. Unitization will not be a universal practice until required by statutory mandate in fields where a majority of the operators desire to unitize. There are always hold outs who for selfish motives refuse to unitize and insist upon producing under the rule of capture. To many persons compulsory unitization is more important than proration; with unit operation the proper rate of production is apt to take care of itself. Another deterrent to the unitization of pools containing lands of the United States is the insistence by the Secretary of the Interior that he have control over the quantity of production and the rate of development.[44]

JUDICIAL DECISIONS AND THE TOWN
LOT DRILLING ACT

The so-called *Town Lot Drilling Act*,[45] passed by the 1931 legislature to prohibit drilling wells to a greater density than one to an acre in new fields, has run the gamut of scrutiny by the courts.[46] In September 1938 Ivar Larsen filed a petition in the Supreme Court of California for a writ of mandate to compel R. D. Bush, the State Oil and Gas Supervisor, to issue a permit for drilling an oil well.[47] Larsen was the lessee of several lots of land in the Wilming-

is a very excellent piece of reporting. Of especial interest is the section on the oil situation at 47, the natural gas situation at 54 and the material following 77. Numerous charts and statistical graphs are included.

[43] Letter to writer from R. D. Bush, State Oil and Gas Supervisor, Dec. 3, 1947.

[44] The Secretary takes this position notwithstanding the amendment to the Mineral Leasing Act by the Act of Aug. 8, 1946, 60 STAT. 957 (1946); 30 U.S.C. § 226 e. (Cum. Supp. 1947).

[45] Cal. Stat. 1931, c. 586.

[46] Marshall *supra* note 1 at 36 for a description of the Act.

[47] Larsen v. Bush, 29 Cal. App. 2d 43 (1938).

ton Oil Field. His lots were separated by a lot 40 feet in width and a public street 60 feet in width; the entire leased area included little more than one acre. Other wells were being drilled in the vicinity, and Larsen alleged these would drain the oil from beneath his property. The proceeding was transferred by the supreme court to one of the district courts of appeal for hearing and decision. The Town Lot Drilling Act provides that: "No well hereafter drilled for petroleum oil or gas, or both, or any such well hereafter drilled and permitted to produce petroleum oil or gas, or both, which is located within one hundred feet of an outer boundary of the parcel of land on which such well is situated or within one hundred feet of a public street or roadway dedicated prior to the commencement of drilling of such well . . . is hereby declared a public nuisance . . . provided that when a parcel of land contains one acre or more but is less than 250 feet in width, then there may be drilled on said parcel of land not more than one well to each acre of the area if the well is so placed as to be as far from the lateral boundary lines of said parcel of land as the configuration of the surface and the existing improvements thereon will permit. . . ." Larsen conceded he was unable to bring his case within the main provisions of the Act which prohibited drilling within 100 feet of a public street and within 100 feet of a property line, but contended that the provision which permitted drilling within those limits under certain circumstances was discriminatory, and in effect asked the court to rewrite the proviso to permit him to drill his lease. The court pointed out that the Act was a police regulation for the purpose of protecting persons and property against danger from fire and explosion in oil and gas wells operated in proximity to public streets and other wells, that a police regulation is not rendered invalid by the fact that it may incidentally affect the exercise of some right guaranteed by the Constitution, that the courts would take judicial notice that although the operation of oil wells is not a nuisance per se it may create public hazard and danger, and that the legislature has primary power to enact such police regulations as it may deem necessary for the protection of the public and subject private property and business to such regulations in the interest of public health, safety and welfare, but such regulations cannot be arbitrary, discriminatory, or unreasonable. The

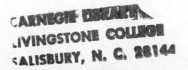

court went on to point out that where there is reasonable relation to an object within the government authority, the exercise of legislative discretion is not subject to judicial review, and the scope of judicial inquiry in deciding the question of power is not to be confused with the considerations dealing with policy. In denying the writ of mandate, the court said: "Being unable to bring himself within the terms of the act proper, the petitioner is forced to the contention that the proviso is arbitrary and discriminatory as to owners of noncontiguous acreage and that we should therefore hold that this proviso should be extended to cover his case. This we cannot do. If the proviso is unconstitutional, it alone falls. . . . We must presume that it [the act] was passed for a lawful purpose as expressed in the title. That it produces inequality in some degree in its application to some property owners must be conceded. But every classification of persons and things for regulation does not offend the constitutional rights for that reason. . . ." Although the decision in the *Larsen* case was doubtful, it served for several years as a slight deterrent to the reproduction of another "Hell's Half-Acre" such as existed earlier in the Santa Fe Springs Oil Field, where wells were drilled to such a density that the legs of the derricks interlocked.[48]

In March 1947 Bernstein and others filed a petition with the supreme court for a writ of mandate compelling the Oil and Gas Supervisor to issue an oil and gas drilling permit upon leaseholds and properties in the Long Beach harbor area of the Wilmington Oil Field.[49] The facts disclosed that the field was subdivided into town lots of approximately 3000 square feet each intersected by streets and highways; that certain of the petitioners were owners of isolated noncontiguous lots in the field and had entered into a community oil and gas lease of those lots with Bernstein; that other producers in the field, by leasing strategic parcels, had effectively isolated the petitioners and cut them off from participation in the leases and royalties from oil produced on adjacent property. The Town Lot Drilling Act was directly attacked as being in contravention of both the Federal and State Constitutions. By 1945 the Act had been amended to include two additional war emergency

[48] Marshall, *supra* note 1, 33.
[49] Bernstein et al. v. Bush, 29 Cal. 2d 773 (1947).

exceptions. One permitted slant drilling outside the boundaries of
a parcel containing an acre or more whose surface was unavailable
for the location of wells, and the other excluded from the prohibition against drilling within 100 feet of any public street or highway,
areas where drilling had commenced prior to opening the street or
highway. These amendments are referred to (not on account of
any adverse effect they had in the litigation) but because California
urged they had enlarged the legislative purpose to include waste
prevention and conservation of natural resources, as well as protection against danger from fire and explosion. Recognizing that legislation may be constitutional per se but invalid in its application,
the court said that although the intendments favor constitutionality of legislation enacted to prevent waste of natural resources, the
courts ". . . are repeatedly called upon to determine whether they
violate the fundamental rights of those adversely affected." [50] Disregarding the *damnum absque injuria* doctrine of the *Larsen* case
and ultimately disapproving that decision in its entirety, the court
found that in the legislation oil and gas wells would be drilled on
private property overlying common sources of supply, and that if
". . . discrimination results from the fact that the enforcement of
the regulations permits some owners of lands overlying the oil basin
to exercise and enjoy their property right to take oil from the field
while the petitioners, who are property owners overlying the same
oil supply, are deprived of the use and enjoyment of their co-equal
right," the legislation, at least upon the facts, amounted to a denial
of the equal protection of the law and a taking of private property
without due process. In this conclusion the court distinguished
statutory regulations dealing with the location and spacing of wells,
which included provisions for pooling and proration of interests
such as those enacted in Texas, Oklahoma, New Mexico, Arkansas,
Louisiana, Michigan, Illinois, Georgia, and Mississippi, pointing
out that mere opportunity for voluntary pooling is not sufficient.
The court said: "In the absence of statutory prohibition, the right
to drill an offset well was commonly resorted to as a means of protection by an owner whose property was being drained by a well
drilled on adjoining land. The wasteful use of offset wells was recognized as one of the evils sought to be minimized by the enact-

[50] *Ibid.* at 777.

ment of well spacing regulations." The court held that equal protection is denied where (as in the California Act) the law, in its
application, does not afford an adequate means of protection as a
substitute for the right to drill an offset well. Although the writ of
mandate was denied upon technical grounds, the clear import of
the decision was that the Act had become meaningless.

Fortunately the decision was rendered at a time when the legislature was in session. Legislation was immediately introduced and
passed as an emergency measure,[51] effective July 18, 1947—just four
months after the *Bernstein* decision. The Act, with the 1945
amendments, was reenacted with a new section. Its effect is to
grant the owner of a tract of land containing less than one acre the
right to have his land included with contiguous lands containing
more than one acre upon which a well is to be drilled, and to participate on an areal basis in the landowner's royalty payable under
the greater than one acre tract. In no case shall the owner receive
less than his pro-rata share of the value of ⅛th of the oil and gas
produced from the unit; that where the land with less than one
acre is contiguous to two or more parcels containing more than one
acre each, then such lot shall be included within and joined to the
leasehold with which it has its longest common boundary. Compulsory unitization of the less than one acre tract is accomplished
by filing a notice of intention to drill upon the more than one acre
plot together with a statement of ownership and description of that
land less than one acre, and the recordation by the State Oil and
Gas Supervisor of his declaration that such land is included in the
oil and gas leasehold of the lands upon which drilling is to occur.
This legislation has not been subjected to the courts, but it is generally considered constitutional.[52] Conservative development continues for the town lot areas with "wells spaced one to the acre,
with the width of the streets and alleys included in the measurement of the acre and the acre still an acre no matter how elongated
or checkerboarded with intervening acres." [53]

From a production of less than 650,000 barrels daily in 1940,

[51] Cal. Stat. 1947, c. 1559; CAL. PUB. RES. CODE § 3600–08 (Supp. 1947).
[52] See Maars v. City of Oxford, 32 F. 2d 134 (C.C.A. 8th 1929), cert. denied
280 U.S. 573 (1929).
[53] Marshall, supra note 1 at 36.

some 38,000 barrels more than market demand, California has in 1948 reached an oil production of approximately 932,000 barrels a day with market demand exceeding that figure.[54] Today there is little or no talk of effort to secure passage of an oil conservation act, although the need is probably greater than ever before.

[54] Daily production Feb. 1948, 931,800 bbls. per day; Bur. Mines market demand Feb. 1948, 963,518 bbls. per day.

CHAPTER 6

Colorado, 1862–1948

～

Although Colorado has been deficient in adopting an effective conservancy measure, it has not been deficient in conservation practice. Colorado has much to boast of concerning its oil and gas resources, more perhaps than any other state. While the state had an early start in locating oil, only within the last few years has Colorado come into its own as an oil producer, now ranking eighth in point of oil reserves, in 1947 surpassing Arkansas, Mississippi, and Illinois.[1] In addition the state had, as of 1939, 316,000,000,000 tons of bituminous coal, ranking second to Wyoming.[2] The Bureau of Mines indicates that in Colorado there is a possibility of recovering some 200,000,000,000 barrels of shale oil.[3] It is probable that there is much undiscovered oil in the state.[4]

The first oil field developed in Colorado was near Florence— site of the Florence Field and the second oldest production in the United States.[5] In March 1862 the first prospecting was begun

WARWICK M. DOWNING, WRITER; F. M. Van Tuyl, Roy C. MacGinnis, Lawrence Hinkley, Advisers. (See app. B.)

[1] AMERICAN PETROLEUM INSTITUTE, ESTIMATE (Jan. 1, 1948).

[2] REP. ENERGY RESOURCES COMMITTEE, NATIONAL RESOURCES COMMITTEE (Jan. 1939).

[3] REP. SEC. OF INT., SYNTHETIC LIQUID FUELS ACT, pt. IV (1947).

[4] Olborne, Address Before Wichita Regional Meeting, American Association of Petroleum Geologists, Jan. 1947 said that in eastern Colorado there has been only one adequate test to every two million acres or three thousand square miles.

[5] Ingraham, *Geologists Visit Florence Field, Second Oldest Oil Discovery*, Oil and Gas Jour. 156 (Apr. 19, 1928) says: "The Florence Field, which now embraces what has become known as the Canon City Pool, afforded the geologists an interesting outing. The district comprises Colorado's oldest and youngest fields. Florence, furthermore, has the distinction of being the second oldest oil discovery in the United States. . . It has produced to date 11,875,423 bbls. of oil, all of which came from shale in a deep basin and every barrel of which was pumped to the surface. 43 COLO. SCHOOL OF MINES, Q. 68 (1948) gives a road log for a field trip to south central Colorado wherein reference is made to an oil seep on the bank of

when six wells were drilled to a depth of 60 to 90 feet and two to a depth of 400 feet. Oil found in these wells was crudely refined and shipped to Denver and other territorial markets where it sold for $1.25 to $2.85 a gallon, the price once reaching $5. Sales up to 1876 are said to have amounted to 3000 gallons. In that year oil was found in fissured shale of the Montana cretaceous group and oil is still produced in small amounts from those strata. One of the first wells which initially made 100 barrels a day still produces. Curiously enough, the present organization of the Continental Oil Company traces its development to the early history of the oil business in Florence.[6] The field now pumps approximately 75 barrels of oil daily and its total production to date exceeds 14,000,000 barrels. A small discovery was made in the DeBeque Field in western Colorado in 1900 starting an oil boom, but further production did not materialize. Another boom—wild but not as wild as DeBeque—took place when oil was found near Boulder in 1901. A number of small wells were located, some still produce. During 1923 important finds were made in the Craig area and about the same time in the Wellington and Fort Collins Fields. The Wellington discovery well (developed by Union Oil of California) was a gasser with an initial flow of 80,000,000 cubic feet of gas a day. The field later became an important oil producer. Max W. Ball, now Director, Oil and Gas Division, Department of the Interior, was responsible for locating and favorably reporting this area assisted by John C. Bartram and A. T. Spring. At the time there was no other well within 100 miles. Greasewood Field, discovered in 1931, had a number of wells encountering oil, about half of which are active today. The Rangely deep sand—the Weber or Pennsylvania—was found in 1933, although shallow cretaceous production began in 1910. Wilson Creek was located in 1937. The three largest Colorado areas today are the Rangely Field producing some 36,000 barrels a day, the Wilson Creek Field with 7800 barrels, and the Iles Field with around 1500 barrels daily. Production from Rangely will

---

Oil Creek which marks the site of the first oil production in Colorado and the second in the United States. The Florence Field is the second field in which wells were drilled, oil produced and marketed.

[6] St. Historical and Natural History Society of Colo., 2 History of Colorado, 749 (1927).

be greatly increased upon the completion of a second pipe line now being built.

LEGISLATIVE HISTORY IN COLORADO

The first legislative act dealing with conservation was the enactment of 1915.[7] It established the office of the State Inspector of Oil charged with the duty of inspecting fluid substances produced wholly or in part from petroleum, paint, varnish, filler, stain, linseed oil, turpentine, and similar products. By this Act it was the responsibility of owners of a bore hole which penetrated workable coal seams to immediately notify the State Oil Inspector and the State Coal Mine Inspector; the law made it unlawful for a person to permit the flow of gas or oil from any well to escape into the open air, and provided that any well sunk for oil or gas purposes later abandoned must be securely plugged and proof thereof made and filed with the county clerk. Other provisions stated that no bore hole penetrating gas or oil bearing formations should be within 200 feet of a shaft or entrance to coal mines not abandoned or sealed, that holes penetrating workable coal seams must be cased to shut off surface water and to prevent gas or oil from contacting the seam whether coal bearing or worked out.

A law creating the Colorado Gas Conservation Commission was passed in 1927.[8] This enactment is still in force without amendment and is the principal conservation statute of Colorado. It is the result of the efforts of a committee headed by W. H. Ferguson, Denver, now Executive Vice-President of the Continental Oil Company. At that time there was little to guide the committee in its draft. The group decided the proposed enactment would be on safer ground if it covered only gas, and that an act providing for gas conservation would (because gas and oil are almost always produced together) enable the Commission to assure oil conservation as well as save Colorado gas resources. The Act of 1927 declares waste and wasteful use of gas produced in the state—whether natural or casinghead-gas—unlawful and prohibited. After this declara-

---

[7] Colo. Laws 1915, c. 126; COLO. STAT. ANN. c. 118 § 38, 39, 45–51 (1935).
[8] Colo. Laws 1927, c. 138; COLO. STAT. ANN. c. 118 § 64 (1935). See *Gas Conservation Law, to Aid Oil Recovery, Passed in Colorado,* Nat. Pet. News 30 (July 6, 1927).

tion of legislative standard, the Commission is authorized and empowered to adopt reasonable rules and regulations proper for the conservation of gas and waste prevention.[9] Findings of the Commission are prima facie evidence in civil or criminal proceedings under the Act. It is the duty of the State Oil Inspector at the direction of the Commission, as well as the Attorney General of Colorado and the district attorneys, to initiate proceedings to punish violations of the law. The Commission on behalf of the state or private parties claiming injury by infraction of the law, rules, regulations and orders of the agency may sue in courts of competent jurisdiction for injunctions and pursue available remedies. In addition to injunctive relief the Act declares any violation a misdemeanor punishable by fine of not less than $50 nor more than $100. Each days infraction constitutes a separate offense. Where oil and gas are produced together in a well the Commission holds it has power to prevent waste in producing the well's oil and gas.

A further Act passed in 1927 requires persons drilling for oil and gas to keep accurate and complete well logs filing a copy with the Colorado Secretary of State, the Department of Geology at the University of Colorado and the Colorado School of Mines.[10] Failure to obey this provision is a misdemeanor. Since 1927 many efforts have been made to provide Colorado with more effective oil and gas conservation laws. An Act approved in 1929 makes it the duty of the Gas Conservation Commission to prescribe rules for proper closing of wells drilled for oil and gas.[11] Operators file affidavits of plugging in the State Oil Inspector's office. Violation of the law is a misdemeanor.

Though a baby among those states forming the Interstate Com-

[9] Singularly enough the body adopted a concept frequently used in the F. D. Roosevelt administration and since followed in the Federal and State Governments. The Colorado Gas Conservation Commission first met July 20, 1927. Present were the three gubernatorially appointed members, Sidney H. Keoghan, Chairman, the Continental Oil Company, Charles H. Sherman, Vice-Chairman, from the Union Oil Company of California, Fred W. Freeman, the Texas Company and James Duce, State Oil Inspector. R. C. Bretschneider replaced Sherman in 1929. Warwick M. Downing took Freeman's post in 1932 and George T. Bradley succeeded Keoghan in 1934. Lafayette M. Hughes took Bradley's place in 1940 and W. Roy MacGinnis was appointed Oil Inspector and ex-officio secretary to the board the same year. John R. Cronin became Oil Inspector in 1947 and Max P. Zall succeeded Hughes upon his retirement.

[10] Colo. Laws 1927, c. 139; COLO. STAT. ANN. c. 118, § 52 (1935).

[11] Colo. Laws 1929, c. 137; COLO. STAT. ANN. c. 118, § 40 (1935).

pact to Conserve Oil and Gas in 1935, Colorado ratified the agreement by a Senate Joint Resolution offered by Senator Hudson; [12] and in 1937 a later statute [13] sponsored by the senator and Representatives Fordham and Hoefnagels, extended Colorado's membership for two years and authorized the governor to further approve the agreement at the end of that period or to modify its terms.

In 1933 a bill modeled after that act proposed by the Oil States Advisory Committee passed both houses of the legislature, but was vetoed by Governor Ed Johnson. The governor did not state his reasons for the veto; however, the proposal had been openly opposed by a major oil company and its interdiction urged on the governor by two other major oil companies. Passage of the bill was strongly desired in the Conservation Commission. Another bill was offered by the agency before the 1935 legislature, but it was not actively supported by any element in the petroleum industry. In 1943 a determined effort was made to pass a conservation enactment. The Commission called a state-wide meeting of the operators and presented a suggested statute prepared by the Interstate Oil Compact Commission's Legal Committee. Violent opposition developed to this act. It was unanimously agreed that a short simple bill would be better wherein the legislative arm declared standards and objectives and an administrative agency would make rules and regulations effectuating the stated legislative policy. Such an act, drafted by a committee headed by Roland V. Rodman, L. L. Aitken, Jr. and others, was adopted without any objection. There was delay both in the bill's preparation and in urging its passage in the Colorado Legislature. During the closing days of the session opposition developed from an unexpected source. The House Rules Committee refused to put the bill on the calendar, and on a motion to override this action the decision was sustained by one vote. Had the time interval been longer the result might have been different. The Commission supported an identical bill in 1945, but it had no advocacy from any major company and nothing was done.

A general state meeting was convened in 1947 by the Commission to consider conservation legislation. During its first session a unanimous resolution called for a law based upon the 1943 pro-

---

[12] Colo. Laws 1935, p. 1174, SJR No. 18.
[13] Colo. Laws 1937, c. 202; Colo. Stat. Ann. c. 118, § 68 (Cum. Supp. 1947).

posal. At a second meeting one of the major oil operators in the Rangely Field opposed the bill—not because it was bad—but because in the opinion of its attorney the proposed enactment failed to contain express statutory authority for the exercise of Commission power. The agency in disgust ceased further efforts. At the last session a proposed law imposing a severance tax was carefully considered, debated, and rejected. It is the intention of interested persons to present to the 1949 session of the Colorado Legislature a conservation act which it is hoped will meet all objections. Failure of the legislature to enact a better and more comprehensive law is due to the indifference and hostility of some major companies. In our neighbor state, Wyoming, these same corporations have been active and vigorous in attempting to pass a conservation law; there the opposition comes from independent operators. In Colorado production is almost entirely controlled or owned by the majors. Nearly all wildcatting is done by them. Naturally they are not unduly concerned with conservation legislation where they control production and make every effort to practice the better conservation principles. The Commission pursues a policy of helpful assistance but has not sought to interfere in operations where improvements were not needed or perhaps impossible. Nevertheless, it is believed that if Colorado had possessed unitization statutes, operators in the Rangely Field would have saved millions of dollars in drilling costs for unnecessary wells and have better conserved the reservoir energy. The board supervises operations in the Rangely Field though the operators do such a good conservation job that there is little occasion for governmental action. The Commission never has considered proration or limitation of production.

COLORADO OIL SHALES

In future shortages of petroleum in this country, Colorado is blessed with oil shales constituting a liquid fuel reserve 10 to 15 times greater than present known petroleum reserves. Other large shale deposits are found in Wyoming and Utah. Because of the clear and remarkable vision of Senator Joseph C. O'Mahoney of Wyoming, Congress passed the Synthetic Fuels Act.[14] Secretary of

[14] 58 STAT. 190 (1944); 30 U.S.C. § 321–325 (Supp. 1946).

the Interior Krug, through the Bureau of Mines, has made progress in developing the mining and retorting of oil shale; in fact, the Bureau now produces and uses shale oil. Synthetic oils are produced by the Bureau and the Department from coal. It is confidently predicted that eventual costs of synthetic petroleum products will be less than that of petroleum. The Federal Government, the Congress, and the oil industry take the unanimous view that America must develop adequate domestic local fuels for times of war and peace, for our continued existence may depend upon this. Colorado oil shales cover an area of 1,200,000 acres. Sixty-three thousand acres are in a naval reserve and approximately one hundred thousand more have been patented and acquired by major oil companies. A large part of the acreage unpatented is covered by oil placer locations based upon valid discovery. Annual labor has not been performed on these claims. The United States Supreme Court holds that under existing law failure to perform annual work does not entitle the Federal Government to a forfeiture of the locations.[15] Unfortunately the Department of the Interior has withdrawn from oil shale entry the unappropriated public domain within the area. The production of materials for liquid fuel from oil shale, coal, and tar sands does not present a conservation problem comparable to that for oil and gas. Nevertheless, problems of importance will arise; by way of illustration physical wastage in the production of oil shales may arise from a failure to utilize their by-products.

COURT DECISIONS

While there have been numerous appellate court decisions on oil and gas law, the Supreme Court of Colorado has not passed upon any questions of novel character or handed down any decisions on conservation.

CONCLUSION

It is the consensus of opinion at the present time that a new conservancy law for Colorado should be one in which the legislature

[15] Ickes v. Virginia-Colorado Development Corp., 295 U.S. 639 (1935).

enacts standards and gives the regulatory body power to adopt rules to carry into effect the stated policy. It may be advisable to ask for express provisions for compulsory unitization, gas cycling, and secondary recovery methods. Authority to prevent waste in mining and retorting of oil shales should be granted. It is likely the legislature will pass laws to adequately conserve Colorado mineral wealth. Governor W. Lee Knous and Attorney General Lawrence Hinkley take active interest in the work; the State of Colorado strongly favors conservation. No state in the union has a better conservation record.

CHAPTER 7

Florida, 1939–1948

Florida has not suffered the deplorable conditions undergone by many oil producing states where conservation and proration law came as a result of chaotic conditions of waste and concurrent oil market panic. Profiting from these experiences Florida, having six producing wells, set its foundation on solid rock by enacting a model conservation law. With an area of approximately 35,000,000 acres, about five-sevenths of Florida is under lease. Here a total of 192 wells is unimpressive.[1] It cannot be said production will not follow continued exploratory efforts. Those carrying on the search for oil have hope that Florida wildcat territory with its ample thicknesses of sedimentary formation will yield oil as favorable traps are found. Testing now in progress may give some answers to problems of source bed position and extent, conditions of permeability, involved lithologic variations and questions of structure and stratigraphy present in new regions.

FLORIDA LEGISLATIVE HISTORY

In 1939, four years before oil was discovered in Florida, a group of farsighted men, to obtain a law making waste in the production, storage and transportation of oil or natural gas unlawful, drafted an act for presentation to the legislature. Drafted by men not trained in the technicalities of petroleum legislation, the proposed act was sketchy and incomplete but it undertook to: (1) prohibit waste of

D. WALLACE FIELDS, WRITER; Herman Gunter, Julius Parker, Frank Bezoni, Advisers. (See app. B.)

[1] For an extensive account of the history of these wells see GUNTER, EXPLORATION FOR OIL AND GAS IN FLORIDA (1948). This volume is obtainable from the Florida State Board of Conservation, Tallahassee.

oil and gas, (2) define waste of oil and gas as did the Texas law, specifically including market demand provisions and authorizing regulation of well spacing, (3) require notice of intent to drill, deepen, or plug wells, (4) require that a log and plugging record for each well be filed with the administrative agency, (5) authorize prescription and enforcement of rules and regulations for conservation, (6) provide proper forms, (7) make valid orders except where overcome by clear and satisfactory evidence, and (8) assess penalties from $25 to $500 and imprisonment for six months (or both) for violations with each day of infraction a separate offense. The proposal was introduced in the Senate April 22, 1939 [2] and a companion bill offered in the House of Representatives May 8.[3] On second reading the Senate placed the bill on the calendar without reference, where it died. The accompanying measure was read the first time, referred to the House Committee on Phosphates, Oil and Minerals, and never reported out. Those opposed to the legislation were at work and their strength apparent. Thus the first attempt was given up as hopeless, and as Florida's legislature meets biennially, those interested in conservation had to wait for 1941 to make further efforts.

When the legislature convened in April 1941 the same conservation minded men submitted another bill. This time they presented their proposal first to the opposition to see if a compromise could be reached. Those against the measure took advantage of the opportunity, mutilated the bill to destroy its purpose and had a substitute proposal introduced.[4] After the obstructionists completed their alteration, the bill no longer dealt with conservation of oil and gas or the protection of correlative rights; it prohibited pollution of water supplies that resulted from negligent drilling, completion or operation of wells, or from failure to properly plug prospective oil or gas wells. Many original definitions left in the modified offering were inappropriate to its restricted subject matter. Some provisions concerning rules which the agency might make in administering the act did not apply. It allowed recycling of gas, called for pooling and mentioned oil-gas ratios, but these sections were meaningless. The bill as drawn probably would have been in-

---

[2] SB No. 394, 1939 Fla. Legis. Sess.
[3] HB No. 1078, 1939 Fla. Legis. Sess.
[4] SB No. 792, HB No. 1711, 1941 Fla. Legis. Sess.

valid, and was defeated in the House, dying on the calendar after passing the Senate.

With passage of time the number of persons interested in conservation increased. The state geologist lined up impressive forces and the major oil companies and many independents offered help; yet the proponents lacked strength to beat down obstacles to proper conservation. Those against saving oil and gas easily defeated any measure establishing further boards or commissions, as members of the legislative body and their constituents were weary of boards, commissions, bureaus, and governmental control; indeed many members had run on platforms pledged to do away with Florida bureaucracy and reduce the cost of state government by halting creation of new agencies. These men had to be sold on conservation. A majority of the legislators and the public knew little concerning oil and gas production or the necessity for spacing, maintenance of water-oil and gas-oil ratios, proration, repressuring, cycling and known methods of conservation protecting correlative rights. Soon after the legislature met in 1943 the proponents girded for a fight at the state capitol. The bill exposed to the opposition in 1941 was excellent, but long, technical in terminology, and difficult to expound to legislators, so the sponsors reverted to the brief proposal used in 1939. This was introduced in the House May 25, 1943,[5] read the first time by title and referred to the Committee on Phosphates and Minerals which on May 27 reported the measure out and recommended its adoption. The latter part of the session the Rules Committee, appointed as is customary in the Florida legislature to decide which bills should be considered, asked that the House take up the conservation act as the order of the day June 3. The House was so engrossed in tax legislation the remainder of its term that there was no vote on the proposal and the session closed with the bill on the calendar.

At the same time another bill was introduced in the Senate [6] which, although not strictly a conservation measure, sought to protect fresh water and minerals within subsurface formations from pollution and intrusion by requiring plugging of wells drilled deeper than 200 feet. The state geologist was given authority to adopt

[5] HB No. 961, 1943 Fla. Legis. Sess.
[6] SB No. 216, 1943 Fla. Legis. Sess.

and enforce reasonable rules and regulations necessary to the Act. An operator before drilling was to furnish the state geologist with the well location, depth to be drilled, commencement of drilling date, name and post office address of the contractor and of persons, firms or corporations responsible for its cost and expense, as well as the purpose for which the well was to be drilled. The contractor was ordered (where directed by the state geologist) to keep formation samples from intervals of not more than 20 feet the entire depth of the well delivering them not later than six months after completion or abandonment. Examples of encountered water were furnished by the contractor. This information was confidential and the private property of the operator for one year. The proposal passed the Senate by 19 to 12, but was not included in any Senate message to the House nor acted upon by that body. There was no organized force against this bill even though the small vote indicates otherwise; lack of interest by its sponsors caused its failure.

September 1943 the first oil and gas was discovered in Florida.[7] Had oil been found prior to or during the legislative meeting, a conservation measure might have passed. By late 1943 more than 15 major oil companies and numerous independents held leases on all available Florida tracts. Principal newspapers began carrying columns of oil news with the conservation program finding its way into these writings. Millard F. Caldwell took office as Governor of Florida January 1945, and immediately appointed an Oil Advisory Committee [8] to study the laws and practices relative to production of oil and gas in other states, instructing them to report to him before the April legislative session. J. Tom Watson, Florida Attorney General, invited the Committee, members of the State Planning

---

[7] Sept. 26, 1943, Humble Oil & Ref. Co. completed its Gulf Coast Realties Corp. No. 1 well at a total depth of 11,626 feet, the first Florida oil well. The first and second wells did not flow although four later wells did. Initial production was 97 barrels of oil with 425 barrels of salt water. The well produced until May 14, 1946, when it was converted into a disposal well. There are now six wells producing in the Sunniland Field whose total production at the end of 1947 was 359,740 barrels. Florida had offered a bonus of $50,000 and a five year paid up lease on 40,000 acres of state lands to the first operator discovering oil or gas in commercial quantities. Fla. Laws 1941, c. 20,667; FLA. STAT. ANN. § 253.49 (Cum. Supp. 1947).

[8] George Couper Gibbs, former Attorney General of Florida, Chairman; S. Van Wickle, Sam D. Fitzgibbons, D. Graham Copeland, Walter C. Sherman, Carl W. Smith, Don Register, F. E. Bayless and E. D. Treadwell.

Board, the State Board of Health, the state geologist, representatives of major companies and independents operating in Florida, to assemble at the Capitol Building February 1, 1945 to discuss possible legislative programs. The meeting was attended by a large and representative audience. Numerous speakers for and against conservation voiced opinions.[9] March 10 the Oil Advisory Committee reported strongly recommending that Florida become a member of the Interstate Compact to Conserve Oil and Gas and that legislation making waste unlawful in production be adopted.[10] Soon after Caldwell created his committee, the State Bar Association of Flor-

[9] Minutes of Atty. Gen's. meeting obtainable from his office, Capitol Building.

[10] "Report of Committee on Proposed Oil and Gas Legislation. Introduction. Your committee to study the law and the practise relative to the development and production of the natural mineral resources of oil and gas, their taxation, and the sale of leasehold interests in the lands of the State for such development and production, that the result of our labors might be beneficial in the enactment of appropriate legislation in Florida concerning these subjects, respectfully makes the following report. We have had a number of meetings of the committee in Tallahassee, many conferences among ourselves and with others, and considerable correspondence. We had the opportunity to hear the Attorney General and others at a meeting called by him to discuss such matters as we have had under consideration. We have studied present and suggested laws, particularly suggested legislation by the Interstate Oil Compact Commission, the laws of Arkansas and Mississippi and Texas. We have by sub-committee had our work translated into the proposed enactments we are sending you. Insofar as they relate to conservation and control they have been examined by Judge Earl Foster, who is Executive Secretary of the Interstate Oil Compact Commission and who came upon our invitation from Oklahoma to advise and help us and have met with his approval as covering the Florida situation even better than the proposed enactment of the Commission. We present to you the following documents and pamphlets: (1) Draft of a Proposed Act concerning Conservation and Control with a pamphlet copy of suggested legislation by the Interstate Oil Compact Commission; and a pamphlet concerning the Interstate Oil Compact.

"As to the Proposed Conservation and Control Act. We have found that great advances have been made within comparatively recent years in a better understanding of the extraction from the land of these resources. We know now better than ever before of how the oil and gas lies in the ground, thus permitting a far better opportunity than ever before of the recovery of these resources. This knowledge makes it easier to control and conserve both oil and gas, thus preventing waste so prevalent and so expensive in times past. Better ways have been found to prevent "wildcatting." Better ways have also been found for protection from injury and damage resulting from development and production. By means of integration of the interests of the owners of adjoining tracts of land under which such minerals lie, their rights are preserved and protected. By providing for allowables and the limitation of product to meet reasonable market demands, further financial loss is prevented and each producer, whether his area of production is large or small, is treated equally. We have benefitted by the trial and errors of others and by their ultimate solution of problems which greater knowledge with the years has made available. Your attention is called to the ease of oppor-

ida appointed an Oil and Gas Committee [11] to study oil state legislation and prepare a suitable conservation bill. The Governor's
Committee invited this body to work with it, and the two groups,
after making detailed comparisons of the conservation statutes of
other jurisdictions and the suggested forms prepared by the Legal
Committee of the Interstate Oil Compact Commission, developed
the present Act—a composite of the better features found in their
research—similar to the Arkansas conservation law.

April 19 Peters of Dade, Dowda of Putnam, Carlton of Duval,
Beasley of Walton, and Kelly of Collier County introduced the
Act [12] in the House with the sponsorship of Governor Caldwell, his
cabinet, the state geologist, his staff, the State Board of Health,
the major oil companies, and a substantial number of those independents doing business in Florida. From the sessions start it was
apparent that those favoring conservation had won their fight for
with this strength behind the proposal, the bill could not fail. The
Act was read the first time by title in the House and referred to the
Committee on Oils. Mr. Peters, chairman of this committee,

---

tunity given interested persons to be heard, both before the Board, in the course
of its administration of the provisions of the Act, and before the Courts, judicially.
We have suggested placing the administration and enforcement of the provisions
of the Act with the already created and established State Board of Conservation,
consisting of the Governor and all of the members of the Cabinet. We have done
this because we have felt that we were dealing with what may some day become
one of the great industries of Florida. We have felt that as such it should have
in its formative period the benefit of the wisdom and experience of every department of the State. We did not feel that the work would be heavy until there
was a greater production of the resources within the State, at which time the
Board may ask legislative relief in the formation of a special commission. We did
not feel that at the present time such commission was necessary. Interstate Oil
Compact. We feel and so recommend that the State of Florida join in the Interstate Oil Compact authorized by Congress and now having in its membership
the majority of the oil and gas producing States. We feel that it is important
and essential that the State of Florida follow other oil and gas producing states.
in the enactment of appropriate statutes covering its oil and gas resources and
in the Compact just mentioned by appropriate legislation that joint action may
be taken whenever necessary for the best interests of the respective states and
their citizens. Conclusion. May we express the hope that from all the work which
will have been done in the furtherance of the subjects of our report before their
enactment by the Legislature there may arise laws just and equitable to all which
will promote the common good and prevent evil practise."

[11] Doyle E. Carlton, formerly Governor of Florida, Chairman, Onan Whitehurst,
Vice-Chairman, James A. Dixon, Ed. R. Bentley and Lawrence A. Truett.

[12] HB No. 284, 1945 Fla. Legis. Sess.; Fla. Laws 1945, c. 22,819; FLA. STAT.
ANN. § 377.06–377.40 (Cum. Supp. 1947).

moved the same day that 250 copies of the law be printed, which
was agreed and so ordered. A companion bill [13] to the House measure was introduced in the Senate May 11 by the Senate Committee
on Oil and Natural Resources and read the first time by title, then
placed on the bill calendar for second reading. In addition to the
conservation statute, the administration sponsored a bill to ratify
the Interstate Compact to Conserve Oil and Gas making Florida
a member of the Compact Commission, a bill for the taxation of
oil and gas produced in the state, one requiring that all leases on
state land be offered for sale by sealed bid, and other provisions un-
related to conservation. New and unexpected hostility arose to the
bills from Florida west coast cities keynoted by the Chambers of
Commerce and large citizen delegations. These people were not
against conservation, but contended provisions must be inserted to
protect their beaches against pollution and from unsightly operations to prevent destruction of beauty and commission of irreparable damage to tourist trade. Newspapers clamored for beach protection.[14] The Committee on Oils in the House and the Committee
on Oil and Natural Resources of the Senate held joint public hearings April 24 inviting those interested in the program as well as the

[13] SB No. 467, 1945 Fla. Legis. Sess.
[14] Tampa Tribune, April 17, 1945, p. 2, col. 4: "The first of Gov. Caldwell's
oil bills was distributed to members of the house oils committee by Chmn. C. W.
Peters, of Miami, today and another will be ready Wednesday, but neither definitely covers the protection of resort areas or beaches, as urgently requested by
West Coast cities. A third bill by M. M. Ingraham, of Arcadia, would put a
privilege tax on all minerals, and Peters named a special committee to consider
it. Only bill introduced so far to protect resort and beach areas was put in the
senate last week by Sheldon of Hillsborough and referred to committee. Gov.
Caldwell's conservation bill follows closely recommendations of the governor's oil
committee, which made a study of the state's legislative needs, should explorations
continue or oil be discovered in quantity. The committee worked with Attorney
General Watson and a committee of the state bar. Following are high points of
the bill: Unnecessary waste of oil or gas is prohibited; the state board of conservation is designated to enforce oil conservation and control production, should a
field be brought in; under ground water resources are protected from pollution by
supervision of drilling and plugging unproductive wells; the industry would be
responsible for fires and "blow-outs"; wells must be properly spaced; permits to
drill would cost $50, to plug a dry hole, $15; the board would have control of
areas to be drilled and quotas of oil to be taken out, proration of oil, and limitation of production when necessary; the chancery court of Leon county would
give precedence to oil case, and penalties of $100 a day are set forth for each
violation of the law, if an oil operator continues to fail to do his duty under the
law the state may take over."

defense of the beach resorts to attend.[15] Senator Sheldon, Hillsborough County, took the lead for the west coast and prepared a proposal governing leasing of state land, which protected the beach areas. He was ready to submit this bill to the hearing and urge its adoption.[16] A large crowd attended; all were given opportunity to

[15] Tampa Tribune, April 19, 1945, p. 1, col. 2, cont. on p. 8, col. 4: "A house and senate hearing for the public was set today for Monday night at 7:30 o'clock in the senate chamber on Gov. Caldwell's oil bill, and all interested in the state program, including protection of resorts and beaches, were invited to attend. Although beach protection is not covered directly in the governor's bill, Sen. N. Ray Carroll, of Kissimmee, and Rep. C. W. Peters, of Miami, chairmen of the oil committees of the senate and house, suggested that those interested in beach protection be represented. A bill by Sen. Sheldon, reviewed in detail in this article, does provide beach protection, but they said it probably will not be taken up at the hearing. However, Sheldon's bill will be before the two committees for consideration along with the governor's bills, and the two chairmen said it would be given full consideration. A fourth oil bill, introduced in the house by Rep. J. Morgan Ingraham, of Arcadia, is now before a subcommittee. It is essentially a taxation bill. Peters said he would introduce the administration bills tomorrow. But Carroll said he would not put them in the senate before the hearing. Both were prepared with the help of a committee of citizens, Attorney General Watson and members of the state bar. The principal bill offered by the governor is written to protect state interests, including the underground water supply, during oil explorations and development, and to conserve oil after it has been discovered in quantities, but it does not cover beach drilling, as contemplated in the West Coast Arnold lease now pending."

[16] United Press Dispatch, appearing in major newspapers in Florida April 23, 1945. "With administration proposals to add more taxes to beer and cigarettes well on their way toward adoption, the Florida legislature is prepared to tackle controversial bills this week to regulate the state's infant oil industry. Two measures—one sponsored by Gov. Caldwell and another by anti-administration Sen. Sheldon of Tampa—are slated to be thrashed out at a public hearing Tuesday night at 7:30. The Governor's proposal, drafted by his citizens' advisory committee, would place supervisory control of the petroleum industry in the hands of the state cabinet, sitting as a conservation board, and would levy a five cents per barrel tax on production. Sheldon contends that Caldwell's plan fails to provide adequate safeguards for Florida beaches. He said his measure had been drawn to meet the demands of coastal areas which feared oil pollution would cripple the state's $100,000,000 tourist industry. Opposition to the control bill centered in the contention that too many restrictions would discourage oil speculation and the eventual discovery of 'black gold' in paying quantity under Florida's soil. Administration forces were on the other hand aiming at discouraging just that sort of speculation. Sheldon's bill, which he slipped into the legislative hopper before Caldwell supporters had a chance to get an administration measure on the books, would prevent speculators from tying up large tracts of land. The measure would limit the extent of an oil lease to 10,000 acres and would provide that no lease may be sold or transferred until a test well of 6000 feet has been drilled, that is, unless oil is reached at a lesser depth. The Sheldon bill would also provide that trustees of the internal improvement fund could not lease lands within a city without permission of the governing body, and rights from the board of county commisssioners would be needed before securing land in or adjacent to a bathing beach or

express their ideas. The committees agreed to appoint a sub-committee [17] to amend the oil bills or to write new legislation affecting the beaches. Amendments were submitted to the oil code sufficient to save tourism; however, these were not favored on the west coast,

---

park. Representatives of all major oil companies in Florida are expected to be on hand at the joint senate-house hearing. Humble Oil Co. is the only one with a paying well thus far."

[17] Tampa Tribune, April 26, 1945, p. 1, col. 1, cont. on p. 2, col. 3: "Rep. Neil C. McMullen, of Tampa, was named chairman of a subcommittee today to prepare an amendment to Gov. Caldwell's oil conservation bill, or write a new bill to protect West Coast beaches and resorts from damage by oil explorers or developers. Other members are Thomas B. Dowda, Palatka; Mabry A. Carlton, Jacksonville, and C. H. Taylor, Wauchula. The group was named by C. W. Peters, of Miami, chairman of the house oil committee, now studying the administration program for conservation and taxation of oil resources. Peters promised a delegation from the West Coast headed by Truman Green, president of the Tampa Chamber of Commerce, at a joint hearing last night by the house and senate committees on oil that he would name a committee to write a beach bill. Two other questions were brought up at the meeting, the allocation of oil tax receipts, and the exemption of oil properties from other taxes. Peters named sub-committees to study both questions, as follows: For allocation of revenues—H. B. Kelly, Naples, chairman; A. Morley Darby, Pensacola; James L. Hardin, Lakeland, and Thomas D. Beasley, DeFuniak Springs. For study of exemption of oil properties from taxes other than the special oil tax—Joe C. Jenkins, Gainesville, chairman; Fred Andrews, Lake Butler; Charles E. Sheppard, St. Augustine; and N. D. Wainwright, Jr., Starke. The meeting lasted only a few minutes and Peters did not go into the beach question, although a number of members of the Tampa committee remained over for his meeting and oil interests were represented. He asked McMullen and his committee to try to report within a week, so the beach bill could be considered along with the governor's conservation and tax bills. At the meeting last night he said he would not proceed with the other bills until the beach bill was ready. At that time he said a beach bill was being prepared. Only person heard was S. Graham Copeland, of Gov. Holland's citizens' committee, which took the lead in preparation of the tax and conservation bills. Copeland, who said he was speaking as chairman of county commissioners of Collier county, said he had studied the oil question a year and a half and visited oil producing states to get data on the kind of legislation needed in Florida. 'My county is the first in Florida to get oil,' Copeland said, 'and I found Florida had no statute governing the production of oil and gas.' "

Tampa Tribune, April 26, 1945, p. 1, col. 2: "Gov. Caldwell assured members of the Pinellas delegation tonight that the west coast would have cooperation in its fight to protect resorts and beaches from damage by oil prospectors and developers. He met for a short conference with Sen. Henry S. Baynard, and Reps. S. Henry Harris and Archie Clement, of Pinellas, and discussed proposed legislation to protect the beaches. Baynard reported after the meeting the governor said he would go along with the West Coast cities in the preparation of a beach bill, and that he agreed to hold up the administration oil conservation and taxation bills until a leasing bill is prepared to protect fully resort cities and beaches outside of corporate limits. Baynard reported Caldwell in favor of such a bill. The governor's position has caused a good deal of satisfaction here in the light of his statement at an internal improvement board hearing some weeks ago the West Coast cities were 'unreasonable' in asking that no leases be given on waterfront properties between Naples and the Pinellas-Pasco line."

and Attorney General Watson, furthering the objections of the cities, asked for a hearing to consider his substitute bill.[18] Dislike of the first amendments impelled redrafting, and May 8 new proposals were made a part of the conservation measure.[19] These changes

Tampa Tribune, April 27, 1945, Editorial, p. 10. "We are pleased to read that Governor Caldwell says he is willing to 'go along' with the West Coast communities and organizations in providing for beach protection in the oil bill. These interests are preparing to introduce either an amendment to the Governor's bill or a separate bill to take care of the beach and resort properties of this coast in whatever oil exploration and exploitation may be done under leases granted by the Internal Improvement Board. We are wondering why the Governor did not include this highly important item in his own bill. The people of this section have acquired the idea that he is not favorable to their protests, due mainly to his comment when a delegation representing West Coast communities appeared at Tallahassee and were told by the Governor that their objections were 'unreasonable.' Whatever legislation is necessary to give proper protection to our beaches and resorts, whether in the form of an amendment or a separate bill, ought to be presented, pushed and passed. It is a matter of vital concern to every citizen and property owner along this coast."

[18] Tampa Tribune, May 4, 1945, p. 4, col. 2: "A sub-committee on oil headed by Rep. McMullen of Hillsborough county submitted an amendment today to Gov. Caldwell's oil code for the protection of beaches, but consideration of it was held up at the request of Attorney General Watson, who said he wanted to be heard on the beach question. The McMullen amendment proposes: 'That no permit shall be granted by the conservation board for the drilling of a well for oil and gas, or either of them, at a location within the tidal waters of the state and within five miles of the line of mean high tide without a hearing of which the board of county commissioners of the county opposite the shore line of which such proposed well will be located shall be given 30 days written notice by the board. Similar notice shall be given the governing body of any incorporated municipality whose corporate limits are located within three miles of a point on the shore line of the state nearest the location of such well.' The proposed amendment asks further that newspaper notices be published of intention to drill an off-shore well, giving its approximate location, and the time and place of the hearing. The board of county commissioners and other governing boards affected would be heard 'as well as all other persons who may be affected by the drilling and production of such well.' The board of conservation would have authority to refuse a permit to drill 'should it appear that unavoidable injury to persons or property' might result. Watson said he was preparing bills to cover oil taxation, competitive sale of oil lands and the protection of beaches, and he would like to appear before a joint meeting of the oils committees of the house and senate. He said the proposed McMullen amendment approached the beach question from a different angle from the bill he proposed, and although he was not opposing it but wanted the committees to know his point of view. 'Mr. McMullen's amendment is good,' he said, 'from the angle from which he approaches the problem, but this is a matter that involves more than a prohibitory regulation. It involves the rights of people over certain kinds of waters.' Rep. C. W. Peters, of Miami, chairman of the oil committee, said he wanted to get the administration's conservation bill on the way and would ask that this be done tomorrow, but he said he would give Watson his hearing as soon as the attorney general is ready to be heard."

[19] Tampa Tribune, May 8, 1945, p. 20, col. 2: "Rep. Neil McMullen's subcommittee on oil tonight approved an amendment to a proposed state oil code,

were adopted by the Committee on Oils May 10 and reported to the House with the statement that the bill had been carefully considered, amended, and recommended for passage. May 11 when the House approved the amendments, the bill was put on the calendar

said to have the okeh of Gov. Caldwell, for the protection of Florida beaches from damage by exploration or drilling. The amendment prohibits drilling in a city or in adjacent waters outside of a city without approval of county commissioners. The amendment: No permit to drill a gas or oil well shall be granted within the corporate limits of any municipality, unless the governing authority of the municipaity shall have first duly approved the application for such permit by resolution. No permit to drill a gas or oil well shall be granted at a location in the tidal waters of the state, abutting or immediately adjacent to the corporate limits of a municipality or within three miles of such corporate limits extending from the line of mean high tide into such waters, unless the governing authority of the municipality shall have first duly approved the application for such permit by resolution. No permit to drill a gas or oil well shall be granted on any improved beach, located outside of an incorporated town or municipality, or at a location in the tidal waters of the state abutting or immediately adjacent to an improved beach, or within three miles of an improved beach extending from the line of mean high tide into such tidal waters, unless the county commissioners of the county in which such beach is located shall have first duly approved the application for such permit by resolution. For the purpose of the amendment an improved beach outside of a city is defined as having no fewer than 10 hotels, apartment buildings, residences or other structures used for residential purposes to the mile. This amendment will go immediately to the house oil committee and C. W. Peters, of Miami, chairman, said he would call a meeting tomorrow to consider it, or any other matters affecting the proposed state oil code. The meeting was attended by Truman Green, president of the Tampa Chamber of Commerce and chairman of an oil committee representing 17 West Coast cities; Lewis T. Wray, city attorney of St. Petersburg, and John C. Blocker, Pinellas county attorney. No mention was made of an earlier amendment proposed by McMullen's committee that drew criticism from a number of West Coast cities, or a third proposal prepared by Attorney General Watson, who has asked the oil committee for opportunity to present it along with other oil legislation. Sen. Henry S. Baynard, of St. Petersburg, and Rep. Archie Clement, Tarpon Springs attended the hearing and took part in the discussion. Baynard announced Caldwell had approved the amendment and said the senators and representatives from west coast counties had a grave responsibility in protecting the established tourist industry from the new oil industry. 'I don't think the oil industry wants to do any harm to our resorts or beaches,' said Baynard, 'but the beaches are our responsibility. 'This amendment has been approved by the governor and it will protect the cities and beaches from pollution by drilling wells. 'We have defined an improved beach. The governor has asked this because some beaches are not improved, and for which no objection would be raised.' He said the amendment should be tacked to Caldwell's conservation bill, and at the same time a companion bill covering leasing should be amended to conform. 'If we don't get some amendment,' said Baynard, 'we are not going to be able to go back to our people. This is of the utmost importance, and I am going to fight these bills until I see that they contain sufficient protection.' Baynard said a city or county commission should be better able to decide on oil drilling than someone up here in Tallahassee. Green said the West Coast cities had asked only that no additional leases be granted pending protective legislation, and pointed out that the amendment would protect resort centers of the East Coast as well as the West. Clement asked if the oil committee would approve the amendment. He was as-for second reading and read by title only. The rules were waived, the bill read the third time in full and passed 79 to 2. A last ditch stand was made by those antagonistic to conservation in the Senate. At their instance Senator Lewis offered on May 11 a change to the Senate proposal: "No proration or allowable under the terms of this Act shall be made effective or applied anywhere in this State until such time as the full aggregate production of petroleum oil in this State shall have been, for a continuous period of 90 days, in excess of 30,000 barrels of oil per day. No proration or allowable under the terms of this Act shall be made effective or be applied to any producing petroleum field in this State until such time as such oil field shall have produced petroleum oil for a continuous period of 90 days in excess of 3,000 barrels per day." This carried. Senator Baynard then suggested amendments to safeguard state beaches as in the House offering which were adopted. On motion of Senator Carroll the rules were waived, the amended bill read in full and passed, 36 to 0 and after engrossing in the Senate certified to the other chamber. To defeat the amendment restricting application of the act, every effort was used to obtain adoption of the House measure. This was successful for on May 24 the Senate passed the House bill, 31 to 0 and June 1 the bill went to Governor Caldwell who signed it June 5. The administration bill making Florida a member of the Interstate Oil Compact Commission passed without a dissenting vote in either house and became effective with the governor's approval.[20]

THE FLORIDA CONSERVATION ACT

After six years of bitter debate oil and gas conservation law in Florida was a reality.[21] Though long and prolix the enactment is in

sured by several that it would, and that the subcommittee would recommend it. McMullen said he hoped the amendment would be satisfactory to all communities, and Green said he was authorized to speak for them, and he was sure it would be satisfactory. Blocker said it would be satisfactory 'to the vast majority of the people of Pinellas county.' Wray said he thought it satisfactory, and he would check a proposed leasing bill to see there is no hitch. Green thanked the committee, and Clement said he did not think newspaper reports of criticism were fair to McMullen, who had worked hard to get a satisfactory amendment. Peters arrived a minute after the meeting had adjourned, and said he would call a meeting of his oil committee tomorrow to push the legislation through."

[20] Fla. Laws 1945, c. 22,823; FLA. STAT. ANN. § 377.01–377.05 (Cum. Supp. 1947).

[21] Daily Democrat, Tallahassee, May, 24, 1945, p. 1, col. 8.

language easy to understand. In substance the statute prohibits the waste of oil and gas,[22] defines reasonable market demand,[23] and allocates to the State Board of Conservation jurisdiction and control over persons and property necessary to administer and enforce the Act. It is the duty of the Board to make proper inquiries to determine the existence of waste and take action to stop its continuance. The Board is given the right to provide by rules and regulations for the proper administration of Florida law to prohibit wells being drilled or operated in a manner causing injury to neighboring leases and property, to prevent drowning by water of strata capable of producing oil or gas in paying quantities and restriction of irregular and premature water encroachment, to require efficient gas-oil ratios, to regulate secondary recovery, to allocate and limit production of oil or gas to prevent waste, to regulate gas cycling, to require certificates of tender, to regulate spacing and establish drilling units, to forbid reasonably avoidable unequalized drainage from developed units, and to provide for ratable taking from pools. In the prevention of waste the statute commands the Board to create drilling units for pools after hearings. These areas are defined and wells must be centered geographically in a unit unless this direction be burdensome. If exceptions are granted by the Board, any advantages gained must be offset. Should two or more owners of separately

---

[22] Waste in addition to its ordinary meaning means physical waste as that term is generally understood in the oil and gas industry, and includes: A. The inefficient, excessive or improper use or dissipation of reservoir energy; and the locating, spacing, drilling, equipping, operating or producing of any oil or gas well or wells in a manner which results, or tends to result, in reducing the quantity of oil or gas ultimately to be recovered from any pool in this state. B. The inefficient storing of oil; and the locating, spacing, drilling, equipping, operating or producing of any oil or gas well or wells in a manner causing, or tending to cause, unnecessary or excessive surface loss or destruction of oil or gas. C. Producing oil or gas in such a manner as to cause unnecessary water channeling or coning. D. The operation of any oil well or wells with an inefficient gas-oil ratio. E. The drowning with water of any stratum or part thereof, capable of producing oil or gas. F. Underground waste however caused and whether or not defined. G. The creation of unnecessary fire hazards. H. The escape into the open air, from a well producing both oil and gas in excess of the amount which is necessary in the efficient drilling or operation of the well. I. The use of gas for the manufacture of carbon black. J. Permitting gas produced from a gas well to escape into the air. K. Abuse of the correlative rights and opportunities of each owner of oil and gas in a common reservoir due to non-uniform, disproportionate and unratable withdrawals, causing undue drainage between tracts of land.

[23] That amount of oil reasonably needed for current consumption, together with a reasonable amount of oil for storage and working stocks.

held tracts within a unit agree to integrate their interests in one unit the law legalizes their conduct. Where these owners do not agree to bring together their holdings for waste prevention purposes, the Board may order forcible integration. To halt waste the agency permits or requires gas cycling for repressure purposes to carry out secondary recovery projects and maintain pressures. Pooling is ordered if necessary to implement cycling operational orders, after notice and hearing. When the total amount of produced oil or gas exceeds reasonable market demand requirements, the Board limits total production by establishing an allowable among pools in a manner to avoid discrimination and prevent waste. It is believed that the commission is authorized to regulate disposal of salt water and contaminated brines. There are no provisions respecting establishment of oil or gas well head prices nor restrictions upon the exportation of natural gas from Florida, due to insufficient production in the state.

THE STATE BOARD OF CONSERVATION

The State Board of Conservation created by the conservation Act consists of the governor, the secretary of state, the attorney general, the state comptroller, the state treasurer, the superintendent of public instruction and the commissioner of agriculture and is vested with power to administer and enforce the law. These constitutional Florida officials are elected for four year terms and with the exception of the governor may succeed themselves in office. As the group's duties require much time these men may not be able to assume increased responsibilities, if Florida becomes a large oil and gas producing state. An amendment to the existing statute substituting another agency may then become needful. The Act creates the post of Secretary to the Board who is to keep records and minutes of the agency, collect and remit to the state treasurer monies collected, account to the Board for funds received, and perform varied requirements. He need not be a member of the body. The agency determines the number, qualifications, duties and compensation of employees assisting in administering and enforcing the law. No one in the employ of the administrative organization may hold official connection or position with a person or entity buying or selling mineral leases, drilling for oil or gas, producing, transporting, refining, or distributing petroleum. All appointments of employees are made by the governor. None have been hired at this date. The Board incurs necessary expenses in the performance of its responsibilities, but no provision is made to pay salaries to its members. Tallahassee has been established as the location of the Board's office where its records are maintained.

No rule, regulation or order, including changes, renewals or extensions absent an emergency are made by the Board except after a public hearing with at least seven days notice publicly given in a form and manner prescribed by agency procedure. Where an emergency exists in the opinion of the commission it issues rules, regulations or orders as valid as if hearing and notice had been had which remain in force 30 days. These temporary provisions expire when rules, regulations or orders made after notice and hearing become effective. The Board prescribes its rules of order and procedure. Rules of legal evidence are applied. Erroneous findings by the agency with respect to admissibility of evidence do not vitiate its action. The right exists by written request to have a called hearing of the agency. The commission, its members or specified persons hold hearings, conduct inquiries and make investigations at times, places and in a manner as they determine. When a meeting of the entire membership is called, a majority constitutes a quorum with power to act. Findings and determinations of less than a quorum or made by people designated by the agency are final and conclusive unless modified upon Board or judicial review. Less than a quorum cannot adopt, amend or repeal general rules, regulations or orders. November 9, 1945 after notice and public hearing, the agency adopted general rules and regulations governing Florida oil and gas conservation.[24] These rules provide that all hearings be held in the office at Tallahassee unless otherwise noted in its procedure. Notice of hearing gives date, place and subject matter of the meeting and is served upon interested persons by mail and through public announcement in the press. Waste is defined in the rules as it is in the conservation statute. Suitable provision is made for the following: applications to drill or deepen, spacing, identifying wells,

[24] Fla. State Board of Conservation, General Rules and Regulations, 1945. Obtainable through the Secretary of State, Capitol Building, Tallahassee.

well reports, sealing oil, gas and water strata, notice of intention to plug, plugging methods and procedure, plugging of seismic, core and exploratory holes, casing requirements, blow-out prevention, drilling fluids, well head fittings, tubing, chokes, ratable taking, gas-oil ratios, certifications of compliance and authority to transport, potential gauges and gas measurement, metering of gas, gas utilization, use of gas for purposes other than light or fuel, transportation and related subjects. No mention is made of: repressuring, cycling, secondary recovery, disposal of salt and contaminated waters, restrictions on carbon black manufacture and market demand, as these are unimportant in Florida's infant industry. The Board will not promulgate rules until needed for waste prevention and market demand stabilization.

The commission or its members are empowered to issue subpoenas for witnesses, require their attendance, the giving of testimony and the production of books, records and papers material to lawful questions of the Board. Subpoenas are served by a sheriff or authorized officers handling process in the state. Refusal to comply with the subpoena, to testify, or to answer lawful interrogations permits the agency to apply to state circuit courts to compel obedience. Failure thereafter subjects the recusant to punishment for contempt as in case of contumacy to like orders or requests of Florida courts. The Board is authorized to sue persons violating or threatening to disobey the statutes respecting conservation of oil or gas in the Circuit Court of Leon County or in a circuit court where the well is located to restrain the continuance of the threat or infraction. The Board obtains injunctions—prohibitory and mandatory—including temporary restraining orders and injunctions, as the facts warrant, including when appropriate injunctions restraining persons from moving or disposing of illegal oil, gas or product. The non-lawful commodities are impounded or placed in the control of a receiver. In case the Board fails to present its suit within ten days after giving of notice any interested person adversely affected may sue. Where the court holds injunctive relief proper the Board is made a party and substituted for that person bringing the action. An injunction then issues as though the Board were the complainant. Penalties for non-compliance with the enactments and administrative regulations are $100 a day for each violation.

Making misleading entries or statements of fact in required reports and destroying records are misdemeanors punishable by fines not exceeding $500, imprisonment of not more than six months, or both.

Authority to require (generally or locally) certificates of clearance and tender in connection with the transport of oil, gas or product lies in the agency. Until the commission provides for these certificates in a manner giving persons opportunity to determine the lawfulness of contemplated transactions or administrative provision is made to identify the characteristics of the commodity, no damages are imposed, unless these people know illegal oil, gas or product is involved. Seizure and condemnation of illegal oil, gas or product is provided in the statutes together with agency procedural rules. Interested persons adversely affected by the enactments, rules, regulations or orders made or threatened to be made by the administrative body—who have first exhausted their agency remedies—may obtain court review and relief by suits for injunctions against the agency or its members in chancery courts of the county or counties where their property is situated or the Chancery Court of Leon County. These suits take precedence on the docket. Trial is *de novo*. Burden of proof rests with the plaintiff. The court is not bound by factual findings of the agency and all legal evidence with respect to validity and reasonableness is admissible. Provisions of the law, and the rules, regulations or orders complained of are prima facie valid. Such a presumption is not overcome by verified bill or affidavit. No temporary restraining order or injunction is granted unless due notice is given at least one Board member, or its secretary, and a hearing had where legal evidence demonstrates that the act done or about to be performed is without lawful sanction, invalid and unreasonable and causing irreparable harm. Temporary injunctions against the Board, its members, agents, employees, and representatives are ineffective until the plaintiff gives a bond in the amount and conditions ordered by the court. Though this bond is for the use and benefit of those injured by the acts done under the injunctive order, it is payable to the Governor of Florida. Persons claiming injury must sue within six months after final determination of validity, otherwise recovery is barred. Appeals are taken in accord with general state appellate law, and agency actions take precedence over other causes on the supreme court docket.

FLORIDA JUDICIAL HISTORY

Florida courts have had no cases before them for decision covering oil and gas conservation. Similar conservancy laws of Florida have been held constitutional.[25] Common law is Florida law except where abrogated by legislative act or in conflict with the Constitution and laws of the United States.[26] Therefore, irrespective of the conservation statutes, a land owner must use due care to avoid negligent wastage or destruction of oil and gas which lies in a common accumulation under another's land.[27] Rules and regulatory actions of administrative agencies have been upheld in the state where the power to make and enforce such activities is lawfully conferred. Courts approve giving of authority by commissions to subordinate employees where the delegation is by legislative fiat.[28] The Bar generally believes the Act constitutional and that the Florida courts will sanction Board actions unless palpably invalid.

AN APPRAISAL OF CONSERVATION

Reaction of the major companies and the independents to the conservation statute is good, and the public accepts the measure of necessity. Florida is not unaccustomed to conservation statutes, as the state has had a program to preserve forests, soil, game, fish, and other products for many years. Protection of oil and gas from waste follows a usual local course. Florida is an outstanding example of a state that set out to gain the ultimate in benefits from natural resources. Florida adopted a conservation law at a time when there was no assurance of large commercial oil and gas production. Our legislation is good and perhaps better than in other jurisdictions. The administrative officers made a proper start by adopting satis-

[25] As to the State Board of Conservation, Fla. Laws 1937, c. 17,917; FLA. STAT. ANN. § 373.01–373.26 (1941); see Coleman v. State, 144 Fla. 488, 198 So. 695 (1940); the State Plant Board, Fla. Laws 1927, c. 12,291; FLA. STAT. ANN. § 581.01–581.14 (1941); see Richardson v. Baldwin, 124 Fla. 233, 168 So. 255 (1936).

[26] FLA. STAT. ANN. § 2.01 (1941).

[27] Eliff v. Texon Drilling Co., Tex., 210 S.W. 2d 558 (1948).

[28] State v. Apalachicola Northern R.R., 81 Fla. 394, 88 So. 310 (1921).

factory rules and regulations of general import, and no doubt will strictly administer the law in fairness with the aim of obtaining the highest efficient recovery. Our judicial background demonstrates a predisposition to approve saving of natural resources and regulations made of the public benefit. We are ready for large scale production of oil and gas in Florida.

CHAPTER 8

Georgia, 1915–1948

~/~

Nineteen hundred and fifteen saw the beginning of interest in Georgia as a potential oil and gas state. In that year the United States Geological Survey and the Georgia Geological Survey [1] issued papers showing the geological formations in the coastal plains (which compose some 60 per cent of Georgia) favorably comparing them with known oil producing structures. This gave renewed hope that Georgia might become a producing state. With such a wealth of technical data to draw upon, major oil companies and independents investigated possibilities of oil in the state. Activities began in geophysical and geological field work and in the securing of leases and land holdings.

THE PASSAGE OF CONSERVATION LEGISLATION IN GEORGIA

June 1, 1923 S. W. McCallie, State Geologist, filed with Governor Hardwick a report on the possibilities of petroleum and natural gas production within Georgia.[2] As the Georgia General Assembly convened in regular session, Senator Moore (of the 17 Senatorial District) on July 10, 1923 offered S.B. No. 41: "A bill to be entitled an Act to regulate the drilling of oil and gas wells, and to provide for the preservation of the logs and other data of oil and gas wells, to prevent the unnecessary waste of oil and gas, to regulate the spacing of wells and to provide the right of eminent domain

ROYAL ALFRED McGRAW, WRITER; George M. Bazemore, C. W. Deming, Vance Custer, Liston Elkins, Advisers. (See app. B.)

[1] DEPT. INT., UNITED STATES GEO. SURVEY, PROFESSIONAL PAPERS 90, 90J, 95F, 95I. STATE OF GA. GEO. SURVEY BULL. No. 26.

[2] STATE OF GA. GEO. SURVEY BULL. No. 40, 56.

in the construction of pipe lines, and for other purposes." This bill passed the Senate by a vote of 42 to 0 and was transmitted to the House. Due to congestion of business in the last days of that session, the House failed to take action and the project did not become law. Little information relating to the reasons for the introduction of S.B. No. 41 can be now obtained. Recorded fact fails to show any interested group sponsoring passage. The plan's provisions indicate that the proposed enactment was intended for protection of correlative rights, conservation of natural resources, and preservation for future use of drilling information. Senator Moore may have been influenced by the drilling in 1921 of a test well 12 miles west of Hazlehurst, and another in 1923 in Wheeler County, Georgia, and the growing possibility that oil and gas would be discovered.

Under the terms of this bill, had it become law, prior to drilling an oil or gas well, one must file with the state geologist written notice of intention to drill.[3] A like requirement applied where it was desired to deepen or redrill wells. Change of the numerical designation of a well was barred without first obtaining consent of the state geologist. Other provisions required the owner or operator to sample borings at stated intervals of ten feet. These samples were to be kept by the owner or operator, subject to inspection by the state geologist or his assistants. An accurate drilling log was necessary and filed with the same official. The enactment prevented drilling of wells at points nearer than 200 feet from property lines, and called for spacing so as to extract oil at minimum cost. No new well could be nearer producing or drilling wells than 200 feet. It was unlawful for owners or operators in possession or control of natural gas or oil wells to allow gas to escape into the open air; this provision applied primarily to gas wells. Upon abandonment or cessation of drilling, the owners, operators, and land owners were to properly and securely plug the well using methods found in the law. A uniform lease form for oil and gas interests to be used in Georgia was inserted in the bill, designed to protect the landowner and public. Right of eminent domain was assigned to persons and

---

[3] The notice included: statement of location and sea level elevation, estimate of the depth at which water would be shut out with method used, size and weight of casing and estimate of oil and gas depth.

corporations operating oil or gas wells to secure right of ways for pipe lines for transportation of oil and gas. Before this power could be exercised, it was necessary that the state geologist find there existed sufficient supplies of oil and gas to warrant construction.

After the failure of the general assembly to pass the 1923 bill, little interest in the discovery of oil and gas in Georgia remained. However, sporadic drilling was carried on in the vast coastal plains from 1923 to 1939. Major companies and independents evinced interest in the information there developed. Citizens of the state and civic organizations persisted in their belief that oil and gas would be discovered. In 1939 and 1940 the Georgia Resources Company (financed by citizens of Homerville and Waycross) reported it encountered live oil at 385 to 410 feet [4] in Clinch County near Homerville.

The Waycross and Ware County Chamber of Commerce had been active in accumulating information and data relating to the prospective formations. In 1939 on the strength of the experience assembled and the test made by the Georgia Resources Company, an oil and gas consultant [5] was sent to the Oklahoma City meeting of the Mid-Continent Oil and Gas Association, where he had ample opportunity to reveal his knowledge. This led to further conferences in Tulsa, Pittsburgh, and other cities with representatives of the oil companies. Out of these sessions grew a new and revived interest in Georgia. Majors and independents increased Georgia leases and land holdings. Encouraged by the backing of the Waycross and Ware County Chamber of Commerce, and the sympathetic interest of Governor Ellis Arnall, the Ware County Representatives—Jack Williams, Wayne Hinson, and Senator Minchew of Pearson—agreed to introduce and sponsor at the 1945 regular session a law to prevent waste and to provide for the conservation of oil and gas. C. W. Deming (oil and gas consultant for the Waycross and Ware County Chamber of Commerce) was called upon by Arnall to study oil and gas laws of producing states and compile these codes for use in drafting proper laws for the state. Deming spent two or three months assembling these laws which he turned

---

[4] This test was drilled to 1507 feet and abandoned for lack of funds. Payton, *Progress of Oil Search in Georgia*, Oil Weekly (Sept. 16, 1946) 92.

[5] C. W. Deming, Director, Ga. Oil and Gas Comm.

over to Arnall and the Ware County legislative representatives. R. A. McGraw was asked to prepare a bill for submission in 1945. This Act modeled upon the Arkansas statutes,[6] with one or two minor amendments, the general assembly adopted.

THE CONSERVATION ACT

The enactment—H.B. No. 284[7]—is entitled: "An Act to prevent waste, foster, encourage and provide conservation of crude oil and natural gas, and products thereof, and protect the vested, coequal or correlative rights of owners of crude oil or natural gas, as defined in this Act and in furtherance thereof, creating an Oil and Gas Commission; authorizing it to prescribe rules, regulations and orders; authorizing it to provide for the spacing of wells and to designate drilling units; providing penalties for the violation of the provisions of this Act, and of the rules, regulations and orders of the Commission; providing that the provisions of this Act are severable; repealing all laws in conflict herewith, and for other purposes."

Section One containing the declared purpose for adoption of the statute reads: "Section 1. The General Assembly having knowledge that gas and oil leases are being entered into over a large area of the State, that oil wells are being drilled in different sections seeking the discovery of oil, and recognizing the evils that would become imminent on the discovery of oil in the State were the State without legal means of regulation, therefore, enacts this law for the protection of the public and private interests against such evils as would likely result under such circumstances."

Created under the Act is the Georgia Oil and Gas Commission composed of three members [8] appointed by the governor and with its offices located at Waycross, the Act providing that the headquarters be established in a county seat in the state. Governor Arnall appointed as members of the Commission: George M. Bazemore, Chairman, Waycross; Paul H. Ploeger, Sr., Darien, and J. A. Pope, Alamo, members. The agency organized selecting C. W. Deming

[6] Ark. Acts 1939, Act 105; ARK. DIG. STAT. § 1–27 (Cum. Supp. 1944).
[7] Ga. Laws 1945, No. 366.
[8] Ga. Laws 1945, No. 366, § 2 provides their terms shall be two, four and six years initially and thereafter six years. Each Commissioner must be a citizen and resident of Georgia.

and Liston D. Elkins, both of Waycross, as director and assistant director. Powers given the Commission are broad and comprehensive. It may meet and hold necessary sessions at any time or place. The Commission appoints a director of production and conservation who also acts as its secretary. The board employs assistants, engineers, and other personnel needful to administer and enforce the Act. It is empowered to promulgate rules and regulations for the control of oil and gas production. Investigations, collections of data, examination of properties, leases, papers and records, tests and gauges of oil and gas wells, the making of inspections of tanks, refineries, and means of transportation, and the keeping of records are within its jurisdiction. Authority over persons and property necessary to the proper enforcement of the Act is assigned this group. It may make determinations administratively of the imminence of waste and act to control and prevent its occurrence.

By rules or orders made after hearing the Commission may require the submission of reports, the filing of logs, the fixing of gas-oil ratios, and order operation within those computations, prevent drowning of wells, blowouts, cavings, seepages, fires, ask for identification of ownership of all wells, leases, refineries, tanks, plants, structures, and equipment. The agency regulates shooting, perforation and chemical treatment of wells, the use and operation of secondary recovery techniques, and limits and prorates production and spacing. Drilling, casing, plugging, and making rules to prevent escape of gas and oil between strata are regulated by the Commission. No one may drill without permits issued from the Commission. With the power to hold hearings goes the right to subpoena and swear witnesses, require their attendance at hearings, and the production of papers and records. The Act invokes the aid of the superior court judges in providing that a judge of the superior court may issue attachments against witnesses or parties failing to obey subpoenas or orders to produce documentary evidence. The court may punish for contempt.

Section 15 of the statute provides for court review of the Act, and of rules, regulations or orders adversely affecting interested parties. This review is available by suit, injunction or other appropriate actions filed in the superior court of the country wherein the property is located. Under other sections of this bill the Commission is permitted to sue, collect penalties, condemn and confiscate illegal product and restrain parties seeking to violate the Act. The Attorney General of Georgia represents the Commission as its legal officer. In case of emergency the Solicitor General of the Superior Courts of Georgia acts for the agency until such time as the attorney general takes over the litigation.

Oil [9] and gas [10] are defined in the Act. The enactment prohibits waste [11] of oil and gas.

THE RULES AND REGULATIONS

Proposed rules and regulations were drafted and public hearings convoked to consider these administrative matters. After public notice the agency met in Waycross June 26, 1945. This session was well attended by counsel from both the majors and the independents. A second hearing held August 27, 1945 brought about the adoption of these governing precepts.[12] The rules follow the Act

[9] Ga. Laws 1945, No. 366, § 8c: ". . . . crude petroleum oil, and other hydrocarbons, regardless of gravity . . . produced . . . in liquid form by ordinary production methods, and which are not the result of condensation of gas after it leaves the reservoir."

[10] Ga. Laws 1945, No. 366, § 8d: ". . . all natural gas, including casing-head gas, and all other hydrocarbons not defined as oil. . . ."

[11] Ga. Laws, No. 366, § 8i: " 'Waste' in addition to its ordinary meaning shall mean 'Physical waste' as that term is generally understood in the oil and gas industry . . . (1) The inefficient, excessive or improper use or dissipation of reservoir energy; and the locating, spacing, drilling, equipping, operating or producing of any oil or gas well or wells in a manner which results or tends to result, in reducing the quantity of oil or gas ultimately to be recovered from any pool in this State. (2) The inefficient storing of oil; and the locating, spacing, drilling, equipping, operating or producing of any oil or gas well or wells in a manner causing, or tending to cause, unnecessary or excessive surface loss or destruction of oil or gas. (3) Abuse of the correlative rights and opportunities of each owner of oil or gas in a common reservoir due to non-uniform, disproportionate, and unratable withdrawals causing undue drainage between tracts of land. (4) Producing oil or gas in such manner as to cause unnecessary water channeling or zoning. (5) The operation of any oil well or wells with an inefficient gas-oil ratio. (6) The drowning with water of any stratum or part thereof capable of producing oil or gas. (7) Underground waste however caused and whether or not defined. (8) The creation of unnecessary fire hazards. (9) The escape into the open air, from a well producing both oil and gas, of gas in excess of the amount which is necessary in the efficient drilling or operation of the well. (10) The use of gas for the manufacture of carbon black. (11) Permitting gas produced from a gas well to escape into the air."

[12] State of Ga., Ga. Oil and Gas Comm., General Rules and Regulations Governing the Conservation of Oil and Gas in Georgia. Adopted Aug. 27, 1945, effective Nov. 9, 1945.

and are framed to confer the administration of its sections upon the board. These regulations deal with drilling and production, spacing, well records and logs, gas and water protection, plugging, and items essential for the protection of the public and interested parties. The Act and the adopted rules and regulations are clear, understandable, and have met with approval and favorable comment from those working under their provisions. These regulatory powers are ample to conserve oil and gas, to prevent waste, and to give needed protection. The rules adopted August 27 are general rules and regulations. Special regulations and orders may be issued as required and prevail over general statements of policy. The Act provides that no rule, regulation or order of the agency is valid except after public hearing upon seven days notice. In emergencies the Commission may make, renew, change, or extend an order, rule or regulation not to exceed ten days at a time without hearing. Emergency regulations are supplanted when the Commission holds a regular hearing and issues other instructions. Principal duties of the agency since its creation have been the receipt and issuance of applications for drilling permits, supervision of drilling and plugging, and the requiring of the filing of data and well logs. All drilling is done under control of the Commission.

The Act and the rules, regulations and orders of the Commission have never been challenged in a court.

In 1946 the Interstate Compact to Conserve Oil and Gas amended its By-laws to permit Georgia to become an associate member.[13]

Georgia has had only 32 tests while Florida has drilled 139 wells, Alabama made more than 200 explorations, and Mississippi 300 searches for petroleum before finding oil in commercial quantities. The people of Georgia, the officials in charge of the administration of the oil and gas laws, and the state geologist earnestly believe commercial oil and gas discoveries will occur. Then the passage of this Act will be of advantage to Georgia and to the oil and gas industry.

[13] Interstate Oil Compact Comm., By-Laws, art. IX. Murphy. *The Administrative Mechanism of the Interstate Compact to Conserve Oil and Gas: The Interstate Oil Compact Commission, 1935–1948,* 22 TULANE L. REV. 384, 386 (1948).

CHAPTER 9

Idaho, 1931–1948

Occasional accounts of oil and gas leasing in the State of Idaho appear in the industry press and newspapers, but no oil or gas has been located within the area. Available reports record the fact that as of June 30, 1947 there were in force some eleven oil and gas leases covering 4935 acres of state owned lands.[1] Even with this paucity of interest and development, the Legislature of the State of Idaho has enacted statutes dealing with the drilling and plugging of oil and gas wells. An Act, adopted during the 1931 session,[2] states as its expressed purpose the prevention of improper methods of drilling, and the prohibition of needless waste or destruction of natural gas. It further orders that wells should be *incased* before drilling into the oil or gas bearing formations with specified casing and in a manner to exclude all surface or fresh water from the well and the petroleum formations.[3] Wells to be plugged, upon abandonment or the cessation of further operations, must be filled with "sand or rock sediment . . . and a round, seasoned, wooden plug, at least two feet in length and in diameter equal to the full diameter of the well. . . ." A set of requirements obtains to complete this plugging program.[4] The wasteful use of natural gas is forbidden. Violation of the Act is a misdemeanor.

The same session of the legislature adopted a further enactment [5]

Blakely M. Murphy, Writer. (See app. B.)

[1] Letter from Burton W. Musser, Utah Oil Building, Salt Lake City, Utah, June 23, 1948.

[2] Idaho Sess. Laws 1931, c. 111; Idaho Code Ann. § 46–310–313 (1932).

[3] Idaho Sess. Laws 1931, c. 111, § 2.

[4] *Id.* § 3. The top of the plug was to be filled in to a depth of 5 feet, another sharpened wooden plug driven and the remainder of the hole filled to a depth of 20 feet with rock and sand.

[5] Idaho Sess. Laws 1931, c. 115; Idaho Code Ann. § 46–301–309 (1932).

making it mandatory to keep an accurate log for all oil and gas wells drilled in Idaho, to file a log and samples of formations encountered with the Bureau of Mines and Geology, the University of Idaho, Moscow. All information is required to be kept in a confidential status by the Bureau until (1) the well is abandoned or drilling ceased for at least 90 continuous days, (2) consent in writing of disclosure is filed by the land owner, where unleased, or the owner and lessee if under lease agreement.[6] Failure to comply with this requirement or any portion of the enactment constitutes a misdemeanor punishable by a fine of not less than $25 nor more than $300. Each week the offense continues is a separate offense. With these enactments further legislative interest in the matter of oil and gas control and conservation has ceased in Idaho.[7]

[6] Idaho Sess. Laws 1931, c. 115, §§ 8a, 8b.
[7] Idaho Sess. Laws 1923, c. 96, § 4; IDAHO CODE ANN. § 46–704 (1932).

CHAPTER 10

Illinois, 1889–1948

Oil was first discovered in commercial quantities in 1889, but production was negligible or nonexistent until 1905 when discoveries in Clark, Crawford, Lawrence, and adjoining counties in the eastern part of the state resulted in a production of 181,000 barrels of oil. From 1907 through 1915 the average annual production from this field exceeded 27,500,000 barrels, its highest production in 1908 being 33,500,000 barrels.[1]

THE HISTORY OF LEGISLATIVE ACTIVITY RELATIVE TO CONSERVATION OF PETROLEUM IN ILLINOIS

The only conservation legislation adopted during the flush production period of this field was a well plugging and casing statute enacted in 1905.[2] This Act, similar to the statutes of other oil and gas producing states of its era, prescribed the manner of plugging abandoned wells, required the filing of affidavits of compliance with the law, provided for casing off fresh water strata, and assessed penalties for violations. The Act was amended in 1911 by adding sections relative to drilling of wells near mine openings and through coal seams.[3] It was again changed in 1923 as to the method of well plugging and in holding that these operations be supervised by a mine inspector.[4] In 1933 after the field had become practically depleted by primary recovery, the casing section of the original Act

W. L. SUMMERS, WRITER. (See app. B.)

[1] Petroleum Facts and Figures, 4th ed. 110 (1931).
[2] Ill. Laws 1905, p. 326.
[3] Ill. Laws 1911, p. 426.
[4] Ill. Laws 1923, p. 462.

was revised to permit secondary recovery through the introduction of air, gas, water, or other liquid into producing formations.[5] The old Illinois field was developed in accordance with the practices of its day. Operators drilled as they pleased, moved by the urge to obtain oil as quickly as possible. Thousands of wells were drilled, many unnecessary, and produced at full capacity, resulting in great physical and economic waste. During the flush production period 1906 to 1912 conditions were favorable for an advancing market due to the increasing demand for petroleum products, but the trend of posted crude prices was downward, and large quantities sold below these levels. It was not until the field's production began to decline, caused in a large measure by wasteful practices, that the crude price advanced. In 1910 Illinois operators and royalty owners sold 33,000,000 barrels of oil for less than $20,000,000; by 1920, they sold 10,000,000 barrels for almost $40,000,000. If the supply had been conserved during the period following discovery, the ultimate production and financial return would have been much greater.[6]

The statement that history repeats itself is strikingly applicable to the business of producing oil and gas. Many oil fields in the Illinois Basin have been discovered, produced, and gone into decline during the last decade in the absence of conservation legislation adequate to prevent immeasurable physical and economic waste. The land owners and the people of Illinois have suffered the major burden of this loss, yet presumably they had the power to prevent it. In future years their failure to act may be difficult to explain. The events here detailed which offer an explanation may fade from memory and seem insignificant; but the basic reason is found in the instinct of human beings with respect to the acquisition of property, for "in the production of oil we have an element which finds no counterpart in any of the other major productive adventures. The novice in the business—the man who, without previous experiences of any kind whatever, enters the business overnight, finds production the second night, and the third night ranks as an oil producer who must be reckoned with. Admittedly, these men have both the ethical and economical right to enter the industry. No one

[5] Ill. Laws 1933, p. 715.
[6] Oil & Gas Jour. (Feb. 2, 1939) 15.

would be foolish enough either to deny or impede their taking advantage of what they conceive to be their opportunity, perhaps their only one for a place in the sun. But it does seem within the bounds of reason that when they become producers they should subscribe to the rules accepted by at least 90% of the members of the industry, which rules had their origin in many years of bitter experience, and came to their present state through trial and error. . . . From the days of Pithole through all of the later oil states, the failure of general cooperation for stabilization in time of need through the resistance of the few might be pointed to. This same element has opposed every conservation measure that ever has been offered in the Legislature of any State save, perhaps, New Mexico. . . . But what is the explanation of the attitude of these small minorities? We simply turn to Aristotle's second principle of human nature in relation to the acquisition of property. *Undue and unbridled selfishness, the desire and intent to gain whatever can be gained, without regard to the rights of neighbors and without regard to the common weal.*" [7]

The first move in the direction of oil and gas conservation legislation was made in 1935 when the Interstate Compact to Conserve Oil and Gas was ratified, pledging Illinois to enact conservation laws in conformity with the compact.[8] At that time the average daily production was 12,000 barrels from stripper wells in the oil field and there seemed no pressing need for such legislation. Late in 1936 the initial wells of the first three pools in the Illinois Basin were drilling. Early in 1937 discoveries came in quick succession. By the end of September six pools had been found and the production for that month exceeded 800,000 barrels. An extensive leasing

[7] Veasey, *Compulsory Pooling*, Address delivered before the Section of Mineral Law, American Bar Association (1938). Harold L. Ickes, Secretary of the Interior and Petroleum Coordinator for War, in an address before the St. Louis section of the A.I.M.E. St. Louis, Oct. 1, 1942, speaking of oil and gas production practices in the early days of the industry said: "Those were the days when the watchword in the oil fields was 'Drill on, Macduff, and damned be he who first says "think of the future"—enough!' We may all thank Heaven that those days, in large measure, are gone—not gone entirely, as I used to be reminded when the train carried me through Illinois—but gone so far as the overwhelming majority of oil people is concerned. But, I wonder very seriously and very solemnly, as I stand before you this evening, whether the lesson has been learned *in time.*"

[8] Ill. Laws 1935, p. 1418.

campaign by major companies and independent operators resulted, placing approximately 5,000,000 acres under lease.[9]

At the annual meeting of the Petroleum Division, the Illinois Mineral Industries Conference, held October 8 and 9 at the University of Illinois, William Bell, president of the Illinois-Indiana Petroleum Association and Illinois representative on the Interstate Oil Compact Commission, spoke of the need for state regulation to prevent physical waste of oil and gas. Mr. Bell stated that in view of the new Illinois discoveries and the prospective production in the state, serious consideration must be given to enactment of waste prevention laws. He expressed a belief that support from Governor Horner and the oil industry was forthcoming to secure passage of statutes conforming to the requirements of the Interstate Compact.[10] As a result of his address and the discussion that followed, W. L. Summers was commissioned by the Illinois-Indiana Petroleum Association to draft a conservation act to present to the Illinois legislature. The act, prepared in collaboration with Robert E. Hardwicke, Fort Worth, Texas, and aided by the suggestions and criticisms of many industry lawyers, incorporated what appeared then to be the better features of the conservation laws of New Mexico, Texas, and Oklahoma. It defined and prohibited physical waste, created a commission with jurisdiction and authority over all persons and property necessary to administer and enforce the act and specific authority to make and enforce rules and regulations for certain purposes, including the limitation and proration of produc-

[9] Bell, *Petroleum Developments this Year in the Illinois Basin*, Oil & Gas Jour. (Oct. 21, 1937) 26.

[10] Oil & Gas Jour. (Oct. 14, 1937) 28. Mr. Bell said, in part: "Our treaty with the other oil-producing states binds us in effect to provide, within a reasonable time, appropriate laws for accomplishing the purposes of the compact in this state in cooperation with the other states. The reason we now have no such is that when we had the large flush production here in the early part of the century, control measures of the present nature had never been dreamed of and since our production declined to the stripper stage we have not needed such laws. Now, however, that new fields are being developed and large wells found in Illinois, serious consideration must be given to these changed conditions. The high character of those who represent the producing interests in our new fields, leads us to believe that they will cooperate to protect the interests of the new fields closely along the lines set up by the Interstate Oil Compact and these other producing states. We feel that we will have the very efficient support of our governor in obtaining conservation legislation similar in purpose to that enacted in other oil-producing states, through which will be protected the interests of the state, the industry and the public."

tion, well spacing and the use of reservoir energy. With minor changes this statute was enacted in Arkansas [11] in 1939, and in a number of other states.[12] During the early months of 1938 while the Summers bill was being drafted, criticized and perfected through consultation with representatives of the Illinois-Indiana Petroleum Association, various drafts of it received wide circulation. Some persons, against conservation legislation of any sort, attacked it as a proration act, without regard for the fact that it was a comprehensive conservation measure for waste prevention, which gave the commission authority to limit and prorate production only after a hearing and finding that limitation of production in any pool was necessary for waste prevention.

A special session of the legislature was called May 20. June 7, persons representing the chambers of commerce and civic bodies of some 30 municipalities in the Illinois Basin met at Flora, Illinois, at the call of the Flora Chamber of Commerce, to arouse sentiment against conservation proposals. Mr. Clarence T. Smith, president of this organization, and the principal speaker, said, "Illinois has a right to produce without restriction its own crude oil up to its consumptive requirements. Let no one be fooled that under the guise of 'conservation talk' the budding industry in Illinois should be hampered and stopped by restrictive legislation at this early stage." [13] A resolution was adopted opposing state regulation of the oil industry.[14] The Summers bill was not offered at the special session of the legislature, although a bill embodying all of its provi-

---

[11] Ark. Laws 1939, Act No. 105; Ark. Dig. Stat. § 1–27 (Cum. Supp. 1944).

[12] This proposed legislation, with changes in the sections dealing with the enforcement agency, was introduced in the Mississippi legislature in 1938 as SB 317 and HB 537, but not passed. See Legal History of Conservation of Oil and Gas, 96 (1938). The conservation acts of the following states follow rather closely the provisions of the proposed Illinois statute. Ala. Laws 1945, Act No. 1; Ga. Laws 1945, Act 366; Fla. Laws 1945, c. 22819; La. Acts 1940, Act 157; Laws N.C. 1945, c. 702. A number of conservation bills presented to the Illinois legislature from 1938 to 1941 closely followed the proposal.

[13] Centralia Evening Sentinel, May 8, 1938, gives a full report of this meeting headlined *Illinois Must Not Have State Oil Proration.* See also Oil & Gas Jour. (June 16, 1938) 33, for report of the meeting.

[14] This resolution as published in the Centralia Evening Sentinel, May 8, 1938, was: "Be it resolved by a group of citizens of the State of Illinois assembled in meeting at Flora, Ill., this 7th day of June, 1938, as representatives of the various present and future oil producing areas of the state that: "First—We are unalterably opposed to any legislation seeking to control or regulate the production of crude oil within this state until such time as our state production shall have attained a volume

sions and giving the Illinois Commerce Commission jurisdiction to enforce them was introduced, but did not pass.[15] A number of other bills and resolutions affecting the oil industry were presented,[16] but all failed except the one authorizing municipalities to grant permits to drill wells within their corporate limits.[17]

During the summer of 1938 the Illinois Legislative Council[18] made an extensive survey of the oil and gas industry in Illinois and the conservation laws of other states.[19] Governor Horner was reported in favor of adequate statutes and hopeful of their enactment.[20] Late in November the Council met in Springfield, presumably to draft a program for presentation at the 61st General Assembly in January 1939; but it merely voted to submit its report

---

equal to at least the consumptive requirements of the state; "Second—Be it further resolved that copies of this resolution be sent to the Honorable Henry M. Horner, Governor; the Honorable Lieutenant Governor, John Stelle, and all members of the Legislature of the State of Illinois."

[15] HB No. 65, introduced by Representative Boyle June 14 and tabled June 27. Speaking of this bill and HB No. 64, defining common purchases of oil and requiring ratable taking, it is said in Oil & Gas Jour. (June 30, 1938) 31, "The measures have met with such opposition that they may either die in committee or be reported unfavorably at this session. Many members are unfamiliar with the complexities of the oil business and appear to be giving ear to the slogan, 'No proration until Illinois' production equals Illinois' consumptive demands.'"

[16] Bills and resolutions introduced at this session favorable to oil and gas conservation were as follows: HB No. 64, introduced by Representative Boyle, defining common purchasers and requiring ratable taking of oil; HB No. 52, authorizing pooling of tracts to prevent unnecessary wells; HB No. 84, creating a commission to investigate the need for oil and gas conservation legislation; HR No. 5 creating a committee to investigate the need of conservation legislation. Bill and resolutions introduced which were unfavorable to oil and gas conservation were as follows: HB No. 51, requiring the drilling of offset wells; HJR No. 9, declaring it to be unjust, discriminating and contrary to public policy for any agency or authority to prorate the production of crude oil until such time as the production at least equals the consumption of oil in the state.

[17] Ill. Laws, 1st Spec. Sess. 1938, p. 16.

[18] The Legislative Council, consisting of ten senators and ten representatives, with the lieutenant governor and the speaker of the house as ex-officio members, was created by Ill. Laws 1937, p. 211.

[19] Professor Charles M. Kneier of the University of Illinois, director of research, and J. F. Isakoff, assistant director, prepared the report.

[20] See Oil & Gas Jour. (Sept. 8, 1938) 35, quoting from a written statement made by Governor Horner as to his views on conservation. After mentioning complaints of discrimination by pipe line companies against small producers, close drilling and sales of crude under posted prices, he said: "You may be assured, however, that as long as I am governor of Illinois every effort will be put forth to obtain fair legislation on the subject. Revenue for the state is a matter of secondary importance— since it is so small a matter in this case—but conservation of our resources and protection of the citizens of our state against reckless exploitation is all important."

without recommendation for legislation. This action came after Lieutenant Governor John Stelle vigorously opposed any restriction on oil production, stating there should be no limitation on production until it equalled state consumption.[21] Those against such legislation made the first move in the impending struggle, again resorting to the mass assembly technique. At a meeting sponsored by the Illinois Independent Oil Operators and Royalty Owners Association, Stelle stated that the motive of those urging proration under the guise of conservation was to make it impossible for smaller operators to continue, and that the enactment of conservation legislation would retard and destroy development, resulting in business depression and unemployment.[22] While lines of battle were being drawn on this issue, the oil industry and producers had become disturbed over marketing problems resulting from excessive and steadily rising Illinois Basin production. In 1938 this totaled 23,601,000 barrels, a gain of 200 per cent over 1937.[23] The forecast for 1939 more than doubled that amount.[24] Pipe line proration had been in full operation for some time in the more productive pools and more than 30,000 barrels daily were marketed to independent refineries at prices 16 to 25 per cent below the posted figure of $1.15.[25] These were the conditions that caused the Illinois Independent Oil Operators and Royalty Owners Association to change its policy and announce through its president, John Pugh, that it had taken a "definite stand for orderly development of the oil resources of Illinois." But a new group, the Petroleum Association of Illinois, was soon created to stalemate all conservation proposals.[26]

In his message to the legislature Governor Horner urged careful consideration of the statutes governing the oil industry, but made

[21] Oil & Gas Jour. (Dec. 1, 1938) 21.

[22] Oil Weekly (Dec. 12, 1938) 55. Oil Weekly (Dec. 19, 1938) 69. In announcing the meeting, the association sponsoring it said that oil conservation legislation "will limit production and thus force producers and landowners in Illinois to wait years for oil money which they are entitled to receive now, and will hamstring Illinois' development to the advantage of other oil producing states and certain oil interests."

[23] Oil Weekly (Jan. 30, 1939) 195.

[24] Oil Weekly (Feb. 13, 1939) 71.

[25] Oil & Gas Jour. (Dec. 15, 1938) 16, Oil & Gas Jour. (Jan. 12, 1939) 25.

[26] Oil & Gas Jour. (Mar. 9, 1939) 32, Oil & Gas Jour. (Mar. 30, 1939) 55. Mr. Pugh stated that "some operators were able to sell 20 to 50 barrels a day from each well at the posted price of $1.15 but other operators were selling several hundred barrels a day per well from offset wells for as little as 50 to 65 cents."

no specific recommendations, stating "it should be kept in mind that the daily consumption of these products in our state is still many times our present production." [27] From this it seems he may have been influenced by the slogan of those against conservation.[28] Before the session opened Governor Horner became ill and Lieutenant Governor Stelle, the most outspoken opponent of conservation, took over as acting governor.[29] In March a legislative committee was created to investigate the oil industry in Illinois and report its findings.[30] The committee held hearings during April at Salem, Champaign, Centralia, and Mattoon where many persons expressed their views relative to the need for regulatory oil and gas laws. At Salem most of those giving testimony favored the enactment of legislation to include limitation of production, proration, and well spacing.[31] A representative of the Pure Oil Company was opposed to limitation of production until consumption exceeded production. At the Champaign hearing nineteen witnesses were examined, a great majority of whom strongly favored statutes to establish restrictions on production, proration, and well spacing; [32] only two witnesses expressed contrary views.[33] Independent producers, refiners, pipe line owners, lawyers, and business men gave testimony at the Centralia hearing, where most of those witnesses

[27] Oil Weekly (Jan. 23, 1939) 74.

[28] See note 13 *supra*.

[29] Oil Weekly (Feb. 27, 1939) 193.

[30] HJR No. 28. For the personnel of this committee see Oil & Gas Jour. (Feb. 16, 1939) 34.

[31] The following is a partial list of the witnesses who testified at the hearing: W. C. Neal, Texas Company; William A. Watkins, Carter Oil Company; C. F. Buchner, W. C. McBride, Inc.; Robert McIlvain, Jr., Pure Oil Company; Ernest G. Robinson, Shell Oil Co., Inc.; E. J. Bergundthal, Continental Oil Co.; E. E. Welch, Illinois Pipe Line Co.; C. C. Carroll, Ohio Oil Co.; Frank Wilson, Sohio Pipe Line Co. See Oil & Gas Jour. (Apr. 13, 1939) 22 for report of this conference.

[32] The following is a partial list of the witnesses who testified at the hearing: Dr. John W. Frey, U.S. Department of the Interior; G. H. Blankenship, independent producer; Dr. A. H. Bell, geologist, Illinois State Geological Survey; Dr. W. F. Voskuil, mineral economist, Illinois State Geological Survey; Prof. Frank W. DeWolf, Head of the Department of Geology, University of Illinois; Prof. W. L. Summers, University of Illinois College of Law; Clarence T. Smith, lawyer; Lynn K. Lee, geologist, Pure Oil Company; Russell B. Brown, Washington Counsel for the Independent Petroleum Association of America; Maxwell Miller, geologist, Texas Company; William K. Kneale, geologist, Texas Company; Vernon Jones, geologist, Magnolia Petroleum Co.; C. J. Hares, geologist, Ohio Oil Co.; Ernest G. Robinson, Shell Oil Co. See Oil & Gas Jour. (Apr. 20, 1939) 76 and Oil Weekly (Apr. 17, 1939) 56 for reports of this hearing.

[33] Clarence T. Smith, lawyer; Lynn K. Lee, geologist, Pure Oil Co.

were opposed to conservation legislation, although some independent producers spoke in favor of it.[34] At Mattoon independent producers favored and independent refiners were against it.[35] May 17, 1939 the committee made its report,[36] one paragraph of which stated: "A close, deliberate study of all the evidence by the committee has led to the conclusion that there is no necessity at this time of enacting laws regulating proration, economic conservation and ratable taking. It is the belief of this committee that such laws would be more harmful than beneficial . . . and would operate without justification to curtail an expanding industry. The committee bases its conclusion upon the fact that there is definitely no evidence either of overproduction of oil or disruption of the price market and no immediate fear of either . . . it appears that refineries will not come to this State . . . unless there exists reasonable assurance that they could purchase sufficient crude to operate at full capacity. This necessary insurance is lacking if laws are enacted providing for proration, conservation and ratable taking." It seems incredible that the committee, charged as it was with a special public duty, could have made such a report in face of the great preponderance of evidence favorable to conservation proposals and the facts of physical and economic waste known in production practices.

When the committee made its report, daily average production

[34] See Oil & Gas Jour. (Apr. 27, 1939) 20, for a report of this hearing. A partial list of those who testified is as follows: Sam D. Jarvis, independent producer; L. B. Manley, independent pipe line owner; E. C. Hines, Eagle Oil Co.; George Harsh, Jr., Frontier Oil Co.; John Pugh, independent producer; J. J. Taxman, Advance Refining Co.; C. A. Sheppard, independent producer; A. E. Groehe, Centralia Refining Co.; Lee H. Jonas, lawyer; J. C. Belmont, independent producer; L. A. Matthew, independent producer; John H. Wall, independent producer. John Pugh and C. A. Sheppard, independent producers, favored regulation of production.

[35] See Oil & Gas Jour. (May 4, 1939) 19, for a report of this meeting. A partial list of those testifying is as follows: A. R. Thompson, independent producer; C. C. Cummings, independent producer; Ben Loomis, independent driller and producer; C. F. Buckner, W. C. McBride, Inc., independent producer; George M. Pfau of Texarkana, Tex., independent refiner; Cotterman Production Co., East Texas independent refiner.

[36] ILL. SEN. JOUR. 1939, p. 586. Clarence T. Smith, of Flora, Illinois, one of the outstanding opponents of conservation legislation at the time, is reported to have characterized the report of the committee as "definite encouragement to independent operators, refiners and crude oil purchasers to extend and enlarge their operations, and is an open invitation to outside independent operators, refiners and purchasers to enter the Illinois fields, thereby assuring further exploration and development of known fields and also many new areas." Oil Weekly (May 22, 1939) 63.

had reached a new high of 221,000 barrels, the posted field price had been reduced from $1.15 to $1.05 and 54,200 barrels daily were sold, most of it to the skimming plants, at 33 cents under posted figures.[37] Apart from considerations of economic waste, great physical wastage was also taking place due to the drilling of hundreds of unnecessary wells, permitting wells to flow unchecked (with a resulting high gas-oil ratio), wasting reservoir energy, and decreasing amounts of ultimate production.[38] In addition, casing-head-gas, apart from small quantities used in drilling and processed in natural gasoline plants, was burned in flares. During the year of the committee report, it was estimated that 95 percent of the gas produced with oil in the new fields, some 134,000,000,000 cubic feet, was flared. Gas wastage in this year was equivalent to more than 5,000,000 tons of bituminous coal in heating value and that

[37] Oil & Gas Jour. (June 15, 1939) 82, Oil & Gas Jour. (June 22, 1939) 29.

[38] See Chicago Journal of Commerce, (Mar. 29, 1943) p. 8, where it is said, in part, "There has been and there continues to be physical waste in the production of oil in Illinois, according to the State Geological Survey. This waste is mainly of two kinds: (1) the drilling of too many wells in and adjacent to small tracts and (2) the waste of gas by burning it in flares because of lack of facilities for transporting and marketing it. It is estimated gas equal in fuel value to 16,000,000 tons of bituminous coal have been wasted in six years from 1937 through 1942. However, loss in fuel value of the gas is not nearly so important as loss of a valuable agent in the recovery of oil. In most Illinois pools the only gas present is dissolved in the oil under pressures in the reservoir rocks. In the process of withdrawing oil through wells, the pressure is released as oil comes to the surface and gas comes out of solution. It is therefore impossible to avoid producing some gas along with oil. However, it has been found experimentally in some fields that when wells are permitted to flow unchecked the gas-oil ratio (no. of cu. ft. of gas produced per barrel of oil) is excessively high. Another practice found worth while in many areas is to pump gas back into oil sands to maintain reservoir pressure." The information upon which this article was based was furnished by the State Geological Survey. Bell and Cohee, *Oil and Gas Development in Illinois in 1939,* Illinois Petroleum (July 13, 1940) 35. On page 38 the authors say: "Unlike most of the major oil-producing states, Illinois does not have any comprehensive law providing for the conservation of oil and gas. Although the greater number of the oil-producing operations are being carried on efficiently, the existence of wasteful practices in some areas must be recognized. The burning of large quantities of natural gas in flares, particularly in the Salem pool, represents a loss of reservoir energy, which if utilized by returning the gas to the oil sand would result in a substantially greater ultimate recovery of oil. The drilling of many wells in a small area, as for example in parts of the Salem pool and on town lots in Centralia, is not only an economic loss but will also result in physical waste through the premature abandonment of wells." At the Champaign hearing of the legislative committee the men who furnished this information to the Chicago Journal of Commerce, including Dr. Alfred H. Bell, petroleum geologist, State Geological Survey, were witnesses. This same information could have elicited from them had the committee really been concerned with finding the facts relative to physical waste of oil and gas.

waste in 1939 and 1941 was more than the total Illinois gas consumption in the same years with consumer value of $120,000,000. The entire waste of gas flared from 1937 through 1942 amounted to 416,000,000,000 cubic feet, the equivalent in heating value of 16,000,000 tons of bituminous coal. Greatest wastage occurred in 1939; [39] this was no secret, for the burning flares of these fields could be seen at night for fifty miles. Much of this waste could have been prevented by the enactment of a statute defining physical, underground and surface waste, authorizing an administering agency to make rules and regulations for well spacing, use of efficient gas-oil ratios, and utilization of oil field gas by processing it for natural gas or reintroduction into formations to maintain reservoir energy.

In its report the committee recommended passage of two bills having some conservancy value—one to amend the existing well plugging statute and the other to require filing of drilling reports with the geological survey and the department of mines and minerals. Also recommended for passage was a bill which required drilling of offset wells, despite the fact that one of the principal causes of physical waste was the drilling of such wells. Approximately 40 bills and joint resolutions respecting oil and gas were introduced in 1939. Two identical measures defined and prohibited waste, created a commission to administer the law, giving it authority to make rules and regulations for waste prevention, and included the establishment of drilling units and restriction of production. [40] Two further identical bills defined common purchasers and required them to buy without discrimination. [41] Seven bills sought to regulate the drilling, casing, and plugging of wells. [42] Numerous additional measures were introduced which affected the production and marketing of oil, some of which would have increased rather

[39] Peterson, *Natural Gas Operations in Illinois*, I Interstate Oil Compact Q. Bull., 58 (1942). Oil & Gas Jour. (Oct. 8, 1942) 25. Statement made by Harold L. Ickes, in an address before the A.I.M.E. Oct. 1, 1942. Oil & Gas Jour. (Oct 8, 1942) 39. Statement made by William B. Heroy.

[40] These two measures, HB No. 999 and HB No. 1034 were substantially the proposed act drafted by the writer in 1938 for the Illinois-Indiana Petroleum Association. The language of the important sections is practically identical.

[41] H.B. No. 1000 and HB No. 1033. Six other bills, HB Nos. 397, 450, 981, and SB Nos. 27, 85 and 255 sought to regulate pipe lines and other purchasers of oil.

[42] HB Nos. 397, 1079, 1080 and SB Nos. 82, 192, 511 and 519.

than prevented waste.[43] The only proposals enacted into law which could be regarded as conservation measures were H. B. No. 1079,[44] requiring drilling logs be filed with the State Geological Survey, and H. B. No. 1080,[45] amending existing statutes relating to plugging abandoned wells. The Interstate Oil Compact was extended to September 1, 1941.[46]

Failure of the Illinois legislature to enact a conservation law during the 1939 session brought forth a storm of criticism [47] and

[43] SB Nos. 83, 448, and 450 required the drilling of offset. SB No. 83 was passed but was vetoed by Governor Horner. HB Nos. 170 and 223 provided that if a driller did not produce oil within 60 days after the commencement of drilling he be required to abandon and plug the well. HB No. 108 provided that if a lessee did not commence drilling within 90 days after the date of his lease, or the effective date of the act, the lease would be void. HB No. 169 prohibited landowners from selling more than 50 per cent of their royalty interests. SB No. 451 required lessees to pay royalty owners the posted market price for oil without regard to the price received by lessees. SB No. 546 required purchasers of oil not to purchase other production until that of "strippers wells" had been sold or disposed of. HB No. 386 required state inspection of wells to determine the quantity and quality of oil produced. HB Nos. 171 and 397 required operators to post bonds to insure compliance with the terms of their leases. SB No. 512 required the metering of oil and gas between the well and pipe line or storage tank. SB No. 607 sought to create a commission to study oil and gas laws. HJR No. 10 encouraged the use of petroleum products manufactured from crude oil produced in Illinois.

[44] Ill. Laws 1939, p. 806.

[45] Ill. Laws 1939, p. 792.

[46] Ill. Laws 1939, p. 795.

[47] Secretary of the Interior Ickes said: "When the California law becomes effective 90 per cent (of oil produced in the United States) will be subject to conservation laws. Illinois, now ranking fifth in production and producing about 5 per cent of the national out put, will remain as the only large oil-producing state which has not adopted legislation to conserve the oil and gas resources within its borders." Oil & Gas Jour. (July 6, 1939) 16. See also Oil & Gas Jour. (Sept. 7, 1939) 37, where it is said: "Secretary Ickes last week bitterly excoriated forces in Illinois which are opposing oil proration legislation. In doing so he absolved Gov. Henry L. Horner of any blame in the failure of the state to act, alleging that major blame should be fastened on Lieutenant Governor John Stelle and the Pure Oil Co. He admitted, however, that Pure has now withdrawn its opposition to state legislation." See Oil & Gas Jour. (Oct. 12, 1939) 28 to the effect that on Oct. 6, 1939, Henry M. Dawes, president of Pure Oil Company, issued a statement favoring a conservation law for Illinois. McIntyre, Oil & Gas Jour. (July 27, 1939) 60, said: "Efforts were made by conservative and experienced Illinois producers to induce the legislature to pass a conservation law, as in New Mexico, Kansas, Oklahoma and Texas, but without success, as the opposition was able to out talk those in favor of such a measure, and the legislators, knowing little of the many problems surrounding the petroleum industry, appeared to think they were doing the state a favor by exhausting its oil resources as rapidly as possible." Smiley, Oil & Gas Jour. (July 27, 1939) 68, reporting the meeting of the Interstate Compact Commission at Santa Fe, New Mexico, said: "It was inevitable that Illinois should be a target of criticism because of its failure to enact a conservation law; but though resentment flared at times during the session,

a period of pessimism among the advocates of conservation. It was not long, however, until hopes for the enactment of conservation legislation revived. Daily Illinois production of crude by August 1 was approximately 275,000 barrels; the market was tight as evinced by the posted prices for 40 degree gravity oil in newly discovered field ranging from 80 to 85 cents per barrel.[48] While production in Illinois continued to increase, shut downs of wells in Texas, Oklahoma, Kansas, Louisiana, Arkansas, and New Mexico, decreased average daily production in the United States about 1,500,000 barrels.[49] The reduction in crude prices in Illinois and the market effect of the shut downs elsewhere at last convinced certain opponents of conservation of the necessity of regulating production in Illinois.[50] Associations of Illinois producers were reported to agree upon the need for conservation law; they drafted a proposal and circulated petitions asking Governor Horner to call a special session of the legislature.[51] Even Lieutenant Governor Stelle was said to have made four suggestions which included

---

there was nothing but friendly regard for Dr. Bell [Illinois representative]." An editorial in Oil & Gas Jour. (Aug. 17, 1939) 32, discussing price cuts in crude and the market situation, stated: "In the matter of controlling production from these reserves, the application of conservation regulations must be based on an equitable withdrawing among leases, fields and states. Illinois has been the outstanding violator of these rules. In insisting on maintaining the position of an outlaw, the state has much to answer for in the unsatisfactory market developments of the past two years, affecting not only its own operators but the entire industry. Its blind policy has given the supporters of federal control a strong argument."

[48] Oil & Gas Jour. (Aug. 3, 1939) 18.

[49] Oil & Gas Jour. (Aug. 24, 1939) 23.

[50] An editorial in Oil & Gas J. (Sept. 21, 1939) 65, said: "It has taken a near debacle in which the entire country shared, to cause Illinois to see the light. It is now considered probable that the state will shortly enact a law which will materially contribute to the stabilization of the operations in Illinois and directly benefit the Mid-Continent and middle western area."

[51] Oil & Gas. Jour. (Aug. 31, 1939) 16, (Sept. 7, 1939) 30 and 37, (Sept. 14, 1939) 30. The associations involved were the Illinois-Indiana Petroleum Association, which had favored conservation from the beginning, Independent Oil Producers Association of Illinois and the Petroleum Association of Illinois. See Oil & Gas Jour. (Oct. 12, 1939) 28, for a statement issued Oct. 6, by Henry M. Dawes, president of Pure Oil Company, favoring the enactment of a conservation law. The following is the concluding paragraph of Mr. Dawes' statement: "As matters now stand, it is my opinion that the total amount which will be recovered from the oil resources of the state will be much larger and the costs much less if reasonable regulations are adopted, and of course, the prosperity of the state and the individuals engaged in or affected by the industry will be increased. Conditions which prevailed only a short time ago were not such as to necessitate an action which now seems to be imperative!"

restriction of production and ratable taking as the basis of a conservation act.[52] Governor Horner favored conservation legislation, and considered adding it to the call of a special session of the legislature.[53] It seemed that Illinois would soon fulfill its repeated pledge made to the other states of the Interstate Oil Compact by enacting adequate conservation legislation.

This apparent unanimity of view among representatives of the oil industry and government respecting oil and gas conservation was destined to be of short duration. When the three associations completed and made public their draft of a conservation measure to present at the proposed special session of the legislature, protest arose. The newest of the oil industry organizations, Illinois Producers Equity Association, adopted a resolution which it sent to Governor Horner asking that no oil control legislation be considered at the special session, on the ground that Illinois production was not a threat to the stability of the national crude markets.[54] Another oil organization, the Illinois Protective Oil League, organized to combat conservation legislation, maintained that producers should be free of state interference.[55] On October 19 when the

[52] Oil & Gas Jour. (Sept. 7, 1939) 37.
[53] Oil Weekly (Oct. 23, 1939) 49, Oil & Gas Jour. (Oct. 19, 1939) 32, Governor Horner is reported to have said in a press conference that if a conservation bill could be drafted which would meet the approval of Illinois oil men generally he would call a special session of the legislature making the conservation measure a subject of the call. This report quotes him as having said, "Illinois is the only big producing state without a regulatory program and I favor such a program." See also Oil Weekly. (Oct. 16, 1939) 46.
[54] Oil Weekly (Oct. 16, 1939) 46. George Harsh, Jr., Frontier Oil Company, Centralia, was president of this organization and Dorsey Hager, Centralia, its technical adviser. In explaining the stand of his organization Mr. Hager is quoted in Oil Weekly (Oct. 23, 1939) 50, as saying: "Conservation of resources is a strong appeal, but *in Illinois there is little real waste of gas and none of oil,* as is well understood, none of the states now under strict proration produce their oil more efficiently than oil is now being produced in Illinois." (italics added) This statement with respect to waste of oil and gas is quite a contrast to that made by John Pugh, president of the Independent Oil Producers Association of Illinois, as reported in Oil & Gas Jour. (Nov. 17, 1939) 90, where he estimated that a proper conservation measure would prevent an annual loss of $27,000,000 per year. He said: "Last spring when this program for oil conservation was first started by our association, the daily loss from wasteful production methods exceeded $20,000 a day. With the increase in daily production we can add to that loss today $10,000 a day from one field alone—Salem-Lake Centralia—and another $45,000 a day from natural-gas gasoline wasted in this state. We can add more than $2,500,000 a month to Illinois' present oil revenue."
[55] Oil Weekly (Oct. 23, 1939) 49.

three industry organizations presented their proposed conservation measure to the Budgetary Commission, they were opposed by the officials of the Illinois Oil Producers Equity Association, and the commission delayed recommending it to Governor Horner.[56] A week after this measure was presented to the Budgetary Commission, Lieutenant Governor Stelle bitterly assailed it as a proration and not a conservation measure in an address before the Illinois Oil Producers Equity Association.[57] The proposed act appears to have been a comprehensive conservation law administered by a commission given broad powers to limit and prorate production for the prevention of waste, establish drilling units, and require purchasers of oil to take ratably from all producers.[58] Opposition to the measure drafted by the industry representatives seems to have been one of the causes of the delay of Governor Horner in issuing a call for a special legislative session, as he hoped to find an act upon which all factions in the oil industry could agree. With this in mind he had an administration measure drawn by the legislative reference bureau,[59] and held a conference with representatives of the industry to consider it, but no conclusions were announced.[60] Apparently this bill did not meet with satisfaction, for the governor sought aid

[56] The proposed act was presented by Alex W. McCandless, president of the Illinois-Indiana Petroleum Association, who stated that it was supported by his organization the Independent Producers and Royalty Owners Association and the Petroleum Association of Illinois, representing producers of more than 90 per cent of the Illinois oil output.

[57] Oil Weekly (Oct. 30, 1939) 49. Mr. Stelle stated that the threatened break in crude prices in previous months was a plan of the major companies to force proration. "They waged," he said, "such a thorough campagn through advertising and news publicity they had the people of Illinois believing a drastic cut in crude prices was pending, and the fear thus created was transferred to we officials in Springfield through requests for regulation. My position has not changed one bit on proration. There is a difference between proration and conservation and many people who have accused me of changing my position on the proration subject have done so in error."

[58] See Oil Weekly (Oct. 30, 1939) 48, for a summary of the act.

[59] Oil & Gas Jour. (Nov. 23, 1939) 16, Oil & Gas Jour. (Nov. 30, 1939) 20, Oil Weekly (Nov. 27, 1939) 45. At his press conferences during this period Governor Horner is reported to have made the following statements: "The terrible thing about nonregulated production is that so much is wasted. A bill is being drafted by the legislative reference bureau which I think will be agreeable to all honest fellows. What we are going to do is to send copies of it to all oil interests and let them point out their complaints with the idea of reaching a harmonizing point. I want a measure that will not regulate oil production so much as it will conserve. Producers are being told that such a measure can't be passed and in preparing a bill I had in mind one that will not be smashed."

[60] Oil & Gas Jour. (Dec. 7, 1939) 22, Oil Weekly (Dec. 4, 1939) 47.

elsewhere in preparing another act.[61] In early 1940 opposition to the consideration of the subject of oil conservation in a called session of the legislature crystallized and took on a political hue. The April primary and the November general election caused political leaders of both parties to be wary of the conservation fight.[62] The Republicans, with a majority in the House and 20 of the 50 Senate members, were expected to oppose conservation as a matter of policy, since their 1938 platform contained such a plank. Some of their gubernatorial candidates did not favor it, and the party's political leaders in off the record statements expressed the view that the issue put the November election in the bag. Governor Horner strongly favored conservation, but Lieutenant Governor Stelle was just as strongly hostile. A number of Democratic members of the legislature viewed support of conservation as political suicide. Three industry organizations favored conservation; two did not, and another, the Southern Illinois Inc., had been recently created to fight conservation with the blessing of Stelle.[63]

By February oil conservation became an open political issue, and all hopes of a special session before the primary election in April were gone.[64] Governor Horner withdrew as a candidate due to ill health; Harry B. Hershey was selected by the party as the Democratic candidate, and Stelle became the independent Democratic choice.[65] As the campaign progressed, the four leading contenders for governor, Dwight H. Green, Richard J. Lyons, Republicans, and Harry B. Hershey, John Stelle, Democrats, announced their policies as to oil control. Hershey said he was "for the prevention of waste in the natural resources and the stimulation of that initiative which is obviously necessary to the growth of the industry."

[61] Governor Horner had Professor Neil Jacoby of Northwestern University prepare a conservation bill which was referred to Attorney General Cassidy in January 1940; there is no further available information as to it. See Oil & Gas Jour. (Feb. 1, 1940) 18.

[62] See Oil Weekly (Nov. 6, 1939) 44, where it is reported that Hugh W. Cross, speaker of the house and Republican candidate for lieutenant governor, had urged caution in adopting conservation legislation and expressed the view that the state should not be stampeded into hasty and ill considered action. See Oil Weekly (Dec. 25, 1939) 46, where Robert J. Branson, Majority house leader, was reported as being opposed to the consideration of conservation measures in a called session.

[63] Malden Jones, *Conservation in Illinois a Political Football*, Oil & Gas Jour. (Jan. 11, 1940) 8.

[64] Oil & Gas Jour. (Feb. 1, 1940) 18.

[65] Oil & Gas Jour. (Feb. 22, 1940) 44.

Green reportedly expressed like views. Lyons and Stelle were out-spokenly contrary to conservation.[66] In the progress of this bitter primary, marked as it was by inter-party strife and the crossing of party lines in the oil counties, Governor Horner was urged to call a special session,[67] but not until after the election, in which Green and Hershey were nominated, did he accede and then he did not include conservation legislation as there was no possibility of its passage in the short special session.[68]

By June 1940 daily production of Illinois crude reached its high-est level—518,000 barrels.[69] After the general election Representa-tive Oral P. Tuttle, chairman of the investigating committee, which reported in 1939 that there was no need of a conservation law, issued a statement saying Republican leaders had agreed that Illinois must enact such a law to forestall federal control.[70]

In his inaugural address January 13, 1941 Governor Green said: "One of the most vital and irreplaceable of natural resources of our state is a bounteous supply of oil. This treasure must be carefully conserved. Our duty to coming generations as well as the immediate advantage of our people must be seriously and impartially con-sidered by the general assembly. I urge that the study of the problem of regulation and conservation be continued." [71] On March 18 the initial conservation measure of the 1941 session, H. B. No. 365, was introduced, defining and prohibiting waste, creating a commission to administer the act with authority to

[66] Oil & Gas Jour. (March 14, 1940) 28. Secretary Ickes, in an address in Wash-ington, speaking of the situation as to oil conservation in Illinois, said: "In that state we find a lieutenant governor, theoretically elected to serve the interest of the whole people of his state, blocking a much needed and sound conservation law while being at the same time financially interested in oil properties. Unfortunately, not only in Illinois but elsewhere, we find a nauseous mixture of oil and politics."

[67] A front page edtorial of the Chicago Daily News, March 19, 1940, urged the governor to call a special session of the legislature, saying: "The subject of oil pro-ration is acute and demands immediate attention. There is only one body competent to deal with that subject—the state legislature." This editorial may have been prompted through some political motive or it may have been the fact that on March 15 the average daily production of oil in Illinois was 455,755 barrels. Illinois had become the third oil producing state in the nation. See Oil & Gas Jour. (Mar. 21, 1940) 25.

[68] Oil & Gas Jour. (Apr. 11, 1940) 16.

[69] Oil & Gas Jour. (July 4, 1940) 5.

[70] Oil & Gas Jour. (Dec. 5, 1940) 10.

[71] Oil & Gas Jour. (Jan. 16, 1941) 28, Oil Weekly (Jan. 20, 1941) 37.

determine the existence or imminence of waste after a hearing, make rules and regulations for its prevention, including power to establish drilling units, and to reasonably limit and prorate production.[72] With administration leaders opposed to this bill as unwarranted, Governor Green announced the administration would support a measure in preparation.[73] According to press reports unanimity existed among legislators and industry for the enactment of a measure to avoid federal regulation. The elected representatives were not faced with elections as in the previous year, and the industry pressure groups seemed quiescent.[74] Hostility to H. B. No. 365 soon developed. At an operators meeting Stelle disapproved it because it was a proration measure. The Illinois Oil and Farm Owners Equity Association, led by George Harsh and Dorsey Hager, organized resistance, sponsoring a series of addresses by Stelle. Another group, the Illinois Oil Conservation Committee, was hastily created to fight the enactment of such legislation. Sponsors of the bill, representing producers of more than 75 per cent of Illinois oil, were not idle and urged Green to lend his support to the law, pointing out that in the past four years 25,000,-000 to 40,000,000 barrels of oil had been wasted through premature escape of gas. Antagonism to the bill from a small minority in the industry—mostly independent refiners and operators—grew intense as it was predicted that unless a compromise could be effected the law would suffer the same fate as in the three previous sessions.[75]

May 7th, 1941, Senator Benson, Republican majority leader,

[72] HB No. 365 was introduced by Representative Harris, Democrat, of Granite City. A synopsis of this bill, as it appears on page 409 of Legislative Synopsis and Digest of the Sixty-second General Assembly, indicates that it was closely modeled after the conservation act prepared by the writer for the Illinois-Indiana Petroleum Association in 1938.

[73] Oil & Gas Jour. (Mar. 20, 1941) 30, Oil & Gas Jour. (Apr. 3, 1941) 20.

[74] Oil & Gas Jour. (Apr. 3, 1941) 20.

[75] Oil & Gas Jour. (Apr. 10, 1941) 22, Oil & Gas Jour. (Apr. 17, 1941) 52. Oil & Gas Jour. (Apr. 24, 1941) 28, Oil Weekly (Apr. 14, 1941) 50. In Mr. Stelle's addresses he charged, among other things, that Texas and Oklahoma producers wanted production of oil restricted in Illinois because Illinois oil was 23 cents a barrel closer to market and that major operators were sponsoring Governor Green's production tax bill for the purpose of gaining the governor's support for their conservation measure. See Oil Weekly (May 5, 1941) 10, for expression of views of Dorsey Hager against a conservation law in Illinois and a reply by Ray L. Dudley, publisher of Oil Weekly.

introduced S.B. No. 522, the long awaited administration sponsored measure.[76] Characterized as an *anti-physical waste act* Governor Green stated it was "a conservation plan and not a proration bill." [77] There was justification for his statement, because the proposal eliminated from the definition of waste, "waste incident to the production of oil or gas in excess of transportation or marketing facilities or reasonable market demands," as well as a section from former acts authorizing the enforcement agency to limit the total production of oil or gas in Illinois and its pools, to distribute the allowable among pools, and to prorate pool allowables among wells on a reasonable basis. Clearly the commission did not have authority to regulate and prorate production for the prevention of market demand waste. Section 5 did allow the commission "to determine, regulate and limit the production of oil or gas, or both, from any well, well leases or properties, in this State, for the prevention of waste." This proviso was undoubtedly intended by the bill's proponents to permit limitation and regulation of production for the prevention of physical waste. If by avoiding the use of *prorata* they hoped to appease or delude their opposition they failed, for Stelle, appearing before the senate committee's first public hearing, branded it a "strict proration measure menacing the economic life of southern Illinois," and a "vicious move toward federal control and price fixing." While his statement was without foundation in fact or reason, it aroused hostility by some of the independent producers and refiners and their legislative supporters.[78]

[76] SEN. JOUR. ILL. 543 (1941), Legislative Synopsis & Digest 216 (1941), Oil & Gas Jour. (May 15, 1941) 32.

[77] Oil & Gas Jour. (May 15, 1941) 32, Oil Weekly (May 12, 1941) 147.

[78] Oil Weekly (May 19, 1941) 41. Oil & Gas Jour. (May 22, 1941) 48. At this first public hearing on the bill the most outspoken opponents, other than John Stelle, were Dorsey Hager, technical adviser of the Illinois Oil and Farm Owners Equity Association, and Charles Vurcell, Salem newspaper publisher. Hager said: "There is no difference between proration and conservation, and this bill is a proration bill. The only reason for conservation is scarcity, and there is no scarcity of oil today in Illinois." Vurcell stated that the bill was the product of the major oil companies aimed directly at the small independent producers, and branded it "camouflage." He further stated that its passage would adversely affect business in southern Illinois. Supporters of the bill included Illinois-Indiana Petroleum Association and the Independent Producers Association of Illinois. Three members of the state geological survey, Dr. M. M. Leighton, survey chief, Dr. A. H. Bell, head of the oil and gas division, and Dr. H. H. Voskuil, mineral economist, all testified to the effect that scientific methods of limiting Illinois production would add longer life to

Despite opposition to their proposal, administration leaders were confident of its passage,[79] but with the introduction May 22 of S.B. No. 632,[80] a counter offering (eliminating well spacing, limitation of production to prevent physical waste, and common purchaser ratable taking) which was little more than a revised well plugging and casing statute, Green announced he was willing to compromise on the objectionable features of the administration act.[81] The governor then submitted three amendments to S.B. No. 522 as a compromise. The most important of these restricted the power of the commission to limit the production of wells for the prevention of physical waste below a minimum number of barrels a week. At a meeting held in the office of Lieutenant Governor Cross to effectuate a compromise between the bills' supporters, Stelle and the officers of the Illinois Oil and Farm Owners Equity Association, rejected the amendments, insisting upon the adoption of S.B. No. 632. Abettors of the administration act refused to yield further to this stubborn minority and the effort to enact conservation legislation was deadlocked.[82] On May 29 Governor Green stated he would not insist upon the passage of the administration supported measure,[83] due to the necessity of passing important appropriation laws before the legislative adjournment. Thus ended in failure the latest attempt in four successive sessions of the Illinois general assembly to enact adequate oil and gas conservancy statutes.

Throughout the four year struggle a majority of the representatives of the oil industry continuously urged state regulation to avoid federal control. When it became apparent the legislature would not enact a satisfactory law at the 1941 session, the fear of federal regulation, with good reason, became real. Administration leaders in Washington, owing to an urgent demand for petroleum products

---

the state's oil reserves and that there could be effective conservation without limitation of production and proration. See Oil Weekly (May 26, 1941) 44, for a report of the second committee hearing. One of the most vocal of the witnesses against the bill at this hearing was A. K. Swan of Evansville, Indiana, secretary of the Tri-State Petroleum Association.

[79] Oil Weekly (May 19, 1941) 41.
[80] Sen. Jour. Ill. 754 (1941).
[81] Oil & Gas Jour. (May 29, 1941) 18.
[82] Oil & Gas Jour. (June 5, 1941) 34.
[83] Oil Weekly (June 2, 1941) 49, Oil & Gas Jour. (June 5, 1941) 34.

for national defense and to the failure of Illinois and California to enact sufficient legislation, threatened to reintroduce the Cole bill.[84] Green appointed a sub-committee of five senators, headed by Senator Charles F. Carpentier, to confer with Secretary Ickes, Petroleum Coordinator, and made public a telegram from Mr. Ickes urging the enactment of a conservation law.[85] After the Washington conference, Senator Carpentier reported to the legislature,[86] "I came back from Washington firm in the belief that the Government wants increased production in Illinois, but not proration or the curbing of market demand. We are determined to cooperate in every way with the Government in order to prepare a simple measure to prevent waste." [87]

Basing their action on his interpretation of the Washington meeting, the senate sub-committee abandoned S.B. No. 522 and 632 and drafted S.B. No. 694, which passed June 20 unanimously. The House amended the bill so that it defined physical waste and gave the Department of Mines and Minerals— the enforcement agency—authority to make rules and regulations for physical waste prevention. Even Stelle, against every adequate

[84] Oil Weekly (June 2, 1941) 49.

[85] Oil & Gas Jour. (June 12, 1941) 28. The telegram of Secretary Ickes' was as follows: "For several years I have been advocating the necessity of petroleum conservation by the oil-producing states. While oil conservation is essential at all times, in the emergency which the country now faces it is imperative. I urge that you give this problem your immediate personal attention to the end that Illinois enact a law to eliminate as far as practicable the waste of oil and gas and at the same time eliminate the drilling of unnecessary wells."

[86] The report of Senator Carpentier was as follows: "After receiving and conferring with a legislative committee from the State of Illinois, Coordinator Ickes said the state's representatives 'voluntarily offered to do their best to cooperate with the Government in the petroleum emergency.' The committee said that all parties in Illinois are primarily in favor of stopping waste. The problem is how to procure this result. Secretary Ickes said: 'The State of Illinois occupies a highly strategic position in the petroleum defense requirements of the nation. Because it is located in the heart of the country close to great central markets, there is no problem of transportation to get the production into the hands of the ultimate consumer. The oil production of Illinois can be used to great advantage at this time when there will be a heavy demand generally on transportation facilities.' Petroleum Coordinator Ickes told the members of the committee that any legislation they advocated both from a national and a state point of view should, in his opinion, be directed toward stopping waste and not to the stopping of the production of oil. He told the committee that he did not intend to offer them a draft of legislation or attempt to dictate in any way what form that legislation should take. That would be a matter for Illinois to decide when properly informed on all facts through its regular legislative process."

[87] Oil & Gas Jour. (June 19, 1941) 20.

conservation act introduced into the last four sessions, supported the amendments, but the Senate refused to concur. The bill passed and became a law without Governor Green's signature.[88]

THE ILLINOIS OIL AND GAS CONSERVATION ACT

A casual reading of the Illinois Oil and Gas Conservation Act [89] demonstrates how completely its preparation was dominated by a small minority of the industry—principally independent producers and refiners, hostile to every form of conservation. Although Senator Carpentier reported his group told Secretary Ickes "that all parties in Illinois are primarily in favor of stopping waste," and even though the heart of an oil and gas conservation law is its definition and prohibition of waste, yet the law neither defines nor prohibits waste. The Act in Section 1 says: " 'Waste' means underground waste or surface waste, or both: (1) 'Underground waste' means unreasonable damage to underground or surface fresh or mineral water, workable coal or other mineral deposits from operations for the discovery, development, production, transportation or handling of oil or gas. (2) 'Surface waste' means the unreasonable damage to or destruction of surface, soil, animal, fish or aquatic life or property from or by oil or gas operations." Underground waste is defined to include damage to practically all underground natural resources except oil and gas. "Unreasonable damage to . . . other mineral deposits" cannot be said to mean unreasonable damage to oil and gas formations. If this was the legislative intent, it is

[88] Oil & Gas Jour. (June 26, 1941) 28. Oil & Gas Jour. (July 2, 1941) 28; Ill. Laws 1941, p. 934.

[89] Ill. Laws 1941, p. 934, as amended by Ill. Laws 1945, p. 1091; ILL. REV. STAT. c. 104, § 62–88 (1945). Harold L. Ickes, Secretary of the Interior and Petroleum Coordinator for War, in an address before the St. Louis section of the A.I.M.E. at St. Louis, Oct. 1, 1942, speaking of the oil fields in the Illinois Basin, said: "Under an orderly, conservative development program, these fields might have been expected to produce at moderate and sustained rates over a period of many years. But there hasn't been an orderly, conservative development. There has not been an effective State conservation law in Illinois—and there still isn't. The result is that more than half of the reserves have already been produced—in only five years. Another result is that the eventual total yield now will be very substantially below what it might have been if conservative practices had been followed. An oil supply that *could* and *should* have been a source of wealth, and, more important still, of National strength, for many years has been tragically exploited, and is now far on the road to exhaustion."

strange that such harm to oil and gas pools was not expressly included, since in the same section a pool is defined as "a natural underground reservoir containing, in whole or in part, a natural accumulation of oil and gas." The interpretation of surface waste in no way concerns waste of oil and gas. If all of the oil wells in the state were set on fire and allowed to burn until exhausted, it would not be waste under this definition. Even if the provision quoted actually defined waste of oil and gas, it would be ineffective for nowhere in the Act is waste prohibited; nowhere is the Department of Mines and Minerals given express power to act or make and enforce rules and regulations to prevent waste as set out in the Act.

Section 6 gives the Department the right to make rules and regulations: "(1) to require the drilling, casing and plugging of wells to be done in such a manner as to prevent the escape of oil or gas out of one stratum to another; to prevent the intrusion of water into oil or gas . . . strata; . . . (4) to prevent 'blow outs,' 'caving' and 'seepage' in the same sense that conditions indicated by such terms are generally understood in the oil and gas business. (5) to prevent fires. . . . (7) to regulate the plugging of wells." Here the express authority given the Department to prevent such acts is effective to prevent certain types of underground and surface waste. Section 25 says: "All powers herein granted to prevent waste are limited to the prevention of physical waste. No power herein granted to prevent physical waste shall be interpreted or construed as authorizing the limitation or production of any well, wells, lease, leases, pool, field or properties to prevent or control economic waste or limit production to market demand." This seems an exercise of unnecessary caution in view of the fact that the Act nowhere defines or prohibits physical waste of oil or gas and nowhere expressly grants powers to prevent physical waste.

Sections 21, 22, 23 and 24 [90] regulate spacing of wells and are

[90] The Department of Mines and Minerals adopted and promulgated Rules and Regulations for the administration of the conservation act Oct. 16, 1945. Rule 18 provides, in part: "A. In the development of all limestone producing pools, the unit of surface area for each well to such limestone producing horizon is fixed at twenty (20) acres of land, comprising, where possible, a half-quarter-quarter section of land, except where, due to irregular sections of land or irregularity of ownership, complete conformity to a unit of twenty (20) acres consisting of such half-quarter-quarter section cannot be had, and except where otherwise permitted by Sections 21 or 22

unduly prolix. The basic plan for well spacing appears to be 20 acre units for wells producing from limestone horizons, 10 acres for wells producing from sands and one well per block in incorpo-

---

of•the Act. . . . B. No person shall drill or deepen any well in a sand pool or horizon on a drilling unit of less than ten (10) acres, except under the following circumstances:" §§ 21, 22, 23, 24 of the Act which regulate the spacing of wells are: "82. *Issuance of permits—Refusal of permit authorized when*. Sec. 21. When the applicant has complied with all applicable provisions of this Act concerning application for and issuance of permits for the drilling of a well for oil or gas purposes the Department shall issue the permit; provided, however, that the Department is authorized and empowered to refuse a permit for the drilling of a well for oil or gas purposes within the State of Illinois, on application as in this Act required, under any or all of the following circumstances:

(a) When the application made is for the drilling of a well on a tract with dimensions of six hundred sixty (660) feet or more in width and length to be drilled nearer to a boundary of said tract than three hundred thirty (330) feet; except that where such tract is directly or diagonally offset by a well producing oil or gas nearer than three hundred thirty (330) feet of the boundary of the tract on which the permit is requested, the Department shall have the power to prescribe, in its discretion, the distance from the boundary of the tract concerned at which the proposed well may be drilled in order to give just and reasonable protection to the premises concerned against drainage from the offsetting producing well;

(b) When the width or the length of the tract on which the well is proposed to be drilled is less than six hundred sixty (660) feet and the well is proposed to be drilled other than in the approximate geographic center of the tract concerned; except that if said tract is offset by a well producing oil or gas so situated that the drilling of said well in the approximate geographic center thereof would not provide reasonable protection against drainage by the offsetting well, the Department may prescribe another or different location;

(c) When the well for which application for permit is made is to be a second or additional well to the same producing horizon from which a well previously drilled thereon is producing on a tract whose dimensions are less than six hundred sixty (660) feet in width or length, or both; provided, however, that this provision is not intended to prevent the issuance or to authorize the Department to refuse the issuance of a permit for a second or additional well to be drilled to and completed in another or different producing horizon; or when such second or additional well is necessary to protect the land or tract involved from drainage by a well or wells located on contiguous or adjacent property;

(d) When a second or additional well is proposed to be drilled to the same producing horizon, in which a well has been originally completed and is productive of oil or gas, if such second or additional well is proposed to be drilled on the same tract to the same horizon from which the previously completed well is productive and within three hundred thirty (330) feet of the well previously completed on such tract; provided, however, that this sub-division shall not apply to a permit requested for the drilling and completion of a second or additional well on such a tract to another or different horizon; or when such second or additional well is necessary to protect the land or tract involved from drainage by a well or wells located on contiguous or adjacent property;

(e) When a well is proposed to be drilled on a tract whose longest dimension is in excess of six hundred sixty (660) feet and less than thirteen hundred twenty (1320) feet and the proposed well is to be a second or additional well in the same producing horizon from which a well previously drilled thereon is productive of oil

rated municipalities not having spacing ordinances.[91] The proposals are so laden with exceptions that there is no utility to them as waste prevention measures unless operators follow them voluntarily. The

---

or gas and said well is proposed to be located either within three hundred thirty (330) feet of the previous well or within one hundred sixty-five (165) feet of the boundary farthest from the first producing well; provided, however, that the Department may grant such permit under such circumstances if in its opinion oil or gas is being unreasonably drained from beneath the tract in question by an offsetting producing well on adjacent property; and provided further, that this subdivision is not intended to apply to a second or additional well proposed to be drilled on such a tract to another or different producing horizon;

(f) When the longest dimension of the tract on which the well is proposed to be drilled is thirteen hundred twenty (1320) feet or more and the second or additional well is proposed to be drilled to and completed in the producing horizon from which the previously completed well is productive and less than six hundred sixty (660) feet from the well previously completed thereon; provided, that this subdivision is not intended to apply to a permit requested for a second or additional well which is to be drilled to or completed in another or different horizon; or when such second or additional well is necessary to protect the land or tract involved from drainage by a well or wells located on contiguous or adjacent property;

(g) When the tract on which the proposed well is to be located is a subdivided portion of an oil and gas lease on a larger tract or body of land covered by an oil and gas lease under the terms of which lease the well is proposed to be drilled, when the subdivision of such oil or gas leasehold estate has occurred after the effective date of this Act and since the effective date of such lease, when such a subdivision has a length or width less than six hundred sixty (660) feet and contains less than ten (10) acres of land in area; except that the Department may grant such permit on condition that the owner of subdivided portions of the original leasehold estate, subdivided after the effective date of such lease, and after the effective date of this Act shall pool or communitize ten (10) acres or more in area into one drilling unit to the common interest of the owners of said subdivided portions for the purpose of drilling one well to each producing horizon;

(h) When a well is proposed to be drilled upon any portion of the land covered in the deed, contract or dedication to the State of Illinois or a political subdivision thereof or any municipal corporation or other governmental unit therein for public highway purposes or upon any portion of a public highway maintained by the State of Illinois or a political subdivision thereof or any municipal corporation or other governmental unit therein and currently kept open for public use and which has been used and travelled by the public for more than fifteen (15) years, consisting of the travelled portion of the highway, the shoulders maintained contiguous to the roadway and the ditches or drainage facilities which are maintained and used as part of the highway system of which such road is part; provided, that this subdivision shall not prohibit the drilling or operation of any well, so situated, under a permit heretofore granted.

83. *Spacing of wells in limestone pool or horizon—Additional permits—Deepening wells.* Sec. 22. When the proposed well may be completed for production in any limestone pool or horizon, after the discovery of oil or gas therein, the Department, in its discretion, may require the future location or spacing of wells completed in such horizon or pool on the basis of one well to each twenty (20) acre unit of land, the exact shape and dimensions of which shall rest in the discretion of the Department; provided, however, that if the unit of land so established shall be owned in severalty in separate tracts, the owners, subject to the other provisions of this Act, shall be permitted to drill not more than one well to such limestone pool or horizon,

right of the Department to enforce its rules and regulations with respect to spacing by injunctions,[92] or the exaction of penalties,[93] has not been tested in the courts. It is dubious if the authority is

on each such separately owned tract; and provided further, however, that this section shall not be construed to prohibit the Department from granting an additional permit, and it shall be the duty of the Department to grant such additional permit, when an additional well is, in the sound discretion of the Department, necessary to give reasonable protection to the owner or owners of such tract of twenty (20) acres or less against drainage from offsetting producing wells in such limestone pool or horizon.

When, after discovery of production in any such limestone pool or horizon, a well based on ten (10) acres spacing shall have been drilled to another or different producing horizon with the announced intention of completing such well therein, and such horizon is not productive of oil or gas, the Department may, in its discretion, permit the deepening of such well to such known limestone producing pool or horizon, or the shooting, ripping or perforation of the oil string of casing for production, in an upper limestone producing formation, on conditions as to the manner of completion which will comply with the other provisions of this Act with respect to the manner of drilling or completing wells.

84. *Alteration of drilling requirements.* Sec. 23. The drilling requirements hereinabove set forth requiring the location of wells in the geographic center of tracts, may be altered by the Department upon a proper showing of reasonable necessity and after notice and hearing and the issuance of a written order, to authorize the drilling of a well at such other location as the circumstances may require.

85. *Permits in cities, villages or towns—Conditions precedent—Bond of applicant.* Sec. 24. *The provisions of this Section shall not apply to any city, village or incorporated town which has enacted or hereafter enacts an ordinance or resolution limiting the locating or spacing of wells.*

Not more than one permit per pool for each block shall be issued for any city, village or incorporated town in which oil or gas is discovered on or after the effective date of this Act. In any city, village or incorporated town in which oil or gas is discovered prior to the effective date of this Act, not more than one permit per pool for each block shall be issued for any block in which no oil or gas well has been or is being drilled to any such pool prior to said date.

As a condition precedent to the issuance of any permit as aforesaid, the Department shall require the applicant to agree to apportion the net production of his well (after deducting therefrom such amount as will compensate him for the cost of production, as determined by the Department in accordance with its rules and regulations) among all of the owners within said block on an acreage basis, or, in lieu of such agreement, to file a copy of a voluntary communitization contract signed by all of the owners within said block.

When two or more applicants apply for a permit within the same block, the Department shall issue the same to the owner of the greatest acreage.

Each applicant shall submit a bond or other proof of financial responsibility to the Department to guarantee the performance of his agreement for the benefit of other owners."

[91] § 11 provides that the department may restrain violations of the act or of its rules and regulations by injunction.

[92] § 26 punishes violations of the act or the rules and regulations of the department by fine.

[93] § 6. The prohibition in this section is as follows: "The drilling of any well is hereby prohibited until such notice is given and such permit obtained as herein provided."

supportable on the theory that the rules and regulations are made
to prevent physical waste, since the Act does not define or prohibit
waste or give the Department authority to make rules and regulations with respect to spacing for waste prevention. The Act does
provide, however, that the agency may make rules and regulations
requiring notice of intent to drill and the securing from the
Department of a drilling permit, prohibiting drilling until compliance is obtained.[94] The agency is empowered to refuse a permit
until requirements as to the location of the well are satisfied.[95]
Therefore, if a permit is refused and the applicant commences
drilling without it, he could be enjoined or penalized for violation
of the regulation, provided a constitutional basis for the prohibition
be shown.

As a conservation law, the Illinois statute is distinguished by its
lack of the provisions found in other conservancy statutes by which
waste of oil and gas may be prevented and greater production
secured. No express terms of the Act authorize or require the
preservation or augmentation of reservoir energy through maintenance of efficient water-oil or gas-oil ratios, the cycling or recycling
of gas, or the injection of water, gas, air or other substances into the
producing formation.[96] There are no restrictions on the open flow
of oil or gas wells, no power in the administrative body to limit
the amount of oil or gas produced in the state from any pool or
well, nor any restrictions on the utilization of dry or casinghead-gas
for the manufacture of carbon black or other uneconomic uses.
The only clause relative to the disposal of salt water and contaminated brines is found in the definition of waste. A single provision
for unit operation is found in Section 21 g which authorizes the
grant of a permit to drill on a unit of 10 acres in a subdivided tract
on the condition that separate owners pool their interests. There
is no basis for implying the existence of any of the conservation
principles not expressly found in the statute for the reason that it
does not define or prohibit waste.

[94] § 21.
[95] Ill. Laws 1933, p. 715, permitted the introduction of air, gas, water or other
liquid into a producing formation for repressuring purposes, but this was repealed by
the present statute. Rule 9 of the Rules and Regulations of the Department recognizes repressuring practices by requiring operators to secure permits for repressuring
operations.
[96] Ill. Laws 1941, p. 934, § 3.

The Illinois Act provides that it shall be administered by the Department of Mines and Minerals,[97] one of the thirteen departments of the state government.[98] Prior to the enactment of this statute, the powers and duties of the Department were exercised with relation to the mining of solid minerals, principally coal.[99] The statutory qualification of its officers—a director, assistant director, mine officers and miners' examining officers—is experience in coal mining.[100] A majority of the oil industry wanted a conservation act directed by persons acquainted with the production of oil and gas, and thus were not in favor of making this body the administrative agency. After the enactment of the statute, an oil and gas division was created to administer it;[101] its principal officers are a supervisor and petroleum engineer. Although these persons are appointed to the post and their qualifications are not prescribed by statute, some of the personnel of the division appear well qualified. The power and duties of the Department to administer and enforce the statute are set out in detail. It has jurisdiction and authority over all persons and property necessary for effective enforcement of the Act,[102] to make rules and regulations including those for stated purposes,[103] the right to inspect oil and gas properties,[104] the right to determine the existence or imminence of waste over which it has jurisdiction by means of hearings, collection of data, investigations, inspections, examinations of properties, drilling records and logs, and such other action as required in enforcement.[105] Rules and regulations are made only after a public hearing upon ten days notice, except in case of an emergency rule. These rules are made without hearing but can be in force only fifteen days and expire when a rule made after notice and

[97] ILL. REV. STAT. c. 127, § 3 (1945).
[98] ILL. REV. STAT. c. 127, § 45 (1945).
[99] ILL. REV. STAT. c. 127, § 7 (1945).
[100] The oil and gas division seems' to have been created under the authority given by § 5 of the conservation statute which provides as follows: "The Department shall have authority and it shall be its duty, to employ all necessary personnel to carry out the provisions of this Act; to fix their compensation; to designate their headquarters and to define their duties. The aforesaid personnel shall be exempt from the provisions and regulations of the State Civil Service Act."
[101] Ill. Laws 1941, p. 934, § 4.
[102] Ill. Laws 1941, p. 934, § 6.
[103] Ill. Laws 1941, p. 934, § 7.
[104] Ill. Laws 1941, p. 934, § 8.
[105] Ill. Laws 1941, p. 934, § 9 (b) and (c).

hearing covering the same subject matter becomes effective.[106] Rules and regulations must be in writing and entered in a book kept in the Department. This book is a public record open to inspection. Certified copies of rules and regulations are received in evidence in all state courts.[107] Notice of rules and regulations is given by publication by the Department, or by registered mail and return receipt.[108] Hearings within its jurisdiction are called upon the volition of the agency or upon the request of interested persons.[109] The group has statutory authority to prescribe rules of procedure followed in hearings before it, to determine the form and manner of giving notice, and to fix the time and place of hearings.[110]

The Department first exercised its authority to make rules and regulations on October 15, 1942, more than a year after its effective date.[111] The rules and regulations were revised October 18, 1945. They do not define waste of oil or gas, although five of them make reference to waste. Rule 4 states that if a gas sand is penetrated in the drilling process, it must not be left open, to permit avoidable escape of gas, which in the opinion of the Department constitutes physical waste. Rule 8, governing salt water and liquid waste disposal, requires that these substances be disposed of in the manner set out for prevention of surface or underground waste. Rule 9 provides that for prevention of surface or underground waste, persons desiring to use or deepen existing wells, or drill a new well for the purpose of injecting water, salt water, or other substance into an underground formation, must secure a permit. The Department may deny this permit if in its judgment the operation will result in waste. To prevent fire hazards, underground and surface waste, Rule 10 details the manner of disposal of surplus

[106] Ill. Laws 1941, p. 934, § 9 (d).

[107] Ill. Rule 13 of the department's Rules and Regulations.

[108] Ill. Laws 1941, p. 934, § 8 and 9 (e).

[109] Ill. Laws 1941, p. 934, § 9 (a) and 9 (b). Rule 12 of the department's Rules and Regulations prescribes the manner in which notice of hearings may be given.

[110] These rules were sent to Illinois oil operators with a letter from the director of the Department which said: "This booklet represents months of study and repeated conferences by and between Oil Operators, Coal Operators, members of the State Oil and Gas Division, members of the State Geological Survey, and others, to all of whom I wish to express my appreciation and thanks."

[111] Notice of these rules and regulations is given to oil operators in the state by registered mail. Copies may be obtained upon request sent to the Department of Mines and Minerals, Oil and Gas Division, Springfield, Illinois.

oil and gas. Waste oil must be collected in pits and burned, surplus gas vented and burned. Rule 11 recites that plugging is required to prevent surface and underground waste. In making its rules and regulations the agency appears to have remained within the limits of its statutory grant. Since the Act does not define and prohibit waste, but only gives authority to govern certain practices which may be wasteful, the waste prevention power is extremely limited. Its rules are concerned with the granting of drilling permits, casing and plugging wells, filing drilling logs, identifying leases and wells, disposal of saline waters, regulation of injection of substances into underground formations, disposal of waste oil and surplus gas, prohibition of vacuum pumps, protection of workable coal beds, and the spacing of wells.[112]

Interested persons affected by the Act, or the rules or regulations of the agency may file suit in the circuit court of the county wherein is situated all or a part of the land which is the subject matter of the action to test the validity of the statute, rule or regulation. Such suits must be tried promptly. The burden of proof is on the complainant and the rules and regulations presumed valid until proved otherwise. Appeals are taken as in other civil actions.[113] The Department has authority to seek injunctions to restrain actual or threatened violations of the statute or its rules and regulations.[114] Persons violating the Act or rules and regulations of the Department are subject to fine.[115] If any suits have been brought contesting the validity of the Act or the rules and regulations of the Department, they have not reached the appellate courts. In view of the fact that under the statute and rules, the regulation is so innocuous, it is unlikely that litigation will arise.

The Illinois oil and gas conservation law is not a true conservation measure within the generally accepted meaning of the term. It neither defines nor prohibits waste, the basic concept upon which state regulation of production of these natural resources must be grounded. It contains but a few of the many terms of other modern enactments through which physical and economic waste may be prevented and greater production achieved. The most

[112] Ill. Laws 1947, p. 1250.
[113] Ill. Laws 1941, p. 934, § 10.
[114] Ill. Laws 1941, p. 934, § 11.
[115] Ill. Laws 1941, p. 934, § 26.

important of these sections in the Illinois statute—spacing—is so fraught with exceptions and its enforceability so clouded with doubt, that it is in a large measure ineffectual as a conservancy device, except through voluntary producer action. Illinois is still a member of the Interstate Compact to Conserve Oil and Gas,[116] but its pledge to the other compacting members, first made in 1935, to enact a waste prevention enactment curtailing wasteful production practices, remains unfulfilled. At the present time oil operators are discussing the need for legislation in aid of secondary recovery operations, but whether additional measures will be enacted in the near future only time and circumstance will tell.

[116] See c. 39 supra n. 6.

CHAPTER 11

Indiana, 1876–1948

In 1876 near Eaton, Delaware County, Indiana, a well was drilled to a depth of six hundred feet by persons seeking a coal deposit. By 1886 the first commercial gas well in this area was completed near Findlay, Ohio, in the Trenton limestone. Soon thereafter the Eaton well was deepened to the Trenton lime obtaining the first gas well in Indiana. Later a well was drilled near the town of Kokomo, which became a large producer. The next well was in Jay County, and after its completion wildcatting became intense in north central Indiana. Identity of the first oil well is problematical as oil was often found immediately below the gas zone in drilling for gas. It is certain, however, that the following counties began oil production in late 1886 or early 1887: Jay, Wells, Huntington, Delaware, Grant, Madison, and Miami. Legal problems developed from gas and oil discoveries, and Indiana's legal history of the conservation of oil and gas began shortly after the discovery well in 1886.

THE LEGISLATIVE HISTORY

In the year following the finding of gas in Indiana, the General Assembly of Indiana incorporated into a statute on voluntary associations a provision for the organization of groups "for the purpose of operating oil and gas wells, and of selling the product of such wells." [1] It is probable that a company for drilling oil and gas wells could have been formed under the prior laws. [2] In 1889

AQUILLA W. GROVES, WRITER; A. C. Colby, Adviser. (See app. B.)
[1] Laws Ind. 1887, c. XXVI, § 1.
[2] OP. ATT'Y. GEN. Apr. 14, 1887.

the legislature attempted to forbid the sale of natural gas beyond state limits,[3] but the statute was held to be invalid as repugnant to the commerce clause of the Federal Constitution.[4] It contained provisions preventing waste,[5] which the court held were not separable; the whole act failed.[6] During the 1889 session the general assembly passed over the governor's veto an act establishing the Department of Geology and Natural Resources [7] in Indiana, providing for a chief of the division of natural gas to enforce laws regarding gas, gather information on the number of wells drilled, increase and decrease of pressure, and information relative to the gas industry. Having failed to prevent the transportation of natural gas from the state, the assembly adopted a new measure in 1891 calculated to accomplish that purpose indirectly by prohibiting the use of sufficient pressure to carry the gas beyond state lines.[8] Section 2 declared it unlawful to employ any device for pumping or other artificial process or appliance "that shall have the effect of increasing the natural flow of natural gas from any well, or of increasing or maintaining the flow of natural gas through pipe lines used for conveying and transporting the same." [9] The state supreme court upheld the Act in *Manufacturers Gas and Oil Co. v. Indiana Natural Gas and Oil Co.*[10] The first legislative act devoted solely to conservation of petroleum was passed in 1891 forbidding the burning of natural gas in flambeau lights.[11] It expressly permitted jumbo

[3] Laws Ind. 1889, c. CCIII.

[4] State ex. rel. Corwin v. Ind. & Ohio Oil Co., 120 Ind. 575, 22 N.E. 778 (1889), Manuf. Gas & Oil Co. v. Ind. Nat. Gas & Oil Co., 155 Ind. 545, 58 N.E. 706 (1900).

[5] Laws Ind. 1889, c. CCIII § 2.

[6] State ex rel. Corwin v. Ind. & Ohio Oil Co., 120 Ind. 575, 22 N.E. 778 (1889).

[7] Laws Ind. 1889, c. XXXIII.

[8] Laws Ind. 1891, c. LXXIV § 1 as amended by Laws Ind. 1903, c. XLIII § 1; IND. ANN. STAT. § 46–304 (Burns 1940 rep.)

[9] Laws Ind. 1891, c. LXXIV § 2.

[10] 155 Ind. 461, 57 N. E. 912 (1900). See Jamieson v. Ind. Nat. Gas & Oil Co., 128 Ind. 555, 28 N.E. 76 (1891) where the 1891 act was upheld as a public safety measure, and Man. Gas & Oil Co. v. Ind. Nat. Gas & Oil Co., 156 Ind. 679, 59 N. E. 169 (1901), *rehearing denied* 156 Ind. 681, 60 N. E. 1080 (1901) where the court denied an injunction under the 1891 act to prevent the transportation of natural gas through pipes at a pressure in excess of rock pressure because the complaint failed to state facts showing any injury to plaintiff.

[11] Laws Ind. 1891, c. XLVII § 1; IND. ANN. STAT. § 10–2407 (Burns 1942 rep.) repealed by Acts Ind. 1947, c. 277 § 28.

burners but limited their use to the hours of 5 P.M. to 8 A.M.[12] The statute was sustained as a valid exercise of the police power in the case of *Townsend v. The State.*[13]

The 1893 session of the Indiana general assembly adopted an enactment making it unlawful "to allow or permit the flow of gas from any such well to escape into the open air, without being confined within such well or proper pipes, or other safe receptacle for a longer period than two (2) days next after gas or oil shall have been struck in such well. . . ."[14] Section 2 provided the state with its first regulation for well plugging.[15] Section 4 stated that upon the failure to plug an abandoned well as in Section 1 of the Act, neighbors in possession of adjacent lands might plug the well and recover their costs from its owner.[16] Section 1, calling for confinement of gas or oil within two days,[17] was tested in a case famous in the annals of the legal history of conservation of oil and gas—*State v. Ohio Oil Company,*[18] in which the Indiana Supreme Court upheld the law's constitutionality, and this decision was affirmed by the United States Supreme Court in *Ohio Oil Company v. Indiana*[19] holding the Act a valid exercise of the state police power.[20]

In 1903 the first law on plugging[21] was repealed and a new law governing abandonment of gas and oil wells adopted.[22] The Indiana legislature in 1909 passed a more comprehensive plugging measure[23] which served as the basis for controlling plugging of abandoned wells until 1947.[24] These laws were never challenged in the

[12] Laws Ind. 1891, c. XLVII § 2; IND. ANN. STAT. § 10–2408 (Burns 1942 rep.) repealed by Acts Ind. 1947, c. 277 § 28.

[13] 147 Ind. 624, 47 N.E. 19 (1896).

[14] Laws Ind. 1893, c. CXXXVI § 1, amended Acts Ind. 1913, c. 37; IND. ANN. STAT. § 46–306 (Burns 1933).

[15] Laws Ind. 1893, c. CXXXVI § 2 repealed by Acts Ind. 1903, c. 115 § 5.

[16] Laws Ind. 1893, c. CXXXVI § 4; IND. ANN. STAT. § 46–307 (Burns 1933).

[17] See note 15 supra.

[18] 150 Ind. 21, 49 N. E. 809 (1898) reaff'd on second appeal 150 Ind. 698, 50 N. E. 1125 (1898).

[19] 177 U.S. 190 (1900).

[20] See Given v. State, 160 Ind. 552, 66 N.E. 750 (1903) where the validity of the statute was again upheld.

[21] See note 16 supra.

[22] Laws Ind. 1903, c. CXV.

[23] Acts Ind. 1909, c. 92 § 1–9; IND. ANN. STAT. § 46–309 to 46–314 (Burns 1933) repealed by Acts Ind. 1947, c. 277 § 28.

[24] Acts Ind. 1947, c. 277.

appellate courts of the state, even though they provided in detail the method of plugging and required that the work must be supervised by a state agent.[25] The year 1919 was important in Indiana's legislative history, for the general assembly created the Department of Conservation with one of its arms, the Division of Geology, assigned to "recommend and secure the enforcement of laws for the conservation and development of the natural resources of the state," [26] and transferred to it those powers previously exercised by the natural gas supervisor and the state geologist.[27] Although the commission was given general powers to adopt rules and regulations "authorized by this act and such others as may be necessary, in their judgment, to carry out its provisions," [28] lawyers disagreed as to whether or not the commission had power to make rules regulating the issuance of permits, spacing, plugging and like operations. As a matter of practice the Department adopted rules requiring drilling permits, submission of logs and plugging which were generally ignored by operators and leaseholders. No legal decisions testing the rule making authority of the Department of Conservation prior to the 1947 Act [29] have been found.

Two historical milestones in oil and gas conservation in Indiana were passed in 1947 when the Indiana general assembly authorized the state to join the Interstate Compact to Conserve Oil and Gas [30] and adopted the state's first comprehensive oil and gas law.[31] The sum of $1000 annually was appropriated to the support of the Interstate Oil Compact Commission.[32] The governor takes an active interest in the work of the compact through his official representative, and the state has members on several of the Commission's working committees.[33] The Indiana conservation law is

[25] See note 23 supra.
[26] Acts Ind. 1919, c. 60 § 15; IND. ANN. STAT. § 60–715 (Burns 1943 rep.).
[27] Acts Ind. 1919, c. 60 § 24; IND. ANN. STAT. § 60–726 (Burns 1933).
[28] Acts Ind. 1919, c. 60 § 6; IND. ANN. STAT. § 60–706 (Burns 1933).
[29] Acts Ind. 1947, c. 277; IND. ANN. STAT. § 60–752 et seq. (Burns Supp. 1947).
[30] Acts Ind. 1947, c. 349; IND. ANN STAT. § 60–779 (Burns Supp. 1947).
[31] Acts Ind. 1947, c. 277; IND. ANN. STAT. § 60–752 to 60–778 (Burns Supp 1948).
[32] Acts Ind. 1947, c. 349.
[33] The governor has designated A. C. Colby, Supervisor of Oil and Gas, Indiana Department of Conservation, Indianapolis, as his official representative. Colby is also a member of the Public Lands Committee and the Research and Coordinating Committee. Aquilla W. Groves, Deputy Attorney General, is an official member

patterned after that of Georgia.[34] There had been attempts in years past to secure a conservation statute, but certain interests had prevented passage. In 1947 Charles F. Deiss, State Geologist, and A. C. Colby, Assistant State Geologist in charge of oil and gas, took the initiative in securing a conservation measure. B. C. Kennedy, Assistant Director and Special Counsel for the Department of Conservation, worked with them and the state is indebted to these three for the statute. The Interstate Oil Compact Commission was consulted, and its model oil and gas law used in making the original draft of the bill submitted to the general assembly. Meetings with the Indiana Oil and Gas Association were held to study this proposal. Several changes were made in the original draft and a bill was agreed upon for submission to the legislature. The members of the association supported the spacing provisions in the proposed measure.[35]

Highlights of the new conservation statute are: (1) the creation of an Oil and Gas Division within and under the control of the Indiana Department of Conservation, constituting the board members of the Department as the Oil and Gas Commission. The oil and gas supervisor is the administrative head of the division.[36] (2) The prevention of physical waste,[37] and (3) its definition.[38] (4)

---

of the Legal Committee. O. L. Sturbois, Vincennes, is a member of the Regulatory Practices Committee and A. B. Barrow of Evansville, a member of the Engineering Committee.

[34] Ga. Laws 1945, c. 366.

[35] See 22 IND. L. J. 385.

[36] Acts Ind. 1947, c. 277 § 1–4.

[37] Acts Ind. 1947, c. 277 § 4H.

[38] The definition of waste is: H. " 'Waste,' in addition to its ordinary meaning, shall mean 'physical waste' as that term is generally understood in the oil and gas industry. It shall include: (1) The locating, spacing, drilling, equipping, operating or producing of any oil or gas well drilled after the effective date of this Act in any manner which results or tends to result in reducing the quantity of oil or gas ultimately to be recovered from any well in this State, or which is contrary to the spacing provisions which may be adopted by the Commission under the terms of this Act. (2) The storing of oil in earthen reservoirs except in the case of an emergency to prevent the total loss of oil. (3) Producing oil or gas in such manner as to cause unnecessary water channeling or zoning. (4) The drowning with water of any stratum or part thereof capable of producing oil or gas, except for secondary recovery purposes by methods approved by the Commission. (5) Allowing salt water to flow from any producing horizon located in a producing pool, except for secondary recovery purposes by methods approved by the Commission or except that flow of salt water which occurs in the normal operation of the well. (6) Allowing gas from any gas well producing gas only to escape into the open air except

The grant of power to the Commission to make rules and regulations to prevent waste,[39] to regulate well spacing,[40] and to establish

such escape as is necessary in making or changing connections or completing and placing on production or reconditioning a well producing only gas. (7) The escape into the open air of gas from a well producing both oil and gas, except as an incident to the production of oil from such well and when there is no market at the well for the gas being produced with such oil; and the escape into the open air, from a well producing both oil and gas, of gas produced with oil when there is a market available at the well for such gas. (8) The use of gas for the manufacture of carbon black when there is a market at the well in the field for the gas in its natural state; PROVIDED, HOWEVER, that the Commission shall have the authority to issue a special permit for good cause for the use of gas for the manufacture of carbon black. (9) Notwithstanding waste, as above defined, it shall not be unlawful for the operator or owner of any well producing both oil and gas to burn such gas in flares when such gas is, pursuant to the other subdivisions hereof, lawfully produced and where there is no market at the well for such escaping gas; and where the same is used for the extraction of casing-head gas, it shall not be unlawful for the operator of the plant, after the process of extraction is completed, to burn such residue in flares when there is no market at such plant for such residue gas."

[39] Acts Ind. 1947, c. 277 § 7 authorizes the making of rules to administer the act. § 9 rules for reports on location of oil and gas wells, preventing drowning of any stratum by water except for secondary recover and to regulate well spacing. § 12 to regulate disposal of salt water or sulphur bearing water. § 13 to establish drilling units. § 13-a to establish integration orders. § 18 to require bond. § 23 to protect coal seams.

[40] *Id.* § 9. "The Commission shall have the authority to adopt such rules, regulations and orders as may be necessary from time to time to administer the provisions of this Act and the powers hereby expressly granted to the Commission, but not in enlargement of the powers granted the Commission hereunder, including, without limiting the foregoing general provisions, the making of rules and regulations or orders for the following purposes: . . . (C) To regulate the spacing of wells for oil and gas purposes and the issuance of permits for the drilling of wells. But no spacing regulation shall be adopted which requires the allocation of more than twenty acres of surface area to an individual well for production of oil from a limestone horizon or more than ten acres of surface area to an individual well for production of oil from a sandstone horizon. The spacing rule adopted by the Commission effective May 9, 1947, follows: Locating and spacing of wells shall be in accordance with the following: (a) The minimum drilling unit for limestone production shall be 20 acres, unless otherwise specified by the Commission. No well for limestone production shall be located less than 330 feet from any lease line, property line, or subdivision which separates un-consolidated property interest and 660 feet from any drilling or well capable of production. (b) The minimum drilling unit for sandstone production shall be 10 acres, unless otherwise specified by the Commission. No well for sandstone production shall be located less than 330 feet from any lease line, property line, or subdivision which separates un-consolidated property interest, and 660 feet from any drilling or well capable of production. (c) Should 5 acre spacing be established, no well shall be located less than 165 feet from any lease line, property line, or subdivision which separates un-consolidated property interest, and 330 feet from any drilling or well capable of production. (d) The Old Trenton limestone producing area, consisting of the following counties: Howard, Grant, Blackford, Wells, Jay, Adams, Delaware, Madison, Randolph, Tipton, Hamilton, Henry, Hancock, Fayette, Rush, Shelby, and

drilling units.[41] (5) The authorization given the Commission to force unitization of two or more separately owned tracts of land "for the prevention of waste or to avoid the drilling of unnecessary wells."[42] (6) The requirement of a state issued drilling permit before a gas or oil well is drilled or deepened,[43] with a permit fee of $25.00.[44] (7) Authority is given the Commission to require by rule or regulation a bond with the application for a permit to drill,[45] and the agency has adopted a rule making mandatory the filing of a bond[46] in the sum of $1000 for each well or a blanket bond of $5000 for all wells drilled during its term. The law authorizes the board to require that a bond (conditioned upon compliance with the statute and rules) accompany applications to plug and abandon a well; however, if a drilling bond is in force covering the well to

Decatur, is hereby declared to be an exception to the above rule and it is hereby ordered that the minimum drilling unit for such area is 5 acres. (e) When geological and pool conditions justify, smaller drilling units may be approved and staggered locations at lesser distances may be permitted in the discretion of the Commission. (f) Exceptions to the general spacing rules herein established or to the special rules and orders hereafter to be promulgated by the Commission establishing spacing and/or drilling units for particular fields or pools, shall be made only upon notice and hearing. Such hearing shall be at the time and place designated by the Commission in its notice.. Such notice shall be by publication or by mail or both and in such manner as shall be reasonably calculated by the Commission in its discretion to give notice to all interested parties of the time, place, and purpose of the hearing, and shall conform to all statutory requirements. Any meeting of the Commission held for the purpose of such hearing may be continued to a later time and other place without the necessity of a new notice. Any person desiring the Commission to make a special rule or an exception to any general spacing rule herein established or to the general rule or special rules and orders herafter to be promulgated by the Commission establishing spacing and/or drilling units for particular fields or pools, shall file a verified petition with the Commission setting forth the desired rule or exception, the reason therefor, and giving in detail the action the petitioner has taken in the matter. Nothing herein shall prevent the Commission itself from initiating the hearing provided for herein. In case of emergency a temporary rule or order may be made by the Commission to be effective only until notice may be given and hearing had as herein provided. (g) The above rules in this paragraph are subject to the following modification: In order to avoid locating a well in a ditch, stream, or other impracticable location, the Oil and Gas Supervisor, upon receipt of a request accompanied by such proof of necessity as he shall deem proper, is authorized to allow a variation in the location of any well of not more than thirty (30) feet from the location shown in the survey or plat in the application for the permit."

[41] *Id.* § 13.
[42] *Id.* § 13-a.
[43] *Id.* § 19.
[44] *Ibid.*
[45] *Ibid.*
[46] Rule 6 adopted May 8, 1947 and effective May 9, 1947.

be plugged, another is not needed. In adopting this rule, the Commission has taken the view that a bond must cover operations from the issuance of a drilling permit to the last plugging operations.[47] (8) A comprehensive plugging provision.[48] (9) The specific provision that the Commission may not limit the production from any well in its unitization orders.[49] Proration would be of doubtful value in the state because of its great refining capacity and low pressure.

The Commission adopted rules and regulations which cover the application for and issuance of permits, bonds for drilling and plugging operations, well logs, the location and spacing of wells and exceptions, plugging and the disposal of salt water and waste liquids. They were presented to the Indiana Oil and Gas Association for suggestions and criticisms prior to promulgation. The Legal Committee of the Interstate Oil Compact Commission gave advice of great benefit to the board in its rule making deliberations.Up to the present the rules and regulations have not been challenged; both the statute and the rules and regulations are respected by the oil and gas operators in Indiana. Although initially some misunderstanding existed as to the law's effect and regarding the rules, a very general cooperation now obtains between the operators and the Division. One of the greatest changes effected by the new law is the scientific spacing of wells.

Other measures adopted in 1947 related to oil and gas conservation are: (1) an Act to govern the leasing of public lands for exploration or production,[50] (2) and an Act creating a one per cent severance tax on crude oil produced in Indiana.[51] The monies received are used to pay the expenses of administration of the Act

---

[47] *Ibid.*

[48] Acts Ind. 1947, c. 277 § 22.

[49] *Id.* § 13-a.

[50] Acts Ind. 1947, c. 302; IND. ANN. STAT. § 46–1601 to 46–1624 (Burns Supp. 1947).

[51] Acts Ind. 1947, c. 278; IND. ANN. STAT. § 64–3101 to 64–3127 (Burns Supp. 1947) reads: "A tax at the rate of one percent of the value of all petroleum is hereby imposed as of the time of the severance of such petroleum from the land, upon all producers and owners thereof as an excise for the privilege of severing the same from the land and producing the same from the well, except when the gas from any well is used to pump or treat the same or when such gas is piped to landowners private buildings for this own use."

by the Oil and Gas Division, and to the Geology Division of the Department of Conservation for operating expense and research.[52]

THE ADMINISTRATIVE HISTORY

Prior to 1947 there was no solid basis for the activities of an oil and gas conservation agency in Indiana. As early as 1896 the police power of the state had been determined broad enough to prevent waste of oil and gas,[53] but it was not until more than fifty years later that the Indiana general assembly formed a state agency with powers to deal effectively with oil and gas conservation.[54] The Indiana Department of Conservation was established in 1919 with divisions of geology, entomology, forestry, lands and waters, including state parks, fish and game, and engineering.[55] A new division, water resources, was later added. The creating law gave the Department power "to secure the enforcement of laws for the conservation and development of the natural resources of the state." [56] In 1945 the law was amended [57] establishing the "Indiana Department of Conservation which shall consist of four (4) members who shall be appointed by the governor, to serve at his pleasure, and for a term of four (4) years, not more than two of said members shall be adherents of the same political party . . . The members . . . shall serve without compensation, except . . . they shall receive fifteen ($15.00) per day for the days actually and necessarily spent on duty and actual and necessary traveling and other expenses when engaged upon their official duties. . . ." The director of the Department is appointed by the governor for four years at a salary not to exceed $6000.[58] The administrative head or chief of the Oil and Gas Division, the oil and gas supervisor, is appointed by the director of the department with the approval of the governor, and his salary is fixed by the director.[59] Active man-

[52] *Id.* § 27.
[53] Townsend v. The St., 147 Ind. 624, 47 N. E. 19 (1896).
[54] Acts Ind. 1947, c. 277.
[55] IND. ANN. STAT. § 60–701, 60–712 (Burns 1933).
[56] *Id.* at § 60–715.
[57] IND. ANN. STAT. § 60–702 (Burns Supp. 1947).
[58] *Id.* at § 60–703.
[59] Acts Ind. 1947, c. 277.

agement of the business of the division is done by the supervisor, who processes all applications for permits to drill, deepen or plug, for bonds, and exceptions to spacing rules, as well as managing the administrative business. He has two assistants in the field to make inspections and reports. Direction of plugging is under the control of twelve pluggers who work on a contractual basis. The administrator cooperates with the state geologist in reporting to the Interstate Oil Compact Commission and the United States Bureau of Mines, and in coordinating and disseminating technical and geological information to the industry.

The Commission is charged with the duties of carrying out and enforcing the provisions of the conservation law.[60] Pursuant to power given to adopt rules and regulations,[61] the agency adopted 20 rules effective May 9, 1947.[62] These rules were promulgated in accordance with the general statute governing fixing of rules by state administrative agencies [63] requiring a public hearing be held on the proposed measures. Perhaps the most important rule of the 20 is that governing spacing.[64] Separate provisions are made for limestone, sandstone and Trenton lime production. Exceptions to spacing can be made only after publication of notice and a public hearing. Provision is made to meet emergency situations or instances necessitating slight variations from the spacing rule. At present the rules do not establish drilling units although the law authorizes their creation.[65] To date the agency has conducted the few hearings requested for exceptions to spacing rules. The Commission may designate one of its members or any officer, agent or employee to hold a hearing and make proposed findings of fact, which would not be valid or binding until approved by the whole Commission.[66] The agency is authorized to subpoena witnesses for lawful hearings under the law.[67] The Commission brings suit against persons violating the law or any valid rule adopted there-

[60] IND. ANN. STAT. § 60–753 (Burns Supp. 1947).
[61] Id. at § 60–758, 60–760.
[62] Copies of the rules may be obtained by writing the Oil and Gas Division, Indiana Department of Conservation, Indianapolis 9, Indiana.
[63] IND. ANN. STAT. § 60–1501 to 60–1511 (Burns Supp. 1947).
[64] See note 40 supra.
[65] IND. ANN. STAT. § 60–764 (Burns Supp. 1947).
[66] Id. at § 60–761.
[67] Id. at § 60–762.

under to restrain such action.[68] Infractions of the conservation law and the valid rules are misdemeanors punishable by a fine of not more than $50 for each day of violation.[69] Although the board may force unitization of separately owned tracts for development,[70] the occasion has not arrived when the exercise of this power is necessary. The Commission has arranged with the Indiana Oil and Gas Association for the selection by it and the association of an unofficial advisory committee to advise and counsel the supervisor on new or unusual technical administrative problems.

THE JUDICIAL HISTORY

The judicial history of oil and gas conservation in Indiana began and ended within three years—1897 to 1900. Professor Walter L. Summers wrote of this era: [71] "The first real controversy between the policy of conservation and the policy of production began in the 1890's through attempts to enforce Indiana Conservation statutes . . . the issue was clearly defined. The opponents of conservation claimed legal privileges to produce oil and gas from their lands, limited only by duties not to commit surface nuisances. In other words, they relied upon the so-called law of capture. The proponents of conservation insisted that such legal privileges to produce were further limited by duties to the public not to waste these natural resources. The statutes were attacked as unconstitutional on many grounds, principally that their enforcement resulted in the taking of private property without due process or just compensation. In Townsend vs State a statute forbidding the burning of gas in flambeau lights was held constitutional as a proper exercise of the police power of the state to prevent injury to the public through waste, although, to fortify the result of its decision, the court mentioned the wild animal analogy for the purpose of showing that a land owner has no property in the gas subject to deprivation without due process. In

[68] *Id.* at § 60–776.
[69] *Id.* at § 60–777.
[70] *Id.* at § 60–765.
[71] Summers, *The Modern Theory and Practical Application of Statutes for the Conservation of Oil and Gas*, Legal History of Conservation of Oil and Gas— A Symposium 1, 7 (1938).

State vs. Ohio Oil Company a statute for the prevention of waste through the escape of gas from an oil well was also held constitutional on a similar theory and against similar objections, although the case again indulged in the wild animal analogy. This latter case was appealed to the Supreme Court of the United States. The decision of this court was stated in the memorable opinion of Chief Justice White supporting the constitutionality of the statute on two grounds: the police power of the state to legislate for the prevention of waste of natural resources for the protection of the public interest, and the power of the state to legislate for the protection of the rights of owners in a common source of supply of oil and gas. It was in these decisions that courts first began to give recognition to the peculiar physical facts of oil and gas, and to base the legal relations of land owners respecting them thereon. Chief Justice White exposed the fallacies of the wild animal analogy, and pointed out that land owners' privileges to take oil and gas actually constitute a property interest. But he also explained that all land owners in a common source of supply of oil and gas are equally privileged to take, and that an unlimited exercise of such privileges by one '*may result in an undue proportion being attributed to one of the possessors of the right, to the detriment of others, or by waste by one or more, to the annihilation of the rights of the remainder.*'" Two and one half months after in the case of *Manufacturers' Gas and Oil Company v. Indiana Gas and Oil Company*,[72] the Indiana Supreme Court adopted the theory of protection of correlative rights in a common source of supply as a basis for the exercise of the state's police power and cited the United States Supreme Court as authority for its decision.[73] Since that time there has been no legal holding in Indiana testing or developing state police power to prevent waste of oil and gas or to protect correlative rights.[74] It has been pointed out by Walace Hawkins ". . . in fact the 1899 decision of Ohio Oil Company v. Indiana . . . was not improved upon as to funda-

[72] 155 Ind. 461, 57 N. E. 912 (1900).
[73] *Id.* at 470 and at 915.
[74] In Given v. St., 160 Ind. 552, 66 N. E. 750 (1903), the Indiana Supreme Court held that the 1893 statute making it unlawful to permit gas or oil to escape into the open air for longer than two days constitutional with the decision based upon police power to protect public health and safety.

mentals by the Champlin Refining Company case. . . ." [75] it seems reasonable to assume that the provisions of the 1947 Act on spacing [76] and unitization [77] will be held valid if challenged in the state or federal courts.[78]

[75] Quoted with permission from a letter to William A. McAfee Nov. 10, 1947.

[76] Acts Ind. 1947, c. 277 § 9.

[77] *Id.* at § 13-a.

[78] See 22 IND. L. J. 385–389 where it is pointed out that statutory provisions similar to these in the law of 1947 have been upheld.

CHAPTER 12

Iowa, 1939–1948

Although not classed as a commercial oil producing state, Iowa enacted certain control laws relating to oil and gas drilling during the 48th session of the Iowa General Assembly in 1939.[1] The Act provides that notice of intent to drill must be given the State Geologist of Iowa at Des Moines at least five days prior to the commencement of drilling operations for oil or gas.[2] The driller or owner of the well is required to use pipe, cement, or other scientific method in common use to shut off all contiguous underground fresh water strata to a depth of 300 feet to prevent its pollution or contamination; this requirement does not apply to geological core holes drilled for informational purposes.[3] A report must be made to the geologist of compliance with this section. Dry or abandoned oil and gas wells are ordered plugged in accordance with processes which confine all oil, gas, or water in the strata where found by the use of mud laden plugs or cement.[4] Before a well may be plugged it must be cleaned out, and prior to the removal of its casing, a fluid of mud and water must be used to close the hole. The geologist may direct the type of fluid used in plugging. Notice of intent to plug is required to be given the geologist

BLAKELY M. MURPHY, WRITER. (See app. B.)

[1] Iowa Acts 1939, c. 63; IOWA CODE § 84.1–5 (1946). The Act, in addition to dealing with the topics mentioned, takes up offset drilling in § 2, the duty to release forfeited leases and affidavits of non-compliance in § 6, an action to obtain releases which provides for costs, attorney fees, and damages in § 7, extensions of leases upon certain contingencies in § 8, liens for laborers, contractors, subcontractors, and materialmen for labor and supplies furnished oil and gas wells or lines in § 9, and authorizes the State of Iowa or any municipality to enter into oil and gas leases upon the giving of certain notices in § 10.

[2] Iowa Acts 1939, c. 63 § 3.

[3] *Id.* § 1.

[4] *Id.* § 4.

and the available adjoining lease and property holders, but plugging need not wait where there is delay in delivering notice to the lease and property owners. Section 5 calls for filing with the geologist, upon the completion of a well or its plugging, a report and log signed and sworn to on blanks furnished by the state. A written report of well potential is due ten days after the completion of its initial test.

CHAPTER 13

Kansas, 1937–1948

~/~

Prior to 1935 little consideration had been accorded in Kansas to the conservation of natural gas. The motivating force which brought oil men into the state was the hope of finding oil. Although the existence of gas was recognized, its possibilities and powers were greatly overshadowed by these dreams of oil. Early discoveries and production of petroleum were carried on in the eastern part of Kansas, where oil was found by 1915 in the El Dorado Field. Production and development were phenomenal and expansion was very rapid. Although oil was located in western Kansas November 24, 1923—in the Fairport pool of Russell County—not until ten years later was that area's productivity fully known. Activity expanded throughout 1937, when economic conditions which lasted until 1941 caused a slight decline.[1] Most of the oil and gas in Kansas comes from the western part of the state—a significant fact when it is realized that it was here that a new chapter in the history of Kansas petroleum development was to be written—the story of the Hugoton Gas Field.

The discovery and the subsequent production of oil and gas in western Kansas was undoubtedly a principal factor enabling people living in this area to weather the economic storms of the 1930's. A world wide depression coupled with unprecedented drouths made it impossible for many people to make their customary living from agricultural pursuits. The money which came into their hands from the production of oil and gas was their salvation, a fact very dramatically stated by Governor Ratner in 1939 when he said, "An oil chariot lugged $20,000,000 into Western Kansas in 1937.

JAY C. KYLE, WRITER; Andrew F. Schoeppel, George Stallwitz, T. A. Morgan, Ennis D. Harris, Advisers. (See app. B.)

[1] Wichita Eagle, Jan. 15, 1938.

138

It relieved economic conditions arising from drouth, depression, and regimentation. And so in gratitude and admiration, Western Kansas humbly bows to the miracle industry which pays so generously for revealing to us the hidden wealth of our own possessions."

The shift in emphasis from oil to gas and in the location of fields from eastern to western Kansas brought with it a number of problems inherent not only in the transition, but in the rapid growth of the industry. Foremost among these difficulties was the conflict between the protection of the lessor's interests through a rapid exhaustion of the land's capability and the logical necessity for conserving and regulating production of Kansas' natural resources.

Development of the petroleum industry during 1938 revealed new quantities of oil in the 45 new producing areas discovered in western Kansas; 21 were gas pools and 24 were oil pools. In 15 of the established pools oil was found in new producing horizons during the year. Based on daily potential capacity these finds built up the reserves by 1,220,000 barrels, and 60,064,000 barrels of oil were produced. The number of wells drilled in that year totaled 1569 and nearly three-fourths of them (or some 1107) were commercial oil wells; 915 were in western Kansas, where in the same period 46 gas wells had been completed. Many years of experience were needed to develop the ideal methods of coping with the problems incident to this production.

It was realized that if the troubles accompanying discovery and production of oil and gas were to be kept at a minimum while preserving these vast resources, appropriate conservation statutes would have to be adopted and enforced. Enactment was comparatively easy. The problem of making the laws work was difficult. Kansas in 1937, still an infant in the field of petroleum regulation and conservation, had untried statutory controls; the path to a practicable application of these standards was not an easy one.

THE BACKGROUND OF CONSERVATION IN KANSAS

The gas statute passed in 1935 [2] provided: "That the production of natural gas in the State of Kansas in such manner and under

[2] Kan. Laws 1935, c. 213, § 1; KAN. GEN. STAT. ANN. § 55–701 (1935).

such conditions as to constitute waste is hereby prohibited." The term waste was then defined as ordinary waste, and in addition included "economic waste, underground waste, and surface waste." [3]

The first action in the administration of the gas Act by the State Corporation Commission—the agency empowered with authority to enforce the conservation statutes—came with an investigation into possible gas wastage at the Otis Field in May 1937. The Commission had been informed of unnecessary waste in the production, sale and use of oil and gas in the Otis Field of Barton and Rush Counties and it found that gas was wasted in the operation of combination wells and that the available production of gas from the common sources of supply exceeded market demands. Gas was not marketed from the wells in the proportion that their open flow potential bore to the total open flow potentials of all wells in the common source of supply. The Commission established a gas-oil ratio for the Otis Field, not to exceed 5000 cubic feet of gas to a barrel of oil.[4] In its tenth finding it stated: "That the requirement for ratable taking would be satisfied if the gas purchased from said field were first taken from the combination wells, and, thereafter, from such other well or wells as may be convenient if the gas taken from said combination wells is insufficient to provide for the total market demand, provided, that the producers of all wells in the field are compensated for the gas taken, in proportion to the gas potentials of each and every well in the field, the same as if the total amount of gas purchased had been taken ratably from each and every well separately." In July 1937 a gas-oil ratio investigation was started in the Burrton Field, Reno and Harvey Counties, which resulted in orders covering gas wastage.

While the Commission's power to enforce statutes was present in the law, it had not been accepted by the producers and land owners who questioned not only the regulatory authority of the Commission and the legality of agency orders, but even the constitutionality of the enabling statutes. It was not uncommon for the Commission to find itself in a court defending its oil and gas orders. The agency was uniformly successful in defending not only the statutes but the orders entered under their direction, thus

[3] *Id.* § 2.
[4] Dockets No. 14,534 (1937) and No. 16,028 (1937).

demonstrating that there was ample jurisdictional precedent to sustain the constitutionality of the statutes and the legality of the orders issued by the Commission. The Commission in 1940 issued this declaration: "It is our firm belief that the oil proration act is constitutional and will be so declared by the highest court of this nation. If this rule can be obtained, not only can physical waste be avoided in the production of crude oil, but the economic welfare of this primary industry of the state can be preserved so that all the people of Kansas may reap innumerable benefits which flow from it. When it is realized that crude oil production contributes in excess of twenty-five million dollars annually to the farmers and royalty owners in Kansas and that the annual value of the petroleum produced in the state exceeds the annual value of our wheat crops, it is not difficult to realize that a vital interest of Kansas is involved in these lawsuits." [5] At the time this statement was issued two gas cases were pending in district courts involving the constitutionality of the oil proration act. The hope of the Commission that these causes would reach the Supreme Court of the United States was never realized, but an answer was given regarding the primary question of their constitutionality.

The first case, *State Corporation Commission of Kansas v. Wall,*[6] arose from these facts: the legislature of Kansas, at its 1939 session, enacted a statute [7] relating to the production of crude oil, defining and prohibiting its waste, and conferring regulatory powers upon the Commission. Subsequent to the adoption of the Act, the petitioner, as receiver of the estate of C. E. Skiles, was allowed to use in May 1939, 4254 barrels of oil from the Campbell well on the west 40 acres of his lease. The petitioner also had a well on the east 40 acres of the lease with a monthly allowable of 2760 barrels. The Commission, pursuant to notice given in May 1939, held a hearing to fix the Kansas allowables for June, July, and August 1939. At the hearing the nominations of the Cushing Refining and Gasoline Company were presented. June 1, 1939 the Commission reduced the allowable for the Campbell well on the west 40 acres from 4254 to 2267 barrels per month, charged it with

[5] Kan. Corp. Comm. 15th Biennial Rep. 18 (1940).
[6] 113 F. 2d 877 (1940).
[7] Kan. Laws 1939, c. 227.

overproduction for April (which left no allowable production for June), and reduced the allowable for the well on the east 40 acres from 2760 to 1781 barrels. The petitioner alleged that other wells in the Campbell Pool were owned by companies (large producers and purchasers of oil) or by oil producers who had pipe line connections and a ready market; that the order of June 1, 1939 was contrary to the provisions of the statute, and if it were in accordance therewith it violated the constitution of Kansas and the Constitution of the United States. The petitioner averred it would be unprofitable for Cushing to continue to take the small amount of oil which he might run in compliance with the order and that his market for the oil would thus be lost. On June 7, 1939 the court entered an *ex parte* order directing the receiver to take the necessary steps to rehear and to review the order of June 1, 1939 and enjoining the Commission, pending these proceedings and until further order, from interfering with the production and sale of oil by the receiver in stated amounts. The Commission June 16, 1939 moved to modify the order. On November 10, 1939 the court entered a judgment ordering the injunction dissolved as of August 15, 1939, but saying that all oil produced and sold by the receiver from June 7, 1939 to and including August 15, 1939 must not be charged by the Commission as overproduction. The Commission appealed this order. The petitioner contended that an order charging overproduction during the time the injunctive order was in force was in the nature of a penalty for a violation of Chapter 227. The court answering this claim stated: "The property right of the owner and lessee of land in and to the gas beneath the surface is not an absolute one. Those substances, *because of their peculiarity in the natural state, partake more in the nature of common property, title to which becomes absolute only when they are captured and reduced to possession. Because they are natural resources, the public has a definite interest in their preservation from waste, and the state has the power to regulate the production of oil and gas for the purpose of preventing waste and protecting the correlative rights of owners producing oil or gas from a common pool.*" (Italics supplied). As to the oil production during the time the injunction was effective, it was held that deducting "as overproduction from further allowables, the amount of oil produced in excess of the order of June 1, 1939, during the time the injunction was in force did not inflict a penalty. . . . It would only right, to some degree, the wrong done to the other owners producing oil from the common pool whose allowable production was restricted during that period by the Commission's order, resulting in the lessor obtaining more than his share of the oil from the common pool."

The second case, *Bay Petroleum Corporation v. Corporation Commission of the State of Kansas,*[8] arose from a complaint challenging the right of the police power of the state under Chapter 227 (the statute attacked in the *Wall* case) to impair the freedom of contract by denying a producer of oil the right to produce and sell, and a purchaser of oil the right to purchase, on terms mutually agreeable where there was neither waste nor impairment of correlative rights within the pool where the oil was produced. Here the court said: "We think the state may in its effort to attain these objectives [prevention of waste and protection of correlative rights] consider the oil industry of the state as a whole, restrict allowed production to predetermined market demands, prorate the allowed production among the several pools in the manner authorized by the statute, and forbid production in a given pool in excess of the amounts allowed, even though a larger amount might be produced without physical waste in that particular pool. If excess production is allowed in one prorated pool, even without physical waste there, total production will exceed total market demands, and that condition contributes to physical and economic waste as well as industrial instability."

Two principles were definitely formulated in these cases which the state might use as a basis for the development of its policy of conservation. The *Wall* case established the fact that the state had the power to regulate the production of oil and gas to prevent waste and to protect correlative rights. The *Bay Petroleum* case gave the state the authority to prevent physical waste in a given pool and to view the oil and gas industry of the state as a whole in preventing economic waste irrespective of conditions in a particular pool. The court held that oil and gas were not absolute property rights, but rather rights partaking of the attributes of common property, title

[8] 36 F. Supp. 66 (1940).

to which became absolute only when captured and reduced to possession. This theory had long been the Kansas judicial approach to conservation. It has been under severe attack since its inception, more particularly so in the years since conservation has grown to maturity. The first attack upon the principles arose under the Statute of Frauds, where the sixth section reads: "No action shall be brought whereby to charge a party upon any obligation, promise to answer for the debt, default or miscarriage of another person; . . . or upon any contract for the sale of lands, tenements, hereditaments, or any interest in or concerning them. . . . ; unless the agreement upon [which] such action shall be brought, or some memorandum or note thereof, shall be in writing and signed by the party to be charged therewith, or some other person thereunto by him or her lawfully authorized in writing." [9] The court, in trying to apply the principle that oil and gas are personalty and not part of the land, emerged with decisions abounding in inconsistencies. To understand fully the judicial concept, it is necessary to notice the prior cases which form a basis for later decisions.

The first case before the Kansas court involving the application of the statute to an oil and gas lease came in 1918 with the case of *Gross v. Rothrock*.[10] A group of buyers negotiated an oral agreement for an oil and gas lease which was executed to one of their members (Lucas) for the benefit of all. Lucas advanced the purchase price and drew drafts on the others of the group for their respective shares. He assigned the lease to the defendants who took with notice of the fact that he held title as trustee for plaintiffs, thus putting them on inquiry and preventing their obtaining the royalty rights then held by Lucas. The court found that the Statute of Frauds interposed no obstacle to the claims of the plaintiffs since the transaction did not amount to an oral contract for the sale of interest concerning land, and each was said to be the owner of his respective interest in the lease. It then applied the general principle that a trust results in favor of the person for whom the property is to be purchased where he furnishes the consideration for the conveyance. The facts may be proved by parol.

Since this case the court has set out the following principles:

[9] Kan. Gen. Stat. Ann. § 33–106 (1935).
[10] 102 Kan. 272, 169 P. 1161 (1918).

(1) an oil and gas lease is not a conveyance and raises no interest in the land as it creates an incorporeal hereditament, and contracts for the sale of incorporeal hereditaments are within the sixth section of the Statute of Frauds,[11] (2) an oil and gas lease may be inherited, and law and good public policy require it to be in writing,[12] (3) the Statute of Frauds does not apply to the personal relation and obligations created by an agreement to deal in oil and gas leases and divide the profits,[13] (4) a contract for the acquisition and sale of leases is a personal relation of joint adventure and not affected by the Statute of Frauds,[14] (5) an oral contract where the defendant agrees to pay plaintiff's labor bills against a contractor who at defendant's request undertook to drill an oil and gas well, but failed to complete it or pay his laborers, is not promise to answer for the debt of another,[15] and (6) a parol contract to transfer an interest in an oil and gas lease is within the Statute.[16]

In *McCrae v. Bradley Oil Company*[17] an action was brought by the lease producers to recover under an oral contract for their services in procuring the sale of an interest in oil and gas leases. Plaintiffs were to be paid for their services $4000 and 20,000 barrels of oil out of any oil produced from the land described in the lease. The question presented was whether the oral agreement, as it related to the 20,000 barrels of oil, was within the Statute of Frauds. The court stated:[18] "Not every contract that touches or concerns the land is within the statute. The general rule is that things attached to and forming part of the realty which are agreed to be severed therefrom before the sale or promptly after the formation of the contract are not an interest in the land within the statute. Minerals, though part of the realty, may be severed, and when severed become goods. A contract to sell severed iron ore would be a contract to sell goods even though the ore which the parties expected, or even contracted, should be the subject of the sale, was not yet mined." Thus the agreement did not create an interest

---

[11] Robinson v. Smalley, 102 Kan. 842, 171 P. 1155 (1918).
[12] White v. Green, 103 Kan. 405, 173 P. 974 (1918).
[13] Bird v. Wilcox and Sternburg, 104 Kan. 799, 180 P. 774 (1919).
[14] Sawtelle v. Cosden Oil and Gas Co. et al., 128 Kan. 220, 277 P. 45 (1929).
[15] Gates v. Syndicate Oil Corp., 132 Kan. 272, 295 P. 649 (1931).
[16] Shoemake v. Davis, 146 Kan. 909, 73 P. 2d 1043 (1937).
[17] 148 Kan. 911, 84 P. 2d 866 (1938).
[18] *Ibid.*

in the land, but merely a lien on the oil when it was separated from the soil. "The contention is made that the agreement to give plaintiff 20,000 barrels of oil out of any oil produced from the land, granted to plaintiffs an overriding royalty; that an overriding royalty is an interest in the lease, and that an agreement to buy or sell an oil or gas lease or any interest therein is within the Statute of Frauds . . . The Texas courts hold that an overriding royalty is an interest in land and cannot be alienated except by an instrument in writing. As we hold the agreement before us does not purport to assign or transfer an overriding royalty, we find it unnecessary to determine whether such royalty is real or personal property." The court did take notice that under its decision in *Robinson v. Jones*[19] an overriding royalty was personal property for the purpose of taxation. The opinion in the *Robinson* case adhered to a distinction made by the court that while oil royalty was real property, *royalty oil* was personal property.

Ruppenthal concluded from the court decisions to 1940[20] that the following transactions were within the Statute of Frauds: "1. An oral agreement to execute and deliver an oil and gas lease. 2. An oral agreement to assign an interest in an oil or gas lease. 3. Where a series of writings or memoranda concerning an oil or gas lease require parol proof to show the essential elements of a contract. 4. Where there has been performance under the terms of parol contract to assign an interest in an oil or gas lease, and the damage can be compensated in money," and that these matters were not within the Statute: "1. Purchase of an oil and gas lease by one of a group for the benefit of all under an oral agreement. 2. An oral partnership agreement to engage in buying and selling leases. 3. An oral agreement to procure, develop and share in oil and gas leases. 4. Joint adventures and partnerships under oral contracts concerned with acquiring oil and gas leases. 5. An oral contract to execute an oil and gas lease from another. 6. An oral contract to share in oil if, as and when produced. 7. An oral agreement to answer for the debt of another, where the consideration is sufficient, since it then becomes an independent binding

---

[19] 119 Kan. 609, 240 P. 957 (1925).
[20] Ruppenthal, *The Effect of the Statute of Frauds on Oil and Gas Transactions*, 9 J. B. A. KAN. 129 (1940).

obligation of the promisor." In the 1945 case of *Riffel v. Dieter*[21] it was held that a contract to execute an oil and gas lease was within the Statute as to the sale of lands, tenements and hereditaments, also that payment alone (under the contract) would not constitute a performance sufficient to avoid the Statute. The court apparently is still trying to apply the principles applicable to minerals in place —principles inadequate to meet the needs of oil and gas.

The second attack upon the maxim that oil and gas (because of their peculiar natural state) partake of the nature of personalty arose under the Kansas doctrine of implied convenants. From the beginning in construing oil and gas leases, the court has been motivated by a *policy of development*. The attitude of the court has been one of preventing delay and promoting rapid development, said to be based upon three primary assumptions. These principles were well stated in an article by Eberhardt written in an effort to show the injustice of enforcing implied covenants in the face of wartime regulations.[22] He said: "One . . . is that the very essence of oil and gas leases is production of oil and gas and by the same token, payment of royalties to the lessor." He noted that it was possibly technically incorrect to refer to royalties as the essential consideration for a lease, inasmuch as the bonus payment, even if only one dollar, was the supporting consideration; nevertheless, it must be admitted that the principal objective of the lease was production and the payment of royalties. It has been stated that the law was adverse to implying a covenant unless the lessor's *rent* was dependent upon the amount of the lessee's production. If this angle were considered alone, it would hardly explain the covenant. The implied covenants doctrine was analogous to decisions relating to leases covering mills, farms, and solid minerals where the rental was based upon the production realized from the leasehold by the lessee. In such cases the courts have often implied and enforced covenants to explore, develop, and market. Eberhardt's second and third premises were: "a second . . . which played an important part during the nascency of implied covenants is that oil and gas are fugacious, freely migrating beneath the earth's surface much in the manner of subterranean waters. . . .

[21] 159 Kan. 628, 157 P. 2d 831 (1945).
[22] Eberhardt, *War on Implied Covenants*, 11 J. B. A. KAN. 102 (1942).

A third factor, which either ignored or was ignorant of fundamental physical and economic considerations, was a belief that oil and gas are of no possible value until captured and marketed; ergo they should be developed and used as quickly as possible. In this the courts undoubtedly sought to further not merely the financial aims of the lease parties, but also a general public interest in the development of natural resources." An additional proposition, which has played an important part in creating the policy of development, was a desire to prohibit speculative trades by lessees inclined to withhold their drilling activities until others defined the field. At any rate it is now well established that in the absence of an express covenant in an oral gas lease, these covenants will be implied and enforced: "(1) A covenant to explore, that is to drill an initial or test well within a reasonable time; (2) a covenant, conditioned upon the exploratory well's indicating the presence of oil or gas in paying quantities, reasonably and fully to develop the leased land—to drill sufficient additional wells fairly to exhaust the land's capability to produce these minerals; (3) a covenant to protect the leased premises from substantial drainage by drilling offset or productive wells, and (4) a covenant to 'market' the product of the wells drilled." These implied covenants ostensibly come from the court's misapprehensions as to the physical and economic truths regarding petroleum and were motivated by a policy of development which no longer retains its verity. Especially did the courts overestimate the migratory nature of oil and gas. It is now known that (except when disturbed and released by drilling) neither oil nor gas migrate far, since its fugitive movements are checked and hindered in all directions. The Kansas court—thinking of oil and gas only in terms of light and heat—did not foresee that with the perfection of the internal combustion engine these substances would become the world's principal source of motive power. The court was interested primarily and exclusively with furthering development; those first concerned with the problem did not foresee the place of conservation in combating the evils of competitive drilling.

Although reluctant to recognize the necessity of enforcing a conservation program, in recent decisions the courts have indicated that the policy of development is no longer paramount.[23] Under modern leases the lessor receives a substantial cash bonus upon the execution of the lease, and sizeable periodic delay rental payments where drilling is postponed. It would seem, when all the factors are considered together, that implied covenants no longer embody a correct approach to the problem of oil and gas leases. It is illogical and unreasonable to believe that oil and gas leases must be so construed as to prevent delay and promote development, regardless of the resultant injury. The courts surely realize that the policy of development has been superseded by a program of conservation to prevent economic and physical waste.

A lessee is under a duty (implied in law) to develop the leasehold estate; neither he nor the lessor is the sole arbiter of what constitutes diligent operation or development.[24] This is up to the discretion of a court in determining what is prudent operation under the particular facts of each case. One of the first Kansas cases to pass directly on the question of prudent development where governmental and state regulations were involved was *Fischer v. Magnolia Petroleum Company.*[25] This was an action to cancel an oil and gas lease for the violation of an implied covenant to develop after the primary term expired. There was no allegation that there were producing wells immediately adjacent to the leased land on any side, or that there was oil drainage, or any threat of drainage. There was no claim of violation by a failure to drill offset wellls. In its answer the defendant said that the intent of the parties in making the contract was to develop the lease in a prudent and businesslike manner. As a part of the Kansas policy and plan for conserving petroleum resources, the state enacted proration and conservation laws by virtue of which it became neither prudent nor reasonable to require further present developments on the leased premises. In its decision the court said: "It may frankly be conceded that our own decisions are wholly harmonious, though such lack of harmony as may appear will be found, upon analysis, to

[23] Davis v. Sherman, McIntyre and Cummings, 149 Kan. 104, 86 P. 2d 490 (1939).

[24] Meyers v. Shell Pet. Corp., 153 Kan. 287, 110 P. 2d 810 (1941); Harris et al. v. Morris Plan Co. 144 Kan. 501, 61 P. 2d 901 (1936).

[25] 156 Kan. 367, 133 P. 2d 95 (1933).

arise in large part at least from an emphasis placed upon isolated sentences from opinions, or from failure to give due weight to divergence in factual situations involved. Some of the differences perhaps may be accounted for by the fact that through comparatively recent years there has been, generally, a shifting of emphasis from *production* to *conservation* of our natural resources. This trend, evidenced by conservation and proration statutes and in other ways, is so well recognized as to require no comment. Courts naturally reflect this trend by stressing the mutual interest of both the lessor and the lessee rather than the special interest only of the lessor, in securing production." (Italics supplied).

Schoeppel [26] gained the impression from this case that the Kansas Supreme Court definitely recognized for the first time that valid proration and conservation orders would be considered in determining whether there was a breach of an implied covenant. The lessor, who alleged a breach of an implied covenant to develop, had the burden of submitting substantial evidence that the covenant had been in fact broken, that the lessee did not act with reasonable diligence, and that regulations and production through governmental agencies must be considered. Schoeppel then cited from Merrill's *Covenants Implied in Oil and Gas Leases*, where the holdings of the court are summarized thus "The Kansas court, in the latter cases, has shied off from the absolute duty theory. First, it held that the absolute duty obtained only in cases wherein cancellation of the lease was sought, and the damages could be recovered only upon proof that the lessee had failed to attain to the standard of the reasonably prudent operator. Then it expressly repudiated the idea of an absolute duty to drill, even as the foundation of a right to cancellation. In fact, the opinion rather indignantly repudiates the motion that there has ever been any justification for deducing the absolute duty from the Kansas decisions, saying that such statements as appear contrary to the rule (of the ordinarily prudent operator) lose much of their authority when viewed in the light of the particular facts and issues involved. The attempted distinction of these cases seems to me to be inadequate,

[26] Schoeppel, *The Effect of Proration Upon Implied Covenants*, 16 KAN. B. J. 13 (1947).

however, and I submit in all respect that, until these last two decisions, one was justified in concluding that there was an absolute duty in Kansas to drill."

It has been settled that statutes providing for proration and conservation of natural resources are a valid exercise of the state police power to protect its citizens and its natural wealth. The law protects not only the land owners property but also his property rights, that is the right to reduce to possession the oil and gas underlying his land or lease. The protection afforded any lease by proration is the same, irrespective of whether it be operated by the owner of the property or his lessee. The allowables established for wells located on a lease are identical regardless of the manner in which title to the property is held. The correlative rights spoken of in judicial opinions are not only those of the lessee, but include those of any person having a right to drill into and produce oil or gas from a given source of supply; the correlative rights doctrine thus includes in most instances protection of the rights of lessors. Whenever correlative rights are impaired, the implied covenants of the lease are not protected and royalty owners are deprived of their rights. If the regulations issued under a conservation statute fail to preserve correlative rights, the implied covenants of leases are not safeguarded. In such instances the royalty owners may have a good cause for action against their lessees. Proration where properly applied serves to make secure the implied covenants to reasonably develop, insofar as they relate to the rate at which drilling of added wells occurs. Even under proration there is an obligation to drill offset wells. Except for economic considerations, proration probably would not affect the rate at which a lessee is obligated to develop a lease. The smallness of the allowable obtained by drilling a well evidences the time at which he must drill. Assuming that the allowables are sufficient to justify drilling, the operator must proceed to develop the productive portions of the lease at a reasonable rate. The *Fischer* case [27] may then be construed as an about face by the court in interpreting and enforcing implied covenants in oil and gas leases, departing as it did from the earlier statements which impliedly imposed an affirmative duty upon a lessee to rea-

[27] See note 25 *supra*.

sonably drill and develop the leased premises. This conclusion was, however, vigorously questioned by Veeder: [28] "Governor Shoeppel's interesting paper suggests the thought provoking proposition that the implications of the Fischer-Magnolia Petroleum case are that the lessee no longer has an absolute duty to drill and develop the premises but instead the emphasis is now upon conservation and prevention of economic and physical waste, requiring consideration of proration and conservation orders effecting the leased premises when cancellation is sought for breach of implied covenant to reasonably develop. The Court in the Fischer case clearly stated that limitation or restriction of production or marketing enforced under lawful governmental orders, constitutes a factor to be considered along with other facts, and circumstances bearing upon the question of prudent development of the oil and gas lease the Court was considering. In view of the extent to which governmental regulation of oil and the production thereof existed prior to such decision, it is perhaps natural and proper that this additional factor is considered in determining the question of prudent development. . . . In view of the record in the case, it may be subject to debate whether the Court did more than to recognize the additional factor or element of lawful governmental orders in determining an extremely weak case for cancellation. In other words, it seems open to question whether the governmental proration orders affecting the lease were all-persuasive or simply a factor which, in the light of the weak case made out by Fischer, resulted in the decision denying cancellation."

The court in *Bennett v. Corporation Commission* [29] apparently followed its previous course to recognize the policy of conservation, as it ruled there that it was illegal to produce oil under conditions which injured the correlative rights of others in a pool and exceeded the allowables fixed by the Commission under the statutes [30] and valid rules and regulations. In the same case it was held that the enactment [31] imposed a duty upon the State Corporation Commission to regulate the production of crude oil in a manner

---

[28] Veeder, *Comments on Effect of Proration Upon Its Implied Covenants*, 16 KAN. B. J. 13 (1947).

[29] 157 Kan. 589, 142 P. 2d 810 (1943).

[30] KAN. GEN. STAT. ANN. § 55–604 (Cum. Supp. 1941).

[31] *Id.* § 55–603.

which prevented inequitable or unfair taking. The only definite conclusion drawn was that the court looked either to development or to conservation, depending upon the facts in each case, and protected whichever party the court believed had the greater equity.

THE OIL INDUSTRY IN KANSAS

In the years spanning the close of the 1930's and the start of the 1940's situations developed in the Kansas oil industry incapable of solution; to understand the causes and magnitude of these problems one must review the Kansas history as compared with that of other states. The number of wells drilled in western Kansas in 1939 totaled 1075, of which slightly more than three-fifths of the total or 824 were completed as commercial oil wells, 24 were completed as gas wells and 200 test wells were abandoned as dry holes. Estimates based upon daily potential capacity showed that the new wells added 1,158,827 barrels to daily productivity raising the total above 4,000,000 barrels.[32] The oil industry in Kansas moved forward at a steady pace during the first six months of 1940 and, while no records for development were shattered, activity approached that of the peak year of 1937. The production of crude oil during this period totaled 30,706,266 barrels compared with 29,406,850 for a like time in 1939. While at the beginning of 1940 there were 245 active operations in the state, at the end of June there were 320. Kansas then produced daily approximately 180,000 barrels of crude oil, and it was thought that before long the figure would reach 200,000 barrels. Up to January 1, 1940, the year of largest production had been 1937, when 70,761,000 barrels of oil were produced; the total oil production through 1939 reached 1,028,469,000 barrels. There were 60 counties having oil or gas production with an area of 2,391,000 miles. The vast reserves in Kansas were greatly increased from 1937 to 1940 and while this might indicate that the state had a tremendous oil income and that conditions were satisfactory in the oil industry, actually the outlook was dismal. The main problem was that of a market. Kansas produced more petroleum products than its market could absorb. Kansas producers were un-

[32] VER WIEBE, EXPLORATION OF OIL AND GAS IN WESTERN KANSAS DURING 1939 (1940).

able to sell enough oil to meet their operating and overhead expenses, let alone to realize a profit. Too many wells were drilled and too much oil was piped to refineries. There was not enough purchasing power to maintain the industry at its then producing levels. The problem of obtaining a more equitable division of the oil market was placed directly in the lap of the state, and Kansas was powerless to act because its powers were limited.

In point of time among the States of Kansas, Texas, and Oklahoma, oil was first discovered in Kansas. Later it was found to a greater extent in Oklahoma and Texas. Big oil and gas companies built pipe lines and refineries in Oklahoma and Texas, but these refineries refused to buy Kansas oil; this left Kansas a market of less than 5 per cent of its daily potential production. The independent producers carried a big load as pioneers in Kansas; in 1937 among the 45 pools newly discovered, 30 were found by independents. The reason for this may be traced to the fact that the big companies had a sufficient supply of oil and were content to regard Kansas oil as *goods on the shelf*—ready to be tapped when the need arose, but not at that time necessary to profitable operation. The problem with all its implications was discussed in 1938 by John F. Jones, then assistant general attorney for the Kansas Corporation Commission: [33] "In 1931 the Legislature empowered the Corporation Commission to administer the Oil Conservation Act. The Commission was authorized to do two things; namely, to restrict and regulate the production of crude oil so as to prevent waste and in this restriction to prevent unreasonable discrimination or drainage between leases. . . . The act states that production of crude oil in excess of the reasonable market demand, or transportation and marketing facilities therefor, constitutes waste. By market demand, the legislature meant that production in excess of the amount which the consumers of Kansas would purchase was wasteful, as gasoline or crude oil when stored in tanks loses a great deal of its quality and quantity by reason of evaporation and shrinkage ·. . ."

The Oil Conservation Act set out a formula for the Commission to apply when it was established that the full production of a pool exceeded its market demand or transportation facilities. Production

[33] Jones, The Kansas Oil Problem, Progress in Kansas (1938).

was to be restricted or prorated so that each well in a field might produce that portion of the market demand which its potential bore to the total field potential. Potential was defined as the amount of oil a well could produce in 24 hours. The use of the formula and the restriction of production was termed ratable taking; the purpose of the formula was to prevent unequalized drainage of the oil from one's land to another's. The Commission received from the legislature a grant of two distinct powers: (1) the right to regulate production to prevent waste, and (2) the authority to prevent undue drainage between leases by the establishment of ratable taking and equitable withdrawal. Nothing was said about regulating drilling of wells or the marketing and sale of oil. Thus it may be assumed that the legislature chose to reserve to private initiative the *problem of finding a market for petroleum*, except where it might have a bearing on waste prevention.

Kansas in 1938 was capable of producing daily 10 times as much oil as in 1933, when the percentage of allowable production was more than half of the potential of all its wells. By 1938, in spite of a tremendously increased potential production, the market for Kansas oil was greater by only some 25,000 barrels. Wells capable of producing 3,000,000 barrels daily were restricted to 175,000 barrels, because of the decreased market demand and as a consequence each well's allowable production was only 5 per cent of its maximum daily production. In 1938 the oil producing states were capable of producing each day many times the market demand; Kansas wells alone could have supplied practically the entire market demand of the nation. Even though the delivery price of crude was the same in all states, Kansas oil was not sold elsewhere due to differences in transportation costs, caused—not by discrimination in rates—but by greater distances. Seaboard states received most of their oil by tanker at rates much lower than by pipe line. Kansas could obtain these markets enjoyed by the southwestern states only by price cuts. The producers did not want this, preferring that the price remain at its then level. The only manner in which Kansas oil could compete was through the price of oil delivered at the wells.

Oklahoma and Kansas together supply practically all of the market demand in the Mid-Continent area, and as the pipe lines were constructed in Oklahoma before the western Kansas fields were known, oil companies built their refineries there. Oklahoma transported refined petroleum in materially larger quantities than could Kansas; in fact Kansas pipe lines were capable of transporting daily only 215,000 barrels of oil. New oil fields were discovered about this time in Illinois and Michigan adding some 85,000 barrels of oil daily to the supply. These states in the Kansas marketing territory were much closer to the heavier industrial and consumption centers and as a result operated at peak capacities, thus absorbing a large part of the former Oklahoma and Kansas market. The only way to secure more of the market for Kansas oil was to acquire a part of Oklahoma's market. Oklahoma produced around 85 per cent of its potential production and many of its fields were operating at 100 per cent of capacity. Kansas producers thought that, since Oklahoma was drawing 85 per cent of its potential at a time Kansas was restricted to 5 per cent, there was an inequitable distribution of markets between the two states. Kansas producers would not submit to a continuance of these conditions because it was economic suicide.

Kansas, involved in the general unfavorable condition of the oil industry, was imperiled by excessive amounts of crude oil and gasoline in storage. During 1937, 45,000,000 barrels of oil were produced in excess of market consumption which was reflected in excessive inventories of refined products. From January 1, 1938 to March 31, 1938 stocks of gasoline increased 15,910,000 barrels. The consumptive demand for 1938 approximated that of 1937. Based on that assumption a continuation of crude oil production at the 1937 level could have resulted only in an excessive inventory, depressing the industry economic conditions and Kansas producers. On April 2, 1938 there were 308,237,000 barrels of crude and an added 92,-000,000 barrels of gasoline in storage. If a sound inventory was to be reached by September 30, 1938, the gasoline stocks would have to be cut to 62,000,000 barrels, and to accomplish this the production level east of California might not each day exceed 2,700,000 barrels. Excessive oil stocks in storage were caused by the fact that the state conservation agencies relied upon the nominations of the oil purchasers to arrive at the state allowables. The oil purchasers in 1937 stated at the monthly allowable hearings that they would purchase more oil than the facts showed necessary to supply market demand or consumption. While their estimate of future consumption was optimistic and erroneous, those compiled by the Bureau of Mines came within 1 per cent of actual consumption. During 1937 Kansas did not materially overproduce the Bureau of Mines estimates. Faced with a situation caused by mistakes of other oil states and sharing the burden of these errors, the state realized a need and a desire to produce and sell more oil at a time when the refineries and pipe lines could supply market demand from stored stocks. The answer was, it seemed, for Kansas producers to increase their markets and thus automatically take care of the situation. It was not that simple. It was mere buck-passing to lay the blame on any one state administration, because none had in any way or at any time decreased the market demand for Kansas oil. During the first 10 months of 1938 purchasers of Kansas crude oil did not buy the granted allowables. Production and consumption of Kansas crude oil fell a million barrels below these figures. The oil was unproduced. In those cases where the Kansas market increased, the Commission immediately raised the state production figure.

The Kansas oil industry desired any aid the state might give. The governor and the Corporation Commission indicated they were willing to go the limit to secure a larger market for Kansas oil, although they might have refused to aid private enterprise in seeking a market. The legislature had given the governor and the Commission no authority to enter private enterprise, as it had merely said the Commission must prevent waste in the production of oil by restricting production to market demand and halting drainage between leases. The legislature never imposed upon the agency the burden of securing a market for Kansas oil, coal, wheat, or any other product.

The pipe line companies, because of their failure to purchase allowables, brought into being pipe line proration, a practice recognized as unsound and which was condemned by the Commission. The questions were: Could the Commission order pipe line companies to purchase greater amounts of Kansas oil? Could any agency or individual in the state order them to purchase the oil? Any act giving a regulatory body the power to order a private individual or company to purchase a stated quantity of oil at a specified place would have been held unconstitutional. It was admitted that the regulatory body under the Conservation Act might legally say to a producer: you don't have to produce any oil if you don't want to, but if you do, you must produce and take it ratably. This solution was not altogether feasible, as a company might purchase and produce ratably in a Kansas field and even then not take the field's total allowable. The Commission had authority through its power to prevent drainage to demand that a purchaser take 100 per cent of the granted allowable. This assumed that unratable purchases defeated ratable production and could be prevented. The question arose as to what happened if the purchaser decided not to buy at all.

The Bureau of Mines (in fixing market demand as its basis for state allowables) only considered past consumption; a practice which failed to account for the tenfold production increase in Kansas within four years. The Commission and the governor attempted to get the oil states and the Bureau to use this information when setting state allowables. If this had been done, market demand gradually would have moved to states with newly found fields, resulting in a more equitable distribution of the market. One effect of conservation was to freeze the oil markets in the states which had enjoyed them in 1933. The price of crude oil was the same in all states, and whereas the purchasers, pipe lines, and refineries might obtain all necessary oil in those areas where the purchases took place in 1933, the market for crude did not shift. No inducement existed to build pipe lines to new fields when established fields and lines could supply a company's market. This huge investment in pipe lines and the uniformity in oil price resulted in oil companies saving money by purchasing in those states where their lines and refineries were found—thus decreasing the Kansas market. If oil and oil markets had shifted freely though channels of trade, the price of oil in established territories following laws of supply and demand might have been higher than the delivered price of oil in fields of new production. Oil marketers then would have desired to purchase oil from the new areas. Fixing of allowable production to current market demand had a tendency to stabilize price, evidenced by the fact that the price of crude oil has been as constant as any other commodity, such as gold. This fact is not to be condemned, because it had a good effect as it made for economic certainty and permitted a reasonable profit over and above exploratory and production costs. This helped the industry and the entire population of a producing state. Its tendency was to stabilize the market in a sense of freezing the channels of trade and in offering no inducement to purchasers to extend present facilities to other sources of production; this was detrimental in a state with recently discovered large potential sources of production. Thus Kansas was faced with a dilemma. If it produced in excess of consumptive demand the price of oil would fall; if it did not so produce, the producers would not be allowed to pump their permissible allowables causing drainage and waste to occur, a thing the Commission was empowered to prevent. The only legitimate aim of conservation (as far as Kansas was concerned) was waste prevention and protection of correlative rights. If conspiracies existed which kept a commodity market from shifting in accord with economic law, they violated the federal and state statutes.

The fact that many wells were drilled at a time when existing fields could easily supply consumptive demand aggravated the situation. Oil producers might have saved considerable sums of money if drilling had been restricted and had a plan of wider well spacing been adopted. However, persons who owned property which had been leased and upon which no wells were drilled desired to enjoy the immediate benefits of their oil. The Commission was without authority to restrict drilling except as it might affect the problem of waste. Those companies which continued to spend money drilling wells slowly moved toward a time when such a great percentage of their capital would be invested in production that capital itself must flow into such enterprises.

The governor called a conference, at Topeka April 25, 1938, of representatives of all major purchasers in an effort to secure a satisfactory solution to the problems of overdevelopment. The companies were in part responsible for the 3,000,000 barrels potential caused by the rapid development of the western Kansas fields. For that reason they were urged to increase Kansas purchases, thus giving the state a bigger share of the crude oil market. The companies felt it unreasonable to ask them to take more Kansas oil, and at the end of the conference the solution was as far away as ever. April 29,

1938 the governor and members of the Corporation Commission attended a meeting of the Interstate Oil Compact Commission at Wichita, where the governor declared he would not hesitate to advocate federal control "if that becomes necessary to preserve the interests of the Kansas oil producers." He thought there should be a reallocation from time to time of the crude oil markets between the states, saying that Kansas could not operate at a profit when its crude market was based on 1933 figures. The question of determining a fair share of market for Kansas was left directly to the Interstate Oil Compact Commission. The problem was not settled at the Compact meeting. During the four succeeding years the question of (1) whether the state had the power to demand that purchasers take oil, and (2) whether the state could protect the prices producers received for their crude remained unanswered. While the acts of the state and the Commission directly benefited the Kansas producers, no solution to market need was realized until the first months of 1941 brought the war emergency.

A part of the struggle for new markets was the purchasers' refusal to take oil from the Kansas stripper wells. There were some 13,000 of these wells producing from one to ten barrels of oil a day; most had produced for ten or thirty years. The Sinclair-Prairie Oil Purchasing Company in May 1938 refused to take oil from a number of strippers thus raising a question as to whether or not it might legally abandon the wells. The state based its authority to enforce continued operation of stripper wells on the right to prevent loss of a natural resource. It was felt that Kansas (through the governor and the Corporation Commission) had the right to intervene to conserve natural resources. State officials thought that the oil business was invested with a particular public interest to an extent that their intervention was apropos. Operation might be compelled so long as profit resulted.

If the state could require continued production from wells under the Conservation Act, might it also properly act in the capacity of an interested party to block the development of new fields? The threatened premature abandonment of eastern Kansas oil fields came when new developments were making still greater recovery feasible. Flooding or water repressuring was in its initial stages in the Kansas stripper fields. Oil men estimated that at least 20 per cent of the total oil in the strata was recovered by primary methods, and with water flooding an additional 40 per cent might be secured. Wells so treated might produce for 10 or 20 years. If they were to be saved by flooding and water repressuring, it had to be done at once, because a flooded stripper well closed in for any length of time was lost.

Kansas was faced with a four part problem. (1) The allowables for the State of Kansas remained unchanged since 1933, although production had increased tenfold. (2) The purchasers and pipe line companies did not even take the allowables granted by the Commission. (3) The pipe line companies, realizing more immediate profit could be made in flush production fields, abandoned the stripper oil wells. (4) New fields rapidly came into production in the western part of the state. Kansas was in a most precarious and paradoxical situation in that it had more oil than it could market, more new wells, and an increasing need to preserve and recover the oil from its stripper wells. If the state allowed maximum production of the flush oil fields and unrestricted development in new oil fields, there would be no need for the stripper wells. The immediate effect of stripper well abandonment caused economic loss to many land owners; what was more important from the conservation standpoint was that once the wells were abandoned the oil could never again be recovered. If this were allowed to happen, the very premises of conservation would have been defeated. This was true for two reasons. (1) The only way the future supply of natural resources might be preserved was to exhaust to the fullest degree all known production before moving into new fields. If conservation principles were carried to their logical conclusion all stripper wells would have to be completely exhausted before oil could be taken from any other field—this was especially so before new fields were developed. (2) If the stripper wells were let go and the state either did nothing or admitted its inability to prevent the premature abandonment, a precedent would be established which would take years to overcome. The state recognized it was in no position to demand complete exhaustion of stripper wells before the producers moved on to other fields, as its duty was to protect equally the state's interest in natural resources and the correlative rights of land owners and producers. Immediate relief could come only through an increase in the market to allow greater withdrawal from both flush and stripper fields. Governor Huxman proposed to the Bureau of Mines that it attempt to balance the market more equitably between Kansas and Oklahoma, complaining that his state did not get a fair share of the petroleum market. The Bureau rejected his proposal saying that the determining factor here was consumer preference—a situation over which it had no control. In July 1938 Huxman again told the State Corporation Commission that unless state action could be taken to provide a fair allowable based upon potential production, Kansas must force the issue.

There started a state-wide movement to buy only Kansas petroleum products as a method of combating the adverse market condition. The Kansas Attorney General held that state departments might specify that only Kansas manufactured oil products be purchased for their use. While no order to this effect was issued, Oklahoma was doing this to favor Oklahoma oil. If Kansas had adopted a like policy, the state and the oil business would have benefited.

The eventual climax began to take shape when in September 1938 the Phillips Petroleum Company announced that it would not obey an order [34] of the State Corporation Commission fixing the amount of oil to be purchased, but rather would cut that quantity by 15 per cent in the current allowables. Phillips refused to take any of the previous underage, in effect creating a 35 per cent cut involving daily some 3400 barrels. This refusal affected 62 pools, and by the end of the month Phillips would have fallen short of its allocated share by 100,000 barrels. The action of Phillips was followed by the Sinclair Consolidated Oil Company's withdrawal from the eastern Kansas stripper fields. The Corporation Commission searched for power to force Phillips to take its allocation.

During the middle of September 1938 Governor Huxman again pleaded with the oil producing states to join in a program of joint federal and state production and marketing control to insure the distribution of a portion of the market demand to each state. He pointed out that the conservation of oil and gas involved two general principles: (1) the prevention of waste, and (2) the prevention of unreasonable discrimination.

In the meantime the purchasing cut dropped runs from the

[34] Docket No. 14534, Order No. 38–09–16 (Sept. 9, 1938).

stripper wells to about half of normal. A majority of leases could not operate under those conditions. Producers had their option to operate at a loss or to shut-in wells; where the latter policy was adopted, wells were ruined for future production. It was generally felt that the only answer to the purchasing policies of the major oil companies was more rigid state supervision. The independent oil producers of Kansas held that the buying reduction could only result in unwanted Federal Government regulation. These producers were seeking any effective solution other than a boycott which it was realized would operate to hurt everyone. The cry of the independent oil producers hit a crescendo when on October 31, 1938 Alf M. Landon [35] declared that if the states lacked power to prevent physical waste of the type caused by Sinclair Consolidated Oil Company's withdrawal from the Kansas stripper fields, then that authority must be given them; further saying that a moral obligation existed because the Commission had encouraged producers to drill wells in the stripper area. Landon charged the Sinclair Company with being ruthless, unjust, arrogant, and short-sighted in its action. Land owners and oil producers in the area in which the company operated complained of its action. Sinclair's refusal to buy meant immense waste in Kansas. At the time of Mr. Landon's statement the Sinclair-Prairie Marketing Company made further slashes in purchases from new stripper wells in southern Kansas. Kansas was *Sinclairized* with a vengeance.

The State Corporation Commission ordered the company to continue its purchases until a hearing in November. Now it was thought the real test of the present stripper situation had come. In an effort to bring Sinclair under the provision which empowered the state to prevent waste, the Commission asserted that a failure to take oil, or the production of more oil than the market could absorb, was waste. Though Kansas' proration law was enacted to prevent this latter waste, state officials believed that the law could be applied to waste arising as a result of a refusal to take oil from settled production. W. G. Skelly, then president of Skelly Oil Company, placed the blame on the Commission, asserting that while the Kansas proration laws were adequate, their administration was responsible for the then present conditions. The answer came

[35] *Kansas City Star*, Oct. 31, 1938, p. 2, c. 2.

in February 1939 when the state established that a common carrier of oil could not go into a flush field during high profit periods and later withdraw from activity, when production subsided, if this action resulted in a loss of all reserves. It was reasoned that all fields would one day be strippers. The state (acting in the public interest) must protect its natural resources. The state had the power to keep purchasing companies in the stripper fields and to have them take ratably from the wells until their oil was exhausted. Purchasing companies were to resume buying retroactive to September 1, 1938.

Concomitant with the marketing problem a further emergency arose—this time in all of the oil producing states. The price of crude oil had steadily decreased until it was no longer possible for any investor to expect a return from his capital. Crude had sunk to a low of 20 cents a barrel. Production at less than cost would have been wasteful, and to allow unrestricted flow would only aggravate the situation. It became necessary to act immediately and on August 15, 1939 by an emergency order [36] the State Corporation Commission closed in 19,268 producing flush production and stripper wells for 15 days to remove from the market 2,460,000 barrels of oil. Kansas joined Oklahoma, Texas, Arkansas, and New Mexico in an effort to take up the slack in the price of crude oil. This description appeared in a newspaper after ten days of shut down,[37] and traced the reaction of Kansas oil men going across the area of some 20,000 wells during the shut-in period. "Men who travel regularly through the oil field territory have been awed by the great silence. They hear no thud thud of the pump and the pipe lines along the road side. They drive to the top of a hill and there is an oil field spread out before them. But there is no putt putt of the gasoline engine, no whirr of the electric motors which drive the pumps; no movement of the walking beams under the derricks, no crews working around and about to keep the wells and pumps and the pipe line shipshape and working in rhythm with the pulse beats of the industry as a whole. 'It's uncanny' said one field man. 'It's weird, almost ghostlike,' said another. Nothing like it ever has happened in the oil industry before. Most of those in the oil industry blink

[36] Docket No. 14534, Order No. 39–8–16 (Aug. 18, 1939).
[37] Kansas City Star, Aug. 18, 1939.

their eyes in amazement now. They did not believe that an industry, composed of so many conflicting elements and made up of so many rugged individuals ever could join with the state government in the cooperative effect such as is now under way in 6 states. . . . The silence of the great producing machinery of the oil industry is complete. But they did it apparently willingly, without scratching or biting and without a single attempt at subterfuge. It has been done without policing the oil field. The cooperation has been 100% from every single interest in the industry."

In 1947 the legislature, to insure against premature abandonment of stripper wells, adopted a concurrent resolution[38] requesting Congress to enact legislation providing for conservation payments for the benefit of stripper wells.[39] The legislature was cognizant of the fact that oil was one of the principal sources of taxable revenue for funds used in building and maintaining roads and schools. There were thousands of independent oil operators who did not own gathering lines, pipe lines, refineries, or marketing systems, but who depended upon the sale of crude to maintain their businesses.

THE HUGOTON AREA

The westward movement of the Kansas oil and gas industry culminated in the discovery and development of the Hugoton Field; a field which contains more than 2,250,000 acres and with an estimated gas reserve of 13,000,000,000,000 cubic feet. Wellman[40] describes the field as a "bubble beneath the whole dust bowl . . . the biggest bubble in the world . . . a bubble of natural gas." Today it furnishes fuel to hundreds of our industries—some over a thousand miles away—sending its gas through the longest pipe line in the world to Michigan, Minnesota, Illinois, Oklahoma, Indiana,

[38] Kan. Laws 1947 c. 497.

[39] "Be it resolved that the house of representatives of the state of Kansas, the senate concurring therein; 'That the Congress of the United States be and is hereby memorialized to enact such laws as will provide reasonable conservation payment to protect and preserve the stripper wells of the United States and will protect and preserve for the benefit of our nation the millions of barrels of crude oil that otherwise would be lost to the great detriment and deterioration of our natural resources, the producing wealth therefrom, the improvement afforded for the taxation therefrom derived."

[40] Wellman, Bubble Beneath the Plains, SAT. EVE. POST (Dec. 12, 1942).

Ohio, Missouri, Kansas, and Nebraska. Most gas and oil deposits are found in anticlines, faults in the rock strata, forming domes beneath which gas or oil gathers. The Hugoton structure is a gigantic monocline (a single great plane of rock) sloping gently upward toward the west which never would have trapped gas had it not been for a geological accident closing off its upper end with impervious rocks and shales. The gas cannot move upward toward the west, and it is trapped at the bottom by water.

The discovery well in the Hugoton Field was the Crawford No. 1, Stevens County, Kansas, drilled by W. L. Sidewell in 1926. The nearest producing well then was the Boles No. 1 completed July 2, 1920 as a gas well. It was located some 4 miles from Liberal, Kansas, and approximately 35 miles southeast of the Crawford well. The discovery well was drilled as an oil well, but as oil was not found, it was plugged back as a natural gas producer. Early development in the Hugoton Field was carried on by Sidewell and William McKnab of Winfield, Kansas, who later organized the Stevens County Oil and Gas Company, now succeeded by other companies operating in the field. From 1920 until 1930 few regulatory problems were present; it was still in infancy and the problems of regulation grew up with its development. When Sidewell drilled the initial well, there was no market for petroleum products. Natural gas was produced and sold some 100 miles away from that part of the field located in Southmoore County in the State of Texas. After the Crawford well was drilled, the Argus Production Company was organized and from 1927 to 1930 drilled approximately 88 wells in the field. Development by producers from 1930 to 1939, while gradual, was continuous. Republic Natural Gas Company succeeded to the interest of the Argus Production Company. From 1935 to 1938 the Columbian Fuel Corporation drilled 16 wells in Grant County, Kansas, the northern part of the field. Natural gas from 10 of these wells was sold to Panhandle Pipe Line Company and the remaining 6 sold to the Carbon Black Company. Panhandle Eastern Pipeline Company became active in the Hugoton Field in 1935 and contracted to purchase from Argus 13 wells.

During primary drilling the size of the tracts upon which the wells were located varied from 80 to 240 acres; the majority were on 160 acre tracts. Land owners refused to give leases larger than

160 acres—a practice which continued through the developmental and drilling stages by the Argus Company. But by 1934 producers of gas were able to hold a larger acreage by production from individual wells. Practically all wells drilled in the Kansas portion of the Hugoton Field were in the center of a quarter section; however, by 1936 some producers were drilling one well to a section. Some tracts were under one ownership and others made up of two or more tracts (belonging to different owners) unitized by agreement. There had been drilled by 1939 in the Kansas portion of the field, 274 wells, some 22 of which had no connection with pipe lines, and 117 on acreages to the extent of 640 acres. Efforts were made by various producers to unitize and pool lands in addition to the 160 acre tracts; due to a number of reasons these efforts in unitizing met with failure. Republic Natural Gas Company had drilled and operated all of its wells on 160 acres. Panhandle Eastern Pipeline Company's original holdings were extended to unitize larger areas; its average was 542 acres to one well. Stevens County Oil and Gas Company's producing wells were on 160 acres. McLumbrein had 16 wells drilled on 640 acres and in some instances was able to unitize larger tracts.

A question arose as to whether or not Kansas had the power under the gas statute to establish ratable taking from the field. The first act of the Commission came September 1, 1938.[41] Then the following finding regarding waste was made—"Due to the fact that oil has not been found to exist in the reservoir, there is no evidence of waste of reservoir energy, and due to the fact that water has not appeared in the reservoir, and withdrawal of gas has not caused waste by premature encroachment of water, there is no evidence of substantial waste, as practically all the gas produced is marketed, and in those instances where the producer has not had a market for his gas, the wells have remained shut in."

With the active development of the Hugoton Field, the Commission's power to force connections to unconnected wells and to break unsatisfactory contracts by operation of law was considered. If the agency had the power, it must be found in the authority conferred upon it by the provisions of its creating act. Section 55–701 of the Kansas statutes stated: "That the production of natural gas

41 Docket No. C-164.

in the state of Kansas in such manner [and] under such conditions as to constitute waste, is hereby prohibited." Section 55–705 read: "That the State Corporation Commission is hereby authorized and directed to promulgate rules and regulations to carry out the spirit and purpose of this act, . . ." and Section 55–702 said: "That the term 'waste' as herein used, in addition to its ordinary meaning, shall include economic waste, underground waste and surface waste. . . . "

Economic waste was defined as the use of merchantable fuel gas in a manner or process other than for light, fuel, carbon black manufacture, efficient chemical, or repressuring processes. The Act did two things: it defined and prohibited waste. Section 55–703 purported to enter the field of production restriction, current production, and proration by providing that: "Whenever the *available production* from the wells drilled into any common source of supply or natural gas in this state is in excess of the *market demands* . . . any person . . . may produce therefrom *without waste* as will permit each well or developed lease to ultimately produce *approximately the amount of gas* underlying the land on which such well is located and currently producing proportionately with the other wells in such common source of supply. The state corporation commission is directed to so regulate the taking of natural gas to prevent the *inequitable or unfair* taking from a common source of supply by any person, firm or corporation, and to prevent *unreasonable discrimination* in favor of any one *common source of supply* as against any other and in favor of *any producer* in any such common source of supply. In promulgating the rules and regulations and formula to attain such results, the commission shall give equitable consideration to the well open flow owned or controlled by the respective producers in such common source of supply under the *existing conditions and circumstances* . . . provided, however, that the daily take of gas from any well shall not exceed 25% of its open flow provided further, provisions of this act shall not apply to any well with an open flow of 750,000 cubic feet or less." [42]

The question of the Commission's power to force a pipe line connection with unconnected wells was first presented to it in Feb-

[42] Italics supplied.

ruary 1938, when Joe E. Denham of Dodge City, Kansas, voiced concern over the fact that the agency had not ordered Panhandle Eastern Pipeline Company to connect to his Warner well in Haskell County and to the Hyde No. 1 in Seward County. Denham stated: "I will be interested in knowing whether proration is going to be practiced in this field under authority of the Corporation Commission. As you know during the past few months the operators in the field have been using 640 acres as a unit for well locations. I have been in sympathy with this as a matter of good field practice, regardless of the fact that it would be less expensive and much more profitable to have proration in the Hugoton Gas Field; it would seem to me that all the rules should be observed by everyone connected with the field. If Panhandle Eastern does not have in mind the connection of wells when the gas is put to their line and in turn the Commission does not see that they do not connect them, I see no good reason why a lot of us should follow the other rules for certainly proration can't be practiced without ratably taking at the pipe line when the gas is put to the trunk line. Panhandle Eastern seems to be disregarding the Commission in all of their plans." The Commission referred Denham to its orders entered in the Otis and Burrton Fields, saying that certain irregularities there corrected would be changed in the Hugoton Field, and that an investigation would be started (not as complicated as in the Otis and Burrton Fields), because Hugoton did not have a gas-oil ratio difficulty. Regarding Panhandle Eastern the Commission hoped for an amicable settlement. A letter was sent to Panhandle Eastern referring to the agency order in the Otis Field; the agency was then assured that Panhandle Eastern would connect these wells in order that there be equitable taking under the Kansas gas proration laws.

March 14, 1938 the Farmers Royalty Protective Association wrote the Conservation Division of the Commission asking that wells be prorated in the Hugoton Field. The letter stated that royalty checks were out of proportion to the open flow output of the wells; that the checks were irregular, varying in amount from $30 to $130 at the same well from month to month. The members asked that a key to the meter houses be given them in order that it might be determined when and how much the wells were running, saying this request had previously been refused by at least two of the companies. A permanent state representative at the field was asked. The Commission (recognizing the need of a field man) assured the land owners a man would be sent in April. J. H. Page, gas engineer for the Commission, did not think it practical to give land owners keys to the meter houses. The locks were to protect the gas companies' property as mercury thieves frequently stripped the meters. For this reason and because an unscrupulous land owner might bend the pen arm of his meter, greatly increasing the apparent amount of gas passing, it was decided that keys should not be given. The presence of a field man to take potential tests of all the wells and check the meters where the accuracy of the measurement was questioned was held to be sufficient.

In June 1938 a complaint was laid with the Commission that certain pipe line companies were striving to complete a monopoly in the field by attempting to defeat the leases of many land owners. At the same time Denham and L. F. Meyers served notice of intention to file petitions asking that the gas proration law be invoked. The petitions were filed July 2, 1938 and a hearing set for July 21, 1938 at Hugoton, Kansas. Meyers withdrew his complaint and Denham's was dismissed. August 24, 1938, prior to the issuance of an order, the hearing was reopened at which time one witness testified.

Before the hearing J. H. Page set out certain features which he felt should be considered by the Commission. No waste was then occurring in the field. There was evidence of unratable taking of gas from developed leaseholds as indicated by a variation in shut-in pressures of wells throughout the field, particularly noticeable in wells with heavy withdrawals where lower pressures turned up than in wells in areas of lesser withdrawals. Wells without pipe line connections showed shut-in pressures considerably below the original known field pressure. Approximately 135,000,000 MCF of gas had been produced to July 1, 1938 with many wells having flowed from 1,000,000 MCF to 3,000,000 MCF. Owing to the large size of the Hugoton Field it would appear best to adopt 640 acre spacing for purposes of ratable taking, in order that the largest number of land owners might benefit from the market. Since there was far more gas than the market demanded, it was necessary to prorate the existing market among developed leaseholds to promote ratable taking. In setting a proration formula it was suggested that three factors be employed: acreage, rock pressure, and open flow. Acreage and rock pressure were to have equal weight, with open flow minimized to some extent as certain wells had been acidized which greatly increased their open flow Page mentioned that although the field was discovered in 1920, the peak of development occurred after 1930. There were in 1938 seven pipe lines purchasing gas within the field. From the standpoint of the owner of a well on a 160 acre tract, a 640 acre spacing plan was unjust. A great many 160 acre wells had produced more gas than in all probability originally existed beneath their leaseholds, since the older portion of the field from which most of the gas had been marketed was in 160 acre developed tracts.

An order was adopted in August 1938 which followed Page's formula and allotted three-fourths to the acreage and pressure factors and one-fourth of production to the open flow potential. The ninth finding of the agency's order was: "That the production of gas in accordance with the foregoing formula has a reasonable relation to the prevention of inequitable and unfair production of gas from the common source of supply, and to the prevention of unreasonable discrimination in favor of one producer in said field, and against another producer therein, and the production of gas in such manner will in fact accomplish the purposes for which Article 7, Chapter 55, General Statutes of Kansas, 1935, was enacted." The tenth finding of the order set forth that the acreage used in the formula: "Shall be contiguous to that which contains the wells and shall be determined by the number of acres in the leased tract on which a well is situated, provided: *'That there is only one well on the lease and [that it] does not contain more than 640 acres, and in the event more than one well is located on any one lease, the acres allotted to each of said wells.'*" In an effort to substantiate the acreage factor in the formula the order in its eleventh finding recited that "acreage is an important factor in determining the amount of gas which a well may produce so as to prevent drainage and permit the owner of a developed tract to ultimately produce approximately the amount of gas which underlies the tract for the reason that it represents two of the dimensions of the reservoir underlying the tract.

In the early stages of the development of the field, most of the wells were drilled on 160-acre tracts, but for some time past most of the wells had been drilled on 640-acre tracts, some of these tracts being all one ownership and others made up of several who had joined in unitization agreements. It has been demonstrated and the Commission finds that a well will efficiently drain an area containing 640 acres and that a maximum acreage factor of 640 acres should be used."

Immediately after issuing the proposed order the Commission had complaints from land and royalty owners; many were based upon the eleventh finding relative to the acreage factor of 640 acres. The complaints (all of a general character) recited that if the rule were adopted, it would make worthless prior contracts and work a great hardship on small land owners. It was contended that the order would allow many larger gas companies to drill on 640 acres and to produce a larger percentage of gas than wells on 160 acres. Most land owners believed every well should be gauged the same. They alleged that the larger companies were allowed to drill on the corner of 640 acres and produce gas from adjoining lands not leased. One complainant wrote: "The complaint is against the taking, against the landowner's wish, [of] 640 acres as a drilling unit. This is most unfair and bitterly objected to by perhaps 98% of the landowners and royalty holders in the field. Ownership varies from possessing large numbers of quarter sections to one or two or a few quarters of land; therefore, the farmer with one or two will likely never get production, though his land is under perpetual contract without any rental." Most land owners' objections were based on an erroneous understanding and interpretation of the proposed order. The Commission time after time pointed out that the acreage factor was necessary in order that the land owner might receive a fair share of the gas beneath his land, and that the order as proposed prevented the owner of a quarter section of land from getting as much gas as the owner of a full section. The order provided 640 acres as the maximum acreage allowed to one well. It did not state that wells should or could not be drilled on smaller tracts. Further, if one had a contract to develop his land on a 160 acre basis, there was nothing in the order modifying the agreement. If the acreage factor had not been adopted, these same people would have found their gas being drained from under their land without any way in which they could participate in production. The proposal, with slight modification, was effective September 1, 1938 with the market demand fixed at 2,177,000 MCF.

Immediately following issuance of the orders, applications requesting a hearing were filed. These stated the order was unenforceable because the statute under which the Commission acted was unconstitutional, as violative of the Kansas bill of rights and in particular Section 18.[43] The statute was assaulted because it gave the Corporation Commission power to make and enforce an order of the kind, character, and nature which delegated legislative powers. It was further asserted that the order was unsupported by evidence. September 17, 1938 a partial rehearing was held and a further hearing was set in Hugoton for October 15. By the terms of the order granting a rehearing, only evidence bearing on the formula and acreage used was to be heard.

During October, November, and December 1938 no allocation orders were issued by the Gas Division of the Corporation Commission. December 31, 1938 the Commission reinstated its order of September 1 and made that order effective January 1, 1939. This was received by the producers January 17. By its terms information was required from each company as to its acreage in the Hugoton Field to aid in compiling the monthly allowable report for the field. Many producers furnished this information under protest, reserving the right to contest the validity and legality of the orders in all particulars by court action or otherwise, and a right to test the validity and legality of the statutes upon which the proposals were based, as well as jurisdiction of the Commission in connection with the promulgation and enforcement of the orders of December 31 and September 1, and any order made thereunder. The requested information was furnished to avoid penalties provided by the statutes of the State of Kansas for failure to comply with the orders. Written objections were filed with statutory applications for rehearing.[44] March 10, 1939 the applications came before the Com-

[43]"All persons, for injury suffered in person, reputation, or property, shall have remedy by due course of law."

[44] Columbian Fuel Corporation, filed Jan. 24, 1939; Stevens County Oil and Gas Company, filed Jan. 25, 1939; Republic Natural Gas Company, filed Feb. 28, 1939; Panhandle Eastern; Saturn Oil and Gas Company; Southwest Kansas Oil and Gas Company.

mission and the rehearing was set for trial June 12, 1939 at Wichita. Consolidated with the hearing was the agency's original investigation. The rehearing convened and after several recesses introduction of testimony concluded June 29, 1939. Argument by counsel was set for July 31, 1939 at Topeka, where the producers, purchasers, land and royalty owners presented an impressive argument as to why the Hugoton Field should not be prorated.

One assertion alleged the Kansas Corporation Commission was confined to that jurisdiction conferred by the legislature. The statute,[45] it was said, gave the Commission jurisdiction to prohibit waste in production by restriction or proration and that the only factor to be considered in creating a proration formula was a well's open flow under existing conditions and circumstances. These conditions and circumstances were held to involve: the extent of market demand and available production, existing contracts, private requirements, investments, reserves under development or lease, the area under the well, number and thickness of pay sands, their porosity and permeability, pressure, common productive practices, existence or imminence of waste, and the effect and result of any proposed order. Since it was contended that the statute did not contain such terms as correlative rights, ratable take, drainage, uniform pressure, common carrier, or common purchaser, these were improper considerations. Although the constitutionality of the statute was not pressed, the parties stipulated that they did not waive that question.

The Commission considered the statute as mandatory, compelling it to take the initiative in promulgating rules, regulations, and formulas for the proration of gas and to enforce them in the Hugoton area. This was strongly protested; it was frequently asserted that the law was not mandatory but merely directory. The protestants argued that to confer jurisdiction upon the Commission, it must appear that waste in one form or another as described and defined in the statute was present or imminent. It was further claimed that there was a standard of measurement for authority provided for the Commission to determine what was inequitable or unfair taking as between sources of supply, or among producers. In the absence of sufficient information enabling the Commission

[45] KAN. GEN. STAT. ANN., c. 55, art. 7 (1935).

to determine the approximate amount of gas underlying the leases, it was said that the record showed a probability of error factor (up to 300 per cent or more) could be introduced into any formula that might be promulgated.

The statute referred to the available production from wells drilled into a common source of supply. There was no contention that this law tried to protect any lease upon which there was no development. Available production from the wells drilled did not necessarily mean all wells drilled as such must be equipped and connected with pipe lines and have a purchaser or taker. Connected wells produced subject to the statute, that is, not exceeding 25 per cent of their open flow and in a manner not constituting actual or potential waste. There was some doubt whether or not unconnected wells were protected by the statute.

It was stated there was no evidence that any waste had been committed, or was being permitted in the gas common sources of supply in Kansas. The total available production from the wells there exceeded the market demand of the purchasing companies connected with the wells, but there was no showing that production from these wells was above the market demand of all the companies purchasing from the common source of supply in Kansas, Oklahoma, and Texas. Purchasers in the Texas part of the field sold to markets and to consumers in Kansas, and those connected with the Kansas wells could meet market demands supplied by Texas or Oklahoma wells drawing from this gas common source of supply. Except for contractual commitments with producers these companies could have then purchased Texas gas for 2 cents a MCF instead of 3½ to 7 cents which they paid in Kansas. These contracts covered approximately 100,000 MCF daily. The loss in price which would occur from breaking the contracts averaged around 2 cents a MCF or $2000 daily, one-eighth of which went to land and royalty owners. The argument was proposed that a contract is property and might be condemned in eminent domain proceeding, but the agency formula and plan when put into practical operation would result in taking a substantial part of the contract market and distributing it to others without compensation to the involved producers or land owners. The right of the state to adopt such a formula was held an abuse of the right of the police power by making the state the guardian and protector of those who do nothing to protect themselves. It was condemned as being wholly for the benefit of the unconnected wells and their owners, that these owners did not ask for a new market, but wanted a part of the old established market for which no compensation would be paid to those who had acquired the older markets. The rule, that when a gas well is drilled on an owner's land the land owner becomes the owner of all gas produced regardless of the source of the gas, was involved. When gas or oil is found, the right to produce it is a vested right and the lessee is protected in exercising it agreeably to the terms of the contract.[46] It was asserted that the companies, when drilling their wells, relied upon this rule and entered into contracts for the sale of gas. The law in existence when the leases were executed and delivered and the contracts made then became a part of these leases and contracts. The argument continued that rights obtained by law under a contract were not confined to those created by statute, but included those conferred by common law. Hence Kansas had no right to say that the lessee could produce only the gas underlying the leased premises, because the state or its agencies cannot determine that amount of oil or gas.

A final order was entered by the Commission January 30, 1940.[47] In answering the land owners' attack that the Conservation Act did not authorize it to enter the field of regulation in the Hugoton area because there was no present evidence of waste, the Commission in the order said: "Since the gas conservation act has not been construed by the courts of this state, it is necessary to make an administrative interpretation of its provisions. The intent or purpose of the statute is clear. Section 55–701 prohibits waste, while 55–702 defines what is meant by waste and authorizes the Commission to make rules for its prevention. While the statute contemplates future waste prevention, as well as the prevention of present waste, the Commission is also authorized and directed to prorate the production of gas, to prevent the inequitable or unfair taking thereof regardless of waste. This authority is found in Section 55–703. The rights of the parties owning interests in any common source of sup-

---

[46] Dickey v. Coffeyville Vitrified Brick and Tile Co., 69 Kan. 106, 76 P. 398 (1904).
[47] Docket No. C-164.

ply of natural gas are set out in the first sentence of this Section." [48] Available production, the agency said, meant gas production available from completed wells whose owners were ready to tender gas to a gas pipe line. The words "and currently producing proportionately with the other wells in such common source of supply" made no distinction between connected and unconnected wells whose owners were ready, willing, and able to tender gas, and expressed emphatically the requirement that production between leases having completed wells be ratable and current. Prior to the statute's enactment, the rights of the parties were protected only by the rule of capture which permitted them to take as much gas as possible in an effort to protect themselves from drainage by their neighbors. The rule accelerated production at rates in excess of demand and compelled well owners in many instances to blow gas into the air. The practice of drainage across property lines resulted in untold waste. The state, however, to afford the property owners protection, replaced the rule of capture by an act of the legislature which imposed upon the Commission a duty and an obligation of protecting a well or developed lease against drainage and depletion of its reserves. Thus under a modified rule of capture the state recognized the doctrine of *sic utere tuo ut alienum non laedas*, which is the principle of correlative rights. It conformed more closely to the physical facts relating to the production of oil or gas from a common source of supply than to the outmoded rule of capture.

The requirement, that each well or developed lease produce currently and proportionately with the other wells and leases, expressly authorized the Commission to prevent undue drainage between developed leases. This concept was found in the words "to prevent

[48] "That whenever the available production of natural gas from any common source of supply is in excess of the market demands for such gas from such common source of supply, or whenever the market demands for natural gas from any common source of supply can be fulfilled only by the production of natural gas therefrom under conditions constituting waste as herein defined or whenever the commission finds and determines that the orderly development of, and production of natural gas from, any common source of supply requires the exercise of its jurisdiction, then any person, firm or corporation having the right to produce natural gas therefrom, may produce only such portion of all the natural gas that may be currently produced without waste and to satisfy the market demands, as will permit each developed lease to ultimately produce approximately the amount of gas underlying such developed lease and currently produce proportionately with other developed leases in said common source of supply without uncompensated cognizable drainage between separately-owned, developed leases or parts thereof."

the inequitable or unfair taking" and "to prevent unreasonable discrimination in favor of any producer." The Commission pointed out that nowhere in those parts of the statute dealing with ratable taking, the protection of correlative rights, or the prevention of undue drainage was there any requirement that regulation must be imposed solely for the prevention of waste. The phrase—"that may be produced therefrom without waste as will permit each well or developed lease"—was construed to mean that gas might not be produced in quantities which caused waste, even though produced ratably and without undue drainage. In no case was waste permitted. Ratable taking or proration could be required in any situation whether or not waste was present or imminent.

The Commission inserted the quoted parenthetical phrase taken from Section 55–703 [49] saying "the spirit, the purpose, and the intent of the sentence standing alone as said in these words are obvious; and when this section is considered with the act as a whole, the meaning of the whole is even more evident." The Journals of the Legislature of 1935 show that the Act in the House of Representatives as H.B. No. 279 contained the parenthetical clause; that it remained in the measure after it was approved by the House (both as a committee and as a whole) but that in engrossing the house bill for the third and final reading thereof, the printer inadvertently omitted the clause. The bill with this omission was passed by the House and the Senate, signed by the governor and was then duly enacted into law. The Commission then applied a general rule (which is the rule in Kansas) that words inadvertently omitted from a statute passed by both houses might be supplied by the courts to give effect to legislative policy. Here the omission was obvious. The identical words could be supplied from the journals of the legislature and the meaning and intent of the statute were clear without the phrase. The Commission relied upon various decisions of the supreme court [50] in holding that such an obvious omission might be supplied. The Commission determined that it could examine the journals of the legislature to learn the history of the legislation.

[49] KAN. GEN. STAT. ANN., § 55–703 (1935).
[50] Landrum v. Flannigan, 60 Kan. 436, 56 P. 753 (1899). Cole v. Dorr, 80 Kan. 251, 101 P. 1016 (1909). State v. Horn, 126 Kan. 591, 270 P. 597 (1928).

The Commission (in answer to the statement that it should not enforce the statute, due to the field's size which made the tremendous amount of gas already produced an infinitesimal portion of the ultimate recoverable reserve) reasoned that if it accepted this view, it must wait until it was too late to take effective action. In response to the further contention that the statutes be interpreted to protect leases with no present wells, the agency said that if this construction were adopted, it would become impossible to produce any gas until every tract in the field had a well. The Commission concluded the statute was mandatory, that it authorized and directed the Commission to prevent waste in any common source of supply of natural gas, and independent of waste, to establish ratable production to halt undue drainage from developed leases and to preserve correlative rights.

The order's eighth finding reversed the Commission's prior stand on spacing one well to each 640 acres. It said that one completed well would adequately and sufficiently drain 640 acres without waste; but that considering the cost of drilling, equipping, and operating one well in comparison with the estimated acre recovery and the slow rate at which fuel production could be ratably and non-wastefully marketed, the basic acreage unit used in the proration formula should be 160 acres. This factor would be increased or decreased by 5 per cent for each 10 acres (greater or less than 160 acres as the case might be) but in no instance would more than 640 acres be considered as attributable to a well for the purpose of calculating the acreage factor. Attributable to a well meant that the acreage must be contiguous to a tract adjoining the acreage containing the well. The tract was to be, where possible, a square or rectangle with the well placed as near the center as practicable. Leases or tracts unitized in compliance with the basic order of September 1, 1938 were deemed to comply with the order in regard to contiguous acreage attributed or area; further unitization must conform to the new order. In the event two or more wells were located on any one lease, the area used in calculating the acreage factor for each well would be determined by dividing the total number of acres by the number of wells, with the quotient becoming the acreage used in making the calculation. The lease was not developed until a gas producing well had been completed and its owner or operator had tendered gas to a purchaser at the purchaser's pipe line. Before a well was entitled to an allowable, the owner or operator had either to tender the gas to a pipe line company or to others purchasing in the zone where the well was located, or demonstrate that he would and could produce the gas allowable for lawful purposes. Because of the size of the common source of supply and to enable gas purchasers to readily adjust their purchases to the allocation of the well's allowable, the field (in accordance with the development of the production and the location of the pipe lines) was divided into five zones.

The tenth finding of the order recited: "Acreage is one of the most important factors in estimating or computing gas reserves under the land covered by the lease, and that to enable each developed lease to produce its share of the gas in the pool or zone, the acreage factor has to be considered and duly weighed; that the pressure factor is of importance in the prevention of drainage inequalization by counter drainage from developed property to developed property so as to permit the owner of developed tracts to ultimately produce the amount of gas which under lies the tracts; that by the use of the well pressure factor, calculation can be made from time to time in the allocation of the allowed current production in order to prevent or diminish such drainage. The relative open flow capacities of the wells is of importance in determining the respective productivities of the various developed tracts in that it is indicative of the porosity, permeability and productive thickness and formation where the various wells are located." The Commission then adopted this formula: four-fifths of the allocation to an acreage factor determined by the observed well pressure, and one-fifth to the open flow potential of the well. The larger fraction was allocated to a well in the proportion that its acreage factor and pressure bore to the sum of these in all the fields in a zone, and the smaller was allocated to each well in the proportion that its open flow bore to the sum of the open flows of all the zone wells. If the zone were judicially determined invalid, all wells in the pool would produce in accord with the formula as though the field had not been zoned. Each well was to produce during the proration period only the allocated amount under the formula. There were two allowable periods for each year.

In 1942 a further basic order was established for the Hugoton Field [51] laying down a new formula: "To determine the well's quota for a given proration period, determine first the proration factor for the field by dividing the total field allowable for such period by the sum of the products of deliverability times the acreage factor of all the wells in the pool, then multiply the field proration factor by the product of the deliverability times the acreage factor for the well. The result reached by this calculation shall constitute the well's allowable in cubic feet which it may produce for such proration period."

The order of October 28, 1942 was then amended March 21, 1944.[52] The order of 1944 shifted the basic acreage unit from 160 to 640 acres, and provided that in no instance might there be more than 640 acres attributable to a well in calculating an acreage factor unless by specific order of the Commission. The acreage factor was to be the number of acres held under production by a well, divided by 640. The order of 1944 stated that where two or more tracts within the unit acreage were properly joined in a production unit by the owners and these persons later failed to agree upon a division of the royalty within the unit, a proper apportionment of royalty among land owners and holders of mineral rights and direct holders would be made by the Commission. Paragraph H of the 1944 basic order was amended January 10, 1946.[53] The amended order stated that the 1944 provision was equivalent to compulsory unitization; that any such power, if exercised, must apply to the lessee's right or working interests as well as to royalties and mineral rights in the land; that there was no expressed legislative investment of the Commission with any compulsory unitization power. The provisions of paragraph H were not in harmony with the remainder of the order or with Chapter 233 of the Laws of Kansas 1935. This paragraph was substituted for old paragraph H: "It shall be lawful for the owner of two or more separately owned contiguous tracts of land, or, of the minerals located thereunder, to be appropriately contracted between such owners, to cause such lands or minerals to be consolidated as one production

[51] Order No. 42–10–28 (Oct. 28, 1942).
[52] Order No. 44–3–21 (Mar. 21, 1944).
[53] Order No. 46–1–10 (Jan. 10, 1946).

unit and to apportion the royalties accruing from the production of the well or wells to be divided among them as they may agree, and when such agreement shall have been made, the royalties arising from the production of the well or wells shall be allocated as the parties thereto shall agree. It shall further be lawful for any operator or owner to agree with the owners of lands or minerals to become part of a production unit and to share the royalties upon such basis as the operator and land owner or mineral owner may agree." The order of 1944 remains the order for proration in the Hugoton Field and is known as Basic Order No. 44-3-21. It is generally accepted and adhered to throughout Kansas by land owners, royalty owners, producers, operators, pipe line companies, and the general public.

In the summer of 1947 it was determined that certain companies had violated the shut-in provision of the order by illegally overproducing 93 wells in the field. On July 31, 1947 the Commission entered appropriate orders directing that these wells be shut-in and directed all producers to show cause why they had failed to observe the shut-in provision of the basic order. All wells with illegal overproduction remained shut down under the order directing compliance until the illegal overproduction was made up by a deduction from the current monthly allowable of each respective well. Some wells were still closed in the early part of 1948.

The immensity of the Hugoton Field has been proved in the last eight years of development. A new high record was established in the 1941 production of gas when more than 93,000,000 MCF of gas were marketed increasing to some 99,000,000 MCF by 1942. The building of additional pipe lines encouraged this advance; nine were started during 1941, some of which were completed in 1942. During 1943 one half of Kansas' 122,000,000 MCF of gas came from the Hugoton Field, while 60 per cent of gas produced in 1944 was drawn from the area. The amount of gas produced in 1945 approximated 10,000,000 MCF less than that produced in 1944. There was a comeback in 1946, when 143,000,000 MCF were produced in the state; again most of this gas came from Hugoton. The outstanding production was insufficient to meet the needs of the state in that year, when actual consumption in Kansas exceeded 150,000,000 MCF. While 87,000,000 MCF were exported, 94,-000,000 MCF had to be imported from Texas and Oklahoma to meet the local deficit. In 1946 and 1947 the Hugoton area supplied more than 10 times as much gas as any pool in Kansas even though in 1947 some 140,000,000 MCF were produced. Even with an increased sale to eastern cities the present known reserves in the field will permit continued production of gas for many years. The Hugoton Field's influence in the economic life of Kansas was tremendous in the past decade; it will wield even greater influence in the future.

USE OF GAS FOR CARBON BLACK PURPOSES

Kansas policy has been to encourage the use of natural gas for the manufacture of carbon black. The section of the Kansas statute [54] prohibiting the waste of natural gas in defining economic waste says waste is "the use of natural gas in any manner or process except for efficient light, fuel carbon black manufacturing and re-pressuring, or for chemical or other processes by which such gas is efficiently converted into a solid or a liquid substance." The use of natural gas for the manufacture of carbon black is held by statute *not to be waste*. The Commission has adopted a strict measure as to what is economic waste where natural gas is consumed in the manufacture of carbon black. In two recent orders [55] the State Corporation Commission granted permits for furnace type plants, stipulating that the ultimate recovery must not be less than five pounds of carbon black a MCF. The use of gas for the manufacture of carbon black has been important in establishing a market for gas. It is estimated that more than 10 per cent of Kansas gas is now used for this purpose, while 15 per cent goes for domestic purposes, 9 per cent to electric plants, and 8 per cent for petroleum products. From April 1937 to September 1945 at least 80 per cent of the Hugoton gas production exported through Kansas produced 122,-929,931 pounds of carbon black.

DISPOSAL OF SALT WATER AND CONTAMINATED BRINES

The problem of salt water disposal has always plagued oil producers. Disposal of salt water is recognized as a necessary expense

[54] KAN. GEN. STAT. ANN. § 55–701 (Cum. Supp. 1947).
[55] App. United Carbon Co. Inc., Docket No. 25, 229-c (Feb. 9, 1943). App. Columbian Carbon Co., Docket No. 28, 198-c (May 2, 1945).

in producing oil and is included in the cost of production. An article appearing in a state paper [56] said: "Salt water disposal is the greatest headache that oil men have. One major oil company spent $50,000 on a conditioning plant . . . to treat the mineralized water so that the receiving well will not clog and be of no further use as a disposal well." The immensity of the problem in Kansas becomes readily apparent when it realized that some 1,600,000 barrels of water are produced with every 650,000 barrels of oil.[57] There are four methods of handling brine; all are expensive. These are: (1) plug the water in the earth, (2) pump it back into the ground in intake wells, (3) store it in earthen tanks to evaporate, and (4) erect plants to remove the salt from water. Since the first permit issued May 1, 1935 (in accordance with 1935 legislative action) for underground brine disposal or repressuring, some 35,-000,000 barrels of mineralized water had been returned to underground formations by January 1937.

The protection of fresh water from pollution by mineralized water and oil field brines is regulated by the State Corporation Commission and the State Board of Health under legislative provisions which fall into three general categories: the prohibition of waste, the casing of oil and gas wells, and the disposal of oil and gas field brines. The State Corporation Commission was authorized to make rules and regulations to halt waste and to protect all fresh water strata encountered in any well.[58] These statutory provisions, with one exception, were prohibitory in nature requiring that owners or operators refrain from doing certain things. The sections which regulate the disposal of salt water require owners or operators desiring to dispose of salt water or oil field brines (who have the right to return water or brines to the horizon from which produced or to other horizons containing or previously producing water or brines to an appreciable degree) to make written application to the State Corporation Commission to dispose of salt water or oil field brines. This permission is granted after an investigation conducted by the Commission or its agents.[59] The State Corporation Commission was directed to prescribe just and equitable rules and

[56] Wichita Eagle, July 25, 1947.
[57] Forbes, Flush Production 123 (1942).
[58] Id. §§ 55–602, 55–702.
[59] Id. § 55–901.

regulations to carry out the disposal of salt water or oil field brines. This section of the statutes was amended in 1937 by the legislature to direct the Commission to assess costs incurred under the disposal provision against the applicant. Any violation of the statutory provision is punishable by a fine of $500, or by six months in the county jail, or both.[60] Statutory authority is also given the State Board of Health [61] to protect generally the fresh water supplies and to issue rules and regulations pertaining to the discharge of foreign matter into state waters. Complaints, investigation of complaints, and correctional orders are permitted. Rules and regulations [62] of the State Board of Health may not prohibit the storage of salt water, oil or refuse in tanks, pipe lines, or ponds. These legislative enactments have stood the test of time well with few additions, deletions, or amendments.

The 1935 legislature ordered by statute the casing of oil and gas wells [63] to exclude fresh water or salt water from oil and gas bearing formations and to exclude brines or oil from fresh water.[64] The legislature assessed a penalty of $1000 for each violation.[65] A further remedy provided that "All persons, companies or corporations, private or municipal, owning or controlling a supply of water for domestic purposes, injured or threatened with injury by a violation of the provisions of section 1 (55–118) of this act, shall be entitled to a remedy by injunction, mandatory or prohibitive, in any court of competent jurisdiction against any person, company or corporation, causing or threatening to cause such injury." [66] The legislature followed this action with a separate statute which declared that it was unlawful for any person in control or in possession of a well drilled or being drilled for oil and gas to permit salt water, oil, or oil refuse to escape and flow from the immediate vicinity of such well. It was further declared the duty of any such person to keep salt water, oil, or oil refuse safely confined in tanks, pipe lines, or ponds. The statute did not apply to circumstances beyond the control of the person in possession, or that could not

[60] *Id.* § 55–902.
[61] *Id.* §§ 66–164 to 66–169.
[62] *Id.* § 65–171 d.
[63] KAN. GEN. STAT. ANN. § 55–15 (1935).
[64] *Id.* § 55–118.
[65] *Id.* § 55–120.
[66] *Id.* § 55–119.

have been reasonably anticipated and guarded against.[67] Penalty for a willful and knowing violation is $1000, one year in prison, or both; each day of violation is a separate offense.

From the time of the enactment of these laws to date there have been no criminal proceedings of record; there have been frequent civil actions for damages to adjoining land owners injured by escaping salt or mineralized water. The problem of pollution of surface streams and of ground water continues. In 1941 in an effort to remedy this damage, an enactment made further provision for the disposal of oil or gas field brines [68] saying that any company or corporation engaged in the production of oil or gas or organized to dispose of oil or gas field brines, or mineralized water, might own, lease, construct, operate and maintain pipe lines, reservoirs, treatment plants, disposal wells, and other disposal facilities. These companies or corporations were permitted to exercise the power of eminent domain in acquiring necessary right-of-ways, but not for the disposal of such brines and mineralized water. Such companies or corporations might provide for financing and acquiring the necessary land easements and right-of-ways necessary for disposal. All plans and specifications for the disposal of oil or gas field brines and mineralized water must be submitted for approval to the State Corporation Commission and the State Board of Health. The legislature laid a duty on the State Corporation Commission [69] that ". . . in giving its approval, [it] shall determine that the proposed method of disposal will not result in the loss or waste of gas or petroleum resources." The burden laid on the State Board of Health [70] required that, ". . . in giving its approval, [it] shall determine that the proposed method is a feasible method to be employed in protecting the water resources of the state from preventable pollution." While the 1945 legislature repealed the 1941 laws identical statutes were passed which added that after the State Board of Health found that the most feasible method for the prevention of pollution was by disposal well, it was required to certify its finding to the State Corporation Commission. The State Corporation Commission gives notice of the findings of the

[67] *Id.* § 55–121.
[68] Kan. Gen. Stat. Ann. § 55–1001 (Cum. Supp. 1941).
[69] *Id.* § 55–1002.
[70] *Id.* § 55–1003.

Board of Health to those owning the wells producing brines and mineralized water. If the owner or operator desires to contest the findings of the State Corporation Commission and the State Board of Health, procedures are fixed. An owner or operator is authorized to exercise the right of eminent domain to secure necessary right of ways and sites for the disposal of brines and mineralized waters.

PLUGGING AND ABANDONMENT

The 1935 legislature provided that operators must shut off and exclude all water from oil or gas bearing sands or formations and use every effort to prevent the pollution of suitable domestic or irrigation waters, in accord with methods, rules and regulations promulgated by the State Corporation Commission. A further requirement was the giving of notice to the State Corporation Commission or its designated agent of (1) intent to abandon any oil or gas wells, (2) the date on which abandonment work would commence, and (3) the facts concerning the plugging of the well in compliance with the rules and regulations. The final section orders the owner or operators to file an affidavit with the State Corporation Commission within 15 days after the plugging of any well, setting forth in detail the method used. Certified copies of such affidavits are available upon request and the payment of a fee set by the Commission.

The State Corporation Commission was directed (by the 1935 legislature)[71] to adopt necessary rules and regulations to provide for a method or methods by which oil or gas wells would be plugged or abandoned. It was authorized to assess the costs [72] of abandonment or plugging in a fair and equitable manner. It could, if in its judgment it was deemed necessary, require a cash deposit or bond to cover these expenses prior to abandonment or plugging. To assure compliance with these statutory provisions, the legislature set as a penalty a fine of not more than $500, or imprisonment not to exceed six months, or both, assessed upon conviction of an infraction of the rules and regulations. The section [73] calling for

[71] *Id.* § 55–130.
[72] *Id.* § 55–131.
[73] *Id.* § 55–116.

filling and plugging wells before drawing gas was repealed by the 1937 legislature.[74] However a like provision was left to the discretion of the State Corporation Commission in adopting rules and regulations.

The 1947 legislature enacted statutes governing the completion or abandonment of any well drilled with rotary or cable tools or equipment. It made abandonment unlawful unless surface or drive pipe be cemented in below the fresh water strata and above all inferior salt water strata in keeping with the rules and regulations adopted and promulgated by the State Corporation Commission.[75] If any well was completed as a dry hole and plugged below the fresh water strata in accord with the law and the rules and regulations of the State Corporation Commission, it would be unnecessary to leave surface pipe in the well.[76] Any person, firm, association, or corporation violating these sections was subject to a fine of not less than $300 or more than $5000 upon conviction. The person in possession or control of the well being drilled must file, within 15 days after the cementing in of the surface or drive pipe, an affidavit with the State Corporation Commission in which is set out in detail the method used. Failure to file subjects the person to a fine not less than $5.00 nor more than $100.

PROTECTION OF FRESH WATER

The problems of fresh water protection are of such vital importance to the citizens of Kansas that not only the state but private industry as well have expended vast sums of money in research and experimentation. Ogden S. Jones [77] of the Kansas State Board of Health pointed out that the Kansas supply of available good water is on the decline because: "Chronological data accumulated over the past one hundred years show a decrease in annual rainfall and a gradual increase in the gradual mean temperature which results in reduced stream flows and a higher evaporation rate on ponds and lakes throughout the state. The accumulated effect of these factors limits the present and perhaps the future water supply expectancy." In a study made in 1945 by two veteran Kansas legislators to de-

[74] Kan. Laws 1937, c. 263, § 1.
[75] Id. §§ 55–136, 55–137 (Cum. Supp. 1947).
[76] Id. § 55–137.
[77] JONES, A REVIEW OF LEASE HOUSEKEEPING PRACTICES 123 (1942).

termine if it was necessary to pass additional legislation, it was found that the greatest amount of property damage and water pollution was caused by the inadequate disposal methods then utilized in the oil and gas industry. Disposal of salt water made into man made ponds from which the sun evaporated the moisture left a deposit of concentrated salt which filtered down through the ground. It was estimated that salt water pollution would travel as far as 300 miles, although the salt content decreased as the distance increased.[78] The Kansas legislature of 1945 amended the laws relating to the disposal of oil or gas field brines [79] to allow condemnation by eminent domain for the purpose of acquiring disposal sites.[80] At the present time the Committee on Labor and Industries is studying the problem of pollution of surface and underground fresh water in an effort to place before the Kansas legislature (at its next session) intelligent and helpful proposals for legislation. This committee reported at Topeka, Kansas, March 19, 1948 that: [81] ". . . there exists in Kansas a considerable amount of pollution of fresh water from abandoned oil wells which were either improperly plugged, or in which the plugging is no longer effective by reason of the deterioration of the pipe, or from other cause. In many instances the person who would normally have the responsibility to rectify this situation had either died, removed or become insolvent, so that no means presently exists to correct this evil. The committee believes that a fund should be created from a small tax on the oil industry of one-tenth of one cent "per barrel the fund to be used by the conservation division of the corporation commission for the purpose of cleaning out and properly plugging suspect wells where no one can be found who has the legal responsibility to do so. The Committee requests authority to draft a bill along these lines which would provide in substance that upon complaint being made to either the state board of health, or the conservation division that an investigation be undertaken and if it is found that there is reason to believe that a suspect well is causing pollution that the corporation commission undertake the proper plugging of such wells and for that purpose a fund be created from a tax of one-tenth of one cent per barrel on oil produced in Kansas

---

[78] Kansas City Times, Jan. 26, 1945, p. 4, c. 2.
[79] See note 68 *supra*.
[80] See note 70 *supra*.
[81] Jour. Kan. Leg. Council (Mar. 19, 1948).

and that such tax be levied and collected by the director of the conservation division for such period of time as he deems necessary in order to provide adequate funds for the purposes above enumerated." The problem has been dealt with adequately but not completely. The seriousness and the necessity of immediate action is recognized by the urgent plea of Jones that [82] "The Plains States are not only situated in a hard water belt but seldom during the years have they had adequate supplies of usable surface or ground waters. The accumulative effects of industrial expansion, war plants, population increases and dry hot summers with consequential accelerated evaporation rates have placed a premium on the water supplies. Fresh water is one of our ranking natural resources and water can conceivably be the controlling factor in economic growth and industrial expansion. It is, therefore, increasingly evident that the protection of this vital resource from pollution should be of concern to all of us. It is readily granted that oil is of paramount importance in this age and increasingly so while we are at war, as we are called upon to supply not only this nation but several of our allies. However, it must be borne in mind that oil even in these times should not be produced with a total disregard to other natural resources and in particular water. Farms and municipalities have a right to expect their respective water sheds to be kept free from contamination. Farms and cities have an economic life expectancy of much longer duration than an oil field. It is, therefore, unjust to allow that expectancy to be jeopardized by the improper handling of oil field brines."

Kansas has developed and grown in an industry which defies delay. Scientific and physical development as applied to the oil and gas industry progressed in the earlier stages beyond the ability of the state to adjust its social concepts. The position of the state has been one of protection of the interests of land owners and lessors. New development and rapid progress in the oil and gas fields make it necessary to keep step by putting into effect a theory of conservation to meet these new problems as they arise. Kansas has been and still is a member of the Interstate Compact to Conserve Oil and Gas. The task has not been easy, but the State of Kansas has done admirable work in the field of conservation.

[82] JONES, DISPOSITION OF OIL FIELD BRINES 7 (1945).

CHAPTER 14

Kentucky, 1819–1948

The history of oil and gas development in the Commonwealth of Kentucky is more impressive than that of conservation legislation. The commonwealth may properly claim the distinction of having the first commercial oil well in the United States—the famous Old American well drilled in 1829 near Burkesville, Cumberland County. That well was drilled for the production of salt and not for oil, as was the Drake well near Titusville, Pennsylvania, thirty years later. Oil from the Old American widely sold for medicinal purposes under the name *American Oil* at 50 cents a half pint, or $336 a barrel. The well operated until 1880 and produced an estimated 50,000 barrels of oil.

In the early nineteenth century, many salt wells were drilled in Kentucky to depths of 200 or 300 feet. The first oil discovery of which the Kentucky Department of Mines and Minerals has any record was made by Martin Beatty in 1819 in what is now McCreary County, then a part of Wayne County, while drilling for salt brine. Apparently there was a substantial flow from the well, but production from this and other early salt wells in which oil was encountered was not sold or used commercially. Much oil was permitted to flow into streams and was so troublesome that it was known as devil's tar. Gas was encountered in some early salt wells, but the first well drilled as a gas well was completed in 1859 in Meade County. The Civil War brought a halt to drilling for gas. In the latter 1860's development was resumed, and since that time there has been continuous activity in the drilling of wells for oil and gas. By the end of the century Kentucky was one of the leaders

George W. Hazlett, Writer; Martin J. Holbrook, Daniel J. Jones, Advisors. (See app. B.)

in the production of oil and gas. In recent years there has been a decline, and in 1947 the commonwealth produced approximately 9,500,000 barrels of oil and 95 billion cubic feet of gas.[1]

CONSERVATION LEGISLATION IN KENTUCKY

Early regulatory legislation enacted in 1892,[2] and still in force, required that a well in which oil, gas or salt water had been found

[1] Further information on history of development is obtainable from the State Geologist, Ky. Geol. Sur., Univ. of Ky., Lexington.

[2] Ky. Acts 1891–93, c. 39; KY. REV. STAT. ANN. § 353.150 (1943). See Common. v. Trent, 117 Ky. 34, 77 S.W. 390 (1903), Calor Oil Co. v. Franzel, 128 Ky. 715, 109 S.W. 328 (1908), Monarch Oil Co. v. Richardson, 124 Ky. 602, 99 S.W. 668 (1907). [Editor's Note. The earliest regulatory acts passed in the state seem to be in Ky. Acts 1889–1890, c. 1187, where plugging of wells was outlined for the Counties of Breckenridge, Grayson and Hancock. In connection with § 353.150 a most shocking factual situation was presented in Louisiana Gas Co. v. Ky. Heating Co., Calor Oil and Gas Co., v. McGehee, 117 Ky. 71, 77 S.W. 368 (1903). The facts were that: "That there is a natural gas field in Meade county, from which the gas is piped to Louisville by the Kentucky Heating Company, and there sold for heating and illuminating purposes. The Louisville Gas Company claimed the exclusive privilege of selling illuminating gas in the city of Louisville. There was a long litigation between it and the Kentucky Heating Company, resulting in a judgment of this court on June 20, 1901, that the heating company has the right to sell natural gas for heating and illuminating purposes, also the right to make and sell artificial gas for fuel, but not the right to sell artificial gas alone or in mixture with natural gas for purposes of illumination without violation of the gas company's exclusive privilege. On September 3, 1901, or about three months after this judgment was rendered, the Calor Oil & Gas Company was incorporated. Its capital stock was fixed at $1,000, divided into 100 shares of $10 each. John A. Gray, Harry Wirgman, and W. A. Jones were the incorporators, subscribing for the entire stock of the company; but neither of them paid anything therefor, or really owned the stock. They subscribed for it for A. Hite Barrett, the chief engineer of the Louisville Gas Company, Udolpho Sneed, the president of the gas company, and Will Speed, and J. B. Speed, who were the real organizers of the company. The money which was paid in for the stock was placed in bank to the credit of the company thus formed, and has since remained there. In the winter before this corporation was formed John H. Trent, a lawyer living in Meade county, who seems to have been in the employ of the gas company previous to that began taking leases of land for gas in the gas field, and took quite a number. In doing this he acted it appears, as the agent of Barrett, Sneed, and Speed, and after they organized the Calor Oil & Gas Company these leases were assigned to it. It is also shown that for some time before the organization of this company they had been considering the gas field in Meade county, from which the Kentucky Heating Company obtained its gas, and one of their objects in getting the leases and organizing the Calor Oil & Gas Company was to interfere with the supply of that company, and thus cripple it as a rival of the Louisville Gas Company. They put up between them about $10,000, which they spent in Meade county in boring wells and in erecting what is called a 'lamp black factory.' In addition to this, when the depositions were taken they had incurred liabilities for about

be kept closed until production from the well was utilized, except that gas produced with oil or water might be permitted to escape. The Act ordered the plugging of wells abandoned as dry holes or no longer productive, and specified the manner in which they be closed. In 1906 these requirements were amplified and extended.[3] Efforts to require the furnishing of well reports were made through the introduction of H.B. 537 at the 1920 session of the State Legislature and H.B. 188 of the 1922 session. Under the provisions of these measures an operator would file with the state geologist, before commencing a well, a sworn statement showing the nature, kind, location and probable depth and, within ten days after completion or abandonment of the well, a second statement showing the location, depth, production, and ownership, with an accurate log of all strata penetrated. Both failed of passage. A fairly comprehensive law was enacted in 1932 to regulate the drilling of oil or gas wells in lands known to be underlaid with coal bearing strata. This Act,[4] still effective, is designed primarily for the protection of the commonwealth's extensive coal deposits. A well

---

$10,000 more, which were then unpaid. They succeeded in getting several good gas wells from which the gas was piped to their lamp black factory. When they began operations, the Kentucky Heating Company had a gas pressure of something over sixty pounds. In five or six months this was run down to less than thirty. On these facts the chancellor on the petition of the Kentucky Heating Company, enjoined the operation of the lamp black factory on the ground that it was operated only to waste the gas, and thus destroy the Kentucky Heating Company. . . . A close fence twelve feet high, was built around the lamp black factory, and no one was admitted within the inclosure. It stood on a half acre of ground leased for that purpose, and no one was permitted to come on this half acre. Firearms were discharged there to deter the neighbors from coming about. The structure was out in the country where such inclosures are unusual, and, as shown by the evidence, unnecessary. The man in charge of the factory was the lawyer Trent, who lived at the county seat, and knew nothing of the manufacture of lamp black. There were only two other persons employed—one, the day man, was a boy sixteen years old; the other, the night man, somewhat older, but both entirely ignorant of the manufacture of lamp black. During the five months the factory operated they manufactured about 300 pounds of lamp black, worth four cents a pound. In this time they burned all the gas they could obtain, the total amount being about 90,000,000 of feet. No lamp black was shipped away from the factory. The gas was burned night and day, and it is evident from the proof that in a short time more the pressure upon the pipes of the Kentucky Heating Company would have been so low as to destroy its usefulness."]

[3] Ky. Acts 1905–06, c. 47; Ky. Rev. Stat. Ann. § 353.180 (1943). See Seaboard Oil Co. v. Common., 193 Ky. 629, 237 S.W. 48 (1922); Palmer Corp. v. Collins, 214 Ky. 838, 284 S.W. 95 (1926); East. Carbon Black Corp. v. Stone, 229 Ky. 68, 16 S.W. 2d 492 (1929).

[4] Ky. Acts 1932, c. 98; Ky. Rev. Stat. Ann. § 353.050 et. seq. (1943).

operator, before drilling in coal bearing land, must notify the Department of Mines and the owners and operators of coal strata in the tract of land on which the well is to be drilled. If any objection to the drilling is filed, the Department holds a hearing and determines whether or not the drilling may be permitted. The Act specifies the precautions the well operator must take in drilling through coal beds and imposes special requirements with respect to plugging of wells so drilled. With the exception of the authority of the Department of Mines to regulate drilling in coal-bearing lands, the statutes of Kentucky still do not provide for administrative control over the drilling or operating of wells for the production of oil or gas. Except when wells are drilled in such lands, drilling permits are not required and well operators need not furnish any reports or information about wells drilled or abandoned. The Division of Geology attempts to collect well logs and facts through voluntary cooperation.

The nearest approach to conservation legislation was enacted in 1936. This Act[5] prohibits the waste or escape of natural gas from a well or pipe line when at all possible to prevent it after a reasonable time. When it is necessary to permit gas to escape while a well is drilling or cleaning out, the work must be prosecuted with due diligence to prevent waste for a period longer than needed. Where gas is produced with oil, the owner or operator must "use all reasonable diligence to conserve and save from waste so much of the gas as it is reasonably possible to save." This law has been of little assistance in waste prevention.

Secondary recovery operations through injection of gas or air and by water flooding have been conducted to a considerable extent, the first in the Paint Creek Uplift Field in 1926.[6] Secondary recovery legislation enacted in 1938[7] does no more than exempt injection wells from the earlier plugging requirements. It permits "the owner or operator of any well that produces oil or gas [to] allow the well to remain open for the purpose of introducing air, gas, water or other liquid pressure into and upon the producing strata for the purpose of recovering the oil. The introduction of

[5] Ky. Acts 1936, c. 35; Ky. Rev. Stat. Ann. § 353.160 (1943).
[6] Wilder, *Secondary Recovery in Kentucky*, Secondary Recovery of Oil in the United States (1942).
[7] Ky. Acts 1938, c. 151 § 1; Ky. Rev. Stat. Ann. § 353.170 (1943).

such pressure shall be through casing or tubing, which shall be so anchored and packed that no other oil-bearing sand or producing stratum above or below the producing strata upon which the pressure is put shall be affected thereby."

The first effort to obtain an adequate conservation law for the commonwealth was made January 1940 when S.B. 66 was introduced by Senator Lee Gibson. It provided for an oil and gas conservation commission and a director of conservation with broad regulatory powers, including authority to promulgate spacing rules, limit and prorate production on the basis of market demand. The bill prohibited waste of oil and gas, contained a comprehensive definition of waste (both underground and surface), and made production in excess of market demand waste. The Gibson bill, largely drawn from conservation laws adopted in Michigan and New Mexico, had been prepared and introduced at the instance of leading members of the Kentucky Oil and Gas Association, and had the support of many operators. After its introduction, the measure was considered at a special meeting of the association held in Louisville, where it met with vigorous opposition and equally vigorous support. The meeting ended in complete disagreement, after it became impossible to obtain approval of a substantial majority of the association members for the proposal or any other adequate bill. A senate committee to which the bill was referred held a hearing where these divergent views were presented, after which it died in committee. A modified form of the 1940 bill prepared for the 1942 session had the support of many operators; because it was concluded that the political situation offered little hope for passage, the presentation was not made. In 1942 Kentucky became a member of the Interstate Compact to conserve Oil and Gas.[8]

During World War II Kentucky experienced well spacing under limitations imposed by the War Production Board on the materials used in well drilling. Most operators found that the spacing rules worked to their advantage. In the years before the war several pools discovered in or near towns and villages were subjected to town lot drilling. Like situations during the war were prevented by the WPB rules. As a result of this wartime spacing experience,

[8] Ky. Acts 1942, c. 207.

at the 1946 session of the legislature, a modified spacing bill was introduced in the House as H.B. 422 by G. I. Drury. The proposed law required the obtaining of a permit before commencing operations for drilling a well and prohibited drilling within specified distances of lease boundary lines, which varied with the well's depth, and, where necessary for compulsory consolidation of royalty and working interests, to comply with the limitations. No spacing was provided for wells drilled in the interior leases beyond the prescribed distances from boundary lines. A companion measure introduced in the House by T. A. Gilliam as bill 423 created a Kentucky Geological Survey under a director and state geologist, to replace the Division of Geology in the State Department of Mines. The two laws were sponsored by the Kentucky Oil and Gas Association, with the endorsement of a majority of its members. The spacing proposal was approved by the House Oil and Minerals Committee and passed the House unanimously. In the Senate it was referred to the Rules Committee and favorably reported. Although every effort had been made to keep the legislation on a non-political basis, both bills became involved in a political controversy and perished without being brought to a vote in the Senate.

The 1948 session of the Kentucky legislature enacted S. B. 303 [9] which created the Kentucky Geological Survey within the Department of Geology at the University of Kentucky and transferred to the newly created survey the Division of Geology from the Department of Mines and Minerals. The Act provides for the gathering of information and the making of periodic reports on the mineral resources of the state.

The absence of conservation legislation in Kentucky is attributed to the traditional individualism of its citizens, their inherent distrust of governmental regulation, and to the nature of the oil and gas development in the commonwealth. Oil and gas have been found in formations ranging in age from Ordovician to Pennsylvanian, but the pools are small and the wells shallow in comparison with the prolific areas of the nation. Commercial production has been encountered at depths of as little as 100 feet; few wells have been drilled deeper than 3000 feet, so that drilling is comparatively

[9] S. B. No. 303, 1948 sess. Ky. Legis.

inexpensive. Production has not been in a volume having any marked effect on market conditions and the entire supply finds a ready sale at prices which reflect lower transportation costs resulting from its location. While nearly all Kentucky operators appreciate the advantages derived from reasonable well spacing, these factors make the need for adequate conservation measures difficult to impress upon the legislature and the public.

CHAPTER 15

Louisiana, 1938–1948

The nation is confronted with the problem of getting maximum recovery from its oil and gas reserves. We produce oil in the United States about as fast as it is discovered. Today's needs for petroleum and its products are greater than ever before, and all indications are that domestic requirements will continue to increase at a rapid rate. In the north and east many industries and homes are discontinuing the use of coal and converting to fuel oil and natural gas, which presents a serious problem, because according to published figures of the Bureau of Mines, known natural gas reserves in this country are less than 1 per cent, and coal more than 98 per cent of our national fuel supply. Each winter for the past few years has seen shortages of fuel oil and natural gas, especially in those areas where there has been a rapid conversion from coal to fuel oil and natural gas. Demand for natural gasoline increases each year, and there is no sign that future requirements will lessen. Press reports from Washington record Secretary of the Interior Krug's recommendation that enormous sums be appropriated by Congress for developing synthetic petroleum products. Confronted with these problems in times of peace, the situation would become even more complex in the event of war.

According to a forecast prepared by the Economics Advisory Committee of the Interstate Oil Compact Commission, the American petroleum industry must supply approximately 6 per cent more oil and refined products to meet the public needs in 1948 than in the record breaking year of 1947. Their estimate of demand for petroleum in the United States for 1947 and 1948 as compared with that for 1941 graphically demonstrates the gain. In 1941 the

E. LELAND RICHARDSON, WRITER; Gordon Keane, Eugene A. Nabors and Dixon Carroll, Advisers. (See app. B.)

daily domestic requirements were 4,071,000 barrels, in 1947 5,410,-000 barrels, and by 1948 the Committee predicts that 5,795,000 barrels will be needed. This report shows a daily export in 1941 of 298,000 barrels, in 1947 459,000 barrels, and it is thought the needs for this purpose in 1948 will reach 400,000 barrels. Thus the Committee estimates the increase in 1947 over 1941 was 1,500,000 barrels daily and that demand will rise to 1,826,000 barrels in 1948. It can readily be seen that the public interest requires that we recover the maximum oil and natural gas from known reserves. This can be accomplished only through proper and adequate conservation laws and their efficient administration.

Before 1940 the rule of capture reigned in Louisiana, as it does today in a number of states, and as a result several large gas distillate fields were produced too rapidly, tremendous quantities of natural gas flared, and the maximum ultimate recovery not realized. In 1940 the Louisiana legislature adopted Act 157 (as its comprehensive conservation enactment) containing provisions revolutionary in the conservation field at that time, and many of which are still unique in administrative law. It was one of the first state statutes providing for compulsory unitization. It represents a step forward in administrative endeavor as well as in the conservation of oil and gas in Louisiana. Under the authority vested in the Conservation Commissioner great strides have been made in the matter of spacing, unit operations, and compulsory pooling, giving Louisiana an effective conservation program. In Louisiana the Conservation Commissioner may require unit operations in any field where production under ordinary methods would constitute waste. Louisiana has keynoted compulsory unit operations since the adoption of Act 157. There has been no great opposition from any quarter to the Act's unitization feature, and the fact that it has not been materially amended since adoption indicates that it generally meets with public approval. The views of informed persons writing on the subject of unitization [1] substantiate Louisiana's position with

[1] Duff, Oil and Gas Jour. (Feb. 12, 1948): "The current record demand for petroleum and its products and efforts of the industry to maximize production have again drawn attention to the need in Texas for oil unitization legislation, which could conceivably add as much as a billion barrels to the state's recoverable oil. . . . A bill for permissive pooling of oil properties failed to pass the last legislature, but indications are that a similar measure will be placed before the state's lawmakers early next year. Clear-cut legislative authority sanctioning oil field unit-

reference to forced unit operations. Since its creation the Interstate Oil Compact Commission has been interested in the important field of secondary recovery. At present a special division of the Commission has been set up to consider the question and to co-ordinate the studies on this subject that have been and are being made by other agencies in the United States. To successfully in-augurate systems of secondary recovery throughout the nation it is

---

ization is considered to be a necessary initial step toward the greatly improved recoveries, which, in many reservoirs in Texas, are economically and technically possible only under joint operation. . . . One indication of the possibilities was given by engineers in testimony during hearings on the unitization bill in the last legislature. Statements were made that if a field-wide repressuring program was conducted in Fullerton Field in West Texas, ultimate production would be in-creased by some fifty million barrels. Proportionate good results could be obtained in many other fields, according to the testimony." The writer quoted W. J. Murray Jr., member of the Texas Railroad Commission as saying: "In many fields, we are not putting into practice techniques of pressure maintenance, repressuring, water injection, and reservoir control which we know would increase recovery and be economically sound . . . Most of these failures to adopt proven conservation mea-sures relate, I believe, the need for a more enlightened public opinion. If the public can be informed of the need for conservation and can have a reasonable under-standing of the process, they will,—while standing firm against abuses and against any real anti-trust violations—nevertheless see to it that no unreasonable federal or state regulation stands in the way of true conservation." Kaveler, World Oil (Feb. 1948): "It is a striking fact that no one has successfully maintained in public or in private communication, that the unitized operation of an oil and gas field did not accomplish a very substantial increase in ultimate recovery, did not achieve the ultimate in conservation of both oil and gas, or did not give to every owner a greater production of oil and gas than would have otherwise been recovered. When the case for unitized management of common sources of supply is examined from an operating, engineering, regulatory, and conservation point of view, it is very preponderantly in favor of that practice. It is not difficult, therefore, to state the case in favor of the need for the unitized method of production of oil and gas. There is good reason to urge that the barriers to more general acceptance of the principle should be eliminated . . . The objectives of unit operation of a common source of supply of oil and gas are to accomplish the following: "1. Maximum recovery of oil and gas. 2. Conservation of natural gas and crude. 3. Elim-ination of unnecessary and wasteful wells. 4. Maintenance of capacity to produce. 5. Maintenance of efficient rates of production. 6. A fair and equitable distribution of oil and gas as between the parties entitled to share it. 7. Removal of 'correla-tive rights' from primary consideration in the allocation of production . . . It must be conceded that through unit operation of a common source of supply, the oil recovery can be materially increased, often doubled, or even trebled, and the waste of gas prevented. The increased recovery of oil, through unitization, is measured in millions of barrels. That is oil which otherwise could not be recovered. Every competent engineer, geologist or practical oil operator, particularly those who have had some experience with unitized operation, will testify to the benefits derived. The agencies of the federal government, the Interstate Oil Compact Com-mission, and the various associations within the industry recognize and urge unitiza-tion as a means of obtaining the greatest ultimate recovery of oil and of preventing the waste of oil and gas."

necessary to have unit operation, as very little can be accomplished without the complete cooperation of all the owners of a reservoir. While this may be done through voluntary agreement, it is not right for the system to fail in any reservoir because of the lack of cooperation by some owners. Statutes similar to Louisiana's are essential to bring about the ultimate in production. Unit operation in the production of oil and gas from common reservoirs or sources of supply is recognized as the most efficient operational method. Many examples of increased recovery are found in those states where unit operation is practiced, and the growing number of voluntary cooperative endeavors provide additional evidence that unit operations greatly augment ultimate recovery. According to figures from the Conservation Department of Louisiana, the increase of recovery in unitized fields [2] is 30 per cent or better over that from the same fields operated under ordinary conditions and methods.

ACT 157 OF 1940

Now to analyze the provisions of Act 157 of 1940 which make compulsory unit operation in the state possible. The Act is full, complete, and comprehensive, protects private property rights, provides for unit operation, and establishes compulsory pooling. The

---

[2] To show how unit operation affects conservation, reference is made to some outstanding projects unitized under Act 157. The Benton Field, Bossier Parish, a cycling project, was developed as such from time of discovery. The entire field is unitized, having a cycling plant with a daily capacity of 50,000,000 cubic feet of gas and a production of some 4000 barrels of liquid hydrocarbons. Some 17,-000,000 barrels of these will be produced, more than 4,000,000 barrels more than under ordinary methods. The Mamou Field, Evangeline Parish, is unitized for water injection. Here production is from 10,000 feet and the high pressure and nearness to bubble point of the reservoir liquid makes some type of pressure maintenance necessary. More than 4,000,000 barrels of oil will be added to the primary recovery. An interesting project in the Tensas and Concordia Parishes, is the Lake St. John Field covering some 13,000 acres and having a rich gas-distillate cap and an oil band. The entire field is unitized, and has a cycling plant with a capacity of 100,000,000 cubic feet of gas daily which saves each day 15,000,000 cubic feet of gas formerly flared. It is thought that in excess of 15,000,000 barrels of liquid hydrocarbons will be recovered which would have been lost under primary methods. In view of the great number of royalty owners in the Lake St. John Field it is doubtful if its unit operation would have taken place without compulsory unitization. The Haynesville Field, Claiborne Parish, is estimated to produce more than 30,000,000 added barrels of oil by unit operation.

primary purpose of the enactment is to prevent waste,[3] defined in language broad and all inclusive.[4] Waste, in addition to its ordinary meaning, includes physical waste as that term is understood in the industry, the inefficient, excessive or improper use or dissipation of reservoir energy, and the locating, spacing, drilling, equipping, operating, or producing of any oil or gas well in a manner which results, or tends to result, in reducing ultimate recovery of oil or gas from any pool. Also included are the inefficient storing of oil, the production of oil or gas in excess of transportation, marketing facilities or reasonable market demand, and unnecessary surface loss or destruction of oil and gas. Waste is not limited in its scope as were previous usages in other enactments.

The legislature gives the Commissioner of Conservation jurisdiction and authority over all persons and property necessary to enforce the Act and all other state statutes relating to conservation.[5] It is his mandatory duty to make inquiries for determining whether or not waste exists or is imminent. He is authorized to collect data, make investigations, and examine properties, leases, papers, books and records, survey and gauge oil and gas wells, tanks, refineries and modes of transportation. The Act empowers the Commissioner to hold hearings and provide for the keeping of records, the making of reports, and to take any action needed to enforce the statute. He may, after hearings, make reasonable rules, regulations, and orders to administer and enforce the law (which includes similar rulings for certain stated purposes).[6]

[3] La. Acts 1940, Act No. 157, § 1; La. Gen. Stat. Ann. § 4741.11 (Cum. Supp. 1947).

[4] Id. § 2.

[5] Id. § 3.

[6] Ibid. (a) To require the drilling, casing and plugging of wells to be done in such a manner as to prevent the escape of oil or gas out of one stratum to another; to prevent the intrusion of water into oil or gas strata; to prevent the pollution of fresh water supplies by oil, gas or salt water; and to require reasonable bond with good and sufficient surety conditioned for the performance of the duty to plug each dry or abandoned well. (b) To require the making of reports showing the location of all oil and gas wells, and the filing of logs, electrical surveys and other drilling records. (c) To prevent wells from being drilled, operated and produced in such a manner as to cause injury to neighboring leases or property. (d) To prevent the drowning by water of any stratum or part thereof capable of producing oil or gas in paying quantities, and to prevent the premature and irregular encroachment of water which reduces, or tends to reduce, the total ultimate recovery of oil or gas from any pool. (e) To require the operation of wells with efficient gas-oil ratios, and to fix such ratios. (f) To prevent "blow outs", "caving"

The Act, in regulating the manufacture of carbon black,[7] makes it a violation for any person to build or operate a carbon black plant without first securing a permit.

One of the statute's unusual features is Section 4 where it is stated that to prevent waste and avoid drilling of unnecessary wells, the Commissioner (after notice and hearing) is authorized to determine the feasibility of, and to require recycling in any pool or its portions producing gas wherein condensate or distillate may be separated or natural gasoline extracted. Rules to unitize separate ownership and to regulate the production and reintroduction of gas into productive formations after separation or extraction may be established, and under these powers unit operation of numerous gas condensate reservoirs for cycling has been effected.

and "seepage" in the sense that conditions indicated by such terms are generally understood in the oil and gas business. (g) To prevent fires. (h) To identify the ownership of all oil or gas wells, producing leases, refineries, tanks, plants, structures, and all storage and transportation equipment and facilities. (i) To regulate the "shooting" and chemical treatment of wells. (j) To regulate secondary recovery methods, including the introduction of gas, air, water, or other substance into producing formations. (k) To limit and pro-rate the production of oil or gas, or both, from any pool or field for the prevention of waste as herein defined. (l) To require, either generally or in or from particular areas, certificates of clearance or tenders in connection with the transportation of oil, gas, or any product. (m) To regulate the spacing of wells and to establish drilling units, including temporary or tentative spacing rules and drilling units in new fields. (n) To require interested persons, firms or corporations to place uniform meters of a type approved by the Commissioner wherever the Commissioner may designate on all pipe lines, gathering systems, barge terminals, loading racks, refineries, or other places deemed necessary or proper to prevent waste and the transportation of illegally produced oil or gas; such meters at all times shall be under the supervision and control of the Department of Conservation, and it shall be a violation of this Act, subject to the penalties provided in Section 17 for any person, firm, or corporation to refuse to attach or install such meter when ordered to do so by the Commissioner, or in any way to tamper with such meter so as to produce a false or inaccurate reading, or to have any by-pass at such a place where the oil or gas can be passed around such meter, unless expressly authorized by written permit of the Commissioner. (o) To require that the product of all wells shall be separated into so many million cubic feet of gaseous hydrocarbons and so many barrels of liquid hydrocarbons, either or both, and accurately measured wherever separation takes place. Gaseous hydrocarbon measurement shall be corrected to ten (10) ounces above atmospheric pressure. Liquid hydrocarbons shall be measured into barrels of forty-two (42) gallons each. Both measurements corrected to 60 Fahrenheit.

[7] *Id.* § 4. "In order to prevent waste of natural gas, the Commissioner shall have authority to grant to bona fide applicants permits for the building and operation of plants and to burn natural gas into carbon black for such period of time as may be fixed by the Commissioner in such permit, not to exceed twenty-five years and subject at all times to the provisions of laws of the state and rules and regulations of the Department of Conservation . . ."

The law permits the Commissioner to prescribe the rules of order and procedure at hearings or proceedings held before him. No rule, regulation or order, including its change, renewal or extension (absent an emergency) is made by the administrator except after public hearing upon at least 10 days notice given in a manner and form prescribed by him.[8] A party in interest is entitled to be heard. If an emergency exists in the Commissioner's judgment which requires the making, changing, renewal or extension of a rule, regulation or order without a hearing, the emergency measure is given equal validity as though a hearing had been had after notice. These remain in force no longer than 15 days from their effective date, and expire when a rule, regulation or order made with notice and hearing which deals with the same subject matter becomes effective. The Commissioner may give notice through personal service made by any officer authorized to serve process, or by any agent of his in the manner provided by law for the service of citations in civil actions in the state district courts. Proof of service by the agent is by affidavit.

All rules, regulations and orders made are written and entered in a book kept for that purpose, which is a public record open to inspection during reasonable office hours. Copies of rules, regulations or orders when certified by the Commissioner are received in evidence in all Louisiana courts with the same effect as the original.

Any interested person may have the Commissioner call a hearing for the purpose of taking action with respect to matters in the administrator's jurisdiction by making a written request. Upon receipt of this petition the Commissioner is required to call a hearing and to act upon the matter with convenient speed; in any event within 30 days he must take appropriate action. If there is any failure or refusal to issue an order within this period, mandamus lies at the suit of any interested person.

All orders fixing or making changes in allowables for the production of oil or gas are issued on or before the 23d day of the month preceding that for which the orders are effective, and are promulgated by immediate publication in the official journal of the state.[9] No order establishing an initial schedule of allowables is issued

---

[8] *Id.* § 5.
[9] *Id.* § 6.

until after notice and hearing, except in the older fields where allowables have been previously set, unless a written request is made by an interested party. This section permitting the fixing of allowable schedules for old fields without a hearing is an exception to the normal rule. When a schedule is promulgated without notice and hearing, any aggrieved producer of oil or gas may file with the Commissioner (at his office) within 72 hours after publication, a sworn written complaint alleging in detail his grievance. The Commissioner holds a hearing in not less than 48 hours, where oral or documentary evidence is received for and against the complaint. After the hearing a decision is summarily rendered, but should this not be done on or before the order's effective date, it is suspended until judgment is rendered. During this suspensory period, the prior order remains in force.

The Commissioner may subpoena witnesses, require their attendance, and the giving of testimony before him.[10] He has authority to require the production of books, papers, and records material to any question lawfully before him. The subpoenas are served by a sheriff, any agent of the department or other officer authorized by law to serve process in Louisiana. No person is excused from attending and testifying, producing books, papers and records, or from obedience to a subpoena from the Commissioner or court, on the ground or the reason that his testimony or evidence (documentary or otherwise) tends to incriminate or subject him to a penalty or forfeiture. Nothing in the Act is construed as requiring any person to produce books, papers or records, or to testify in response to any inquiry not pertinent to a question lawfully before the Commissioner or a court for determination. No natural person is subject to criminal prosecution nor to a penalty or forfeiture by reason of any thing concerning which he was required to testify or produce evidence, or in obedience to its subpoena, except the commission of perjury in giving evidence. Where there is a failure or refusal to comply with a subpoena of the Commissioner, or a case of recusancy as to matters in which a witness is lawfully interrogated, any district court in the state, at the Commissioner's application, may issue out an attachment forcing compliance with the subpoena and attendance before the agency, the production

[10] *Id.* § 7.

of documents, and the giving of testimony lawfully required. The court has the power to punish for contempt as it would disobedience to its subpoenas, or refusals to testify.

Whether or not the total pool production is limited or prorated, the Commissioner may issue no order making it necessary for the producer or owner of a tract to drill a greater number of wells on that tract than will recover (absent waste) its fair share of oil and gas; nor may the administrator permit net drainage from a tract unless the drilling and operation of added wells would result in waste.[11] To prevent waste and avoid the drilling of unnecessary wells, the Commissioner establishes drilling units for each pool, except in those developed to an extent before the enactment's effective date which makes it impracticable and unreasonable to form drilling units. A drilling unit is the maximum area efficiently and economically drilled by one well, and constitutes a developed area as long as its well is capable of producing oil and gas in paying quantities. Each well in a unit is located approximately in the center, although exceptions are granted where it is found that this point is partly outside the pool, that a well so located would be non-productive, or topographical conditions make the use of the central location unduly burdensome. When exceptions are granted, the Commissioner offsets any advantage secured so that drainage from other areas to the excepted tract is prevented or minimized. The producer of such a well is allowed to produce no more than his just and equitable share of the oil and gas in the pool.

Subject to waste prevention and to structural adjustment a producer's or a tract's just and equitable share of the pool oil and gas is that part of the authorized pool production (whether the total produced without restriction, or a lesser amount where limitation is imposed) which represents the proportion that the quantity of recoverable oil and gas in the tract's developed area bears to all recoverable oil and gas in the pool as far as it can be practically ascertained. The administrative rules, regulations and orders must prevent or minimize reasonably avoidable net drainage from developed areas—that is, drainage not equalized by counterdrainage—and give each producer the opportunity to use his just and equitable share of the reservoir energy. In determining this share the

<hr>

[11] *Id.* § 8.

Commissioner considers the productivity of the well as determined by flow and bottom hole pressure tests, other practical methods of testing wells and producing structures, as well as pertinent factors, geological and engineering tests and data.

The Act provides that two or more separately owned tracts of land embraced within a drilling unit (as established by the Commissioner in Section 8) may be validly pooled and developed as a unit.[12] Where the owners do not agree to pool their interests, the Commissioner shall (where necessary for the prevention of waste or to avoid the drilling of unnecessary wells) require the development of their lands as a drilling unit. All orders which call for pooling are made (after notice and hearing) upon reasonable terms and conditions, to afford each tract an opportunity to receive its just and equitable share of oil and gas without unnecessary expense, preventing or minimizing concurrently reasonably avoidable drainage unequalized by counter drainage. That production allocated the owner of each tract in a unit formed by a pooling order is considered as produced from the tract by a well thereon. If pooling is forced, the cost of development and operation of the unit chargeable to the interested owner or owners is limited to the reasonable actual expenditure, including a fair charge for supervision. In the event of a dispute about these costs, the Commissioner determines the proper amounts. Should the owners of separate tracts fail to agree to pool their interests and to the drilling of a well on the unit, and it be established by final and unappealable judgment of a court of competent jurisdiction that the Commissioner is without authority to order pooling, then (subject to the other applicable provisions of the Act) the owner of each tract within the unit might drill; his allowable production would be in the proportion that the area of the separately owned tract bears to the full unit.

Whenever the Commissioner limits the total amount of oil or gas produced, he allocates this allowable among the fields [13] on a reasonable basis, giving, where practical under the circumstances to each field of small wells with settled production, an amount preventing their general premature abandonment. Where the total amount of oil or gas produced in any pool is limited to an amount

[12] *Id.* § 9.
[13] *Id.* § 10.

less than its total production without restriction (which limitation may be imposed incidental to or without a limitation of the total amount of oil or gas produced in Louisiana), the administrator prorates the allowable among the producers in a pool on a reasonable basis, preventing and minimizing avoidable drainage, so that each producer produces or receives his just and equitable share from the reservoir, subject to the necessities of waste prevention. After the effective date of any rule, regulation or order of the Commissioner fixing the allowable production of oil or gas, no person may produce from any well, lease, or property in a pool more than his allowable, nor in a manner different from that authorized.

Ample redress is given those aggrieved by an order of the Commissioner.[14] Any interested party adversely affected by an oil and gas conservation statute of Louisiana, any provision of Act 157, or rule, regulation or order made under the Act, and any act done or threatened, who has exhausted his administrative remedy may obtain court review and relief by a suit for an injunction against the Commissioner as defendant, instituted in the district court of the parish where the principal office of the administrator is located. Such suit is tried summarily and the attorney representing the Commissioner may have the case set for trial at any time after 10 days notice to the plaintiff or his attorney. The burden of proof is the plaintiff's, and all pertinent evidence with respect to the validity and reasonableness of the order is admissible. The rule, regulation or order complained of is prima facie valid, and this presumption is not overcome in any application for injunctive relief or temporary restraining order by a verified petition or affidavit in behalf of the applicant. The right of review accorded by the Act is inclusive of all other remedies.

No temporary restraining order or injunction of any kind is granted against the Commissioner of Conservation, the Attorney General of Louisiana, or any agent, employee or representative of the agency restraining these persons from enforcing any statute of Louisiana relating to the conservation of oil and gas, any of the provisions of Act 157, regulation or order, except where, after notice and hearing, it is clearly shown the court that the act done or threatened has no sanction in law, or that the provisions of Act

[14] *Id.* § 11.

157, or the questioned rule, regulation or order is invalid, and if enforced will cause irreparable injury.[15] The nature and extent of the probable invalidity of the statute, provision of the Act or the rule, regulation or order involved must be recited in the order or decree granting a temporary injunction, as well as a clear statement of the probable damage relied upon by the court to justify relief. No temporary injunction of any kind becomes effective until the plaintiff executes a bond in an amount and condition as the court directs.

Whenever it appears that any person violates or threatens to violate a statute of Louisiana with respect to conservation of oil and gas, or any rule, order or regulation, the Commissioner brings suit against such person either (1) in the district court in the parish of the defendant's residence, (2) in the parish of the residence of any defendant if there be more than one, or (3) in the parish where the violation occurs or is threatened, to restrain the violation or threat.[16] In his action the Commissioner may obtain injunctions (prohibitory and mandatory) including temporary restraining orders and preliminary injunctions, as the facts warrant, including, when appropriate, one restraining any person from moving or disposing of illegal oil, gas or product; any or all of these commodities may be impounded or placed under the control of an agent appointed by the court if such action is advisable. All proceedings brought under the Act, or any oil or gas conservation statute of the state, or rule, regulation or order may be appealed in accord with the general laws of the state relating to appeals; [17] appeals from judgments or decrees entered in suits contesting the validity of any section of Act 157, or any rule or regulation issued in connection with the Act, when docketed, are placed on the preference docket. If the Commissioner fails to bring suit within 10 days to enjoin actual or threatened violations of any statute respecting conservation of oil and gas, or rule, regulation or order, then persons or parties interested or adversely affected by the violation, who have notified the Commissioner in writing of such violation or threat, and requested him to take action, may sue in the district court of

[15] *Id.* § 12.
[16] *Id.* § 13.
[17] *Id.* § 14.

the parish where the Commissioner could have sued to prevent violation.[18] Here, if the court holds injunctive relief should be granted, the Commissioner is made a party and substituted for the person bringing the suit, and the injunction issues as if he had at all times been the complainant.

Penalties are assessed for intentional false entries or statements of fact in reports required by Act 157, or any rule, regulation or order.[19] Any person knowingly and willfully violating the statute, rule, regulation or order (in the event no penalty is otherwise provided) is subject to a fine not to exceed $1000 a day for each day and act of violation.[20] The payment of a penalty does not change illegal oil into legal oil, illegal gas into legal gas, or illegal product into legal product, nor does it legitimatize the purchase, acquisition, sale, transportation, refining, processing or handling of the illegal oil, gas or product. The sale purchase, acquisition, transportation, refining, processing or handling of illegal oil, gas or product is barred.[21] Until the Commissioner provides certificates of clearance or tenders, or a method giving a person an opportunity to determine whether contemplated transactions involve illegal oil, gas or product, no penalty is imposed. If a person knows or could have known or determined from facts within his knowledge by the exercise of reasonable diligence that illegal oil, gas or product is involved, penalties are assessed. Regardless of the lack of actual notice or knowledge, the penalties apply to any transaction involving illegal oil, gas or product where administrative provision is made for identifying the character of the commodity as to its legality. It is likewise an infraction of the law for which penalties are levied for any person to sell, transport, or refine oil, gas or product without complying with the applicable rules, orders and regulations of the Commissioner. In addition to all the remedies afforded the Commissioner, illegal oil, gas or product may be treated as contraband, seized, sold, and the proceeds distributed as set out in the Act.[22] Whenever the Commissioner believes that illegal oil, gas or product is subject to seizure and sale as contraband, he acts through the Attorney General of

[18] *Id.* § 15.
[19] *Id.* § 16.
[20] *Id.* § 17.
[21] *Id.* § 18.
[22] *Id.* § 19.

Louisiana, to bring an in rem civil action in the district court of the parish where the commodity is found, or the action may be maintained in connection with a suit or reconventional demand for injunction or for a penalty relating to any prohibited transaction involving illegal oil, gas or product. Any party adversely affected by the seizure and sale may intervene to protect his interests.

Act 157 is cumulative of and in addition to all laws of Louisiana not in direct conflict with its provisions,[23] except Act 134 of 1924 and Act 225 of 1936 which are repealed. The repeal of Act 225 of 1936, or any prior law of Louisiana does not affect the rules, regulations or orders made under their authority as these measures remain valid and effective, unless amended, rescinded or superseded to the same extent as if made and promulgated under the authority of Act 157.

THE COMMISSIONER OF CONSERVATION AND THE ADMINISTRATION OF ACT 157

Pursuant to the power delegated in Act 157 the Commissioner of Conservation July 15, 1941 issued Order No. 29 which created necessary rules and regulations to conserve the natural resources of the state, prevent waste of oil and gas, and carry out the provisions of the Act.[24] The rules governed the drilling and producing of oil and gas in Louisiana, except where in conflict with orders issued on specific fields. Order No. 29 concerning applications constituted an adequate procedural background for drilling, completion and operation of oil and gas wells in Louisiana. The Commissioner next issued Order No. 29-A [25] May 20, 1942, a revised compilation of rules and regulations controlling the drilling for oil and gas and the completion of wells; on July 19, 1943, Order No. 29-B, a reworking of the previous orders was adopted, governing drilling and producing of oil and gas, except where in conflict with specific field orders.[26]

Order No. 29-B defines those procedures applicable to drilling

[23] *Id.* § 21.
[24] La. Dept. Cons. Order No. 29 (July 15, 1941).
[25] La. Dept. Cons. Order No. 29-A (May 20, 1942).
[26] La. Dept. Cons. Order No. 29-B (July 19, 1943).

for oil and gas [27] and to filing applications for certain permits.[28] The operator is required at the Commissioner's request to supply the department with field maps showing lease lines and well locations

[27] *Id.* § II. A. All applications for permits to drill wells for oil or gas or core test wells below the fresh water sands shall be made on Form MD-10R or revisions thereof, and mailed or delivered to the District Office. These applications, in duplicate, shall be accompanied by plats, preferably drawn to a scale of 500 feet to the inch. The plats shall be constructed from data compiled by a registered civil engineer or surveyor and shall definitely show the amount and location of the acreage with reference to quarter-section corners, or other established survey points. There shall also be shown all pertinent lease and property lines, leases and offset wells. When the tract to be drilled is composed of separately owned interests which have been pooled or unitized, the boundaries to and the acreage in each separately owned interest must be indicated. Plats must have well location certification either written on or attached to the well location plats and this certification must be signed by a registered civil engineer, qualified surveyor or a qualified engineer regularly employed by the applicant. If possible the application card shall give the name and address of the Drilling Contractor, otherwise the information, as soon as determined, shall be supplied by letter to the District Manager. B. When dual completion applications are granted, each well shall be considered as two wells. The production from each sand shall be run through separate lead lines and the production from each sand shall be measurable separately. The Department's agents shall designate suitable suffixes to the well number which will serve as references to each producing sand. C. No well shall be drilled, nor shall the drilling of a well be commenced, before a permit for such well has been issued by the Department of Conservation; furthermore, any work, such as digging pits, erecting buildings, derricks, etc., which the operator may do or have done, will be done at his own risk and with the full understanding that the Department of Conservation may find it necessary to change the location or deny the permit because of the rules and regulations applying in that instance. D. No well shall commence drilling below the surface casing until a sign has been posted on the derrick and subsequently on the well, if it is a producer, showing the ownership and designation of the well, name of lease, section, township, range and the serial number under which the permit was issued. The obligation to maintain a legible sign remains until abandonment.

[28] *Id.* § III. A. All applications for permits to repair (except ordinary maintenance operations), abandon (plug and abandon), acidize, deepen, perforate, perforate and squeeze, plug (plug back), plug and perforate, plug back and side-track, plug and squeeze, pull casing, side-track, squeeze, squeeze and perforate, workover, cement casing or liner as a workover feature, or when a well is to be killed or directionally drilled, shall be made to the District Office on Form MD-11R and a proper permit shall be received from the District Manager before work is started. A complete record of all work done shall be filed with the District Office after said work is completed. At least 12 hours prior notice of the proposed operations shall be given the District Manager and/or an offset operator in order that one of them may witness the work. If the District Manager fails to appear within 12 hours the work may be witnessed by the offset operator, but failing in this, the work need not be held up longer than 12 hours. This rule shall not deter an operator from taking immediate action in an emergency to prevent damage. When a service company, other than the drilling contractor, cements, perforates or acidizes, either before or after completion of a well, the service company shall furnish the District Manager with legible exact copies of reports furnished the owner of the well.

for producing areas, and to furnish driller's and electrical logs of all test wells, or wells drilled in search of oil, gas, sulphur and other minerals, as well as cutting samples.[29] Sections V, VI, and VII establish stringent rules for setting casing, casing-heads and blow-out preventers.[30] To prevent fires wells must be cleaned into a pit,

[29] *Id.* § IV.

[30] *Id.* § V—Casing Program. A. Conductor Pipe. Conductor Pipe is that pipe ordinarily used for the purpose of supporting unconsolidated surface deposits. The use and removal of conductor pipe during the drilling of any oil or gas well shall be at the option of the operator. B. Surface Casing. (1) Where no danger of pollution of fresh water sources exists, the minimum amount of surface or first-intermediate casing to be set shall be determined from TABLE NUMBER ONE hereof:

TABLE NUMBER ONE

Total Depth of Contact Casing Required		*Number of Sacks Cement*	*Surface Casing Test Pressure Lbs. Per Sq. In.*
0–2500	100	200 or circulate to surf.*	300
2500–3000	150	500 " " " "	600
3000–4000	300	500 " " " "	600
4000–5000	400	500 " " " "	600
5000–6000	500	500 " " " "	750
6000–7000	800	500 " " " "	1000
7000–8000	1000	500 " " " "	1000
8000–9000	1400	500 " " " "	1000
9000–deeper	1800	500 " " " "	1000

* *Circulate to the Surface* shall mean the calculated amount of cement necessary to fill the theoretical annular space plus ten per cent.

In known low-pressure areas, exceptions to the above may be granted by the Commissioner or his agent. If, however, in the opinion of the Commissioner, or his agent, the above regulations shall be found inadequate, an additional or lesser amount of surface casing and/or cement or test pressure shall be required for the purpose of safety and the protection of fresh water sands. (2) Surface casing shall be tested before drilling the plug by applying a minimum pump pressure as set forth in TABLE ONE after at least 200 feet of the mud-laden fluid has been displaced with water at the top of the column. If at the end of 30 minutes the pressure gauge shows a drop of ten per cent of test pressure as outlined in TABLE ONE the operator shall be required to take such corrective measures as will insure that such surface casing will hold said pressure for thirty minutes without a drop of more than ten per cent of the test pressure. The provisions of D-7 of this section, for the producing casing, shall also apply to the surface casing. (3) Cement shall be allowed to stand a minimum of twelve (12) hours under pressure before initiating test or drilling plug. "Under pressure" is complied with if one float valve is used or if pressure is held otherwise. C. Intermediate Casing. (1) Intermediate Casing is that casing used as protection against caving or heaving formations or when other means are not adequate for the purpose of segregating upper oil, gas or water-bearing strata. (2) If an intermediate casing string is deemed necessary by the District Manager for the prevention of underground waste, such regulations pertaining to a minimum setting depth, quality of casing, and cementing and testing of same, shall be determined by the Department after due hearing. The provisions of D-7 of this section, for the producing casing, shall also apply to the intermediate casing. D. Producing Oil String.

barge, or tank located at least 100 feet from any fire hazard.[31] Before a well is perforated, its drilling fluid must be conditioned and brought to a weight necessary to hold normal hydrostatic pressure at the point perforated allowing a margin for safety, and proper

(1) Producing or oil string is that casing used for the purpose of segregating the horizon from which production is obtained and affording a means of communication between such horizon and the surface. (2) The producing string of casing shall consist of new or reconditioned casing, tested at mill test pressure or as otherwise designated by the Department, and set at a sufficient depth to cut off all gas formations above the oil-saturated horizon in which the well is to be completed. The position of the oil horizon shall be determined by coring, testing or electrical logging, or other satisfactory method, and the producing string of casing shall be bottomed and cemented at a point below the gas/oil contact, if determinable and practicable. (3) Cement shall be by the pump-and-plug method, or another method approved by the Department. Sufficient cement shall be used to fill the calculated annular space behind the casing to such a point as in the opinion of the District Manager local conditions require to protect the producing formations and all other oil and gas formations occurring above, but in every case, no less cement shall be used than the calculated amount necessary to fill the annular space to a point 500 feet above the shoe. (4) The amount of cement to be left remaining in the casing, until the requirements of Paragraph 5 of this Section have been met, shall be not less than 20 feet. This shall be accomplished through the use of a float-collar, or other approved or practicable means, unless a full-hole cementer, or its equivalent, is used. (5) Cement shall be allowed to stand a minimum of twelve (12) hours under pressure and a minimum total of thirty-six (36) hours before initiating test or drilling plug in the producing or oil string. "Under Pressure" is complied with if one or more float valves are employed and are shown to be holding the cement in place, or when other means of holding pressure is used. When an operator elects to perforate and squeeze or to cement around the shoe, he may proceed with such work after twelve (12) hours have elapsed after placing the first cement. (6) Before drilling the plug in the producing string of casing, the casing shall be tested by pump pressure, as determined from TABLE TWO hereof, after 200 feet of the mud-laden fluid in the casing has been displaced by water at the top of the column.

TABLE NUMBER TWO
(Intermediate and Producing Casing)

Depth Set	No. of Sacks of Cement		Producing String Test Pressure (Lbs. Per Sq. In.)
2000–3000'	200	but in every case no less cement shall	800
3000–6000'	300	be used than the calculated amount	1000
6000–9000'	500	necessary to fill the annular space to a	1200
9000' and deeper	500	point 500' above the shoe.	1500

If, at the end of thirty minutes, the pressure gauge shows a drop of ten percent of the test pressure or more, the operator shall be required to take such corrective measures as will insure that the producing string of casing is so set and cemented that it will hold said pressure for thirty minutes without a drop of more than ten percent of the test pressure on the gauge. (7) If the Commissioner's agent is not present at the time designated by the operator for inspection of the casing tests of the producing string, the operator shall have such tests witnessed, preferably by an offset operator. An affidavit of the test, on the form prescribed by the Department of Conservation,

connections for lubricating the gun in and out of the hole must be installed. All drill stem tests must be started and completed during daylight hours except in fields where it is known the pressure does not exceed that of a column of oil from the hole's top to the producing horizon. No boiler, open fire, or electric generator may be

signed by the operator and witness, shall be furnished to the District Office of the Department of Conservation showing that the test conformed satisfactorily to the above mentioned regulations before proceeding with the completion. If test is satisfactory, normal operations may be resumed immediately. (8) If the test is unsatisfactory, the operator shall not proceed with the completion of the well until a satisfactory test has been obtained. E. Tubing and Completion. (1) All flowing wells shall be produced through tubing not larger than two and one-half (2½) inches, unless otherwise allowed by the Department, upon application. (2) A valve, or its equivalent, tested to a pressure of not less than the calculated bottomhole pressure of the well, shall be installed below any and all tubing outlet connections. (3) When a well develops a casing pressure, upon completion, equivalent to more than three-quarters of the internal pressure that will develop the minimum yield point of the casing, such well shall be required by the District Manager to be killed, and a tubing packer to be set so as to keep such excessive pressure off of the casing. F. Well-Head Connections. (1) Well-head connections shall be tested prior to installation at a pressure indicated by the District Manager in conformance with conditions existing in areas in which they are used. Whenever such tests are made in the field, they shall be witnessed by an Agent of the Department. Tubing and Tubing-heads shall be free from obstructions in wells used for bottom-hole pressure test purposes. § VI—Blowout Preventers. A. All wells drilling or running casing or tubing are to be equipped with a master gate and a blowout preventer having the correct size rams or plugs installed and in first class condition, together with a flowline valve of the recommended size and working pressure. If a "fill-up" line is connected to the blowout preventer, this line shall be equipped with such valves and fittings of at least the same working pressure as the blowout preventer. If the preventer is hydraulically operated, adequate pressure shall at all times be available for efficient operation. B. The entire control equipment shall be in good working order and condition at all times and shall meet with the test or inspection requirement of the Department. C. If, at any time, evidence indicates that the preventer is not efficient, the casing shall be blocked off below the preventer by some effective method and such repairs to the preventer shall be made as to allow it to hold the originally designated pressure test. D. Drill strings shall be equipped with a stop-cock or some other type of drill-stem back-pressure valve for the purpose of controlling back-flow. E. No casing shall be perforated until adequate control equipment has been installed and in good working order. Such control equipment shall consist of Master Valve and Lubricator, or their equivalent. § VII—Casing Heads. A. All wells shall be equipped with casing-heads with a test pressure in conformance with conditions existing in areas in which they are used. Casing-head body, as soon as installed, shall be equipped with proper connections and valves accessible to the surface. Reconditioning shall be required on any well showing pressure on the casing-head, or leaking gas or oil between the oil string, and next larger size casing-string, when, in the opinion of the District Managers, such pressures or leakages assume hazardous proportions or indicate the existence of underground waste. Mud-laden fluid may be pumped between any two strings of casing at the top of the hole, but no cement shall be used except by special permission of the Commissioner, or his agent.

[31] *Id.* § VIII.

operated within 100 feet of a producing well or oil tank. Each permanent tank or battery must be surrounded by a dike or fire wall at least the capacity of the tank or battery, except where fire walls are impossible, as in water areas. The Department is given the right to inspect the mud records of any drilling well and to conduct essential tests on the mud used in drilling.[32] When conditions indicate a need for a change in the drilling fluid program to insure proper control of the well, the Department may require the operator or company to use due diligence in making corrections. Comprehensive rules and regulations respecting well allowables and conditions are contained in Section X of the order,[33] as are

[32] *Id.* § IX.

[33] *Id.* § X—Well Allowables and Completions. A. 1. Upon completion or re-completion of a well, immediate notice within 24 hours from the time of completion (Sundays and Holidays excepted) must be filed in writing with the District Office on forms provided by the Department. Notice of completion or recompletion of a well may be made by telephone or telegram to the District Manager if supplemented by written notice on proper form within three days from the date of completion or re-completion. Wells shall be considered completed when turned into the tanks, a potential and gas/oil ratio test shall then be conducted by the operator or company, and witnessed by an Inspector of the Department within five (5) days from the date of completion or re-completion (Sundays and Holidays excepted). 2. After receipt of the completion reports and reports or tests required by the Commissioner, a completed or re-completed well shall be given a daily allowable, determined in the same manner as was used in computing the schedule of daily allowables for the months in which such completion is made. 3. The daily well allowable when determined shall be effective from 7:00 A.M. on the date of completion or re-completion if the well is completed or re-completed before 7:00 P.M.; and from 7:00 A.M. of the following day if the well is completed or re-completed after 7:00 P.M.; provided the completion or re-completion report has been filed in accordance with the above mentioned provision, and if the initial potential and gas/oil ratio test has been made within five (5) days from the date of completion or re-completion. If the completion or re-completion is not reported as provided, then the daily well allowable shall be effective from the date of receipt of the completion or re-completion report, with a one day tolerance. If the initial potential and gas/oil ratio test is not made within five days from the date of completion or re-completion, the daily well allowable shall be effective five days before the date of the initial potential and gas/oil ratio test. B. Allowables given to wells for oil produced on drill-stem tests, production test and any miscellaneous production of oil shall be in accordance with the following rule: All operators are required, within five days, to file three signed copies of the record of the daily production from the well, showing the number of hours the well produced and the interval of production; as "from 8:00 A.M. August 5th to 3:00 P.M. August 8th, 1941." C. Gas/oil ratios. All leases are to be so equipped as to permit the determination of gas/oil ratios on individual flowing and gas-lift wells. Gas/oil ratio data on all wells shall be available to the Inspector of the Department at all times. D. No. flowing and/or gas-lift oil wells shall be permitted to produce with excessive gas/oil ratio, except where special orders are operative. Wells that are gas-lifted with gas from gas wells shall be prorated in the same manner as are hi-ratio naturally flowing oil wells, the G.O.R. being defined for this

elaborate requirements with respect to the production of oil and gas, the keeping of records, the making of production [34] tests, and the measurement of oil and gas.[35]

Under the rules and regulations of the Department the Commis-

purpose as the total output gas less the total input gas divided by the number of barrels of oil produced. The uneconomic or unreasonable use of gas for gas-lift will not be permitted. E. 1. Each lease shall be provided with sufficient tankage or meters to permit proper gauging of the oil produced. The tanks or meters must be identified by a sign, showing the ownership of the tanks or meters and name of the lease from which the oil is being produced. In no case shall meters be the sole means of measuring oil runs from any field. There must be used at least one gauge tank to check the readings of meters. Applications for the use of oil meters, in lieu of gauge tanks, shall be the subject of open hearings until rules are formulated. 2. All flowing and gas-lift oil wells are to be produced through efficient operating separators, except in the case of low-pressure heading or gas-lift wells with low-gas output. 3. All oil and gas meter and by-pass settings shall be provided with the necessary connections to permit the installation of Department of Conservation Official Seals, and such seals shall be affixed by a representative of the Department. 4. When it becomes necessary to use a by-pass or other flow-line connection which has been sealed by the Department, permission to use same must be obtained from the District Manager. In the event that an unforeseen emergency requires the use of by-pass or flow line connections before notification to the District Office, a detailed, written report, in duplicate, setting forth the occasion for such action must be given, and the by-pass or other connection shall forthwith be re-sealed. F. In the event that any operator considers that his well has not had a fair determination of its gas/oil ratio, or that its gas/oil ratio has changed due to natural causes or to corrective work on his well, he may make application in writing to the District Manager for a re-test or a special test of the gas/oil ratio of his well, and for an adjustment of the allowable of his well. If, upon re-testing a well, the District Manager finds that the new gas/oil ratio justifies a change in the allowable, he is authorized to make such change. G. Changed or corrected allowable shall be effective from the date of completion of such work, but in no case shall the effective date be more than five days prior to the date of re-testing. H. Gas wells shall not be tested by the "open-flow" method. The back-pressure method of determining the open flow, as outlined by the Bureau of Mines in their Monograph 7, "Back Pressure Data on Natural-Gas Wells," shall be used. When, for any reasons, the back-pressure method is not feasible, an acceptable method, not entailing excessive physical waste of gas, may be used, upon recommendation of the technical staff of the Department.

[34] *Id.* § XI—Production, Production Records, Production Tests. A. All oil tendered to any transportation system shall be gauged and tested for B.S. & W. and temperature. For each and every transfer of oil from the lease tanks the number of the "on-seal" and "off-seal," observed temperature, and the percent of B.S. & W. shall be recorded on each and every run ticket, and each party of any transfer of oil from lease tanks shall receive a copy of the run or delivery ticket or tickets. B. 1. There shall not be any simultaneous movement of oil into and out of any lease tank that is being used for delivering oil to a gatherer or transporter. Transfer of oil or gas from the possession of one lease to the possession of another lease, except when properly accounted for, is hereby prohibited. The possession of improper mechanical means for transferring oil from one lease tank or well to the lease tank or well of another lease is hereby prohibited. 2. All pipe line outlets from lease tanks shall be kept sealed at all times except when a pipe line run is being made from the tank, and the number of the "on-seal" and "off-seal" shall be recorded on each and every

sioner or his agents have the right to change the monthly production and proration orders where reasonably necessary for safety, conservation, waste prevention, or the maintenance of proper oil-gas ratios.[36] The Commissioner may require bottom hole pressure surveys at times designated by him.[37] When a well starts to produce salt water, that condition is reported to the Department, and permits must be secured before disposing of the salt water underground.[38] Where the well lacks the capacity to produce its total allowable, then it produces that amount of oil and gas it is able to make, but the deficiency is not made up by the overproduction of any other well.[39] Order No. 29-B governs the drilling of directional wells and the making of well surveys.[40] All oil and gas wells in the

---

run ticket. 3. B.S. & W. bleed-off lines of lease tanks shall be sealed or locked at the time any pipe line run is being made. 4. Oil produced from separately owned leases, not pooled, unitized or consolidated shall not be co-mingled in lease tanks. 5. All leases having more than one producing well shall be equipped with a test line, so as to obviate the necessity of spudding in wells when taking individual well tests. C. Producers shall keep the following records in the main office for a period of three years and the current records in the field office for three months. 1. The daily production in gross barrels produced from each lease and tanks into which oil was produced. A record of choke, % B.S. & W., tubing pressures, casing pressures, of each well on that particular lease shall be recorded on a daily basis. 2. A record of opening stock and closing stock on hand each 24 hour day. 3. A record of all deliveries of oil from the lease, to whom made, and the identity of the means of transportation, and the transporter. 4. Gauge tickets, and run tickets, as made by the employees actually performing or directing the operations recorded on such records. 5. When crude oil or distillate is moved by trucks each transaction shall be evidenced by a manifest form which will be issued by the Department of Conservation. Such forms shall bear the appropriate data as to origin and destination of the oil, ownership of the oil at point of receipt and delivery, ownership of truck and name of driver. D. 1. Every producer shall make and report to the District Managers production tests of each of his oil wells by the 15th of each month. The data collected shall include the daily rate of production, size choke, % B.S. & W., tubing pressure, casing pressure, gravity at 60 degrees Fahrenheit, or observed gravity and temperature, gas/oil ratio and volume of gas produced, which shall be recorded on the daily gauge report on or before the above date. A signed record of such tests shall be filed with the District Manager. 2. When any well or wells shall go off production, other than because of ordinary maintenance operations, same shall be reported to the District Office immediately and a letter of cancellation of allowable for that well shall be issued.

[35] *Id.* § XII—Oil and Gas Measurements.
[36] *Id.* § XIII.
[37] *Id.* § XIV.
[38] *Id.* § XV.
[39] *Id.* § XVI.
[40] *Id.* § XVIII—Directional Drilling and Well Surveys. No well shall be drilled in the State of Louisiana in which the well bore shall deviate laterally at any point a distance greater than that determined by a three (3) degree angle from a vertical line passing through the center of the surface location of the well bore; provided, however, that in the event the operator desires to whipstock or intentionally deflect

state must be abandoned in accordance with the requirements of the Department.[41]

Any operator is given an opportunity to show that the rules and regulations contained in Order No. 29-B prejudice his interests,[42]

---

said hole more than said three degrees from vertical, except to straighten the hole or to side-track junk in the hole or other mechanical difficulties, then and in that event, said operator shall first obtain a special permit from the District Manager to so deflect said hole and shall furnish the Department a copy of the survey of said hole when the drilling has been completed and before the casing has been set if an objection has been filed. Nothing in these rules shall be construed to permit the drilling of any well in such a manner that it crosses property lines. The Department shall have the right to make or to require the operator to make a directional survey of any hole, on its own initiative or at the request of an offset operator, and at the expense of said offset operator, prior to the completion of the well; and it shall have the authority to make or to require the operator to make, a directional survey of any hole at any time, and at the expense of the offending party, i.e., if the operator contends his hole is in a certain condition and it is found so to be, then party requesting survey should pay. In cases of directional drilling, the Department shall assess appropriate allowable penalties to prevent undue drainage from the offset properties. All new wells that have surface locations 300 feet or less from any property or unit line and that reach a depth of 4,000 feet or more shall, beginning with the effective date of this order, have directional surveys made to the total depth of the hole before setting final string of casing. Three certified copies of such directional surveys made to the total depth of the hole before setting final string of casing. Three certified copies of such directional surveys shall be filed with the District Manager by the well owner or by the service company which made the survey.

[41] *Id.* § XIX—Abandonment and Casing Pulling. A. All wells which are to be abandoned shall be filled with a mud-fluid of sufficient weight to offset the hydrostatic pressure of any of the formations penetrated. Substantial cement plugs must be efficiently placed in sufficient number and at proper locations as to prevent the commingling of oil, gas, salt water and fresh water from one formation to another (mud is not permanently efficient for this purpose). Before the work of abandonment is begun, a permit must be secured and a detailed plan of abandonment must be submitted to the District Manager for approval or modification to meet the local and specific needs. Any drilling well which is to be temporarily abandoned and the rig moved away, shall be mudded and cemented as it would for permanent abandonment, except a cement plug at the surface may be omitted. B. The District Manager or his representative will inspect the work of abandonment as it progresses, check the location and quality of plugs, check the amount of casing pulled, check the demonstration of movement, if any, of oil, gas or water, and finally submit to his superiors a complete report on the work. C. The plan of abandonment may be altered after the work has started, provided new or unforeseen conditions arise but only after approval by the District Manager. D. For wells that have produced, the producing formation shall, where practicable, be protected by a cement plug extending from well below the bottom to well above the top of the reservoir and the cement shall be made to bond with the walls of the hole where possible. E. All cement plugs shall be placed by the displacement method unless exception is granted by the Department. F. The Commissioner or his Agent may require the posting of a reasonable bond with good and sufficient surety in order to secure the performance of the work of proper abandonment. G. The District Manager shall be immediately notified by the vendor whenever a change of title occurs as to lease, well or equipment appertaining thereto.

[42] *Id.* § XX.

and that the drilling and production methods provided for securing well tests, or in any part of the order as applied to his operations result in waste, or to him are unreasonable. If the Commissioner finds the complaint well founded, he makes an exception which prevents the waste or eliminates the unreasonable restraint. Before the operator is allowed a change he must establish that the privilege, if granted, will not result in field waste or give him an inequitable and unfair advantage over other operators in the field. No special exception is granted except upon written application which fully states the facts alleged and a hearing.

Fortified by the broad and comprehensive provisions of Act 157, and the complete rules and regulations contained in Order No. 29-B, the Department of Conservation of Louisiana has progressed in the conservation of oil and gas. Numerous fields have been unitized for cycling, pressure maintenance, and repressuring. Louisiana has reached the stage where secondary recovery is an important item in its conservation program and the present law gives full authority to proceed in this important field in a manner resulting in the greatest ultimate recovery from its reservoirs.

THE DEPARTMENT OF CONSERVATION

In Louisiana the Commissioner of Conservation is a constitutional—not a statutory officer.[43] The constitution of Louisiana authorizes the governor, by and with the advice and consent of the senate, to appoint for a four year term such an official and to fill the post should a vacancy occur.[44] Prior to 1944 the constitution of Louisiana, in providing that the natural resources of the state be protected, conserved, and replenished,[45] placed their management under a Department of Conservation created and established in the same document,[46] giving departmental control to a Commissioner of Conservation exercising such authority and power as prescribed by the legislature. The legislature was to enact all necessary laws to protect, conserve, and replenish the natural resources of the state and to prohibit and prevent their wasteful use. Act 328

[43] State. Maestri, 199 La. 49, 50 So. 2d 199 (1941).
[44] *La. Const.* Art. V, § XVIII (1921).
[45] *Ibid.*
[46] *Id.* Art. VI, § I.

of 1944 (adopted by popular vote November 7, 1944) amended Article VI, Section I, the Louisiana Constitution of 1921, separating the mineral division of the old Department of Conservation from the wild life division. The amendatory act provided that the wild life, game and non-game quadrupeds, oysters, et cetera would be regulated by the Department of Wild Life and Fisheries.[47] All other natural resources were placed in the Department of Conservation.

The Commissioner has his office at Baton Rouge, where the general administrative division of the Department is found. His staff includes an executive assistant, the departmental attorney, chief engineer, state geologist; these persons usually assist in conducting hearings and formulating policy matters. A technical and statistical force is maintained to provide expert assistance in connection with the work of the Department. District offices are located in Monroe, Shreveport, Lake Charles, Lafayette, Houma, and New Orleans, each directed by a manager vested with the supervision of drilling and production operations within the district. All applications for permits to drill or to do work are lodged in these offices, and all permits there issued. The field offices provide the contact with the well and the operators.

Act 157 does not attempt to mark out the limits of administrative procedure, but simply says that the Commissioner prescribe the rules of order and procedure in hearings or proceedings. No rule, regulation or order (absent an emergency) is made except upon public hearing and notice of its time and place, given in a manner as established by the Commissioner. Any person having an interest in the subject of the hearing is entitled to be heard. An exception to the statutory requirement for hearing relates to emergencies, where an order may be promulgated without notice and hearing; [48] even this is limited by the proviso that it is not to remain in force more than 15 days from the effective date. Notwithstanding the safeguards in the statute for hearings, a large portion of the departmental operations are necessarily handled without them. The agents of the Department, the district managers, and even the Commissioner daily make decisions and interpretations having the

[47] La. Acts 1944, Act No. 328.
[48] La. Acts 1940, Act No. 157, § 5.

force and effect of rules and orders, and unless the party in interest is aggrieved or prejudiced, there is no need for a hearing; as a practical matter, these decisions often could not be preceded by notice and hearing without undue delay.

Rules and regulations which govern the Department and orders issued in connection with specific fields are always preceded by notice and hearing. The statute gives any interested person the right to request a hearing in respect to any matter within the administrator's jurisdiction. Usually hearings for unit operations or exceptions to general regulations are conducted only after written applications made by an interested operator or company, although the Department initiates these where necessary. Hearings for the establishment of the monthly allowables are held bi-monthly without request. The statute provides that public notice be given of the hearing in a manner and form set by the Commissioner; the present practice is to publish it in the official state journal and in a newspaper or newspapers in the parish where the regulation or order is to take effect. A regular mailing list is maintained for the sending of notices of hearings. There has been some criticism of the statute for its failure to clearly prescribe what constitutes reasonable notice. Although the Louisiana Department of Conservation is domiciled in Baton Rouge, the Commissioner often conducts hearings elsewhere in the state. Where feasible he makes a practice of holding them in the parish where the field involved is located. Witnesses are usually sworn by the Commissioner and their testimony subject to cross examination by him, the members of his staff, proponents, and interested parties. The Commissioner is required by statute to take such action he deems apropos within 30 days after the hearing's conclusion. Should he fail to do so, he may be compelled to act by mandamus at the instance of any interested party.

The orders of the Department are divided into two general classifications—state-wide and special field orders; the broad coverage of the former is illustrated by Order No. 29-B. Another state-wide order is that designated as the proration order, which is far reaching and applies in a varying degree to most producing wells in the state. The Act authorizes the prevention of waste; this includes production in excess of market facilities, transportation, and demand.[49]

[49] *Id.* § 2.

It has been the practice of the Commissioner to balance the monthly proration requirements against the departmental idea of reasonable market demand. Since the passage of Act 157, the need for crude has been so great there has been little difficulty in fixing monthly allowables. Considerable trouble might ensue should the requirements for oil materially decrease. In establishing the state allocations the Commissioner is confronted not only with the quoted waste definition, but must keep before him that section of the Act which directs the reasonable allotment of production by fields when the total amount of oil or gas produced in the state is limited.[50] The proration of a pool allowable must be accomplished in a manner insuring against unreasonable drainage and permitting each producer to receive his just and equitable share subject to the necessities for waste prevention.[51] Since the Act fails to set out a manner to determine reasonable market demand and does not establish a method of proration, the Department receives purchase nominations to derive their total demand figure. From this computation they then subtract non-proratable liquid hydrocarbons (gasoline plant and stripper production, condensate produced with gas), add an allowance for new production, and the resulting figure becomes the Louisiana allowable. The Department then resorts to the depth bracket method of proration—all wells of a particular depth are assigned a quota, and cannot exceed this allocation. The amount may be less where the well is incapable of producing this allowment, or where that amount would damage the reservoir. In Louisiana no additional allocation is given wildcat wells, as they must participate as other wells in a field. Where producing the allowable fixed by the depth bracket method injures the reservoir, production is fixed at a special allowable determined by the circumstances and conditions in each instance.

WILD OR UNCONTROLLED WELLS

Louisiana is one of the few oil and gas producing states with a comprehensive statute which authorizes a governmental agency to take charge of the capping of a wild or uncontrolled gas well where the owner or operator fails, refuses, or neglects to effect its harness-

[50] *Id.* § 10.
[51] *Id.* § 8.

ing.[52] To protect the natural gas fields it is unlawful and a nuisance for any person, firm, or corporation to negligently permit a natural gas well to go wild, become uncontrollable, or wastefully burn. In the event owners of wild wells fail, refuse, or neglect to close the well within five days after notice, the governor of the state may direct the State Board of Engineers to take charge and plug the well. The costs and expenses of such plugging are a lien upon the property and its production until recovered. In case the returns are insufficient to defray the expenses, the owner's property may be seized and sold to satisfy the amounts due. It is a misdemeanor to set fire to a natural gas well, or negligently permit it to catch fire, go wild, or become uncontrollable. While Act 157 grants broad powers to the Commissioner of Conservation covering almost every phase of the production and sale of oil and gas, this was declared in addition to existing powers, and it is believed that Act 71 of 1906 and Act 283 of 1910 are in full force and effect.[53]

LOUISIANA AND NATURAL GAS

During the past six years Louisiana's position on natural gas has created much public interest in this irreplaceable natural resource, and the basis for its stand can be found in part in an investigation and report made by the Federal Trade Commission to the 70th Congress, 1st Session, transmitted to the United States Senate December 31, 1935.[54] The FPC in its 20th annual report [55] sent to

[52] La. Acts 1906, Act No. 71, La. Acts 1910, Act No. 283.

[53] Hunter Co. v. McHugh, 202 La. 97, 11 So. 2d 495, 506 (1942).

[54] Rep. FTC 70th Cong. 1st ·Sess. pt. 84–a, 200 (1935). "That the subject of natural gas conservation is one which the Federal Government must approach with caution is understandable to anyone at all familiar with the jurisdictional problems involved. On the other hand, anyone equally familiar with the economic importance of the commodity itself as a truly national resource, and the shocking and irreparable waste that has attended its exploitation in private hands, can hardly condemn an anxious national concern as to conditions that exist, or deny the national importance of their correction. . . Conservation is the first problem that demands attention. Vast acreage is being drained and natural gas is being subjected to profligate and wanton waste and uneconomical uses. . . Such a valuable nonreplaceable natural resource of general country-wide use or need should, in the public interest, be conserved and utilized to the highest economic and social advantage. . . Natural gas must be used practically as soon as produced. Therefore, the public concern is not that it be produced only as needed, but that it be produced and delivered when needed, and then that it be used to the highest economic and social advantage. There are no precise parallels in the utility fields for such a situation."

[55] 20 FPC ANN. REP. 9 (1940). "The Commission has before it the first pro-

Congress December 1, 1940 said "the Natural Gas Act and the work which the Commission is doing under it should be considered as a first step in dealing with thc conservation of one of the country's exhaustible resources." These two reports, together with numerous applications for certificates of public convenience and a necessity to construct new and additional gas lines from the southwest to the eastern seaboard, brought about Senate Concurrent Resolution No. 7. Senate Concurrent Resolution No. 7, June 2, 1942, which passed in the Louisiana legislature with but few dissenting votes,[56] imposed certain duties upon the Louisiana Public Service

posal to tap the Southwestern reserves of natural gas to supply the tremendous markets of the industrial Northeast. This proposal, which will probably be planned initially to deliver more than 150,000,000,000 cubic feet of gas annually to the New York City Area, has already raised the question whether the proposed use of natural gas would not result in displacing a less valuable fuel, creating hardships in an industry already supplying the market, while at the same time rapidly depleting the country's irreplaceable reserves of natural gas. . . This first proposal to tap the Southwestern reserves of natural gas to supply the tremendous markets available in the Northeastern States poses the country with a serious problem of energy resource conservation. The Natural Gas Act as presently drafted does not enable the Commission to treat fully the serious implications of such a problem. The question should be raised as to whether the proposed use of natural gas would not result in displacing a less valuable fuel and create hardships in the industry already supplying the market, while at the same time rapidly depleting the country's natural gas reserves. Although, for a period of perhaps 20 years, the natural gas could be so priced as to appear to offer an apparent saving in fuel costs, this would mean simply that social costs which must eventually be paid had been ignored. . . Careful study of the entire problem may lead to the conclusion that use of natural gas should be restricted by functions rather than by areas. It is especially adapted to space and water heating in urban homes and other buildings and to the various industrial heat processes which require concentration of heat, flexibility of control, and uniformity of results. Industrial uses to which it appears particularly adapted include the treating and annealing of metals, the operation of kilns in the ceramic, cement, and lime industries, the manufacture of glass in its various forms, and use as a raw material in the chemical industry. General use of natural gas under boilers for the production of steam is, however, under most circumstances of very questionable social economy. . . There is an even more important question which should be answered before Government sanction is given to large scale delivery of natural gas to the great Eastern industrial areas. That is the question as to whether rapid depletion of the country's natural gas reserves may not reduce for all time the country's potentially recoverable reserves of oil. In view of the tremendous importance of petroleum products in both peace and war, it would be a grave mistake to allow the quest for quick profits and temporary convenience to cut into our available petroleum supplies."

[56] Passed in the senate with 1 dissent, none in the house. The text of the resolution reads: "WHEREAS, it is estimated by federal departments and agencies that of the nation's reserves of mineral fuel resources, in terms of British thermal units, coal constitutes 98.9 per cent, petroleum one-tenth of one per cent, natural gas one-tenth of one per cent, and oil in shales nine-tenths of one per cent; and WHEREAS, from 40 to 50 per cent of these mineral fuel reserves are located in that portion of

Commission and the Department of Conservation to appear in all certificate cases pending before the FPC affecting Louisiana. Expert testimony was offered by the state, and at times the governor

---

the country lying north of the Ohio and Potomac Rivers and east of the Mississippi River, and but three and two-tenths per cent of such reserves are located in that area usually referred to as the Southwest, comprising the states of Arkansas, Louisiana, Oklahoma and Texas; and WHEREAS, federal agencies report that for the year 1940 Louisiana produced 343,191 millions of cubic feet of natural gas, of which 174,366 millions of cubic feet, or 50.80 per cent of the total production, were exported to other states; and WHEREAS, it is estimated by various federal authorities and agencies that at the 1940 rate of consumption of mineral fuels, the nation's coal reserves are sufficient to last for several thousands of years, while based upon the consumption in the same period the natural gas reserves of the nation will be exhausted in from twenty to thirty years; and WHEREAS, there are presently on file with and pending before the Federal Power Commission numerous applications for certificates of public convenience and necessity for authorizations to construct and operate new and additional natural gas pipe lines having aggregate capacities of many hundreds of millions of cubic feet of gas per day, whose function it will be to transport gas from the fields of the Southwest, including Louisiana, to the great industrial sections of the North and East, located in areas in or closely adjacent to the great coal deposits of those sections of the country, which have for many years been supplied with their fuel requirements by said coal fields; and WHEREAS, the Federal Power Commission in its report for the year 1940 expresses deep concern with the constantly increasing rate of natural gas withdrawals from the fields of the Southwest, questioning not only the economic wisdom of such unrestricted withdrawals of gas and its transmission for great distances as a substitute for coal, but expressing apprehension as well as to the effect of such withdrawals of gas on the potentially recoverable reserves of petroleum, through geologic processes; and WHEREAS, the accelerated depletion of the natural gas reserves of Louisiana will constitute a most serious handicap and bar to the normal industrial development of the state, now, therefore BE IT RESOLVED by the Senate of the State of Louisiana, the House of Representatives concurring, that cognizance is hereby taken by the Legislature of Louisiana of the official utterances of the Federal Power Commission, the United States Geological Survey, the National Resources Committee, as well as of other recognized federal authorities, expressing concern over the present unrestricted, unrestrained and indiscriminate withdrawals of gas from the nation's natural gas reserves; and, be it further RESOLVED that the Legislature of Louisiana hereby approves and commends the announced policy of the Federal Power Commission to inquire into the economic need and justification for, and the geologic consequences of, construction of additional natural gas pipe lines, and especially those projected to areas and sections of the United States lying immediately in or reasonably adjacent and accessible to the great coal deposits of the nation; and be it further RESOLVED, that the Department of Conservation of the State of Louisiana and the Louisiana Public Service Commission be and they are hereby directed and authorized to appear before the Federal Power Commission in any and all proceedings before said Commission involving application for certificates of Public Convenience and Necessity for the construction of additional natural gas pipe lines, or for authority to enlarge the capacity of existing pipe lines, where the supply of gas for transmission by such pipe lines, in whole or in part, originates in the State of Louisiana; and to make such representations to the Federal Power Commission in respect of such applications as may be consistent with this declaration of policy by the Legislature of Louisiana."

appeared and opposed the issuance of certificates of public convenience and necessity (under the Natural Gas Act) that broadened the markets supplied by Louisiana gas.

One case in which the state intervened created comment throughout the nation, involving an application filed with the FPC in which the Memphis Natural Gas Company asked to complete looping its line from the Monroe Gas Field in Louisiana to Memphis, Tennessee.[57] After exhaustive hearings the FPC denied the application, saying: "In view of the limited natural gas reserves shown by the record to be available to Applicant, their present rapid rate of depletion, and the effect of excessive rates of withdrawal on the ultimate recovery of gas therefrom, it is necessary and appropriate in the public interest that such natural gas resources be conserved insofar as possible for domestic, commercial and superior industrial uses. The record does not contain a sufficient showing that the proposed construction and operation are or will be required by the present or future public convenience and necessity. Dismissal of the instant application . . . is appropriate in the public interest." Denial precipitated a hard and lengthy fight between the pipe line companies and the state. The Memphis company asked for and was granted a rehearing. During the course of the case, the FPC announced an immediate national investigation of the natural gas business.[58] The fight that Louisiana was conducting to limit market expansion for natural gas had a great deal to do with this announcement.

In the *Memphis Case* the applicant showed at the rehearing that it had added gas reserves at its disposal and the FPC, reversing its original decision, granted the certificate to complete the looping of the line from Monroe to Memphis, as well as the construction of a line from the Lisbon Field to Monroe.[59] Their opinion concluded: "While we are not unsympathetic with the effort of the producing State of Louisiana to protect and conserve its natural gas resources for the benefit of its citizens, it is apparent that denial of Applicant's request for these certificates will not afford the State of Louisiana a satisfactory solution of the problem posed by it.

[57] In the matter of Memphis Nat. Gas Co., FPC Docket G–522 (1944).
[58] FPC, Docket G–580, Natural Gas Investigation.
[59] See note 57 *supra*.

Such problems cannot be determined within the limit of these proceedings. It is reasonable, however, to condition the certificates so
that the facilities herein authorized shall not be used for the transportation or sale of natural gas to any new customers . . . except
upon specific authorization by this Commission." Louisiana reviewed this decision in the United States Circuit Court of Appeals,[60] where the issues raised in the petition for review are best
stated in the Louisiana assignment of error.[61] The court affirmed

[60] Dept. of Conservation v. FPC, 148 F. 2d 746 (1945).

[61] "ASSIGNMENTS OF ERROR. 1. That Opinion 119 and the Order issued in
connection therewith by the Federal Power Commission on November 21, 1944, is
in direct contravention to sound conservation practices, constitutes another step toward an unwarranted dissipation of the limited and irreplaceable natural gas reserves
of the United States, and is contrary to the spirit, if not the letter, of the Natural
Gas Act and the record fails to disclose substantial evidence to justify the issuance of
the certificates of public convenience and necessity herein. 2. That said opinion and
order are in error for the reason that approximately ninety-eight (98%) per cent of
the nation's fuel supply is coal, and approximately one-tenth ($\frac{1}{10}$) of one (1%)
per cent of the nation's fuel supply is natural gas, and it is in direct contravention to
sound conservation practices to authorize and permit, and, by the issuance of certificates of convenience and necessity, encourage the use of natural gas, an irreplaceable
natural resource, as boiler fuel, especially in territories far distant from the natural
gas fields and in territories where there is a bountiful supply of coal as is found in
the State of Tennessee, and the issuance of a certificate of convenience and necessity
under these circumstances constitutes a gross abuse of discretion on the part of the
Federal Power Commission, and its order should be reversed. 3. That said opinion
and order are erroneous and should be reversed for the further reason that approximately eighty-eight (88%) per cent of all the natural gas sold in Memphis for industrial purposes is burned under boilers, and approximately seventy-six (76%) per
cent of the volume sold for commercial purposes is used for boiler fuel which is an
inferior and un-economic use and is in contravention to sound conservation practices
especially where other fuels are available; that for these reasons, there is not substantial evidence to justify the finding that the general public interest and the general public convenience and necessity require or justify the issuance of certificates of
convenience and necessity in this cause. 4. That said opinion and order issued herein
on November 21, 1944, are erroneous and should be reversed for the further reason
that the record does not disclose substantial evidence to show that the general public
convenience and necessity require the granting of said certificates because, if the proposed facilities are not constructed, curtailments would have to be made only in
service to consumers using gas for boiler fuel purposes, which is an inferior purpose,
and to use natural gas for such purpose is in direct contravention to sound conservation practices, and such uses of natural gas are in derogation of the general public
interest within the meaning of that term as used in the Natural Gas Act, and the
record fails to disclose substantial evidence to show that the general public interest
and the convenience and necessity of the general public require the building of the
pipe lines involved herein. 5. That the Applicant has failed to show adequate reserves in place available to applicant under firm contracts to justify the construction
of the proposed pipe line from the Lisbon gas field to the Guthrie Compressor Station and the completion of the looping of the line from said compressor station to
Memphis, Tennessee. 6. That said opinion and order rendered by the Federal Power
Commission in this cause on November 21, 1944, is in error and should be reversed

the opinion and order of the FPC, in effect holding that since the
Natural Gas Act did not define public convenience and necessity,
it was within the province of the Commission to determine when
these factors required the building of an interstate natural gas pipe

---

for the reason that said Commission had no right to include natural gas reserves as
being available to Applicant, when to make such reserves available, additional intrastate pipe line facilities must be constructed, and no application has been filed for a
permit to construct such lines. 7. That said opinion and order should be reversed
for the further reason that, in truth and fact, the gas reserves in fields available to
Applicant were shown to be less at the second hearing than were the natural gas
reserves available to Applicant, as shown on the original hearing, in that the estimate
of reserves available in the Monroe field was reduced by Applicant's own witness to
a far greater extent than the additional reserves shown to be available in the Lisbon
field. 8. The said opinion and order issued herein by the Federal Power Commission
in both applications should be reversed for the reason that most of the additional
gas sought by Applicant for delivery to its principal customer, the Memphis Light,
Gas and Water Division, would be used as boiler fuel in an area where there is an
adequate supply of coal, which use of said natural gas would be for an inferior purpose, all in contravention to elementary principles of sound conservation; that the
record for this reason, does not disclose substantial evidence to show the general
public interest will be served by the issuance of said certificates of convenience and
necessity, and to the contrary, the issuance of said certificates of convenience
and necessity are in conflict with and in derogation of the general public interest and
will not serve the present or future public convenience and necessity. 9. That said
opinion and order are erroneous and should be reversed for the reason the Lisbon
gas field, referred to in said proceedings, has a very limited reserve of natural gas in
place, as shown by the record, yet is served by two major interstate pipe lines which
are adequate to transport the total known production of the Lisbon gas field, based
on the present known reserves, under proper conservation practices and allowables;
that the record does not disclose substantial evidence for this reason to justify the
issuance of said certificates of convenience and necessity and that the issuance of said
certificates is in derogation of the general public interest and will not serve the present or future public convenience and necessity. 10. That the opinion and order rendered herein on November 21, 1944, are erroneous and should be reversed for the
further reason that it is not sound conservation practice and is grossly uneconomic
and unfair to permit the transportation of gas from an area where no coal is found
to an area where there is an ample supply of coal, especially when the main purpose
of transporting such gas to such coal-producing area is to convert coal furnaces under
boilers to gas-burning furnaces under boilers; such practices are contrary to the purpose and intent of the Natural Gas Act; that the record does not disclose substantial
evidence to show that it is to the general public interest to construct the lines involved in these applications and, to the contrary, the record shows that the issuance
of said certificates would be in derogation of the general public interest and will not
serve the present or future public convenince and necessity. 11. That the opinion
and order rendered herein on November 21, 1944, are erroneous and should be reversed for the further reason that the record in this case clearly shows that the greatest gas field ever discovered in Louisiana, and the largest in the world at the time of
its discovery, namely, the Monroe gas field, has practically been depleted since the
installation of the present pipe line from Guthrie to Memphis, and that said Monroe
gas field had an original reserve in place of approximately five and one-half trillion
cubic feet of natural gas, and the total present gas reserves in place in the entire
State of Louisiana are estimated to be eight and one-half trillion cubic feet and the

line.[62] Under the Act considerations of conservation and whether or not natural gas be put to an alleged wasteful use are not determinative of the authority of the FPC to grant certificates to appli-

entire natural gas reserve in place in the State of Louisiana, based on present withdrawals, would be depleted in approximately seventeen (17) years; and to grant additional permits to withdraw additional amounts of natural gas from Louisiana's present reserves will reduce the life of the present known reserves much faster, all of which is an uneconomic dissipation of the nation's supply of natural gas, especially when the natural gas is piped a considerable distance to be used as boiler fuel in a coal-producing territory that the record does not disclose substantial evidence to show that it is to the general public interest to construct the lines involved in these applications, and, to the contrary, the record shows that the issuance of said certificates would be in derogation of the general public interest and will not serve the present or future public convenience and necessity. 12. That the opinion and order rendered herein on November 21, 1944, are erroneous and should be reversed for the further reason that, while said opinion and order condition the certificates provided for therein so that the facilities authorized shall not be used for the transportation or sale of natural gas to any new customer of either Applicant or of natural gas to any new customer of either Applicant or United Gas Pipe Line Company except upon specific authorization by the Commission, yet the principal advocate of the building of the new lines, the Memphis Light, Gas and Water Division, as the record shows, is advocating the conversion of industries from the use of coal to the use of natural gas to burn under boilers, which constitutes an inferior and uneconomic use of this irreplaceable natural resource which constitutes only one-tenth (1/10) of one (1%) per cent of the nation's fuel supply; that the record does not disclose substantial evidence to show that it is to the general public interest to construct the lines involved in these applications, and, to the contrary, the record shows that the issuance of said certificates would be in derogation of the general public interest and will not serve the present or future public convenience and necessity. 13. That said opinion and order are erroneous for the reason that the limited present known supply of natural gas in place should be conserved for use as a raw material and for other superior uses, rather than be transported to areas where coal is produced, there to be used as boiler fuel, for the principal reason that natural gas is a cheaper fuel as compared to coal; that the record does not disclose substantial evidence to show that it is to the general public interest to construct the lines involved in these applications and, to the contrary, the record shows that the issuance of said certificates would be in derogation of the general public interest and will not serve the present or future public convenience and necessity. 14. That the opinion and order rendered herein on November 21, 1944, are erroneous and should be reversed for the further reason that, as stated by the Commission in its order of June 10, 1944, dismissing application in Docket No. G–522, 'In view of the limited natural gas reserves shown by the record to be available to Applicant, their present rapid rate of depletion, and the effect of excessive rates of withdrawal on the ultimate recovery of gas therefrom, it is necessary and appropriate in the public interest that such natural gas resources be conserved insofar as possible for domestic, commercial and superior industrial uses. . . The record does not contain a sufficient showing that the proposed construction and operation are or will be required by the present or future public convenience and necessity.' That the situation has not been substantially changed since the original hearing; that the record does not disclose substantial evidence to show that it is to the general public interest to construct the lines involved in these applications and, to the contrary, the record shows that the issuance of said certificates would be in derogation of the general public interest and will not serve the present or future public convenience and necessity. 15. That the

cants desiring to provide natural gas service.[63] The Supreme Court of the United States October 8, 1945 denied an application for a writ of certiorari.[64]

January 3, 1945 the Board of Liquidation of the State Debt met in Baton Rouge with all but one of its members present and adopted a resolution providing the governor with funds to be expended in the court battle and the national gas investigation.[65] The

---

opinion and order rendered herein on November 21, 1944, are erroneous and should be reversed for the further reason that Applicant failed to show that the public convenience and necessity requires the issuance of either or both certificates issued herein. 16. That the Commission was correct when it said in its first opinion rendered in this cause on June 10, 1944, that, 'In view of the limited natural gas reserves shown by the record to be available to Applicant, their present rapid rate of depletion, and the effect of excessive rates of withdrawal on the ultimate recovery of gas therefrom, it is necessary and appropriate in the public interest that such natural gas resources be conserved insofar as possible for domestic, commercial and superior industrial uses.' That the record does not disclose substantial evidence to show that it is to the general public interest to construct the lines involved in these applications and, to the contrary, the record shows that the issuance of said certificates would be in derogation of the general public interest and will not serve the present or future public convenience and necessity. 17. That estimates of possible requirements shown at the second hearing are greatly exaggerated when compared to the possible requirements shown at the original hearing. 18. That the opinion and order issued hereon on November 21, 1944, are erroneous and should be reversed for the reason that the construction of the twenty-inch (20″) line from Lisbon to Guthrie is, in effect, the construction of two lines, one for the Applicant and one for United Gas Pipe Line Company, without United Gas Pipe Line Company filing an application therefor and obtaining a certificate of convenience and necessity as provided for in the Natural Gas Act, and without the proper showing that twenty-inch (20″) line is necessary and proper."

[62] See note 60 supra.

[63] 15 U.S.C.A. § 717 f (Cum. Supp. 1947).

[64] 326 U.S. 717 (1945).

[65] 1. to defray expenses in connection with litigation now pending on behalf of the State in the United States Circuit Court of Appeals for the Fifth Circuit, seeking to set aside and enjoin recent order and opinion, No. 119, of the Federal Power Commission authorizing the Memphis Natural Gas Company to increase substantially its pipe line facilities for the further withdrawal of natural gas from certain North Louisiana gas fields. 2. To set up the proper organization, consisting of an overall director, geologic, chemical engineering and other technical assistance, including legal aid and the necessary staff to participate properly and effectively in a nationwide investigation recently announced and now pending before the Federal Power Commission, under its Docket G–580, designed to determine, among other things, (a) the extent and probable life of natural gas reserves; (b) the present and prospective measures for preventing waste and prolonging the life of such reserves; (c) the present and probable future utilization of natural gas for domestic, commercial and industrial purposes; (d) the extent, character and results of the competition of natural gas with other fuels; and (e) such related matters as may seem helpful in the administration of the Natural Gas Act or in determining what additional legislation, if any, should be recommended. 3. To continue with all possible

appropriation was approved by an overwhelming majority of the membership of both houses of the Louisiana legislature, causing the governor January 9, 1945 to issue an executive order creating a natural gas conservation committee.[66] August 10, 1945 Commission Joseph L. McHugh issued a six point program on natural gas conservation,[67] and in view of the proposals there made, the Louisiana Natural Gas Conservation Committee at its August 13 meeting requested the governor to dissolve it, as the pronunciamento of the Commissioner covered the principles for which it was working. Thereafter the governor issued Executive Order No. 14,[68] August 15, dissolving the group and transferring its functions to the Director of Natural Gas Conservation—a post within his executive office. With the organization and creation of a staff consisting of a director, engineer-geologist, attorney, petroleum engineer, and a clerk,

---

vigor efforts being made to protect and conserve the natural gas reserves of the State and to assist and augment the efforts of the Louisiana Public Service Commission and the State Department of Conservation looking to that end.

[66] Exec. Order No. 10 (Jan. 9, 1945) reads: "January 9, 1945 Executive Order No. 10 Pursuant to the authority vested in me by law there is hereby created a committee to be hereinafter designated as Louisiana Natural Gas Conservation Committee. Members of said committee shall be: P. A. Frye, Chairman, Sam H. Jones, B. A. Hardey, Scott Heywood and John Huner, members. The said Committee shall serve as advisory to the Governor. It shall study and recommend procedures relating to the conservation of natural gas in Louisiana."

[67] 1. Call a statewide hearing as early as possible for the purpose of determining the feasibility of putting into effect a system of statewide gas proration in order to equitably prorate the market demand among all producing fields. 2. It is my opinion that the use of natural gas in areas where there is an existing adequate supply of coal or hydro-electric power, constitutes waste, and for this reason it will be my purpose to decline approval of all future proposed market requests for natural gas in such areas. All parties affected by this policy are hereby placed on notice. 3. Continue to call hearings with the view of issuing orders for ratable takings in all the producing gas fields of the State. 4. Institute further investigation to determine the advisability of issuing orders reducing the maximum amount of flared or vented gas presently allowed for use in lifting oil. 5. Continue the practice of conducting hearings to bring about cycling or pressure maintenance practices in all fields where there is a possibility that such methods may be economically feasible, which program to date has already achieved excellent results. 6. To keep the public fully informed as to the progress being made with respect to the program.

[68] Exec. Order No. 14 (Aug. 15, 1945) reads: "August 15, 1945. Executive Order No. 14. Pursuant to authority vested in me by law and based on resolution recently adopted by unanimous vote of the Louisiana Natural Gas Conservation Committee, which is attached hereto and made a part hereof, the Louisiana Natural Gas Conservation Committee is hereby dissolved, its functions and responsibilities to be assumed by P. A. Frye (and members of his staff) attached to this office as Executive Director of Natural Gas Conservation. So much of Executive Order No. 10. dated January 9, 1945, as is in conflict herewith is hereby revoked.

the agency embarked upon a three phased program of activity.[69] The Executive Director of Natural Gas Conservation produced a volume of testimony and evidence before the FPC at New Orleans in the course of their investigation,[70] and later made recommendations to the governor and members of the legislature, January 1, 1946.[71]

[69] 1. Prosecution of the pending litigation in the Memphis Natural Gas Company Case, 2. Preparation for effective participation in the nationwide investigation of the natural gas situation ordered by the Federal Power Commission under its Docket G–580. 3. A study of ways and means of making more effective Louisiana's local program of gas conservation within Louisiana.

[70] 1. Historical review of the discovery and production of natural gas within Louisiana. 2. Explanation of gas produced with oil. 3. Present picture: (a) Number of parishes in the State that produce gas. (b) Number of dry gas wells. (c) Number of wells producing gas and oil, including condensate. (d) Pipe lines operating within and from the state to other territories. (e) Number of individuals and companies producing gas. (f) Approximate number of gas royalty owners, separated as to residents and non-residents. (g) Number of fields and wells without markets. (h) Number and percentage of municipalities within Louisiana not served with natural gas. (i) Number and percentage of farms in Louisiana not served with natural gas. (j) Number and history of exhausted gas fields in Louisiana. 4. Production figures. (a) Past. (b) Present. (c) Potential. 5. Figures to show: (a) Imports of gas from other states. 6. Reserve figures: (a) Total for state. (b) Present rate of production. (c) Estimated remaining life. (d) Same information as to individual fields. (e) Availability of reserves. (f) Relation to centers of population. 7. Consumption and use: (a) To pipe lines for use within the state, separated as to major use classifications. (b) To pipe lines for movement beyond the state. (c) Flared, exclusive of that used in gas lift. (d) Used for gas lift. (e) Lease operations. (f) Returned to earth (cycled). (g) Burned to carbon black. (h) Miscellaneous use, plant fuel, shrinkage, and leakage. 8. Anticipated effect of depletion of natural gas resources on potentially recoverable oil reserves. 9. Possibilities of converting natural gas and its constituent hydrocarbons to chemicals, etc., which may be utilized in the public interest to greater advantage than if the gas from which such chemicals may be made is used for other purposes. 10. The relative cost of natural gas used industrially as compared with other fuels within Louisiana. (a) Absence of other forms of mineral fuel in Louisiana. (b) Absence of water power, present or potential. (c) Effect of the depletion of its gas reserves on the State's general economy. 11. Conservation practices: (a) Outline of conservation statutes. (b) Explanation of the State's conservation agency and its administration. (c) Relation of price and market to conservation. (d) Methods, practices and economy of cycling. (e) Current efforts to improve conservation practices. 12. The State's policy respecting natural gas conservation, as reflected by Senate Concurrent Resolution No. 7, dated June 2, 1942, also Section 1 of Article VI of the Constitution of Louisiana. 13. Recommendations.

[71] 1. That a statewide system of gas proration and ratable take, based on market demand, be made effective at the earliest possible date. 2. That more vigorous efforts be made to eliminate the flaring or venting of gas in oil fields. 3. That the use of gas for gas lift, followed by venting, be discontinued. 4. That better policing and control of producing gas-oil ratio to a figure not in excess of twice the original gas-in-solution ratio; also, that the present 15,000 cubic feet per barrel upper gas-oil ratio limit for oil wells be reduced to 5,000 cubic feet per barrel. 5. That the continued and increased cycling of all gas condensate fields be fostered, encouraged and made mandatory, where at all feasible. 6. That more accurate metering and report-

When the public press indicated the Commissioner of Conservation was not in accord with the position taken by Senate Concurrent Resolution No. 7, the Lieutenant Governor of Louisiana, February 20, 1947, addressed a letter to the Attorney General of Louisiana requesting a ruling on the validity of a proposed order under Act 157 to effect the position set out in the resolution. The ruling approved the proposed order.[72] The Executive Director of Natural

---

ing of gas production and transmission be required. 7. That our principal Conservation Statute, Act 157 of 1940, be amended to more specifically define and to prohibit "economic waste" of natural gas. 8. That the Gathering Tax be re-enacted on a permanent basis and increased to a minimum of three cents per thousand cubic feet, to be paid in all instances, and in its entirety, by the gatherer. 9. That appropriate legislation be enacted declaring natural-gas public utilities and placing them under the jurisdiction of the Louisiana Public Service, as to their intrastate operations. 10. That funds be provided Louisiana State University to set up and maintain a laboratory dedicated to research in the hydrocarbons of Louisiana's natural gas. 11. That continued active participation be maintained in the affairs and deliberations of the Interstate Oil and Gas Compact Commission, including proper financial support to its maintenance and operation. 12. That this office or similar organization be continued at the Executive Department level for at least the ensuing biennium.

[72] In your letter of February 20, 1947, you inquire if under the laws of Louisiana it is permissible for the Commissioner of Conservation to issue the following order relative to the conservation of natural gas: "STATE OF LOUISIANA DEPARTMENT OF CONSERVATION, BATON ROUGE, LOUISIANA, STATEWIDE ORDER PERTAINING TO THE SEVERANCE AND PRODUCTION OF NATURAL GAS IN THE STATE OF LOUISIANA. ORDER NUMBER Pursuant to the power vested in me by Section 1 of Article 6 of the Constitution of the State of Louisiana for the year 1921, as amended by Act No. 328 of the Legislature of Louisiana for the year 1944, approved November 7, 1944, and all laws applicable hereto, and after public hearings held at Baton Rouge, Louisiana, on February, 1947, following publication of notice of hearing not less than ten (10) days prior to said hearing in the official journal of the State of Louisiana, namely, the "State-Times" in Baton Rouge, Louisiana, and in order to protect, conserve and replenish the natural resources of the State, and to prohibit and prevent the waste and wasteful use of natural gas severed from the soil in Louisiana, and in order to prevent the wasteful utilization of natural gas severed from the soil in Louisiana, and to prevent the use of natural gas in such a manner as will threaten with premature exhaustion, extinction and destruction of the common supply and common reservoirs in the State of Louisiana from which natural gas is severed, and to prevent the use of natural gas in such quantities as will threaten with premature exhaustion, extinction and destruction of the common supply or common reservoirs, and to prevent the improper use of such natural gas in order to prolong the life of the supply of natural gas severed from the soil in Louisiana, and to prevent the severance of natural gas from the reservoirs of the State of Louisiana to be used in a manner and in such quantities as to threaten with premature exhaustion, extinction or destruction the common source or reservoir from which said natural gas is being drawn in the State of Louisiana, and to prevent the undue uses of natural gas, and to prevent waste, and considering the known reserves of natural gas in Louisiana and the rate of present production and withdrawal from such reservoirs, and considering the present and contemplated rapid expansion of natural gas pipe lines from Louisiana to areas al-

Gas Conservation of Louisiana did his utmost to have the take of natural gas prorated in the same manner as oil, thus giving every well a share in the market where economically feasible. Agitation, fomented in the Spider and Lucky gas fields which were without

---

ready supplied with adequate fuel and the resulting threat to the natural gas reserves of the State of Louisiana: IT IS HEREBY ORDERED by the Commissioner of Conservation, that the existing markets supplied and serviced by natural gas produced in Louisiana as of June 1, 1946 are adequate, and to further expand said markets would seriously jeopardize the availability of natural gas for such markets for a reasonable length of time; that in order to assure the consumers of natural gas in Louisiana and other areas now depending on Louisiana gas of a reasonable amount of natural gas for a reasonable length of time, the severance and production of natural gas from natural gas reservoirs of the State of Louisiana for shipment and transmission through pipe lines to new markets not now served with Louisiana gas, in new areas, adequately supplied with other fuels, or the expansion of markets as they existed on June 1, 1946, in areas adequately supplied with other fuels, constitute waste, and would threaten with premature exhaustion, extinction and destruction of the common supply and common reservoirs of natural gas, is hereby prohibited. IT IS FURTHER ORDERED that in all nominations for allowables on natural gas wells, the following information shall be specifically set forth: name of the purchaser, name of transporter, and the ultimate destination. IT IS FURTHER ORDERED that no natural gas severed from the soil of Louisiana under an allowable fixed by the Department of Conservation shall be transported through or sent to a destination other than that named in the nomination, without first obtaining a permit after a hearing, as provided for in Act 157 of 1940." Although the constitutionality of the order has in principle jurisprudential support (Walls v. Midland Carbon Company, 254 U.S. 300, 65 L. Ed. 276, 41 S. Ct. 118; Henderson v. Thompson, 300 U.S. 258, 81 L. Ed. 632, 57 S. Ct. 447), we may disregard its constitutionality vel non under the well recognized rule that an administrative officer, whose private rights are not adversely affected by the operation of a statute, may not raise the question of its constitutionality. His mere interest as a public officer is not sufficient to entitle him to question the validity of the statute. 16 C. J. S. p. 172, Section 82; Bossier Parish School Board v. Louisiana State Board of Education, 168 La. 1033, 123 So. 665. His duty is to obey the legislative mandate. Act 157 of 1940 was adopted for the purpose of conserving the oil and gas resources of the State, and to prevent waste and depletion of such resources. In Section 2 (a) of the statute "waste" is defined as follows: '(a) 'Waste,' in addition to its ordinary meaning shall mean 'physical waste' as that term is generally understood in the oil and gas industry. It shall include: (1) the inefficient, excessive or improper use or dissipation of reservoir energy; and the location, spacing, drilling, equipping, operating or producing of any oil or gas well or wells in a manner which results, or tends to result, in reducing the quantity of oil or gas ultimately recoverable from any pool in this state; and (2) the inefficient storing of oil; the producing of oil or gas from any pool in excess of transportation or marketing facilities or of reasonable market demand; and the locating, spacing, drilling, equipping, operating or producing of an oil or gas well or wells in a manner causing, or tending to cause, unnecessary or excessive surface loss or destruction of oil or gas.' It is evident that 'waste,' as used in the statute is not solely physical waste because the statute says that the word, in addition to physical waste, shall also be understood in its ordinary meaning. That ordinary meaning, as stated in Webster, includes a needless or extravagant use, so that the statute is concerned with economic as well as with physical waste. Indeed, the only kind of waste other than physical that we can conceive of is economic waste. The

markets even though in close proximity to pipe lines, was largely responsible for the repeal of the Senate resolution at a special session in 1947.

The fight that Louisiana made during these years placed natural gas—an irreplaceable natural resource—in its proper focus in the affairs of the nation, and did much to emphasize in the public mind the importance of this natural resource.

THE WELL HEAD PRICE OF NATURAL GAS

There has been considerable agitation in Louisiana for a better well head price for natural gas; the average price in 1936 was 3.1

---

jurisprudence recognizes the right of a State to prevent economic as well as physical waste. See cases cited in 24 American Jurisprudence, p. 631, Section 148 under Footnotes 14–19. The Constitution of Louisiana, Article VI, Section 1, requires the protection and conservation of the natural resources of the State, and directs the Legislature to enact laws to that end. It there expressly makes it the duty of the Legislature 'to prohibit and prevent the waste or any *wasteful use*' of the State's natural resources, and it provides that the Commissioner of Conservation '*shall* have and exercise such authority and power as may be prescribed by law.' It will be observed that the Constitution not only directs the Legislature to invest the power in the Commissioner to protect and conserve the State's resources, but it directs the Commissioner to exercise all invested power to that end. Section 3 of Act 157 of 1940 invests the Commissioner with authority and provides that 'it shall be his duty' to determine if waste exists or is imminent, and further invests him with authority after hearing and notice to make rules and regulations for the purpose of administration and enforcement of the act, including the right to limit and prorate the production of oil and gas to prevent the waste thereof. Section 21 of that statute provides that the act shall be cumulative of and in addition to all existing laws not in direct conflict with its provisions except certain laws adopted in 1924 and 1936. Among the laws then existing was Act 268 of 1918, Section 1 of which makes it unlawful 'to permit the waste of natural gas or to use natural gas for any purpose whatever in such manner as will threaten with premature exhaustion, extinction or destruction the common supply or common reservoir from which said natural gas is drawn.' The proposed order is not designed to interfere with interstate commerce. On the contrary, its purpose is to prevent production for a wasteful use. For other uses it may move freely in commerce and for wasteful purposes it never enters commerce. The control of production, both as to quantity and use, is purely a state matter, Henderson Company v. Thompson, supra, and the fact that the production may be intended for interstate shipment does not affect the State's power to control the use to which it may be put. Champlin Refining Company v. Corporation Commission, 286 U.S. 210, 87 L. Ed. 1062, 52 S. Ct. 559, 86 A.L.R. 403, 413. Section 10 of Act 157 of 1940 authorizes the Commissioner to limit the total amount of oil and gas production in the State and to distribute the allowable production among the fields and in turn among the producers if the field allowable is less than the field could produce if no restrictions were imposed. We think that the Commissioner has authority to issue the proposed order and that, in order to give proper effect to it, it should be followed with another issued pursuant to the provisions of Section 10 of Act 157 of 1940.

cents per MCF and in 1943 3.3 cents. S.B. No. 200, introduced in the regular session of the 1946 legislature, would have given the Commissioner the right to fix a minimum well head price for which natural gas could be severed from the state reservoirs. The Commissioner in arriving at this figure was to take into consideration the BTU content of natural gas, as well as its other properties, and the comparable prices of other major fuels at the point of production. The minimum price when fixed would control, regardless of any agreement or contrast to the contrary; gas severed and sold for less than the minimum constituted economic waste and violated the act. The bill received an unfavorable report. Again in the 1948 legislative session an attempt was made to increase the well head price of gas by fixing the minimum at 7 cents a MCF, but this bill was likewise defeated.

Some people have misunderstood Louisiana's position in the matter of conservation in that they believed Louisiana favored federal control of conservation of oil and gas; nothing is further from the truth. The state has and will continue to oppose federal control of conservation of its natural resources, as Louisiana is convinced that this matter is best handled by local government. A further misconception was that Louisiana advocated the cessation of exportation of natural gas, which was incorrect. The state simply opposed the expansion of the natural gas markets to the extent that known reserves would not serve any area for a reasonable time.

JUDICIAL INTERPRETATIONS OF ACT 157 OF 1940

The decisions of the Louisiana Supreme Court interpreting Act 157 of 1940 and the administrative action taken under it reflect a wholesome judicial understanding of the legislative purpose behind the statute's enactment. The court in the majority of instances exhaustively explores the evidence to assure the land owner adequate protection against arbitrary administrative action. The supreme court has given the decisions of the Louisiana Conservation Commissioner that reasonable judicial respect necessary if administrative action is given those presumptions established by law.

The statute was declared constitutional in *Hunter Company Inc.*

v. McHugh.[73] Order 28-B, issued by the Commissioner to regulate the production of gas from the Jeter zone in the Logansport Gas Field, prescribed drilling units of 320 acres with the requirement that the well locations be approximately in the center of each unit. Plaintiff's well, completed in 1938, was located on a 190 acre lease. It contended that so far as Order 28-B required unitization of the 190 acre lease with other acreage to conform to the 320 acre unit, the order was unconstitutional. The constitutionality of Act 157 of 1940 was directly at issue on the ground that it constituted an unauthorized delegation of legislative power. All of the court were in accord in approving the validity of the statute, although not equally so as to the question of the use of the authority granted under its provisions. On the question of legislative delegation the court held that the authority of the legislature to delegate to administrative boards the power of ascertaining and determining the facts upon which the laws were applied and enforced could not be seriously disputed. The statute was as specific as it could be and reasonable standards for administrative action under the Act were present. In answer to the contention that there was a deprivation of property without due process of law, the court said there was a co-equal right in common owners to take from the common source of supply, and that the legislative power might be exercised to protect all collective owners. In referring to the question of waste, the language of the court is pertinent: "The fact that there may have been no waste or wasteful use of gas in the Logansport field, in the ordinary sense in which the word 'waste' or the term 'wasteful use' is used, is no reason why the commissioner should not have taken steps for the prevention of waste and to avoid the drilling of unnecessary wells in that field. The purpose of establishing drilling units, as expressed in section 8(b) of the statute, is not merely to stop the wasting of gas which is already going on. The purpose is said to be to prevent waste and to avoid the drilling of unnecessary wells . . . ,"[74] further adding: "It goes without saying that the drilling of more wells than are necessary to drain a gas field efficiently and economically causes waste; it is a waste of valuable material and skill and labor; a waste of gas for fuel in the drilling

[73] 202 La. 97, 11 So. 2d 495 (1942).
[74] *Id.* at 507.

of unnecessary wells; and a waste of gas in allowing the unnecessary wells to clean themselves out before being placed on production . . ." [75]

A strong dissent voiced by Mr. Justice Fournet said that there was no necessity for invoking the statute where there was no waste in 'the ordinary sense and where no unnecessary wells were being drilled. The dissenting justice found no present need for unitization of the field and was of the opinion that these sections of the statute could be invoked only where present need was evident. The court permitted the complainant due reimbursement for his proper share of the well and production costs, by recognizing that the company could retain all of the proceeds from production "until the drilling of the well and putting it on production" was entirely paid for.

On appeal to the United States Supreme Court,[76] that body found that Order 28-C had in the meantime been promulgated by the Commissioner and that the cause, insofar as Order 28-B was concerned, was moot. On the bare question of constitutionality, the Court stated: "On this appeal, absent from the record an operative order implementing Act No. 157, we cannot say that the application of the Act can be enjoined as invalid on its face, for we cannot say that no order could be made by the Commissioner which would apportion the production and distribute the costs of production and of the apportionment in a manner which would be consonant both with the requirements of the statute and the Federal Constitution. . . ." [77] Referring to former decisions upholding the constitutionality of mineral conservation laws, the Court pointed out that a state has constitutional power to regulate production of oil and gas to prevent waste and to secure equitable apportionment among landholders of the common supply.

Hood v. Southern Production Company [78] involved a suit by a landowner lessor seeking to annul a lease on 100 acres of land on the ground that the lessee failed to comply with the provisions of a lease agreement requiring the drilling of an offset well "in the

[75] *Id.* at 508 (1943).
[76] Hunter Company v. McHugh, 320 U.S. 222 (1943). Appeal dismissed for want of substantial federal question.
[77] *Id.* at 228.
[78] 206 La. 642, 19 So. 2d 336 (1944).

event a well or wells producing oil or gas in paying quantities should be brought in on adjacent land." This lease had been entered into January 10, 1941 prior to any unitization order covering the Logansport Field of which the land was a part. The order as issued divided the entire gas field into drilling units of 320 acres and forbade the drilling of more than one well on any drilling unit; subsequently, the drilling unit was increased to 640 acres. Thirty-five acres of plaintiff's land had been made a part of a drilling unit in Section 2, but the remaining 65 acres were not a part of any recognized unit, and it was plaintiff's contention that the defendant's failure to drill satisfactory offset wells constituted a breach of the lease agreement. (After the judgment by the lower court the 65 acre tract was made a part of another unit.) The Supreme Court of Louisiana decided that the drainage clause did not apply, since the well draining plaintiff's premises was on land within a 640 acre drilling unit of which the leased land was a part. Since the lessee was forbidden by orders of the Department to drill additional wells, it would be unfair to annul the lease for failure to drill, when the defendant was prevented from drilling necessary wells under the Commissioner's order. In answer to the plaintiff's contention that should prohibitory law render the performance of a contract impossible, both parties were discharged, the court said: "There is no obligation to drill an offset well in the circumstances of this case, according to a fair and reasonable interpretation of the contract of lease. If the contract should be annulled the plaintiff could not drill a well on his 100 acres of land, because a part of it is in one 640-acre drilling unit, on which the Lewis well is producing gas in paying quantities, and the other part of the 100 acres of land is another 640-acre drilling unit on which a well is producing gas in paying quantities." [79] The court took the position that the orders of the Commissioner of Conservation establishing drilling units were made after due notice and hearing, and that orders validly issued under the state laws superseded private agreements to the contrary. It was pointed out that Hood was fully aware of the fact that the Conservation Commissioner could and might establish compulsory drilling units when he granted the lease.

A similar question was before the court in the case of *Hardy v.*

[79] 19 So. 2d 336, 341 (1944).

Union Producing Company.[80] Here the plaintiffs brought suit to annul an oil and gas lease, predicating their cause of action on the failure of the lessee to drill a well on the leased premises within the primary term of the lease. Since the lease agreement had been executed prior to the passage of Act 157 of 1940 and the issuance of unitization orders for the Logansport Field of which the land was a part, plaintiffs took the position that the conservation order in effect annulled the contract, or if the contract was not abrogated the orders issued for unitization were subject to the existing contracts in the field. Since plaintiff's land was part of a unit on which there was a producing well, the court held this argument untenable and said that the defendants in reality had not failed to perform any obligation of their contract. The conclusion of the court is summed up thusly: ". . . The right of defendants to drill a well on the forty-seven acre tract covered by the lease was in effect taken away from them by order of the Commissioner of Conservation, with, however, the right reserved to them, as well as to the plaintiffs, to share in the production of the gas produced from the unit in proportion to their ownership. Defendants' hands were literally tied as the result of the orders issued by the Commissioner of Conservation and they could do nothing whatsoever to prevent the primary term of the lease from expiring without drilling a well thereon." [81] The court again took the logical view that should the contract be annulled, the plaintiffs could not drill on their 47 acre tract as it was already a part of a unit on which there was a producing well, and it would be grossly unfair to terminate the lease agreement where defendants had done all that they could do under the existing law and orders. The clause in the lease requiring defendants to drill a well on the leased premises within a primary term of five years was superseded and made inapplicable by the orders of the Department of Conservation validly issued under Act 157 of 1940.

The case of *Placid Oil Company v. North Central Texas Oil Company, Inc.,* [82] decided interesting questions of notice and unitization in a part of the Cotton Valley Oil Field. The Commis-

[80] 207 La. 137, 20 So. 2d 734 (1945).
[81] *Id.* at 737.
[82] 206 La. 693, 19 So. 2d 616 (1944).

sioner of Conservation, acting under the authority of Act 225 of
1936, issued an order establishing drilling units of 80 acres, composed of any two adjacent 40 acre subdivisions, for the production
of oil and gas from the Bodcaw sand or from a depth of 8000 feet
or more. The Hunt Oil Company, a lessee owning the producer's
share of $7/8$ths in an 80 acre tract in the Cotton Valley Field, wished
to drill to the Bodcaw formation under the Department's order.
Hunt applied to the Commissioner of Conservation for permission
to unitize two 40 acre tracts, and the order was granted without
notice or hearing. J. R. Parten, the real complainant in the action,
owned a $3/32$nd royalty interest in the 40 acre tract, upon which the
producing well was actually drilled, and a $1/64$th interest in the
other tract unitized to make up the drilling unit. He claimed that
since he had been given no opportunity to be heard, he was entitled to a $3/32$nd interest in the well's production, and that those
owning a share in the acreage not drilled were not entitled to participate in the distribution of proceeds. In answer to Parten's contentions, the court took the position that the original order under
which unitization had been effected was properly preceded by notice and hearing and, therefore, became the law governing the drilling for oil or gas to the Bodcaw sand in the Cotton Valley Field.
The language of the court follows: ". . . The effect of the order
was to substitute for the right of every owner of a mineral interest
in a tract of land having an area less than 80 acres—to receive all of
his proportionate share of any oil or gas that might be produced
from the Bodcaw sand through a well drilled upon the land in
which he owned the mineral interest—the right to receive only his
proportionate share of any oil or gas produced from the Bodcaw
sand through a well drilled upon an 80-acre drilling unit embracing
the land in which he had his mineral interest." [83] Although the
court pointed out that the field order became the law of drilling
operations in the Cotton Valley Field, the right of a royalty owner,
who had no notice of the intention to unitize, to afterwards show
that the order was prejudicial to him, was not foreclosed. The court
then found that Parten had suffered a technical harm by the failure
of notice, because it could be presumed that had he received no-

[83] *Id.* at 619.

tice, he would not have objected since the drilling permit could not have been secured without the assemblage of the unit. It was to his advantage that the additional 40 acres included a tract in which he held an interest. Since it was impossible at this juncture to undo what had happened without affecting the rights of others in the unit, the complainant's request for an increased share in the production was denied, and it was pointed out that the failure of notice was unintentional and harmless and that: ". . . All the king's horses and all the king's men could not reinstate the status quo ante again." The *Placid Oil Company* case, on the question of notice, is primarily important because the court held that the Commissioner by issuing a field order does not have authority to grant unitization orders without giving "to all parties having mineral rights in any part of the area to be unitized due notice and an opportunity to be heard." The court added: ". . . Such notice is due particularly to parties having a mineral interest in only a part of the area intended to be unitized, or having a greater mineral interest in one part than in another part of the area intended to be unitized. Whether such notice is due to parties having the same mineral interest in one as in the other or the others of the two or more tracts intended to be unitized is a matter which we are not obliged to decide in this case, because, as we stated in our original opinion in this case, the parties having such uniform mineral interests in this instance are not complaining." [84] Since Act 157 of 1940 does not provide specific provisions of notice, this problem is left within the discretion of the Commissioner, which gives rise to considerable speculation as to what actually constitutes adequate notice under the statute. The *Placid* case seems to indicate that there are instances where all royalty owners must be given notice, but the impracticability of such a task is apparent. The *Placid* case decides questions arising under the 1936 statute, as the original field order was issued while that statute was in effect. Since the procedure under the 1940 Act is to notify as many of the interested parties (those as to whom the Department is advised) as possible, and at the same time to give notice in the official state journal and in a journal of the parish where the order is effective, it appears that a

[84] *Id.* at 621.

royalty owner alleging a lack of adequate notice would have to make out a clear case of prejudice to come within the rule established in this case.

The case of *Alston v. Southern Production Company, Inc.*,[85] discussed the validity of an order of the Conservation Commissioner increasing the size of drilling units from 320 to 640 acres. The effect of the ruling was to supersede pooling agreements made between owners of the land and the lessees under authority of a previous 320 acre order. The majority of the court sustained the new orders on the ground that they were valid in the absence of a showing by the plaintiff that the Commissioner's findings were incorrect and that 640 acres was a larger area than one well could drain efficiently. The order, being validly issued, superseded contracts made between land owners or leaseholders in the field, even though these agreements were made under the authority of the previous departmental order. The constitutional exercise of the police power was not subject to an objection that there was an impairment of the obligations of contracts. Justice Fournet, in a vigorous and impressive dissent, pointed out that the effect of the Commissioner's action was to create confusion and uncertainty as to valuable property rights. He was of the opinion that when the original 320 acre units had been fixed, the information on which such units were established was either incorrect, or the evidence adduced at the second hearing at which 640 acre units were ordered was not entitled to much credence by the Commissioner.

In connection with the question whether valid orders of the Conservation Commissioner do or do not supersede private contracts, the case of *Dillon v. Holcomb* [86] raises interesting issues of royalty rights where two tracts of land have been pooled for the purpose of drilling a well. The lease by the plaintiff to the defendant lessee provided for overriding royalties, in addition to the usual ⅛th land owner's royalty. The producing well on the unit was not on plaintiff's land but on the adjoining tract. The original lease in the latter acreage provided only for the ⅛th land owner's royalty. The defendant contended that the plaintiff was entitled to royalties only in accordance with the terms of the lease covering

[85] 207 La. 390, 21 So. 2d 383 (1945).
[86] 110 F. 2d 610 (C.C.A. 5th 1940).

the land where the well was drilled. The circuit court of appeals reversed the conclusions of the federal district court in holding that (with regard to royalties, overriding royalties and oil payments) the authority of the Conservation Commissioner, or of a lessee, to pool or allocate acreage was subject to the terms of the lease contract between the lessor and lessee. Since the plaintiff had not consented to a reduction in the amounts due to him under his contract, he was entitled to the royalties and oil payments. The *Dillon* case was cited as authority for the plaintiff's contention in *Hardy v. Union Producing Company.* The Supreme Court of Louisiana distinguished the *Dillon* case on the ground that there was no question of an overriding royalty raised by plaintiff in the *Hardy* case. The issue has not been squarely before the Louisiana court, but in light of the distinction made in the *Hardy* case, it would appear a different treatment might be given to ordinary lease stipulations as contrasted with royalty and oil payments.

The case of *McHugh, Commissioner of Conservation, v. Placid Oil Company* [87] deals with an action to enforce penalties for alleged willful and intentional violation of the provisions of Section 17 of the 1940 statute. It was alleged that oil was produced by the defendants between the dates of December 1, 1941 and June 1, 1942 in excess of the allowable fixed by the orders of the Commissioner. These unlawful acts first became known to the Commissioner August 20, 1942 but suit was not filed until May 27, 1943, or a little more than nine months after he learned of the violations. The defendants pleaded prescription of six months under Act 67 of 1926, which reads in part: ". . . Nor shall any person be prosecuted for any fine or forfeiture under any law of this state unless the prosecution for the same shall be instituted within six months of the time of incurring such fine or forfeiture." The plaintiff contended that the action was civil in form and did not fall within the intendment of the 1926 statute, which was entitled "An Act Relative to the Prescription of Criminal Offenses." The majority of the court, deciding that the "nature of the cause of action is a test" in determining the applicable prescriptive period, sustained the plea despite a logical and thoroughly convincing dissent based on the strained interpretation of the criminal prescriptive statute.

[87] 206 La. 511, 19 So. 2d 221 (1944).

The effect of this decision was to permit illegal oil to be run out of the state with safety, so long as it was undiscovered and a suit was not instituted within six months from the illegal act. That such a public policy was both dangerous and inconsistent with the meaning of the conservation statute was immediately recognized by the legislature through its passage of Act 273 of 1944, providing a prescriptive period of three years to run from the time that a violation is known to the Attorney General of Louisiana.

The case of *Crichton v. Lee*[88] raised the routine problem of whether a lease entered into before the effective date of Act 157 of 1940 would be superseded by a valid unitization order issued under provisions of the statute. The court again held that the order under which the tracts were unitized was issued to prevent waste and depletion of the natural resource; hence it was a valid exercise of the authority granted the Commissioner. The important point of the *Crichton* case is not in the answer given regarding the validity of the Commissioner's order—rather it is in the questions remaining unanswered, due to the maladroit pleading in the lower court. The contested order had reference to two sands. In the supreme court upon his appeal, plaintiff contended that since the lease operated as to all sands, the unitization order validated it only as to the sands specifically designated in that order. Since this issue was not urged below, it was improperly before the supreme court and this question was unanswered.

In *Ohio Oil Company v. Kennedy*[89] the land owners had sold 10 acres in dispute December 27, 1932 to the defendant reserving all the minerals. The land was then covered by a lease made March 18, 1919. Operations maintained this lease in effect, but not within the preceding ten year period. February 6, 1942 the Commissioner of Conservation issued an order providing special rules for the area of which the acreage was a part, and subsequently it was made a part of an 80 acre drilling unit. A producing well was brought in April 12, 1942 within the unit but not on the 10 acres in question. Kennedy's position was that when the land was sold, the reservation created a new servitude which had expired, that the order deprived him of his constitutional rights, and that the articles of the

---

[88] 209 La. 561, 25 So. 2d 229 (1946).
[89]   La.   , 28 So. 2d 504 (1946).

Civil Code of Louisiana pertaining to prescription had been repealed by the provisions of Act 157 of 1940. The court held that the servitude had been used within the period and was interrupted by drilling on the unit as effectively as though it had been done on the acreage in controversy. As to the question of inadequate notice, the court pointed out that certified copies of the two hearings indicated proper notice had been given and that "unless the record in this case shows, which it does not, that such notice is insufficient, then we take it that the notice is good and sufficient." From this statement it appears that the court does in fact accord the record as it comes from the Commission a general presumption of validity, and places on the plaintiff the burden of showing that proper notice and hearing were not granted.

The important case of *Hunter, Inc., v. Shell Oil Company* [90] involved a question stated by the court thusly: ". . . When an oil and gas lease covers land both within and without a drilling unit pooled by order of the Commissioner of Conservation during the primary term of such lease, and when production in paying quantities is secured while such lease is in effect by payment of delay rentals from a well within the pooled unit, but not on any portion of the leased land, does such production maintain the lease beyond its primary term as to the part of the land leased which lies outside such unit?" [91] The plaintiff contended that the order of the Commissioner in effect segregated that part of the lease covering the land within the drilling unit from the remaining leased acreage outside the unit. Under plaintiff's contention the order divided the leased premises; two leases were created, and the well drilled on the unit did not have the effect of holding that part of the property without the unitized area. The majority declined this argument stating the real question was whether the Commissioner, by his issuance of the order, had divided the "obligation of the lease." The court held it had not. Since the obligation to drill a well is indivisible, the lessor's corresponding duty is to deliver the land as a whole. If the duty of one of the parties to the contract had been fulfilled, the duty of the other contracting party must likewise be carried out in whole. Since the defendant had drilled a well and

[90] 211 La. 893, 31 So. 2d 10 (1947).
[91] *Id.* at 12.

the plaintiff was receiving its proportionate share of the royalties from this well, the remaining question was whether the well constituted adequate development of the leased premises; and the court pointed out that this issue was not raised. Mr. Justice Hamiter, in his dissent, was unable to agree with the application of the indivisibility theory and urged that to interpret the order as binding plaintiff's property without the unitized area would constitute deprivation of property without due process of law. The dissenting justice did not see how the acreage could be divided and the lease maintained indefinitely by payment of a minute fractional part of the production from the unitized area. As a purely legal proposition the decision is sound. Certainly, it finds support in the jurisprudence dealing with adequate development. From a practical standpoint the right to rescind a lease for failure to adequately develop is a circuitous and expensive remedy for the average lessor. In view of the expressed desire of the court in previous cases to prevent a tying up of valuable mineral property and circuity in litigation, the court (in the interest of public policy) might have found a means of giving the lessor relief without leaving the matter to be corrected by legislative action.

O'Meara v. Union Oil Company of California [92] involves questions of administrative procedure. The plaintiff in a letter dated April 11, 1947 had requested the Commissioner of Conservation to call a public hearing, under the provisions of Act 157 of 1940, to determine whether or not there had been an excess production of the legal allowable oil and gas from any of the wells of the defendant company during the three preceding years within the meaning of the 1940 statute. The attorney for the Conservation Commission advised the plaintiff that an investigation of the matter indicated purely technical violations and that the Commissioner felt hearings were unnecessary. When plaintiffs insisted on public hearings, the Commissioner issued an order for a hearing July 1, 1947. On June 30, 1947, the day before the hearing was to be held, plaintiffs instituted the present suit under Sections 13, 14 and 15 of Act 157 of 1940. The defendant there interposed an exception of no cause or right of action, based on the plaintiff's failure to exhaust the administrative remedies granted it under the statute. The

[92] 212 La. 745, 33 So. 2d 506 (1948).

court sustained this defense and in the following language judicially recognized the need for an administrative sifting of facts in these difficult questions of oil and gas law: "We quoted at some length the communications passing between the plaintiffs and the Commissioner and referred to the general allegations contained in the petition in order to show the wisdom of the legislature in placing preliminary sifting process of matters peculiarly within the competence of the administrative authority in the Conservation Commissioner which will prevent attempts to swamp the court by resorting to them in the first instance. We also recited these facts in order to show the uncertainty existing. In other words, it has not been determined what wells are over-producing and what wells are under-producing. These, as well as all the other indefinite matters, should be thrashed out and relief denied before resort is made to the courts. . . . The doctrine of exhausting the administrative remedy before relief can be sought from the courts is well recognized in this State."[93] The Supreme Court of Louisiana and the lower courts have indicated their willingness to uphold administrative action in the absence of a positive showing that such action is arbitrary and unreasonable. Act 157 of 1940 expresses the public policy in regard to oil and gas conservation, and the liberal attitude of the courts in supporting this statement of public policy is appreciated by the administrative agency and the industry with which it works. On the other hand, although the courts have generally sustained the administrative action, the exhaustive study which they make of the evidence indicates the private rights have not been disregarded. Constitutional rights of the individual are protected if each common owner is given an ample opportunity to share equitably in the common source of supply.

[93] *Id.* at 509.

CHAPTER 16

Michigan, 1938–1948

~/~

After the passage of the Michigan Oil and Gas Regulatory Act in 1929,[1] production of petroleum in the United States increased rapidly, and in the southwestern areas to an extent that a number of producers and governmental officials looked with favor on detailed and stricter state regulation. While Michigan did not overproduce[2] so far as demand for products was concerned, nevertheless, such activity elsewhere resulted in depressed prices below cost of production. Through the flow of interstate commerce from the great producing centers into Michigan, these economic price waves extended out from the southwest reaching the state and the eastern markets. By 1933 and 1935 proposed oil and gas conservation or control bills were presented to the state legislature asking increased supervision over the Michigan oil industry. These bills died.

THE 1937 GAS CONSERVATION LAW

In 1937 producers, gas purchasers, and some public officials proposed the Michigan Gas Conservation Bill. This Act was patterned

FLOYD A. CALVERT, WRITER; Burke Shartel, Virgil W. McClintic, Advisers; Research Assistant Mearle D. Mason. (See app. B.)

[1] Mich. Acts 1929, c. 15; MICH. COMP. LAWS § 5696–5722 (Mason 1929), MICH. STAT. ANN. § 13.121–137 (Henderson 1937). There have been laws enacted, regulations adopted and decisions rendered, affecting oil and gas conservation in Michigan since publication of Calvert, Legal History of Conservation of Oil and Gas in Michigan, LEGAL HISTORY OF CONSERVATION OF OIL AND GAS, A SYMPOSIUM 75–91 (1938) and this paper supplements the 1938 monograph.

[2] As of January 1, 1948, Michigan had produced over 273 million bbls. of oil and 164 billion cubic feet of gas; it had over 3500 producing wells in 125 pools and about 900 gas wells in 40 pools. Oil production declined from 16,628,344 bbls. in 1937 to 16,215,213 bbls. in 1947. Natural gas production increased from nine billion cubic feet in 1937 to twenty-three billion cubic feet in 1947. Michigan oil reserves are about 70,000,000 bbls. and gas reserves around 168,000,000,000 cubic feet.

generally after the 1929 law where gas was concerned, giving detailed jurisdiction to the Supervisor of Wells, and containing many modern regulatory provisions found in the statutes of Oklahoma and New Mexico. The producers, both independent and major, consider the Act good. Neither the Federal Government nor the public exhibited any deep feeling for or against its passage. There was little opposition to this gas statute, although some individual gas producers were against it, saying the 1929 Act was sufficient to control gas production. The impelling reasons for the passage of the 1937 statute were to protect the correlative rights of land owners, particularly in gas pools or fields, to aid orderly development, to prevent wastage of gas, and possibly to forestall federal control of the gas industry. Michigan oil and gas producers now feel that the price of Michigan gas at the well is too low, that it should be increased in line with prices received in other eastern states and the prices received here for southwestern gas.

Another bill had been offered giving almost exclusive jurisdiction to the Supervisor and the Conservation Department (except as to transportation, distribution, and public utility rates), but was killed. Act No. 326 of 1937 [3] passed in its stead, which gave the

---

[3] Mich. Acts 1937, c. 326; MICH. COMP. LAWS. § 5712–1 to 33 (Mason Supp. 1940), MICH. STAT. ANN. § 13.138(1)–(32) (Henderson Cum. Supp. 1947). Calvert *supra* note 1 at 80, said "This statute (1937 Act) reenacts generally the provisions of the 1929 oil and gas conservation statute and, in addition thereto, grants additional powers to the Supervisor of Wells to subpoena witnesses, hold hearings, and to require the production of books, papers and records of all producers in order to obtain evidence with reference to the drilling, operating and plugging of natural gas wells in the State. It further grants full powers to the supervisor to obtain data and facts with reference to the production of natural or dry gas from all wells in the State, their rock pressure, open flow volume, and other production matters. It provides that the Supervisor of Wells may allocate the allowable natural gas production between the fields and pools of the State if he deems it necessary to prevent waste. It is made a criminal offense for an operator or owner of a well to fail to plug same properly when abandoned, and civil liability is impliedly placed upon said operator for failure to plug properly and abandon any well. All logs, drilling data, etc., furnished by the well owners or operators to the Supervisor of Wells remain confidential for a period of ninety days after the completion of the well or test hole, the same as provided in the 1929 Act. The pooling or unitization of properties is authorized and incorporated with a provision that in case of small tracts of land of irregular shape and containing less acreage than the usual drilling unit, the owner thereof shall be limited in his production to that amount of gas only equal to the owner's just and equitable share of the total gas in the entire pool. The Act defines 'legal gas' as being gas produced from a well within an allowable take, as determined by the supervisor, and prohibits the production of illegal gas in excess of such take. It further provides for the Supervisor of Wells

Supervisor power over the conservation of natural or dry gas, except that already assigned the Michigan Public Service Commission under the common carrier and common purchaser gas pipe line law.[4] Hence the 1937[5] and 1929 Acts must be read together to determine the Supervisor's jurisdiction and that of the public utility commission, now the Michigan Public Service Commission. The Supervisor ordinarily has authority over drilling of gas wells, well spacing, pooling or unitization of acreage, and the plugging of wells, and in some instances, all production matters. The duty of the Public Service Commission begins when the well is connected to the pipe line selling or delivering gas to public utilities, or when sold for public use. The Commission exercises control over the sale of gas, proration of production, ratable take, transportation, distribution, and rate matters. On many things the Supervisor and the Commission work together, and in a way, have a concurrent jurisdiction—for example, over well spacing where the operators do not agree to an adopted spacing plan in a pool or field.

Waste[6] as here defined in the 1937 law is very broad and in-

---

to prosecute suits against persons violating the Act, and for heavy penalties. It also provides that all persons, corporations and associations exercising the right to carry or transport natural gas by pipe lines for hire, compensation, or otherwise, within the limits of this State, or engaged in the business of purchasing and selling natural gas, shall be common purchasers, subject to certain exceptions. The Supervisor of Wells is authorized to make rules and regulations covering the drilling and operating of natural gas wells in the State; all operators are prohibited from taking more than 25 per cent of the daily natural open flow of any gas wells (rules specify exact allowables) unless expressly authorized to do so by the Supervisor of Wells, provided, however, that all wells may at all times produce at least 2 per cent of their daily natural open flow, unless the field as a whole is being prorated. Section 30 of the 1937 Act specifically grants authority to the Supervisor of Wells to prorate natural gas production when the field involved is producing more gas than can be marketed without waste. An appeal may be taken from all orders and rules of the Supervisor of Wells to the Conservation Commission. . . ."

[4] Mich. Acts 1929, c. 9; MICH. COMP. LAWS § 11632–51 (Mason 1929), MICH. STAT. ANN. § 22.1311–30 (Henderson 1937).

[5] Mich. Acts 1937, c. 326; MICH. COMP. LAWS § 5712–13 (Mason Supp. 1940), MICH. STAT. ANN. § 13.138 (13) (Henderson Cum. 1947).

[6] The complete definition of waste in § 4 of the Act is: "The term 'waste' as used in this act, in addition to its ordinary meaning shall include, (a) surface waste which shall include the escape of natural dry gas in commercial quantities into the open air from a stratum recognized as a natural dry gas stratum and any unnecessary or excessive surface loss, including leakage, fire-loss and loss or destruction incident to the manner of spacing, equipping, operating or producing such well or wells, or by inefficient handling thereof. All waste of gas is hereby prohibited and it shall be the duty of the supervisor to prevent such waste and said supervisor is hereby empowered to make and enforce such rules, regulations and orders, subject to the

cludes surface waste, blowing gas into the air, intentional drowning with water of commercial gas strata, underground waste, wasteful burning of gas at the well, and wasteful use of gas. Economic waste is mentioned only in Section 4 and says: "It shall be the duty of the Supervisor of Wells . . . to visit from time to time operations for the discovery or production of gas, to inspect such operations with a view to preventing . . . economic waste; and to issue . . . rules and regulations to owners, operators, well contractors and drillers as will effectively prevent such waste. . . ."

(a) *Proration, Ratable Take and Maximum Take of Natural Gas*

Section 18 provides the Supervisor with power "to limit and prorate production of natural dry gas, such proration to be upon the basis of a minimum allowable take regardless of open flow and a further authorized take in proportion to tested open flow"; and "to establish drilling or prorating areas or units." Sections 29 and 30 state: "All persons, firms, associations and corporations, whether producing gas or receiving gas from other producers, in any production field, are hereby prohibited from taking more than 25 per cent of the daily natural open flow of any gas well or wells, unless for good cause shown under the exigencies of the particular case, the Supervisor of Wells shall establish a higher or lower per centum under rules and regulations to be by him prescribed: Provided, however, That except when it is necessary so to do in order to prorate a field, the Supervisor of Wells shall not make any order or regulation prohibiting the taking of at least 2 per cent of the daily

---

approval of the commission, and to require such surety bonds and do whatever else may be reasonably necessary to carry out the purpose of this act and to prevent such waste. Upon the verified complaint of any interested person that such waste is taking place or is imminent, or upon his own motion, the supervisor may call a hearing to determine whether or not such waste is taking place or is reasonably imminent, or what action should be taken to prevent such waste, (b) the intentional drowning with water of a gas stratum capable of producing gas in commercial quantities, (c) underground waste which shall include inefficient, excessive, or improper use or dissipation of the reservoir energy, including gas energy and water drive, of any pool, and the locating, spacing, drilling, equipping, operating, or producing of any well or wells in such a manner as to reduce or tend to reduce the total quantity of gas ultimately recoverable from such pool, and the unreasonable damage to underground fresh or mineral waters, oil, natural brines or other mineral deposits from operations for the discovery, development, and production of gas, (d) the permitting any natural gas well to wastefully burn, (e) the wasteful use of such gas."

natural open flow of any well. Whenever the full production from any common source or field of supply of natural gas in this State is in excess of the market demands, then any common purchaser of such natural gas as herein defined, receiving production or output from such source or field, shall take therefrom only such proportion of the available supply as may be marketed and utilized without waste, as the natural flow of the well, or wells, owned or controlled by such common purchaser bears to the total natural flow or production of such common source or field, having due regard to the minimum allowable provided in Section 29 hereof, and the provisions of Section 26, and to the acreage drained by each well, so as to prevent any common purchaser from securing an unfair proportion therefrom; and it shall be the duty of the Supervisor, and he is hereby empowered, to regulate and enforce the above provision; Provided, That the Supervisor may by proper order, permit the taking of a greater proportion by any common purchaser whenever or wherever he shall determine a taking of such greater proportion reasonable and equitable or conducive to public convenience or necessity."

Though the Supreme Court of Michigan has passed twice upon the conservation features of Michigan gas statutes,[7] in neither of these cases was their constitutionality attacked. In the *Wolverine Natural Gas Corporation v. Consumers Power Company*[8] case certain gas producers in the Six Lakes Field entered into gas purchase contracts with predecessors of the defendant Consumers Gas Company, whereby it was to buy a minimum quantity of natural gas each year, and required to pay for that amount, whether or not it was actually taken, receiving a stipulated credit on future gas for that not actually run. Under the rules of the public utilities agency, Consumers could lawfully take annually $17\frac{1}{2}$ per cent of the open flow of plaintiff's wells. It argued that this ignored the effect of the Commission Rule No. 13 limiting annual take to a pro rata equivalent of the total annual gas withdrawn from the field; that Wolverine's wells were in a common field and constituted approximately $\frac{1}{7}$th of the open flow there and this was the total gas Con-

[7] Mich. Acts 1929, c. 9 *supra* note 4. Mich. Acts 1937, c. 326 *supra* note 3. Nelson v. Galpin, 277 Mich. 529, 269 N.W. 586 (1936). See Calvert *supra* note 1 at 89.

[8] 296 Mich. 500, 296 N.W. 660 (1941).

sumers could take. Under Commission proration orders, lawful withdrawal from a given well constituted a fixed percentage of gas actually taken annually from the entire field. Wolverine admitted Consumers took the full prorata amount from its wells allowed on the basis of the field's ratings (percentage wise) assigned by the Commission to the Six Lakes Field wells, but claimed that Consumers took only about ½ the amount required under the minimum take clause in the purchase contracts. The court, denying plaintiff's claim, held that it could deliver only its proportion of the allowed ratable take for the entire field. The court further found that permitting plaintiffs to compel Consumers to purchase the minimum agreed gas under the contracts amounted to a price discrimination in favor of Wolverine as against other field sellers.

(b) Pooling

Section 20 covers gas well pooling.[9] So far, the Supreme Court of Michigan has not decided any cases construing these clauses. Since the section in this Act is similar in principle to that in the 1939 Oil Conservation Act,[10] there is no reasonable doubt that the court would interpret it other than as it did under the oil well pooling law.[11]

(c) Well Spacing

Section 18, among other things, provides that the Supervisor of Wells shall have power "to fix the spacing of wells." In case of any controversy between producers, the Supervisor and the Public Service Commission exercise concurrent jurisdiction with reference to the proper spacing to minimize litigation. The statute allows the

[9] "The pooling of properties or parts thereof shall be permitted, and, if not agreed upon, the supervisor may require such pooling in any case when and to the extent that the smallness or shape of a separately owned tract would, under the enforcement of a uniform spacing plan or prorating unit, otherwise deprive the owner of such tract of the opportunity to recover his just and equitable share of the gas in the pool: Provided, That the owner of any tarct that is smaller than the drilling unit established for the field, shall not be deprived of the right to drill on and produce from such tract, if the same can be done without waste, but in such case the allowable production therefrom of such tract, as compared with the allowable production if such tract were a full unit, shall be in the ratio of the area of such tract to the area of a full unit. Such order for pooling shall be made only after due notice and hearing."

[10] Mich. Acts 1939, c. 61, § 13.

[11] Smith Pet. Co. v. Van Mourik, 302 Mich. 131 4 N.W. 2d 495 (1942).

Supervisor to fix spacing so that the drilling unit is the maximum area efficiently and economically drilled by a single well. The discovery gas well in the Six Lakes Field, Montcalm County, was completed in 1935; [12] this field was drilled upon a 40 acre pattern like other gas areas in the state at that time. After the passage of the 1937 gas measure, the Public Utilities Commission, upon recommendation of the gas producers, adopted a basic 160 acre gas well spacing. The Commission's Rule No. 15 gives a well drilled upon such a tract a producing factor of four. No well is drilled on a unit less than 40 acres in size. A well upon such a unit has a producing factor of one, or ¼th that of a 160 acre tract. Wider spacing will be granted if justified, and in one instance, a 640 acre pattern was adopted in the Kawkawlin area. At the outset of World War II the PAW ruled that one gas well be spaced to each 640 acres, later amended to allow one well to each 160 acres. Gas producers agree today that this latter unit is, with certain exceptions, the most economical and efficient in shallow Michigan gas fields.

ADMINISTRATIVE HISTORY

(a) *Natural Gas Wells*

Under the 1937 Act the Supervisor of Wells and the Michigan Public Service Commission adopted rules covering the drilling, producing, and operating of lands for natural or dry gas purposes. The Supervisor's rules cover, among other matters: (1) Well Per-

---

[12] Most dry natural gas comes from the Michigan Stray formation; however, there are a few commercial wells in the Traverse, Dundee and Richfield, and in the Salina. For several years all gas consumed in Michigan came from local wells, until a great expansion in the use of gas exceeded production. In 1942 Panhandle Eastern Pipe Line Company completed its 24 inch line bringing gas from Kansas to the state as well as from Texas and Oklahoma. Now some 75% of natural gas consumed is imported from those three states. Michigan Consolidated Gas Company is bringing in additional natural gas in its line scheduled for completion in 1951. Gas is injected and stored in at least four underground basins during the summer for winter use, the same as has been done in ten other states and Canada for many years. Casinghead plants have been abandoned in the Porter and Temple Fields; one now operates in the Reed City Field, one in the Coldwater Field and one is being built in the Kimball Lake Field. There is not much casinghead gas in Michigan. Only one condensate well of any size has been located, the Pure Oil Company's Freer Well in Clare County which has declined to a point where it is no longer commercial production. There are some wet gas wells in the Norwich Field similar to condensate wells.

mits. Like oil producers, every gas producer must apply to the Supervisor (on forms prescribed by him) for a gas well permit, paying a fee of $25 a well before issuance and prior to drilling. He must also file with the Supervisor and have approved a bond in the sum of $1000 for a single well, or a blanket bond of $2500 covering several wells, both conditioned on compliance with state law. (2) Sealing and Casing off Wells. Every operator or producer must case and seal off oil, gas, brine, or fresh water stratum above the producing horizon effectually preventing migration of these substances to other strata or the surface. No well drilled for gas in a proved or semi-proved gas field may drill into the producing formation, until casing has been set as closely as practicable to its top and cemented by the pump and plug method with sufficient cement to fill annular spaces behind the casing from shoe to surface. (3) Drilling Through Oil or Gas Formations. No well may be drilled into any formation known to contain oil or gas until the innermost string of casing is equipped with a blowout preventer, control head, or high pressure mastergate valve to keep the well under control. Producers must secure written permission to deepen wells below the depth mentioned in the original application. Steel measuring lines are required, and operators must keep accurate logs and records of wells, and file them with the administrator. When requested by him, formation samples, drill cuttings, and fluid samples must be taken and preserved. No well is permitted to produce either oil or gas from differing strata through the same casing without first having the Supervisor's written permission. (4) Well Locations. All well locations must conform as nearly as possible to the requirements of the Supervisor's rules and those of the public service body. (5) Well Plugging. No operator or producer may plug or abandon any well or test hole until filing with the Supervisor—on his forms—notice of intent to abandon and receiving permission to proceed. Plugging operations on dry or abandoned wells must start within 15 days after drilling or production ceases; extensions of time are granted upon a proper written showing. Mud laden fluid, cement, or suitable substance is used in the plugging, and all materials and operations are under the supervision of the administrator or his representatives. Complete records of the work are made on agency forms and filed with the Supervisor. (6) Penalties. There are strin-

gent penalties for intentionally violating the provisions of the Act
—fines and imprisonment.

The Supervisor and the Oil and Gas Association of Michigan—
through its practice committee—now are considering alteration of
the oil well drilling rules concerning drilling with rotary as compared to standard drilling tools. The separate gas well spacing rule
may be combined with general regulations, the minimum drilling
unit may be increased to 160 acres, and the rules for both oil and
gas wells modernized. Action on proposed changes will not be effective before August 1948 or later.

(b) *Michigan Public Service Commission Rules*

Section 5 a, Rules of the Michigan Public Service Commission,
provides: "The jurisdiction of this Commission . . . over all gas
wells and over the production of gas from such wells, shall begin at
the time the production or preparation for production is started
and shall continue and remain with the Commission until production is abandoned. The operations of drilling, deepening, plugging
and abandoning, and in fact all underground work on gas wells, is
under the jurisdiction of the Supervisor of Wells of the Department of Conservation. . . ." Section 5 b states that any gas well
will be considered as producing or preparing for production at the
time an application for a well connection permit is filed with the
Commission, or if a connection is already made, the jurisdiction
begins when the installation is started. In its exercise of concurrent
authority over production, transmission, and distribution (including rates of natural gas), the Commission promulgates separate
rules and regulations which relate to gas production and distribution involving gas utilities or common carriers and at times producers. Present rules published by the agency in its Order No.
2883 cover: (1) Private Pipe Lines. Section 3, the 1929 statute,
excepts those pipe lines of oil and gas producers, factories and
industries in the state transporting their gas for use in drilling
wells and certain plants from the authority's control, in these
terms: ". . . nothing in this Act shall be construed to prevent oil
and gas operators or producers of gas from laying pipe lines to
transport or transmit gas to drilling wells within this State . . .
factories or industries in this State may transport or transmit gas

through pipe lines for their own use in plants located wholly within this State without constituting themselves a common purchaser." In a recent case, *Michigan Consolidated Gas Company v. Sohio Petroleum Company*,[13] the Supreme Court of Michigan held that Sohio, in constructing and maintaining a gas pipe line from its gas wells in Osceola County and transporting its gas to Midland, Michigan, for sale to the Dow Chemical Company, was not a common carrier for hire; therefore not required to secure approval of its transmission system or a certificate of convenience and necessity from the Service Commission under the Act. Michigan Consolidated, it was held, could not interfere with Sohio constructing and maintaining a pipe line to privately market its gas. (2) Waste. Section 7[14] prohibits waste of natural gas defining the term in essentially the same manner as in the 1937 enactment. (3) Determination of Well Capacity—Proration. The producing or open flow capacities of wells used as a basis for proration are determined by the Commission at its discretion. The method of finding this capacity, where practicable, avoids the open flow test plan and makes use of the United States Bureau of Mines productive capacity test, based on observations of shut in well pressure and the admeasurement of gas production volume at varying well head pressures together with any improved methods adopted by the Commission.[15] Capacity tests may be made by producers, purchasers, or transmit-

[13] 321 Mich. 102, N.W. 2d (1948).
[14] Mich. Pub. Ser. Comm. Rule 7 (1940) reads: "The term 'waste' as used in these rules in addition to its ordinary meaning shall include (1) the permitting of any gas to wastefully burn, (2) the wasteful use of gas including the use of gas in its natural state in engines or pumps where its pressure is the main or direct operating force, unless such gas can be consumed after discharge from such engines or pumps for normal use for fuel purposes, (3) surface waste, which shall include the unnecessary blowing, release or escape of natural gas into the open air, and any unnecessary or excessive surface loss, including leakage, fire loss and loss or destruction incident to the manner of equipping, operating or producing of such well or wells, or by inefficient handling thereof, (4) underground waste, which shall include inefficient, excessive, or improper use or dissipation of the reservoir energy, including gas energy and water drive, of any pool; and the equipping, operating, or producing of any well or wells in such a manner as to reduce or tend to reduce the total quantity of gas ultimately recoverable from such pool, and the unreasonable damage to underground deposits from the operation, maintenance or production of gas; and (5) the intentional drowning with water of a gas stratum capable of producing gas (except that temporary drowning may become necessary as an exigency of drilling or repairing wells)."
[15] Mich. Pub. Ser. Comm. Rule 11 a (1940).

ters with approval of the board.[16] (4) Unmetered Gas. Lessors using unmetered gas from wells on their lands for domestic purposes, or well operators utilizing unmetered gas from their wells for drilling fuel on the same lease, must operate without waste subject to the regulations of the agency. (5) Permit for Well Connection. Section 14 a provides the operator of each well must apply, before producing gas, to the Commission on its forms [17] for permission to sell gas from the well. An application and permit are not requisite for connection to pipe lines used exclusively for transporting fuel gas to drilling wells, or gas used in lessor's homes where wells are located. (6) Taking of Gas—Maximum Withdrawal—Acreage Factors. Section 15 says the maximum withdrawal during any 12 months period from gas wells may average daily not more than 17½ per cent of the current approved absolute daily open flow capacity of the well; this is the allowable maximum annual take. To provide for variable seasonal demand, percentages of the last determined allowable maximum annual withdrawal may be taken, but not exceeding, in six consecutive months 66 per cent, one month 12½ per cent, and any one day ⁶⁄₁₀ths of one per cent. The acreage area from which any well is considered to produce or draw gas enters into the determination of the well gas take. A well in the center of a 40 acre square of land is a unity with an acreage factor of one. The factor for a well producing from a square or rectangular tract of an area other than 40 acres is that in alloted well acres divided by 40. No side of the allotted well area may be farther from the well than the length from the center point to its most distant side, excepting that in the case of a discovery well this may be increased by as much as 330 feet for a well on 40 acres, or 900 feet for a well on 160 acres. Where a well is drilled off center because of topographical or physical conditions the distance may be increased not to exceed 25 per cent upon presentation to the Commission of satisfactory proof, supported by a map and a written statement showing a center location was barred. Every reasonable effort is made to drill centered wells. (7) Minimum Take. Subject to exceptions, the minimum monthly allowable take of gas from a well is a 500,000 cubic feet. The allowable from a well not capable

[16] Mich. Pub. Ser. Comm. Rule 11 b (1940).
[17] Mich. Pub. Ser. Comm. Form 15 a (1940).

of producing its minimum under the operating factors in its field is the total gas the well is capable of producing under those conditions. For fields or pools, where reservoir status and gas withdrawal operations do not permit the practical use of Rule No. 15 c 1, special applicable procedures are authorized.[18] (8) Ratable Taking or Gas Proration. Rule No. 15 d 1, e 1, 2 holds that all gas produced from a field or pool in excess of the minimum allowable be taken ratably from all wells capable of producing more than their minimum; the excess is divided among them in proportion to their modified open flow capacities determined by the agency, except that in no case shall total gas from a well be more than provided in Rule No. 15 a. Proration schedules and orders are prepared and issued by the Commission, and revised not more than once a month. No schedule or order affecting a well is made until the well connection permit is issued. (9) Production Reports. All gas operators are required to file producers' monthly reports, upon Commission forms, giving full information as to well production.[19] (10) Proration Among Pipe Lines and Fields. Rule No. 21 says the allowable gas withdrawal rates for proration among producers and purchasers, transmitters, or pipe lines from the same field, as well as prorating withdrawals among fields, are subject to Commission approval. It is the agency's duty to ascertain that production is not abandoned or unreasonably curtailed until recovery of all economically produced gas is assured. (11) Discrimination. Rule 22 b expressly forbids common purchasers and carriers from discriminating in amount of gas taken, its price, or rates charged for like grades of natural gas or facilities. If a common purchaser or common carrier is also a producer, it must not favor its own or any production in which it is directly or indirectly interested. The agency has authority to relieve any common purchaser or carrier, after application, notice, and hearing, from purchasing or receiving gas from wells which (due to variation in quality and pressure, or for economic reasons) are not a practicable source of supply. (12) Miscellaneous. The regulations cover many matters in detail, including availability of producers' records, fire prevention and control, well head heaters, fittings and meters and their installation and testing,

[18] Mich. Pub. Ser. Comm. Rule 15 c 1 a, b, c, 2 and 3 (1940).
[19] Mich. Pub. Ser. Comm. Rule 16 (1940).

well conditioning, pumps or compressors, approval for pipe line projects, requirements to connect gas wells, transmitters maximum take of gas, patrolling of pipe lines, filing of rates, contracts, regulations, reports, and records of transmitters or purchasers.[20] Under Act 35 of 1947 [21] all rules and regulations of the Supervisor (and other officers, boards, departments, agencies, and commissions), with stated exceptions, must be approved before becoming effective by the legislature of Michigan if in session, otherwise by its joint committee on administrative rules. The Michigan legislature abrogates such rules and regulations, or suspends them in the joint committee prior to their approval during the session interim.

The Chief Engineer of the Commission is its executive officer carrying out rules and regulations. One of his principal responsibilities is to determine the percentage of usable open flow capacity of gas wells when in his opinion such action is needful to protect the productive formation.[22] The Commission employs a gas engineer, a field engineer, and a stenographer.

1939 OIL CONSERVATION LAW

Prior to the adoption of the 1939 Act there had been a small number of producers opposed to government control or proration of oil production, holding that they should be permitted to produce any amount of oil from their wells—regardless of whether or not reservoir energy was lessened, salt water intruded, or the lives of other wells shortened, resulting in a smaller pool recovery. These were the minority; the great majority of producers, including major companies, believed in reasonable, scientific engineering control. Where members of the Oil and Gas Association lined up on different sides, that body did not sponsor one theory against the other. With dissolution of the Michigan Producers Proration Committee in 1935, and to the beginning of World War II, federal officialdom had little to do with oil and gas conservation in the state, although the Secretary of the Interior continually urged passage of strong conservation acts either by the Federal Government or the states.

[20] See Mich. Pub. Ser. Comm. Rules and Regulations Covering the Production and Transmission of Natural Gas (1940).
[21] Mich. Acts 1947, c. 35;
[22] Mich. Pub. Ser. Comm. Rule 5 c 1–4 (1940).

Michigan is unique in its control of the production of oil and gas in that it has an active oil and gas industry board (Advisory Board), that studies and considers oil and gas problems and meets with the Supervisor of Wells for the purpose of investigating and hearing all matters relating to proration, well spacing, and other important operations affecting the industry, and makes recommendations to the Supervisor as to what orders, rules or regulations the Board believes should be promulgated.

By 1939 after the oil producers had for several years observed the effects of overdrilling, unreasonably close spacing, and resultant low prices accruing from overproduction in other parts of the country, the industry and members of the Conservation Department worked out the basic conservation law of Michigan.[23] To protect the interests of its citizens and land owners from unwarranted waste of gas and oil, and to foster development of industry along most favorable conditions with a view to the ultimate maximum recovery of these natural products is the declared state policy in this statute.

The law, like the 1929 oil statute and the gas statute of 1937, makes the Michigan Director of Conservation the Supervisor of Wells. The Director is chosen by the State Conservation Commission (whose members are gubernatorial appointees holding office for six years) and serves at its pleasure. Under the Oil Act the Supervisor of Wells, with the approval of the Conservation Com-

---

[23] Mich. Acts 1939, c. 61; MICH. COMP. LAWS § 5712–41–5712.67 (Mason Supp. 1940), MICH. STAT. ANN. § 13.139 (1)–(27) (Henderson Cum. Supp. 1947). There were many conflicting ideas and cross currents presented in consideration of this bill before it passed. Some felt sole jurisdiction to regulate the industry should be in the Conservation Department, while others held the industry should have an equal voice. The legislature's final decision was to create the Advisory Board to sit with the Supervisor of Wells. Many producers argued that the very nature of the oil and gas business, its many economic and operating hazards, dictated that the operators and producers should be given wide latitude in controlling their own industry. Others felt that state should act as an umpire preventing larger and major operators from infringing upon the smaller or independent producers. Still a third group argued the state should have greater control. The result, a merging of all ideas, allows the state to have the advice and recommendation of producers in regulating the oil and gas production in Michigan. As the case in the passage of the 1937 Gas Act, waste prevention, avoidance of overproduction, a desire to forestall federal control, protection of landowners' correlative rights and a desire to avoid bankruptcy prices were the underlying motives for passage of the law. Both the public, the majors and the independent producers look on this law as fair and reasonable and one that has encouraged oil development.

mission, appoints six persons constituting the Advisory Board. Three members are chosen from independent oil and gas producers or operators, their managing agents or representatives, whose ownership, production, or operations are chiefly within Michigan; the other three are selected from among oil and gas producers or operators, managing agents or representatives, whose ownership, production or operations are chiefly interstate, and who are directly or indirectly through controlled subsidiaries engaged as actual producers in five or more states, including Michigan. No one company, its subsidiaries or affiliates, may have more than one representative on the Board. This group is selected with reference to training, experience, and standing as oil and gas producers and operators. Members must have been residents of Michigan at least two years preceding appointment and have five years practical or technical producing or operating experience. Appointments are for three years.

Section 2 of the 1939 law defines oil,[24] gas,[25] pool,[26] field,[27] and market demand.[28] The Act interprets waste.[29] Section 4 specifi-

[24] Natural crude oil, petroleum or other hydrocarbons, regardless of gravity, produced at the well in a liquid form by ordinary methods not the result of condensation of gas after it leaves the reservoir.

[25] Casing head gas or that produced incidental to oil.

[26] Underground reservoir containing a common accumulation of oil, gas or both.

[27] Field and pool are the same when only one pool is involved; however, a field means in instances two or more pools.

[28] "The words 'market demand' as used herein shall be construed to mean the actual demand for oil from any particular pool or field for current requirements for current consumption and use within or outside the state, together with the demand for such amounts as are necessary for building up or maintaining reasonable storage reserves of oil or the products thereof, or both such oil and products and shall not be less than the actual purchasing commitments for oil from such pool or field." Market demand covers the demand for petroleum products within as well as without Michigan for Michigan oil and gas.

[29] "(1) 'Underground waste' as those words are generally understood in the oil business, and in any event to embrace (1) the inefficient, excessive, or improper use or dissipation of the reservoir energy, including gas energy and water drive, of any pool, and the locating, spacing, drilling, equipping, operating, or producing of any well or wells in a manner to reduce or tend to reduce the total quantity of oil or casinghead gas ultimately recoverable from any pool, and (2) unreasonable damage to underground fresh or mineral waters, natural brines, or other mineral deposits from operations for the discovery, development, and production and handling of oil or casinghead gas. (2) 'Surface waste' as those words are generally understood in the oil business, and in any event to embrace (1) the unnecessary or excessive surface loss or destruction without beneficial use, however caused, of casinghead gas, oil, or other product thereof, but including the loss or destruction, without beneficial use, resulting from evaporation, seepage, leakage or fire, especially such loss or

cally outlaws waste.[30] Section 5 assigns the Supervisor jurisdiction over administration and powers necessary for enforcement of the statute's provisions.

The Supervisor, acting directly or through his authorized representatives (after cosultation with the Board), under Section 6 is empowered to make and enforce rules and regulations, subject to Commission approval, to issue orders and instructions for enforcement of these rules and regulations and to do whatever is needed to carry out the purposes of the Act, whether indicated, specified, or enumerated or not in this or other sections.[31] Under Section 16 no

---

destruction incident to or resulting from the manner of spacing, equipping, operating, or producing well or wells, or incident to or resulting from inefficient storage or handling of oil, (2) the unnecessary damage to or destruction of the surface, soils, animal, fish or aquatic life or property from or by oil and gas operations; and (3) the drilling of unnecessary wells. (3) 'Market waste,' which shall embrace the production of oil in any field or pool in excess of the market demand as defined herein."

[30] It is unlawful for any person to commit waste in exploration, development, production, handling or use of oil, gas or product.

[31] Collect data, make inspections, studies, and investigations, examine properties, leases, papers, books and records, check, test and gauge oil and gas wells, tanks, plants, refineries, and all modes of transportation and equipment, hold hearings, provide for the record keeping, making reports, and checking of the accuracy; to require the locating, drilling, deepening, redrilling or reopening, casing, sealing, operating, and plugging of wells drilled for oil and gas or for geological information or as key wells in secondary recovery projects, or wells for the disposal of salt water, brine, or other oil field wastes, to be done in such manner and by such means as to prevent the escape of oil or gas out of one stratum into another, or of water or brines into oil or gas strata; to prevent damage to or destruction of fresh water supplies and valuable brines by oil, gas, or other waters, to prevent the escape of oil, gas, or water into workable coal or other mineral deposits; to require the disposal of salt water and brines and oily wastes produced incidental to oil and gas operations, in such manner and by such methods and means that no unnecessary damage or danger to or destruction of surface or underground resources, to neighboring properties or rights, or to life, shall result: Provided, however, That any such well may be plugged to a fresh water level and not to the surface in case such well is desired to be used as a water well. To require reports and maps showing locations of all oil and gas wells, the keeping and filing of logs, well samples, and drilling and operating records or reports: Provided, however, All well data and samples furnished the Supervisor shall, upon request of owner of well, be held confidential for 90 days after the completion of a well and not open to public inspection except by written consent of the owner: Provided further, however, That no producer shall be required to submit or file logs or reports of core or test wells drilled for geological purposes only, nor required to furnish well samples of such core or test wells. To prevent the drowning by water of any stratum or part thereof capable of producing oil or gas, or both oil and gas, in paying quantities, and to prevent the premature and irregular encroachment of water, or any other kind of water encroachment, which reduces, or tends to reduce the total ultimate recovery of oil or gas, or both such oil or gas, from any pool. To prevent fires or explosions.

rules, regulations, or orders are made, revoked, changed, renewed or extended, except in an emergency, until after public hearings. These hearings are held at a time, place and manner as prescribed in the general rules and orders, upon notice of not less than ten days. The Supervisor puts into effect emergency rules, regulations, or orders without a public hearing where necessary; the rules then remain in force not more than 21 days.

With reference to hearings upon complaints involving waste, Section 7 states that upon the initiative of the administrator, the Board or a verified complaint from any interested person alleging that waste is taking place or is imminent, the Supervisor calls, or directs the Board to call, a hearing to determine whether or not waste is taking place or is imminent. The Board holds a hearing, promptly makes findings and recommendations which the Supervisor considers in promulgating rules, regulations, or orders necessary to prevent waste.

When to prevent waste the administrator limits the amount of oil produced from any pool or field, he (after consulting with the Board and considering its recommendations) allocates and distributes the production on a reasonable basis, giving where possible to each small well of settled production an allowable to save it from general or premature abandonment.[32] Section 13 sets forth the basis and method of proration.[33] Naturally well allowables vary.[34]

To prevent "blow-outs," "seepage," and "caving" in the sense that the conditions indicated by such terms are generally understood in the oil business. To regulate the "shooting" and chemical treatment of wells. To regulate the secondary recovery methods of oil and gas, including the pulling or creating a vacuum, the introduction of gas, air, water, and other substances into the producing formations. To fix the spacing of wells. To require the operation of wells with efficient gas-oil ratios and to fix such ratios. To require by written notice immediate suspension of any operation or practice and the prompt correction of any condition found to exist which is causing or resulting or threatening to cause or result in waste. To require either generally, or in, or from, particular areas, certificates of clearance or tenders in connection with the transportation of oil, gas, or any product thereof. To identify the ownership of oil and gas producing leases, properties, and wells. To make rules, regulations, or orders for the classification of wells as oil wells or gas wells; or wells drilled, or to be drilled, for geological information, or as key wells for secondary recovery projects, or wells for the disposal of salt water, brine, or other oil field wastes. To require surety bonds of owners, producers, operators, or their authorized representatives in such reasonable form, condition, term, and amount as will insure compliance with this Act and with the rules, regulations, or orders issued thereunder.

[32] Mich. Acts 1939, c. 61 § 12.

[33] "Whenever, to prevent waste, the total allowable production for any field or pool in the State is fixed in an amount less than that which the field or pool could

After the issuance of a proration order, no producer is allowed to produce more than his allowable. Producers follow proration orders, and there is no overproduction in Michigan.

In December 1943 after public hearing and over the protests of practically all producers (supported by the testimony of various geologists and petroleum engineers) and contrary to the recommendation of the Advisory Board, the Supervisor reduced the allowables in the Reed City Field from 125 barrels daily per well to 100 barrels for wells on 20 acre locations. Two engineers from the University of Michigan, specially hired by the Geological Survey, testified that the allowable should be 80 barrels daily a well for like areas. The producers appealed the order to the Conservation Commission where it was sustained. No appeal was taken to the courts. On the whole, producers have felt that most of the orders of the Board and Supervisor have been fair and reasonable.

During World War II the Petroleum Administrator for War issued Conservation Order No. 68 which limited the drilling of one well to 40 acre tracts, the minimum being 35 acres, save where applications for exceptions were granted. This was replaced by Order No. M-81. A general exception was made by the PAW for the

---

produce if no restriction were imposed, the supervisor, after consulting with the Board and considering its recommendations, shall prorate or distribute on a reasonable basis the allowable production among the producing wells in the field or pool, so as to prevent or minimize reasonably avoidable drainage from each developed area which is not equalized by counter drainage. The rules, regulations, or orders of the supervisor shall, so far as it is practicable to do so, afford the owner of each property in a pool the opportunity to produce his just and equitable share of the oil and gas in the pool, being an amount, so far as can be practicably determined and obtained without waste, and without reducing the bottom hole pressure materially below the average for the pool, substantially in the proportion that the quantity of the recoverable oil and gas under such property bears to the total recoverable oil and gas in the pool, and for this purpose to use his just and equitable share of the reservoir energy: Provided, That a well in a pool producing from an average depth of 1,000 feet or less, shall, on the basis of a full drilling unit as may be established under this section, be given a base allowable production of at least 100 barrels of oil per well per week; for a well in a pool producing from an average depth greater than 1,000 feet, the base allowable production shall be increased 10 barrels per well per week for each additional 100 feet of depth greater than 1,000 feet; Provided further, That such allowable production is, or can be, made without surface or underground waste, as defined herein."

[34] In the Deep River Field the discovery well flowed without being prorated at around 700 to 800 bbls. a day for a time, and then 500 to 250 bbls.; the Supervisor then issued his order for 100 bbls. daily production. At the producers' request this was amended to allow 4000 bbls. a day for the field. This stabilized field pressure and remained in force a few months when amended to allow 80 bbls. a well a day.

shallow Traverse wells in southwestern Michigan to allow 20 acre spacing for all wells less than 2000 feet deep. An exception was granted gas drilling units, permitting drilling of gas wells on 160 acres instead of 640. In 1942 and 1943 after the Reed City Field had been half drilled upon 40 acre patterns by most operators, the producers petitioned PAW for an exception permitting further development on 20 acres. Their petition was denied. PAW insisted steel was more essential for ships and other war material than for oil. A number of well qualified geologists and petroleum engineers testified that this spacing would result in a loss of 3,000,000 to 4,000,000 barrels of oil that could have been produced under the smaller pattern.

The general concept of oil conservation in Michigan, as developed by the proration orders recommended by the Board and put into effect by the Supervisor, is that flat well allowables serve conservation better than pool or field quotas or their equivalents based on potential producing ability using open flow, bottom hole pressure, and like factors. When a discovery well is completed, it is the Supervisor's practice to permit an operator to produce what he considers a safe, conservative daily amount of oil from the well, based upon open flow for several hours, bottom hole pressure, gas-oil ratio, et cetera; as a rule, proration orders [35] are not entered until a few wells are completed, so long as the production schedule is within safe bounds. This is a sound theory when dealing with experienced, responsible producers.

The pooling of leases [36] is allowed, although the Supervisor has

[35] Typical daily proration schedules (in force at various times in the past few years) were: Reed City, 175 barrels for wells on 40 acres, 100 barrels for 20 acres; Adams Field, 262.50 barrels from ten acre locations, later reduced to 125; Coldwater Field, 40 acre spaces 100 barrels; Kimball Lake Traverse 20 acre locations 50 barrels; Deep River, 80 barrels for 10 acre spacing; Fork, 20 acre locations, 125 barrels; Evart, 20 acre spacing, 100 barrels and Stony Lake with 40 acre locations, 100 barrels.

[36] "The pooling of properties or parts thereof shall be permitted, and, if not, agreed upon, the supervisor, after conference with and recommendations by the Board, may require such pooling in any case when and to the extent that the smallness or shape of a separately owned tract or tracts would, under the enforcement of a uniform spacing plan or proration or drilling unit, otherwise deprive or tend to deprive the owner of such tract of the opportunity to recover or receive his just and equitable share of the oil and gas and gas energy in the pool: Provided, That the owner of any tract that is smaller than the drilling unit established for the field, shall not be deprived of the right to drill on and produce from such tract, if same can be done without waste, but in such case, the allowable production there-

no power to compel it. Where a well is drilled upon a tract smaller than the fixed drilling unit, its production is reduced in the ratio the smaller area bears to the authorized unit. Prior to the 1939 Act there were instances where producers drilled upon tracts smaller than the usual voluntary units adopted by others. Under the law of capture then in force they obtained more oil from their tracts than others from larger areas. This practice was not as prevalent in Michigan as in other oil states, due to the fact that Michigan had a lesser number of producing fields. The pooling statute prevents drilling of wells upon one acre school sites, town lots, and small areas. Today owners usually enter into pooling or unitization agreements.

---

from as compared with the allowable production if such tract were a full unit, shall be in the ratio of the area of such tract to the area of a full unit, except as a smaller ratio may be required to maintain average bottom hole pressures in the pool, to reduce the production of salt water, or to reduce an excessive gas-oil ratio. All orders requiring such pooling shall be upon terms and conditions that are just and reasonable, and will afford to the owner of each tract in the pooling plan the opportunity to recover or receive his just and equitable share of the oil and gas and gas energy in the pool as above provided, and without unnecessary expense, and will prevent or minimize reasonably avoidable drainage from each developed tract which is not equalized by counter drainage. The portion of the production allocated to the owner of each tract included in a drilling unit formed by voluntary agreement or by a pooling order shall, when produced, be considered as if it had been produced from such tract by a well drilled thereon. Each well permitted to be drilled upon any drilling unit or tract shall be drilled approximately in the center thereof with such exception as may be reasonably necessary where it is shown, after notice and upon hearing and the supervisor finds that the unit is partly outside the pool, or for some other reason, a well approximately in the center of the unit would be unproductive, or that the owner or owners of a tract or tracts covering the central part of such unit refuses to permit drilling in or near the center of the unit, or where topographical or other conditions are such as to make drilling approximately in the center of the unit unduly burdensome or imminently threatening to water or other natural resources, or property or life. Whenever any exception is granted the supervisor shall take such action as will offset any advantage which the person securing the exception may have over other producers in the pool by reason of the drilling of the well as an exception, and so that drainage from the developed areas to the tract with respect to the exception granted will be prevented or minimized and the producer of the well drilled as an exception will be allowed to produce no more than his just and equitable share of the oil and gas in the pool as such share is set forth herein, and to that end the rules, regulations and orders of the supervisor shall be such as will prevent or minimize reasonably avoidable drainage from each developed area which is not equalized by counter drainage and will give to each producer the opportunity to use his just and equitable share of the reservoir energy. Minimum allowable for some wells and pools may be advisable from time to time, especially with respect to wells and pools already drilled when this act takes effect, to the end that the production will repay reasonable lifting cost and thus prevent premature abandonment of wells and resulting wastes."

The Supervisor has authority to issue certificates of clearance or tenders whenever required for the purposes of the Act. This provision was inspired by the Connally Hot Oil Act but has not been used. Section 15 makes it unlawful for any person to sell, purchase, acquire, transport, refine, process, handle, or dispose of illegal oil or product.[37] No penalty or forfeiture is imposed until certificates of clearance or tenders are required. All illegal oil, products, storage containers, and conveyances used in their transportation, except railroad cars and pipe lines, are subject to confiscation. The Supervisor is empowered to seize them, instituting an in rem proceeding for condemnation in the circuit court of the county where seizure is made or in the Circuit Court of Ingham County. Upon trial, if the court finds the oil, products, containers, or conveyances are illegal, it orders a sale under terms and conditions as it directs.

Section 23 provides no well may be begun or drilled for oil or gas purposes, geological information, a key well for gas, air or water secondary repressuring, or for disposal of brines and oil field wastes, until the owner makes a written application and files with the agency a satisfactory surety bond. The permit upon receipt must be posted in a conspicuous place at the well. A fee of $25 is charged for an oil and gas permit and a fee of $1 for the others. Upon receipt of application and fee, the Supervisor within five days issues a permit to drill. No permits are issued to owners not in compliance with the rules, regulations, and orders of the agency or the Department of Conservation, or to violators of the Act. Information and records with reference to the issuance of permits for drilling core or test wells, or for geological information, including the permit, are held confidential for six months after the well's completion.

Nothing in the law prevents exploration for new pools by drilling wildcat wells, but in the event oil or gas production is obtained,

---

[37] Illegal oil is that produced within Michigan from any well or wells in excess of the amount allowed by valid rules, orders and regulations of the Supervisor. " 'Illegal product' shall mean any product of oil or gas or any part of which was processed or derived in whole or part knowingly from illegal oil as distinguished from 'legal product' which is a product processed or derived to no extent from illegal oil. 'Illegal conveyance' shall mean any conveyance by or through which illegal oil or illegal oil products are being transported. 'Illegal container' shall mean any receptacle which contains illegal oil or illegal oil products. 'Tender' shall mean a permit or certificate of clearance for the transportation of oil or products, approved and issued or registered under the authority of the supervisor."

then the new pool and well or wells drilled are subject to the Act. Section 27 states the enactment does not apply to drill holes for exploration and extraction of iron, copper, brine, water wells, mine and quarry drill and blast holes, nor to coal test holes, seismograph or other geophysical exploration tests.

Sections 19 and 20 provide penalties for violation of the law by fine and imprisonment, which includes a fine of $1000 a day for each day of violation. The Circuit Court of Ingham County is granted exclusive jurisdiction of all suits brought against the Commission, the Supervisor, the Advisory Board, any agent or employee thereof, by or on account of any matter or thing arising under the provisions of the Act. No temporary restraining order or injunction is granted in any suit, except after due notice and for good cause. The Supervisor is empowered to bring proceedings at law or in equity for the enforcement of the statute and all rules and regulations adopted thereunder, or for the prevention of infractions thereof; in such matters he is represented by the attorney general. The Circuit Court of Ingham County has concurrent jurisdiction in all suits brought by the Supervisor.

June 1939, soon after the Act's effective date of May 3, 1939, the Supervisor of Wells, his staff and the members of the Advisory Board met with the oil producers and the Directors of the Oil and Gas Association of Michigan and formulated a set of rules and regulations governing drilling, producing, operating, plugging, and general oil and gas field operations in the state.[38]

New rules, regulations, or orders entered by the Supervisor are first considered by him and the Advisory Board in a public meeting, except emergency orders which are heard at public or private sessions. Ten days personal notice by mail [39] is given to the interested parties, and published notice [40] is given the public prior to the hearings involving the orders, rules, or regulations.

At least one regular meeting each month is held at the Capitol as a rule, in the office of the Supervisor. When public hearings are

[38] Copies of the Supervisor's rule may be obtained by writing him at Lansing, Michigan. The same is true as to the rules of the Michigan Public Service Commission.

[39] Personal notices are mailed directly to parties interested in the properties or field or pool involved.

[40] Notice to the public is published in a daily or weekly newspaper of general circulation, or oil trade journal of wide circulation.

held, they meet in the public hearing room of the service commission, the state senate room, if available, or other large meeting places in the building. At the hearings the Supervisor and the Board sit *en banc* with the former presiding. As a rule industry managing officers, their counsel and assistants attend the public hearings, which are conducted like those before the average state administrative board or commission. Witnesses are requested to state an opinion of the matter under consideration and the reason therefor. While they may be examined by friendly counsel, under general practice the Supervisor and members of the Board ask the questions which may be offered by interested parties or counsel through the Supervisor or Board. Under the law parties have the right to examine and cross examine all witnesses through counsel as though appearing before a judicial body. Testimony is taken from a reasonable number of witnesses; briefs or written arguments may be submitted to the Supervisor, but seldom are required. No set rules of evidence are followed. Voluntary statements from the producers and parties interested are received as well as whatever testimony or written evidence having relevancy the parties offer. Any oil producer concerned may appear and testify. The Supervisor is authorized to compel by subpoena the attendance of witnesses, production of books, papers, records, or articles necessary in any proceeding before him, the Advisory Board, or the Conservation Commission. No person is excused from obeying the subpoena for the reason that his testimony or evidence, documentary or otherwise, tends to incriminate or subject him to a penalty or forfeiture. No witness is compelled to produce books, papers or records, or to testify in response to a question not lawfully before the Board, Supervisor, or Commission, or a court for determination within the purposes of the Act; any incriminating evidence (documentary or otherwise) may not be used against the witness in a prosecution or action for forfeiture. No person testifying is exempt from prosecution and punishment for perjury. In case of failure or refusal to comply with a subpoena issued by the Supervisor, or to testify or answer as to matters on which one is lawfully interrogated, any circuit court in Michigan, or their judges, on application of the Supervisor, may issue an attachment and compel obedience with the subpoena and attendance before the Board or Supervisor, the production of documents, and the giving of testimony. The court or judge has the power to punish for contempt as in case of disobedience to a like subpoena issued by or from a court, or a refusal to testify. Witnesses summoned are entitled to the same fees and mileage as those attending circuit court. Heavy penalties are provided for perjury or false reports.

Although the Supervisor is compensated for his time as Director of Conservation, he is ex-officio Supervisor of Wells; the members of the Advisory Board serve without pay but are allowed their actual expenses. The Supervisor has a well qualified staff of assistants who spend all or a good part of their time carrying on conservation work. The staff consists of an assistant director, commission secretary, the state geologist, two petroleum geologists, a petroleum engineer, a lands division chief, assistant lands division chief, the supervisor of state land sales from the lands division of the Commission, several petroleum engineers and geologists at Lansing, as well as district petroleum engineers, district clerks, and a number of field agents engaged in oil field hazard reduction work. An assistant attorney general of Michigan handles the legal work of the Supervisor and the Board, and a petroleum geologist on the Supervisor's staff serves as Secretary of the Advisory Board. The state furnishes a court reporter to take the evidence at public hearings and transcribe same when needed.

The provisions in the Act for voluntary and compulsory pooling and unitization of leases and portions of leases enable the Supervisor and the Board to work out well spacing problems in the interests of the lease owners as a whole, protecting their correlative rights in individual pools or fields. In urging producers to pool or unitize their properties where necessary, owing to the smallness of the acreage or the irregularity of tracts involved, the administrators have so far worked out these problems satisfactorily and without much litigation. There are no specific written rules on this matter other than the rules with reference to location and spacing of wells. Unit operation and cooperative development plans are encouraged. Rule 14 provides that the drilling upon a tract less than 10 acres shall not be permitted until the lease owner has made a bona fide effort to pool his lease or tract to form a full drilling unit and has failed. Proof of his effort must be submitted before the operator is permitted to drill the smaller tract and receive his proportionate allowable in the ratio his land bears to the regular drilling area.

In *Smith Petroleum Company v. Van Mourik* [41] defendant, Gruenbauer, was the fee owner of 1.75 acres, (treated as two acres) of land on which a producing oil well was operated by defendant lessee, Van Mourik. Plaintiffs were the lessors and lessees of the remaining eight acres, comprising a ten acre tract. Because the lessees of the two acre and the eight acre tract had entered into a pooling agreement, the plaintiffs claimed that it bound Gruenbauer, the fee and royalty owner of the two acre tract, who had refused to execute the agreement. It was further asserted Gruenbauer was estopped to refuse the pooling agreement, because he had verbally agreed to it which he denied. The trial court found that Gruenbauer had so agreed, and that his lessee, Van Mourik, entered into the community agreement with the owner of the lease on the eight acre tract in reliance upon this statement that they would sign the pooling agreement, which was never executed. The supreme court, reversing the decree of the trial court, held that the defendant did not agree to or execute the pooling or communitization agreement, and further that they were entitled to the full ⅛th (royalty) of the oil and gas produced from the well on the Gruenbauer two acre tract, notwithstanding the fact that the Supervisor of Wells issued a permit for the drilling of the well on the two acre tract assuming that a binding community agreement had been consummated. Such contract between the lessees did not bind Gruenbauer. [42] Under the Van Mourik case, it is necessary that all

---

[41] 302 Mich. 131, 4 N.W. 2d 495, (1942).

[42] The defendants did not raise the question of the statute of frauds as to the pooling agreement, and that defense was not discussed by the court in its opinion. The supreme court, in discussing the pooling or communitization clause said: " 'The pooling of properties or parts thereof shall be permitted, and, if not agreed upon, the supervisor after conference with and recommendations by the board, may require such pooling in any case when and to the extent that the smallness or shape of a separately owned tract or tracts would, under the enforcement of a uniform spacing plan or proration or drilling unit, otherwise deprive or tend to deprive the owner of such tract of the opportunity to recover or receive his just and equitable share of the oil and gas and gas energy in the pool.' It is not claimed that a community agreement was required as a matter of law under the above-quoted statute. The permit to operate on the basis of a 10-acre unit was not granted by the supervisor or department of conservation on the ground that it was being so ordered under the authority of the statute; but instead the permit so to operate was issued on the assumption that a binding community agreement had been consummated. Clearly such assumption as applied to the Gruenbauers was erroneous.

royalty owners join in the execution of pooling agreements (unless pooling is authorized in the lease) [43] otherwise, those owning under the separate tract where the well is located are entitled to receive their entire ⅛th royalty in the proportion their royalty acreage bears to the separate tract upon which the well is drilled.[44]

Nor do we find that the defendant appellants were estopped from denying any pooling or community agreement because, without their being in any way a party thereto, Van Mourik obtained a permit to operate the well at the rate of 100 barrels per day, and that the well was so operated after November 1, 1939. That the well was so operated did not work to the disadvantage of any of these litigants, but in fact was quite to the contrary. Before Van Mourik secured the permit to operate at the rate of 100 barrels a day he had entered into an agreement with the other lessees as follows: 'It is understood and agreed that Van Mourik hereby accepts the responsibility for the development, operation and management of said 10 acres as a unit for the production of oil and gas and the payment of royalty to the various lessors as their interests appear (and also to the other lessees).' Van Mourik was already under contract obligations to account for royalties to the parties who owned the 2-acre parcel, and by the agreement just above quoted he obligated himself for 'payment of royalty to the various lessors as their interests appear.' Under the circumstances the main controversy in this case is in effect between Van Mourik and the Gruenbauers. Under the record we think he was obligated to pay royalties to the Gruenbauers on the basis of ⅛ of all the oil produced by means of the well on the Gruenbauers' 2 acres, notwithstanding Van Mourik had obtained a permit to operate the well as one located on a 10-acre unit."

[43] It has been the practice in Michigan for oil and gas lessees to secure the execution of a proper pooling agreement by all lessors and lessees involved, or insert in the lease a definite pooling clause authorizing the lessee to pool lands or any parts with other lands or leases and, provide that drilling of a well upon any portion of the unit constitutes drilling or completion of a well upon all of the leases so pooled, regardless where the well is drilled. Some pooling clauses provide for abatement of rentals upon all leases after completion of a well, and others abate rentals on lands in the drilling unit. Some pooling agreements in Michigan leases further provide that the lessees, when agreed upon certain pooled drilling units, file a declaration with the Register of Deeds of the County where the land is located, explicitly describing the various pooled drilling units, and no further notice need be given to the lessors of such pooling in order to make it effective.

[44] As an aftermath to the Smith-Van Mourik litigation, the lessees owning the lease upon the 8 acre portion of the above 10 acre tract completed a producing well and the Supervisor of Wells reduced the daily allowable production from the Gruenbauer 2 acre tract, allowing the latter well to produce less than the allowable from a 10 acre drilling unit. The production from the 2 acre tract was then so small as to make it a noncommercial well, and when the lessees attempted to abandon the well, Gruenbauer refused to let them remove the casing and other equipment from the well, in order that they might abandon same, and Gruenbauer stopped them and ordered them from the premises. The lessees secured an injunction restraining the landowner, Gruenbauer, from interfering with the removal of the equipment, and the supreme court sustained the circuit court, holding that a bill in equity for enforcement of lessees' specific contract rights under the lease to remove lessees' equipment and property from the lands upon the abandonment of the well, was proper and held that Gruenbauer should be enjoined from interfering with such removal. *See* Thurmes v. Gruenbauer, 310 Mich. 507, 17 N. W. 2d 732, (1945).

While the Michigan pooling statutes definitely provide for voluntary pooling, they also authorize drilling upon small tracts less than ordinary units, if it can be done without waste. All wells drilled upon lesser tracts are prorated in their allowable production in the ratio of the smaller tracts acreage to the entire drilling unit. In view of this explicit statute and the holding in *Hunter Co., Inc. v. McHugh*,[45] the Michigan pooling statute is constitutional and can be upheld under the state's police power and conservation policy.

The State of Michigan under the 1939 Act may enter pooling agreements similar to those made by fee and royalty owners. Pooling or unitization of government-owned lands for oil and gas mining purposes has been an approved policy of the Federal Government for over 17 years. Under the Act of July 3, 1930 [46] and later acts lessees are permitted to unitize their interests in a unit plan of development, when determined and certified by the Secretary of the Interior as necessary or advisable in the public interest.[47] The Act of August 21, 1935 [48] authorizes the Secretary of the Interior to require development and production of oil and gas deposits under a unit or cooperative plan where expedient; the prior acts had authorized the Secretary to approve a unitization plan with the consent of the holders of permits or leases involved. A 1946 amendment [49] also permits pooling government-owned lands with private or state-owned lands to comply with well spacing requirements.[50] The Secretary of the Interior may authorize pooling or unitization agreements between various operators and lessees of federal or state-owned lands.[51] The Secretary, in addition to issuing regulations covering unitized operations, has prepared a suggested form of unit agreement for all parties in interest to execute. The form is

[45] 320 U.S. 222 (1943). King, *Pooling and Unitization of Oil and Gas Leases*, 46 Mich. L. Rev. 311–40 (1948) and Shank, *Some Legal Problems Presented by the Pooling Provisions of the Modern Oil and Gas Leases*, 23 Tex. L. Rev. 150–163 (1948); Patterson v. Stanolind Oil & Gas Co., 305 U.S. 376 (1939); See Handbook on Unitization of Oil Pools, Mid-Continent Oil and Gas Association, Tulsa.

[46] 46 Stat. 1007 (1930), 30 U.S.C. § 226 (1940).

[47] 46 Stat. 1523, 30 U.S.C. § 194 & 226 (1940); 49 Stat. 674, 30 U.S.C. § 185, 221, 223, 226; Act of Aug. 8, 1946, Pub. L. 696, U.S.C. Cong. Serv. § 5.

[48] 49 Stat. 674 (1935), 30 U.S.C. § 185, 221, 223, 226 (1940).

[49] Act of Aug. 8, 1946. Pub. L. 696, U.S.C. Cong. Ser. 85.

[50] See the Secretary's regulations governing pooling and unitization.

[51] Act of Aug. 8, 1946 supra note 49.

not mandatory as operators and producers are given opportunity to submit their own agreements if they substantially follow the regulations.[52]

The Supervisor's Rule 14, subparagraph A, provides that the minimum drilling unit for oil in Michigan is a 10 acre tract which conforms to ¼th of each 40 acres in a governmental survey section of land, allowance being made for differences in the shape and size. As a rule no permit is granted for drilling an oil well unless the location is 330 feet from an adjoining lease or property line and 660 feet from an adjacent or adjoining well. However, the Supervisor may grant exceptions to the rule. In Michigan each well is placed in the approximate center of the unit unless the Supervisor finds (after notice and upon hearing) that the unit is partly outside the pool, or that a well drilled in the center of the unit would be unproductive, or that the owner of the unit's central part refuses to permit drilling near the center, or that topographical or other conditions make drilling there unduly burdensome or imminently threatening to water, other natural resources, property, or life.[53] For about seven or eight years after commercial production was first obtained in Michigan, the usual oil well spacing pattern was one well to 10 acres.[54]

[52] King *supra* note 45 at 311–344.

[53] Drilling units should be fixed by rules approved by the Conservation Commission. Ops. Att'y. Gen. Mich. 1941–42 393 (Oct. 30, 1941).

[54] About 1933 the Pure Oil Company inaugurated a 20 acre pattern in the Yost-Jasper Field—each well being in the approximate center of the north or south half of a governmental surveyed 40 acre tract, and thereafter, up until World War II, a number of other fields were drilled up on this pattern. Presently most new wells are drilled on either a 20 or 40 acre spacing except the Shallow Traverse pools in the state where the plan is ten acres. About 50% of the pools have been drilled on a ten acre spacing, one on a five and the remainder on twenty to forty acres. The following oil fields have 40 acre spacing patterns: Ashton (Traverse), Belly Achers (Dundee), Cedar (Dundee and above), Coldwater (Dundee), Dwight (Monroe), East Norwich (Richfield), Enterprise (Richfield), Essexville (Dundee), Evart (Dundee), Fork (Dundee), Goodwell (Traverse), Harrison (Dundee), Hatton (Dundee), Mt. Forest (Dundee), Prosper (Dundee), Richfield (Richfield), Rose City (Richfield), Rose Lake (Traverse), Stony Lake (Traverse), Wise (Dundee), and Woodville (Traverse). Bloomer (Traverse), Douglas (Dundee), Headquarters (Traverse), Kawkawlin (Dundee), Kimball Lake (Traverse), Winterfield—East (Dundee), and Winterfield—West (Dundee) have 20 acre spacing. Reed City (Dundee, Monroe and Traverse) has part 20 acre and part 40 acre spacing; Rockford (Traverse)—in City of Rockford, has 10 acre drilling units; and the Southwestern Michigan area (Generally Traverse) has 20 acre units with exceptions for 10 acres usually granted. In a number of gas fields of the State, including the Austin, Six Lakes, New Haven, Sumner, West Vernon, Crystal, Broom-

Section 6 of the 1939 Act authorizes secondary recovery methods including pulling or creating a vacuum, introduction of gas,
air, water, or other substances into the producing formations.
There have been no water flood operations in Michigan, because
most oil comes from a limestone formation (Traverse, Dundee,
Monroe and Richfield oil producing formations) generally too
tight to permit successful water flooding. Oil production from the
Berea sandstone in the Saginaw, Birch Run, and Tuscola pools is
small, and it is doubtful they will ever be water flooded. The Supervisor encourages the underground disposal of brine or salt water;
paragraph 2 of his Production Rule reads: "Brine or salt water
produced in the drilling for or the production of oil shall not be
run to earthen reservoirs or ponds, except for such reasonable time
and under conditions as may be approved by the Supervisor, or his
authorized representative, after which it must be returned to some
underground formation or otherwise disposed of as approved by
the Supervisor where it cannot do damage to any fresh water, oil,
gas or other minerals."

field, McKay of Clare County, Vernon, and others, the Commission has generally
approved 40 acre gas well spacing programs, and in some fields it has approved
a mixed spacing plan of one well to 40 acres or one well to 160 acres or one
well to 80 acres, but of course each well is subject to the acreage factor above
mentioned, and is allowed to produce only in the amount that the well acreage
bears to the ordinary 160 acre unit. Most of the 40 acre spacing patterns provide
for the drilling of one well in the center of a governmental surveyed quarter-
quarter section of land; for instance, in the Coldwater field, each well is located
in the center of the North half of each governmental surveyed quarter-quarter
section of land. Sometimes it is in the East half of the 40 acres (Goodwell-
Traverse pool), sometimes in the center of the South half of the 40 acres (Fork-
Dundee pool). In the Reed City field, the 40 acre units in the North half of the
field were drilled in the center of the South 20 acres of each unit, and in the
South part of the field they were drilled in the center of the North 20 acres
of each 40 acre drilling unit. In some fields, such as the Wise pool, diagonal
well spacing patterns are in effect; that is, in each governmental surveyed quarter-
quarter (40 acres) section of land, the wells are located in the center of the
NW¼ or the center of the SE¼ of the drilling unit. The same is true in the
Essexville and Kimball Lake fields, which have 20 acre spacing units, but the wells
are located either in the center of the NW¼ or the center of the SE¼ of each
governmental surveyed quarter-quarter section of land. Of course, there are numerous exceptions in various fields where the Supervisor, for sufficient reasons
under the statute, has permitted the drilling of wells off center or at locations
not conforming to the general spacing patterns in effect in the fields involved.
This is particularly true in the Deep River field and the Pinconning field, which
appear to be located along a fracture or fault line. The Deep River field is generally
drilled on a 10 acre spacing pattern, with many exceptions.

Neither have there been any successful secondary recovery operations in Michigan, other than recycling of gas in the Norwich Township, Missaukee County field (Sun Oil Company and the Pure Oil Company lease owners).[55] While there are no specific written rules as to repressuring, cycling, or recycling, such operations are subject to the approval of the Supervisor under his general power. The Dow Chemical Company of Midland receives a large amount of salt water from the Midland County fields and manufactures it into chemical compounds; (one of its salt water products is aspirin, of which it is probably the largest manufacturer in the world). Operators are permitted to run salt water into earthen reservoirs for a reasonable time under conditions approved by the Supervisor. Most salt water produced from oil wells in Michigan is now returned to a receptive formation. The Supervisor and his staff keep in touch with gas-oil ratios, but as a rule a producer exercises his discretion here as long as the amount of gas produced is not extremely great or does not injure adjoining wells. The facts in each case generally determine the allowed gas-oil ratio. Individual proration orders issued by the Supervisor provide for the ratable taking of oil and gas from certain wells in the field or fields involved. In fixing daily production allowables the Board and the Supervisor try to preserve reservoir energy by conserving the maximum gas energy possible, thus preventing early water intrusion without injury to the operator or the field. Most of the larger oil fields in Michigan have a water drive as their propulsive agency, although some have had gas expansion or dissolved gas drives.

The producer of oil from a lease that is prorated and his purchaser are allowed tolerance to produce and overrun not to exceed

[55] Repressuring experiments were made over a period of years with several wells in the Dundee formation in the Yost-Jasper pool of Midland County, and the Mt. Pleasant field of Isabella and Midland Counties, without successful results; air was also injected into at least one well in the Saginaw field (Berea formation) without results; casinghead gas was injected for several months into several wells in the Buckeye pool, Gladwin County; and gas and air injected into the Diamond Springs pool of Allegan County and Monterey pool of Allegan County (Traverse formation); gas was also injected into the Walker field of Kent and Ottawa Counties for several months; all without appreciable results. Some water pressure experiments were also made in the Sherman pool of Isabella County, without results. See Survey of Secondary Recovery Operations, Research and Coordinating Committee Interstate Oil Compact Commission, I, Interstate Oil Compact Q. Bull. 47–48 (1942).

one days allowable production from each well on the lease over the amount calculated for the calendar month; such overproduction is made up during the next calendar month.[56]

The Supervisor's rules prohibit the production of carbon black within the State of Michigan, except with his written approval.

The general regulations do not refer to market demand for oil or gas, but in issuing oil proration orders, the Board and the Supervisor take into consideration market demand for oil; in recent years, particularly since the end of World War II, the demand for petroleum and petroleum products in Michigan has greatly exceeded the local supply and production. The Board and the Supervisor take for granted a strong demand for all oil produced in Michigan. The same is true with reference to production of dry or natural gas. The fact is, Michigan produces only about 20 to 25 per cent of the oil it consumes, and not over 20 to 25 percent of the natural gas used. Michigan is a big importer of oil and gas and petroleum products, rather than an exporter. There are no restrictions on the exportation of oil or natural gas from Michigan. The natural gas imported and consumed in Michigan is piped here from Oklahoma, Kansas, and Texas.

A producer, lease owner, or the Advisory Board may appeal to the Conservation Commission from any rule, regulation, or order of the Supervisor deemed unduly burdensome, inequitable, unreasonable, or unwarranted. On appeals taken by the Board, the decision of the Commission is final. Any producer or owner may seek further relief by bringing a separate suit or action in the Circuit Court of Ingham County, Michigan, against the Commission, the Supervisor, the Board, or any agent or employee thereof, and either side may appeal from the circuit court to the supreme court. No temporary restraining order or injunction is granted except after due notice and for good cause shown. The supreme court would probably advance appeals involving the Supervisor's orders upon its docket, although there are no rules to that effect. It would be necessary for the Supervisor or the producers to file and present a motion to advance a cause on the ground that same was a case *publici juris*. General rules of practice and procedure apply

[56] Tolerance Rule adopted by the Supervisor of Wells, Oct. 27, 1941, effective Nov. 15, 1941.

on an appeal from the circuit court to the supreme court. While the Supervisor is not required to file an appeal bond, it would be required for the complainants suing the Supervisor or Advisory Board or Commission to file and have approved proper supersedeas bond, in the event the complainants desired to stay or supersede the judgment of the circuit court or to stay the order of the Supervisor, Board, or Agency.

STATE-OWNED LANDS

A part of the state-owned lands are held in fee simple and in a part the state owns the minerals only, the surface belonging to homesteaders or others. By statute the state is authorized to lease its mineral interests for oil and gas mining purposes. It is the policy of Michigan not to sell, but to lease its mineral interests; at this time the state has under lease over 400,000 acres.[57] All oil and gas leases are offered at public auction after published notice and sold to the highest bidder for a cash bonus and a prescribed rate of rental and royalty. The practice of the Conservation Department is to retain ⅛th of the area in each township, and not offer same for lease until approximately the entire township is proven, except as leasing is necessary to protect any tract from drainage. Not more than 2560 acres are included in any one lease. The lease term is for a period of five years and so long thereafter as oil or gas is produced in paying quantities. Upon proper and sufficient showing in exceptional cases, this primary term may be extended.[58]

[57] Since the rendition of the decisions in Krench v. State, 277 Mich. 168, 269 N.W. 131, and Rathbun v. State, 284 Mich. 521, 280 N.W. 35, no further serious attacks have been made upon the state's right to reserve the minerals in state lands acquired on account of nonpayment of taxes where the surface rights were afterwards sold by the state and the minerals reserved.

[58] At the time of the sale, areas are declared to be either wildcat or proven, and the Department of Conservation will hold to this classification when later issuing leases, even though subsequent events between the time of the sale and the issuing of the leases may change the status of certain areas. Ordinarily, it takes about one month after the sale before the leases are actually delivered. Applications to have any particular tracts of land offered for lease are required to be on file with the Department of Conservation at least 10 days prior to the regular monthly meeting of the Commission, which falls on the second Friday of each month. Lessees are required to file individual bonds guaranteeing that they will faithfully carry out their lease or leases, ranging from $500 covering up to 240 acres, to $2000 for 2560 acres, or may file proper blanket bonds covering $5000.00 up to 10,000 acres and ranging up to $10,000 for over 25,000 acres. There is no limit to the

PUBLIC UTILITIES

Act 356, 1947, provides gas public utilities may condemn lands, easements, right of ways, gas royalties, dry natural gas leaseholds, and other property, and any and all interests therein (other than lands lying within a known mineral zone of iron ore, copper or coal) necessary for pipe line right of ways or for underground natural gas storage field or fields, located in strata down to and including the Marshall (shallow gas formation), but not lower. The Act prohibits one public utility from condemning the properties of another natural gas or public utility.

total acreage that any one lessee may lease, except no single lease shall contain over 2560 acres. Producers are required to file monthly production reports and no assignment of any lease or interest therein is valid, except after written approval of same by the Department of Conservation; no assignment will be approved where there are overriding royalty interests, unless such interests conform to the schedule in Rule 19 governing State leases, such overriding royalty ranging from ½nd to ⅛th, according to the daily production per well for each calendar month. Successful bidders are required to deposit ⅒th of the bonus bid on proven descriptions, together with the entire application fee, amounting to $1 per description; no operations shall be commenced until the lease is executed and delivered; normally, this takes about one month. The Department reserves the right to reject any and all bids. When leases are granted on lands where the state owns only the mineral rights, and does not own the surface, the lessee is required to reimburse the surface owner for all damages caused by his or its operations. Lessee is required to secure the written approval of the Department covering division order and sale contracts for the sale of oil or gas and copies of such sale contracts or division orders must be filed with the Supervisor. Lessee may surrender at any time all or any part of the leased premises, but must file and have recorded a proper release in the Register of Deeds' office of the county where the land is located, and also with the Department. The rules and regulations and any changes made from time to time become a part of all state leases, but any change in such regulations after the execution of any lease shall not operate to affect the term of the lease, rate of royalty, rate of rental or acreage leased, unless agreed to by both lessee and lessor. The special form of lease furnished by the Department covers the above and many other matters mentioned in the rules, and copies of said rules, together with the regulations governing the development and operation of private lands for oil and gas mining purposes, may all be obtained from the Supervisor's office at Lansing. The minimum annual rental is 50¢ per acre a year, payable quarterly in advance, except when the annual rental is $100 or less when it is payable annually. Each producing oil or gas well abates the rental on 80 designated acres chosen by the Supervisor. The lessee commences drilling within one year or pays an additional 50¢ rental. Royalties vary according to whether the well is in wildcat or prove territory. The gas royalty is one-eighth.

CHAPTER 17

Mississippi, 1938–1948

∼

Since the publication of the original Mississippi monograph, there has been a tremendous change in the oil and gas industry in the state. At that time production of gas was from only two fields and one of them, the Amory Gas Field, had been abandoned. The Jackson Field reached its peak production in the first six months of 1939, then declined sharply; now the field is expected to be depleted and abandoned for commercial use January 1, 1952.[1] There had been no commercial production of oil in Mississippi prior to the discovery of the Tinsley Field, Yazoo County, September 1939. The initial well in the Pickens Field, Madison and Yazoo Counties, was completed in March 1940, and that for the Cary Field, Sharkey County, in July 1941. No new finds were made in 1942, but each year thereafter witnessed expanded activity and increased production[2] of oil and gas. Latest reports put March 1948 production of gas condensate and oil at 3,678,674 barrels from 21 areas, and April 1948 gas production at 3,288,946 million cubic feet from four fields.[3] Two gas fields are not available for use due to lack of pipe line facilities and because unexpired producer's contracts furnish present commercial needs of distributors.

EDWARD L. BRUNINI, WRITER: II. M. Morse, W. H. Watkins, Greek L. Rice. (See app. B.)

[1] STATE OIL AND GAS BOARD, NATURAL GAS IN MISSISSIPPI (1946) prepared for a hearing of the Federal Power Commission.

[2] Technical data, details of locations, completions, and production are secured through the State Oil and Gas Board and the publications of geological services. The Dixie Geological Service, Tower Building, Jackson, Mississippi has published a weekly bulletin since April 24, 1941. The Mississippi Oil and Gas Engineering Committee, Tower Building, Jackson, publishes bulletins at intervals for use of its subscribers since March 1945.

[3] Production records are maintained in the office of the Supervisor of Oil and Gas, Jackson. These are the latest figures.

LEGISLATIVE HISTORY

Oil and gas conservation laws in Mississippi are embodied in Sections 6132 to 6179, *Mississippi Code Annotated*, 1942.[4] An amendment in 1946 required that all gas produced from a well and purchased or sold there be measured and reported to the agencies or subdivisions of the state in multiples of a standard cubic foot of gas, and defined the system of measurement. This Act made violations punishable after 1936 and except for the one change effected in 1946, the laws dealing with conservation were unchanged until the enactment of the present conservation Act at the 1948 session of the Mississippi legislature. At the regular sessions of the legislative assembly for 1940, 1942, 1944, and 1946 efforts were made to enact comprehensive conservancy statutes,[5] but all resulted in failure. Prior to the first producing well in the Tinsley Field, the need for laws and a specialized administrative board for enforcement was not generally thought—except within the industry—to be essential, and this attitude was justifiable. It might easily have seemed that the bills offered in 1938 and 1940 set up laws to meet contingencies having no immediate application to existing Mississippi conditions. But the real obstacle in the path of an exhaustive conservation law was a fear of production limitation and the encroachment upon private property rights incident to conservation. Most persistent opposition to legislation during the period since 1938 has been grounded upon an allegation that each so called conservation bill was in fact only a *proration bill*. The prevalence of this notion is demonstrated in a resolution approved by the 1940 legislature, following the discovery of the Tinsley Field in House Concurrent Resolution No. 25, which after acknowledging a fear of laws limiting production, resolves that no law "adversely affecting" the oil industry be adopted. In 1944 at the regular session an endeavor was made to curtail the existing power of the State Oil and Gas Board, weak as it was, by repealing Section 9 g.[6]

[4] Miss. Laws 1932, c. 117 as amended by Miss. Laws 1936, c. 305, Miss. Laws 1946, c. 345.

[5] SB No. 517, Miss. Leg. 1940, HB No. 36, S. B. No's. 93 and 153, Miss. Leg. 1942, HB No. 39, SB No. 24, Miss. Leg. 1944, SB No. 84, Miss. Leg. 1946.

[6] Miss. Laws 1932, c. 117 as amended by Miss. Laws 1936, c. 305. Senate Bill No. 268.

This measure died in the Senate Conservation Committee. On the other hand, H.B. No. 39, introduced in the same legislature, contained an attempt to broaden the definition of waste [7] then current, but this died in committee. The acts during this period varied in certain particulars. Their definitions of waste were broader than in the 1938 proposal, and the powers of the State Oil and Gas Board granted by S.B. No. 84 even more extensive than those given under H.B. No. 80. This law passed both the House and Senate in 1948 and was approved by the governor on April 9, 1948, effective 30 days from passage. There had been no comprehensive oil and gas conservation laws in Mississippi before H.B. No. 80 was adopted. Those previous enactments, found in Chapter 8 of the Mississippi Code of 1942, were entirely inadequate. The small amount of control they effected was accomplished only by the State Oil and Gas Board under Section 5 a, Chapter 117, Laws of Mississippi, 1932, which permitted adoption of rules and regulations "for the drilling, development, sinking, deepening, abandonment and operations of oil and gas wells as may be necessary to prevent the waste of such products and to protect the common source of supply." The efforts to control gas production failed. No real contest of any Board rule or regulation was made until an order dated August 11, 1947, relating to well spacing and productive allocation of gas in the Gwinville Field was unsuccessfully attacked.[8] From the agency's creation in 1932 until the appeal from this order, the operators in Mississippi were fairly well satisfied that their rights were not infringed. During this time the Board entered orders and made rules relating to the fields in Mississippi, which dealt with spacing and exceptions, permits for drilling, specifications of equipment used on wells, manner of well completion in detail, filing of reports, minimizing fire hazards, and a number of other matters.[9]

The Mississippi Supreme Court has held that the land owners' interest in oil and gas is based upon the absolute ownership

[7] Miss. Laws 1932, c. 117.

[8] State Oil and Gas Bd. v. Sup. Oil Co.,   Miss.   , 30 So. 2d 589, sug. error overr. 32 So. 2d 200 (1947).

[9] Conservation Laws, 1932, 1934, 1936, Affecting Oil and Gas, a collection of current laws, rules, orders and regulations in effect November, 1947. Copies may be obtained upon request addressed to the Oil and Gas Supervisor, New Capitol, Jackson, Mississippi.

theory.[10] The policy of the current Mississippi law as laid down in Section 1 is to encourage and promote production of petroleum natural resources, to protect public and private interests against waste, to safeguard and enforce coequal and correlative rights of owners in a common source or pool of oil and gas, and to obtain full development of resources as soon as practicable and consistent with waste prevention. The maximum efficient rate of production assigned owners is that needed to prevent waste; any intent to prorate or restrict production to market demand is negatived by the Act. This law does not ignore or override the absolute ownership of oil and gas by the land owner, but limits his use of these resources by preventing irreparable damage of the oil and gas supply to protect equal rights of adjoining land owners in a common pool or reservoir. Within certain limits the Act effectively carries out its purpose. The law embodies a broad and comprehensive definition of waste.[11] Section 6 confers jurisdiction upon the administrative agency to put into practice and enforce the Act and all other measures relating to the conservation of oil and gas, and grants the Board authority to make inquiries it thinks proper to determine whether waste over which it has power exists or is imminent. Subdivision c of this section contains the rights of the agency to make reasonable rules, regulations, and orders necessary in proper ad-

[10] Moss v. Jourdan, 129 Miss. 598, 92 So. 689 (1922), Stern v. Great. Sou. Land Co., 148 Miss 649, 114 So. 739 (1927). See 13 Miss. L. J. 427 (1941) and 18 Miss. L. J. 243 (1947).

[11] Waste, which is unlawful, means and includes: inefficient, excessive or improper use or dissipation of reservoir energy; locating, drilling or operating either oil or gas wells in a manner resulting in a reduction of the quantity of oil or gas ultimately to be recovered from any pool; inefficient storing of oil; operations causing unnecessary or excessive surface loss or destruction; abuse of correlative rights of landowners by reason of disproportionate or unratable withdrawals causing undue drainage between tracts or resulting in the recovery by one landowner of an unjust and inequitable share of the production from a pool; production causing unnecessary channeling of water or gas or both, or coning of water; operation with an inefficient gas-oil ratio; drowning of a stratum or part thereof with water; creation of unnecessary fire hazards; allowing the escape into the open air of an excessive amount of gas or an amount more than that necessary to the efficient operation of the well; permitting gas from a gas well to escape into the open air; and the use from any gas well of other than sour gas for the manufacture of carbon black unless the Board finds that no adequate pipeline connections are available otherwise to market gas. Subsurface waste of particular kinds is specifically prohibited although there is no general definition which will include underground waste. Economic waste is not specifically covered, and the act declares that no proration will be made on the sole basis of market demand.

ministration and enforcement, specifying without limiting purposes for which these rulings may be adopted.

Section 9 concerns the power of the Oil and Gas Board to regulate drilling, locating of wells, and spacing. Subdivision a permits the Board to control the drilling and location of wells for the prevention of reasonably avoidable net drainage from each developed unit, assuring the owner his equitable share of recoverable oil and gas in the pool. Drainage is defined as that unequalized by counter drainage. Subdivision b empowers the Board to establish a drilling unit or units for each pool to prevent waste as well as preserve the correlative rights of owners in a pool, and to avoid that risk incident to drilling excessive numbers of wells or the reduced recovery which comes from too few wells. Subdivision c permits the agency to grant exceptions to spacing patterns and drilling units. The unit referred to is an area for drilling purposes and the paragraph in effect accords the Board a right to fix spacing patterns.

The Act does not define water-oil or gas-oil ratios, but declares that waste includes the operation of any oil wells with an inefficient gas-oil ratio and the drowning with water of any stratum or part capable of producing oil or gas, and gives the Board sanction to halt drowning by water and control premature or irregular encroachment of water which tends or reduces total ultimate recovery. The Board requires operation of wells with efficient gas-oil ratios and fixes their limits by appropriate rule promulgation. Inefficient, excessive, or improper use or dissipation of reservoir energy is barred. The general waste prevention provisions are flexible enough to enable the Board to pass necessary rules for preserving reservoir energy. No power conferred upon the Board *requires* repressuring, cycling, recycling, or any action on the part of producers aimed toward secondary recovery of oil and gas. Section 6 c 10 assigns the Board the right to *regulate* voluntary secondary recovery methods, including introduction of gas, air, water, and other substances into producing formations. Sections 10 c and e hold the agency may *permit* cycling of gas, introduction of gas or substances into an oil or gas reservoir for repressuring, maintaining pressure, carrying out secondary recovery operations, and where reasonably necessary for these purposes, the pooling or integrating of separate tracts. Subparagraph e, Section 10, excludes these projects from the provisions of Mississippi law relative to trusts, monopolies, contracts and combinations in restraint of trade, where the action and agreements are first approved by the Board.

Specific jurisdiction is not conferred upon the agency to require salt water disposal processes. Section 6 c 1, which states that drilling, casing, and plugging of wells shall be done in a manner that prevents the intrusion of water into an oil or gas stratum, keeping fresh water supplies unpolluted by oil, gas or salt water, seems sufficiently broad to authorize the agency to make necessary rules for stopping damage of fresh water, oil or gas by a failure to properly dispose of salt water and contaminated brines.

Section 10 a calls for compulsory pooling (by order of the Board) of separately owned tracts of lands into established drilling units comprising 40 acres or less in area; any drilling unit of greater size is excluded from the terms of compulsory pooling procedure. No method exists to recover the proportionate expense of drilling from unwilling or non-consenting owners.[12]

Disposition of gas is controlled by subsections 8 through 10 of Section 4 k by including certain acts in the definition of waste. The escape of gas into the open air in excess of that amount required to efficiently drill or operate a well producing both oil and gas, together with blowing it in the open air from a gas well, are forbidden. The use of sweet gas from gas wells in the manufacture of carbon black (except where market conditions allow no adequate pipe line connection to dispose of it) is prohibited. This Act places no open flow restrictions upon gas wells, nor upon gas production. However, broad proration powers are given the agency to prevent waste as set out in the Act to insure the pool or field owners their fair share of oil and gas. The Board will, by rules and orders, regulate production where necessary for purposes enumerated in the law; but these are limited to an extent. Section 6 c grants authority to make rules, regulations, and orders, and subsection 12 provides for them where the purpose is oil and gas allocation and apportionment between pools, fields and separately

---

[12] The only property chargeable with a reasonable share of drilling expense is the production interest from the unitized tract that belongs to the unacquiescent parties. In the event of a dry hole, the operator has no right to charge these persons.

owned tracts of land. This subsection holds that the owners and producers of a field or pool discovery well are permitted to operate it without restriction while recovering drilling costs. Section 11 a allocates and apportions allowable pool production among producers where allowables are fixed at less than the pool's productive capabilities. Those parts which deal with proration are limited in Section 9 d by the requirement that production allotment be made on the basis of, and in proportion to, the areal content of the drilling unit for the pool producing horizon; so that each such unit has equal opportunity to make an equivalent daily allowable. Any special unit of lesser acreage than the norm is allowed to flow only in that proportion its spatial content bears to the regular unit; no well may operate in a manner resulting in waste or which is detrimental to the whole field. Where waste or detriment result, the quota is adjusted.

The present law does not establish prices for oil or gas at the well head, or halt exportation of natural gas from Mississippi, nor does it consider market demand. Section 1 in its declaration of policy states it is not the purpose of the law to require or permit proration or distribution of production on the basis of market demand.

The Mississippi Act differs from others by protecting each owner's coequal and correlative rights allowing him a fair and equitable share of production. The abuse of this right is waste. It is impossible to evaluate the effectiveness of the Act at present on any basis other than its probable usefulness. The industry as a whole, particularly the major integrated companies, and a majority of independents, though realizing the Act has imperfections, regard it as effective. In fact, it appears to be as good, if not better than any current law. Those who opposed passage are not satisfied, but it is accurate to state that any effective legislation would have been objectionable to them. The current Act is adequate except at a few points. General enforcement powers are given the State Oil and Gas Board to prevent waste and to protect owners' correlative rights in a common field or pool. Details of administration are left to the Board with a directive that they, by the promulgation of rules and orders, provide for the effectuation of the law's purpose. Some terms are not defined; this is not serious, since most if not all have generally accepted meanings. Criticism is directed at the law largely because it fails to provide compulsory pooling for drilling units of more than 40 acres, compulsory cycling, repressuring and unitization in the discretion of the Board. At the same time, this Act is a tremendous improvement over statutes prior to its approval. As a comprehensive measure it should prove workable.

Mississippi became a member of the Interstate Oil Compact Commission on April 29, 1948 through action of the governor, and authorized by the Mississippi legislature at the regular 1948 session.[13]

ADMINISTRATIVE HISTORY

The first administrative agency dealing with conservation of oil and gas in Mississippi was the State Oil and Gas Board, created by the legislature in 1932 and composed of the governor, the attorney general, the state land commissioner, and a state oil and gas supervisor, (a gubernatorial appointee with consent of the Senate for a period of four years). The supervisor was the only Board member devoting his entire time to the agency and the sole person required to do so under the Act. The post was filled either by a qualified petroleum engineer or geologist with five years or more experience in the development and production of oil and gas, or a practiced oil operator with five years work in the oil and gas fields. This agency continued in operation until May 1948. The first Board was seriously handicapped by having as members three persons whose time was occupied with other official duties. While it functioned efficiently, insufficient authority and the rapid expansion of the petroleum industry in Mississippi obstructed effective Board action.

The second and present State Oil and Gas Board was established by House Bill No. 80 of the regular session of 1948, approved by the governor April 9, 1948, becoming effective 30 days following passage. The agency is composed of five members, one appointed by the lieutenant governor for four years, one by the attorney general for four years (these persons must come one each from the two United States District Court Districts in Mississippi), and

[13] S. B. No. 33, Miss. Leg. 1948.

three members selected by the governor, one from each supreme court district, their terms being: first district, two years, second district, four years, and third district, six years. Upon expiration of the original terms of the governor's appointees, subsequent appointees will serve for six years. Additional qualifications required are: (1) no more than two members may come from any one Mississippi Supreme Court District, (2) each member must be a citizen of the United States, a resident of Mississippi, and a qualified elector of integrity with sound, nonpartisan judgment, (3) no Board member (or person employed by or connected with the Board in any manner) may be associated with any phase of the oil and gas industry in Mississippi or any other state. The agency selects from its number a chairman and a vice-chairman.

Under the Act's provisions the Board appoints as oil and gas supervisor, an experienced petroleum engineer or geologist with five or more years of experience in his profession. The supervisor is the executive officer of the Board and its ex-officio secretary, charged with enforcing the law and all rules and regulations promulgated by the Board. The supervisor, with the agency's concurrence, employs all necessary personnel. Presumably the Board and its supervisor will employ engineers, geologists and other professional groups; provision is made for their payment out of funds in the hands of the supervisor. No civil service proposal is designated for the employee selection, and it is not believed any such requirements will be made. Employees may not be hired on a permanent basis unless residents and qualified electors of Mississippi. No particular employees are listed in a table of organization. The Board selects an official reporter, sworn by and subject to its control and authority, in the same manner as official reporters for the circuit and chancery courts of the state are under the direction of the judiciary; the reporter's duties are those of court reporters insofar as the statutes are applicable. The attorney general is counsel for the Board, but permission is given to employ special attorneys in emergencies or unusual cases at the request of the attorney general. A majority of the five board members constitute a quorum; three of whom must concur in an affirmative vote before a rule, regulation, or order is made. The State Oil and Gas Board prescribes its procedural rules for hearings and furnishes copies of these without charge. Ten days notice of public hearing for making a rule, regulation, or order is given, except in cases of emergency, where the Board makes, changes, renews or extends rules, regulations, or orders without notice. Any emergency rule, regulation, or order remains in force no longer than fifteen days from effective date and expires when the same subject matter is regulated after due notice and hearing. Notice is given by publication in state and county newspapers of general circulation in the area in which the affected pools are found. Where the Board elects to issue notice by personal service, the notice is written by the supervisor or agency member and served in the same manner as are summonses in civil actions in the circuit ·courts of the state. All rules are permanently recorded, and copies must be furnished upon demand. In the past rules have been first mimeographed and periodically printed. The Board, its members, or the supervisor issues summonses to require witnesses' attendance and the production of books, papers and records. Witnesses give testimony on subjects properly before the Board, but are excused from criminal prosecution by reason of any transaction, matter or thing about which they are required to testify by the subpoena. The Board has no power to punish a failure to obey its orders to appear and testify. Rather the agency applies to a judge of the circuit court of the recusant's county, if a Mississippi resident; otherwise to a court in the county where the land in controversy or any portion lies. In the latter event the circuit court issues an attachment for the person compelling attendance and testification before the Board and production of requisite documents. The court has authority to require attendance and, by the Act's provisions, to punish for contempt any disobedience of subpoenas.

The State Oil and Gas Board is without power to levy fines or inflict punishment for infractions of its orders, rules, and regulations. The law makes the alteration, falsification, or concealment of reports or records required under the Act, or falsification of any statements by a person for the purpose of evasion, a misdemeanor punishable by fine not to exceed $500 a day or imprisonment for a term of not more than six months, or both. The Act subjects persons knowingly and willfully violating its terms, or the rules or orders of the Board to a penalty not to exceed $500 for each day, or for each act of disobedience, recoverable by suit at defendants' residence, or in the county where the infraction took place. In addition, the statute makes the knowing and willful aiding and abetting of any person in infringing a provision of the Act an offense, subject to those penalties provided for the principal offender. The Board has the authority to require certificates of compliance prior to permitting shipments of oil and gas. The Act prohibits the use, in any manner, of illegal oil, gas, or products and the agency seizes and condemns illegally produced oil, gas, and products.

Since no rules of procedure have been promulgated by the Board the methods of hearing are unknown. In the past legal rules of evidence and procedure have been followed generally, with hearings conducted in an informal fashion. Litigants were accorded the right to appear before the agency, personally or through attorneys, and to cross examine witnesses and present testimony in their own behalf. All hearings of the new administrative body are public, and it is believed the agency will not limit those rights of litigants existing under the old Board. At present the new organization is forming. Under Section 21 of the Act, which does away with pre-existing laws, provision is specifically made for continuing for six months from the law's effective date all rules, regulations, or orders previously made. The rules, regulations, or orders may be amended, rescinded, or superseded during the six months. The new Board has made no orders or rules; those issued and in effect are still in operation.[14] The new law has its own definition of waste and the agency cannot limit or broaden this definition. The commission regulates spacing. Rules of the old agency called for 40 acre spacing of oil wells and 320 acres for gas wells, with exceptions for cause shown. Under the new Act the group has no power to issue orders or pass rules requiring compulsory repressuring, cycling, recycling, secondary recovery, unit operation and cooperative development plans as to units greater than 40 acres. The Board has the jurisdiction to make orders and rules governing these actions by reason of their power to approve voluntary plans of the property owners in a field or pool. The new Board has ample authority to fix water-oil and gas-oil ratios, to preserve the reservoir energy by conserving

---

[14] See note 9 *supra.*

water and gas drive, to restrict the open flow of natural gas, to dispose of salt water and mineralized contaminated brines, and to require ratable taking of oil and gas. No right is given to regulate or establish well head prices for oil and gas, restrict exportation of natural gas from the state, or to prorate production or make orders based on market demand. The Board allows use of gas for the manufacture of carbon black where no adequate pipe line connections are available to market the gas; however, the utilization of other than sour gas for the manufacture of carbon black is generally prohibited. The agency controls well completion and requires proper plugging for abandoned wells.

Under the new law appeals by interested aggrieved persons from final rules, regulations, or orders of the Board (regardless of the amount involved) are made to the Circuit Court of the First Judicial District, Hinds County, Mississippi, or the circuit court of the county where all or a part of the appellant's property is situated. These appeals are disposed of promptly by the court as preference cases, at term time or in vacation. Appeal from the court decision follows normal appellate channels from the circuit to the supreme court. The appeal from the Board to the court selected is commenced by filing a petition with the agency 30 days from the date of the final rule, regulation or order. After petitioning the appellant files a bond for $500 to pay the costs. Notice is given the Board's reporter to transcribe his notes within ten days after the adjournment of the Board; the reporter is then given 30 days to so do and to file a transcript of the record with the Board from and after approval of the appeal bond. After the petition is docketed, the Board files as promptly as possible (in any event within 60 days after approval of the appeal bond) a copy of the petition and of the rule, regulation, or order appealed from with the transcript of the pleadings and evidence before it with the clerk of the circuit court. Supersedeas is not automatic, but authority is granted the judge of the court to award the writ after five days notice to the Board and a hearing. The order or judgment staying operation of any rule, regulation, or order of the Board must contain specific findings based upon evidence submitted the court that great or irreparable damage will result to the appellant if denied relief. The stay is ineffective until a supersedeas bond is executed, filed, and approved by the clerk of the court or judge, payable to the state, conditioned as directed.

JUDICIAL HISTORY

There has been little occasion for court review of the State Oil and Gas Board's activities. Records of appeal to the supreme court exist from only two orders of the agency; no rules, regulations, or orders have been set aside. The scope of court review is very limited, the court confining its action to inquiring "whether or not the decision of the Board is supported by substantial evidence or is arbitrary or capricious or beyond the power of the Board to make, or whether it violates any constitutional right of the complaining party." *California Company v. State Oil and Gas Board,*[15] decided under Section 5, Chapter 117, Mississippi Laws of 1932, provided for trial *de novo* on appeal to the circuit court. The Supreme Court of Mississippi declared a complete trial *de novo*, ignoring entirely matters placed before the Oil and Gas Board, would be unconstitutional, as calling for legislative action on the part of the court substituting its opinion for that of the agency, and for this reason disregarded the *de novo* portions of the original Act. The transcript can be used, but is not the sole source of matter examined upon appeal, and in any case the court is not authorized to substitute its opinion on completely different facts from those shown the Board. The supreme court refused to state how the complainant informs the court of facts upon which the Board acted other than to say that the court could not hear evidence different than that presented to the Board or substitute its findings or judgment in the premises for the tribunal's from which appeal was taken. Judge Griffith dissenting, said that the court should announce it would not permit duplication of effort in the lower court and the inferior tribunal, nor would it allow reception of secondary and inferior evidence, but rather would rely upon the transcript as made before the Board. *State Oil and Gas Board v. Superior Oil Company,*[16] was an appeal from an order of the Board establishing a 320 acre spacing pattern

[15] 200 Miss. 824, 27 So. 2d 542 (1946) sug. error overr. 200 Miss. 847, 28 So. 2d 120 (1946).
[16] Miss. , 30 So. 2d 589 (1947) sug. error overr. Miss. , 32 So. 2d 200 (1947).

in the Gwinville Gas Field, Jefferson Davis County. The supreme court held that the lower court had no jurisdiction as a timely appeal was not taken. The appellant had failed to appeal within ten days, but had petitioned the Board asking it to review and revoke its earlier ruling, and then attempted to appeal from the refusal to re-hear and reconsider the order on substantially the same evidence as before. The court said there was no need that the agency re-examine its former decision upon the same evidence, and an appeal from a refusal to so do did not comply with the requirement as to time.

On appeal to the circuit court under the terms of the new Act no trial *de novo* is specified, rather it provides for a hearing "on the record, including a transcript of pleadings and testimony, both oral and documentary, filed and heard before the Board." Whether the Supreme Court of Mississippi will limit the review on appeal to the record before the Board is uncertain. Section 12, providing for further appeal from the lower court to the supreme court, adopts those provisions of law respecting notice to the reporter and the allowance of bills of exception in force at the time of the Act's passage or thereafter, with respect to like petitions. It is difficult to determine whether the Act is intended to limit evidence on appeal, as it appears there would be no need for bills of exception if review by the lower court is limited to the record made before the Board.

In discussing judicial review of the action of an administrative agency in Mississippi, Professor Wade, considering the *California Company* decision and the additional case of *Dixie Greyhound Lines, Inc. v. Mississippi Public Service Commission* [17] suggests that it may be indicated that the court is adopting the test there used to determine whether to set aside a verdict and grant a new trial.[18] A portion of the controlling opinion in the case of *Tri-State Transit Company v. Gulf Transport Company* [19] seems to move toward this general end. In summarizing the court had this to say: "Having in view then the testimony disclosed by the record, the rules under which this Court has announced it will or will not disturb the finding of the Commission, the powers and duties of the

---

[17] 190 Miss. 704, 200 So. 579, 1 So. 2d 489 (1941).
[18] 18 Miss. L. J. 243, 261–266 (1947).
[19]   Miss.   , 29 So. 2d 825 (1947).

Commission, and the public policy of the State, we think it cannot be said that the action of the Commission in this case was without substantial evidence to support it, or that such action was capricious and arbitrary." And at a later point the court repeated it should not substitute its judgment for that of the Commission and reverse the action "unless it is beyond the powers of the commission, or not supported by substantial evidence, or is arbitrary or capricious." The same general language has been used by the court in all cases noted, and the Court admitted in the *Tri-State Transit* case that it entered into a review of all the testimony made before the Public Service Commission to evaluate the action taken by the Commission in the light of the matters submitted to it.

Two separate and distinct methods of enforcement are provided. The first of these is Section 13, which authorizes an injunction upon application of the Board to the chancery court of the county of defendant's residence, or in the county where the violation of the Act, any rule, regulation, or order of the Board occurs, to restrain continuance of or carrying out of the threatened infraction. In the event the Board fails to bring suit after ten days notice of a violation or threatened infraction and a request to sue, the moving person may bring suit. The second is Section 19, where seizure and sale of any illegal oil, gas, or product as defined in the Act is authorized. After seizure and sale the money received is applied to payment of costs of the case and to reimburse any intervening interested royalty owner for his share, provided he establishes his title, and the remaining sums are paid the state oil and gas fund. This seizure and sale is made under a proceeding instituted in the circuit court of the county where the contraband is found, or maintained in connection with a suit or cross-action for an injunction or penalty which relates to prohibited transactions involving illegal oil, gas, or products. Sale is conducted in the manner provided for sales of personal property under execution. The right of action, which a royalty owner, lien holder, or other claimant has because of a forfeiture of illegal oil, gas, or product against the person whose action resulted in the loss, is preserved.

No attack upon any conservation measure of the state has reached the Supreme Court of Mississippi or the federal courts involving the constitutional or statutory power of the state to enact measures for the purpose of oil and gas conservation. The theory of conservation in general appears to have been accepted by oil and gas operators as a proper function of the state, and the delegations of authority by the legislature to the State Oil and Gas Board under the new enactment are much more extensive than those held by the old agency. There is no way to predict if this fact will result in increased litigation. The only serious attack (which was timely) made against the previous action of the Board in attempting to prorate gas production from the Jackson Gas Field under the old laws resulted in the agency agreeing to a permanent injunction restraining enforcement of its order. The new Act has a broader foundation for enforcement of an order of this type, and similar action of the Board would possibly be sustained if contested.

CHAPTER 18

Missouri, 1948 [1]

The slight current production within the State of Missouri has not warranted the adoption of any oil and gas conservation legislation in that jurisdiction. In 1938 it was thought that sufficient oil and gas were about to be discovered in the Forest City basin in northwest Missouri to make it worthwhile to establish such laws. A preliminary draft was prepared for presentation to the legislature, in order that any oil or gas encountered might be preserved through good conservation practice. The introduction of this statute was deferred pending determination of the tests and when oil was not discovered, no further attempt was made to present the enactment. Since then no steps have been taken toward adopting a conservation statute in Missouri, and in the words of a state official, "nor has there appeared to be any justification for its introduction."

Possible membership in the Interstate Compact to Conserve Oil and Gas has been considered, but due to the limited production in Missouri it has not been deemed advisable to join this effort.

There have been no judicial decisions in Missouri dealing with the conservation of oil and gas.

BLAKELY M. MURPHY, WRITER. (See app. B.)

[1] The Committee on Special Publications, Section of Mineral Law, requested Lester G. Seacat, Esq., Jefferson City, Missouri, to undertake the preparation of a paper on Missouri. He enlisted the services of Edward Clark, State Geologist, Rolla, and Prof. H. H. Lesar, Law School, Univ. of Missouri, Columbia, in examining the situation. From their reports and his investigation it was concluded that insufficient material existed to prepare a paper of the scale contemplated by the Committee. Accordingly Mr. Seacat submitted his research to that group for its use. The work of Messrs. Seacat and Clark and Prof. Lesar is acknowledged and it has been the partial basis of this short statement.

CHAPTER 19

Montana, 1913–1948

Montana oil and gas production dates from 1913 with the discovery of natural gas near Hardin in Big Horn County. Thereafter natural gas discoveries were made at widely separated areas, as the Elk Basin Oil and Gas Field on the Montana-Wyoming state line. The industry assumed little importance in the state until the 1920 discovery of the Cat Creek Oil Field in central Montana. Though the initial well was of slight commercial importance, it was followed by very productive wells located principally on land included in Federal Government prospecting permits. About that time the Department of the Interior issued drilling, operating and producing regulations applicable to wells, leases and permits in which the United States had an interest thus affecting two-thirds of the pre-1940 wells drilled at the Cat Creek Pool. In 1922 crude oil was found in the Kevin-Sunburst area in Toole County on a large geological structure containing approximately 88,000 acres. After this development extensive wildcatting resulted in the location of oil and natural gas in divergent areas east of the Rocky Mountains. Steady development followed until by 1947 more than 850,000,000 barrels of oil and 31,000,000,000 cubic feet of natural gas had been produced. Widespread prospecting and development work continues unabated in Montana.

OIL AND GAS CONSERVATION LEGISLATION

The problem of conservation legislation in Montana is complicated by the fact that oil and gas are produced from five classes of land ownership: (1) public lands owned by the United States;

E. K. CHEADLE, WRITER: J. E. Hupp, G. S. Frary, R. P. Jackson, Advisers. (See app. B.)

(2) Indian reservation lands (allotted to Indians who are wards of the Federal Government, the Secretary of the Interior or held by tribal governments subject to disposition with the approval of the Secretary); (3) Fee lands; (4) State lands included in grants from the United States for the use, support or benefit of state schools and institutions; and (5) Railroad lands granted by the United States as bonuses for construction of transcontinental railroads. Legislation first aimed at conservation of oil and gas was enacted in 1917 requiring an operator before drilling into oil or gas bearing rock to case a well to prevent surface or fresh water from penetrating oil and gas formations, and to exclude salt water from intruding oil and gas strata.[1] It provided for the filling of wells to be abandoned. In 1921 an enactment of the legislature[2] declared as waste and unlawful the use, consumption or burning of gas from gas wells (or borings from which natural gas is produced) for the purpose of manufacturing carbon black, without its heat being fully and actually used for manufacturing or domestic purposes. This was declared unconstitutional by the state supreme court.[3] Another 1921 law required that upon the abandonment of a prospective oil or gas well an operator file with a county clerk a sworn statement setting out the well's location and the manner in which it had been plugged.[4] In addition during this 1921 session the Board of Railroad Commissioners of Montana was authorized to make rules and regulations (general or particular in nature) to prevent waste of oil, and regulate field operations dangerous to life or property.[5] Legislation seriously attempting the conservation of oil and gas originated in the 1925 session, which provided that the Board of Railroad Commissioners prescribe and enforce rules and regulations governing drilling, casing and abandonment of oil and gas wells and the waste of oil and gas in Montana, except on certain public lands.[6] This enactment repealed prior acts adopted in 1917

---

[1] Mont. Laws 1917, c. 43; Mont. Rev. Code § 3547–3549 (1921). Repealed by Mont. Laws 1925, c. 56; Mont. Rev. Codes Ann. § 3552.1–3552.4 (1925).

[2] Mont. Laws 1921, c. 125; Mont. Rev. Code § 3550–3552 (1921).

[3] Gas Products Co. v. Rankin, Att'y Gen., 63 Mont. 372, 207 Pac. 993 (1922).

[4] Mont. Laws 1921, c. 244; Mont. Rev. Code § 3553–3554 (1921). Repealed by Mont. Laws 1925, c. 56; Mont. Rev. Codes Ann. § 3552.1–3552.4 (1925).

[5] Mont. Laws Ex. Sess. 1921, c. 8; Mont. Rev. Codes Ann. § 3552.1–3552.4 (1935).

[6] Mont. Laws 1925, c. 56; Mont. Rev. Codes Ann. § 3552.1–3552.4 (1935). This legislation was proposed by a resolution of the Rocky Mountain Oil and Gas

and 1921. The extraordinary session of the 1933 legislature created an Oil Conservation Board prescribing its duties and authority.[7] Upon complaint to this Board by a producer of crude
petroleum, or by the agency itself, where it appears waste—as defined in the Code of Fair Competition for the Petroleum Industry
—is committed, or that violations of the rules, regulations or orders
of the Board occur, hearings are held in each of the counties where
the violation or waste takes place.[8] If at the hearing the Board finds

Association in 1924 and supported by the legislative committee of the Association,
members of which testified in its support, interviewed members of the Montana
Legislature and arranged publicity. The bill was drafted by a committee headed by
A. Judson Findlay. Because of lack of knowledge of oil and gas conservation law
precedents the Committee's draft was based on the Federal Oil and Gas Leasing
Act of February 25th, 1920, 41 Stat. 437, 30 USC § 181 et seq. (1940).

[7] Mont. Laws Ex. Sess. 1933, c. 18; MONT. REV. CODES ANN. § 3554.1–3554.19
(1935). This legislation received the recognition of the then Governor of Montana,
and the approval of the Attorney General, necessary for its consideration in an extraordinary session. The bill was supported by members of the Independent Petroleum Association, Montana Division, and by the representatives of some of the large
independent operators. An impelling reason for passage was the inclusion of the oil
and gas regulatory sections in the National Industrial Recovery Act of 1933 (§ 9a,
9b, and 9c, Act of June 16th, 1933, 48 STAT. 195 (1933)) and in the Code of Fair
Competition for the Petroleum Industry, together with the fear that lack of an adequate state oil conservation law would expose the industry to regulation, allocation
of production, etc., by agencies under the National Industrial Recovery Administration. The life of the regulatory body was coterminous with that of the Code of Fair
Competition for the Petroleum Industry, this Code being approved by President
F. D. Roosevelt in Exec. Order No. 6256 (1933). Invalidation occurred in the
Amazon Petroleum Corp. v. Ryan, 293 U.S. 388 (1935) and the Panama Refining
Co. v. Ryan, 293 U.S. 388 (1935) cases. Mont. Laws 1935, c. 136; MONT. REV.
CODES ANN. § 3554.2 (1935) amended the previous enactment to provide for a permanent administrative board to take the place of the agency whose power expired
with the invalidation of the National Industrial Recovery Administration authority
over petroleum. Waste prevention was not an important issue, the main problem
being one of marketing and producing in competition with products imported from
other states. Production control was not regarded as needful to prevent waste; neither was there any economic over supply. The enactment of this legislation was effective in relieving Montana producers of apprehension concerning the importation
of oil and federal control. In view of the large number of operators active in Montana, the highly competitive nature of exploration and production, and, until 1933,
the lack of consistent efficient supervision or regulation of drilling or producing there
were few complaints of wastage since 1925. The most prolific oil pools in Montana
are "low pressure" pools with respect to natural oil-gas production ratios and the
operators were not confronted with difficult production problems involving waste.
The 1933 conservation act while not resulting in important changes in production
practice did assure operators and investors that the state and its governing officials
were interested in maintaining the oil industry on a sound producing basis, and were
prepared to exercise a degree of regulatory control where necessary in the public interest.

[8] Notice of hearing must be published, posted or served five days prior to the date
of hearing. Each member and the designated representatives of the Board conduct

waste is committed or that its rules or orders are violated, an order enters requiring the offender to desist within a specified time. In the event of failure to comply the agency files a complaint in equity —in the name of the State of Montana—against the violator in the district court of the county wherein the affected property is situated or the offense occurs to restrain violation and compel obedience. The court in enjoining the defendant may find the extent of his violation and enter judgment accordingly. If the order of the Board be invalid, the court dismisses the action without prejudice to the right of the Board to hold hearings anew and make orders. No restraining order issues ex parte. The proceedings are governed by the Montana Code of Civil Procedure. Pending an appeal no temporary or permanent injunction shall be dissolved or stayed upon the giving of bond or otherwise. The Act specifically states it shall not be construed to derogate any powers of the Board of Railroad Commissioners or of the Public Service Commission.

STATE-OWNED LANDS

Present state land leasing acts require that state oil and gas leases be subject to these conditions: a lessee conducting explorations or operations must use reasonable precautions to prevent waste of oil and gas, and to halt intrusion of water through wells drilled to oil or gas sands thus preventing their destruction or injury. A violation constitutes grounds for the forfeiture of the lease after hearing by the State Board of Land Commissioners.[9] The statute further says that nothing in the act governing leases of state land prevents the Board of Land Commissioners from entering into agreements for the pooling of oil or gas acreage for unit operations, the apportionment of oil or gas royalties on an acreage or other equitable basis, or from modifying existing and future leases in accordance with pooling agreements and unit plans of operation;[10] this section has been construed and upheld in the Montana courts.[11] Like enact-

hearings, make investigations, take testimony at such sessions and have the power to administer oaths, take affidavits and issue subpoenas for the attendance of witnesses.

[9] MONT. REV. CODES ANN. § 1882.1 (1935) as amended by Mont. Laws 1947, c. 261.

[10] MONT. REV. CODES ANN. § 1882.2 (1935) as amended by Mont. Laws 1945, c. 128.

[11] Toomey v. State Board of Land Com'rs., 106 Mont. 547, 81 P2d 407, (1938).

ments give commissioners of Montana counties acquiring tax title property powers identical with those exercised by the Board of Land Commissioners concerning pooling and unit operation. The county commissioners may modify present and future leases of such lands with respect to rentals, drilling penalties and royalties in accord with pooling agreements and unit plans of operation, provided the county royalties are not changed from those fixed in the lease.[12]

INTERSTATE COMPACT TO CONSERVE OIL AND GAS

In 1945 the state legislature authorized and directed the governor to join the Interstate Compact to Conserve Oil and Gas.[13] The chief executive is empowered to execute agreements for the extension of the compact's expiration date, determine if and when it shall be for the best interest of Montana to withdraw, and take steps effecting such a withdrawal. The governor is the official representative of Montana on the Interstate Oil Compact Commission, having authority to appoint a representative to act for him. The law does not grant the state's representative in private or official capacity or the Interstate Oil Compact Commission power to allocate, regulate or control oil or gas production or refined products in the state or its markets. Neither does the enactment surrender to the Federal Government rights over production, sale or transportation of oil, gas or refined products in Montana and nothing therein binds or obligates the state to enact, amend or alter legislation affecting the oil or gas industry in the state.

PROVISION OF CONSERVATION LAWS

Montana statutes make no specific provision for repressuring, cycling, recycling, maintenance of water-oil and gas-oil ratios, ratable taking of gas, secondary recovery of oil and gas, or the preservation of reservoir energy; nor do particular provisions regulate disposal of salt water and contaminated brines, open flow restric-

[12] Mont. Laws 1945, c. 48.
[13] Mont. Laws 1945, c. 121.

tions, establishment of well head prices, restrictions on the use of gas for carbon black manufacture, limitations upon export of natural gas from the state or market demand. These matters might be partially controlled under general terms of the existing enactments to enforce conservation and prevent waste as these terms are understood in Montana.

LEGISLATIVE PROPOSALS

Two unsuccessful attempts have been made to modify or replace the conservation statutes. In 1937 the Drumheller bill [14] introduced into the state Senate, created a commission akin to the present Oil Conservation Board to be known as the Petroleum Commission of the State of Montana. Without defining waste, the bill declared the production of crude petroleum and natural gas under conditions and in amounts constituting or resulting in waste was opposed to public interest and prohibited. This commission, for the purpose of conserving natural resources of Montana and to prevent waste through negligent and harmful methods of operations, was directed to prescribe and enforce rules and regulations governing drilling, casing, operating and abandonment of oil and gas wells and the prevention of waste of oil and gas except upon public lands in accord with the rules and regulations of the United States Bureau of Mines or the Secretary of the Interior. Persons and corporations drilling or operating oil or gas wells upon patented or state land were to comply with all rules and regulations, file logs of wells, make reports and case, control or plug wells. Section 12 required that before the 20th day of each month, purchasers of Montana produced crude oil or natural gas (for local or export consumption, or for storage and refining of oil within the state) must file with the commission requirements for the succeeding month, designating the pool within the state or the source without the state from which they desired to purchase their needs. Thereafter the commission allocated state producers that monthly quantity of petroleum and natural gas which they might produce and market. Pipe lines except those within a lease were made common carriers required to connect and receive crude petroleum from

[14] SB No. 66.

producers tributary to the line and physically join with other lines to equitably distribute purchases of oil from given pools. This bill was strenuously fought by the industry principally because of Section 12, and under such opposition the author of the proposal withdrew his support; the bill was dropped upon a recommendation of the Montana Senate Committee on Oils and Leases. In 1947 a comprehensive oil and gas conservation bill was offered in the Montana House of Representatives [15] creating a State Oil and Gas Conservation Board of five gubernatorially appointed members subject to removal by the governor at any time for cause. The board was granted exclusive jurisdiction over regulation and enforcement of conservation and waste prevention. It was a well considered offering with adequate provisions, a step forward in adopting modern concepts of conservation and efficient oil and gas recovery. A great deal of study went into its drafting through the efforts of the Secretary of the Oil Conservation Board and a few industry representatives. Although there was no organized force against the bill, an adverse committee report killed it, largely because no thorough preparation had been made for presenting the bill to the legislature.

ADMINISTRATIVE HISTORY

Today two agencies in Montana share the administration and enforcement of conservation statutes—the State Board of Railroad Commissioners and the Montana Oil Conservation Board. Original powers of the Commissioners encompassed the establishment of rates for intrastate carriers. These early concepts of the Commissioners' authority now have been extended to those matters normally considered to include the work of a public service commission charged with the regulation of public utilities. The Commissioners are elective officials, who receive a salary of $4200 a year. General powers of conservation enforcement were given the Commission in 1921 and enlarged in 1925, due to a lack of a suitable agency for oil control in Montana. Printed regulations adopted in 1941 [16] set out the responsibilities of the Commission in the con-

[15] Sub. HB No. 399.
[16] Board of Railroad Commissioners Montana. Operating Regulations, Oil and Gas Well Division, (1941).

trol of conservation and delegate these duties to two supervisors, employed jointly with the Oil Conservation Board. The supervisors have the right to prescribe and enforce measures to prevent waste of oil and gas, damages to oil, gas or water formations, injury to life and property, economic waste and issue instructions to effectuate their purposes. Among the powers delegated to the supervisors is that requiring wells drilled on state and private lands be spaced in accord with the Department of the Interior rules; such authority is questionable, but success in cooperation has been obtained.

Five members—appointed by the governor and removable by him at will—constitute the membership of the Montana Oil Conservation Board. Terms of office are two years. Requirements for membership are that they be bona fide residents of Montana for a year, and that at least four members be Montana producers of crude petroleum. No compensation is allowed other than expenses. As need arises the Board employs a secretary, engineers, geologists and attorneys. Money for its operation is derived from a privilege and license tax of ¼th cent levied upon each barrel of oil produced, saved, marketed or stored in Montana. Funds collected under this tax are deposited in the oil and gas conservation fund of Montana, and expenditures limited to needs of the Board. Powers of the Board extend to that general control, regulation and supervision necessary to govern the operation of wells, conservation, transportation and storage of petroleum for effectively carrying out the laws, regulations and orders. The agency may determine what wells are stripper wells, make orders to protect them, and provide their production allocation. The Board may compel the filing of informational reports from producers, transporters, dealers and storers of petroleum, or act as a regulatory body for the allocation and regulation of crude petroleum and storage under the Code of Fair Competition. Sworn statements are required from producers and operators relative to production of oil wells under their control. Right to inspect wells, measure, test or gauge production is given the administrative body.

Initial rules of the Oil Conservation Board adopted in 1934 [17] provide that the general effect of the act creating the body is to

[17] Oil Conservation Board. Regulations. Jan. 22, 1934.

supplement and strengthen those enactments previously adopted with relation to production, storage and transportation of oil; the act does not repeal or supplant existing laws, rules or regulations and is not to be construed in a manner to curtail, extend or modify powers and duties assigned the Board of Railroad Commissioners. Principal requirements of the rules concern the periodic filing of reports by crude producers, transporters and refiners. Amendments adopted later in 1934 defined stripper and isolated wells.[18] Amendments to the definition of a stripper well came later the same year.[19] A revised set of rules and regulations issued out in 1943.[20] Promulgation of rules, regulations and orders by the Railroad Commissioners or the Oil Board is on an informal basis coming usually after conferences with industry representatives. Interested parties appear before either agency, make their requests, present testimony and file briefs. There are no restrictions upon the rights of appearance. Production of evidence is not held to those strict rules applicable in courts of law.

In the exercise of their concurrent functions the present conservation agencies cooperate well. Educational activities among operators, cooperation with federal commissions and the Interstate Oil Compact Commission highlight the joint programs. The industry feels the Board (or a like agency) should be given exclusive authority over the regulation and enforcement of conservation, and this feeling is strengthened by a conviction that the body governing the industry should be removed from possible political influence.

JUDICIAL HISTORY

The Montana supreme court and the state inferior courts have not been called upon to interpret or determine the validity of present oil and gas conservation laws, the adopted rules and regulations of the administrative boards, or the actions of these regulatory agencies. An Act—indirectly affecting oil and gas conservation—

[18] Oil Conservation Board. Regulations, Mar. 1, 1934.
[19] Oil Conservation Board. Regulations. Sept. 20, 1934. Jackson, Stripper Wells in Montana, I INTERSTATE OIL COMPACT Q. BULL. 62 (1942) states: In 1942 73% of the wells in Montana were stripper wells. Eight refineries out of a total of seventeen in operation in 1942 could not have operated without the stripper well supply.
[20] Oil Conservation Board. Revised Regulations. Sept. 30, 1943.

permitting the Board of Land Commissioners to agree to pool acreage for unit operation and apportion royalties on an acreage or other equitable basis, has been sustained as not in conflict with the enabling Act or the Montana constitution.[21]

CONCLUSION

It is felt that results under the conservation laws now in effect have been adequate. It may be conceded, however, that this situation is not due entirely to the competence of such laws and of their enforcement. Oil and gas operations, development and producing practice in Montana have been efficient and conducted with a view to obtaining a maximum ultimate recovery and waste prevention. This condition may not continue in the future if the present intensive development campaign results in materially increased production from deeper pools with characteristics dissimilar from those now producing, and current high prices continue. Today's satisfactory conservation practices have discouraged wasteful exploitation of Montana resources, and have contributed to the financial prosperity of land owners, operators and state educational institutions. Conservation accomplishments in Montana have been comparatively good; extant statutory law, ostensibly adequate, is deficient. The state conservation program would be strengthened by modification of the statutes to provide: (1) delegation of regulatory power to one agency having no overlapping concurrent powers and duties; (2) a definition of waste; (3) provisions and enumerations of exact practices to prevent waste and promote conservation; and (4) adequate funds for regulation.

[21] See note 11 *supra*.

CHAPTER 20

Nebraska, 1939–1948

Nebraska's first commercial oil well was drilled about three miles west of Falls City [1] in 1939, before Nebraska had a law governing procedures for drilling and producing oil or gas. In 1941 the state legislature provided that a well operator must exclude water from intruding oil or gas bearing strata before abandonment, file notice of intent to abandon with the State Geologist and plug the well according to his regulations.[2] This law is on the statute books and that is all that can be said for it. Experienced contractors and operators plug and abandon wells in accordance with recognized practices, still too many irresponsible operators pull the well casing and go off, or if the test does not justify running pipe, simply leave the hole. Of voluntary conservation, not much has been accomplished either. One company interested in the Falls City Field attempted to obtain consent of all operators in that area for a voluntary working arrangement, however, due to the refusal of one lease owner nothing came of it. The State Geologist directs the Division of Conservation and Survey at the University of Nebraska.[3] Duties of this division are to gather and correlate information on the natural resources of Nebraska. The State Geologist is required to have specimens of strata penetrated in test wells drilled for oil, gas or other purposes; no penalty attaches for refusal to submit these samples.

Four pools were developed near Falls City; two have been profitable. Today there is no further oil and no gas production in the state.[4] A more effective agency is needed to deal with oil and gas

ARCHIBALD J. WEAVER, WRITER; John H. Wiltse, Adviser. (See app. B.)

[1] WRITERS PROGRAM NEB., THE SEARCH FOR OIL IN NEBRASKA (1942).

[2] Neb. Laws 1941, c. 118; NEB. REV. STAT. § 57–213–57–217 (1943).

[3] Neb. Laws 1921, c. 16; NEB. REV. STAT. § 85–163–85–165 (1943).

[4] Reed, *Stripper Wells in Nebraska*, I INTERSTATE OIL COMPACT Q. BULL. 64 (1942). Total production to 1942 was 1.6 million bbls. Reserves were said to be .5 million bbls.

exploration and production and to properly enforce the present plugging law. Once the possibility of enacting a comprehensive conservation law was considerably discussed, but the time was not ripe. Serious thought should be given the introduction of such a measure at the January 1949 session of the Nebraska legislature.

CHAPTER 21

New Mexico, 1938–1948

During the ten years since Hiram M. Dow reported in 1938 for New Mexico, developments of legal significance in the conservation of oil and gas have been almost exclusively in the administrative as distinguished from the legislative and judicial fields. The basic Oil and Gas Conservation Act [1] adopted in 1935 has been amended but once—to require ratable purchase of oil,[2] and Mr. Dow's statement that neither the Act nor any order of the Commission had been challenged in the courts remains true to 1948.

The dearth of legislative and judicial development does not indicate a decrease in the importance of the oil industry in New Mexico in the last decade or in the production of oil and gas. In 1937 the state produced 38,484,630 barrels of oil, and by 1947 annual production had risen to 40,926,163 barrels, while New Mexico's position among the oil producing states was reduced from sixth to seventh by the increase in production in Wyoming, where there is no proration. During the period New Mexico's fields included in the monthly proration schedule grew to a total of 81 with 5080 oil wells. The San Juan Basin in northwestern New Mexico now has 97 wells, and since their output is consumed locally, they are not included in the proration schedules which cover all other state fields.

THE LEGISLATIVE HISTORY

The single amendment to the 1935 Oil and Gas Conservation Act was the Ratable Purchase of Oil Act [3] introduced in the 1941

ROSSER LYNN MALONE JR., WRITER; H. M. Dow, J. O. Seth, Advisers; (See app. B.)
[1] N.M. Laws 1935, c. 72; N.M. STAT. ANN. c. 69, art. 2 (1941).
[2] N.M. Laws 1941, c. 166; N.M. STAT. ANN. § 69–203 et seq. (1941).
[3] Ibid.

session of the legislature by Representative Don G. McCormick from New Mexico's principal oil producing section—Lea County. The Act amends the definition of waste in the basic Conservation Act to include non-ratable purchase or taking of crude petroleum oil. Its stated purpose is to insure each producer an opportunity to produce his just and equitable share of the oil in a reservoir and to prevent discrimination in the purchase of oil between the fields in the state. The Act empowers the Commission to enforce its provisions and to determine the extension of a carrier's pipe line system which will be required to effect a ratable purchase of oil. Violation of the statute or order of the Commission is punishable by a fine of not more than $1000 for each infraction, and specifies that each day of violation constitutes a separate offense. The Act expressly provides that it shall become an integral part of the Oil Conservation Act adopted in 1935, and makes all provisions of that legislation applicable to its administration and enforcement. The constitutionality of this section may be subject to question, but to date it has not been attacked.

Adoption of the ratable purchasing measure was a logical outgrowth of crude oil marketing conditions existing in the state in 1940. The allowable was 32 barrels for a 40 acre proration unit; even then the market for New Mexico crude was unable to absorb the quantity of oil offered. Eddy County, New Mexico, "the Independent's Paradise," had several new fields—principally Loco Hills, Square Lakes and Anderson—each with a large number of small operators who found upon completion of their wells that pipe line connections were unavailable. Charges of discriminatory purchase of oil, particularly at Anderson, were heard frequently. Pressure was brought upon the Commission to remedy the evil and finally became so great that on October 30, 1940 the agency wrote the Lea County Operators Committee (on which all the purchasing companies operating in the state were represented) pointing out the lack of pipe line connections and the inadequacy of the market available to producers. Attention was directed to the fact that New Mexico had at that time the lowest allowable in the country (only $8/10$ths barrel an acre) and that the Commission had held this amount to a minimum to prevent waste. In strong language the agency urged cooperation to remedy the situation and taking advantage of its only available weapon, threatened a substantial cut in allowable unless the matter be corrected. This letter was dispatched by the Operators Committee to all its members, soliciting their cooperation to end the difficulties.

The communication apparently resulted in little improvement, and as an aftermath two bills respectively requiring ratable purchase of oil and gas were introduced in the 1941 legislature. Eddy County operators attended the legislative hearings and urged action. State officials were sympathetic and in the absence of opposition from the oil purchasing companies the oil legislation passed.[4] The ratable gas purchase bill contained regulatory provisions governing gas production. It met strong opposition. The two gas purchasing companies (the principal outlet for gas) actively fought the legislation, and it was killed in the House of Representatives. Similar bills introduced in the 1943 and 1945 assemblies of the legislative body met the same fate. The fact that New Mexico—a state with extensive natural gas resources—has not enacted a statute dealing with purchasing, production and marketing of natural gas, other than its basic oil law, has been the subject of comment on a number of occasions and resulted in embarrassment to state representatives supporting amendment of the Federal Power Commission Act on the premise that regulation of gas production is a state right and responsibility.

During the session of the 1947 legislature, John E. Miles, State Land Commissioner and a member of the Oil Conservation Commission, sought to obtain a natural gas statute. He called meetings of state and industry representatives to consider the need for such an enactment, but after several discussions the group decided insufficient time remained for the preparation and passage of an act at that legislative session. In the course of the meetings a statement was made that the industry would prepare and submit a proposal in advance of the convening of the nineteenth assembly of the legislature, January 1949; it is anticipated that natural gas legislation will be introduced and there adopted, with or without industry approval.

The Oil Conservation Commission of New Mexico, as created by the basic Act of 1935,[5] consists of the governor, the state land

[4] *Ibid.*
[5] *Id.* § 69–204.

commissioner, and the state geologist, each ex-officio a member of the agency. The governor may appoint a "practical oil man, a resident of this State, to serve in the place and stead of the Governor as a member of the said Commission," but none has availed himself of this right. Two attempts have been made to amend the law to change the composition of the agency because in general, the men elected to the offices of governor and state land commissioner have little or no knowledge of the oil industry, and the conflict of official duties prevents the devotion of substantial time to the Commission. The state geologist is in fact the Commission as to most of its functions. The 1941 bill, introduced by the senator from Eddy County, substituted a five man board appointed by the governor to exercise the functions of the present Commission. Industry opinion was not unanimous as to the merits of this proposal. A preponderant number thought the present system worked satisfactorily and that they should let well enough alone. The governor and land commissioner, though not taking a public position on the measure, were reluctant to surrender their added power. The bill failed. To an appreciable extent its support within the industry came from small operators, and the opposition from the larger companies, although the issue did not result in any major conflict. The 1945 bill introduced at the suggestion of the governor would have added to the Commission three experienced oil men, gubernatorially appointed in lieu of the executive being a member of the agency. The state land commissioner opposed the measure apparently feeling that it would tend to reduce his power as a Commission member. The bill passed in the House but was recalled and died in committee. The speaker of the House, in explaining his recall vote said, "it has boiled down to where the Governor is the champion of this bill and former Governor Miles [the State Land Commissioner] is its opponent. I feel that each is sincere in his position. I haven't seen anyone actively supporting or opposing this bill other than state officials or their agents and employees. I feel that the oilmen are entitled to representation on the Commission and it is with the intention of giving the measure fair and impartial consideration that I vote for the recall."

The only further effort of consequence to amend the Oil and Gas Conservation Act occurred in the 1947 session. S.B. 226 would have authorized individual members of the Commission to hear testimony and conduct hearings on behalf of the entire group, with a provision for the testimony to be transcribed and made the basis of the agency's decisions. Conflicting duties and commitments of the governor and land commissioner have made it difficult to secure a quorum in attendance at some hearings. In certain instances the hearings have been held before the director alone, though the three members thereafter joined in the announced decision. Since the present Act requires the participation of a majority of the Commission in any hearing, the director introduced this legislation to meet the situation. In the absence of active support from other members of the agency, the bill died in the Senate.

THE BASIC OIL AND GAS CONSERVATION LAW

The fact that the basic Oil and Gas Conversation Act has never been subjected to judicial scrutiny makes it difficult to evaluate. No order of the agency has been challenged in the courts. At the time of adoption the law was generally recognized as a model and acts of several states were patterned after it in varying degree.[6]

Waste in the production or handling of oil or natural gas is prohibited by the Act and in addition to the amendment which added non-ratable purchase of oil, the definition includes underground waste, surface waste, and the production of oil in excess of reasonable market demand, which is declared to result in waste and is forbidden. Underground waste includes the inefficient, excessive, or improper use or dissipation of reservoir energy, gas or water drive, and drilling or operating a well in a manner which tends to reduce the total quantity of crude or gas ultimately recoverable. This terminology appears broad enough to require compulsory unitization for secondary recovery negatively; that is, by shutting in wells until unitized and secondary recovery operations are provided, but the agency has made no attempt to exercise this power. Surface waste is defined as unnecessary or excessive surface loss or destruction without beneficial use, of natural gas or oil (loss or destruction without beneficial use from evaporation, seepage, leakage or fire), that incident to spacing, equipping, operating or producing wells,

---

[6] Dow, *Legal History of Conservation of Oil and Gas in New Mexico*, LEGAL HISTORY OF CONSERVATION OF OIL AND GAS—A SYMPOSIUM 108 (1938).

and which results from inefficient storage or from production of oil in excess of market demand. The third section of the definition declares the production of oil in excess of reasonable market demand to be waste in addition to the related provision of the surface waste terminology. Such market demand is that for reasonably current consumptive requirements within and without the state in addition to reasonable storage reserves of oil and its products. There is no express provision supporting the agency determination of market demand for New Mexico oil by making its calculation prima facie correct.

Conforming to the Act's general pattern, which gives broad powers to the Commission without detail or erecting specific safeguards, its spacing provisions are general and grant wide powers to the agency [7] to make rules, regulations and orders to "fix the spacing of wells." To avoid the drilling of unnecessary wells, the Commission is authorized to fix proration units for each pool—an area efficiently and economically drained and developed by one well. The owner of a tract smaller than a drilling unit cannot be deprived of his right to drill and produce it if waste will not result, but his allowable is limited by the ratio of the area of his tract to that of a full proration unit. The Commission is authorized to compel the pooling of properties to form a drilling unit where the size or shape of a separately owned tract otherwise deprives the owner of an opportunity to recover his just and equitable share of the oil or gas in a pool. This power to require pooling was exercised for the first time in April 1948 under order 739 at the petition of the Texas Company for a tract in the Monument Pool from which the applicant had produced since 1937.[8] The company, owner of the oil and gas leasehold estate in 36 of the 40 acres embraced in the drilling unit at the well's original completion, had an allowable of $36/40$ths of the normal allocation. It acquired an oil and gas lease on 2 added acres, leaving outstanding 2 acres claimed by a large number of people. After notice and hearing, the Commission ordered the 40 acre tract "be . . . pooled as to all strata or any stratum or strata," making the Texas Company operator and allotting the well a full 40 acre unit of production. The operator is required to make roy-

[7] N.M. Stat. Ann. § 69–211 (1941).
[8] N.M. Oil Cons. Comm., Case 117, Order 739 (Apr. 9, 1948).

alty payments to all owners in the unit in the proportion their interest bears to the full unit, and is permitted to demand satisfactory evidence of title before making payment.

The order is of importance as the first of its kind issued by the New Mexico Oil Conservation Commission and because of the questions which remain unanswered. The dissenting parties were mineral owners and the effect of the ruling requires them to execute a lease to the Texas Company without receiving a bonus. Royalty payments are made to these persons, and though unspecified, presumably it is ⅛th. The owners of the 2 acre interest, though served by publication, were not represented at the hearing, and it is doubtful that the order would have been issued in its present form had they been represented. The effect of the ruling on the legal rights incident to the cotenancy between the Texas Company and the owners provides an interesting speculation. Prior to this proceeding the reduction of the allowable in proportion to a tract's size had provided sufficient inducement to effect voluntary pooling, which the Commission may approve. Provision is made in the Act for the sanction of unusual plans of well spacing for particular pools where the operators have agreed upon it; there is no reference to less than unanimous consent, and for that reason the authority is of questionable value.

The oil proration unit established by the Commission is 40 acres, and this is the uniform basis of distribution of allowable throughout the state. The center of the tract is the customary location, although the only requirement is that no well be less than 330 feet from the boundary of the unit. The Commission may approve unorthodox well locations (less than 330 feet) upon petition, notice and hearing. With the exception of an unusual situation in the city of Hobbs, this has been done only with the consent of the offsetting lease owner affected. Apparently, the royalty owners in these situations have not been consulted, which ultimately may result in litigation. In no instance has any adjustment of allowable been made by reason of the nonconforming location, even though the basis for the application was geologic information indicating that a well in the center of the tract would be unproductive. Presumably New Mexico operators are no more generous than those in other states; the lack of protest is a notable sidelight on the general omission of reference to correlative rights in the state conservation laws. In December 1947 the United States Geological Survey raised the question of an adjustment in allowable to protect correlative rights where a location is more than 330 feet from the unit boundary but does not conform to the area spacing pattern. Informal talks with the Commission were held and the problem was discussed at a meeting of operators called by the USGS at Fort Worth, December 12, 1947. Inability of the operators to agree to the proposal resulted in no action, but the question will undoubtedly arise again in other instances.

With the exception of general provisions authorizing the Commission to approve plans for the development or operation of a pool which prevents waste "and [are] fair to the royalty owners in such pool," the New Mexico Act has no section dealing with repressuring, recycling and secondary recovery operations. Similarly, there is no express provision of the statute governing preservation of reservoir energy, or restricting open flow of natural gas wells. Disposal of salt water and contaminated brines has not been a problem in the state and no legislation covers the matter.

The use and exportation of natural gas is not restricted or regulated by the present Act, although these subjects may be included in the proposed natural gas law under preparation for introduction in 1949. There is no statutory authority relating in any manner to the price of oil or gas at the well head and effort has not been made to control or affect price except that which might indirectly result from the adjustment of allowables. Several aspects of conservation about which the Act is silent have been treated by the Commission in orders under its general terms. Protection of correlative rights is only incidental to the creation of the agency. Throughout the Act the exercise of its powers is predicated upon waste prevention. The only reference to correlative rights appears in Section 12 relating to proration and provides that the rules, regulations and orders of the Commission shall "afford to the owner of each property in a pool the opportunity to produce his just and equitable share of oil and gas in the pool . . . substantially in the proportion that the quantity of the recoverable oil and gas under such property bears to the total recoverable oil and gas in the pool, and for this purpose to use his just and equitable share of the reservoir energy." Increased consciousness of correlative rights is inevitable and their protection may assume added importance as compared to the prevention of waste in future legislation.

THE ADMINISTRATIVE AGENCY

The administrative agencies which preceded the present Oil Conservation Commission are described by Dow in his treatise. The attempts to amend the 1935 Act to reconstitute the agency failed. Present membership of the New Mexico Oil Conservation Commission is: Thomas J. Mabry, Governor of New Mexico, Chairman, John E. Miles, State Land Commissioner, member, R. R. Spurrier, State Geologist and Director of the Commission. The term of office of the governor and the state land commissioner, ex-officio agency members, is two years with a constitutional limitation to two successive terms of office. The state geologist, appointed by the governor, holds office at his pleasure.

Members of the Commission, with the exception of the state geologist, receive no compensation; the actual expenses incurred in the performance of their duties are paid out of a conservation fund. The geologist's salary is adjusted by the governor and a portion paid from the fund. Inasmuch as an old statute limits his salary to $300 a month,[9] the additional amount coming from the fund is allocated for his duties as director and secretary to the Commission. Monies for the functioning of the agency are obtained from the conservation tax (levied in the 1935 Act) which is ⅛th of one per cent of the value of all oil and gas produced in the state, excepting royalties paid to the United States or the state of New Mexico. Expenditure is solely in the hands of the Commission and no legislative action is required to make money available, since a blanket appropriation is made in the levy.[10] Proceeds of the tax are paid the state treasurer, and by him credited to the oil conservation fund. That section appropriating tax proceeds to the agency and giving it unlimited powers to expend money and to employ personnel reads: "Such fund or so much thereof as may be necessary is hereby appropriated to the Oil Conservation Commission to be by it expended in the

[9] N.M. Stat. Ann. § 69–201 (1941).
[10] Id. § 69–231.

enforcement of this Act. The Commission is hereby authorized within the limits of the funds available to employ a secretary and such other employees and agents as may be necessary to enforce the provisions of this Act." To the extent that the monies are actually expended, they are out of the legislative control as well as that of the executive branch, but those sums not used by the Commission are not appropriated under the terms of the statute, and have been treated as surpluses accruing from other departments, including those operating upon legislative appropriations. As a result, when Governor John J. Dempsey in 1945 was seeking funds to remodel the state capitol at an anticipated expense of $1,500,000, some $30,000 in the oil conservation fund which remained from previous years was transferred to the building fund. The money was lost to the Commission and the cause of oil and gas conservation, the express purpose for which the tax was levied. The increase in price of oil and in production in New Mexico during the past two years resulted in the accumulation of a further surplus which by May 1948 amounted to $75,000; this is being eyed covetously by departments which consider themselves residuary legatees of surpluses in the treasury. The Commission, suffering from an office housing shortage in the state capitol, now has under consideration the expenditure of these sums in the construction of suitable offices and a hearing room in Santa Fe, which would materially add to the efficiency of the agency.

The Commission employs agents, engineers, geologists and secretarial assistance as required. Presently, in addition to the director, the roster encompasses twelve employees. The agency maintains four offices: the headquarters at Santa Fe, one at Farmington, New Mexico, for the San Juan Basin representative, one at Artesia, for the Eddy County representative, and an office at Hobbs, in charge of the state oil and gas inspector including on its staff the petroleum engineer, chief clerk and a stenographer. Personnel at the headquarters consists of the director, a purchasing agent, the geologist, a chief clerk and a stenographer. The agency representative is the only employee at Farmington, and a representative and a stenographer make up the Eddy County office. Personnel may be changed as the Commission considers additional assistance necessary.

The agency has its own attorneys. Section 3 of the basic Act which creates the Commission provides the attorney general shall be the attorney for the Commission. This has been honored in its breach. Carl H. Livingston, appointed attorney for the Commission when organized in 1935, was given a commission as an assistant attorney general to conform to the statute, and his compensation was paid from the conservation fund. Mr. Livingston, who continued in this capacity until his death in March 1947 made substantial contributions to the progress of conservation in New Mexico. Political patronage entered into filling the vacancy. The result was the appointment by the governor, the most powerful member of the group, of two part time attorneys who divide between themselves the compensation. One is the counsel for the State Land Office, a resident of Santa Fe, and the other is not a resident of the state capitol. This is a temporary situation as ultimately a return must be made to a single legal representative devoting full time to the agency, residing in Santa Fe, and available at all times. Commissions as special assistant attorney generals have been issued to the present legal representatives.

No discussion of the administrative aspect of oil and gas conservation in New Mexico is complete without mention of the Lea County Operators Committee, which has a quasi-official status unique in the country. Dow relates the original organization of the Hobbs Proration Committee, succeeded by the Lea County Operators Committee, which was to establish a voluntary proration schedule in advance of the basic laws adoption.[11] With the organization of the original Commission under the 1935 Act, it became apparent that should it set up personnel and records to issue a monthly proration schedule, they would duplicate an existing organization which had been established and was operating successfully under the Lea County Operators Committee. A decision was made to allow this committee to handle issuance of the proration schedule and incidental reports under Commission supervision. This arrangement has continued except for a period of two months in the summer of 1938, when due to a controversy between the state land commissioner and the committee, the Commission issued the schedule. Sixty days experience apparently demonstrated

[11] Dow, *supra* note 6 at 106.

that it had taken on quite an assignment, or perhaps the controversy was settled, as the function was returned to the Lea County Operators Committee. The work of the committee is performed at the expense of the committee notwithstanding the fact that increasing percentages of the scheduled wells are in counties other than Lea. The administrative cost of the group, which includes issuing the proration schedule, is paid by the represented operators on a basis of average daily production; thus the Lea County operators actually pay for issuing the state proration schedule. This is done, undoubtedly, on the theory that the added economy and efficiency coming from the absence of political patronage makes it less expensive to the individual Lea County operator than support of a state department prorated among all oil producers in the state. To a great extent the unique position of Lea County Operators Committee, its excellent relationship with the state government and the operators, is attributed to the good judgment, personality and hard work of Glen Staley, since 1930 the conservation engineer and principal administrative officer of the committee. Mr. Staley, State Geologist of New Mexico prior to accepting this position, has been continuously engaged in the conservancy program in New Mexico in a quasi-public capacity longer than any other official. As a result, operators frequently turn to the Lea County Operators Committee for advice and assistance on industry questions of public importance.

Determination of the monthly quota of production and its allocation between fields and wells is accomplished by the joint efforts of the Commission and the Lea County Operators Committee. The Commission holds monthly meetings at which allowables are determined for the ensuing month. The figure is reported to the Lea County Operators Committee for allocation among various state fields and their wells. This allocation is made in accordance with the provisions of the Commission's State Wide Proration Order in effect, which sets the basis upon which the allowable is prorated, and the allocation factors. The committee then breaks down the allowable on the basis of the equation furnished by the Commission, promulgates the prepared schedule and maintains required production records. The monthly "Over and Short" report is made and distributed by the committee. A supplemental schedule embracing wells brought in the first half of the month is issued the 16th of each month.

Under the terms of the state-wide proration order now in effect [12] a unit of proration is 40 acres. An appropriate exception is made in cases where production is obtained from two or more separate pools underlying a single proration unit. For purposes of allocation between fields and wells, all wells are divided into marginal and non-marginal units; a marginal unit can not produce its top unit allowable for the pool. In distributing the daily allowable, cumulative daily production of the marginal units in the state is first subtracted from the whole allotment. The remainder is equally apportioned between all non-marginal wells in the state on an acreage and depth basis. The unit allowable multiplied by the number of non-marginal wells in a field, plus the production of marginal field wells is that field's allowable. Adjustments because of excessive gas-oil ratio, or bottom hole pressure (where a factor) are on a field basis; penalties are given the field's remaining top allowable wells. Division of production among wells in a pool is made on the basis of acreage and depth with the exception of the Hobbs and Monument pools. Case Two of the Oil Conservation Commission was the proration plan for the Monument Field. On July 16, 1936 their order disposing of the case apportioned production—80 per cent on an acreage basis and 20 per cent on static bottom hole pressure. This ratio continues unchanged. Production allotments among wells in the Hobbs pool were initially 50 per cent acreage basis and 50 per cent potential production, and subsequently were changed at the operators' request to 60 per cent acreage and 40 per cent potential.

In 1939 a controversy as to the basis of allocating production in the Hobbs Field developed among operators up and down the structure with the Gulf Oil Corporation and the Stanolind Oil and Gas Company as the principal contestants. Two hearings were held and a substantial amount of testimony taken, which revolved around the question of the effect of existing and proposed basis of proration upon the migration of oil in the structure. The order of the Commission December 30, 1940 [13] settled the controversy by

[12] N.M. Oil Cons. Comm. Order 637 (Mar. 1, 1946).
[13] N.M. Oil Cons. Comm. Order 329 (Feb. 1, 1941).

putting the Hobbs Field on the same footing as the Monument Field, 80 per cent to acreage and 20 per cent to bottom hole pressure. This decision was of significance in that it eliminated potential with its attendant evils as a factor in allowable. The only further exceptions to the uniform acreage and depth allowable are the Langlie, Loco Hills and Maljamar Fields, all of which are operating pressure maintenance units. By agreement of the operators the allowable of these wells is apportioned specially to obtain the maximum benefit from repressuring.

Before February 7, 1948 depth of the producing formation was not considered in allocating production. On that date the Commission issued its Order No. 637 (the state-wide proration order with deep pool adaption) in which graduated allowables increase with the depth of the well. The following unit allowables are specified:

Pool Depth Range	Proportional Factor
From 0 to 5,000 ft.	1.00
Below 5,000 to 6,000 ft.	1.33
" 6,000 to 7,000 ft.	1.77
" 7,000 to 8,000 ft.	2.33
" 8,000 to 9,000 ft.	3.00
" 9,000 to 10,000 ft.	3.77
" 10,000 to 11,000 ft.	4.67
" 11,000 to 12,000 ft.	5.67

Completion of the Mid-Continent Sawyer No. 1 May 16, 1948, the discovery well in the Crossroads pool in northern Lea County, gave New Mexico its first production below 12,000 feet. The Commission had retained jurisdiction to provide in executive session, "an equitable proportional factor applicable to any pool that may be discovered at any depth range below 12,000 feet," and thereafter fixed 6.75 as the proportional factor for such wells. After the discovery well was completed certain operators requested a flat 500 barrel allowable for the Crossroads pool, which was opposed by others on the basis that insufficient information was then available. June 15, 1948 the Commission fixed a 500 barrel allowable for the Crossroads Pool retroactive to May 16, limited to a 90 day period, after which a permanent ruling will be made. The first exception to 40 acre spacing of oil wells in New Mexico may result from the discovery of the Crossroads pool, where by reason of the depth of the producing formation, the expense of drilling, and local conditions, operators in the area have requested to the Commission to establish 80 acre proration units.

Order No. 573 of the Commission dated June 1, 1944 gave a bonus allowable to discovery wells in a new pool or a new producing horizon in existing fields. Extensions of known oil pools qualify for the bonus if two miles or more from any commercially producing oil well. The bonus discovery allowable is determined on the basis of depth:

Up to 1,000 ft.	5,000 barrels
1,000 to 1,500 ft.	7,500 "
1,500 to 2,000 ft.	10,000 "
2,000 to 2,500 ft.	12,500 "
2,500 to 3,000 ft.	15,000 "
3,000 to 3,500 ft.	17,500 "
3,500 to 4,000 ft.	20,000 "

and 5 barrels per foot of depth below 4000 feet. The bonus is to be produced within two years after discovery at a rate not greater than the figure obtained by dividing the bonus allowable "by the number of days in the current year." The general proration order prohibits a well from taking advantage of the deep pool and discovery allowable at the same time, giving the operator the option to waive the latter, if he desires, or to complete its running before receiving additional allocations of production be reason of well depth exceeding 5000 feet. There has been discussion among operators and members of the regulatory body as to the justification and legality of the bonus discovery allowable. It is in derogation of correlative rights as it affects other producers in the pool, and should it be attacked there is little doubt but that it would be invalidated.

The demand for New Mexico crude always has been limited by transportation facilities. Inspection of pipe line maps shows New Mexico's position at the end of the line, in fact at the end of the longest oil gathering line in the United States. Oil from the North Basin pools in Texas flowing through the New Mexico gathering lines to the trunk line also limits the capacity available for New Mexico. Approximately 160,000 barrels daily is the maximum amount of oil transportable with extant facilities. Currently, this amount is further decreased to some 135,000 barrels by lack of capacity available in trunk lines outside the state. Pipe lines from Texas North Basin pools now under construction will remove Texas oil from competition with New Mexico crude and provide substantial added capacity to the state during the coming year. New Mexico's position at the end of the gathering lines has been used as an excuse in times of weak market demand for a reduction in price and amounts of crude purchased, a condition subjected to much protest at times. The chaotic 1939 market resulted in the issuance of Emergency Order No. 196 which recites, "Whereas it appears that the immediate production of crude oil tends to create waste because of unstable conditions in the petroleum industry, an emergency is hereby declared." The order suspended all production for a 15 day period from August 17, 1939. Normal production was resumed on September 1. While the order was protested by a small group of producers, for the most part it was considered justified.

COMMISSION PROCEDURE

The Commission holds public hearings at irregular intervals in Santa Fe, when all pending matters in which service has been completed are considered. Action is initiated by the Commission upon its motion or by petition of interested parties. Practice before the body is informal and free from detailed regulation. Rules of the Commission dealing with operations, hearings and matters of general interest are collected in Circular No. 6 of the Oil Conservation Commission,[14] containing the rules, regulations and statutes with which an operator normally is concerned. The Conservation Act [15] provides that (with the exception of emergency orders) no rule, regulation or order, amendment or extension, is effective until a public hearing is held. Notice of the hearing is given by one publication in a newspaper at the state capitol and in a newspaper in the county where the affected land is located. Ten days must elapse after publication before the hearing. The notice states generally the proposed action subject of the hearing. Personal service may be

[14] Copies are available from Lea County Operators Committee, Hobbs.
[15] N.M. STAT. ANN. § 69–221 (1941).

made. The Commission promulgates emergency orders that remain in force not longer than 15 days, in which time a hearing after notice must be had if the order is to be extended. Rules of evidence are not followed. A quorum of the agency is required at the hearing, where all interested persons are given an opportunity to be heard and to cross examine adverse witnesses.

The Commission or any member is empowered to issue subpoenas and to require production of records. No person is excused from testifying or producing records on the ground that these acts tend to incriminate him, so long as the questions to which answer is required are lawfully before the Commission or a court. No criminal prosecution, penalty or forfeiture ensues for any required testimony given before the Commission. In case of the refusal of a witness to honor a subpoena or to testify, the Commission may have an attachment for his person issued from any district court in the state compelling the desired action. Failure to obey constitutes contempt of court and is punishable as other contempt.

No direct appeal is provided from action of the Commission. A party to a hearing before the Commission aggrieved by the result obtains court review by institution of suit for injunction against the Commission in the District Court of Santa Fe County or a court of the county where the plaintiff resides or the property is situated. Precedence is given these suits over other pending matters, and the case may be set for trial on ten days notice to plaintiff. Burden of proof is expressly placed upon the petitioner and the order or regulation of the Commission is prima facie valid. The Act prohibits issuance of a temporary restraining order or injunction against the Commission without notice and hearing and further requires a bond from the petitioner as a prerequisite before granting an order after hearing. Any person suffering damage from the injunction is permitted to sue on the bond within six months after the questioned regulation is finally held valid or the litigation terminated. Before suit for an injunction is filed to test the agency action, the applicant must exhaust his administrative remedy. Hearing in the injunction suit is de novo.[16]

Fines up to $1000, imprisonment for not more than three years, or both, are assessed upon violation of rules or regulations of the

---

[16] *Id.* § 69–223.

Commission; a penalty not to exceed $1000 a day may be recovered for each act of violation by suit in the district court.[17] The Commission may proceed by injunction against persons violating or threatening to violate its orders or regulations.[18] It may confiscate and sell under court order illegal oil (that produced in violation of an order of the Commission). Violation of the Commission orders in the operation of wells, pipe lines or refineries is ground for the appointment of a receiver to conduct operations under order of the court.[19]

Matters presented to the Commission of general concern are frequently referred by it to an advisory committee of operators representative of all interested parties which seeks to arrive at a unanimous report to the Commission. Recommendations so made have been adopted by the Commission in every case. Commission attaches report an instance where the Commission referred a pending question to an advisory committee which in turn had filed its report with the Commission. At a hearing by the Commission on the proposal, one of the operators asked to be heard in opposition to the recommendation; he was advised by the state land commissioner that if the operators had not reached agreement as to the action, the matter would be returned to the committee, where his dissent might be presented. This plan of operation contributes to the fact that no order of the Commission has been challenged in the courts of New Mexico during thirteen years. It should be observed that most action taken by the Commission has been intitiated by the affected operators and seldom, if ever, has the agency imposed upon the industry any rule or regulation which a majority opposed. While this situation might seem unhealthy, actually the real interests of the operators and of the state are identical in many respects. New Mexico's sparse population, the early adoption of the 40 acre proration unit and the fact that most production is at substantial depth have tended to limit the number of active operators in the state. These conditions in turn contribute to harmonious relations within the industry making possible good feeling and trust between the regulatory body and the operators. It is inevitable that someday

---

[17] *Id.* § 69–228.
[18] *Id.* § 69–225.
[19] *Id.* § 69–227.

a situation will arise in which the industry will be unable to agree; similarly on some occasion, state interest as viewed by the Commission will clash with the viewpoint of the industry, and litigation result. The fact that it has not occurred to date is worthy of comment and demonstrates the actuality of cooperation between the industry and a regulatory body, both seeking ultimate maximum recovery.

SIGNIFICANT ORDERS OF THE COMMISSION

Through June 1, 1948 the Commission issued 771 orders; the great majority have related to allocation of production. The agency has disposed of 146 cases. A significant step in the conservation of oil and gas was the promulgation January 13, 1940 of Order 238 prescribing maximum gas-oil ratios for all fields in New Mexico and penalizing the allowable of any well exceeding its field ratio. Wells exceeding the maximum net gas-oil ratio are limited to that amount of oil produced without exceeding the maximum gas production permitted in the recovery of the daily allowable of the field. Any allowable lost by this penalty is allocated to other producers in the field rather than throughout the state. A lack of adequate technical staff, which handicaps the Commission in several respects, is evident in connection with the maximum gas-oil ratios prescribed. The technical personnel of the operating companies in a field submit estimates of the maximum efficient gas-oil ratio for the field. The Commission uses these figures and by compromise specifies the maximum ratio. The Commission does not have available disinterested scientific advice which would be the basis of independent conclusions as to these figures.

The first pressure maintenance projects in New Mexico were sanctioned by the Commission January 28, 1941, when programs for the Langlie pool in Lea County and the Loco Hills pool in Eddy County were approved.[20] Submission of the plans to the Commission was made under the provisions of Section 12, which provides that where the owners of any pool agree upon development or operation which in the opinion of the Commission will

[20] N.M. Oil Cons. Comm. Orders 339, 340 (Jan. 28, 1941).

prevent waste and is fair to the royalty owners in a pool, the plan may be adopted by the Commission upon hearing and notice. An interesting aspect of the Loco Hills pressure maintenance [21] order was the provision shutting in two producing gas wells in the field and permitting the owners of those wells to produce from oil wells belonging to them having identical royalty ownership, an additional allowable for each shut-in gas well. Pressure maintenance plans in effect are voluntary and provide that the allowable of wells used as input wells may be produced by the owner from other wells having like royalty interests. Langlie and Loco Hills were followed by the Maljamar and Graysburg pressure maintenance project in Eddy County, each of which was submitted to and approved by the Commission.[22]

Prior to World War II, informal inquiries as to permits for carbon black plants in New Mexico met with no governmental encouragement. During the war years when carbon black became critical material, the Commission approved operation of four plants limited to the use of waste gas which cannot be utilized for domestic or commercial purposes. Each plant burns residue gas from gasoline plants. The burning of wet gas to make carbon black is still prohibited. No general regulations have been promulgated by the Commission, but the limitations are incorporated in the order approving plant operation. Actually, there is no provision in the statute or the rules and regulations of the Commission necessitating agency consent, but apparently no one wants to invest the required capital without obtaining prior approval to contribute to the security of his position.

The lack of a natural gas act is responsible for the failure of the Commission to exercise any control over the production of natural gas. There is supposedly a gentlemen's agreement between operators not to produce more than one-fourth the open flow capacity of a gas well, but undoubtedly that limitation is frequently breached. In fact, the Commission would have power to prorate gas production to prevent waste under the basic conservation Act. The contrary has been argued by certain gas producing and distributing

[21] N.M. Oil Cons. Comm. Order 339, (Jan. 28, 1941).
[22] N.M. Oil Cons. Comm. Orders 485, (Nov. 14, 1942) 659 (June 7, 1946).

companies, and the Commission is unwilling to go further without specific legislative authorization. The only significant regulation of natural gas wells undertaken is in the spacing order of the Fulcher Basin, San Juan County, where an original well spacing order of one well to 160 acres adopted in 1943 was extended by the Commission in 1948.[23]

CONSERVATION ON FEDERAL LANDS

Some 41 per cent of the State of New Mexico is composed of Federal Government lands, approximately one half of which are public domain administered by the Bureau of Land Management. In addition the Federal Government owns the minerals underlying thousands of acres of land patented to individuals and institutions where the oil, gas and other minerals were reserved by various acts of Congress. The United States Geological Survey is charged with the supervision of operations under oil and gas leases issued by the Government. In New Mexico, as elsewhere, the USGS through its control of operations on federal lands contributes substantially to conservation. The Southwestern regional office of the Conservation Branch, USGS is in Roswell;[24] its jurisdiction extends to New Mexico, Arizona, southwestern Colorado, southeastern Utah, and acquired lands in Texas west of the 100th meridian. In general the Federal Government is treated as any mineral owner. The state takes the position that its police power extends to operations of federal lands as on private lands, even though it has not exercised this power in its own right. By agreement between the Commission and the USGS drilling permits, bonds and supervision of operations on federal lands is handled by the latter. The Survey cooperates fully with the Commission in having its operators conform to requirements equivalent to those of the Commission. While the Department of the Interior does not expressly recognize the police-power of the state to restrict production of oil from federal lands, it requires its lessees to observe the state proration schedules as a matter of comity.

[23] N.M. Oil Cons. Comm. Order 746, (May 17, 1948).

[24] In addition to the assistance of the New Mexico Advisers the writer expresses his appreciation of the contribution of Foster Morrell, Sup., USGS Conservation Branch, at Roswell, N. Mex. in the preparation of this article.

AN APPRAISAL OF CONSERVATION IN
NEW MEXICO

The promise for sound conservation of oil and gas inherent in New Mexico's early adoption of a model Oil and Gas Conservation Act, and establishment of a uniform 40 acre spacing pattern throughout the state has been borne out by the developments of the last decade. It is doubtful if any state has had more orderly development of its petroleum resources in terms of efficient capital investment and the elimination of unnecessary drilling. Cooperation between the regulatory body and the industry in New Mexico, effected through the liason provided by the Lea County Operators Committee, has demonstrated that two common interests can be welded into a course of action. While no order of the Commission has been challenged in the courts, this is not necessarily a credit to the Commission. It could be indicative of a regulatory body subservient to the industry, in effect, an instrumentality of the industry rather than of the people whose natural resources are being depleted. Fair evaluation of the operations of the Oil Conservation Commission in New Mexico leads to the conclusion that if one is paramount, it is the industry, not the regulatory body. Such a condition is not necessarily undesirable. An industry which has outgrown the adolescence of booms and gushers, which has come to appreciate the dollars and cents value of conservation, and demonstrates this realization by expending millions of dollars annually in research has interests strikingly similar to those of the people whose natural resources are being developed. In New Mexico, to a greater extent than in other comparable producing states, there has been unanimity of opinion among the operators and a freer exchange of engineering experience and technical data. These conditions and the fact that more than two-thirds of the wells in New Mexico are on state or federal lands contribute to the operation of a sound conservation program with a minimum of regulatory compulsion.

There still remain legislative and administrative situations where the cause of conservation in New Mexico might be implemented. The composition of the Oil Conservation Commission could be improved. Neither the governor nor the land commissioner has enough time to devote to his duties as a board member; at times

the Commission has suffered from controversies and feuding between these two officials—the most powerful in the state—frequently jealous of each other. Members should have some qualifications other than that of political success to sit in judgment upon
the important technical problems of the oil industry. Only the
state geologist satisfies this requirement. Additional commissioners
might be appointed one by the governor, and one by the state land
commissioner to forestall a complete abandonment by these officials of their present authority.

While Section 12 of the basic Act authorizes Commission approval of plans for operation of a pool to prevent waste, and the
state land commissioner approves unit operations embracing state
lands which contribute to conservation,[25] legislation expressly exempting these operations from the anti-trust or restraint of trade
laws is needed. Legislation authorizing compulsory unitization and
secondary recovery operations is needed and will become increasingly important as New Mexico fields pass flush production. It is
arguable that the Commission has adequate power to deal with this
subject under the broad provisions of the 1935 Act, but in the light
of agency functions to date no likelihood exists that it will enter
this field without express legislative sanction.

Flaring of New Mexico gas has been decreased as its market increased; the purchasing companies continuously amplify the
amount and percentage of flare gas taken in New Mexico. Construction of gas pipe lines to the west coast is a measurable factor
in reduction of the waste through flaring. In spite of a greater market the amount of gas dissipated remains excessive. It is doubtful
if the cause of conservation can await operation of the law of supply and demand to eliminate further waste of a depletable natural
resource. Action by the Commission is indicated.

In a recent address a competent secondary recovery engineer
pointed out the Monument Field in New Mexico as an example
of a field which through lack of unitization is turning the potential
benefits of water drive into water encroachment which is wasting
the recoverable resources of one of New Mexico's great oil deposits.[26] Other pressure maintenance projects have been considered

[25] N. M. Laws 1943, c. 88; N. M. STAT. ANN. 8–1138 et. seq. (1941).
[26] Knowlton, *Proper Control of Oil Reservoirs*, V INTERSTATE OIL COMPACT Q.
BULL. 21 (1946).

in fields where ultimate recovery would be substantially increased thereby, but are delayed if not prevented by dissenting operators, whose opposition could have been overcome by appropriate legislation authorizing compulsory unitization for pressure maintenance and secondary recovery operations.

Finally it is generally conceded that a program, similar to that undertaken in other oil producing states, whereby the maximum efficient rate of production for each individual well is determined and made the basis for its allowable, would be a great advance in sound conservation. Such a plan is out of the question with the present personnel of the Commission, but since the proceeds of the conservation tax largely exceed present demands, the possibility of adopting the program might be beneficially explored.

The active participation of the State of New Mexico through its representative and its regulatory officials in the program of the Interstate Oil Compact Commission is of inestimable value. New Mexico, the first state to provide by legislative action for representatives to negotiate an interstate oil compact,[27] and the first state to ratify the Compact, continues its interest in and active support of the Commission without abatement. Hiram M. Dow has served as the representative of New Mexico since its organization in 1935, climaxing his contribution by outstanding service as its chairman in 1946–1947. The legislature ratifies each renewal of the Compact promptly, and the state may take just pride in the contribution it has made to the cause of conservation through the Interstate Oil Compact Commission.

In the final analysis, the real test of New Mexico's conservation program is in its achievements. The Hobbs pool offers an opportunity to examine these results. In 1929 its discovery centered the eyes of the country upon New Mexico as a new oil frontier; today, 19 years after the discovery well was drilled in, only 4 of the 256 original wells have been abandoned, and only 34 are pumpers. Such results are obtainable only through a sound conservation program and typical of other examples in the state, they indicate that New Mexico has achieved substantial success in the conservation of its petroleum resources.

[27] N. M. Laws 1935, c. 1.

CHAPTER 22

New York, 1864–1948

New York is the locale of the first surface discovery, in 1627, of oil in America by white men in what later became Seneca Territory.[1] The first drilling for natural gas took place in Fredonia, Chautauqua County, about 1821, with production after two failures brought in from a well 27 feet deep. This gas was transmitted through log pipes to two village stores and used for lighting purposes in greeting General Lafayette.[2] After the Drake well discovery in Pennsylvania in 1859, exploration spread to New York where the first oil well was drilled in 1864; by 1878 there were 250 producing wells.[3] Following this discovery, extensive and systematic exploration of the state's natural gas resources was undertaken.[4] In the pioneer days of oil and gas production, producing practices in the Appalachian states were subservient to the desire to get maximum production. Natural gas when discovered was a disappointment and considered a nuisance. Wells blew the gas into the air and no immediate attempt was made to pipe it for use;[5] not until the later 1880's were lines built to market natural gas in the larger communities of western New York.[6]

WILLIAM A. DOUGHERTY, WRITER; Assisted by James Lawrence White. (See app. B.)

[1] N.Y. STATE MUSEUM BULL. No. 273, THE MINING AND QUARRYING INDUSTRIES OF NEW YORK 67 (1927); GIDDENS, THE BIRTH OF THE OIL INDUSTRY 1 (1938).

[2] Legis. Doc. No. 28, Production, Supply and Distribution of Gas in New York State 3 (1948). Elsewhere it is indicated that the depth of the first well was 70 feet, and the gas transported through lead pipes to a hotel and several stores. In Re: Investigation on rates, charges, practices, etc. of natural gas companies in State of New York, N.Y. Pub. Serv. Comm. Case No. 7091, vol. 1, 175 (1932).

[3] MUSEUM BULL. No. 273, op. cit. supra 68.

[4] Id. at 61.

[5] WILSON, OIL ACROSS THE WORLD 126 et seq. (1946).

[6] Legis. Doc. No. 28 supra note 2 at 4 et seq.

THE LEGISLATIVE HISTORY OF OIL AND GAS CONSERVATION

The absence of a comprchcnsive conservation law is due both to geological and economic factors. There is no large continuous reservoir or field in the Appalachian region and the productive areas are widely scattered and not extensive; oil and gas are found only in the western part of the state. Although criticism has been expressed in regard to competitive drilling practices, no widespread demand has ever been made by producers or state officials for laws limiting such techniques.[7] By the time conservation programs were enacted in the prolific producing Mid-Continent states, New York production of oil and natural gas had greatly declined, except for a temporary increase in oil production brought about by a process characterized by the legislature as flooding[8] and one short spurt of gas production;[9] there have been no new discoveries of consequence.

In one phase of conservation, the plugging of abandoned wells, however, the State of New York was assiduous, first acting in 1879.[10] A number of amendatory acts followed the original enactment of 1879, all occurring at ordinary sessions of the state legislature. The first of this series of legislation provided for plugging in more or less general terms to prevent flooding of the flow of oil or gas and the escape of oil or gas into fresh water. Subsequently, in 1882[11] the original act was amended to particularize the method of plugging before withdrawing the casing. No significant changes were made in the Plugging Act in a 1893 amendment.[12] In 1919[13] a proviso was inserted excepting from the plugging requirements the operation known as flooding, which section was carried over into the presently effective law of 1941.[14] The operation characterized as flooding refers to the method of increasing production by the introduction of water into a well with the column pressure

[7] *Id.* at 6 *et seq.*
[8] MUSEUM BULL. No. 273, *op. cit. supra* at 69.
[9] Legis. Doc. No. 28, *supra* note 2 at 6 *et seq.*
[10] N.Y. Laws 1879, c. 217, § 1.
[11] N.Y. Laws 1882, c. 64.
[12] N.Y. Laws 1893, c. 256, § 1.
[13] N.Y. Laws 1919, c. 252.
[14] N.Y. Laws 1941, c. 167; N.Y. GEN. BUS. LAW § 308.

driving the oil or gas out to adjoining wells. Two methods have developed. By the first, wells are drilled around the water filled well until water reaches them, when they in turn are flooded and new wells drilled at distances of 100 to 200 feet. This is called circular flood. About 1924, another system developed—the line flood. By this second method new wells are drilled to the producing sand in a row 150 feet apart and filled with water. Then, at right angles to a point midway between and on each side of each water well, two producing wells are drilled. As in the circular flood the producing wells go to water and in turn are used as water wells.[15] Injection of water under pressure has developed in recent years with a definite trend toward higher pressures, with 600 to 800 pounds per square inch at the well head in shallow sand areas and up to 1200 pounds per square inch for deeper sands. Cooperation between adjoining lease owners is good and most property lines are drilled with a row of water input wells. One authority has indicated that the flooding proviso first included in 1919 adequately covers such conventional methods of increasing production as secondary recovery, cycling, recycling, repressuring, and pressure maintenance operations.[16] The 1941 Act also provides that an oil or gas operator, upon abandonment or ceasing to operate, in order to exclude water from the producing sand, must plug to a depth of 20 feet from the producing horizon and in case of an oil well insert a wooden, cement, or other appropriate plug of specified dimension, and upon drawing and casing insert other specified plugs. An operator may, in lieu of plugging, flood the well upon making his intention known in a prescribed manner. It seems clear that, aside from considerations of safety, the purpose of the Plugging Acts in New York State is the protection of neighboring owners from damage which might result from the seepage of water into producing sands.

The only other legislative action in New York looking toward conservation has been the entrance of the state in 1941 into the Interstate Compact to Conserve Oil and Gas.[17] Lacking flush production of oil and gas since that time, the legislature has not enacted conservation legislation of the type sponsored by the Inter-

---

[15] MUSEUM BULL. No. 273, *op. cit. supra* at 69.
[16] II INTERSTATE OIL COMPACT Q. BULL. 44 (1943).
[17] N.Y. Laws 1941, c. 501.

state Oil Compact Commission. Joining the Compact has been of small service to the people of the State of New York.

Lack of proper legislation caused unlimited production and early exhaustion of many natural gas pools, true particularly with the development in the 1930's of the Oriskany sands in the southern tier counties. There were no restrictions upon any producer as to practices, quantities, or manner of production. Consequently, the law of capture operated, causing gas to be produced as rapidly as it could be sold. To a great extent sales were made at low prices for boiler fuel, and although the quantities were not large, imposition of ratable production would have given longer life and better economic recovery. Unit operation and cooperative development arose in some cases only from private initiative, especially in the gas developments of the Wayne-Dundee area in the 1930's.

THE ADMINISTRATIVE HISTORY OF OIL AND GAS CONSERVATION

With such a paucity of legislative enactment, administrative bodies in New York State have not been charged with the execution of conservation laws. The Plugging Act contains no provision for supervisory control and violations of the Act carry only criminal penalties [18] with a provision that an adjoining owner may plug and recover the expenses thereof.[19] There is, however, some administrative awareness of the need for conservation. The New York Public Service Commission in its Case No. 7091 [20] in 1931 pointed out that in New York gas reserves were rapidly being depleted because of the overlapping of economic drilling areas. In a later report the Commission expressed doubt as to whether more conservative policies in the past would have helped New York in her current gas

[18] N.Y. GEN. BUS. LAW § 309.
[19] N.Y. GEN. BUS. LAW § 308.
[20] N.Y. PUB. SER. COMM. Case No. 7091 supra note 2 at 219 et seq.; See also N.Y. STATE MUSEUM CIR. 7, RECENT NATURAL GAS DEVELOPMENTS IN SOUTH CENTRAL NEW YORK 5 (1932). In Case No. 7091 the Commission's ninth conclusion was: "Where natural gas wells are drilled so close together that there is an overlapping of their economic drainage areas, the additional wells add nothing to the amount of gas that can be removed from a field; they only increase the rate at which the gas can be withdrawn, add to the possibilities of waste and damage due to flooding by salt water, and cause great economic waste because of the unnecessary investment."

shortage, and decried the enormous use of gas for industrial purposes as well as the indiscriminate drilling practices.[21] Aside from the matter of conservation directed at oil and gas in place, the subject of conservation by controlling end use of gas is being increasingly treated. In a report made in 1931 and again in 1948 the Public Service Commission concluded that natural gas from limited reserves should not be used in an area having artificial service, and that artificial and natural gas should be mixed where feasible to stretch supplies.[22] The latter report ascribed some of the loss of production to low-grade uses, cut throat competition with artificial gas, inefficient burners and like causes.[23] Apparently in line with this policy of limiting use, in the one lease being operated in lands under the jurisdiction of the Conservation Department, it is provided that the "local needs of the public shall be met as far as reasonably practicable before transporting the gas beyond the County of Steuben." Recently the jurisdiction of the Public Service Commission was enlarged to enable it effectively to regulate end use of gas in periods of shortage and emergency.[24]

As to control over production, neither the Public Service Commission nor any other administrative agency has direct jurisdiction. Because the legislature has done nothing except act in matters of plugging and flooding, and has provided no administrative control over these activities, there is no administrative history of produc-

[21] Legis. Doc. No. 28, *supra* note 2 at 6, 8. The Commission stated: "As pointed out in the preceeding, [sic] the industry was characterized by wasteful and unsound practices throughout its development. The impression prevailed that the supply was inexhaustible, and land owners and drilling companies engaged in a wild scramble to cash in on the bonanza. There was frantic drilling, and numerous wells in close proximity dotted the new fields. They were merely draining the same pools in a hurry. Large quantities were withdrawn without an immediate market for their disposal. As a result much of it was thrown into destructive competition with manufactured gas and other fuels, and great quantities were allowed to go to waste. Today we have a somewhat similar situation in Texas fields where gas is being burned at the wells for lack of adequate pipe lines to the east where the gas is sorely needed. In the face of this profligate use of a value natural resource, the Public Service Commission could do little to curb existing abuses. In 1931, this Commission, following a general investigation of the natural gas industry, pointed out the dangers of a rapid depletion and uneconomical development. This warning and the Commission's recommendations were given little heed. Land owners and drilling companies are not under jurisdiction of the Commission."

[22] N.Y. *Pub. Ser. Comm.* Case No. 7091 *supra* note 2 at 222; Legis. Doc. No. 28, *supra* note 2 at 6–7.

[23] Legis. Doc. No. 28 *supra* note 2 at 4–8.

[24] See note 33 *infra*.

tion restrictions. An exception to the statement that there is no administrative control over oil and gas production arises in the case of exploration of the state's reforestation areas. Such areas as of April 30, 1948 contained 510,790.37 acres. In 1933 the legislature authorized the Conservation Department, with the approval of the state geologist, to lease these lands for oil and gas purposes, upon terms and conditions prescribed by the Department.[25] Since only one well has been drilled on the lands,[26] the need for supervision of production practices is slight indeed. The terms of the Act do not place restriction upon production, but leave the conditions to the Conservation Department. The prescribed lease terms, however, provide for the drilling of wells to combat offsetting within 30 days or paying an amount of money in lieu thereof, that the lessee keep accurate logs and records, and that no wells be drilled within 100 feet of any stream or boundary, except offset wells.

THE JUDICIAL HISTORY OF OIL AND GAS CONSERVATION

The courts of New York have had little to do from the standpoint of the conservation of oil and gas. In connection with the Plugging Act a question did arise. In *Davis v. Iroquois Gas Corporation* [27] a lower court granted a temporary restraining order to enjoin the pulling of casing and the plugging of a producing gas well drilled under a lease limited to a definite term of years. The lease was about to expire and its terms provided for the removal of trade fixtures. The parties stipulated that the casing and other equipment were trade fixtures, but the court would not allow removal on the ground that there would be susbtantial damage to the freehold because plugging the well would injure the rights of the reversioner, who owned the oil and gas in place. The court also based its decision on the premise that the oil and gas production in the immediate vicinity would be seriously damaged.[28] The Appel-

[25] N.Y. Laws 1933, c. 207; N.Y. Conserv. Law § 60–b.
[26] Conser. Dept. Bull. No. 20, New York State's Reforestation Program 29 (1942).
[27] 161 Misc. 103, 292 N.Y. Supp. 111 (1936), rev'd 248 App. Div. 670, 288 N.Y. Supp. 927 (1936). App. Div. rev'd 272 N.Y. 572, 4 N.E. 2d 742 (1936).
[28] The lower court stated: "The drawing of the casing and tubing from the well here in question, followed by plugging it, would mean destruction of the well; it

late Division reversed purely on the theory that removal was allowed by the terms of the lease. The Court of Appeals reversed the Appellate Division and the decision of the court of the first instance was reinstated. Additional judicial pronouncements in or concerning New York indicate that the state has power under its present constitution to prevent waste and probably to enact the usual conservation measures. Indicative of this are those cases dealing with correlative rights of common owners in underground reservoirs of percolating waters containing carbonic acid gas. Oil and gas and percolating waters both have been subject to the familiar doctrine of capture, and the court of appeals has likened the two.[29] Withdrawals from reservoirs of carbonic acid waters have been regulated since 1908 [30] in New York. On analogy to *Ohio Oil Company v. Indiana* [31] it was held that the legislative power extends to such a manner of regulation, since there is a common interest of all owning land containing natural deposits as in a common fund, and that the state may protect such common interests and, in addition, has authority to prevent waste of its natural resources.[32]

---

would no longer exist; and I am satisfied that the gas field or area in the immediate vicinity of the well would be seriously damaged thereby." 292 N.Y. Supp 111, 115 (1936).

[29] Wagoner v. Mallory, 169 N.Y. 501, 62 N.E. 584 (1902). The court, after stating the two are found in like accumulations said: "In this respect oil resembles water as it exists in the earth—especially salt and mineral waters, which have a market value—and is largely governed by the same rule of law. It consequently was held at a very early day in the history of the petroleum oil production that a man could not be restrained by his abutting neighbor from boring for oil upon his own premises, although he located his well within a few feet of the line, and would necessarily drain the oil from his neighbor's land, if any existed therein."

[30] N.Y. Laws 1908, c. 429; N.Y. Pub. Lands L. § 90.

[31] 177 U.S. 190 (1900).

[32] Lindsley v. Natural Carbonic Gas Co., 220 U.S. 61 (1911); Hathorn v. Natural Carbonic Gas Co., 194 N.Y. 326, 87 N.E. 504 (1909); The People of New York v. New York Carbonic Acid Gas Co., 196 N.Y. 421, 90 N.E. 441 (1909). In the Lindsley Case, the United States Supreme Court in treating New York's regulation of carbonic acid gas extraction stated: " 'It follows, from the essence of their right and from the situation of the things as to which it can be exerted, that the use by one of his power to seek to convert a part of the common fund to actual possession may result in an undue proportion being attributed to one of the possessors of the right, to the detriment of the others, or by waste by one or more, to the annihilation of the rights of the remainder. Hence it is that the legislative power, from the peculiar nature of the right and the objects upon which it is to be exerted, can be manifested for the purpose of protecting all the collective owners by securing a just distribution to arise from the enjoyment by them of their privilege to reduce possession and to reach the like end by preventing waste.' "

A CRITICAL APPRAISAL OF THE LEGISLATIVE, ADMINISTRATIVE AND JUDICIAL CONCEPTS OF CONSERVATION

It is impossible to criticize a concept never really originated. The plugging legislation has been adequate more from its early (1879) imposition and by becoming a standard practice than from any tenets of conservation. The legislative, administrative, and judicial concepts appear to have been founded in a large measure upon exploitation of property rather than upon any concept of the public good. Apt illustration of this lies in the fact that the extraction and exploitation of carbonic gases have been circumscribed by legislation, but not the extraction of oil and natural gas. It is not only in the protection of the public good in preserving valuable resources that no practicable steps have been taken; there has been nothing done (except in the matter of restraining the plugging of a well) to protect pecuniary and proprietary interests of adjoining and nearby owners.

Recent legislation indicates clearly that the State of New York is now interested in gas conservation, but from the standpoint of market apportionment rather than conservation directed to extractive practices. Effective February 16, 1948 the legislature declared it to be the state's policy that, in localities in short supply of gas, the available gas must be conserved for the use of domestic consumers, and thereafter for others already receiving the service. Meeting needs of those applying for service is postponed accordingly.[33]

New York has not acted effectively in any way to impose production conservation principles and the impelling motive for a general conservation law is now lacking, particularly in the case of natural gas. Secondary oil recovery operations by water flooding present different problems from those found in fields of flush production with a dissolved gas drive. Unless new sources of flush production of crude oil or gas are discovered, conservation legislation is not likely to be enacted. Production of natural gas increased from approximately 2,399,000,000 cubic feet in 1904 to 39,402,000,000 cubic feet in 1938, the zenith, and since then declined to about

[33] N.Y. Laws 1948, c. 7; N.Y. Pub. Ser. Law § 66–a.

9,210,000,000 cubic feet in 1945.[34] Oil reserves increased from an estimated 35,000,000 barrels in 1940 to 81,000,000 barrels in 1946,[35] not from new discoveries, but from improved technology in production methods and by increasing the yield from secondary recovery operations. Production recently declined from 5,185,000 barrels in 1941 to 4,648,000 barrels in 1945.[36] Although the oil reserves are largely in the stripper well category, increases in price may encourage greater production. There still is an appreciable quantity of oil to be extracted in an area where the demands are constantly growing.

[34] N.Y. STATE MUSEUM CIR. 7, RECENT NATURAL GAS DEVELOPMENTS IN SOUTH CENTRAL NEW YORK 3 (1932); Legis. Doc. No. 28 supra note 2 at 7.
[35] MINERALS YEARBOOK 1050 (U.S. Dep't. Int. 1945).
[36] Id. at 1052.

CHAPTER 23

North Carolina, 1945–1948

↝

The legislative session of 1945 enacted two systems of statutory control over the finding and production of petroleum or gas in North Carolina. Although the state is not at present ranked as a producer of petroleum, its future possibilities appear bright and seem to necessitate the adoption of a substantial code of conservation control to govern in the case of any commercial discoveries.

Persons desiring to make drilling explorations within North Carolina for oil or natural gas are required by a short 1945 statute [1] to register with the Department of Conservation and Development by furnishing names, addresses and the location of proposed operations. A bond in the amount of $2500 which runs to the state must be filed. This agreement is conditioned upon the promise of the applicant to properly plug any wells drilled under the rules and regulations as established in the Department. Upon the completion of any well or its shut down and abandonment the drilling operator must file with the Department a complete log of the drilling. Violation of these requirements is made a misdemeanor.

The more extensive legislation adopted during 1945 was the Oil and Gas Conservation Act. [2] The General Assembly of North Carolina in adopting this modern and comprehensive conservation statute provided that the law was enacted to protect against the evils that occur in the production and use of petroleum in the absence of the protection of coequal and correlative rights and thereafter declared that the public policy of the state was to protect public

BLAKELY M. MURPHY, WRITER. (See app. B.)
    [1] N.C. Sess. Laws 1945, c. 765; N.C. GEN. STAT. ANN. § 113–378 to 113–380 (Cum. Supp. 1945).
    [2] N.C. Sess. Laws 1945, c. 702; N.C. GEN. STAT. ANN. § 113–381 to 113–413 (Cum. Supp. 1945).

and private interests against such evils by prohibiting waste and compelling ratable production. Waste of oil and gas is specifically prohibited in the most modern terms. Provision is made for administrative control by creating a petroleum division within the Department of Conservation and Development. The division is officered by the director of the Department, three members of the Board of Conservation and Development designated by the governor of the state and the state geologist. Ample administrative powers are assigned this agency in its control of oil and gas production. Viewed in the most critical of lights the State of North Carolina has enacted a statute in accord with the most advanced concepts in the field of conservation legislation.

Section 2 of the Act states that if and when oil and natural gas are discovered within North Carolina in commercial quantities and this fact is called to the attention of the governor and his council of state, that he shall then "proclaim and declare this law to be in full force and effect, and shall proceed with the necessary action to see that the provisions of this law are carried out."

CHAPTER 24

North Dakota, 1907–1948

North Dakota looks enviously to the wealth and romance which follow the discovery of oil and gas in sister states. Vast deposits of lignite coal in North Dakota and the arm chair geologist belief that oil and gas accompany coal assure in the absence of commercially profitable discoveries of petroleum a keen continuing interest.

Gas was first found in the state by accident in July 1907 while drilling for water on a farm about nine miles south of Westhope, Bottineau County.[1] The Great Northern Oil Gas and Pipe Line Company, later reorganized as the North Dakota Gas Company, was formed to prospect and develop the field, and a number of villages in the vicinity were supplied with gas for heating, cooking, and lighting from the wells. These gas wells were confined to Bottineau County in north central North Dakota. Gas was found later near Crosby, Williams County, in the northwestern part of the state, and Lamoure County, in the southeast section.[2] In recent years these wells have become more or less obscure with the principal gas producing area now in Bowman County in southwest North Dakota. The Montana-Dakota Utilities Company had fourteen wells in Bowman County in 1943; not all were in production. Latest available figures show that a total of 177,000,000 cubic feet of gas was produced in 1943, some 55,000,000 cubic feet more than in 1942. New unitization agreements signed since have increased production for 1944 and subsequent years.[3]

GORDON V. COX, WRITER; Assisted by Ray R. Friedrich, Maurice E. Garrison, O. H. Thormodsgard, Nels G. Johnson, Alex C. Burr, Advisers. (See app. B.)

[1] LEONARD, NATURAL GAS IN NORTH DAKOTA, U.S. Geol. Sur. Bull. No. 431, 3–6 (1910).

[2] LEONARD, POSSIBILITIES OF OIL AND GAS IN NORTH DAKOTA, N.D. Geol. Sur. Bull. No. 1, 2 (1920).

[3] LAIRD, STRATIGRAPHY AND STRUCTURE OF NORTH DAKOTA, N.D. Geol. Sur. Bull. No. 18, 10 (1944).

Wildcat drilling for oil within North Dakota has not produced petroleum in commercial quantities.[4] The picture is not as discouraging as it might be since the Carter N. P. No. 1 well just over the Montana–North Dakota border, produces oil in substantial amounts, and there is every reason to believe the oil bearing formations extend a few hundred yards east into the state.

CONSERVATION LEGISLATION IN NORTH DAKOTA

In conjunction with the prevailing optimism the matter of conservation of these minerals has not been overlooked, and North Dakota can be classed as conservation conscious. As early as 1911 a statute was enacted providing that any well producing natural gas in the state, to prevent gas wasting by escape, be shut-in and the gas confined until such time as it could be utilized for lights, fuel, or power purposes.[5] This law did not apply to wells operated for oil. There is little information available as to what prompted the North Dakota legislature to pass the second conservation measure in 1929.[6] From the Act it is apparent that strong influences were present. It provided for licensing of any person or corporation desiring to drill a test hole, or an oil or gas well, and required that a permit be obtained from the state geologist, and a detailed log of the drilling operations furnished him. The principal feature of the law, and the one which caused the greatest reaction, was a provision making the drilling log available for examination as a public record to anyone having an interest in land within a radius of six miles of the operation, and giving the geologist of the state the right

[4] *Op. cit. supra.* at 10–11. Wildcat wells drilled: Des Lacs Western Oil Co. No. 1, Ward County, 1923; Davis Well, Adams County, April 27, 1923; Glenfield Oil Co. Well, Foster County, 1928; Prairie Oil and Gas Co's. No. 1 Armstrong, Kidder County, Jan. 15, 1930; A. R. Jones Oper. Co's, No. 1 Gehringer, Renville County, 1934; A. C. Townley Interests No. 1 Robinson Patented Land, Kidder County, 1934; D. J. Carter and Co. Well No. 1, Logan County, 1934; Big Viking Oil Co. No. 1, Williams County, 1935; Calif. Co. No. 1 Kamp, Williams County, 1940; Carter Oil Co. test, Morton County, Oct. 1940; Carter Oil Co's. No. 1 Emma L. Semling, Oliver County, Aug. 26, 1942; Northern Ord. Co. No. 1 Franklin Inv. Co., Emmons County, July 22, 1943. (All dates are completion times.) Well just across the border in Montana: Carter N.P. No. 1 produces oil.

[5] N.D. Laws 1911, c. 195. This was never repealed. Although not a part of the 1941 law, it is included among the statutes by the revisers of the 1943 code and appears as N.D. REV. CODE § 38–0810 (1943).

[6] N.D. Laws 1929, c. 184.

to examine the drilling operations for purposes of testing the well. Large oil and gas interests in the state objected violently to this provision. Obviously, a prospecting corporation which had invested thousands of dollars in search of a new field would be reluctant to disclose its records. A number of wildcat operations took place based on promotional schemes or on wishful thinking, rather than a sound technical basis. A scheme of that nature was the A. C. Townley well in Kidder County. Narratives related in connection with the sale of stock in that project, and the stories about its promoters, while not reliable enough to repeat, have the elements of a western movie. There was no manifest public reaction to this bill nor any response to it from the petroleum associations or the Federal Government. Essentially all of the older wildcats were financed by stock sold within North Dakota. The 1929 enactment did not repeal the 1911 law, and during the period 1929 to 1937 both statutes remained on the books.

The theory of conservation of the natural resources of North Dakota has grown slowly. The reason for passing the 1911 [7] statute was that of protection of adjacent landowners as is indicated in the reports of State Geologist A. G. Leonard writing in 1910.[8] He records that gas from one well escaped in such quantities that a loud roar could be heard in a town four miles distant. Considering the unsettled condition of much of North Dakota at that time, it is apparent that well capping as required by the statute was aimed at curbing escaping gas and incidentally at conserving a natural resource. It is very doubtful that the 1929 law [9] was directed toward the interests of conservation. From available incomplete data the impelling motive was curbing fraud upon innocent farmers and land owners in a primarily agricultural state. The law did achieve that purpose, though there is no indication of a sudden stoppage of the limited operations in view of the necessity for a public record being maintained of all activities. What actually happened where a well was drilled was that the companies simply disregarded the law, and the state geologist did not enforce its provisions. There was, in general, a detrimental effect to large scale operations,

[7] N.D. Laws 1911, c. 195.
[8] See note 1 *supra.*
[9] N.D. Laws 1929, c. 184.

which overbalanced the conservancy benefits. The influence of gas and oil interests upon the state geologist, and the bad effect which the Act had upon prospecting, caused its repeal in 1937. A further statute was enacted which provided that the state geologist prescribe and enforce rules and regulations governing drilling, casing and abandonment of oil and gas wells, and the prevention of waste.[10] As in the 1929 law, all persons and corporations drilling and operating oil wells in North Dakota were required to file a well log with the geologist within six months after completion or abandonment. The former section, that of making a log available to the public, was purposely omitted. This law was designed to and did encourage scientific exploration within North Dakota, but none of the rules and regulations which the Act stated were to be prescribed by the state geologist can be found in the official's office or the Geological Department of North Dakota, and it may be reasonably assumed that none were written.

THE PRESENT ENACTMENT

Unquestionably the biggest step made in the direction of satisfactory petroleum conservation is in the present law.[11] Following the repeal of the 1929 measure, the larger corporations again showed interest in the possibilities of oil and gas in the state. Hope that oil or gas might be found in commercial quantities in North Dakota was higher than ever. It was obvious from the experience of oil producing states that if adequate conservation measures were not on the books prior to the discovery of petroleum, it would be extremely difficult to enact such legislation later, because of the influence exerted upon the legislators. The 1937 law was woefully inadequate to meet large scale drilling programs. The drafting of a conservation law was already under way supervised by Dr. Foley in the fall of 1940, when Dr. Laird assumed his duties. The first proposal drafted by Dr. Laird was found unsuitable and discarded. A suggested statute, compiled by the Legal Committee, Interstate Oil Compact Commission, was then adopted as the proposed statute, and Dr. Laird appeared personally before the Affairs Com-

[10] N.D. Laws 1937, c. 135.
[11] N.D. Laws 1941, c. 170; N.D. Rev. Code c. 38–08 (1943).

mittee of the State Legislature on behalf of the bill. This was its only hearing and no opposition was voiced. The foresight of Dr. Frank Foley, the then State Geologist, and his successor Dr. Wilson M. Laird, the present official must be given credit for this statute. It was introduced and passed unanimously without discussion on the floor of the 1941 session.[12] Though the Act was closely scrutinized by certain coal interests in North Dakota, since it did not infringe upon the coal or coal mining businesses in any manner, no objection was made. The law in North Dakota as it stands today is surprisingly complete, as might be expected from a law incorporating those provisions found most suitable over a period of time by oil producing states. The control of the conservation of crude oil and natural gas is vested in the North Dakota Industrial Commission, which is given authority over all persons and property necessary to enforce the law's provisions. The statute does not provide for extensive conservancy measures, but gives the Commission power to pass such rules and regulations for conservation as are necessary. The agency adopted a complete set of general rules and regulations for the conservation of oil and gas December 19, 1941[13] which are modeled after those approved by the Interstate Oil Compact Commission.

The 1941 Act includes a specific definition of waste,[14] followed by a direct prohibition of waste of oil and gas.[15] After this express

[12] *Id.*

[13] North Dakota Industrial Commission. General Rules and Regulations for the Conservation of Crude Oil and Natural Gas (1941).

[14] "Waste, in addition to its ordinary meaning, shall include physical waste as that term is generally understood in the oil and gas industry and shall include: a. Underground waste and the inefficient, excessive, or improper use or dissipation of reservoir energy, including gas energy and water drive, of any pool; and the locating, spacing, drilling, equipping, operating or producing of any oil well or gas well in a manner which results or tends to result in reducing the quantity of oil or gas ultimately recoverable from any pool; and b. Surface waste and the inefficient storing of oil and the locating, spacing, drilling, equipping, operating or producing of oil wells or gas wells in a manner causing or tending to cause unnecessary or extensive surface loss or destruction of oil or gas."

[15] "Waste of Oil and Gas Prohibited. The production or handling of crude petroleum oil or natural gas in such a manner or under such conditions as to constitute waste is prohibited. If gas production is developed in the course of drilling for gas or oil, the owner within ten days after production commences shall determine whether the well shall be used for the production of gas or drilled further for the purpose of producing oil. If the well is not to be drilled further for oil, the producer shall prevent the waste of gas by shutting and confining the same in the well until such time as the gas shall be utilized for lighting, fuel, or power purposes. The production of

enactment as to waste, implicit directions are given the rule making body to adopt such rules, regulations, or orders as may be necessary from time to time in the proper administration and enforcement of the chapter.[16] Finally the Commission is given supervision and control over crude petroleum and natural gas resources of North Dakota.[17] This gives the agency all the implied powers essential to adequately carry out the legislative intent.

Until the present Act, the supervisory functions of a state agency were in name only. A state geologist was first appointed in 1895, when it was provided by legislation that the Professor of Geology at the University of North Dakota would also fill this post. From the reports available in the office, this official's primary function was the compilation of drilling reports and the granting of permits

---

water, however, insofar as such gas comes from a water bearing formation, shall not constitute waste under the provisions of this chapter if the discharge of gas does not exceed an average of five thousand cubic feet each twenty-four hour period."

[16] N.D. Rev. Code § 38–0804 (1943). "1. Require the drilling, casing, and plugging of wells to be done in such a manner as to prevent: a. The escape of oil or gas from one stratum to another; b. The intrusion of water into oil or gas strata; and c. The pollution of fresh water supplies by oil, gas or salt water; 2. Require a reasonable bond conditioned for the performance of the duty to plug each dry or abandoned well; 3. Require the person desiring . . . to drill any well for gas or oil, before commencing such drilling, to notify the state geologist . . . and to pay to the Commission a fee of twenty-five dollars. The form prescribed by the state geologist shall require: a. The exact location of the well; b. The name and address of the owner, operator . . . . c. The elevation of the well above sea level; and d. Such other relevant information as may be necessary to effectuate the purposes of this chapter. 4. Compel the filing of logs, . . . drilling records, and typical drill cuttings or cores if cores are taken, in the office of the state geologist within six months after the date of the completion of the well; 5. Prohibit wells from being drilled, operated, or produced in such a manner as to cause injury to neighboring leases or property; 6. Prohibit the drowning by water of any stratum or part thereof capable of producing oil or gas in paying quantities; 7. Prohibit the premature and irregular encroachment of water which reduces or tends to reduce the total ultimate recovery of oil or gas from any pool; 8. Require the operations of wells with efficient gas-oil ratios, and fix such ratios; 9. Prohibit 'blow-outs,' caving, and seepage as conditions indicated by such terms are generally understood in the oil and gas business; 10. Require appropriate precautions for the prevention of fires; 11. Require the identification of the ownership of all oil and gas wells, producing leases, refineries . . . ; 12. Regulate the shooting and chemical treatment of wells; 13. Regulate secondary recovery methods, including the introduction of gas, air, water, or other substance into producing formations; 14. Regulate the spacing of wells; 15. Require the filing currently of information as to the volume of oil and gas, or either of them, produced and saved from each and every property; 16. Require the filing with the state geologist of a notice of intention to drill a stratigraphic well, which notice shall specify the location of the drilling; and 17. Require the plugging report to be filed with the state geologist within sixty days after the completion of a stratigraphic well."

[17] N.D. Rev. Code § 38–0802 (1943).

to drill. Other than certain periodical statements, there is nothing to indicate that functions commonly concerned with conservation were performed. Although the 1937 [18] statute specifically provided that the geologist was to promulate rules and regulations for conservation of petroleum, no rules were ever put into operation. Not until the enactment of the present laws and the subsequent issuance of complete rules and regulations under the supervision of the present geologist, Dr. Wilson M. Laird, were proper measures taken to effect conservation of oil and gas. The agency in control of the conservancy program for North Dakota today is the Industrial Commission. The statute, proposed and recommended by the Interstate Oil Compact Commission, placed the administrative functions under a separate agency known as a petroleum board; but since there was little or no oil and gas activity in the state at that time, the governor felt the addition of another administrative agency a needless duplication; so in the conferences preceding passage of the law, all duties as to oil and gas were included with those of the Commission.

THE NORTH DAKOTA INDUSTRIAL COMMISSION

The same session of the legislature enacted a Uniform Administrative Practices Act [19] designed to govern proceedings of all administrative agencies operating on a state-wide basis, which includes the Industrial Commission in its usual capacity and provides it with a complete directive for procedure. Another set of rules is furnished by the oil and gas laws regulating this function of the Commission when administering these laws. That the legislature intended the Industrial Commission should be governed by one set of rules when acting in its capacity to conserve oil and gas, and another type of rule in its common capacity, is improbable. Since, however, a completely independent system is given in the chapter on conservation of oil and gas, it seems doubtful that the Administrative Practices Act repeals the procedural sections of the chapter on oil and gas. The following discussion assumes the provisions of the latter chapter prevail.

[18] N.D. Laws 1937, c. 135.
[19] N.D. Rev. Code § c. 28–32 (1943).

The North Dakota Industrial Commission performs duties within the state in connection with the conduct and management of utilities, industries, enterprises, and business projects, the best known of which is the state-owned flour mill. The Commission consists of three members—the governor of North Dakota, acting as chairman, the attorney general and the commissioner of agriculture and labor. These members obtain their posts by election and maintain their positions in the agency as long as they hold office. No additional compensation is given for serving on the body. Department heads are appointed by the Commission and these in turn hire needed employees for their work. Whenever the Industrial Commission deems it essential, it may employ technical personnel such as geologists, engineers, attorneys and the like. The state geologist under the present law is an assistant to the Commission with regard to conservation of oil and natural gases and is required to assist that body in every way. Compensation of employees and appointees is governed by the appropriations and earnings provided by the legislature. The Industrial Commission may discharge any of its personnel to promote the efficiency of public service. The present employees would be only a skeleton force if drilling operations should suddenly develop on a large scale.

The Commission passes such rules and regulations as needed at any of its current meetings. At these sessions the North Dakota attorney general is the counsel for the agency and procedure is generally informal.[20] In the absence of an emergency, no rule, regulation, or order may be made unless a public hearing has been held after ten days notice is given. This notice may be in such form and manner as the agency prescribes.[21] The hearing may be before the agency, any member of the agency, or before the state geologist at such time and place as is opportune.[22] But in case of emergency, the board may enforce a rule or regulation without first having a hearing as provided, however, these rules or regulations cannot remain effective more than 15 days and in any event expire when a rule or regulation made after due notice and hearing be-

---

[20] N.D. Rev. Code § 54–1703 (1943).
[21] N.D. Rev. Code § 38–0806 (1943).
[22] See note 23 supra.

comes effective.[23] Any interested party making a request to the Commission in writing may have it call a hearing for taking action on any matter within its jurisdiction. At the hearings, procedure is usually informal; up to the present no set of rules or regulations governing the appearance of parties has been adopted nor have any particular rules of evidence been followed. It is provided that any person having business with the agency may be represented, file briefs, cross examine witnesses, and present testimony. Upon the passage of a rule or regulation, it is entered in full by the state geologist in a book kept by the Commission for such purposes, which is a public record available for public inspection.[24] Only the *General Rules and Regulations for the Conservation of Crude Oil and Natural Gas* have thus far been adopted and published, and are available at the office of the state geologist, University of North Dakota, Grand Forks. The Commission with the state geologist is given power to require witnesses to attend, give testimony and require the production of books, papers, and records material to the issue before it at a hearing.[25] If such witnesses fail or refuse to obey the subpoena, the district court of a judicial district in North Dakota, on application of the Commission, its members or the state geologist, issues a subpoena.[26] Failure to comply with this order subjects the party to contempt proceedings.[27] An examination of the general rules indicates the Commission has promulgated adequately for conservation purposes. A slightly different definition of waste is given the code provision.[28] It is not necessary to detail every rule and regulation; the more pertinent

[23] N.D. Rev. Code § 38–0807 (1943).
[24] N.D. Rev. Code § 38–0808 (1943).
[25] N.D. Rev. Code § 38–0812 (1943).
[26] N.D. Rev. Code § 38–0813 (1943).
[27] See note 26 *supra.*
[28] "Waste in addition to its ordinary meaning, shall mean waste as that term is ordinarily used in the oil and gas industry. The meaning of waste shall include, (1) the inefficient, excessive, or improper use or dissipation of reservoir energy; and the locating, spacing, drilling, equipping, operating or producing of any oil or gas well or wells in a manner which results, or tends to result in reducing the quantity of oil or gas ultimately recovered from any pool in this state under production operations, and (2) the inefficient storing of oil; the producing of oil or gas in excess of transportation or marketing facilities or of reasonable market demand; the locating, spacing, drilling, equipping, operating, or producing of a well or wells in a manner causing or tending to cause, unnecessary or excessive surface loss or destruction of oil or gas, and the use of gas from a well producing gas only for the manufacture of carbon black or chemicals, unless otherwise authorized by the Commission."

ones deal with spacing,[29] pressure maintenance,[30] repressuring with gas or oil,[31] gas-oil ratio,[32] proration units,[33] equitable distribution of production,[34] disposal of brines or salt waters,[35] and flowing wells

[29] "1. SPACING—Unless a different well-spacing plan is adopted the State Geologist will, simultaneous with the establishment of proration units for each pool, prescribe well-spacing plans therefor, the boundaries of which shall coincide, if possible, with the boundaries of such proration units, which plan shall require a minimum of ten (10) acre spacing."

[30] "2. PRESSURE MAINTENANCE—means (1) the reintroduction (in the early stages of field development) of gas or fluid produced from an oil or gas well to maintain the pressure of the reservoir; (2) the introduction of gas or fluid for the same purpose but obtained from an outside source."

[31] "3. PRESSURE MAINTENANCE OR REPRESSURE WITH GAS OR OIL AND GAS PROPERTIES—The owner or operator of any well may inject gas under pressure into the formation containing oil or gas from the reservoir, upon application to and approval by the State Geologist. No gas shall be injected into a well for pressure maintenance or repressuring purposes until so ordered by the State Geologist pursuant to application, and notice as herein required. The application shall be verified and filed with the State Geologist showing; (for example) (a) the location of the intake well (b) the formations from which wells are producing or have produced. (c) the log of the intake well or such information as is available."

[32] "4. GAS-OIL RATIO—shall mean the relation of the gas in cubic feet to the production of oil in barrels as accepted by pipe lines. By special order the State Geologist will authorize periodic gas-oil surveys and reports to be filed on forms furnished by the Commission and including thereon for each well: Pool, reservoir and county in which the well is located; lease name and well number; elevation, producing formation; size and length of tubing; size and length of casing (oil string); size choke (if pumping well so designate); tubing pressure, casing pressure and trap pressure; production of water; oil and gas (in thousands of cubic feet) during the test; gas-oil ratio; and the A.P.I. gravity of the oil; duration of the test. The data shall be furnished for each well separately and the gas-oil ration shall be determined according to the following procedure."

[33] "5. PRORATION UNITS—Immediately upon the discovery of any pool or after the effective date hereof, the Commission may prescribe proration units for each pool which shall include shape, size and location thereof."

[34] "6. EQUITABLE DISTRIBUTION OF PRODUCTION—PURPOSE OF ACT A. Whenever the total amount of oil which all the producers in the state can produce exceeds the amount reasonably required to meet the reasonable market demand for oil produced in the state, then the Commission in order to prevent waste may limit the total amount of oil which may be produced by fixing a state allowable. The Commission may then allocate or distribute the allowable production among the pools in an equitable, reasonable and nondiscriminatory manner. B. In prorating the production allowed to each pool among the proration or drilling units therein, the Commission shall first deduct from the total pool allowable the quantity of oil which will be produced by the minimum or unprorated wells in such pool during such proration period and the balance shall be distributed pro rata among the remaining proration or drilling units in an equitable and reasonable manner, insofar as the same can be practically done."

[35] "7. DISPOSAL OF BRINE OR SALT WATER—A. Brine or salt water produced in the drilling for or the production of oil or gas shall not be run to earthen reservoirs or ponds, except for such reasonable time and under such conditions as may be approved by the State Geologist, after which it must be returned to some underground formation or otherwise disposed of as approved by the State Geologist

continuously produced.[36] Where it appears that the Commission is unable to prevent a violation or threatened infraction of its rules, regulations, or orders, it may, through the attorney general, bring suit in the name of North Dakota to restrain the acts done or threatened in the district court where the defendant resides or in the county where the violation occurred, or in any event in Burleigh County.[37] An appeal by either party to the Supreme Court of North Dakota may be taken from such restraining order.[38] An appeal lies also from the decision by interested parties testing the validity or enjoining the enforcement of any provisions of the law, the rules, regulations, or orders of the Commission.[39] The manner of presenting this appeal is governed by the regular judical review sections.

North Dakota has in the past adopted a very restrictive view as to the weight to be given to administrative findings, giving a trial *de novo* on appeal from administrative orders.[40] This policy has

---

where it cannot do damage to any fresh water, oil, gas or other minerals. B. Application approval and place of disposal. Salt water or other water containing minerals in such amount as to be unfit for domestic, stock, irrigation, or other general uses, upon application to, and approval by the State Geologist may be disposed of by injection into the following formations: 1. Nonproducing zones of oil or gas-bearing formations that contain water mineralized by processes of nature to such a degree that the water is unfit for domestic stock, irrigation, or other general uses. 2. All nonproducing formations containing water mineralized by processes of nature to such a degree that the water is unfit for domestic, stock, irrigation, or other general uses; Provided, that before any such formations are approved for disposal use, it shall be ascertained that they are separated from fresh water formations by impervious beds which will give adequate protection to such fresh-water formations, and that fresh-water supplies contained by the proposed disposal formation near its outcrop shall be at such a remote distance as not to be endangered by addition of mineralized water in the proposed disposal wells."

[36] "8. FLOWING WELLS CONTINUOUSLY PRODUCED—The oil flow shall be stabilized during the 24 hour period immediately preceding the test at a rate fixed as nearly as possible to its allowable as shown on the Commission's current oil proration schedule. Major adjustments in the rate of flow shall be made during the first 12 hours of the stabilization period and only minor adjustments made during the last 12 hours. No adjustments shall be made during the time in which the well is being tested and the rate of production during the test shall not be less than the well's daily allowable. Should gas be withdrawn from the casing in an attempt to maintain a fluid seal, or for any other reason, this volume of gas must be added to gas produced through tubing in computing the gas-oil ratio."

[37] N.D. REV. CODE § 38–0819 (1943).

[38] N.D. REV. CODE § 38–0820 (1) (1943).

[39] N.D. REV. CODE § 38–0820 (2) (1943).

[40] Gotchy v. Work. Comp. Bur., 49 N.D. 915, 194 N.W. 663 (1923); Weisgerber v. N.D. Work. Comp. Bur., 70 N.D. 165, 292 N.W. 627 (1940); Starkenberg v. Work. Comp. Bur., 73 N.D. 234, 13 N.W. 2d 395 (1944); In Re Minn.

continued under the Administrative Practices Act[41] and it is assumed would greatly influence the court in the scope of review given findings of the Industrial Commission in its control of oil and gas.

In spite of the interest in conservation in North Dakota from 1911 to the present, no challenges have been made of the validity of any enactment nor has there been any litigation involving oil and gas conservation.

Throughout this discussion the present law of conservation has been commended, and in a critical appraisal of the legislative, administrative, and judicial phases of conservation, this approval is justified. Either through oversight or insufficient planning by the framers of the present law, the administrative functions of the Industrial Commission are duplicated in differing chapters of the code which causes confusion in determining the exact scope of the Commission in the matter of oil and gas conservation. Overbalancing this administrative difficulty is the fact that, although North Dakota ranks among the lowest in the production of commercial oil and gas, it has a thorough, comprehensive conservation statute. This state may well be proud of the foresight of those who contributed to the present enactment.

St. Paul & S. Ste. M. R. Co., 30 N.D. 221, 152 N.W. 513 (1915); In Re Tri-State Motor Trans. Co., 67 N.D. 119, 270 N.W. 100 (1936).

[41] In Re Nor. Pac. Ry. Co., 74 N.D. 416, 23 N.W. 2d 49 (1946).

CHAPTER 25

Ohio, 1885–1948

~

Ohio, an early oil and gas state, was the next to produce in substantial quantities after Pennsylvania. In the search for gas, oil was discovered in 1885 at Lima, Ohio. Gas had.been found near the neighboring town of Findlay some months previously and the drillers of the first oil well in Ohio who confidently expected to find gas were probably somewhat disappointed when oil appeared in its stead. From 1885 development of both oil and gas readily increased. The production of oil reached a peak in 1896 of 23,941,-000 barrels, and dwindled gradually to 3,120,000 barrels in 1947. Gas production reached its crest later than oil, 80,000,000,000 cubic feet in 1915, and did not go off as rapidly as oil. At present a substantial quantity of gas is being produced, about 60,000,000,000 cubic feet in 1947, or 1 per cent of the total in the United States.

Today oil comes from three principal fields in Ohio—the Lima-Indiana Field, originally centered around Lima and Findlay, which in its heyday accounted for the greater part of Ohio oil production —the Chatham Field centering around Medina, and the Marietta Field in the southeastern part of the state near Marietta, a continuation of the western Pennsylvania oil field, producing the same grade and quality of crude oil.[1] The greater part of the gas production, on the other hand, is in the eastern half of the state, particularly the northeast half. Except for the period of flush production in the Lima-Indiana pool, more importance has been attached in Ohio to the discovery and production of natural gas than crude oil.

WILLIAM A. MCAFEE, WRITER; A. M. Gee, C. C. Hogg, Fred J. Milligan, Advisers. (See app. B.)

[1] Wilson and Faine, *Stripper Wells in Ohio*, I INTERSTATE OIL COMPACT Q. BULL. 68 (1942) states that slightly more than 50% of all stripper wells in the state produce Pennsylvania grade crude.

This is because, after the first decade of the twentieth century, Ohio production of crude oil has been relatively insignificant, and the small wells have required continual pumping. Also, the crude oil from the Lima-Indiana Field has a large sulphur content and is consequently somewhat undesirable. Possibly the small oil and gas production of Ohio accounts for the fact that the state has never paid much attention to oil and gas conservation.

OHIO CONSERVATION LEGISLATION

The Ohio legislature enacted in 1883 a law entitled, "An Act Regulating the Casing of Oil Wells and the Mode of Plugging the Same When Abandoned." [2] Its apparent purpose was to require drillers of oil or gas wells to prevent the pollution of water by these substances and to conserve them by stopping the encroachment of water on their sands. The Act provided that all oil or gas wells before being drilled into oil bearing sand should be encased "with good and sufficient wrought iron oil well casing and in such manner as shall exclude all surface or fresh water from the lower part of such well, and from penetrating the oil bearing rock." On abandonment of an oil well the Act provided that it be plugged in the manner specified before drawing the casing, "for the purpose of excluding all fresh or surface water from penetrating the oil bearing rock or rocks."

"An Act to Prevent the Wasting of Natural Gas and to Provide for the Plugging of all Abandoned Wells" [3] was enacted by the legislature on February 19, 1889, H.R. 813, and it could properly be called Ohio's first conservation measure. While the Act called for the shutting in of gas wells within a reasonable time after completion (not exceeding three months) "in order to prevent the said gas wasting by escape," it was expressly stated that this requirement should not apply to an oil well. The Act further provided for the plugging of abandoned gas wells before drawing the casing in a somewhat different method than that set out in the Act of 1883; and gave neighboring owners the right to shut-in gas wells flowing in violation of the Act, to plug wells which the owner failed to plug upon abandonment, and to recover costs from the violator.

[2] 80 Ohio Laws 190.
[3] 86 Ohio Laws 48.

Effective April 1, 1893 "An Act to Regulate Drilling, Operation and Abandonment of Petroleum Oil, Natural Gas and Mineral Water Wells, and to Prevent Certain Abuses Connected Therewith"[4] repealed the Acts of 1883 and 1889. Section 1 of the law required the owner or operator of any oil or gas well or mineral water well to encase it with "good and sufficient wrought iron casing" in a way to exclude all surface or fresh water from the lower part of the well from penetrating oil or gas bearing rock. Section 2 governed the plugging of abandoned oil, natural gas and mineral water wells before drawing the casing in the manner specified. Section 3 required that gas wells be shut-in within ten days after penetrating the gas bearing rock to prevent gas wasting by escape and to "confine the gas in said well until and during such time as the gas therein shall be utilized for light, fuel or power purposes." As in the Act of 1889, wells operated as oil wells were excepted from this requirement. Section 4 prohibited the use of natural gas for illuminating purposes in flambeau lights. It was expressly provided, however, that this section did not prohibit jumbo burners or other burners consuming no more gas than jumbo burners. Persons using these burners in the open air were required to enclose them in gas globes or lamps and to turn off the gas not later than 8 A.M. and were not permitted to light them again until 5 P.M. This Act was amended March 19, 1896 so as to permit the burning of flambeau lights within the derrick of any drilling well or for the purpose of lighting the streets of towns, villages and hamlets.[5]

Upon the adoption of the General Code of Ohio in the early part of 1910, the Act of 1893 was codified in Chapter 22, "Natural Gas, Oil and Mineral Waters" as Section 6311 to 6319, inclusive. Shortly thereafter, by H.R. 441 passed May 10, 1910[6] Sections 6311, 6312, 6313, 6314 and 6319 of the General Code were amended and new Section 6319–1 was enacted. The amendments were not significant, merely changing in minor respects the sections dealing with casing oil and gas wells, plugging when abandoned, giving the right of self help and recovery of cost to adjoin-

[4] 90 Ohio Laws 24.
[5] 92 Ohio Laws 78.
[6] 101 Ohio Laws 337.

ing owners on failure to plug abandoned wells, and amplifying the penalties for failure to comply. One new type of provision added by amendment to Section 6312 was that no oil well be permitted to stand without diligently pumping or flowing for a period of more than three months, and permitting adjoining owners (after giving notice to the owner either to operate or repair the casing in such well) to sue for a penalty of $1000 any owner, operator or lessee of any oil well allowed to remain for that period without being pumped or flowed, if neglect might cause injury to the adjacent land and well owner "by flooding the oil and gas bearing sand with fresh or salt water from leaks in the casing in such well." The newly added Section 6319–1 required a person before abandoning a well to notify the owner or owners of adjoining land and wells of his intention to plug and fill it and of the time the operation would commence.

For many years the part of the General Code of Ohio containing the laws regulating mining, and especially coal mining,[7] had contained similar provisions to those in Section 6311 and 6319, but originally limited in their application to oil and gas wells drilled on coal lands. The first legislation of this character is found in H.R. 435 [8] passed April 23, 1898 providing, among other things, for casing oil and gas wells drilled upon coal lands and their plugging in a specified manner. These provisions of the law were amended and modified [9] from time to time. By S. 167, passed March 21, 1917,[10] the provisions (then found in Section 973 of the General Code of Ohio) were further amended so as to provide the method of plugging abandoned oil and gas wells, whether or not drilled in coal bearing lands. This section of the General Code repeated the subject matter of Section 6312 of the General Code then in effect, probably through inadvertence. Section 973 of the General Code was further amended in minor respects by H.R. 207, April 4, 1927.[11] By S. 321 passed June 10, 1931 the entire mining

[11] 112 Ohio Laws 144.

[7] Now codified under the heading Mining Law, § 898–898–202 Ohio Gen. Code Ann. (Throckmorton Supp. 1940–1945).

[8] 93 Ohio Laws 237.

[9] S. 287, Apr. 16, 1900, 94 Ohio Laws 379; H. R. 125, Apr. 3, 1902, 95 Ohio Laws 91; S. 91, Apr. 5, 1910, 101 Ohio Laws 52; S. 205, May 31, 1911 (102 Ohio Laws 457).

[10] 107 Ohio Laws 630.

laws of the state were revised, recodified and supplemented. Section 973 of the General Code was repealed and split up into Sections 898–184 to 898–189 inclusive. Section 898–188 prescribed the method of plugging abandoned wells, whether or not in coal lands, and a new paragraph, codified as Section 898–190, permitted the withdrawal of the casing of gas wells, leaving only the tubing and packer in the wells, where filled with mud laden fluid from the top of the packer to the surface as each succeeding string of casing was withdrawn, and provided the written consent of the Chief of the Division of Mines of the State of Ohio was obtained.

There was some duplication in the Ohio mining laws, Section 898 *et seq.*, and the provisions of Chapter 22 of the General Code entitled, "Natural Gas, Oil and Mineral Waters" Section 6311 to 6319–1. In view of this partial repetition and with the evident desire to concentrate the Sections of the Ohio code dealing with regulation of the production of oil and gas in the chapter containing the mining laws, H.R. 695 was passed June 8, 1933.[12] The Act repealed Section 6311 of the General Code requiring the casing of oil and gas wells, but amended Section 898–190 of the General Code to incorporate substantially the same provisions. The Act also repealed Section 6312 of the General Code which called for the plugging of abandoned wells, but since Section 898–188 substantially duplicated this section (except for that part prohibiting oil wells from standing without pumping or flowing for a period of more than 90 days, and compelling repair of leaky casing or plugging of any such well upon notice from the chief of the division of mines). These latter items were enacted as a separate new section of the mining laws, Section 898–188-A. Sections 6313 and 6314 giving the right of self help and recovery of cost to adjoining owners on failure to plug abandoned wells, and Section 6319 prescribing penalties were repealed by this Act. In addition the Act repealed Section 6319–1 (requiring notice to adjoining owners of intention to abandon and to plug an oil or gas well) but incorporated it as an amendment to Section 898–187.

The movement to concentrate all parts of law dealing with the production of oil and gas in the chapter of the Code of Ohio con-

[12] 115 Ohio Laws 428.

taining the mining laws was carried further by the passage on April 7, 1937 of S. 113.[13] This bill repealed Section 6315 of the General Code, that gas wells be shut-in within ten days after completion of drilling, but reenacted the clauses in substantially the same form as Section 898–188-B of the General Code. Section 6316 of the General Code, exempting oil wells from the last mentioned provisions was repealed, but reenacted in its original form as Section 898–188-C of the General Code. The net effect of the foregoing enactments and repeals was to gather the portions of the Ohio statutes dealing with the production of oil and gas in the chapter of the General Code containing the mining laws of the state and to leave ony two paragraphs regulating the production of gas or oil in Chapter 22 entitled, "Natural Gas, Oil and Mineral Waters." These were found in Section 6317 and 6318 of the General Code prohibiting flambeau lights and the use of jumbo burners except between 5 P.M and 8 A.M. and permitting burning of flambeau lights within the derricks of drilling wells or for the lighting of streets of cities and villages.

The Attorney General of Ohio had ruled by opinion July 7, 1930 [14] that the provisions of the General Code of Ohio requiring the plugging of abandoned oil and gas wells, in order to prevent the encroachment of water into the oil and gas sand formations, prohibited the use of the so-called water flooding method for the recovery of oil. As it was thought desirable to authorize this type of oil recovery, H.R. 491 passed March 22, 1939 [15] was enacted. By this Act Section 898–188-C of the General Code was so amended to permit water flooding operations upon the written approval of the Chief of the Division of Mines of the State of Ohio, "provided that the introduction of such pressure of water or other liquid into said oil bearing sand shall be controlled from the ground surface only and shall be through casing or tubing which shall be anchored and packed so that no other oil or gas bearing sand and fresh water strata, above or below, shall be affected by the introduction of such controlled pressure." The section further required furnishing a map of the proposed operations to the chief of the division of mines

[13] 117 Ohio Laws 242.
[14] 2 Ops. Att'y. Gen. Opinion 2061 (1930).
[15] 118 Ohio Laws 100.

showing all existing wells, the location and depth of all proposed wells within the area to be flowed and the location and depth of producing wells on adjoining lands. The section also provided that the chief of the division of mines must give notice of the application for the water flooding permit to adjoining well owners and owners of adjoining lands entitled to object to the granting of the water flooding application. This Act, for the first time in the history of the legislation of Ohio regulating the production of oil and gas, enunciated general principles of conservation by amending Section 898–188-B of the General Code so as to add the following provision: "All owners, lessees, operators or other agents drilling for or producing crude oil or natural gas shall use every reasonable precaution in accordance with the most approved methods of operation to stop and prevent waste of oil or gas, or both." Prior to amendment this section had only required gas wells to be shut-in within ten days after completion of drilling.

No further amendments except of a very minor character have been made since the last mentioned, but the entire mining laws of the State of Ohio were revised and codified by S. 326 passed May 16, 1941 [16] effective September 2, 1941. In this codification the following sections of the General Code contain all of the provisions of the statutes of Ohio which by any stretch of the imagination could be considered as intended for the conservation of oil or gas, save the provisions of Sections 6317 and 6318 dealing with the burning of natural gas in flambeau and jumbo lights. Section 898–192 specifies the method of plugging abandoned wells. Section 898–193 requires an oil well owner or operator of an oil well having a leaky casing or tubing to either repair or plug the well upon notice from the chief of the division of mines, and specifies that unless written permission is obtained from the chief of the division of mines no oil well shall be permitted to stand without pumping or flowing same for a period of more than 90 days. Section 898–195 lays down the general rule that all reasonable precautions be taken and the most approved method of operation used in drilling for and producing oil or gas to prevent waste, and requires that natural gas wells be shut-in within ten days after completion of drilling. Section 898–196 permits water flooding operations for the recovery

[16] 119 Ohio Laws 457.

of oil as described. Section 898–198 requires gas and oil wells to be cased in such manner as shall be affirmed by the chief of the division of mines and in accord with approved practice, and further specifies the manner and under what conditions casing of gas wells or water wells used in the water flooding process may be withdrawn.

ADMINISTRATION OF THE LAW

Section 898–179 provides that the laws relating to oil and gas wells shall be administered by the oil and gas well inspectors under the supervision of the chief of the division of mines. Under Section 898–9 the chief of the division of mines has the power to issue instructions and make rules and regulations for the government of gas and oil well inspectors and deputy gas and oil well inspectors. The Division of Mines is a division of the Department of Industrial Relations of the State of Ohio.

COURT REVIEW

The constitutionality of the laws of the State of Ohio regulating the production of oil and gas does not seem to have been tested by court action. Until 1912 the laws regulating oil and gas production were passed in pursuance of the grant of legislative power to the general assembly made by Section 1 of Article II of the Constitution of 1852, and were valid as a reasonable exercise of the general police power. However, by amendment of the Ohio Constitution adopted September 3, 1912, special power was granted to the legislature in Section 36, Article II, "Laws may also be passed . . . to provide for the regulation of methods of mining, weighing, measuring and marketing oil, gas, and all other minerals."

There are no decided cases of any significance whatsoever involving the interpretation or effect of the statutes regulating oil and gas production, and the only pronouncement of an Ohio court which enunciates any common law principles of oil or gas conservation is found in *Moore v. Barry* [17] where a lessee of land on

[17] 10 Ohio Law Abstract 720 (1931).

which an oil well had ceased to produce, was enjoined by the Ohio Court of Appeals (intermediate court), at the instance of the land owner, from pumping air into the well to drive the oil remaining in the lower strata to other wells located on adjoining lands of which he was also the lessee but which were owned in fee by third parties. In its opinion the court said: "We then come to the question whether the lessee has a right to install a mechanical device which tends to drive the oil from under any part of defendants' premises. In 1st Thornton on The Law of Oil and Gas at page 56, Sec. 31, we find the following: 'While every land owner has the right to bore for gas on his own land, and to use such portion of it as arises by natural laws to the surface in this wells, or flows into his pipes, yet an adjoining owner, at least has no right to induce an unnatural flow into or through his well, or do any act with reference to the common reservoir and the gas in it, injurious to or calculated to destroy it; and an action may be maintained by the owners of the superincumbent lands to enjoin another owner from using devices for pumping, or any other artificial process, that shall have the effect of increasing the natural flow of gas.' "

MEMBERSHIP IN THE INTERSTATE COMPACT TO CONSERVE OIL AND GAS

April 30, 1943 the Ohio legislature passed S. 160 [18] to authorize and *direct* the governor "for and in the name of the State of Ohio, to join with other states in the Interstate Compact to Conserve Oil and Gas, which was heretofore executed in the City of Dallas, Texas on the 16th day of February, 1935, . . . and to enter into and execute an agreement with other states now parties or which may hereafter become parties, whereby said Compact shall be extended with the consent of the Congress for a period of four years from September 1, 1943." Other sections of the Act authorize the governor to execute agreements for the further extension of the expiration date of the Interstate Compact and to determine if and when the State of Ohio withdraw from the Compact, and appoint the governor as the official representative of the state on the Interstate Oil Compact Commission with authority to name an

[18] 120 Ohio Laws 203.

assistant representative to act in his place. The Act further provides that it is not intended and should not be construed to prevent or prohibit the production of oil by water flooding, nor require the enactment of conservation statutes, or the creation and establishment of bureaus or commissions unless and until the legislature should determine by law that such statutes, bureaus or commissions are advisable to prevent the physical waste of oil or gas.

CONCLUSION

To those accustomed to legislation such as is in effect in the great oil producing states in the nature of proration statutes, well spacing, unitization and similar enactments, the provisions of the laws of Ohio may seem trivial. The absence of more important and far reaching conservation legislation is due to the fact that oil and gas production in Ohio has been comparatively insignificant since the first decade of this century.

CHAPTER 26

Oklahoma, 1938–1948

~⁄~

The King is dead. Long live the King. A new ruler has come to the throne in the last ten years. Not by one blow, but by a series of thrusts and jabs, the legislature, the courts and the Oklahoma Corporation Commission have buried individual (I own) property rights, and raised to the throne the greatest good for the greatest number. Oil rights are no longer safely measured by property lines, productivity of wells, a person's desires or needs, nor, for that matter engineer's estimates. The value of each property—unless isolated—depends upon that single property's restricted and allocated production in a shifting panoramic system of regulations designed to meet varying circumstances and to compel the ultimate recovery of oil from a pool, equitably balancing so far as possible individual rights between tracts.

German in 1938[1] vividly described the paths by which the law of oil and gas came out of the jungle and into the area of correlative rights. The law of capture, except as a rule for determining title of oil, had been effectively repealed before Judge German laid down his pen. By 1938 the ranks of the individualists began to thin and the survivors fought less vigorously those laws and regulations designed for the furtherance of public good and the protection of correlative rights. Not all producers liked being told how much they could produce each day; but fewer complained of it, and the majority began to see its underlying justice. By 1938 all persons recognized the right of the Commission[2] to regulate plugging and

T. MURRAY ROBINSON, WRITER; Assisted by Robert A. McCracken, Floyd Green, Barret Galloway: Earl Foster, W. P. Z. German, Advisers. (See app. B.)

[1] German, *Legal History of Conservation of Oil and Gas in Oklahoma*, LEGAL HISTORY OF CONSERVATION OF OIL AND GAS—A SYMPOSIUM 110 (1938).

[2] The Corporation Commission administers the oil and gas laws of Oklahoma. Okla. Laws 1933, c. 131, § 4–7; OKLA. STAT. tit. 52, c. 3, § 87–90 (1941). Pound,

to prevent surface waste, including unnecessary surface storage (the right to restrict production to the market demand).[3] By then the authority of the Commission to regulate underground waste through gas-oil ratios and limitations upon production was accepted by most of the industry. The doctrine of correlative rights and the need for more efficient reservoir control brought on well spacing and acreage as a factor in well allowables, but the power of the Commission to regulate in a manner to insure the greatest ultimate recovery from a pool had not yet been nailed to the masthead as the dominant pennant.[4]

In 1938 where regulation blended the rights of adjoining land owners with duties to the public to protect a reservoir, the former responsibilities were measured exactly and the latter loosely. Conversely, today reservoir protection is the primary objective and the rights and duties of adjoining land owners to one another move to the background.[5]

History of Proration and Conservation in Oklahoma, in a paper read Mar. 15, 1944 before the Ill.-Ind. Basin Chapter, API, with reference to the vesting of authority in the Corporation Commission, said: "The authors of the Oklahoma Constitution had no thought that the Corporation Commission should control the production of oil and gas. Because of that Commission's broad powers, however, the petroleum industry later induced legislatures to place such control in that body. The success of conservation in Oklahoma is at least partially attributable to this fact."

[3] Okla. Laws 1933, c. 131, § 2; Okla. Laws 1935, c. 59, art. 1, § 1; Okla. Stat. tit. 52, c. 3, § 85 (1941).

[4] In 1934, our court said in H. F. Wilcox Oil and Gas Co. v. Walker, 168 Okla. 355, 32 P. 2d 1044, 1047 (1934): "By the provisions of Section 11567, O.S. 1931, the term 'waste' is defined, in addition to its ordinary meaning, to 'include economic waste, underground waste, surface waste and waste incident to the production of crude oil or petroleum in excess of transportation or marketing facilities or reasonable market demands.' When these conditions exist and the same have been properly found by the Commission, then and then only is the Corporation Commission vested with power, authority and jurisdiction to limit the production of crude oil or petroleum by the owner from a common source of supply to 'such proportion of all crude oil and petroleum that may be produced therefrom, without waste, as the production of the well or wells of any such person . . . bears to the total production of such common source of supply.' Section 11568. Then and then only is the Corporation Commission 'authorized to so regulate the taking of crude oil or petroleum from any or all such common source of supply as to prevent the inequitable or unfair taking, from a common source of supply . . . by any person . . . and to prevent unreasonable discrimination in favor of any one such common source of supply as against another. Section 11568."

[5] In 1947 our court said: "Title 52 O.S. 1941 § 86, as amended, Laws 1945, p. 156, sec. 3, 52 O.S. Supp. § 86, provides that the Commission shall have authority and is charged with the duty of preventing the inefficient or wasteful utilization of gas in the operation of oil wells producing from a common source of supply, of pre-

In the absence of a formula for a proper distribution of reservoir value, regulations designed for the ultimate in pool production— true conservation—necessarily favor production from some tracts or areas as opposed to other tracts or areas. When all regulations and orders are designed to bring about the ultimate in recovery and to distribute it on the most equitable basis, then the millennium will have arrived. In Oklahoma conservation has proposed to correlative rights; soon they will be married and live in the same house. Oklahoma remains in the vanguard in the change from jungle law and legal shackles to scientific control and allocations.[6]

By 1938 the definition of waste in Oklahoma as applied to oil had been expanded to include economic waste, underground waste (improper use of the reservoir to reduce ultimate recovery), and production in excess of transportation facilities or reasonable market demand.[7] The Corporation Commission had been vested with the broad power to make orders preventing waste.[8] The structure of enforcement provided by the legislature included a grant to the Commission of legislative, executive and judicial powers needed to control oil pools and production.[9] Although the Commission

---

venting the production of gas in such quantities or in such manner as unreasonably to reduce reservoir pressure or unreasonably to diminish the quantity of oil or gas that might be recovered from a common source of supply, and of preventing the escape of gas from oil wells into the air in excess of the amount necessary in the efficient drilling, completion or operation thereof." and further: "Experience has taught us that the heedless dissipation of gas reservoir energy of oil pools has resulted in the loss of many millions of barrels of oil. We take judicial knowledge of this fact. In most instances it is impossible to use a formula which will apply equally to all persons producing from a common source. In striking a balance between conservation of natural resources and protection of correlative rights, the latter is secondary and must yield to a reasonable exercise of the former," in Denver Producing and Refining Co. v. State, 18 OKLA. B.J. 1335, 184 P. 2d 961 (1947).

[6] For a comprehensive statement on the progressive advancement of the conservation of oil and gas in Oklahoma, see FPC, Natural Gas Investigation, Docket G–580, Hearing II Oklahoma City (1945). See Robinson, A Discussion Concerning the Oklahoma Law of Oil and Gas, 17 OKLA. B.J. 1071 (1946).

[7] See note 3 supra.

[8] See note 2 supra.

[9] Russell v. Walker, 160 Okla. 145, 15 P. 2d 114 (1932). In a statement by Reford Bond, Chairman of the Corporation Commission of Oklahoma, given in opposition to H.R. 7372, referring to the powers of the Corporation Commission of Oklahoma, Judge Bond said: "The Corporation Commission is a constitutional body possessing executive, legislative and judicial powers. No state court, except the Supreme Court, has power to set aside, alter or annul the Commission's orders, rules and regulations, and the Supreme Courts of the State and of the United States have

had been reminded in the *Wilcox* case [10] that its powers were derived from and therefore limited by the legislature, the admonition related to means and not to results or objectives. The Commission was told to travel on the prescribed highways but was not limited in a choice of destination.

The right of the Commission to prevent surface waste in all its phases, to restrict production for the prevention of waste and to pace all operators at the same comparative rate of production through each well bore seemed established in 1938. Ownership of oil in place, determined by the comparative acreage or percentage of reservoir ownership, had been overlooked until 1935 when well spacing or drilling units were created for the first time in any state by the Legislature of Oklahoma.[11] Acreage is only one of the dimensions by which reservoir ownership or percentage of reservoir ownership is measured; even so, the Commission and the courts moved cautiously into this phase of regulation for reservoir protection and adjustment of ownership. This new sprout from the police power had to be cultivated in a manner that tended to increase recovery and yet effect proper division between the owners of the right to reservoir production. This first Spacing Act by express language was limited to oil common sources of supply, although the economic implications of spacing seem to make its application more desirable in gas distillate or pure gas fields. Moreover, the Act, in describing the factors which to be considered by the Commission, did not include the cost of wells.[12] An increased understanding by both the legislature and the Commission of the need for and the usefulness of spacing regulations has been one of the outstanding developments of oil law in the past decade.

In 1945 the legislature added pool-wide compulsory communization or pooling to the weapons provided the Commission to fight waste.[13]

---

upheld the constitutionaity of the Oklahoma conservation laws." Hearings before Committee on Foreign and Interstate Commerce on H.R. 7372, 76th Cong., 3d Sess. (1940).

[10] H. F. Wilcox Oil & Gas Co. v. Walker, 168 Okla. 355, 32 P. 2d 1044 (1934).
[11] Okla. Laws 1935, c. 59, art. 1, § 3; OKLA. STAT. tit. 52, c. 3, § 87 (1941).
[12] *Ibid.*
[13] Okla. Laws 1945, tit. 52, c. 3b.; OKLA. STAT. tit. 52, c. 3, § 286 (Cum. Supp. 1945).

To best achieve continuity in discussing the changes which have occurred during the evolution of oil and gas conservation in Oklahoma from 1938 to now, the subject matter has been broken into the components of a well-rounded conservation program. While there is some overlapping and the classifications are perhaps arbitrary, the following subdivisions are offered: (1) proration (production control), (2) gas-oil ratios, (3) well spacing, (4) spacing unit pooling, (5) pool-wide unitization, (6) conservation of gas, (7) miscellaneous matters of interest, (8) the administrative history of oil and gas conservation.

PRORATION

Orders imposing production control are entered to prevent waste or to equitably divide the available transportation facilities or market. The right of the Commission to prorate as a means of preventing waste was recognized and accepted by 1938. Proration was about the only tool employed for waste prevention before 1938. Many were the trials and tribulations which befell proration before it reached a mature stature.[14] In general the procedure for fixing the state-wide allowable of oil production has been constant since the enactment of the 1933 law.[15] Therein the Commission was authorized to restrict the full production from any common source of supply if such production would constitute waste, and in the event of such restriction or regulation, to permit each individual within the restricted field to take therefrom only such portion of the allowed field production as the unrestricted production from his wells would bear to the total field's unrestricted production. The factors of acreage and drainage were not included in the yardstick furnished the Commission for measuring well allowables. The Commission was authorized to prevent discrimination between common sources of supply. The right to prorate set forth in the earlier act was included verbatim in the 1935 Act.[16]

Under these sections the enforcement officer or the Commission each month, or on occasion every other month, gives notice

---

[14] See note 1 *supra*.
[15] Okla. Laws 1933, c. 131, § 4; OKLA. STAT. tit. 52, c. 3, § 87 (1941). Peppers Refining Co. v. Corporation Comm., 198 Okla. 451, 179 P. 2d 899 (1947).
[16] Okla. Laws 1935, c. 59, art. 1, § 4; OKLA. STAT., tit. 52, § 87 (1941).

of a state-wide allowable hearing to be held the closing days of the month. All state purchasers are requested to file nominations and the enforcement officer (now the director of conservation), by telephone or telegram, fills in the hiatuses in his information. After considering these materials together with the facts gleaned from the Bureau of Mines forecasts and those of industry associations, the director of conservation comes to the proration hearing prepared to recommend a state-wide daily oil allowable for Oklahoma; all this is presumably done without relation to the national picture. Where the several fields within Oklahoma can without waste produce the amount of Oklahoma oil for which the conservation officer has determined there is a firm market demand, that demand fixes his recommendation. If on the other hand the market for Oklahoma crude exceeds that amount of oil producible from the fields without waste, then the daily allowable of oil production is set at the fields' capacities to produce without waste.

In general the per well allowable—or the rates of withdrawal allowed per well—are determined for each pool of consequence at a separate Commission hearing. Here the Commission also fixes the rules required to regulate production practices in that field to preserve and promote its orderly development and protect correlative rights. Sometimes in newly discovered fields or in fields in which the determining factors have substantially changed in the preceding month, the Commission at the state-wide hearing considers changes or amendments to the well production rates for those fields. Thus through the hearing, the Commission allocates its determined state-wide daily allowable among the several fields within ·the state; the allowable for each field is in turn reallocated to individual wells by specified orders or by the general order of the Commission. In most cases the monthly hearings are comparatively brief and seldom is a voice raised in opposition to the recommendation of the conservation officer. On occasion the producers in a field have complained that they were not allowed a fair share of the state-wide allowable, or that the state-wide allowable was set at a figure smaller than reasonable market demand and the capacity of the state to produce oil without waste. Where disagreement is manifested the Commission usually follows the recommendation of its director of conservation.

Within the last ten years three attacks upon well allowable pro-ration orders reached the Supreme Court of Oklahoma. In the case of *Grison Oil Corporation v. Corporation Commission* [17] an attack was made upon the 100 barrel per day flat allowable to Oklahoma City Wilcox wells suffering water encroachment on the ground that this radically departed from a determined percentage allowable based upon well capacities. The Supreme Court of Oklahoma upheld the Commission on the premise that the agency's general authority to prevent waste supported its order. The court said, however, that radical departures from percentage allowables (determined by dividing well capacity by field capacity) would not be allowed to prevent inconsequential waste. In the *Peppers* case [18] appellant challenged the Commission's determination of the reasonable market demand for oil, alleging that it was contrary to the testimony of all purchasers and supported only by the conclusions of the conservation officer based on the Bureau of Mines forecast. The court held the Commission's findings sustained under the substantial evidence rule. In *Denver v. State* [19] the appellants questioned the right of the Commission to establish a flat gas-oil ratio limitation. The Oklahoma supreme court upheld the authority of the Commission to restrict production from high gas-oil ratio wells where the order was calculated to produce a greater ultimate pool recovery.

Determination of a well's proper percentage of the allocated production presents a multi-angled problem. With the advancement of engineering and technical information, engineers take the position that a percentage formula for determing a well's share of the field production arrived at by dividing its potential by the total of all well potentials in the field is basically unsound in that it disregards gas-oil ratios, as here the potentials are merely a measure of the size of the spigot—not a measure of the size of the tank behind it. The taking of well potentials proved costly to operators and their actual determination by production was hard for the Conservation Department to make accurately. Likewise, some engineers do not hold with allowable formulas based upon

[17] 186 Okla. 548, 99 P. 2d 134 (1940).
[18] 198 Okla. 451, 179 P. 2d 899 (1947).
[19] Denver Producing and Refining Co. v. State, 18 OKLA. B.J. 1335, 184 P. 2d 961 (1947).

reservoir voidage as these disregard structural advantages and do not reward good operating practices.

To avoid uncertainty in its formula and attendant difficulties since the *Grison* case, the Commission in establishing per well allowables for newly discovered fields in most instances has ordered a flat daily allowable of oil per well. In the majority of fields, as the result of the adoption of well spacing or drilling units, wells are on a uniform pattern having an equal amount of acreage attributable to each; the operators request a flat allowable. Where the character and thickness of the underlying producing formation varies substantially from well unit to well unit, the Commission uses a formula based upon percentages of total field capacity; today there remain not more than two or three fields within Oklahoma where the Commission fixes the per well allowable on a percentage basis.

In an effort to obtain direct legislative sanction of the Commission's practice of fixing flat well allowables, interested operators introduced H.B. No. 250 in the 1945 legislature. The proposed act provided that, in reservoirs of comparatively uniform conditions within the producing formation, the Commission might allocate the field production by a flat number of barrels a day to the several wells in the field. This bill never reached the floor of the House.[20] In the *Peppers* case [21] the court reminded the Commission that any rule or formula of allocation departing from percentage production must bear reasonable relation to prevention of waste or the protection of correlative rights. In 1947 when the con-

[20] An interesting commentary upon the sentiment concerning this bill made at the time by an outstanding oil news analyst, Claude V. Barrow, in The Slush Pit, The Daily Oklahoman, Feb. 11, 1945, § A, p. 16, col. 1 said: "Some of the oil men following the legislative program ran up the red flag Saturday when they read HB 250, by Rep. Arrington. This bill seeks to legalize flat allowables to oil wells, with minimum allowable of 25 barrels daily. Flat allowables have been granted by the Corporation Commission as a conservation measure, but only upon full agreement of operators in a specific field. In so doing, the capacity of a well to produce was considered secondary or entirely overlooked. The original oil law of 1913 and 1915 provides for ratable-taking when production exceeds demand for oil. That law and subsequent statutes define correlative rights in conservation measures; provide for taking potentials to determine capacity of wells. HB 250 would legalize the penalization of a 5,000 barrel well to the rate of a 100-barrel producer; would contradict the original statutes; would endanger property rights to both producer and royalty-owner."

[21] Peppers Refining Co. v. Corporation Comm., 198 Okla. 451, 179 P. 2d 899 (1947).

servation acts were again upon the remodelers' drafting boards, an act was passed repealing the existent sections most repugnant to flat allowable allocation; [22] these were the parts specifically directing the Commission to make exceptions in cases of wells suffering water encroachment and requiring that well capacities be determined to fix allowables. With repeal of these sections all limitations upon the discretion of the Commission to determine proper field allocation formula, except that of reasonableness, have possibly been withdrawn. The general grant of power to the Commission by the 1933 Act [23] is slightly amended in the 1945 [24] and the 1947 [25] proration Acts where express language authorizes the Commission to consider acreage as a factor in allocating production, proration to prevent waste and to restrict production to prevent drainage uncompensated by counter-drainage.

Production control now has much industry acceptance and although applied without exception to all flush fields, there is little if any *fudging*; oil production speeding laws are less frequently violated than almost any state police measure. Those who acquire leases take them with knowledge that they may be called upon under the general powers of the state to limit production from any strike and to produce unhurriedly whether any questions are involved or not of the rights of offset owners or of correlative rights.

During the period covered by this account the so-called discovery allowable which authorized disproportionate withdrawals in discovery wells, as a financial reward to the operator for the risk taken, has fallen into disfavor; an order promulgated in 1945 by the Commission eliminated discovery allowables. [26]

GAS-OIL RATIOS

Since the 1933 proration law the Corporation Commission has had the right to incorporate within its orders provisions designed to prevent unreasonable dissipation of oil reservoir energy by wells

[22] Okla. Laws 1947, c. 3b.; OKLA. STAT. tit. 52, § 87 (Cum. Supp. 1947).

[23] Okla. Laws 1933, c. 131, § 6; OKLA. STAT. tit. 52, c. 3, § 87 (1941).

[24] Okla. Laws 1945, tit. 52, c. 3, § 4; OKLA. STAT. tit. 52, c. 3, § 87.1 (Cum. Supp. 1945).

[25] Okla. Laws 1947, tit. 52, c. 3a., § 1; OKLA. STAT. tit. 52, c. 3, § 87.1 (Cum. Supp. 1947).

[26] Okla. Corp. Comm. Order No. 17528 (Jan. 24, 1945).

producing with too high a gas-oil ratio. The first order of the Commission based upon this authority was issued to regulate the production from the Oklahoma City Wilcox Field.[27] The order was only partially effective and no one now denies that there was a shameful waste of producing energy in the Oklahoma City Field,[28] a part of which could have been prevented by effective limitation on the use of energy in high gas-oil ratio wells. The order applicable to the Oklahoma City Wilcox zone provided that the limitation upon a well's allowable be found by multiplying the well's oil allowable (determined by its oil potential) by a 10,000 cubic foot per barrel arbitrary limit, and dividing by its gas-oil ratio if more than 10,000. The formula was too complex and too many uncertainties were involved in determining the limiting factors and enforcing the order.

In September of 1937 the Commission issued an order [29] fixing a formula for computing the allowable production from the Moore pool, Cleveland County. Therein the Commission found that a reasonable maximum gas-oil ratio was 4000 cubic feet of gas for each barrel of oil, and provided that any well that produced oil with a gas-oil ratio in excess of that should have its production penalized. To make effective this inhibition against excessive reservoir energy use, the Commission said each well's allowable production of oil would be multiplied by a factor of 4000, the limiting gas-oil ratio, and thereafter divided by the well's actual gas-oil ratio. For example, a well having a gas-oil ratio of 8000 and an allowable production of 100 barrels would only be entitled to produce 50 barrels. This type of limiting formula has been employed by the Commission in most fields discovered since the Moore pool order where high gas-oil ratios indicated the advisability of a restrictive production formula. In certain pools in the state, notably the West Cement Medrano, a portion of the wells drilled to the common source of supply produce gas only, while in other parts of the same common source wells produce oil with a small amount of gas. All engineers recognize that the compressed gas within the gas cap portion of the reservoir drives down against the gas-oil contact as a piston, and furnishes reservoir energy for oil production in the wells located lower structurally.

[27] Okla. Corp. Comm. Order No. 6433 (1933).
[28] See note 1 supra.
[29] Okla. Corp. Comm. Order No. 11623 (1937).

From the standpoint of the greatest recovery of oil it would be proper to shut-in the gas wells. The rights of the owners of the gas wells to use their fair share of reservoir energy could be protected only by permitting them to produce some amounts. The West Cement Medrano Field is one of the pools now fully unitized by order of the Corporation Commission, and these factors entered into the making of such order, but prior to making the order, the Commission faced a difficult problem in writing a proper restrictive formula on gas production. In October 1943 the Commission issued an order [30] dividing the allowable gas production for the West Cement Medrano Field among the wells by a formula which included an acreage, a potential and a pressure factor. Oil wells producing at high gas-oil ratios were limited in their production of oil in the same manner as the wells in the Moore Field.

In some fields the Commission employs a formula which results in allowing a well to produce a given number of barrels of oil where its gas-oil ratio is low or a certain number of cubic feet of gas where the gas-oil ratio is high. The number of cubic feet of gas which the well may produce is determined by multiplying the limiting gas-oil ratio by the fixed well oil allowable. For example, see the orders [31] applicable to the West Edmond Field. In other fields a more stringent penalty has been imposed on the high gas-oil ratio wells (which generally speaking produce smaller amounts of oil) by allowing these wells to produce only that portion of their full productive capacity which the limiting ratio bears to their actual gas-oil ratio [32] (as an example see the Commission's Order No. 17950, July 1945, concerning the Pauls Valley Field). At the hearing where the Commission considers the applicable field formulae, there is much engineering debate. In discussing the effect of gas-oil ratios on the conservation of oil and gas in Oklahoma, it must be said that the industries' recognition of the need for regulation has developed to a point that limiting ratios are now used by the Commission as a matter of course to preserve reservoir energy and to prevent operators from using unfair amounts of

[30] Okla. Corp. Comm. Order No. 16683 (1943).

[31] Okla. Corp. Comm. Order No. 17920, (1945) as amended by Orders Nos. 18174, 18373 and 18822.

[32] For a detailed history of the orders in connection with the Pauls Valley and the West Edmond Field, see a statement by Pound before the FPC, Oklahoma City, Oklahoma 5–6, (Oct. 9, 1945).

that energy. The right of the Commission to limit production by the use of a restrictive gas-oil ratio limitation was recently upheld in the case of *Denver Producing and Refining Company v. Corporation Commission.*[33]

WELL SPACING

In 1935 the legislature amended the waste statutes of the state in passing a Well Spacing Act,[34] the state's first law enacted directly empowering any agency to create spacing units for oil development. By the terms of that Act the Commission is authorized to prevent waste, to establish well spacing and drilling units in any common source of supply of oil. The Act is not broad enough in scope to permit the Commission to fix units for the protection of correlative rights in common supplies of gas or distillate.

The industry immediately arranged a court test of the spacing law—*Patterson v. Stanolind Oil & Gas Company.*[36] Patterson owned the minerals under a divided portion of a spacing unit and protested the constitutionality of the spacing law insofar as it required him to share the oil royalties from a well drilled on his lands with the other unit owners of minerals. The Supreme Courts of Oklahoma and of the United States upheld the law and the Commission's order. Since the decision by the Supreme Court of the United States in the *Patterson* case, there has never been any question of the right of the Commission—in the exercise of its power to prevent waste and in derogation of contractual rights—to establish effective drilling and spacing units for the development of a common source of supply of oil.

The 1935 Well Spacing Act contained two features that have undergone considerable change in the last decade. The Act provided that the consent of a percentage of the lessees was required

[33] 18 OKLA. B.J. 1335, 184 P. 2d 961 (1947); the court in the syllabi said: "The Supreme Court would take judicial notice of fact that heedless dissipation of gas reservoir energy of oil pools has resulted in loss of many millions of barrels of oil." and "The Corporation Commission has power and is charged with duty of conserving gas and oil resources and may, subject to rule of reasonableness, promulgate an order restricting dissipation of natural gas without being utilized to produce greatest quantity of oil."

[34] Okla. Laws 1935, c. 59, art. 1, § 3; OKLA. STAT. tit. 52, c. 3, § 87 (1941).

[35] 182 Okla. 155, 77 P. 2d 83 (1938); appeal dismissed 305 U.S. 376 (1939).

before the units were established, provided a limit on the size of the units and specified uniformity. The limitation upon the power of the Commission to act, except upon the application of 80 per cent of the lessees in number and of area owned in the common source of supply, was inserted by the legislature to protect minority interests. Spacing was permitted only when a substantial majority of the owners of the leases wished to employ drilling and spacing units as a means of protecting their co-equal rights in the enjoyment of the common source of supply. These provisions were immediately made the basis of an attack in the *Croxton* case.[36] In 1938 Gus Delaney completed a well in the Wilcox horizon in the Noble pool. He with other owners holding 80 per cent of the leases within the probable common sources of supply decided that one well to each 20 acres was about the right spacing pattern for the development of that particular area. As the legislature had provided in the spacing Act that each well be drilled in the center of the unit, the operators recommended to the Commission that triangular drilling or spacing units be established by northeast-southwest diagonals intersecting each 40 acre tract. Expediency dictated this pattern, as square sections cannot be regularly divided into 20 acre squares. A group of royalty owners, headed by a man named Croxton, attacked the Commission's order [37] alleging that royalty owners had been excluded in determining the 80 per cent whose consent was required for the establishment of a spacing unit, and that triangular units were not consistent with the legislature's direction to locate wells in the center of units. They further alleged that a well would not uniformly drain the unit upon which it was located but would drain oil from under adjoining units, and that the selected location (the center of the 10 acre tract lying wholly within the unit) was not mathematically the center of the triangular units. The Supreme Court of Oklahoma upheld the order of the Commission in all respects,[38] saying that the legislature did not act unconstitutionally in providing different rights for lessor and lessees, that the spacing units as established conformed to the law's directive, and that it was immaterial that each well might not re-

[36] Croxton v. State, 186 Okla. 249, 97 P. 2d 11 (1939).
[37] Okla. Corp. Comm. Order No. 12474 (1939).
[38] See note 36 *supra*.

cover its oil from under its own unit so long as all wells had an equal opportunity to recover a fair share of the producible oil within the common source of supply.

It is significant that since the two initial attacks upon the spacing order made in the *Patterson* and *Croxton* cases, in which among other things its constitutionality was challenged, only one further attempt has been made through the courts or by appeal from the orders of the Commission to challenge the power of the agency in relation to its authority over spacing units. In 1941 on the application of the Danciger Oil & Refining Company, the Corporation Commission issued a 40 acre spacing order [39] for the development of the Lovell pool covering the Tonkawa, Hoover, Elgin, Lovell and Layton sands, and the Simpson dolomite. In July 1943 on the application of the Davon Oil Company and without reference to the 80 per cent ownership clause as a condition precedent to issuance, the Commission extended the Danciger order [40] to include a substantial area to the south. This extension was subsequently enlarged by an application of the conservation officer [41] and upon an application by Fox and Fox.[42] The Continental Oil Company, owning an 80 acre lease within the extended area, launched two attacks upon the orders of the Commission by an appeal from the last order of extension, on the grounds that 80 per cent of the lessees within the extended area had not consented to 40 acre units, and on the further ground that the extended area was not a part of the same source of supply as that covered by the original spacing order. The court held [43] that the percentage requirement did not apply to an extension of an area covered by a spacing unit order, and that the Commission's determination of fact as to the identity of the common source of supply was controlling upon an appeal. The second attack on the Lovell-Crescent orders was made through an application of the Continental Oil Company to vacate the spacing order as applicable to company acreage on the ground that it could recover more oil if the spacing orders were vacated, in that

[39] Okla. Corp. Comm. Order No. 14134 (1941).
[40] Okla. Corp. Comm. Order No. 16499 (1943).
[41] Okla. Corp. Comm. Order No. 17388 (1944).
[42] Okla. Corp. Comm. Order No. 17702 (1945).
[43] *In re* Lovell-Crescent Field, Logan County, 198 Okla. 284, 178 P. 2d 876 (1947).

addition wells could be drilled for additional recoveries, therefore, the spacing order caused rather than prevented waste. The Commission denied Continental's application and the company appealed to the Supreme Court of Oklahoma. The court sustained the order of the Commission [44] holding that the Commission did not have authority to single out and grant concessions to a portion of the area covered by a spacing order, even to prevent waste, if the exception gave the property owners of that tract an advantage over the others. The court protected correlative rights even though some oil may have been lost by the order's enforcement.

Following the *Patterson* and *Croxton* decisions, a substantial number of the discovered oil pools were spaced. Perhaps drilling and spacing units would have been established in most of the others had it not been for the fact that in some cases the owners of 80 per cent of the leases were not able to get together on the size of the desired pattern. In the period from January 1, 1939 to May 5, 1945 (the effective date of a new spacing act) [45] of the 223 oil fields discovered in Oklahoma, spacing orders were entered in 84.

In 1945 a group of companies, headed by the Carter Oil Company, sponsored the introduction of a new well spacing Act [46] in the Oklahoma legislature. The first Act limited the size of the unit to 40 acres. Since its passage the average depth of new discoveries in Oklahoma has increased. In large areas on the western side of the state it was apparent that existing productive horizons would be encountered at depths unattainable in 1938. Moreover at these depths by reason of formation pressures, the horizons under most circumstances would contain gases in a higher ratio to oil than in the common sources of supply, which were the concern of the Oklahoma legislature when the first spacing Act was adopted in 1935. Such circumstances tended to make 40 acre well spacing uneconomic and indicated a need for larger units. For these reasons the companies wished the legislature would enlarge the area of drilling or spacing units which the Commission might order. The legislative hearings were attended primarily by the outspoken advocates of dense or wide spacing; the in-betweens did not partici-

[44] Application of Continental Oil Company, 198 Okla. 288, 178 P. 2d 880 (1947).

[45] Okla. Laws 1945, tit. 52, c. 3; OKLA. STAT. tit. 52, c. 3 (Cum. Supp. 1945).

[46] See note 11 *supra*.

pate. A subject of bitter debate at the legislative hearings was the question of the percentage of lessees or of lease ownership to be required to give the Commission jurisdiction for the establishment of drilling or spacing units for common sources of supply. Enlargement of the Act to include gas and distillate fields did not bring forth a single antagonist. This in itself is proof positive that the industry had by now without reserve accepted drilling or spacing units as useful tools. At the conclusion of the legislative hearings, the act (drafted by attorneys for the interested companies) was amended by well meaning but unskilled legislators endeavoring to effect a compromise of the divergent views presented. The amendment inserted a spacing paragraph,[47] the focal point of many arguments.

Following the passage of the 1945 Act, the Commission issued an order[48] establishing square sections as drilling or spacing units for Oklahoma's largest and most productive gas field—the Guymon-Hugoton Field—and since then has issued no less than 14 spacing orders in the gas or gas distillate fields with units varying in size from 40 to 640 acres.

In August 1945 the Cities Service Oil Company, Phillips Petroleum Company, and Mid-Continent Petroleum Corporation

---

[47] Okla. Laws 1945, tit. 52, c. 3, § 4 (c); OKLA. STAT. tit. 52, c. 3, § 87.1 (Cum. Supp. 1945), reads: "The Commission shall have jurisdiction to establish well spacing units of more than ten (10) acres in size in oil pools only upon proof that the owners of at least sixty-six and two-thirds (66⅔%) per cent of the acreage covered by leases of record have consented to the size of such spacing unit; provided that, before the Commission shall amend a spacing order so as to decrease the size of the well spacing unit or increase the density of drilling in oil pools, the owners of at least sixty-six and two-thirds (66⅔%) per cent of the acreage covered by leases of record shall have consented thereto; provided further, that in enlarging the area covered by any spacing order, the Commission shall not be required to have the consent of owners or lessees; Provided further, all such units established for the drilling of gas wells, where gas only is found, shall not contain more than six hundred and forty (640) acres or a governmental section of land; Provided further, all such units established for the drilling of oil wells shall not contain more than forty (40) acres when the common source of supply is found above a depth of eight thousand (8,000) feet; and provided further, all such units established for the drilling of oil wells shall not contain more than one hundred sixty (160) acres where the common source of supply is found below a depth of eight thousand (8,000) feet, except where there be short units in a common source of supply containing materially less than the unit acreage established by the Commission for that particular common source of supply the same may be included with an adjoining unit upon approval and order of the Commission after notice and hearing."

[48] Okla. Corp. Comm. Order No. 17867 (1945).

opened a new oil pool in an area now known as the golden trend along the east flank of the Anadarko basin. The producing horizon was the Bromide sandstone zone, comparable to the Wilcox sand in other areas of Oklahoma. The well was completed for a cost of $325,000 at a depth of about 11,000 feet. The industry considered the discovery one of major importance, and the well if fully opened could have produced at a high rate of flow in excess of 25,000 barrels of oil daily. An independent named Frank Russell owned the majority interest in a 10 acre tract located in the same section as the discovery well. He at once started a well on his 10 acre tract and filed an application with the Corporation Commission for the creation of .10 acre drilling or spacing units in the common source of supply. Cities Service and its associates then applied for 80 acre spacing or drilling units for the zone. The two applications were heard together.

Royalty owners in Garvin and McClain Counties formed an organization to fight the wide spacing proposed by Cities Service and its associates. More than 30 days time was consumed in introducing evidence on both sides of the controversy, and the Commission did not ultimately pass on the applications until January 28, 1946 when it denied both. The evidence on behalf of the applicants tended to show that the area could not be developed economically by a closer spacing pattern than one well to 80 acres. The evidence introduced by Russell and by the organized royalty owners urged that the prolific productivity of the sand, as proven by other areas, could economically support a well density of one well to 10 acres. It is obvious that the Commission was not persuaded by the evidence of either of the parties. Russell did not need any percentage of lessees to consent to his proposal of 10 acre spacing as the Act did not require any where the spacing for oil was 10 acres or less. On the other hand, if the spacing pattern were larger than 10 acres, then by the terms of controversial paragraph (c) of the 1945 Act a spacing order required the consent of 66⅔rds per cent of the leases. Cities Service and its associates represented some 80 per cent of the lease ownership, consenting only to a spacing pattern of 80 acres. The opponents of the 80 acre spacing pointed out that if this pattern was adopted and later developments proved the area could support closer spacing, economically recovering additional oil, the

Commission would be powerless to reduce the size of the spacing unit or increase the number of wells without the consent of Cities Service and its associates. Thus the lessees and not the Commission would control the spacing pattern. This fight was closely watched by the industry, the land owners, and the royalty holders, as all concerned felt that the order when entered would establish a precedent probably followed by the Commission in spacing applications through the area overlying the Anadarko basin. Included among the interested mineral owners were influential members of the Oklahoma legislature; as a result of the fight to obtain 80 acre spacing for the production of oil, the spacing law of 1945 was returned to the next legislature for consideration. The 1947 assembly, after ghost hunting for the author of and reasons for paragraph (c), rewrote the spacing law [49] to eliminate the percentage consent requirement as a condition precedent to the order and vested control exclusively in the Commission. To go back, after the 10 acre and 80 acre applications were denied, Cities Service and its fellow applicants returned to the Commission with an application for 40 acre drilling and spacing units in the same area, and this after a short hearing was granted.[50] Since that time 15 spacing orders creating 40 acre units have been issued by the Commission within the trend area, initially discovered by Cities Service Lawson No. 1.

As a result of the continuing evolution of the spacing law, we now find the Corporation Commission of Oklahoma in exclusive and unlimited control of drilling or spacing units for all common sources of supply of oil, gas and distillate.[51] The present law [52] provides for publication of a notice of the hearing in the county where spacing is to be had (in order that those outside the industry be forewarned). Spacing no longer is exclusively predicated upon the prevention of waste, but may now be adopted "to protect or assist

[49] Okla. Laws 1947, tit. 52, c. 3a; OKLA. STAT. tit. 52, c. § 87.1 (Cum. Supp. 1947).

[50] Okla. Corp. Comm. Order No. 19191 (1946).

[51] The first pool spacing by order of a regulatory agency was the Edmond Wilcox Pool spaced for 10 acre units on July 3, 1935, Okla. Corp. Comm. Order No. 9130 (1935). For a tabulation of the number of pools spaced, size of the unit created, and the percentage that each bears to the total spaced pools, see Pound and Frye, *Oklahoma*, VI INTERSTATE OIL COMPACT Q. BULL. 69 (1947).

[52] Okla. Laws 1947, tit. 52, c. 3a., § 1(a); OKLA. STAT. tit. 52, c. 3, § 87.1 (a) (Cum. Supp. 1947).

in protecting the correlative rights of interested parties." The only limitation on administrative control is that proviso forbidding drilling or spacing units of more than 40 acres for common sources of supply of oil lying less than 9990 feet below the surface.[53] The Commission establishes drilling and spacing units upon the application of a royalty owner, a minority lessee, its conservation officers, or any interested party and may at any time upon the petition of these persons, decrease the size of the units or increase the density of well spacing within them if proof discloses that such an order may increase the amount of oil recoverable from the common source of supply and still preserve correlative rights.[54] These changes in the law make the attitude of the Commission more liberal toward large drilling units or wider spacing, because where the development of the area subsequently discloses the first guess as too wide, the Commission has power to rectify its mistakes made in that direction.

No law is perfect, nor is the administration of any law above reproach; yet there is now no undercurrent of dissatisfaction with the law or criticism of its application and enforcement by the Commission.[55]

One further feature of the spacing law should be noted. Attention has been called to the fact that the 1935 Act required that wells be located in the center of the drilling or spacing unit. The legislature in thus specifying no doubt had in mind that each well so placed would as nearly as possible drain its unit. Resulting from

[53] Id. § 1 (c); § 87.1 (c).

[54] *Ibid.*

[55] The same intrepid pioneering spirit that built the state of Oklahoma was infused into the enactment of its laws for the conservation of oil and gas. Consistent with all pioneering activity, opposition was encountered due to fear and apprehension, but experience has justified this courage and beneficial results have sustained these conservation laws as evidenced by a significant statement by Pound, *History of Proration and Conservation in Oklahoma*, in a paper read Mar. 15, 1944, before the Ill.-Ind. Basin Chapter, API, saying: "It will also be observed from what has been said above that before the passage of every law in Oklahoma, there has been agitation by the industry and action taken by the Commission which, while it may have been legally questionable at the time, was later authorized by the laws. Oklahoma again finds itself in this position. And finally it should be observed that at least so far as Oklahoma is concerned in the promulgation of any rule or law governing the proration or conservation of oil and gas, it has been proven that most of the benefits that have been derived therefrom have accrued to the small or independent producer. Though he may have opposed the institution of these rules, after the rule has once been put in force and effect and its results ascertained, the independent producer usually becomes the strongest advocate of the law or rule."

the attention directed to this feature by Croxton's court attack, the 1945 legislature (impressed with the idea that under some circumstances added wells might be permitted in units) included within the 1945 Act a provision authorizing the Commission to permit wells to be located other than in the center of the unit, thus leaving available additional drilling locations in each unit.[56] The court in the Croxton case had approved any formula which provided each well a fair share of the reservoir's total drainage area even though that share might not necessarily underlie the lease on which the well was located. To preserve this essential requirement in the spacing Act, the legislature provided that the spacing pattern, as distinguished from the unit shape and the location of the wells within a unit, be uniform making the wells substantially equidistant, and the well location pattern practically uniform. This feature first adopted by the 1945 legislature was carried forward in the 1947 Act.[57]

Although Gus Delaney's solution to the 20 acre spacing problem was acceptable from the standpoint of providing drainage areas, it complicated ownership determination where the ownership was not uniform in each forty, since the diagonal lines tended to include owners of more than one tract. To permit formation of drilling or spacing units more nearly conforming to property or ownership lines, the 1945 legislature substituted for the words uniform size and shape in the 1935 Act the following: "Power to establish well spacing and drilling units of specified and *approximately uniform size and shape.*"[58] In all spacing orders entered since 1945 where 20 acre drainage units are set as the proper pattern, the Commission, with one or two exceptions, creates rectangular units and provides as the drilling pattern the centers of alternate 10 acre tracts in order that the drilling units and pattern remain approximately uniform.

The original spacing Act provided where the units were on the outside or fringe of the common source of supply, the Commission

[56] Okla. Laws 1945, tit. 52, c. 3, § 4 (b); OKLA. STAT. tit. 52 c. 3, § 87 (b) (Cum. Supp. 1945).

[57] Okla. Laws 1947, tit. 52, c. 3a., § 1 (b); OKLA. STAT. tit. 52, c. 3, § 87.1 (b) (Cum. Supp. 1947).

[58] Okla. Laws 1945, tit. 52, § 4 (a); OKLA. STAT. tit. 52, c. 3, § 87 (a) (Cum. Supp. 1945).

might enter an order permitting the drilling of a well at a location other than the center. This variation from the general plan was granted to allow the owner to move in toward production and thus prevent the drilling of a dry hole. The request for authority to move the well location was an admission that the operator did not own a fully productive unit. The first Act did not direct the Commission to write conditions into the order permitting the move, such as allowable penalties, to protect the owners of the unit in the direction of the shift. In certain areas one can with a degree of certainty predict, in advance of actual drilling, that a well located in the exact center of an inside unit will be dry or commercially unproductive, whereas a commercial well might be drilled at another location within the unit. Flexibility of well locations was needed. The problem was continually arising in the matter of location changes made necessary by surface obstructions. In the 1945 and 1947 Acts the legislature provided that upon proper hearing and a showing that it would be inequitable or unreasonable to require the operator to drill at a prescribed place, the Commission has the right to authorize a move, but in so doing it "shall adjust the allowable production for said spacing unit and take such other action as may be necessary to protect the rights of interested parties." [59]

From the time of the original spacing Act to April 29, 1947 (the effective date of the 1947 Act) after a spacing application had been filed and before an order was granted, operators motivated by self interest occasionally moved in as close as possible to the discovery well. They assumed that wells actually drilling prior to the order's issuance would of necessity be given an exception to the spacing pattern, without the imposition of the production penalties ordinarily levied where such moves were requested after the spacing pattern had been established. The Globe Oil & Refining Company filed an application for spacing in the Antioch Field in March 1946. The Magnolia Petroleum Company appeared at the hearing and obtained from the Commission an exception for a well started after Globe's application was filed. [60] Anderson-Prichard Oil Corporation owned an identical spacing unit with relation to the

---

[59] Okla. Laws 1947, tit. 52, c. 3a., § 1 (*b*); OKLA. STAT. tit. 52, c. 3, § 87.1 (*b*) (Cum. Supp. 1947).

[60] Okla. Corp. Comm. Order No. 18679 (1946).

discovery well, and after the original order was entered applied for an exception, alleging and arguing that Magnolia had obtained a producing advantage, and that they wished to shift their location in the same manner as Magnolia had done without penalty. The application was denied.[61] This and other like incidents focused attention upon the advantage operators had been taking of the lag in time between the application for and the establishment of drilling and spacing units. The 1947 legislature, while considering the spacing law, took notice of these incidents and wrote a proviso into the law designed to prevent *fudging*, reading: "The drilling of any well or wells into a common source of supply covered by a pending spacing application, at a location other than that approved by a special order of the Commission authorizing the drilling of such a well, is hereby prohibited." [62] The interpretation of this clause brought on controversies in determining when a well is drilled into a common source of supply, whether at the well's commencement or completion. To avoid future arguments the conservation officer circularized the industry in 1948 to ascertain its attitude concerning a proposed amendment of the Commission's general rules and regulations providing that a well commences when actual digging operations are begun, and that a well shall not be given an exception to the spacing order without a production penalty unless started before the filing of a spacing application for the area.

SPACING UNIT POOLING

The 1935 law was self executing as to the pooling or unitization of royalty interests. The *Patterson* case,[63] a direct attack upon the constitutionality of that portion of the Act pooling royalty in a unit, sustained that statute in all respects in the Supreme Court of Oklahoma and in the Supreme Court of the United States in 1938. So at the beginning of the period covered by this material there was no longer any legal doubt that all the owners of land owners' royalty within a spacing unit could be required, as a matter of law, to share

[61] Okla. Corp. Comm. Order No. 18936 (1946).

[62] Okla. Laws 1947, tit. 52, c. 3a., § 1 (d); OKLA. STAT. tit. 52, c. 3, § 87.1 (d) (Cum. Supp. 1947).

[63] Patterson v. Stanolind Oil and Gas Co., 182 Okla. 155, 77 P. 2d 83 (1938); *appeal dismissed* 305 U.S. 376 (1939).

on an acreage basis the ⅛th free production. Any controversies which have arisen as to the effect of spacing orders on contracted royalties in excess of ⅛th interest have not reached courts of record. The 1935 spacing law did not operate to pool the lessees' interests within drilling or spacing units. It provided a means whereby the owner of the lessee's interest in a divided tract within a drilling unit (where the owner of the larger tract proposed to drill a well) could compel pooling by paying the party proposing to drill the participating party's proper share of the costs of the proposed development. On the other hand, the owner of the lease on the larger of the divided tracts within the unit had no means of compelling the owner of the lease on the smaller tract to join in the development. The owner of a lease on an undivided interest in the minerals underlying the entire tract had no way of compelling co-tenants to join in development.[64] These factors forced lessees to voluntarily get together on some basis before the tract's development, or one of the lessees had to carry the other lessees' interests in the unit which often retarded drilling. If the owners of the separate tracts did not cooperate, two wells might be drilled within a unit and this led to obstruction of proper reservoir control and made more difficult adjustment of the unit owners' correlative rights. Too, owners of minority interests in a unit felt that well allocation based on unit allowables divided by an acreage factor deprived them of an opportunity to recover their share of unit production and this complicated the Commission's problem as to two well units.[65]

In May 1929 under the authority of the municipal police power and acting in the interest of public safety, to limit the number of oil wells in its bounds, Oklahoma City adopted an ordinance [66] providing that only one well could be drilled in any block. To prevent additional drilling, the ordinance set out a procedure for the adjustment and protection of the rights of unleased owners or non-consenting lessees within the drilling units. A number of other municipalities in Oklahoma have since adopted similar measures. Under these ordinances in the orders granting well permits, the

[64] Meeker v. Denver Producing & Refining Co., 18 OKLA. B.J. 1675, 188 P. 2d 854 (1947).

[65] See note 36 supra.

[66] Oklahoma City Ordinance No. 3615, OKLAHOMA CITY REVISED ORDINANCES, ¶ 25–33, et seq. (1936).

judicial boards, vested with jurisdiction to adjust the rights of the owner of minerals in the drilling unit, gave the outstanding un-leased owner or non-consenting owner alternative rights; the owners either participated in the development by paying or securing the payment of such owner's proportionate share of all the projected costs of development, or executed an oil and gas lease on the min-eral interest, or assigned the outstanding lease and received a lease bonus in line with the fair market value of an oil and gas lease on the interest leased or assigned. Such orders have been upheld sev-eral times by the Supreme Court of Oklahoma.[67]

In 1945 when a revision of the spacing law was considered, inter-ested parties prevailed upon the legislature to include in the re-vised Act a section permitting drilling of but one well to a unit, and to protect the constitutionality of the one well limitation, a re-quirement for the compulsory pooling of the lessees' interests in drilling and spacing units established by orders of the Commission. The authorization of compulsory pooling of the lessee's interest adopted by the 1945 legislature [68] is different from the royalty pool-ing provision in that it is not self-executing, and that the rights of the owner of lessees' interests are not established by the spacing order itself. The law provided that these rights be determined upon application to the Commission, by any person proposing to drill a well within the unit, for an order adjudging and determining the rights of the owners of lessees' interests within the unit. After the Act was passed, applications were filed with the Commission seek-ing adjudication of the rights and equities of the parties within a particular spacing and drilling unit and the order of the Commis-sion granted on this application was appealed to the Supreme Court of Oklahoma and there upheld as proper under the Act.[69] Neither of the parties to that appeal raised any question as to the constitutionality of that portion of the law authorizing the Com-

[67] Amis v. Bryan Petroleum Corp., 185 Okla. 206, 90 P. 2d 936 (1939); Cook v. Westgate-Greenland Oil Co., 185 Okla. 209, 90 P. 2d 940 (1939); Inland Development Co. v. Beveridge, 185 Okla. 174, 90 P. 2d 942 (1939); Phillips Petroleum Co. v. Davis, 194 Okla. 84, 147 P. 2d 135 (1942); Gruger v. Phillips Petroleum Co., 192 Okla. 259, 135 P. 2d 485 (1943).

[68] Okla. Laws 1945, tit. 52, c. 3, § 4 (d); OKLA. STAT. tit. 52, c. 3, § 87 (d) (Cum. Supp. 1945).

[69] Denver Producing & Refining Co. v. State, 18 OKLA. B.J. 23, 182 P. 2d 503 (1947).

mission to make the determination, and the Supreme Court of Oklahoma did not express any opinion in that regard.

Within the months following the passage of the Act, applications for orders defining, fixing and adjusting the correlative rights and obligations of discordant unit owners were numerous, indicating a grateful acceptance by the industry of a tribunal wherein the differences between the parties in any unit could be arbitrated, in the event one owner proposed development within the unit and no common agreement could be reached. Upon application the Commission determines who is to be the operator, how the costs are to be paid, and what lease bonus is to be paid to the unleased mineral interests or lessees' interests if they elect not to participate. After the promulgation of the first orders and the decision in the *Denver Producing & Refining Company* case, it became apparent that the law and its effectiveness obtained. This fact created a realization that it was mutually advantageous for development controversies to be settled between the parties without resort to an order from the Commission. The filing of pooling applications continues in somewhat diminishing numbers, and in numerous cases the disputes are settled before or during the hearings. The number of applications for compulsory pooling of a unit gradually decreased until the number filed with the Commission during the first four months of 1948 amounted to only eleven. The mere filing of an application before a court authorized to determine the equities of the parties seems to have the psychological effect of inducing arbitration. The 1945 Act provides that the pooling application be filed by a person proposing to drill a well within the unit. The matter of arbitrating through the Commission the rights of the owners of the unit in relation to proposed wells worked so well that the 1947 legislature extended the law [70] to permit the Commission to adjust and adjudicate the rights of the owners of a unit in which a well had already been drilled.

The 80th Congress in an Act [71] effective August 4, 1947 revised the provisions of the federal statutes applicable to the control of oil and gas lessees holding leases on land of the Five Civilized

[70] Okla. Laws 1947, tit. 52, c. 3a., § 1 (d); OKLA. STAT. tit. 52, c. 3, § 87.1 (d) (Cum. Supp. 1947).

[71] Pub. L. No. 336, 80th Cong., 1st Sess. (Aug. 4, 1947); U.S. Code Cong. Serv. c. 458, (1947).

Tribes to permit the Commission's orders to be operative as to federal lands. Section 11 of that Act provides: "All restricted lands of the Five Civilized Tribes are hereby made subject to all oil and gas conservation laws of Oklahoma; provided, that no order of the Commission affecting restricted Indian lands shall be valid as to such lands until submitted to and approved by the Secretary of the Interior or his duly authorized representative." Under this provision the Secretary of the Interior has in every application approved compulsory unit pooling orders of the Corporation Commission which involve Indian and adjacent lands.

POOL WIDE COMPULSORY UNITIZATION

The Oklahoma City Wilcox Field in many ways was an outstanding oil discovery. No drilling pattern or spacing was employed in its development except by ordinance as to that part within the limits of Oklahoma City. In its early stages production was unrestricted and the shackles of litigation, accompanied by a fluctuating and often depressed oil price, made difficult the enforcement and policing of production regulations. Moreover, the gas within the zone was wastefully and inefficiently utilized and when passed through the oil and gas separators in most cases was vented into the air. The horse was practically out of the barn when in March 1939 a group of operators, spearheaded by Phillips Petroleum Company and Anderson-Prichard Oil Company, organized the Oklahoma City Wilcox Secondary Recovery Association. This Association, employing a full time engineer and supporting staff, made an engineering study of what was then termed the possibilities of a secondary recovery in the Wilcox zone in the Oklahoma City Field.

Due to the absence of spacing regulations in the development of the field, to drill a well an operator needed only enough ground for his drilling equipment. Wells have been drilled on tracts 50 x 140 feet. There were a large number of independent operators in the Oklahoma City Field, royalty and lease ownership was extremely complex, and it seemed obvious to all, after the first meetings of the Association, that no voluntary unitization of the field or in any workable part was feasible. Legislative assistance was needed to support the kind of unit operation recommended by the engineers of the Association.[72] The Association employed R. M. Williams, an attorney of Oklahoma City, to draft proposed legislation. He had to pioneer, but in the fall of 1940 he delivered to his clients a proposed form of law for compulsory unitization for secondary recovery purposes. Meanwhile, the engineering studies made by some of the companies, and in part confirmed by the reports of the Association's engineers, indicated that the Oklahoma City Field defied prior engineering concepts in that (due to the thickness of the producing sand, its uniform east to west dip, and lack of water drive) the oil was gravity draining downhill. There was a sharp division of engineering opinion as to whether the proposed gas injection would render an additional economic oil return. Those who owned down dip, down hill wells felt they might get the oil without gas injection; therefore, the proposed unitization would only accomplish a division of their structural advantage with the owners of less advantageously located tracts.

A majority of the Association favored immediate introduction of the bill drafted by Mr. Williams. A group of the operators who either objected to unit operation of the Oklahoma City Field or to the form of the bill proposed certain revisions in the measure. These persons in turn wrote a law. The advocates of secondary recovery legislation within the Association believed the bill drafted by the opposition group contained too many restrictions and conditions to be workable. There resulted a writing and rewriting of the proposals, compromises and countermeasures appeared in every new draft; and in all not less than 14 prospective statutes were prepared and dissected. In line with the Association's original conception of the legislation, these offerings divided the recoverable production obtained under unit operation into primary recovery and secondary recovery. All the bills entitled each operator to recover his estimated primary recovery without added cost and the assessment of further expenses would be collectible only from secondary production, which would be the result of the unit's partial restoration of reservoir energy.

Finally on April 28, 1941—although the opposition was still of-

---

[72] See a recent article in which the author reaches the same conclusion as to the need for legislation. King, *Pooling and Unitization of Oil and Gas Leases.* 46 MICH. L. REV. 311, 340 (1948).

fering counterproposals and suggestions—the proponents' last compromise draft was introduced in the 1941 legislature as S.B. No. 298. Probably no bill ever presented to the Oklahoma legislature brought so much pressure upon the members; it came from both sides. Able lawyers were employed to voice opposing viewpoints at the legislative hearings, and in each instance storm ensued. In the closing days of the session Leon C. Phillips, the then Governor of Oklahoma, in a statement to the press about over active lobbying for the passage of the act in effect gave it the executive *boot*, and eliminated all chance of its adoption. Governor Phillips was quoted as saying: "The biggest threat to the present legislature has been the lobbyists' action on this repressuring bill. I have heard enough things about this bill from members of the legislature which smells of improper lobbying. So, I called 'Bob' Kerr and told him to pull all his lobbyists out of the capitol." [73] Having failed in its objective, in October 1941 the Oklahoma City Wilcox Secondary Recovery Association dissolved; but the Oklahoma City Wilcox Pool Engineering Association was formed to carry on its valuable engineering work. The engineering association did not retain as its purpose the enactment of legislative authority for secondary recovery operations. With the death of the Oklahoma City Wilcox Secondary Recovery Association, substantially all efforts to unitize the Oklahoma City Field ceased. Meanwhile, some engineers and certain pioneering individualists within the industry were beginning to *whoop it up* for the adoption of secondary recovery programs. The drum beating included praise for engineering devices and schemes for recovering additional oil, including secondary practices employed after primary or competitive production practices had ceased to recover substantial oil, as well as those types of unit operations initiated in an earlier stage in the pool's life. The drums also sounded for unit operations extending over the entire life span of a pool, tending to limit the decline in reservoir pressures, and expertly and efficiently employ the reservoir energy to greatly increase ultimate recovery. Here it was not contemplated that the oil recoverable by primary methods be taken out before such operations began, rather it was proposed that se-

[73] The Daily Oklahoman, May 16, 1941, p. 16, col. 2.

lective production coupled with the reinjection of gas or water, or both, start early in the pool's history.[74]

Burdette Blue, then president of the Kansas-Oklahoma division of the Mid-Continent Oil and Gas Association, believed the reason failure attended the first Oklahoma effort to pass a compulsory unitization measure resulted from the fact that the backers of the legislature were those primarily interested in the Oklahoma City pool, where technical differences of opinion as to the success of secondary recovery existed. Mr. Blue envisioned a better fate for an act sponsored by an industry wide committee. Under his guidance and under the auspices of the Mid-Continent Oil and Gas Association, a group was organized as a Secondary Recovery Committee for the states of Kansas and Oklahoma in early 1942.[75] This committee at its first meeting agreed to write an acceptable draft and a sub-committee was formed to do the pick and shovel work involved in drafting a bill. W. P. Z. German, Tulsa, and T. Murry Robinson, Oklahoma City, were selected as scriveners by the sub-committee. Again, over a period of months, the bill was drafted and shaped. On March 2, 1943 the final bill approved by a large majority of the committee was introduced in the legislature as H.B. No. 332 by Representative John Steele Batson. The committee and the drafters of the bill inserted a proviso eliminating the Oklahoma City Field from the influence of the bill in an effort to sidestep a large portion of the opposition to the 1941 proposal. These efforts were not altogether successful and cries of communistic doctrine and desecration of property rights were heard so frequently and loudly in the committee rooms that the bill's passage was blocked; it died in the House Committee.

[74] Barnes, *Proposed Unitization and Pressure Maintenance May Treble Oil Production in West Cement Pool,* Oil and Gas Jour. (Dec. 7, 1946) 80 and references. Barnes, *Oklahoma at Important Threshold with New Deep Pools, Need of Wider Spacing and Pressure Maintenance Operations Strongly Shown,* Oil and Gas Jour. (Dec. 8, 1945) 76, and references. Kaveler, *More Efficient Operation of Oil Fields,* an address delivered before the Oil and Gas Division, Oklahoma City Chamber of Commerce (1946). Dahlgren, *Pressure Maintenance Projects on The Increase in Oklahoma,* World Pet. (No. 1946) 74, Andrus, *Secondary Recovery Research an Adventure in Conservation,* V INTERSTATE OIL COMPACT Q. BULL. 16 (1946). Report of Legal Committee, Interstate Oil Compact Commission, *Secondary Recovery Operations and Related Operations,* VI INTERSTATE OIL COMPACT Q. BULL. 73 (1947).

[75] Barrow, *The Slush Pit,* The Daily Oklahoman, Mar. 11, 1943, p. 18, col. 1.

As the education of the public by the industry continued, more and more engineering articles appeared in the trade journals extolling the merits of pool wide unit operations.[76] And so in January 1945 with another state legislature convening, the proponents of field-wide unitization (without the benefit of preliminary fanfare, committee meetings, or any organization as sponsor) again prepared a compulsory unitization bill. At this point in the history of the fight for the enactment of unitization legislation, it is interesting to note that the "Bob" Kerr Governor Phillips directed during the 1941 legislative session to "pull his lobbyists out of the capitol" had become the Governor of Oklahoma, and as Governor Robert S. Kerr, in his message to the legislature of January 2, 1945 recommended the passage of secondary recovery legislation in these words: "Engineers tell us that there are hundreds of millions of barrels of crude oil in presently known and developed oil fields which can never be produced by primary methods but which can most certainly be obtained through secondary production methods. Economic considerations make it impossible to operate under secondary recovery methods in areas where there is diversification of ownership, unless voluntary agreements can be reached. This can not always be done and when it is not, the secondary oil cannot be recovered and great loss occurs, not only to the operators, but also to the royalty owners, the workers and the State. I therefore urge that you give your most serious consideration to the enactment of secondary recovery legislation providing a means whereby oil not recoverable by primary methods can be saved and produced through legalized procedure on a basis of equity and justice."

The bill was introduced February 27, 1945 in the House of Representatives as H.B. No. 339. Again the legislative committee hearings were stormy, vitriolic sessions well attended by individual operators apprehensive as to the far reaching effects of radical legislation. Opponents of the bill visualized all pools as unitized and independent operators eliminated as producers. Again a great por-

[76] Simons, *Unitization Conserves Pressure*, Oil and Gas Jour.(Feb. 16, 1939) 44, Oklahoma City Field Enters Secondary Stage, Oil and Gas Jour. (July 6, 1939) 28, Stanley, *Law to Facilitate Secondary Recovery Will be Sought*, Oil and Gas Jour. (Dec. 19, 1940) 16, Heath, *Unitization of Oil Pools for Secondary-Recovery Development*, Oil and Gas Jour. (July 6, 1946) 66, Deegan, *Wilcox Sand at Oklahoma City May Get Secondary-Recovery Project*, Oil and Gas Jour. (Dec. 16, 1944) 60.

tion of the opposition came from the operators of the Wilcox pool in the Oklahoma City Field, and the stripper well associations; as a result of this hostile reaction the bill after introduction was amended so as to not apply to common sources of supply discovered 20 years or more prior to its effective date. With this major shift and some minor changes the bill was adopted and became the law of Oklahoma.[77] In substance the Commission, if petitioned by the owners of leases covering 50 per cent of the area, may unitize all or a portion of a common source of supply if the proof discloses from an engineering standpoint the portion can be separately operated from the remainder, and that additional amounts of oil or gas are economically recoverable by reason of unit operation. An order based on such a petition does not take effect if within 60 days from its date the owners of 15 per cent or more within the unitized area protest. The Act states that the manner in which the unit owners are organized be set forth in a unitization plan submitted with the petition. After the effective or take-over date, no person is permitted to operate an oil and gas well producing from the unitized portion of the source of supply other than in the manner provided by the unit plan of operation.

Immediately following the Act's effective date proponents of unit operations owning leases in the extensive West Edmond Hunton Lime pool in Kingfisher, Logan, Canadian, and Oklahoma Counties, and the Cement Medrano pool located in Caddo County organized operators' and engineering committees and set about preparing petitions for unitization and plans of unit operation for these fields. The plans were re-worked and the formulas for the division of unit proceeds endlessly debated before the engineering committees. October 23, 1946 the required signatures were obtained and a petition for the unitization of the Cement Medrano Field filed; and January 29, 1947 the petition for unitization of the West Edmond Field was filed with the Corporation Commission. The hearings before the Commission were lengthy and due to the congestion of its docket were continued numerous times before their conclusion. In each case the opponents were a small minority of lessees together with a well organized group of royalty owners

[77] Okla. Laws 1945, tit. 52, c. 3b; OKLA. STAT. tit. 52, c. 3, § 286.1 (Cum. Supp. 1945).

publicly threatening active efforts to repeal the law at the next session of the legislature. While the proceedings for unitization were pending before the Corporation Commission, the 1947 legislature convened and there, in both Senate and House, bills were introduced to amend, to modify, and to repeal outright the unitization law. Although compulsory unit operation had not yet been given a trial, its opponents were aggressive, vociferous, and heated in their opposition. The royalty owners of the Grady and Caddo Counties organized a Red Heart Association and attended en masse legislative committee hearings, filling to capacity the galleries of the House and Senate during the debate and vote on the bills to amend, modify, or repeal the statute. Each royalty owner wore a red cardboard heart upon his or her lapel or dress upon which was printed: "Have a Heart. Repeal 1945 House Bill No. 339. 98% of the People Want It Repealed. Will You Grant Their Wishes? Vote for Senate Bill No. 102." The vote cast in the two houses reflects the formidable opposition: in the House, on H.B. No. 431 to amend, the vote was 20 ayes and 60 noes, and in the Senate, on S.B. No. 245 to amend, the vote was 21 ayes and 15 noes, 4 did not vote and 4 were excused; as the bill failed to receive a constitutional majority of all the members elected to the Senate, the bill failed of passage. On a vote to reconsider S.B. No. 245, there were 24 ayes and 12 noes, thus the bill passed the Senate by 2 votes, and was sent to the House where it died in committee. On a vote for outright repeal in the House, H.B. 313 died in committee; but in the Senate, the bill the Red Hearts strenuously championed, S.B. No. 102, received 20 ayes and 15 noes, the Senate coming within 3 votes of repealing the unitization law.

On July 29, 1947 the Corporation Commission issued an order establishing the West Edmond Hunton Lime Unit,[78] which included all wells producing from the formation at the time the petition was filed. Since then the unit has been extended without opposition to include additional wells completed along its edge Those opposed to the unitization of the West Edmond Hunton Lime pool gave notice of appeal to the Supreme Court of Oklahoma, but no record was filed or prepared nor was the appeal com-

[78] Okla. Corp. Comm. Order No. 20212 (1947).

pleted. September 5, 1947 the Commission ordered unitization of the Cement Medrano formation.[79] Here the opponents of unitization perfected an appeal to the Oklahoma supreme court from the order; the matter is now pending.[80] The appeal attacks the constitutionality and legality of the Act, as well as an assault upon the Commission's acts and determination of equities in establishing the unit operation plan in the field. The decision of the Oklahoma court will, to a great degree, settle all questions of the Act's validity and the correctness of the agency's orders issued thereunder.

Tracing the design of the two earlier unit operation plans, the operators of the Southwest Antioch Field on the December 23, 1947 filed a petition for the creation of a compulsory producing unit for Gibson sand production. Heeding the source of opposition to the preceding applications, these petitioners held many meetings, to which the non-cooperating operators and all royalty owners were invited, primarily to educate the interested parties in the probable benefits obtainable from unitization. The agency's hearing on the petition for the creation of the unit lasted but one day and there was no active opposition, although a number of lessees in the field did not join in the petition. The Commission issued the unit operation order.[81] Following the precedents established in the previously unitized fields, the operators in the Chitwood pool petitioned for separate orders for the creation of compulsory producing units for the production from each of the two common sources of supply—the Spiers and the Cunningham sand. These petitions were approved by all operators, and by a further written agreement 92 per cent of the royalty owners agreed to the plans of unitization. The petition for the Cunningham sand was filed November 13, 1947 and for the Spiers sand November 26, 1947. The methods employed by the Antioch operators were utilized by owners of the Chitwood pool. Numerous meetings of operators and royalty owners were held both before and after filing the petitions. No opposition developed with the exception of one royalty owner who appeared at the hearing with counsel and opposed the petitions. After

[79] Okla. Corp. Comm. Order No. 20289 (1947).

[80] In the Matter of the Petition for the Creation of a West Cement Medrano Unit, Sup. Ct. of Okla. No. 33,336.

[81] Okla. Corp. Comm. Order No. 20827 (1948).

a three day hearing, the Commission issued orders unitizing the Spiers sand [82] and the Cunningham sand.[83] The Cunningham sand contains gas distillate and thus is the first gas distillate field so unitized.

There are now five compulsory field-wide unit operations within Oklahoma which disregard lease ownership and permit operation of the entire field as if covered by one oil and gas lease. Under these orders production is divided among the owners according to a predetermined percentage of the field production, found by applying an engineering formula to the productive formation under each tract, and dividing the total figure for all tracts into the result secured for each tract. The accomplishments in engineering practices, operating costs, economic returns, and the equitable division of the total unit production do not differ from voluntary plans of unitization. The difference is that large areas and tracts, and number of operators and royalty owners have been involuntarily included in unit operation plans, as a result of a law which in the interest of greatest ultimate recovery authorizes the Corporation Commission of the State of Oklahoma to declare these persons in a unitized operation, whether they like it or not. Whether the additional oil and gas will be recovered in the amounts predicted by optimistic engineering appraisals has not been determined, but in the short time these units have operated, it is obvious that one stride toward the ultimate in conservation has been accomplished—that is, that in the unitized fields, actual production practices are designed by the best engineering talent after respective merits have been debated before an operating committee chosen by the operators. The engineers and the operating committees no longer have selfish interests to protect, regardless of how their principals got into the units. All are in the same boat after the effective date of the unit, and no one person recovers additional oil except by making the field as a whole recover additional oil. Therefore, a common interest exists to obtain the greatest ultimate production. The debates (expressions of the selfish viewpoints of competitive operators) before the Commission on the engineering practices to be employed are dumped overboard to lighten the ship. The necessity

[82] Okla. Corp. Comm. Order No. 21066 (1948).
[83] Okla. Corp. Comm. Order No. 21065 (1948).

for argument, engendered by selfishness before regulatory agencies as to proper conservation practices in a unitized field, is ended. Although the regulatory agency might say to the unit operators that certain practices are wasteful, inasmuch as the Commission still retains its power to prevent waste, it is hard to imagine such a situation arising.

The dourest critics of unit operation do not hold there is any possibility of losing ultimate recovery. Regardless of individual inequities which might inadvertently occur in striding toward the greatest good for the greatest number, the total benefits to the royalty owners, to the operators, and to the citizens of Oklahoma cannot be denied.

CONSERVATION OF GAS

The decade from 1938 to 1948 might be termed the time during which the natural gas industry in Oklahoma came to maturity. Although the superior attributes of natural gas as a fuel were well known, development of this industry has been hampered by two serious deficiencies: (1) the lack of development of high pressure pipe lines capable of transporting gas to relatively distant markets efficiently and at a cost warranting the very large investment involved, and (2) the lack of dependable long time reserves which would provide sufficient gas to warrant construction of pipe lines from the field to distant markets. It should be noted that residue gas does not provide a dependable source of supply necessary for the operation of a high pressure pipe line. Production rates of residue gas depend upon oil allowables from the oil fields which supply the refineries and are not geared to the same seasonable demands. Oil fields produce gas at differing rates at each stage of depletion and when gas is efficiently used to produce the more valuable oil, it may be said to be a by-product salable only under proper combinations of market demand and economic delivery costs. The history of gas development within Oklahoma during the past ten years is for the most part a story of that enormous tri-state dry gas field, the Hugoton Field, which in its entirety constitutes the largest known dry natural gas field in the world. That portion of the field located in Oklahoma is referred to as the Guymon-Hugoton Field.

The existence of dry natural gas in large quantities in this area was well known in the 1920's; in fact, most of the field was under lease and sufficient development had occurred to define the general extent of the field. During this period no market existed for the bulk of the gas which might have been produced from the Guymon-Hugoton Field. As a consequence, those pipe line companies extending their facilities into the area secured gas purchase contracts at relatively low prices with a dedication clause for the lives of the leases. These particular contracts are mentioned as they have been the source of much litigation within the past three years. Today's production picture is vastly different. There are in operation the interstate pipe line systems of Cities Service Gas Company, Panhandle Eastern Pipe Line Company, Northern Natural Gas Company, and others serving the large metropolitan markets of Kansas City, Chicago, and the middle west. For the first time in Oklahoma the transportation and sale of natural gas is a first class industry on its own, departing from its usual roll as the unwanted child of oil production.

For the most part proration in dry gas fields relates to the proper pacing of production to market demand and pipe line facilities, and a division of the available market on a fair basis among those prepared to produce gas. The first real attempt of the Corporation Commission of Oklahoma to place the Guymon-Hugoton Field under proration came in January 1945 when the Commission promulgated an order [84] establishing 640 acres as a drilling and development unit, and fixing a formula for each unit's allowable gas production. Considerable doubt existed whether the Oklahoma statutes then in force were sufficiently broad to allow the spacing of a dry natural gas field as distinguished from a common source of supply of oil or gas produced in conjunction with oil. While a record was kept of production under the order and calculations were made as to what allowables would have been, no attempt was made to prorate the field until an order effective June 1, 1945 was issued.[85] In the interim the legislature enacted into law H.B. No. 257 [86] broadening the conservation statutes to allow spacing in

[84] Okla. Corp. Comm. Order No. 17410 (1945).
[85] Okla. Corp. Comm. Order No. 17867 (1945).
[86] Okla. Laws 1945, tit. 52, c. 3; OKLA. STAT. tit. 52, c. 3 (Cum. Supp. 1945).

common sources of supply of dry natural gas. The pattern of proration closely followed that of oil. The order established 640 acres as the spacing unit, provided a workable formula for the allocation of allowables to gas wells in the area and followed the usual outline of effective proration regulations relating to common sources of supply of oil.

The serious problems of proration in the Guymon-Hugoton Field came immediately before and shortly after the promulgation of the order, and dealt almost exclusively with questions of ratable take and common purchase under the applicable statutes. To understand the problem it is necessary to turn back to the statutes and view them in the light of the circumstances existing at their enactment. The 1913 Act [87] purported to make common purchasers of every corporation, partnership, or person claiming or exercising the right to carry or transport natural gas by pipe line for hire, compensation or otherwise, within the limits of the state. Another 1913 Act [88] adopted the theory of ownership of gas in place and provided that a well in the common source of supply reduced the gas to possession. The Act also provided for ratable production from the common reservoirs of natural gas. Among other things these laws provided that transporters of gas (except that used for developmental purposes, the operation of oil wells, or their domestic use) from gas fields must take ratably from each producer-owner in proportion to his interest in the gas, upon agreed terms, or in case the owner and purchaser did not agree, then at a price and upon terms as fixed by the Corporation Commission after notice and hearing. While a more comprehensive gas conservation Act was enacted in 1915 [89] purporting to cure certain defects in the 1913 Act, the 1913 provision allowing the Corporation Commission to resolve price controversies remained on the statute books, for the 1915 Act did not by its terms specifically repeal the 1913 Act in part or in entirety.

The circumstances giving rise to common purchaser and ratable production statutes are relatively simple. In virtually every gas field in Oklahoma, as well as in oil fields, large integrated companies ca-

[87] Okla. Laws 1913, c. 99; OKLA. STAT. tit. 52, c. 3, § 21–35 (1941).
[88] Okla. Laws 1913, c. 198; OKLA. STAT. tit. 52, c. 3, § 231–235 (1941).
[89] Okla. Laws 1915, c. 197; OKLA. STAT. tit. 52, c. 3, § 236–247 (1941).

pable of financing pipe lines constructed lines to their production and to that of a favored few, and by withdrawals effectively drained the other owners in the common source of supply not financially or otherwise able to construct a pipe line to a market outlet, or to secure an outlet. The requirements of the statutes operated to protect the correlative rights of all owners and producers in a common source of supply. With this background, let us now note the developments which took place in the Guymon-Hugoton Field.

In 1944 Peerless Oil and Gas Company asked the Corporation Commission to force a pipe line connection with Republic Natural Gas Company. No aspect of price was raised, the question being simply whether Republic was required under the Oklahoma statutes to take the gas of Peerless. The factual situation differed radically from those situations contemplated by the statute. Both Peerless and Republic were corporations, approximate in size and financial ability. Republic was not an integrated pipe line system in the true sense of the word, as its system was primarily confined to gathering its gas and delivering it to an integrated pipe line company at a point in or near the field. It had no market other than by gas purchase contracts with certain pipe line companies. The Peerless well was located in a section entirely surrounded by wells owned by Republic. The Corporation Commission by its order required Republic to take ratably from Peerless and pay Peerless directly, or to market gas and account for it to Peerless, or to shut in its production from the common source of supply. This order was sustained by the Oklahoma supreme court and thereafter appealed to the United States Supreme Court by Republic.[90] The Commission, incidentally, reserved jurisdiction for the purpose of deciding the terms and conditions of the taking of natural gas by Republic in the event the parties were unable to agree. In a five to four decision the Court arrived at an inconclusive result; the majority held that by reason of the matters left open by the Commission's order, the state court judgment lacked the finality requisite to a review by the Supreme Court. The minority would have sustained the order.

Meanwhile, a dispute arose between Peerless and the Cities

[90] Republic Natural Gas Co. v. State; 198 Okla. 350, 180 P. 2d 1009; 68 Sup Ct. 972, 92 L. Ed. 911 (1948).

Service Gas Company (the latter an integrated, interstate pipe line system with market outlets in Kansas and Missouri, particularly in the metropolitan area of Kansas City, Missouri) following the issuance of the field-wide spacing order June 1, 1945.[91] Under the provisions of paragraph 4 (*b*) of the order a producer seeking to secure a pipe line connection was required to tender gas at the field going price. Peerless tendered production from several of its unconnected gas wells to Cities Service, whereupon a disagreement arose between the parties as to the price. Peerless tendered the gas at prices exceeding four cents a MCF when the price then paid by Cities Service ranged from four to four and one-half cents. Since the parties could not agree, Peerless applied in the broadest terms to the Corporation Commission asking not only a connection with the pipe line system of Cities Service, but also that the price and terms of purchase be fixed throughout the entire field as well as between the two parties. Now for the first time the Commission was launched into a hearing the result of which determined, in one hearing and on the same evidence, the rights of the parties litigant and the rights of all producers and purchasers in the field with regard to the price to be paid for dry natural gas. While the statute referred to by its terms purportedly conferred jurisdiction upon the Commission to resolve price disputes between individual purchasers and sellers, it became necessary to look elsewhere for jurisdiction to establish a field-wide price. This the Commission did when it found that a price of less than seven cents a MCF constituted—among other things—economic and physical waste. The only other order of the agency fixing gas price had been issued in 1920;[92] there the Commission fixed a price under the mentioned statute between individual parties litigant in the Cushing Field at nine cents a MCF. The order was not contested. The Guymon-Hugoton order in the Peerless case is the first effort fixing price field-wide based on the theory that price by itself is reducible to physical or economic waste. This case is on appeal to the Supreme Court of the State of Oklahoma by Cities Service Gas Company, where it is pending.[93] The action of the Commission was attacked

[91] Okla. Corp. Comm. Order No. 17867 (1945).
[92] Okla. Corp. Comm. Order No. 1662 (1920).
[93] Cities Service Gas Co. v. Peerless Oil and Gas Co., Sup. Ct. of Okla. No. 32994.

by Cities Service both before the Commission and in the court on numerous grounds. It appears, from an examination of the existing conservation statutes in force when the cause was heard, extremely doubtful whether economic or physical waste can be defined solely in terms of price.

By summary and with regard to future legislation, it is apparent that the growing pains of the natural gas industry remain. Many proration problems have been solved and those solutions for the most part have been widely accepted. Much yet is to be done toward final solution of the problem of disposition of gas once produced, for as it is well known, an immediate marketing of gas is inherent in the product. While progress has been made toward development of dry gas storage fields, the suitable areas for storage could hold but a very small percentage of the Guymon-Hugoton Field production.

MISCELLANEOUS MATTERS OF INTEREST

In many circumstances the orders of the Commission [94] establishing drilling or spacing units for the development of a common source of supply include regulations governing the drilling and completion practices of the operators in the common source. The tenor of the provisions imposed is usually a specified casing program, directing where casing be set and the manner in which the well be completed for production. Authority to issue these regulations is found in the statutes prohibiting waste. Seldom are such field-wide rules established except in spaced common sources of supply, which leaves many of the older and shallower and some of the newer and deeper Oklahoma fields without field-wide rules applicable to those problems concerning which the Commission occasionally exercises authority. Thus the hiatus, existing between specific field rules and orders and good conservation practices, causes the Commission from time to time to adopt general statewide rules to regulate the manner of drilling and producing in a field prior to the time it is specifically considered by the Commission, and to serve in the event no special field rules are needed. From 1934 to 1945 these orders in force covered production restric-

[94] For example Okla. Corp. Comm. Order No. 17920 (1945).

tions, allocations of production to the several fields and wells, and procedures for the enforcement of such restrictions through proper reports and tests.[95] During this interval the Commission was often confronted with problems which arose from a lack of specific rules governing the acts of the operators in respect to: (a) location of wells in unspaced fields with reference to lease lines and previously drilled wells, (b) methods to be employed in, and the proper control of, salt water disposal, particularly in underground formations, (c) processes to be used in secondary recovery or repressuring operations conducted on individual tracts or a portion of a field, but not on a field-wide basis, (d) plugging of wells in a manner as to prevent a connection between the various strata penetrated, waste of oil or gas, and pollution of fresh water formations, (e) amount wells might properly produce prior to a state-wide order fixing the production for the ensuing month, (f) surreptitious directional drilling, (g) dual completion of wells simultaneously producing from two horizons.

By reason of the frequency with which the problems in these classifications arose, it was apparent to the Commission and to the industry that general rules and regulations supplementing and implementing the statutory regulations prohibiting waste were needed. In July 1943 Walker T. Pound, the Oklahoma Conservation Officer, filed with the Corporation Commission an application for the adoption of state-wide uniform rules and regulations governing the acts of those seeking and producing oil and gas. The conservation officer appointed a committee of 80 individuals to prepare suggested rules and regulations for submission to the Commission at the time his petition would be heard. This group was divided into a number of sub-committees to write rules for production methods, gas production, drilling, directional drilling, well spacing, transportation and purchasing, plugging and abandoning, secondary recovery, the disposal of salt water, and procedural rules for guidance in hearings before the Commission. The sub-committees and the parent body held a number of hearings throughout 1943 and 1944, and prepared a set of suggested rules. At a meeting held January 24 and 25, 1945 the Commission

---

[95] Okla. Corp. Comm. Order No. 6394 (1933), amended by Order No. 6511 (1933) and by Order No. 8229 (1934).

adopted the suggested state-wide rules to be applicable in instances where specific field rules had not been issued.[96]

Operating experience and application proved that the first version contained certain ambiguities and imperfections, and in May 1945 Pound again applied to the Commission for a revision of the general rules; at his instance all suggested changes were discussed and debated by an industry committee and in October 1946 the Commission adopted the revised rules then recommended by the Conservation Department and the committee.[97] The opportunity, which the Commission provides those governed, to write their own rules of government, is a fine example of democracy at work, and demonstrates excellent cooperation between a regulatory agency and those regulated.[98]

[96] Okla. Corp. Comm. Order No. 17528 (1945).

[97] Okla. Corp. Comm. Order No. 19334 (1946).

[98] General Rules and Regulations Governing the Drilling of Oil and Gas Wells and the Production Therefrom in the State of Oklahoma. (1946) "INTRODUC-TION—On July 19, 1943, there was filed by the Conservation Officer an application for an order fixing new general rules and regulations governing drilling and production of oil and gas wells in the State of Oklahoma. Shortly thereafter an invitation was issued to the oil and gas industry to work with the Conservation Department in preparing a set of general rules to be submitted to the Commission for recommended adoption. A meeting of a group of operators and the Conservation Department was held, at which time a general committee was formed with the following officers elected: W. A. Delaney, Jr., Chairman, Ada; E. G. DeParade, Vice-Chairman, Oklahoma City*; Lawrence R. Alley, Secretary, Oklahoma City. The general committee then designated the following sub-committee chairmen and members: *Coordinating Committee*—E. G. DeParade,* Chairman, Oklahoma City; A. M. Bell, Tulsa; C. O. Moss, Tulsa; D. A. Howard, Dallas, Texas; Lloyd Noble, Ardmore; Wm. T. Payne, Oklahoma City; Alvin Richards, Tulsa; W. A. Delaney, Jr., Ada; Walker T. Pound, Secretary, Oklahoma City; J. B. Sledge, Ada; K. R. Teis, Tulsa. *Committee on Drilling and Development*—Wm. T. Payne, Temporary Chairman, Oklahoma City; A. M. Bell, Tulsa; Geo. E. Campbell, Tulsa; A. B. Cook, Shawnee; O. E. Dougherty, Tulsa; H. H. Kaveler, Bartlesville; Harry Mack, Tulsa; D. A. McGee, Oklahoma City; F. M. Porter, Oklahoma City; John Porter, Oklahoma City; T. L. Regan, Oklahoma City; W. J. Sherry, Tulsa; J. F. Smith, Shawnee. *Committee on Gas Production*—D. C. Bothwell, Temporary Chairman, Tulsa; W. B. Berwald, Tulsa; Chas. Binckley, Bartlesville; Richard W. Camp, Oklahoma City; Elmer Capshaw, Norman; J. L. Gere, Bartlesville; E. C. McAninch, Tulsa; Ray Stephens, Oklahoma City; Colin C. Rae, Tulsa. *Legal Advisory Committee*—Alvin Richards, Temporary Chairman, Tulsa; W. H. Brown, Oklahoma City; E. G. DeParade,* Oklahoma City; Earl Foster, Oklahoma City; Vernon Roberts, Ada; T. Murray Robinson, Oklahoma City; George Selinger, Tulsa; W. R. Wallace, Oklahoma City. *Committee on Production Methods*—R. B. Curran, Temporary Chairman, Tulsa; H. F. Beardmore, Tulsa; R. E. Chandler, Oklahoma City; A. B. Imel, Cushing; C. J. Kirwin, Tulsa; Fred Lichtenheld, Oklahoma City; D. R. McKeithan, Bartlesville; Ward Merrick, Ardmore; C. V. Millikan, Tulsa; R. Van A. Mills, Ponca City; Albert E. Pierce, Tulsa; W. M. Saxon or H. F.

The rules, limited to the prevention of waste, contain a preamble stating they are not intended to establish standards as to what constitutes prudent operations for the guidance of any other tribunal in Oklahoma. This obviously for the reason that the Commission did not care to provide a precedent for use in litigation in any other court.

The rules, by set back and interval requirements, provide as a minimum the equivalent of 10 acre spacing in common sources of supply in excess of 2500 feet in depth, and 2½ acre spacing in common sources of supply above 2500 feet in depth.[99] Prior to adoption of this rule many lease lines were crowded so closely that the derrick legs actually rested on the lease boundary line. The owners of the offset leases, to comply with the implied and express covenants of their leases, then had to offset the lease line at a point equidistant. In many places in Oklahoma one may still see these twin derricks with their feet together. The validity of general statewide spacing has not been challenged. In each case where the operators desire to drill wells closer to the lease line, or to other wells than permitted by the rules, applications for an exception to the rules may be filed alleging an unusual circumstance which entitles them to an exception. The applications are presented to the Commission at which hearing the offset operator, who would or might be prejudiced by the granting of such exception, is given an

---

Schaffer, Tulsa; J. H. Stewart, Tulsa. *Committee on Secondary Recovery and Salt Water Disposal*—Jack Abernathy, Temporary Chairman, Tulsa; Jim Arrington, Stillwater; Raymond Carr, Tulsa; Lloyd Gray, Tulsa; W. L. Horner, Tulsa; Donald P. Oak, Tulsa; J. B. Sledge, Ada. *Committee on Plugging and Abandoning*—M. M. Tripplehorn, Temporary Chairman, Tulsa; Del Baker, Shawnee; Fred Bowles, Ada; C. M. Copeland, Tulsa; H. O. Harder, Oklahoma City; J. C. Watkins, Nowata; Jerome Westheimer, Ardmore. *Committee on Oil Transportation and Purchasing*— J. K. McGoldrick, Temporary Chairman, Tulsa; Lawrence R. Alley, Oklahoma City; W. B. Case, Tulsa; A. L. Dade,* Tulsa; J. M. Linehan, Tulsa; F. J. Martin, Tulsa; Gail Nusbaum, Enid; Henry Waters, Tulsa. These committee members, and many other industry representatives, all participated in the drafting of these general rules and regulations. Suggestions and advice as to what rules should be adopted were welcomed from any royalty owner, operator or contractor. Many such suggestions were received. More than one hundred meetings of committees and sub-committees were held. Without the sincere and unselfish work contributed by the oil and gas industry, these rules and regulations could not have been written, and it is to the people who gave so unselfishly of their time that this introduction is dedicated."

* Deceased.

[99] Okla. Corp. Comm., General Rules and Regulations, Order No. 19334, Rule No. 202 (1946).

opportunity to be present and offer evidence against the petitioner's request.

One of the first conservation statutes adopted in Oklahoma was a well plugging statute [100] never expressly repealed. It was only in 1940 that the Supreme Court of Oklahoma held [101] that the Act of 1917, which created an oil gas department under the jurisdiction and supervision of the Corporation Commission, expressly provided that all abandoned oil wells be plugged under the supervision of the Corporation Commission and therefore vested exclusive jurisdiction in the agency to make appropriate regulations unhampered by the prior plugging act.[102] The first Act among other things ordered the use of cedar plugs in plugging operations. From 1917 there existed a regulation, by Corporation Commission order,[103] as to the manner in which wells were plugged, and from 1917 forward an operator proposing to plug a well was required to notify the Corporation Commission in order that their inspector be present to see the well properly plugged. But even with this safeguard, a well frequently would be improperly plugged and would thereafter cause underground waste or pollution of fresh water formations. A lessee abandoning the lease might sell it to an irresponsible individual or junk dealer who would thereafter plug the well in the most economic and convenient manner to him regardless of the hazards or nuisance which might arise. From these experiences grew very specific instructions as to the manner of plugging,[104] and a provision was inserted that no person might plug a well without being licensed by the Corporation Commission.[105] These licensees are under constant scrutiny by the Commission, and upon application of the conservation officer a number of licenses have been revoked. In addition to these safeguards, the Commission upon complaint of its enforcement officers or from any person interested in the property to be drilled or adjacent premises, may require the owner or person drilling the well to post a $2500 bond conditioned upon abandoning and plugging

[100] Okla. Laws 1909, c. XXVI, art. II, § 7a.; Okla. Stat. tit. 52, c. 4. (1941).
[101] Sheridan Oil Co. v. Wall, 187 Okla. 398, 103 P. 2d 507 (1940).
[102] Okla. Laws 1917, c. 207; Okla. Stat. tit. 52, c. 4 (1941).
[103] Okla. Corp. Comm. Order No. 1299 (1917).
[104] Okla. Corp. Comm., General Rules and Regulations, Order No. 19334, Rule No. 604 (1946).
[105] Id. Rule No. 608.

the well in accordance with the agency's rules.[106] In view of the success of the current rules in eliminating improper plugging, this rule is seldom resorted to and very few bonds are required.

All newly completed wells are limited to a top allowable of 150 barrels a day of oil, or a maximum gas allowable not exceeding 500,000 cubic feet of gas (whichever is produced first), until the owners of the property at a special or state-wide hearing obtain a greater well allowable [107] from the Corporation Commission. This rule reverses the burden of proof in debates before the Commission as to the daily allowable of a well. The conservation statutes vest authority in the Commission to issue orders preventing waste; prior to the adoption of the allowable rule, the conservation officer, to obtain a restriction on the allowable of a well, had to show that daily production in excess of certain amounts caused waste. Under the present rules if an operator wishes a daily allowable greater than 150 barrels of oil, or 500,000 cubic feet of gas, he must come before the Commission and prove, in the light of the well's performance (about which he is best informed), that a greater allowable would not cause underground waste of oil or energy.

During the days of small tract development, particularly in the Oklahoma City Field, operators frequently employed the use of a whipstock in drilling to direct the bottom of a well to a better spot; one was bold enough to whipstock a well so that it was actually bottomed under the State Capitol Building. The drilling logs, which under the rules of the Commission had to be filed, did not disclose the location of the hole in relation to its location on the surface, and this lack of information interfered with the Commission's production allocation regulations. Moreover, it destroyed the usefulness of well logs in the study and correlation of sub-surface formations, where admittedly future study would be useful in sustaining production to the economic end, and in the exploitation of oil and gas bypassed for initial production at a lower level. When these facts came before the industry committee, they included, in the recommended general rules adopted by the Commission, a provision that drilling must not be so conducted as to intentionally divert the bottom of the hole from the vertical with-

[106] *Id.* Rule No. 201.
[107] *Id.* Rule No. 304.

out prior consent of the Commission given after notice and hearing. The rule further provides that a survey of the directional hole be made upon completion of drilling operations, and a copy filed with the Corporation Commission.[108]

During the war a shortage of materials as well as of oil made desirable the dual completion of oil and gas wells so that two formations penetrated by one well might be produced concurrently rather than consecutively. A low commodity price or a diminishing recovery enhances the desirability of dual completions in order that the economic life of the well be extended and additional recovery realized before abandonment. The first dual completion in Oklahoma was in the Ramsey Field, Payne County, in August 1941 where a well produced from the Hunton lime and the Wilcox sand. The increasing popularity of this technique indicated the necessity for close supervision by the Commission to halt eventual adverse effect upon the ultimate recovery from either zone.[109] Today in Oklahoma, since the passage of the state-wide rules, a well may not be dually completed until after a permit has been obtained from the Corporation Commission.[110]

The disposal of salt water produced with oil is always a troublesome problem.[111] Under the state-wide rules an operator, desiring to engage in a secondary recovery or pressure maintenance program or the underground disposition of oil well brines, must petition the Corporation Commission for permission.[112] The petitioner must in his application set out the nature of the undertaking, the manner in which it will be conducted, the formations utilized, other pertinent information, and give notice of his request to the owners of all offset properties.

In many instances other interested operators, who understand the nature and magnitude of the project to be undertaken on adjoining leases, are able to get together on a joint plan of operation, possibly increasing ultimate recoveries. Most operations conducted

[108] *Id.* Rule No. 209.

[109] Howard, *Dual Completions in Oklahoma*, III INTERSTATE OIL COMPACT Q. BULL. 59 (1944).

[110] See note 98 *supra*, Rule No. 211.

[111] For a comprehensive discussion of salt water disposal methods see V INTERSTATE OIL COMPACT Q. BULL. 67 *et seq.* (1946).

[112] See note 98 *supra*, Rule No. 501.

under permits granted by this rule are low pressure gas injection or water flooding operations, carried on in a limited area without substantial hazard or injury to adjacent properties. The efficacy of the rule is attested to by the fact that, since its adoption, 86 orders of the Commission have been issued authorizing these operations.

The fact that improper disposition of oil well brines constitutes a nuisance has led to the enactment of many statutes of prohibition and regulation. A state agency known as the Oklahoma Planning and Resources Board has by statute been vested with authority to prevent surface pollution.[113] The legislature charges the Corporation Commission with the duty to halt sub-surface pollution.[114] Authority was assumed by both agencies to regulate with reference to the prevention of pollution of fresh water strata, underneath but relatively close to the surface. As a consequence all operators contemplating underground disposal of salt water brines filed requests for permission to construct and use such disposal systems with the Planning and Resources Board and with the Corporation Commission. In June 1945 the Attorney General of Oklahoma, in rendering an opinion clarifying the spheres of influence and control as between the two agencies, ruled that the Corporation Commission has jurisdiction to protect the fresh water strata encountered in drilling an oil and gas well.[115]

In a number of fields operators form associations which own and operate cooperative brine disposal systems. One of several such systems in Oklahoma is West Edmond Salt Water Disposal Association operating a brine gathering system in the West Edmond Field. The water so gathered is injected into non-oil or gas bearing formations through unproductive oil horizon wells along the west flank of the field. Authority for the operation of this system and for the injection of water into the formation was obtained by the association from both the State Planning and Resources Board, and the Corporation Commission.[116] When injection began the owners

---

[113] OKLA. STAT. tit. 74, c. 12, § 351c–354o (1941). See OPS. ATTY. GEN. OKLA., Sept. 8, 1945, construing this statute.
[114] OKLA. STAT. tit. 52, c. 3, § 85 and § 274 (1941).
[115] See OPS. ATTY. GEN. OF OKLA., June 19, 1945.
[116] Davis, *West Edmond Salt Water Disposal Plant Initiates Service to Member Operators*, The Pet. Eng. (Dec. 1945) 106 *et seq.*

of an adjoining tract filed an action in the District Court of Oklahoma County,[117] seeking to enjoin the operation of the system and recover damages on the grounds that the water injected into the disposal well would travel under and across their lands without their permission; their theory was that this forcible injection of water under their tract constituted a trespass. The plaintiffs sought as damages the value of the use of their lands for salt water storage, whether or not such injection caused any actual damage. As the distance which injected water moves and the place or places where it comes to rest are speculative, it follows that the number of tracts involved and the number of owners who might similarly contend is legion. As a result, the action attracted considerable industry interest. The cause was tried to a jury where a verdict was returned for the plaintiffs in the sum of $12,500 actual and $10,000 exemplary damages. On a motion for new trial, the court struck the exemplary damages. The case is now pending in the Supreme Court of Oklahoma. A judgment sustaining the verdict would be a blow to the industry.

Since 1926 the Bureau of Mines has published salt water disposal reports in cooperation with the State of Oklahoma.[118]

ADMINISTRATIVE HISTORY OF OIL AND GAS CONSERVATION

When Oklahoma became a state in 1907, Article IX of the Oklahoma constitution [119] created a Corporation Commission to regulate transportation and transmission companies and public utilities. Section 15, Article IX, provides that Corporation Commissioners, three in number, are to be elected, one each two years, for six year terms; any case of vacancy is filled by gubernatorial appointment until the next general election. Section 16 sets out the qualifications of Commissioners and Section 17 provides the form of the oath of office a Commissioner takes. Since 1907 the Corporation Commission of Oklahoma has continually regulated

[117] Rosecrans v. West Edmond Salt Water Disposal Association, Dist. Court, Oklahoma County, Oklahoma, No. 111,897, and in the Sup. Ct. of Okla., No. 33,712.

[118] U.S. BUR. OF MINES, REPORT OF INVESTIGATION SUBSURFACE DISPOSAL OF OIL FIELD-BRINES IN OKLAHOMA, R.I. 3603 (1942).

[119] OKLA. CONST. Art. IX, § 18.

transportation and transmission companies, and from time to time special acts of the legislature have conferred additional authority upon it. The constitution states that all orders made by the agency are to be signed by at least two members. The Commission organizes itself by selecting one of its members as chairman and another as vice-chairman; the organization of the group changes with the inclination of the Commissioners. By a recently enacted law [120] the Commissioners' salaries have been supplemented by a payment of $2500 annually, the money coming from the oil and gas conservation fund of Oklahoma. This Act has been tested in court and its validity sustained.[121]

At the time of the enactment in 1933 of the first basic proration law in Oklahoma, there was much discussion whether or not the conservation of oil and gas should be assigned the Corporation Commission of Oklahoma, or go to a state agency created for that purpose. After extended legislative debate, authority was vested in the Corporation Commission, primarily because the constitution gave that agency the power and authority of a court of record together with executive and legislative powers. The legislature was unable to create an agency possessing equally the rights and exercising the functions of all three branches of the government. Continuously since the enactment of oil and gas laws in Oklahoma, the Corporation Commission of Oklahoma has been charged with the duty of administration. Although at practically every session of the Oklahoma legislature the conservation statutes are amended or modified, the question of the wisdom in choosing the Corporation Commission to regulate the oil and gas industry is never raised. Throughout the years the degree of Commission regulation steadily increases. More and more industry shortcomings and bad production practices are being eliminated, and during this era conservation laws, as interpreted and enforced by the Commission, have grown in the esteem of the industry and the public.

Under a legislative Act in 1909 [122] (the nation's first common carrier and common purchaser statute) the Acts of 1913,[123] which

[120] Okla. Laws 1947, tit. 52, c. 3c., § 2; OKLA. STAT. tit. 52, c. 9, § 452 (Cum. Supp. 1947).
[121] Bond v. Phelps, 19 OKLA. B.J. 455, 191 P. 2d 938 (1948).
[122] Okla. Laws 1909, c. xxvi, art. 1, § 3–4; OKLA. STAT. tit. 52, c. 3 (1941).
[123] Okla. Laws 1913, c. 99; OKLA. STAT. tit. 52, c. 3 (1941).

related to the production and transportation of natural gas and the ratable production of natural gas, and the Acts of 1915,[124] extending definitions of waste, the Corporation Commission had to some extent before 1933 regulated the production of oil and gas. This activity consisted mostly of providing for ratable taking of oil and gas, and in seeing that depleted oil and gas wells were properly plugged. A small field force had been provided by the legislature to enable the Commission to carry out its required duties. The Oil and Gas Conservation Department in the agency was originally established in 1917,[125] and greatly augmented with the passage of the comprehensive Act of 1933. As now constituted, there is a director of conservation supervising the operation of the Conservation Department and enforcing the orders, rules and regulations of the Commission. There are two assistant directors of conservation, one whom acts as office manager, and the other as field supervisor. There is a conservation attorney who by statute represents the director of conservation, all departmental employees and members, and who acts as legal advisor to the Corporation Commission and the members of the department. There is an assistant conservation attorney who assists the conservation attorney. In 1947 the legislature passed an Act [126] giving the agency four·oil and gas engineers or petroleum geologists, one of whom is senior engineer or geologist. The same Act added fifteen field supervisors who must have had at least five years practical experience in the production of oil and gas, or be qualified engineers or geologists, or have had five years experience as deputy conservation officers. There are two court reporters, three statisticians, two secretaries and six stenographers or clerks in the department. A tremendous increase in the volume of hearings on oil and gas matters congested the agency trial docket. To assist the Commission in expediting its hearing agency, the Act provides a trial examiner who sits as a referee. The trial examiner now hears many of the cases heretofore heard by the Commission. All Department employees are selected by the Corporation Commission and serve at the will of the Commission.

[124] Okla. Laws 1915, c. 197; OKLA STAT. tit. 52, c. 3 (1941).

[125] Okla. Laws 1917, c. 207, § 1; OKLA. STAT. tit. 52, § 121 (1941).

[126] Okla. Laws 1947, tit. 52, c. 3c, § 8; OKLA. STAT. tit. 52, c. 3, § 127 (Cum. Supp. 1947).

The administrative agency is empowered to make rules and regulations governing the proration of oil and gas with or without a hearing.[127] In no circumstance has the Commission availed itself of the right to promulgate general rules without notice and hearing. The procedure followed in presenting oil and gas matters to the Commission is provided in the statute. Before any order is issued (except in cases of enforcement) notice of the time, place and purpose of the hearing is published at least 10 days before the hearing in a paper of general circulation in Oklahoma County. An Act of the 1947 legislature[128] provides that at least 15 days published notice must be given before the Commission has jurisdiction to enter an order providing for spacing oil or gas pools. The notice is published in Oklahoma County and in the county where the land to be spaced is located. This is the only exception to the 10 day notice section.

Where a person, firm, or corporation violates the then entered rules and regulations of the Commission, the agency has jurisdiction under the law to enter an order of enforcement. Generally these order the person violating the rules and regulations immediately to cease and desist operations by shutting in the well, and set a future hearing, not less than 10 days in advance, at which time the person charged may appear and present evidence to the Commission. No publication of notice is required for this order of enforcement but the person charged must be served with a copy of the order. The director of conservation and the field supervisors are authorized by statute to serve this notice or order.

Under its contempt power, the Commission assesses fines against persons, firms, or corporations charged with violating its rules and regulations; each day the person violates the rules and regulations of the Commission constitutes a separate offense. The minimum fine provided by the statute is $1000, the maximum is $5000, and the person charged may be imprisoned for violating the rules and regulations where charged before the district court in the county where the offense is committed. Compliance with Commission orders is so common that this provision is seldom used. The Attorney General of Oklahoma is authorized to file an action in the

[127] Okla. Laws 1933, c. 131, § 14; OKLA. STAT. tit. 52, c. 3, § 97 (1941).
[128] Okla. Laws 1947, tit. 52, c. 3a., § 1 (a); OKLA. STAT. tit. 52. c. 3. § 87.1 (a) (Cum. Supp. 1947).

district court in the county in which the offense is committed, requesting that a receiver be appointed for the corporation or person charged, and that their properties be kept in receivership until a time when all penalties provided by statute are collected. No occasion for this enforcement section has arisen since enactment.

At hearings, any person interested in the subject matter has a right to present evidence, to be heard, and to cross examine witnesses. Likewise any person has the right to file briefs, provided a request to do so is made before the Commission enters its order. General laws as to the admittance and admissibility of evidence are followed. The Supreme Court of Oklahoma has held in several cases that strict rules of evidence do not apply to hearings before the Corporation Commission [129] except when the agency acts in a quasi-judicial capacity where one is charged with contempt. In these instances, the supreme court specifically holds that strict rules of evidence apply.[130] Otherwise, letters, telegrams, well information, and other statistical data are admitted. The Commission has the right, under Section 18, Article IX of the constitution, to subpoena records and to enforce attendance at hearings.

In oil and gas matters, an appeal from an order of the Commission to the supreme court must be lodged within 60 days. Any person aggrieved by an order of the Commission has the right to appeal by giving notice of his intention to do so within 10 days from the order's date, as provided by Section 20, Article IX of the constitution. The provisions of the order are not stayed unless a supersedeas bond is filed with the Corporation Commission as provided by Section 21, Article IX of the constitution; but when the bond is filed, the agency must stay the order's effectiveness until the time the case is finally determined.

The framers of the Oklahoma constitution wisely provided that the legislature, at any time after 1909, 'might alter or amend those sections of the document which conferred powers on the Corporation Commission.[131] As originally drafted, Sections 20, 21 and 22 of Article IX placed the right of complete review of the Commis-

[129] Hine v. Wadlington, 27 Okla. 285, 111 P. 543 (1910), Muskogee Gas & Electric Co. v. State, 81 Okla. 176, 186 P. 730 (1920).

[130] St. Louis & S.F.R.Co. v. C. H. Cannon & Son, 31 Okla. 476, 122 P. 231 (1912).

[131] See OKLA. CONST. Art. IX, § 35.

sion's orders in the Supreme Court of Oklahoma. The right of legislative review was possibly repugnant to other provisions of the constitution, so in 1941 the legislature [132] amended the article to provide for judicial review only, therein specifically directing that the orders of the Corporation Commission be sustained by the Supreme Court of Oklahoma if supported by substantial evidence.

CONCLUSION

As the drill bit penetrates deeper levels and more complex formations, so do the principles of oil and gas conservation dig deeper into legal phases and legal ramifications. The Corporation Commission of the State of Oklahoma is the focal point of a maze of conservation laws. Each package handed them to open is wrapped in intricately interwoven facts. If the agency had the wisdom of Socrates, the patience of Job, and the heart and inclinations of Santa Claus they could not write orders and judgments which would suit every person interested in the affected area. Hind sight is bound to prove them wrong in a few particulars.

When the Commission makes orders in relation to a field, these orders become the law for that field, making up the bulk of the law of oil and gas conservation in Oklahoma. This law is not found in reported decisions or in statutory compilations, hence the Commission has wisely seen fit to reproduce its orders by multigraphic processes. When the Corporation Commission is called upon to rule, for example, as to the proper spacing in a common source of supply, and issues an order establishing 20 acre spacing units, then it is the law of that field that it be developed on 20 acre spacing units (although the get-it-now element may wish 10 acre, and the economic theorists and reserve accumulators may want 80 acre units).

The scope and importance of administrative law to the owner and operators of oil and gas properties cannot be over emphasized. In nearly every proceeding the Commission is called upon to balance many factors which are not reducible to a common denominator. They measure tangibles against intangibles, interests of the

[132] Okla. Laws 1941, Constitutional Amendments 544; OKLA. CONST. Art. IX, §§ 20, 21 & 22.

haves against the interests of the have nots, and private rights against long range public policy. It is surprising that in working through this ever changing maze, and exercising their functions as legislators, judges, and enforcement officers, they are able to win and hold the respect of those concerned with oil and gas production.[133]

Aided by advancing engineering techniques and understanding, the operators in Oklahoma are back in once harvested oil fields gleaning vast amounts of oil and gas left as unrecoverable by the gold rush boys of the early unrestricted days of the industry. To aid the engineers, lawyers not only fashion new raiment in which to garb the everchanging size of correlative rights, but provide modern vehicles in which the field operators may ride to increased recoveries.[134] This earnest cooperative team work of engineers and lawyers extending through legislative enactments has been the subject of study by others.[135] The *lawgineers* and *enginawyers* in attendance at all Commission hearings seek (with the aid of the Commission) to rationalize applicable engineering equations to legal principles in order to lawfully accomplish the ultimate in scientifically and thoroughly milking nature's structures of black gold and energy. In this phase of cooperation, Oklahoma advances along the front of its twin objectives, conservation and protection of correlative rights, with a cooperative spirit supported by popular approval. In this spirit Oklahoma wholeheartedly supports the Interstate Oil Compact Commission as it has throughout the entire interval to which this history relates. Its industry citizenry pull for greater recoveries of oil and gas for their benefit, for the benefit of Oklahoma and in the benefit of national security.

[133] Robinson, *The Law Applicable to and the Problems Arising Incident to the Establishment of Oil and Gas Well Drilling Units*, 17 OKLA. B.J. 1928 (1946).

[134] A very practical and applied cooperation between lawyer and engineer may be seen in the resolution adopted Dec. 13, 1945 by the Legal Committee of the Interstate Oil Compact Commission. Pursuant to this resolution a sub-committee was appointed in Feb. 1946, to study the organization and functioning of oil-field engineering committees, and to draft provisions thought to be suitable for use in organizing such committees. The constructive work of this sub-committee with forms may be seen in the pamphlet ORGANIZATION AND FUNCTION OF OIL-FIELD ENGINEERING COMMITTEES (1946).

[135] See Oliver, *Cooperation Between Lawyers and Engineers*, 56 A. B. A. REP. 691 (1931), Nyce, *Cooperation Between Engineers and Lawyers*, 17 A. B. A. J. 325 (1931), Myers, *Legal Aspects of the Unitization of Oil and Gas Fields*, Oil and Gas Jour. (May 20, 1948) 229.

CHAPTER 27

Oregon, 1923–1948

~

A combination waste prevention and plugging statute represents the efforts of the State of Oregon to bring about conservation of oil and gas. Chapter 185,[1] adopted February 22, 1923 and still in force, is the sole incursion into conservancy.

Persons in possession of a well, notwithstanding their capacity, are forbidden to waste natural gas by escape into the open air, but must confine the gas until it is used for light, fuel, or power purposes. After striking a producing formation gas may waste four days while a decision is made as to further drilling. Waste or leaks from pipe lines running from gas wells are unlawful. Surface waste is halted by a section which inveighs against permitting the product from any well to run into tanks, pools, or streams used for watering stock and prevents salt water from running over the land. Wells drilled for oil and gas must be cased. No well can be drilled within 200 feet of the boundary of adjoining property. Precautions must be taken to stop waste of oil and gas in drilling, producing, storing piping, and distributing. Upon abandonment wells must be plugged, and a report filed with the clerk of the county where the well is found showing location, name of owner, depth of formations encountered, and plugging technique. This oil and gas well record is accessible for public inspection. Penalties for violations not exceeding $500 are included in the Act.

Administration of the law is under the direction of a County Inspector of Oil and Gas Wells named by the county court of the Board of Commissioners to oversee and inspect drilling, operating, and conservation practices. This appointee must be notified

BLAKELY M. MURPHY, WRITER. (See app. B.)
[1] Laws Ore. 1923, c. 185; ORE. COMP. LAWS ANN. § 108–701 to 108–711 (1940).

in writing of intention to plug in order that he may be present to supervise the proceedings. Power is accorded the inspector to require records, logs, and information regarding wells within his jurisdiction.

CHAPTER 28

Pennsylvania, 1858–1948

The legal history of conservation of oil in Pennsylvania began before the Drake well's completion, when on December 8, 1858 Lewis Peterson sued Samuel M. Kier in trover for the conversion of 50,000 gallons of carbon oil or petroleum of the alleged value of $20,000. Kier had leased land near Tarentum, on the Pennsylvania Canal, Allegheny County, with the privilege of boring salt wells and manufacturing salt. He bored a well in 1839 and manufactured salt until about 1845, when oil came up in small quantities with salt water by ordinary pump operation. The trial judge related: "At first it was regarded not only as an article of no value, but as a great obstruction in the manufacture of salt; because, unless separated from the water, it injured the salt, and consequently they were obliged to pump the water and oil together into large cisterns or basins, and let it remain there several days until the oil, by its specific levity, rose to the surface, when it was conducted, at first into the canal and covered its surface for several rods, when it was set on fire and burned for a number of days." The oil increased in quantity from year to year and Kier finally determined to introduce it to the public as an article of merchandise. He promoted the sale of oil for medicinal purposes, advertising extensively and employing agents in various quarters. Kier pleaded not guilty. At the trial, May 2, 1860, he asserted (contrary to the plaintiff's allegation that large profits had been derived from the oil) that he lost money largely by reason of the heavy expenditures for advertising to establish the value of oil in the public estimation.

The record is enlightening. The oil was not a surface exudation,

James B. Sayers, Writer; Don T. Andrus, Wolf and Wolf, Advisers. (See app. B.)

as the salt well was 465 feet deep. Kier shipped 371 barrels of merchantable oil before 1858, and a substantial part of it was sold in half pint bottles for medicinal purposes at a dollar a bottle. The defendant must have realized some profit for he agreed to a verdict against him in the sum of $5910, subject to the opinion of the trial court upon questions of law reserved. The two problems were—whether the oil in controversy when brought to the mouth of the well was plaintiff's or defendant's, and if it was the plaintiff's property, would trover lie for its value. The trial court determined both issues in favor of the plaintiff and judgment on the agreed verdict was entered September 1, 1860. On appeal a majority of the supreme court found that Kier was "certainly not guilty of either legal or equitable waste because the well through which oil reaches the surface was opened in direct obedience to the stipulations in the lease, and must be continued open and kept in operation in order to prevent a forfeiture." Believing that the petroleum was Kier's property, the court reversed the judgment; one judge dissented. Another filed a separate concurring opinion in which he agreed with the trial court that the oil when brought to the mouth of the well belonged to the plaintiff, but concluded that Kier and his associates were not "guilty of waste in severing petroleum from a freehold, since it was an inseparable consequence from the right granted to them by the landlord. Their actual possession, therefore, of the severed chattel, was in every sense a rightful possession, and because no right of possession existed in Peterson at the moment of severance, trover will not lie." In this unique case the court was first called upon to define petroleum.[1]

Kier's oil had an important part in the drilling of the Drake well, in that it is said that George H. Bissell was attracted by imitation greenbacks displayed in a New York drug store as an advertisement for "Kier's Rock Oil." They bore a picture of a salt derrick at Tarentum which suggested the possibility of boring for oil. Bissell and others had been trenching lands near Titusville and raising the surface oil and water into vats from which the oil was

[1] Kier v. Peterson, 41 Pa. 357 (1861); Lewis Peterson v. Samuel M. Kier, 2 Pittsburgh 191, at 193 (1860); 154 January Term, 1859, Court of Common Pleas No. 2, Allegheny County, Pa., Appearance Docket 33; Paper Books, Allegheny County Law Library, Pa. Supreme Court, 1860, Vol. 4.

skimmed.[2] The influence of Kier's pioneering was recognized by Bissell who was one of the group responsible for the subsequent drilling of the Drake well.[3]

The modern concept of oil conservation rests on the geological and engineering knowledge accumulated since the drilling of the Drake well. Unfortunately for Pennsylvania such essential knowledge was not available in time to enable the commonwealth to profit by the warnings of those who anticipated an early exhaustion of the state's oil and gas reservoirs. In less than three generations Kier's nostrum has become a substance absolutely indispensable to modern living, and its conservation a matter of grave importance. The law had no ready-made answers for the problems which arose simultaneously with the first oil. This was a new res with which to deal. When the state supreme court likened oil and gas to *ferae naturae* and brought forth the rule of capture it expressed concern that the analogy might be "too fanciful," but no one at that time seemed able to suggest anything better.[4] Critics of early judicial decisions must recognize the dearth of valid technical evidence. It is not surprising that doctrines now criticized found their way into the law of property as a result of the early decisions, and resisted change by legislative action. Texts are replete with citations and comment upon the opinions of the courts of Pennsylvania. None bear directly upon conservation.

Many assume the subject of conservation is slighted in Pennsylvania because the only legislative enactments (in the nature of conservation statutes) are the well plugging acts and related aids to secondary recovery. Conservation statutes, such as that suggested by the Interstate Oil Compact Commission, are not suited to today's situation in Pennsylvania. States still enjoying flush production and new discovery do not think in terms of daily production

[2] Ross, THE EVOLUTION OF THE OIL INDUSTRY 35 (1920).

[3] Rep. U.S. Rev. Comm. on Petroleum as a Source of National Revenue, H.R. EXEC. DOC. No. 51, 39 Cong. 1st Sess. 4–5 (1866); GIDDENS, PENNSYLVANIA PETROLEUM, 1750–1872 52 (1947). This volume contains an excellent collection of contemporary accounts of many incidents in the evolution of the industry. See also GIDDENS, THE BEGINNINGS OF THE PETROLEUM INDUSTRY (1941) which contains a comprehensive bibliography.

[4] Westmoreland Natural Gas Co. v. DeWitt, 130 Pa. 235, 249 18 A. 724 (1889).

of 62,000 barrels from approximately 133,000 wells as reported for 1947 for the entire Pennsylvania grade crude oil territory.[5] There is an exaggerated idea of early well potentials in the state. It is estimated that in July 1883, 17,400 wells were producing, whose average daily product was 3.8 barrels; July 1884, 21,844 producing wells were averaging 3 barrels, and a year later 22,524 producing wells were averaging 2.5 barrels.[6] Although the growth of the industry was phenomenal, it never dominated business in the state to the extent prevalent in the jurisdictions where legislative conservation has made greatest strides. Bituminous coal has been mined in western Pennsylvania and anthracite in the eastern part since Revolutionary War days, and much oil and gas territory is underlaid with merchantable bituminous coal. Coal operators object to penetration of coal measures by oil and gas wells, and conflicts of interest are reflected in the annals of the legislature.

STATUTES AIDING DEVELOPMENT

The legislative history of Pennsylvania since the discovery of oil furnishes an interesting chapter in the industry's development. One must take into consideration the conditions existing at the time and in the locality where oil was first discovered. There were no containers in which oil could be stored or shipped except miscellaneous vessels, no standard of measurement greater than the gallon, no means of transportation but wagon or flatboat, no refining processes, no immediate market but for "medicinal purposes." Other things were of more vital importance than oil to many citizens of Pennsylvania, for example, the emergency call of Governor Curtin issued in June 1863 for volunteers to defend the state from invasion by General Lee. Nevertheless, oil excitement and speculation continued. There can be no doubt that the public was attracted to the quest for oil before the completion of the Drake well. On April 7, 1859 Governor William F. Packer approved an Act of Assembly permitting the organization of companies for "the manufacturing of oils" from mineral coal.[7] The following year a

[5] Ring, *President's Report*, 25th Anniversary, *Pennsylvania Grade Crude Oil Association*, Pittsburgh, Pa., June 17, 1948.
[6] Ashburner, I TRANSACTIONS A.I.M.E. 416 (1886).
[7] Act of Apr. 2, 1859, P.L. 347.

statute authorized the formation of companies for mining, manufacturing, and refining carbon oil, and granted them the right to hold lands in the manner and to the extent provided for opening coal mines.[8] The 1861 general assembly incorporated a number of companies by special acts, to explore, search, and bore for mineral oil on sites secured by purchase or lease in described territory, and to dispose of it when found.[9]

Special acts also incorporated railroads to be built along routes "proven by their surveys and explorations to be the most desirable for the accommodation of the oil trade."[10] Despite the new railroad companies, water conveyance was far more important. The early oil fields were on headwaters and tributaries of the Allegheny River, and by creating artificial "pond freshets" in small streams and creeks the oil could be shipped downstream to Oil City and on to Pittsburgh. This boating was hazardous and often disastrous. Fires were frequent. The 1863 legislature passed a bill to prevent running of tar and distillery refuse into certain creeks in producing districts.[11] The same session passed an act granting a bounty of eight cents a barrel for taking up empty oil barrels found floating upon the Allegheny and Monongahela Rivers and their tributaries. Either in recognition of the value of the oil or as an additional reward for extra salvage effort the act fixed the bounty for a filled oil barrel at 16 cents.[12]

Fraudulent practices and indefinite measurement led an industry group to standardize the oil barrel at 42 gallons.[13] The use of tanks at the well and on railroad cars led the adoption of tank tables in August 1865 calculated in 42 gallon barrels.[14] In 1867 the House passed a bill to secure uniformity of gauge in the purchase and sale of crude petroleum in certain counties but it was lost in the Senate.[15] An Act of 1878, in force at present, requires that all statements of bulk petroleum be given in barrels of 42 gallons.[16]

[8] Act of Mar. 29, 1860, P.L. 343.
[9] Acts of Mar. 25, 1861, P.L. 305; May 1, 1861, P.L. 572 and P.L. 654.
[10] Act of Apr. 2, 1860, P.L. 722, amended Jan. 29, 1862, P.L. 5—Oil Creek Railroad Co.
[11] SB No. 975, HB No. 700, Senate Journal 790 (1863).
[12] Act of Apr. 14, 1863, P.L. 388.
[13] THE DERRICK'S HANDBOOK 77 (1859–1898).
[14] SMILEY, A FEW SCRAPS, OILY AND OTHERWISE 48–50 (1907).
[15] HB No. 1653, H.R. Journal 1146 (1867).
[16] Act of May 22, 1878, P.L. 104, § 6; 58 PS § 110.

By 1862 a special act created the first of the corporations "for the purpose of conveying oil through pipes or tubes," [17] and 1864–1865 marked a complete change in the mode of transporting oil to market.[18] (Today oil pipe lines are the third largest carrier of freight in the United States, handling one-ninth of the freight tonnage of the country, and carrying a stream of crude oil through 125,000 miles and finished products through 150,000 miles of various sized pipe lines). Corporations with broader power were created, given the right to condemn lands for tanks and pipes and authorized to collect tolls as determined by the boards of directors for transportation and storage of oil.[19] In 1874 a statute passed to govern the operation of persons engaged in the storage and transportation of crude and refined petroleum by pipe lines, provided penalties for the issuance of fraudulent receipts for oil and called for monthly reports.[20] In 1878 a very comprehensive statute, for the regulation of pipe line transportation, requiring reports, statements, and the appointment of examiners, was enacted and remains effective.[21]

From the Legislative Journals it is apparent that conflicts were violent between business interests. Resolutions introduced in 1878 called for the appointment of a commission to investigate the oil trade and recommend legislation on charges and pipe line transportation. Proposals for additional privileges to pipe line companies were fought vigorously by the railroads.[22] In 1879 an amendment was presented which would have given the right of eminent domain for pipe line transportation and oil storage, but it did not pass.[23] Another law, enacted in 1883 and still current, provides for gauging petroleum in the custody of oil transportation and storage companies, and for inspection of the oil and examination of books and accounts, by persons appointed by the court, upon application of owners of two per cent of the oil in the company's custody.[24]

Up to this time the legislature had displayed little interest in

[17] Act of Feb. 26, 1862, P.L. 60—Oil Creek Transportation Company.
[18] GIDDENS, PENNSYLVANIA PETROLEUM 308 (1947); Lamp, January, 1947 5.
[19] Act of Mar. 22, 1869, P.L. 495—Western Oil and Pipe Company.
[20] Act of May 15, 1874, P.L. 172.
[21] Act of May 22, 1878, P.L. 104; 58 PS § 101–113.
[22] SB No. 245, H.R. Journal 1534 (1878).
[23] HB No. 121, H.R. Journal 72, 1051 (1879).
[24] Act of July 5, 1883, P.L. 186; 58 PS § 131–144.

natural gas. As pipe lines improved, it became possible to move gas from the wells to settlements where it could be utilized. Easy adaptability of gas to iron, steel, glass, and brick businesses tended towards rapid industrial development, but simultaneously incurred antagonism from producers of other fuels who feared displacement. One of the most constructive pieces of legislation dealing with oil and gas was the Act of 1885, which provided for the incorporation of natural gas companies, to satisfy a need the Supreme Court of Pennsylvania had pointed out in Emerson v. Commonwealth.[25] It prescribed an exclusive method of organizing and operating corporations to produce, transport, store, and supply natural gas in a territory described in the articles of incorporation, granted the right of eminent domain for pipe lines, and listed procedure for condemnation. It declared furnishing natural gas a public service, and required that gas be supplied to all applicants along transmission and distribution lines. To permit competition and consumer rate advantages, the territorial franchise was non-exclusive. So well was the Act drawn that, although amended in minor particulars, it is today the governing statute of all natural gas utilities except for administrative provisions of the Public Utility Law.[26]

WELL PLUGGING LAWS

A long series of bills and enactments, known as well plugging laws, have had for their purpose the prevention of drowning by water of strata capable of producing oil and gas. As early as 1867, a member of the legislature from oil producing Venango County introduced a bill to compel the owners of oil wells to keep them cased or plugged. It was tabled.[27] Another unsuccessful effort was made in 1877 to enact a law requiring owners and operators of oil lands to plug all wells upon abandonment "to shut off the water from oil bearing rock, and to exclude the oil and gas from the fresh water." [28] Finally a plugging law was passed and approved by Governor Hartranft in 1878. Further plugging statutes or amendments were passed in 1881, 1885, 1891, and 1921. The Act of 1921 repealed most of the earlier acts and was supplemented by an en-

[25] 108 Pa. 111, 126 (1884).
[26] Act of May 29, 1885, P.L. 29; 15 PS § 1981.
[27] HB No. 1616, H.R. Journal 872 (1867), H. Res. No. 100, 246 (1867).
[28] HB No. 345, H.R. Journal 299 (1877).

actment adopted in 1923, which permitted wells producing from the Bradford, Kane, and Haskell sands to remain open for water flooding, repressuring by air, gas, and other liquids "for the purpose of recovering the oil and gas contained therein."[29] The flooding law recognized a practice which pioneers in secondary recovery had followed for some years despite the plugging laws in effect. A later amendment permitted flooding operations in other sands.[30]

PROPOSED CONSERVATION BILLS

When in 1941 the general assembly of the commonwealth authorized the governor to execute the Interstate Compact to Conserve Oil and Gas, it included in the act a provision that participation in the Compact should not prohibit or prevent water flooding or "require or necessitate the enactment of conservation statutes, unless and until the General Assembly shall determine by law that such statutes are advisable or necessary to prevent the physical waste of oil or gas."[31] On its face this appears inconsistent with the purposes of the Compact, and undoubtedly the underlying reasons for the proviso are those that have caused conflict each time a conservation bill has been introduced. Several measures have been presented, but none, aside from the plugging laws, have been reported out of committee or voted upon by both houses of the legislature.

A House committee in 1887 unfavorably reported a bill to prevent waste of natural gas, and refused to concur in a Senate proposal "to prevent the escape and waste of natural gas, to provide for the closing of gas wells and for compensation to owners of the land in certain cases."[32] In 1913 a bill was introduced to create a petroleum and gas well commission to regulate location, drilling, casing, protection, operation, abandoning, plugging and filling of oil and gas wells, and referred to the Committee on Geological Survey. A similar bill was proposed in 1917 but did not get out of the Judiciary Special Committee to which it was committed.[33]

[29] Acts of May 16, 1878, P.L. 56; June 10, 1881, P.L. 110; June 23, 1885, P.L. 145; May 26, 1891, P.L. 122; 58 PS § 1; May 17, 1921, P.L. 912; 58 PS § 4.
[30] Acts of May 1, 1923, P.L. 115; Apr. 26, 1929, P.L. 821; 58 PS § 7.
[31] Act of July 23, 1941, P.L. 435; 58 PS § 191 and 195.
[32] HB No. 501, H.R. Journal 463 (1887); HB No. 551, 513; SB No. 196, 645; HB No. 794, 1447.
[33] HB No. 1783, H.R. Journal 1715 (1913); HB No. 798, H.R. Journal 628 (1917).

The first modern conservation statute before the legislature was presented in 1933. Article I defined waste as underground and surface waste together with that incident to or resulting from production of oil in excess of transportation, marketing facilities, or reasonable market demand; the Act declared it in the public interest and essential to conservation of Pennsylvania oil resources that oil, not required by the demands of commerce, be kept so far as possible in underground storage and that requirements of commerce be met by production from wells of settled production. These were wells not producing more than one barrel a day. The bill proposed establishment of a Pennsylvania Oil Commission to eliminate waste by preventing premature abandonments; the agency was vested with authority to determine average cost per barrel of settled production in order that it might curtail production when market price was less than average cost. The commission was empowered to fix the quantity of oil produced from each oil pool in the state, having regard to equitable apportionment between pools, the preservation of pools of settled production, and the prevention of monopolies. In addition to its authority to write proration orders, it had power to prohibit drilling of unnecessary oil wells and inlet wells for repressuring of air, gas, or water, but was without jurisdiction to interfere with the drilling of wildcat wells. The bill provided penalties and prohibited connection with pipe lines until the well owner or operator secured from the commission a certificate of compliance with the law.

Article II called for the establishment of an "interstate compact" between New York, West Virginia, Ohio, Pennsylvania, and any other producing states wishing to enter for "prevention of waste of petroleum resources of the compact states and to conserve such resources for the use of the people of the United States in adequate quantities for the longest possible period of time, the object being in all respects to promote the public interest of such state and of the United States." It undertook as a part of this compact to create a "Federal-State Oil Conservation Board" as the interstate fact finding and advisory committee of the compact states. This Board was to make and publish April and October first of each year, or oftener if required, an estimate of the quantities of oil needed the succeeding six months, from production and through storage withdrawals within the United States, to supply the estimated consumer demand in the United States and for export. The bill was committed to the Committee on Judiciary General; the Journals are silent as to its fate.[34] By this time secondary recovery had substantially increased production in the Bradford region, and obviously the Act might have stifled secondary recovery in one area by aiding marginal well operators in other parts of the state. The same bill was introduced to the Senate at the 1935 session, and was referred to the Committee on Mines and Mining which did not report it back.[35]

There is one legislative enactment which passed since the operations in deeper sands started several years ago. It is an Act of 1937 which requires the filing with the State Department of Internal Affairs an advance notice of intention to drill any well over 4000 feet deep and certain records to show the geological formations and conditions encountered in drilling wells more than 2500 feet. This information is available to anyone after a 90 day period of secrecy.[36]

In 1939 an Oil Conservation Act was presented to the House, with a stated purpose of protecting crude oil resources from waste and destruction. It defined waste and created a Pennsylvania Oil Commission to administer the Act. Much of the bill was drawn from the Senate bills of 1933 and 1935, but one new feature was the establishment of an oil conservation fund to pay the commission salaries and expenses, secured by taxes levied on crude oil or by a special appropriation from state general revenue. The powers and duties of the commission were set forth at length as were the procedures and means of enforcing the commission's orders. The bill, referred to the Committee on Corporations and Industry, was not reported out.[37] A supplemental measure, proposing a tax of $\frac{1}{5}$th cent a barrel on the right to produce crude oil to maintain the oil conservation fund, also died in committee.[38]

Another bill not adopted at the 1939 assembly was the Migratory Fuel Control Act. The law declared natural gas a "migratory mineral resource," and one avowed purpose was to compensate

[34] SB No. 1494, 1933 Session.
[35] SB No. 1130, 1935 Session.
[36] Act of July 2, 1937, P.L. 2772; 58 PS § 41.
[37] HB No. 938, 1939 Session.
[38] HB No. 939, 1939 Session.

land owners for gas removed from their land by wells on property owned or leased by others. "In order to prevent an overly rapid depletion of the gas reserves" it made unlawful the drilling of a well deeper than 3000 feet for gas or oil without first notifying the Department of Interior. Any well of this depth or with an original rock pressure of more than 1000 pounds came under the bill. Drilling was banned where the operator did not control a majority of the acreage in a circle with the well head as center and having a radius equal to 30 per cent of the proposed or actual depth of the well. Exceptions were made for wildcat wells. Data was to be furnished immediately upon completion and the department given ten days to make an estimate of recoverable reserves in the pool, field, or producing area tapped by the discovery well, with the assistance (at its election) of a committee of seven producers. Each producer was limited to 15 per cent annually of these recoverable reserves irrespective of the number of wells he had, except that 20 per cent was allowed the discovery well. All acreage within the described circle having a radius of 40 per cent of the well depth around a discovery well was a "royalty pool," and a minimum royalty of $3/16$ths of the market price of oil and gas at the well (not less than 8 cents per MCF for gas or 80 cents per barrel for oil) was payable to owners or lessees of leased lands in the ratio of $2/3$rds to owners and $1/3$rd to lessees, on an acreage basis.[39] This Act remained in the hands of the Committee on Mines and Mining when the legislature adjourned.

STATUTES IN AID OF RESEARCH

We look upon conservation as preservation of an irreplaceable resource obtainable at the well or mine. Its economic value is the enjoyment resulting from use. Necessarily the scheme of sound conservation rests upon empirical knowledge until scientific learning and firmly grounded theory charts a course. The predominant attitude of the rugged individualist willing to assume the speculative risks was unfavorable to sharing or disclosing observed data and information, which resulted from successful drilling operations, to assist competitors. Lack of geological or scientific knowledge

[39] HB No. 1009, 1939 Session.

of what lay hidden and what happened underground when wells were drilled was a serious obstacle. Tribute is due from the entire industry to the ardent efforts of the state government to aid promotion and continuation of the oil industry. As early as 1870 Governor John W. Geary addressed the legislature on the subject, and at the next session in 1871 he said: "A reliable geological and mineralogical survey would be of incalculable value in the State. Without it we have indefinite ideas of our vast undeveloped mineral wealth and the expense attending it would be utterly insignificant when compared with the beneficial results. The old study of 1836–41 did a good work but it is of little value now, except in a few localities. Since it was made wonderful discoveries have taken place, and problems of structure and deposit still remain unsolved, doubtless involving many millions of dollars in value. . . . . Science is cumulative and its advances are slow. It must collect many facts before it arrives at true conclusions . . . Much valuable information has been lost never to be recovered, and but little certain knowledge of past mining and other scientific operations has been preserved to govern and assist the future engineer . . ." [40] The survey was made, and in 1893 Governor Robert E. Pattison told the general assembly: "The Board of Commissioners of the Geological Survey, created by the Act of May 17, 1874, has about completed its labors. . . . There has been a total expenditure of $1,589,491.24. The work of the Commissioners is embodied in eighty volumes of reports, thirty-seven atlases and five grand atlases." [41] The vision of John F. Carll, Geologist in Charge, J. P. Lesley and Henry E. Wrigley, the men who made the oil and gas surveys, is recorded in their reports.[42]

[40] Governor's Message to General Assembly, Senate Journal 11 (1871).

[41] Governor's Message to General Assembly, Senate Journal 11 (1893).

[42] WRIGLEY, 71 SECOND PA. GEOL. SURV. 7–9, 76–78 (1874), "For the past two years, 1873 and 1874 the production of oil has increased so rapidly that even the steady growing consumption, which has from its decrease in cost attained unexpected proportions, failed to maintain a balance essential to a healthful condition of the trade. The result has been that the production was necessarily confined to the largest wells, or rather that such new territory only was developed, as was expected to produce great results; development in the upper region, where the wells were of moderate size, was gradually abandoned, and small wells shut down entirely as the price received would not repay the cost of pumping. When we carefully consider the short life of the best territory that has been found, how comparatively small is the relative proportion of the actual producing area to the entire region, it becomes a serious question, even in the face of the enormous production of today,

In times of crises oil operators have effectively cooperated. Voluntary organizations and agreements have been surprisingly successful in bringing about orderly producing and marketing. The Pennsylvania Grade Crude Oil Association, established twenty-five years ago, is untiring in its efforts to foster and encourage research in the production of crude and the improvement of products.[43] Secondary recovery is supported materially by legislative aid.

whether we shall, in the Commonwealth, continue to supply petroleum to the next generation. Whether any protection to our general interests in this matter as a State is possible or advisable, is a question that present abundance has put out of sight. With a will to meeting the questions: Whether we are over estimating the durability of our oil fields; and what can be done to realize the greatest return and avoid 'waste,' the following points seem to be worthy of remembrance: Our everyday idea of the mining of all minerals is based, to a great extent, upon the older discoveries of coal and gold. The special difference between the mining of coal and other solid minerals, and of this fluid, lies mainly in the fact that the former is not necessarily wasteful, the bed can be measured and estimated; and we know that we can go and get it when we want it, and stop when we please. We also know that operations on the land of one owner may be carried directly to his boundary without affecting the interests of his neighbor. But the oil sand-rocks which stretch under adjacent farms, are not only affected but often absolutely controlled by a few thoughtless operators who own or lease territory adjoining that in which a poor well has been found. Developing a bed of rock is but a race between the owners of the surface above it, as to who shall first exhaust the basin of oil below the surface, common to all parties. All this is highly disastrous; and the result has been that whereas the sand-rock, if kept free from the surface water and pierced only by a moderate number of holes will last eight to ten years, the average life of a well has not practically reached three years. We do not exhaust our beds of sand-rock, but destroy them. We pluck the apple, so to speak, by rooting up the tree. Had it been possible from the start to regulate drilling, it can hardly be questioned that one-third of the wells that have been drilled, would have brought us as great a return as we have had from them all thus far, and at one-third the cost of producing. The production of oil has reached a point at which it becomes our interest to supply, not in wasteful abundance ruinous to the territory, and at a loss to ourselves, but with such restrictions as will not only give better pecuniary results, but enable us to secure the fullest return from every bed of which it is capable, and of spreading the production over a greater period of time. We find that the discovery of petroleum in quantity was so ordered as to be practically coincident with the beginning of the great war which called forth all our resources, that it paid during several years to the National Government a direct tax of over ten millions of dollars, and that as an article of export it has brought a return from abroad of at least three hundred millions. It will not be hard to discern that this great result is due less to any local advantages of fortune than to the untrammeled freedom which our institutions give to American enterprise." LESLEY, 69 SECOND PA. GEOL. SURV. XIV (1883), "The next generation will gather from our oil history, with angry astonishment, a lesson of warning in political economy, only useless because coming too late."

[43] Andrus, *Secondary Recovery Research—An Adventure in Conservation,* V INTERSTATE OIL COMPACT Q. BULL. 16, 20 (1946). Jones, *Testimony before the House Armed Services Committee, Feb. 6, 1948,* Producers Monthly (Feb. 1948) 18.

Since 1929 the general assembly has made annual appropriations to the Pennsylvania State College School of Mineral Industries for such research and experimental investigation. The College conducts studies, assisted substantially by financial contributions from producers in the region.

There can be no question that the development of oil and gas in Pennsylvania would have been carried on differently had present scientific information been available in 1859. Today we see no justification for many of the practices indulged in when the reservoirs of the state were originally opened. The major role of Pennsylvania has been to bring order out of the early chaos by evolving an organized and informed industry anxious to accept and promote sound conservation.

CHAPTER 29

South Dakota, 1881–1948

The discovery of oil and gas in commercial quantities has been an alluring hope in South Dakota since its early history, and though sizeable sums have been expended on exploration and drilling, there has not been a substantial return to show for this investment. Small quantities of natural gas were discovered in South Dakota as a result of drilling for water wells in 1881. In 1890 the Norbeck Company, a well drilling group organized by Perter Norbeck (later Governor and United States Senator from South Dakota), developed machinery and methods for drilling deep low cost artesian wells. These operations, in connection with the drilling of artesian wells, produced natural gas in many parts of the state. In the state capitol at Pierre, and its neighboring city of Fort Pierre across the Missouri River, sufficient natural gas has been produced since 1890 to provide limited domestic consumption, but in no instance has natural gas been produced within the state in commercial amounts.

The first discovery of oil in South Dakota is rumored to have been in the northern Black Hills in connection with the early history of the Homestake Gold Mine. It is reported that while drilling for water near the state line north of Belle Fourche, oil was found in quantities enabling the operators of the mine to use it for lubrication of machinery. Numerous wildcat wells have been drilled at widely separated points in the state, and twenty years ago there was a test well in the southwestern part of the state, near Edgemont, which produced a small quantity of low grade oil. There have been, likewise, showings of oil in non-commercial quantities at other

ROY E. WILLY, WRITER; Karl Goldsmith, M. A. Sharpe, E. P. Rothrock, Advisers.
(See app. B.)

points in the state. Interest in the subject of oil and gas production has been kept alive by a number of oil companies, which have leases on many tracts of land in South Dakota. A substantial portion of these leases are sustained by the payment of annual rents. Beginning in 1938 and continuing for six or seven years thereafter, an extensive leasing and exploratory program was conducted in the state by five to ten major oil companies. Oil and gas leases were obtained on large tracts of land and a number of test wells completed.

LEGISLATIVE HISTORY

In anticipation of the discovery of oil and gas in commercial quantities within the state, the legislature as early as 1923 gave consideration to conservation legislation. In that year the legislature passed an act which provided for the regulation and inspection of oil and gas wells and the prevention of waste of natural gas.[1] This Act was replaced at the ensuing session of the legislature in 1925, by a new measure assigning the state geologist charge of the conservation of natural resources in the state and the prevention of waste therein. The geologist was authorized to prescribe and enforce rules and regulations necessary to carry out the purpose of the Act, to govern drilling, casing, and abandonment of oil and gas wells, and to prevent the waste of oil and gas therefrom.[2] By 1929 there was a considerable showing of natural gas in the state in connection with artesian well drilling. In various sections of the state farmers drilling for artesian water found natural gas. It was felt the possibility of the discovery of natural gas in commercial quantities justified additional conservation legislation. To prevent and prohibit waste of natural gas, the 1929 legislature passed an act prohibiting the use of natural gas in any form without fully utilizing its heat units in manufacture or domestic use.[3]

By 1939 there was considerable demand to lease public lands for oil and gas development which required legislative permission. The legislature passed several acts relating to the rights of public bodies to enter into oil and gas leasing arrangements covering public lands.

[1] S.D. Laws 1923, c. 242.
[2] S.D. Laws 1925, c. 250. S.D. CODE § 42.0603–6 (1939).
[3] S.D. Laws 1929, c. 203. S.D. CODE § 42.0601–2 (1939).

One act authorized the Board of School and Public Lands and the Rural Credits Board to enter into agreements on behalf of the State of South Dakota to pool acreage under their several jurisdictions with acreage for unit operations and to apportion oil or gas royalties on an acreage or equitable basis.[4] For the further purpose of fostering and encouraging the development and exploitation of oil and gas, counties within South Dakota were permitted to sell or lease their public lands for oil and gas purposes.[5]

When the South Dakota legislature met in 1941, sufficient interest had been aroused in the subject of conservation to insure the presentation to the lawmakers of legislative proposals. Large oil companies conducting exploratory work held oil leases in the state. Their local counsel took an active part in preparing the initial legislation. Attorneys for these companies, working in some instances with the company general counsel, drafted legislation. An attempt was made to prepare a bill which embodied the best features of conservation legislation in effect in states where oil and gas was found in commercial quantities. The bill prepared and introduced in the House was H.B. 241. Hearings were held by both houses and little opposition was presented.[6] After this Act had been adopted, active opposition developed from a group apprehensive that the conservation board created in the act would not be fair in its decisions to smaller operators. Referendum petitions were circulated and sufficient signatures were secured to defer the operation of .the bill until after the 1942 election. In the election of 1942, this bill appeared on the ballot and failed of passage by the small margin of some 500 votes.[7]

Those interested in conservation legislation were not discouraged, and spokesmen for both groups worked out a compromise measure which was introduced in the 1943 legislature. This bill met little active opposition and was passed in both houses and signed by the governor.[8] Act 153 created a Conservation Commission consisting of the governor, the secretary of state, the attorney general, the state treasurer, the commissioner of school and pub-

[4] S.D. Laws 1939, c. 164.
[5] S.D. Laws 1939, c. 165.
[6] S.D. Laws 1941, c. 177.
[7] No votes 67,038; Yes votes 66,585.
[8] S.D. Laws 1943, c. 153.

lic lands, and the state auditor. This act is now in force and, pursuant to its terms, the Conservation Commission has promulgated rules and regulations. The state geologist and state engineer are technical advisors of the board. One of the controversial features which led to the defeat of the 1941 bill was fear that the Commission might discriminate in the limitation of oil and gas production. Consequently, one of the features of the 1943 law prohibits the Conservation Commission from adopting rules or regulations which limit the production of oil or gas, except to prevent waste.

As there is little gas produced in South Dakota and no oil, the enactment of legislation is similar to a condition existing in states where a game and fish commission is provided, although there exists little or no wild life. Conservation in South Dakota is academic and not entirely practical. However, the state has conservation legislation, a Conservation Commission, and—in the event of the discovery of oil or gas in commercial quantities—laws are available to control the development of new discoveries. Unquestionably, if oil or gas is found, the Commission would be subject to changes in the present form. Until that time the Commission meets the needs of South Dakota. We are assured that should oil or gas in commercial quantities be found, South Dakota cannot be subjected to the ruthless exploitation occurring in other jurisdictions where the discovery of this valuable mineral product preceded any legislative control.

CHAPTER 30

Tennessee, 1866–1948

~/~

Tennessee bears a common heritage with the eastern oil states in the history of oil discovery and production, having had a period of decline to a point of non-existence, and then with the intensified search of the oil industry for new provinces, a resurgence of importance in the petroleum world. Oil seeps have long been known in the state. Gerard Troost, first state geologist, reported their presence in eastern Tennessee more than one hundred years past.[1] Stories were common in the early part of the eighteen hundreds of disappointed prospectors who found oil instead of the salt so greatly needed and sought.[2] Evidences of surface waste in 1820 are mentioned in reports of conflagrations in the rivers and areas adjoining the salt diggings.[3] In 1837 in a hole dug for salt in Clay County, large flows of oil were obtained.[4] Early geologists spent much time in exploring the oil springs.[5] What is possibly the first commercial oil well in Tennessee was drilled in 1866 in southern Overton County, and another was located in southeastern Pickett County

BLAKELY M. MURPHY, WRITER; H. B. Burwell, Paul S. Mathes, Advisers. (See app. B.)

[1] DEPT. CONSER., OIL AND GAS IN MIDDLE TENNESSEE, OIL AND GAS INVESTIGATIONS No. 1 (1943).

[2] JILLSON, THE OIL AND GAS RESOURCES OF KENTUCKY, 3–9 (1919).

[3] MUNN, PRELIMINARY REPORT UPON THE OIL AND GAS DEVELOPMENTS IN TENNESSEE, TENN. GEOL. SUR. BULL. 2-E, 5–6 (1911).

[4] KILLEBREW, OIL REGION OF TENNESSEE WITH SOME ACCOUNT OF ITS OTHER RESOURCES AND CAPABILITIES: Rep. Bur. Agri., Statistics, and Mines, 63 (1878). At 62–64 he says: "Salt water with some oil was obtained up a hollow . . . The well was bored 178 feet deep, and about 10,000 bushels of salt were manufactured in the year 1867. Sixty gallons of water made a bushel of salt. The cost of making salt was 7½ cents per bushel, but bacon was then selling at 25 cents per pound, labor $1.50 per day."

[5] Id. at 62–64.

about 1896.[6] The most concentrated period of oil and gas production came in the 1920's and continued into the 1930's. After that date new discoveries lagged and production was reduced to infinitesimal amounts. Today the picture is one of exploration. Major companies have carried out lease blocking campaigns and turned their attention to western Tennessee, where fewer than 40 wells in an area of 11,000 square miles have been drilled.[7]

By 1895 the General Assembly of Tennessee found it necessary to curb uncontrolled plugging and abandonment of wells.[8] The small capital needed to drill to a shallow depth then the custom brought about unprecedented wildcatting with a resulting careless attention to plugging and closures. The statute created a procedure for closing patterned after those in force in the eastern oil regions which governed the placing and composition of the plug. Where the owners or operators failed to properly close their wells, adjoining owners could enter and perform the work at the former's expense. A penalty of $200 was assessed for disobedience to the law. By 1905 a more exhaustive measure was called for to govern abandonment and plugging. In that year the general assembly adopted an Act[9] which did not repeal the 1895 enactment, but strengthened and supplanted many of its sections. A further shift in control of oil and gas was the requirement that gas wells were forbidden to allow wastage by escape of gas. All gas was to be securely confined within the well or connecting pipe lines within 90 days after the operator reached the lowest recognized oil or gas sand, or a penalty was levied. In addition, the chancery courts of the state were vested with the right to hear and determine bills filed to restrain waste. Prevention of waste was not required where any well produced both oil and gas and was operated solely as an oil well. This remained the controlling statutory law of Tennessee until 1943, when a law was adopted more nearly representative of the needs of the industry and the state.

The general assembly of 1943 passed the comprehensive oil and gas conservancy code[10] under which control of petroleum is carried

---

[6] See note 3 *supra* at 6–8.

[7] *The Oil Prospects of West Tennessee*, Oil (Nov. 1947) 12.

[8] Tenn. P.A. 1895, c. 217; Ann. Code Tenn. § 6831–6833 (Shannon 1918), Tenn. Code Ann. § 11299–11301 (Michie 1938).

[9] Tenn. P.A. 1905, c. 379; Tenn. Code Ann. § 5234–5240 (Williams 1941).

[10] Tenn. P.A. 1943, c. 64; Tenn. Code Ann. § 5240.1 *et seq.* (Williams 1943).

on in Tennessee today. In 1947 the membership of the state in the Interstate Compact to Conserve Oil and Gas was approved.[11]

Chapter 64 creates an administrative board charged with protecting petroleum natural resources from waste and dissipation. This agency, the State Oil and Gas Board, is composed of the commissioner of conservation,[12] as chairman, the attorney general[13] and the commissioner of taxation.[14] The state geologist[15] serves as state oil and gas supervisor. The Board has jurisdiction to control all persons and oil properties for the prevention of waste in the production of oil or natural gas. Under the waste definition[16] extensive powers are assigned the agency to prohibit waste.[17] The agency may

[11] Tenn. P.A. 1947, c. 44. Murphy, *Tennessee and the Interstate Compact to Conserve Oil and Gas*, 19 Tenn. L. Rev. 551 (1947). Paul S. Mathes, then Commissioner of Conservation, H. B. Burwell, State Geologist, and A. L. Roberts of the Memphis Bar were instrumental in securing the adoption of this measure. In general the law follows those acts adopted by other states joining the Compact but § 6 states that by adopting the act the state is not surrendering any of its rights to the Compact or the Federal Government. The state maintains a representative on the Commission and the committees of that body.

[12] The commissioner is selected by the governor. Tenn. P.A. 1937, c. 33 § 1–2, Tenn. P.A. 1939, c. 11 § 1–2; TENN. CODE ANN. § 255.1–255.2 (Williams 1943).

[13] The attorney general is chosen by the Supreme Court of Tennessee and holds office for a term of eight years. TENN. CONST. Art. VI § 5. Tenn. P.A. 1870, c. 24 § 7; TENN. CODE ANN. § 642 (Williams 1943).

[14] The commissioner of taxation, head of the department of finance and taxation, is selected by the governor. Tenn. P.A. 1937, c. 33 § 1–2, Tenn. P.A. 1939, c. 11 § 1–2; TENN. CODE ANN. § 255.1–255.2 (Williams 1943).

[15] A division of geology was created in 1923 headed by a state geologist. Tenn. P.A. 1923, c. 7 § 36. This department was placed under the department of conservation in 1937. Tenn. P.A. 1937, c. 33 § 56. The qualifications of the office are fixed in Tenn. P.A. 1923, c. 7 § 37; TENN. CODE ANN. § 311–312 (Williams 1934).

[16] In addition to its ordinary meaning waste is defined as ". . . underground waste and inefficient, excessive, improper use or dissipation of reservoir energy, including gas energy, water drive of any pool; . . . surface waste and the inefficient storing of oil and the locating, spacing drilling, equipping, operating or producing of oil wells or gas wells in a manner causing or tending to cause unnecessary or excessive surface loss or destruction of oil or gas. . . ." Tenn. P.A. 1943, c. 64§ 3–4.

[17] 1. To prescribe rules, regulations and orders to carry into effect the pronouncements of the statute. 2. To hold hearings (regular and emergency). 3. To determine the existence or imminence of waste by collection of data and investigation by checking oil and gas wells, tanks, refineries and transportation agencies. 4. To require drilling, casing and plugging of wells for the prevention of escape of oil, gas or water into oil and gas strata. 5. To require the filing of notices of intention to drill, drilling logs, drilling records and electrical logs. 6. To prevent water drowning of structures. 7. To require operation of wells by means of efficient gas-oil ratios. 8. To prevent blowouts, caving and seepages. 9. To regulate the shooting of wells and their chemical treatment, secondary recovery practices and well spacing. 10. To require persons to identify ownership of wells, refineries, storage and transportation equipment.

require the integration of separately owned or leased tracts into drilling units. No production within Tennessee can be limited until its daily average exceeds "50,000 barrels per day for ninety consecutive days."

Power to issue rules and regulations and promulgate orders exists, although to date the administrative group has withheld exercise of this prerogative, preferring to initiate rules only at the time and for purposes needed. The Board stands ready to take effective action under its rule making power. The usual procedures for notice and hearing in the absence of an emergency are followed. Attendance of witnesses and giving of testimony at hearings is required. Witnesses who refuse to testify or to produce documentary evidence called for may, upon application of the agency to a proper circuit court, be coerced to purge themselves of recalcitrance upon pain of being held in contempt of court. Attachments issue to force attendance upon the agency. A penal section subjects violators to a fine of not more than $1000 for each day of infraction and in addition the agency may sue to compel obedience to the law or to restrain violation. No provision is made for appeal, but reviews of Board decisions are obtainable through equitable action. No court in Tennessee has had occasion to consider the 1943 or prior conservation measures.

CHAPTER 31

Texas, 1938–1948

∿

Ten years ago in *Legal History of Conservation of Oil and Gas—A Symposium*, Maurice Cheek and Robert E. Hardwicke undertook to recount in separate articles, one as to gas and the other as to oil, the legal history of conservation of oil and gas in Texas up to October 1, 1938.[1] The history is here extended to cover the ensuing period to August 1, 1948. Among the conclusions Hardwicke stated in the earlier article were: "(1) It is now everywhere admitted that conservation practices, including proration under governmental regulation, were necessary; that these practices are based on scientific principles, and have been highly beneficial to the State of Texas and to the oil industry. The conservation program will likely be continued in some degree for a long time, probably under state laws. (p. 265) (2) Many of the fundamental legal, scientific, economic, and political issues with respect to state regulation have been settled, but only after bitter conflicts, and at enormous avoidable cost to the state and to most members of the industry. The application of some of the principles still presents considerable difficulty, and many other problems are pressing for solution, or at least a better

ROBERT E. HARDWICKE, WRITER; Elton M. Hyrder, Jr., A. W. Walker, Jr., Advisers. (See app. B.)

NOTE: The oil and gas conservation statutes as they existed in 1925 were codified under Title 102 of the Revised Civil Statutes of 1925. No further official codification of the statutes has been made; however, the Vernon Law Book Company in 1926 published VERNON'S ANNOTATED REVISED CIVIL STATUTES of the State of Texas, Revision of 1925, using the official article numbers. This set has been kept up to date. In many instances new article numbers have been assigned to provisions of acts passed since 1925. Although unofficial, these statutes are usually cited as if they were official, and they are cited herein as VERNON'S CIV. STAT. Reference in this paper to conservation laws or statutes means the oil and gas conservation statutes.

[1] Hardwicke, *Legal History of Conservation of Oil in Texas*, LEGAL HISTORY OF CONSERVATION OF OIL AND GAS 214 (1938), and Cheek, *Legal History of Conservation of Gas in Texas* in id at 269.

447

solution, and no doubt others will arise as conditions change. Clearly, however, facts are now available which make possible a rather accurate appraisal of the benefits and dangers involved in lack of any regulation, and in various degrees of state and federal regulation. (p. 265) (9) It is a tribute to the character and patience of our people, and to our system of government, cumbersome though it may be at times, that such drastic and detailed regulation and control of private property and business as outlined in this paper were accomplished with no greater confusion, mistakes or ill will. Great progress has been made toward conservation practices of a high order, and toward orderly production of oil and gas. Surely the evils in the present system can be reduced so that no violent upheaval will be necessary in the search for a solution of the problems which are still confronting us." (p. 268) It was fair prophesy, as this supplemental history will show.

A Texan should not be accused of bragging when he says that what happens to the oil industry in Texas is of national importance. This is so because on January 1, 1948 there were in Texas 1248 oil fields, with 106,738 oil wells scattered through 189 of its 254 counties. These wells produced in 1947 more than 816,000,000 barrels of oil at the rate of more than 2,236,000 barrels each calendar day, or about one-half of the total production of crude oil in the United States. The wells also produced large quantities of gas associated with the oil. In addition, there were 8623 gas wells in 831 gas reservoirs. The total production of gas in 1947 was more than 2,893,-553,700,000 (almost 3 trillion or 3 thousand billion) cubic feet. Moreover, from the natural gas, including casinghead-gas and condensate gas, there was extracted or produced during 1947 a total of more than 73,232,000 barrels of liquid hydrocarbons at the rate of more than 200,000 barrels each calendar day.[2] According to a public statement made July 15, 1948 by Colonel Ernest O. Thompson, a member of the Railroad Commission of Texas, there were approximately 28,000 producing leases in Texas and some 147,000 more awaiting development; there were 3400 small operators or companies, the independents, and 14 large companies, the major companies, operating in Texas. Colonel Thompson declared that

[2] Information obtained from Jack K. Baumel, Chief Engineer, Railroad Commission of Texas, in July 1948.

60 per cent of the oil produced in Texas is refined in the state; that the proved crude oil reserves of the state are more than 12,000,-000,000 barrels; that Texas has one-half of the known oil reserves of the United States, and more than one-half of the known gas reserves —the fuel value of the gas being equal to that of 14,000,000,000 barrels of crude oil.[8]

Although a number of the producing wells are upon lands owned by the state or some political subdivision, all operating rights or leases are privately owned. Over all these fields, wells, and leases— privately owned and of tremendous value—the Railroad Commission of Texas has far-reaching powers for the purpose of preventing waste and protecting correlative rights. The opportunity of the Commission to do good is great, and great good has been done, but there is an equal opportunity to be unwise, to be arbitrary, and to be discriminatory, in spite of what may appear to be elaborate safeguards. The record of regulation in Texas presents an interesting study of the difficulties inevitable in any extensive regulation of private property.

The argument has frequently been made that the control of oil and gas production—particularly the restriction of production so that it will not exceed reasonable market demand—has stifled competition and killed initiative. The argument is not considered sound. These facts are interesting in that connection. When extensive regulation began in Texas in the summer of 1930, the operators were producing without restriction an average of 800,000 barrels of oil a day from about 37,000 wells; in 1939, after nine years of regulation, the daily average production of oil was about 1,400,000 barrels from some 85,000 wells; and January 1, 1948, nine years later (or eighteen years after regulation began), the daily average was about 2,200,000 barrels of oil from some 106,700 wells. There is no official record of production of the other liquid hydrocarbons (natural gasoline and condensate) in 1930, but it was relatively small. Production of those liquids in January 1940 averaged about 80,000

[8] Dallas News, July 16, 1948, § 1, p. 5. For detailed estimates of reserves as of January 1, 1948, see Proved Reserves of Crude Oil, Natural Gas Liquids, and Natural Gas (1948), a joint report of the American Gas Association and the American Petroleum Institute; World Oil (Yearbook Forecast Issue, Feb. 1948) 177; Oil and Gas Jour. (Jan. 29, 1948) 170. For records to January 1, 1947, see 1947 Petroleum Data Book, c. 3–22.

barrels a day and by January 1, 1948 about 220,000 barrels a day. It is logical to say that the search for new fields has actually been stimulated, because oil men in Texas know that their properties will not be ruined by wasteful practices of others, and that the laws contemplate protection of correlative rights.

This article does not purport to be an exhaustive commentary on all, or even a large part, of the legal questions which have been raised or could be raised with respect to the oil and gas conservation laws of Texas and their administration. It is a history, necessarily limited by the space allotted, but it does purport to set forth primary source material so that the reader may understand what has taken place in Texas with respect to the conservation of oil and gas since October 1938.

I. LEGISLATIVE HISTORY

The conservation statutes in force in Texas at the beginning of 1939 were the result of nearly a decade of intensive study, debate, and conflict in the legislature, the courts, the hearing room of the Railroad Commission of Texas, and in other forums. In most of the other important oil producing states, the history was similar. The court decisions and the literature on the subject became voluminous over a period of less than a decade. The power of the state to regulate oil and gas production to prevent waste and protect correlative rights was well established by 1939. Moreover, the fundamental provisions of the statutes had been reasonably well settled in Texas by that date. There remained, however, the need for amendments, largely a process of sharpening or polishing to meet changing conditions and to take advantage of a better understanding of the facts. Emphasis shifted from controversies over the power to regulate to those involving the fairness of the regulation.

(1) New Legislation
(a) EXTENSION OF CONSERVATION ACT

The practice which began in 1932 [4] of providing for the termination of the conservation Act at the end of a short period (two years

[4] Tex. Acts 4th called Sess. 1932, c. 2, § 14 provided for expiration of the act on Sept. 1, 1935.

each after September 1, 1935) continued until 1941; when the section containing the limitation was repealed, thereby removing the necessity of extending the Act every two years, and also avoiding the bi-annual need for industry planning to meet the possibility that the act might not be extended and thus expire by its terms. Without an extension, the authority of the Railroad Commission of Texas to control production effectively would be taken away, a situation with infinite possibilities for confusion and harm.[5]

(b) EXTENSION OF MEMBERSHIP IN INTERSTATE OIL COMPACT

With respect to the Interstate Oil Compact to Conserve Oil and Gas, the practice of limiting the duration of membership by Texas continued partly because the Congress in its authorization provided for a limited term. Texas was a charter member and has continued its participation. The legislature in 1947 authorized the governor to commit the state to membership for the four year period ending September 1, 1951.[6]

(c) REVISION OF MARGINAL WELL ACT

In the process of polishing the provisions of the conservation statutes, the Marginal Well Act, passed in 1931 and amended in 1933, was further amended in 1941. The original Act declared pumping wells of specified capacities within certain depth limits were marginal wells, and that no order should be entered "requiring restriction of the production" of any marginal well. The 1941 amendment made clearer the definition of a marginal well. In part this was done by including specifically not only pumping wells of specified capacities and depths, but also wells producing by gas lift or other means of artificial lift.[7]

[5] Tex. Acts 1935, c. 76, § 20 provided for expiration Sept. 1, 1937; Tex. Acts 1937, c. 15, changed the date to Sept. 1, 1939; Tex. Acts 1939, c. 1, extended it to Sept. 1, 1941; Tex. Acts 1941, c. 559, repealed the section containing the expiration date.

[6] Tex. Acts 1937, c. 217, authorized membership to Sept. 1, 1939; Tex. Acts 1939 (special law) to Sept. 1, 1941; Tex. Acts 1941, c. 63, to Sept. 1, 1943; Tex. Acts 1943, c. 15, to Sept. 1, 1947; Tex. Acts 1947, c. 52, to Sept. 1, 1951.

[7] The orignal act was passed in 1931, Tex. Acts 1931, c. 58; VERNON'S CIV. STAT. art. 6049 b. It was amended by Tex. Acts 1933, c. 97, and then by Tex. Acts 1941, c. 550. The amendments related only to § 1 of the original act which defined marginal wells and declared wells of certain capacities and depths to be marginal wells. The 1933 act changed the number of barrels applicable to

The 1933 and 1941 Acts did not amend Section 2 of the original Act. That section in broad terms seemed to say that the Railroad Commission of Texas was without power to make an order or rule which would restrict directly or indirectly or for any reason the production of a well defined as a marginal well.[8] The meaning of the Act was involved in the *Konowa* case, in which the validity of a water-oil ratio order was questioned. By limiting the amount of water any oil well could produce, the order had the effect of limiting the production of oil from oil wells of the Konowa Company, which the company claimed were marginal wells. The company argued that the marginal well statute deprived the Commission of power to restrict even indirectly the oil production of those wells. The trial court sustained that contention, but its judgment was reversed by the court of civil appeals. The case did not reach the Supreme Court of Texas. The court of civil appeals pointed out that the marginal well statute talked about wells incapable of producing specified amounts "under normal unrestricted operating conditions." This meant, said the court, that a normal unrestricted operating condition was one provided for under the conservation rules of the Commission. The court held that the water-oil ratio order was such a conservation rule, that it did not therefore conflict with the marginal well law, and it was not an order restricting the production of a marginal well contrary to the provisions of Section 2 of the Marginal Well Act.[9] The court used this language: "We hold that the purpose of the marginal well law was to prohibit the passage of orders designed and operating directly to restrict production in marginal wells, such as proration and other like orders, if such there be. That the orders in suit do not come within the

---

various depths as follows: 10 bbl. to depth of 2000 ft.; 20 bbl. between 2000 and 4000 ft.; 25 bbl. between 4000 and 6000 ft.; 30 bbl. between 6000 and 8000 ft.; 35 bbl. if deeper than 8000 ft. The 1941 act did not change these figures.

[8] Such was the opinion in January 1940 of the Texas Attorney General's department copied in full in Texas State House Reporter No. 213 (Jan. 1940). It refers to and quotes from earlier opinions of the Dept. of similar import. § 2 of the Marginal Well Act read as follows: "To artificially curtail the production of any 'Marginal Well' below the marginal limit as set out above prior to its ultimate plugging and abandonment is hereby declared to be waste, and no rule or order of the Railroad Commission of Texas, or other constituted legal authority, shall be entered requiring restriction of the production of any 'Marginal Well' as herein defined."

[9] Railroad Comm. v. Konowa Operating Co., 174 S.W. 2d 605 (Tex. Civ. App. 3rd, 1943) *no app. for writ.*

purview of such prohibition, are therefore not in conflict with the marginal well law, and are valid. This holding concedes, arguendo, the validity of the marginal well law, a question upon which, however, we express no opinion, since it is not essential to this holding and the proper disposition of the case thereunder." (174 S.W. 2d 605, 609)

The validity of the Marginal Well Act was questioned in several other instances, but the cases were disposed of without the necessity of a clear cut decision on the point.[10] It was forcibly argued in those cases that although the marginal well law might be valid, and as a consequence the Commission could not directly restrict the production of a marginal well, it did not follow that the Commission could validly restrict non-marginal wells so drastically that the owners of marginal wells were given great advantage over the owners of non-marginal wells and without reasonable grounds from a waste prevention standpoint. The principle involved is sound, but difficulties arise in its application to the facts in a particular case. Presumably the interpretation of the Marginal Well Act in the *Konowa* case has produced no intolerable results, for the Act has not been amended.

(d) ACTS RELATING TO NATURAL GAS

The Railroad Commission of Texas had many problems in its efforts to control production in the gas fields or gas areas, particularly in the great Panhandle Field where the problems were complicated by the existence of·unconnected gas wells owned mainly by small operators, and the existence of sour gas, sweet gas, and oil in the same formation. Further difficulties arose because of the restrictions, or lack of restrictions, upon the use of gas from gas wells for making carbon black. The legislature appeared unable to write a law and the Railroad Commission of Texas unable to issue orders which would be legally effective and would solve the problems.

In spite of federal court decisions which declared invalid the orders of the Commission relating to natural gas and questioned the right of the Commission to act except to prevent waste, (as Mr.

[10] Rowan and Nichols Oil Co. v. Railroad Comm. and Humble Oil and Ref. Co. v. Railroad Comm. 35 F. Supp. 573 (W.D. Tex. 1940), 311 U.S. 570, (1941); 311 U.S. 578 (1941).

Cheek pointed out) there was still a hope that further legislation was unnecessary. It was hoped that a satisfactory solution could be devised under the terms of the elaborate gas control Act (passed in 1935 and often called H.B. 266),[11] even if the regulation should be based on that part of the statute (Section 10) authorizing the Commission to restrict production and to allocate the total market for gas irrespective of the existence of waste for the sole purpose of effecting an "adjustment of correlative rights and opportunities of each owner of gas in a common reservoir to produce and use or sell such gas as permitted" by law. The Supreme Court of the United States in *Thompson v. Consolidated Gas Utilities Corporation* [12] expressed "grave doubts" of the correctness of the holding by the district court that the statute did not authorize adjustment of correlative rights except as incident to the prevention of physical waste.

In order to give partial relief to those owners of sweet gas wells who had no market for their gas because the gas pipe line companies would not buy it, and since it was very doubtful that the Common Purchaser Act was valid,[13] the legislature in 1941 amended the provisions of the conservation Act. The amended provisions dealt pri-

[11] Tex. Acts 1935, c. 120; Vernon's Civ. Stat. art. 6008.

[12] 300 U.S. 55 (1936).

[13] The original statute, Tex. Acts 5th called Sess. 1930, c. 36, limited to oil, was amended, partly to include gas. Tex. Acts 1st called Sess. 1931 c. 28; Vernon's Civ. Stat., art 6049 a, § 8–8a–8aa. A federal district court enjoined the enforcement of the act in a case involving gas, Texoma Nat. Gas Co. v. Railroad Comm. of Texas, 59 F. 2d 750 (W.D. Tex. 1932) no appeal was taken. No case in Texas involving oil has been found where the question was directly at issue. Cf. Agey v. American Liberty Co., 141 Tex. 379, 172 S.W. 2d 972 (1943). A somewhat similar act was upheld by the Oklahoma Supreme Court, Okla. Nat. Gas Corp. v. State, 161 Okla. 104, 17 P. 2d 488 (1932). Such decisions as Corzelius v. Railroad Commission, 182 S.W. 2d 412 (Tex. Civ. App. 1944) writ ref., discussed in § III, (1), of this article, and Republic Nat. Gas Co. v. Oklahoma, 198 Okla. 350, 180 P. 2d 1009 (1947), 68 S. Ct. 972, (1948), support the argument that in Texas a properly written common purchaser law might be upheld. The argument of Mr. Justice Rutledge in the Republic case is quite persuasive. True, the case involved a statute requiring "ratable taking" rather than purchasing, but the dissenting opinion points out that the real question in the case was "whether a state, as a means of adjusting private correlative rights in a common reservoir, has the power in such circumstances as these to compel one private producer to share his market with another, when otherwise his production would drain off that other's ratable share of the gas in place and thus appropriate it to himself." The majority held that the judgment was not final, so the Court should not discuss the constitutional questions submitted. The minority thought that the judgment of the Supreme Court of Oklahoma sustaining the order of the Commission, was final and should be affirmed. The argument has been made that the need for a "common purchaser" statute is greatly reduced if the allowable production for the state does

marily with natural gas by authorizing the use of sweet gas in carbon black plants having "an average recovery of not less than five (5) pounds of carbon black to each one thousand (1000) cubic feet of gas" without first extracting the natural gasoline if the wells producing the sweet gas be located "in a common reservoir producing both sweet and sour gas." Furthermore, the specifications of permissible use for sweet and sour gas were broadened in 1941 [14] and again in 1947.[15]

Another Act passed in 1947 provided for variations from mixed monthly allowables for gas wells so that fluctuating demands could be met, but with a requirement for periodic adjustments to effect a balance between allowables and actual production.[16] This Act gave authority which the Assistant Attorney General of Texas, Elton M. Hyder, Jr., in Opinion No. R-238 declared did not exist under prior statutes.

(e) CORPORATIONS TO FIGHT FIRES AND BLOWOUTS

Fires and blowouts in oil fields frequently do great damage. The opinions in *Corzelius v. Harrell* and *Elliff v. Texon Company* [17] show how great that damage may be. Few operators have proper equipment or experienced men readily available to control serious fires and blowouts on their own properties, much less on others. No doubt the need for a general service of this sort prompted the legislature to pass H.B. 590 in 1947 to permit the organization of corporations "for the purpose of fighting fires and blowouts in oil wells and gas wells and oil and gas wells." [18]

(2) *Bills Which Did Not Pass*

(a) MISCELLANEOUS

During the period 1938–48 there were, of course, many bills relating to conservation of oil and gas which failed to pass. (Some of

---

not exceed the reasonable market demand, and if the state allowable is allocated among fields and properties without discrimination. Experience in Texas, at least as to oil, appears to sustain the argument. Such a program of fixing and distributing allowables makes almost certain that each operator will get or keep a connection and can sell his allowable at the market price.

[14] Tex. Acts 1941, c. 91, amending TEX. REV. CIV. STAT. art. 6008, §§ 3, 7 (1925), as amended by Tex. Acts 1935, c. 120, cited in note 11 *supra*.

[15] Tex. Acts 1947, c. 351, VERNON'S CIV. STAT. art. 6008a.

[16] Tex. Acts 1947, c. 453; VERNON'S CIV. STAT. art. 6008, §§ 12, 14.

[17] 143 Tex. 509, 186 S.W. 2d 961 (1945); Tex.   , 210 S.W. 2d 558 (1948).

[18] Tex. Acts 1947, c. 408; amending VERNON'S CIV. STAT. art. 1302-F.

them will be briefly discussed herein. Others are merely identified in a footnote). The variety of the proposed legislation is clearly indicated.[19]

(b) REGULATION, PRODUCTION, AND USE OF GAS

Early in the 1939 session of the 46th legislature S.B. 32—drafted in view of what was said in *Thompson v. Consolidated Gas Utilities Corporation* [20]—was introduced to provide adequately for the prevention of waste and the protection of correlative rights in gas

[19] 46TH TEX. LEG. 1939: SB 32, discussed in text; SB 241, providing for use of sweet gas for carbon black; HB 478 (dead-well bill), providing penalty for obtaining allowable on false representations; HB 671, to revise provisions for confiscating illegal oil. 47TH TEX. LEG. 1941: SB 31 and HB 119, creating "Oil and Gas Commission of Texas" to administer the oil and gas conservation laws; SB 319, providing for de novo trial in testing validity of administrative orders; HB 18, to prorate wet gas and HB 179 and HB 415, for proration of condensate or distillate; HB 129, amending statutes with respect to the use of gas for carbon black; HB 163, providing for penalty for making false reports to get allowables for wells; HB 490, defining marginal wells; HB 941, providing in detail for allocation of state allowable and fixing standards to prevent selective purchasing and discrimination (failed to repass after being vetoed, and discussed herein in connection with the Continental case under judicial history). 48TH TEX. LEG. 1943: HB 62, SB 104, and HB 168, providing for proration of distillate or condensate; SB 78, to authorize Commission of the Texas General Land Office to execute pooling agreements; SB 277 and HB 261, providing for pooling agreements; SB 283 and HB 442, for the purpose of validating orders of the Railroad Commission of Texas which had granted exceptions to our spacing rules but the orders had been nullified by court decrees; SB 284, providing for de novo trial in connection with administrative orders; HB 89, providing for use of gas for carbon black; HB 437, to penalize unauthorized exploration for oil; HB 558, called anti-pipe-line-proration bill, to require a purchaser of oil having available transportation facilities to purchase all oil tendered to him which was produced in accordance with allowable regulations, whether or not the purchaser wanted to purchase all the oil tendered; HB 593, which would redefine waste. 49TH TEX. LEG. 1945: SB 185 and HB 470, to amend Art. 6008 of the Rev. Civ. Stat.; HB 112, for prorating condensate; HB 578, for pooling leases from state; HB 582 and 591, undertaking a revision of Art. 6008 of the Rev. Civ. Stat. to require repressuring; HB 683, creating a "Natural Resources Commission" to administer the conservation laws; HB 713, providing for venue in the county where property is situated and for procedure with respect to suits against the Railroad Commission of Texas to invalidate an order issued under the conservation statutes; HB 752, amending definition of waste, setting forth the obligations of common purchasers of oil, gas, and distillate, authorizing voluntary unit operation agreements under certain circumstances, and fixing minimum prices for certain hydrocarbon products. 50TH TEX. LEG. 1947: SB 200, authorizing condemnation for directional drilling; SB 325 and HB 541, defining a cubic foot of gas; HB 59, similar to HB 67 dealing with agreements for unit operations; HB 392, authorizing Railroad Commission of Texas to fix price for gas if owner and prospective purchaser unable to agree; HB 393 and HB 392, to amend statutes to conform to HB 392; HB-sp.544, for regulating natural gas, enforcing ratable taking, and fixing prices.

[20] See note 12 supra.

pools. The bill failed to pass, as did S.B. 241 which would have liberalized the use of sweet gas. The debates on those bills served, however, to make clearer the need for a satisfactory settlement of the problems involving gas fields, particularly the Panhandle Field. As we shall see in connection with the discussion of litigation, the Supreme Court of Texas in 1945 upheld the right of the Railroad Commission of Texas under H.B. 266 to restrict and control the production of gas, either to prevent waste or to protect correlative rights irrespective of waste;[21] so the need for S.B. 32 was not as great as it appeared to be in 1939 when the situation as to natural gas presented so many very live problems.

(c) PRORATION OF CONDENSATE

For many years large quantities of liquid hydrocarbons (commonly called natural gasoline) have been recovered from oil-well gas, known as casinghead-gas. In some particulars this gasoline competed with crude oil or products and to that extent reduced the demand for crude oil, but no one suggested very seriously that natural gasoline or casinghead-gas production should be prorated. One reason was that casinghead-gas production was an inevitable incident to oil production. Quite a different situation was presented with respect to distillate or condensate, the liquid hydrocarbons obtained from pools in which the reservoir hydrocarbons were originally in the gaseous phase. Ordinarily these pools are found at considerable depths. The number of pools of this character steadily grew with the increase in drilling depths, causing the condensate production to mount.

About 1940 the present efficient method of operating these condensate pools was developed. It involves the stripping or extraction of heavier hydrocarbons from the gas produced, and the return of the residue gas to the reservoir for one or more of the following purposes: (a) to maintain pressure so that the heavier hydrocarbons will not liquefy in the reservoir (retrograde condensation) and become difficult or impossible to recover on an economic basis; (b) to avoid wasting the residue gas into the air; or (c) to sweep or push the rich reservoir gas containing heavy hydrocarbons to producing wells so that the rich gas may be stripped of the heavier hy-

[21] Corzelius v. Harrell, 143 Tex. 509, 186 S.W. 2d 961 (1945).

drocarbons. This method of operation is known as cycling, and the liquid hydrocarbons which are recovered or extracted are sometimes called distillate, but more often spoken of as condensate.

Production from condensate pools became considerable by 1941, and, as it absorbed a part of the crude oil or products market, many operators insisted that condensate pools be prorated in a manner similar to oil pools. A number of bills to that effect were introduced, but none became effective.[22]

(d.) COURT REVIEW

The opinions of the Supreme Court of Texas in May 1946 in the *Trapp* and *Thomas* cases [23] undertook to resolve conflicts in the decisions as to the character of court review which was applicable to cases involving the validity of an order of the Railroad Commission of Texas issued pursuant to the conservation statutes. The opinions seemed to say that although the statutes provided for an ordinary injunction suit and a trial in the district court to test the validity of an order, and that evidence must be introduced as in an ordinary case, nevertheless, the courts must sustain the order as far as the facts were concerned if a witness testified to facts, which if true would constitute substantial evidence in support of the order.[24] As might have been expected a bill (S.B. 27) was introduced early in the session of the 50th legislature, which convened in January 1947. The purpose of the bill was to broaden the scope of court review, or as it was argued, merely to provide for the type of review which the court, in *Marrs v. Railroad Commission* [25] and in the cases there cited, had previously held applicable under the same statute involved in the *Trapp* and *Thomas* cases. In short, the bill provided for a trial and a determination of the issues of fact as in any ordinary civil case, taking into account the credibility of witnesses and the preponderance of the credible evidence. The bill

[22] 47TH TEX. LEG. 1941: SB 8, HB 179, HB 514; 48TH TEX. LEG. 1943: SB 104, HB 62, HB 168; 49TH TEX. LEG. 1945: HB 112; 50TH TEX. LEG. 1947: None.
[23] Trapp v. Shell Oil Co., 145 Tex. 323, 198 S.W. 2d 424 (1946); Thomas v. Stanolind Oil and Gas Co., 145 Tex. 270, 198 S.W. 2d 420 (1946).
[24] 10 TEX. BAR J. 238 (1947), the report of the Committee on Administrative Law, State Bar of Texas. The Supreme Court in Texas Co. v. Railroad Commission, 209 S.W. 2d 338, (1948) admitted that the opinions in the Trapp and Thomas cases had been so understood.
[25] 142 Tex. 293, 177 S.W. 2d 941 (1944).

would have done away with the substantial evidence rule in such cases.

The bill caused lively committee hearings and vigorous debates about the process of providing adequate checks and balances for administrative agencies (which still continues) with respect to the proper scope of court review of agencies having far-reaching powers over private property. As often happens in the legislature, the bill became involved or entangled with another bill (H.B. 67), so that neither could actually be isolated and dealt with wholly on its merits without reference to its effect on the other. At any rate S.B. 27 failed to pass. The Supreme Court of Texas has modified, or perhaps it would be more accurate to say clarified, its opinions in the *Trapp* and *Thomas* cases. It remains to be seen whether the clarification which has been made and the actual application by the courts of the clarified rule will forestall efforts to pass a bill similar to S.B. 27 in the 51st legislature (1949).

If the procedure for court review of orders of the Railroad Commission of Texas is not materially changed, the result may be that legislation will be proposed to provide in considerable detail for the exercise of power by the Commission, similar perhaps to what are called modern administrative procedure acts, rather than by statutorily broadening the now applicable scope of judicial review.[26]

(e) VOLUNTARY AGREEMENTS FOR UNIT OPERATIONS

Unusual interest was aroused over what were called pooling bills introduced in the 50th legislature, 1947. H.B. 67 (companion bill to S.B. 127) provided in part that voluntary agreements (among oil operators and others interested in oil pools) to carry on specified activities, if approved by the Railroad Commission of Texas, would not constitute a violation of the anti-trust laws. This lan-

[26] The reports of the Committee on Administrative Law of the State Bar of Texas in 1947 and 1948 recommended a careful study of administrative agencies in Texas, and particularly the Railroad Commission of Texas, with the idea of either writing a modern administrative procedure act applicable to that agency and like agencies, or of changing materially court review provisions to be certain that adequate protection could be had against arbitrary and capricious acts of administrative bodies which had broad power to regulate private property. For an account of the procedure and methods found to exist with respect to the administration by the Railroad Commission of Texas of the conservation laws, see Davis and Willbern, *Administrative Control of Oil Production in Texas,* 22 TEX. L. REV. 149 (1944).

guage appeared in Section 1 of H.B. 67: "It is hereby declared to be the public policy of this State to prevent waste, to promote the conservation of oil and gas, and to protect correlative rights. Therefore, it shall be lawful for persons owning or claiming interests in a field or area which appears from geologic or other data to contain one or more common accumulations of oil or gas, or both, to enter into agreements for establishing and carrying out a plan for the co-operative development and operation of all of such common accumulations, or any part or parts of one or more of them, and for the storage, processing and marketing of gas, including, but not limited to, secondary recovery operations and operations known as cycling, recycling, repressuring, and pressure maintenance, when the agreements will prevent waste or promote the conservation of oil and gas or will protect correlative rights."

The author of H.B. 67 took the lead in pressing for action. Proponents of the measure argued that in many instances the cooperative development or the carrying out of unit operations was necessary to prevent waste and to protect correlative rights. They pointed out that Section 21, Article 6008 of the Revised Civil Statutes as amended in 1935, provided for such activities or operations with respect to natural gas pools; consequently, similar authority should be given concerning oil pools, thereby removing any fear or claim of fear, that such activities or operations necessary from a conservation standpoint might subject the operators to prosecution for violating the anti-trust laws of Texas.

The bill met considerable opposition, some of it was based upon an erroneous belief that the proposal, instead of merely authorizing voluntary agreements binding only those who signed, went further and required operations compelling those who did not sign to join in the operations and be bound by the decisions of the majority. Though some of the reasons for opposing the bill appeared fanciful, there were logical grounds upon which opposition was founded. It was argued, for instance, that the bill undertook to authorize activities not reasonably necessary to prevent waste or to protect correlative rights, and if it should pass, the measure would constitute an unwarranted exception to the anti-trust laws in favor of a group or industry, and therefore endanger the validity of those laws. The

Attorney General of Texas was asked for an opinion, and his department ruled that the passage of the bill as introduced would endanger the validity of the anti-trust laws and would make more difficult their enforcement.[27] The bill was then revised to meet these objections,[28] and as a committee substitute reached the floor of the House late in the session. It passed the House, was amended in the Senate, and there passed, but the conference committee could not reach an agreement. The bill died on the calendar.[29]

II. ADMINISTRATIVE HISTORY OF OIL AND GAS CONSERVATION

(1) Organization of the Railroad Commission of Texas— The Administrative Agency

The Railroad Commission of Texas, composed of three elected members with six year terms, is the administrative agency with respect to the oil and gas conservation statutes.[30] On January 1, 1939 the members of the Commission were Ernest O. Thompson, who first became a member by appointment in 1932, Lon C. Smith, who became a member in 1925, and G. A. Sadler, who succeeded C. V. Terrell as a result of the elections in 1939. Olin Culberson was elected in 1940, succeeding Lon C. Smith who was not a candidate for re-election. Beauford Jester succeeded G. A. Sadler in

[27] Ops. Att'y. Gen. Tex., No. V-97 (March 21, 1947).

[28] Ops. Att'y. Gen. Tex., No. V-97-A (April 9, 1947).

[29] A more extended discussion of the bill and of many legal and economic questions touching voluntary and compulsory unit operations and the anti-trust laws appears in Hardwicke, Antitrust Laws, et al. v. Unit Operation of Oil or Gas Pools (1948) by this writer and recently published by the AIME. In the appendix to that book will be found copies of the two opinions given by the Attorney General's Department with respect to HB 67.

[30] The Commission was created by Tex. Acts 1891, c. 51; Vernons Civ. Stat. Art. 6444 et seq., for the purpose of regulating railroads. The Commission has since been given considerable additional authority. It now performs many of the functions of a public utility commission, regulating common carrier pipe lines, trucks and buses, and gas utilities, as well as many other phases of the oil and gas industry. It was given jurisdiction over common carrier pipe lines for oil by Tex. Acts 1917, c. 30; Tex. Rev. Civ. Stat. art. 6019 (1925), and was first authorized to administer oil and gas conservation statutes by Tex. Acts 1919, c. 155; Tex. Rev. Civ. Stat. art. 6023 (1925). Members of the Commission are elected for six year terms. The administrative processes with respect to the conservation statutes were described by Davis and Willbern in Administrative Control of Oil Production in Texas, 22 Tex. L. Rev. 149 (1944).

1942 under interesting circumstances.[31] When Mr. Jester became Governor in January 1947, he appointed William J. Murray, Jr. as his successor on the Commission. Mr. Murray was nominated in the Democratic primary in July 1948 for the unexpired term. In Texas this is equivalent to election. No special technical qualifications are set forth in the statutes as prerequisites for qualifications for members of the Commission.[32] With respect to the present members, Ernest O. Thompson was a practicing lawyer in Amarillo, and formerly its mayor, when appointed in 1932. Olin Culberson was an employee of the Gas Utilities Division of the Commission when he was elected as Commissioner in 1940. He was the owner of a dry goods business and had been County Clerk and County Judge of Hill County. William J. Murray, Jr., a petroleum engineer, previously an employee of the Commission and connected with the Petroleum Administration for War during World War II, was engaged in the active practice of his profession at the time of his appointment in 1947.

[31] Mr. Sadler resigned, having been tendered a commission in the Army; he announced that the Governor had promised to appoint James E. Kilday as Commissioner; the Governor did not formally accept the resignation of Mr. Sadler; the resignation of Mr. Sadler was tendered in the afternoon of June 1, 1942, being the final date for filing as a candidate in the Democratic primary, 1942; James E. Kilday filed his application late in the afternoon of June 1, 1942; the Democratic Executive Committee declared the office vacant, after Mr. Sadler took oath as a Lieutenant, and declared that any one could file as candidate for Commissioner for the Democratic primary; Sadler, shortly after the action by the Committee, withdrew his resignation, and claimed that, being only a reserve officer in the Army, he could continue to hold the office of Commissioner; the Supreme Court of Texas, in Kilday v. German, 163 S.W. 2d 185, on June 26, 1942, held that all names of candidates were properly on the ballot, but did not pass on the question whether the office was vacant; the Attorney General of Texas refused to give Mr. Sadler an opinion as to the status of Mr. Sadler; Beauford Jester, the successful candidate in the primary election in August, was given an interim appointment on the Commission, and took the oath of office on August 24, 1942, and began to perform duties of the office; Mr. Sadler brought suit in the federal district court at Dallas on Sept. 2, 1942, seeking to enjoin Mr. Jester from acting as Commissioner, and seeking to establish that he (Sadler) was still Commissioner and could legally hold that office while being also an officer in the armed forces. Part of this story is given in the opinion in the Kilday case, cited above. A more detailed account appears in the State House Reporter, Oil Regulation Report, covering the months of June, July, August, and September, 1942. A short chronology appears in the Reporter for Sept. 2. The suit against Mr. Jester was tried in September 1942. The Court dismissed the bill of complaint on various grounds. Sadler v. Jester, 46 F. Supp. 737 (N.D. Tex 1942) no appeal.

[32] A member must be a resident citizen, not less than twenty-five years of age, qualified to vote under the Constitution and laws, must not be interested in any railroad or its securities, and cannot hold any other office or engage in any other occupation. VERNON'S CIV. STAT. art. 6447. The annual salary in 1948 was $7,620,00.

The Commission has a secretary who keeps the records, issues notices, and performs the customary duties of his post for the Commission. Conservation matters are under the jurisdiction of the Oil and Gas Division, one of the five divisions of the agency. The administrative officer with respect to conservation matters is the Chief Supervisor of the Oil and Gas Division, a statutory official.[33] Employees of the Commission are appointed or engaged by the Commission and no civil service rules are applicable. There were approximately 200 employees on January 1, 1948 in the Oil and Gas Division, including technical or professional men such as petroleum engineers, geologists, and attorneys. The Commission has wisely welcomed the opportunity to employ young technically trained graduates of state schools. Many of the men who now stand high in their professions started their careers in the service of the Commission.

(2) Procedure at Hearings as Bases for Orders

The Texas conservation statutes do not prescribe the procedure to be followed in hearings before the Railroad Commission of Texas, and the Commission itself has promulgated no formal set of rules applicable to conservation matters. There are, of course, provisions of the statutes which may be called procedural, such as one requiring notice of a hearing (except in an emergency) as a prerequisite for the making of an order,[34] but actually these provisions do not deal with procedure in hearings before the Commission. The hearings in conservation matters are normally quite informal, but not always so in proceedings which involve particular parties and properties, such as a hearing for an exception to a well spacing rule.

The Commission may require the attendance of witnesses and the production of books and records (including attachment if the subpoena is not obeyed), and there is a provision with respect to a person being forced to give incriminating testimony.[35] There is a provision Article 6024 which in terms authorizes the Commission itself "to punish for contempt or disobedience of its orders as the

---

[33] VERNON'S CIV. STAT. art. 6030.
[34] VERNON'S CIV. STAT. art. 603a is the general statute. It requires 10 days notice of a hearing.
[35] VERNON'S CIV. STAT. arts. 6024–6027.

district court may do," but no case has been found which discusses the power of the Commission in that connection, and no instance is known where the Commission has undertaken to punish for disobedience of an order except by suit in court to collect penalties as prescribed by statute.

At hearings each interested person is given an opportunity to have his say: that is to testify under oath, to present witnesses and documents, to interrogate witnesses or speakers, and to make a statement or a rambling speech. A special hearing, one taking place on an application for an exception to a spacing rule or for a permit to inject water or other fluid into a producing formation, is based upon a written petition or application. The hearing, often being in the nature of an adversary proceeding between the applicant and neighboring operators, frequently is conducted with a formality approaching that of a judicial proceeding. At all of these hearings, general or special, the testimony is taken down by a reporter, though this is not required by law. There is no statutory requirement that the reporter transcribe and file the notes, and frequently he does not do so. Unless a question of procedural due process is involved, the record of the hearing is not made the basis of a proceeding in court to test the validity of the order predicated on the facts disclosed at the hearing. In the judicial proceeding evidence is introduced, not the record made at the Commission hearing, and to that extent the trial is de novo. The evidence upon which the Commission acts may be quite different from that presented in court. Since that is the situation, the informality of the proceedings at the Commission hearing may not be so serious a matter. This is not to say, however, that the proceedings and the practices of the Commission are entirely satisfactory; for they are not, and they have been criticized.[36] Now that the substantial evidence rule is applicable to fact questions in connection with court review of the Com-

---

[36] Davis and Willbern, *Administrative Control of Oil Production in Texas*, 22 Tex. L. Rev. 149 (1944); the report of Committee on Administrative Law, State Bar of Texas, 10 Tex. Bar J. 237 (1947). The report points out that, where a statute requires notice and a hearing as a prerequisite for an order, it is the general rule that a fair and full hearing is contemplated, and the order must be supported by evidence at the hearing, and not upon material which is not disclosed. The report questions the soundness of the opinion to the contrary in Cook Drilling Co. v. Gulf Oil Corp., 139 Tex. 80, 161 S.W. 2d 1035 (1942). In the recent case of Hawkins v. Texas Co., Tex., 209 S.W. 2d 338, 344 (1948) it is intimated that an order may be defective because of lack of proper procedure.

mission's orders entered under the conservation statutes, these criticisms and suggestions are of special significance. There is more need than ever to insist upon as many administrative safeguards as possible to insure fair hearings (with all that the term implies) as well as a need for a more careful consideration of problems by the entire Commission, not by its subordinates or by less than all of the Commissioners. Moreover, it is important that the Commission act as a body with an opportunity for each member to discuss the problems and to vote, otherwise its action does not conform to legal requirements.[37]

(3) *Enforcement of Orders*

There are no provisions in the conservation statutes which authorize the Commission to impose fines or penalties for enforcing compliance with its orders. Violations must be reported to the Attorney General of Texas for appropriate judicial action, by way of penalty and injunction.[38] There are several statutes which have been helpful in obtaining enforcement of orders. One of these, Article 6032 of Vernon's Civil Statutes, provides for the issuance by the Commission of a certificate showing compliance with orders before a pipe line may connect to an oil or gas well, except for a temporary period. Another act, often called the Transportation Act of 1935,[39] elaborately controlled the movement of oil, gas, and products, and called for tenders or other documents to show whether the commodity to be transported was legal. Section 10 of the statute authorized the confiscation by the state of illegal oil, gas, and products—that is oil or gas produced in excess of allowables fixed by the Commission, and products made in whole or in part from illegal oil or illegal gas. The state has confiscated and sold thousands of barrels of oil under the proceedings set forth in Section 10.

[37] Webster v. T & P Motor Co., 140 Tex. 131, 166 S.W. 2d 75 (1942); Sanders v. Midstates Oil Corp., 166 S.W. 2d 716, 718 (Tex. Civ. App. 3rd 1942) *no app. for writ.*

[38] Vernon's Civ. Stat. art. 6036 (1937) is the general statute which provides a penalty of $1000 for each violation; each days' violation is treated as a separate one. There are other penalty statutes which are considered as part of the conservation statutes contained in Title 102 of the revised statutes. References to these other provisions are not considered necessary here. VERNON'S CIV. STAT. art. 6049 (e), § 13 specifically authorizes the issuance of injunctions to prevent actual or threatened violations.

[39] Tex. Acts 1935, c. 246; VERNON'S CIV. STAT. art. 6066 a (1937).

The 1935 Transportation Act and orders thereunder have been upheld.[40] An interesting situation arose with respect to the movement in interstate commerce of illegal oil which had been confiscated by the state. The federal courts held that although the confiscation and sale of the oil had purged it of its illegal taint so that it could move freely in commerce as far as Texas was concerned, nevertheless, under the Connally Hot Oil Act, it was still hot oil, and its movement in interstate commerce was prohibited.[41]

Beyond question, the Connally Hot Oil Act has been a cogent factor in minimizing violations of the orders of the Commission which fix allowables. The Act has served and it should serve to induce the Commission to enter more definite orders so that the operators and the purchasers of oil need not speculate whether any production is in excess of that permitted by the orders.

(4) Methods of Preventing Waste, Including Limitation to Market Demand

The earlier article on the legal history of conservation in Texas pointed out that, subject to specific restrictions or limitations in the statutes, the Railroad Commission of Texas was authorized to adopt any reasonable means or methods to prevent the waste of oil or gas as generally or particularly defined in the statutes. It is now well established that the Commission has the power to regulate spacing, drilling and production activities, the amount of oil and gas to be produced, the water-oil and gas-oil ratios, the injection of fluids into oil or gas reservoirs (cycling, repressuring, pressure maintenance, water flooding, water disposal), and all other activities to the extent reasonably necessary to prevent waste and protect correlative rights. As a part of this program the Commission has promulgated what are called *State-wide Rules* of general application which apply until special field rules are substituted to meet the particular field conditions. The state-wide rules include provisions as to spacing, casing and tubing requirements, construction of slush pits, shoot-

[40] Thompson v. Spear, 91 F. 2d 430 (C.C.A. 5th 1937) cert. denied, 302 U.S. 762 (1938); Skipper-Bivens Oil Co. v. State, 115 S.W. 2d 1016 (Tex. Civ. App. 3rd 1938) writ refused; Dyer v. Railroad Comm., 115 S.W. 2d 1020 (Tex. Civ. App. 3rd. 1938) app. writ dismissed; Carter v. State, 116 S.W. 2d 371 (Tex. Crim. App. 1937).
[41] Hurley v. Federal Tender Board, 108 F. 2d 574 (C.C.A. 5th 1939).

ing and treating of wells, swabbing, keeping of records and books, and making reports. There are hundreds of special field rules or orders.[42]

The history of the development of these provisions of the Texas statutes which broadly define and prohibit waste was given in the earlier article. No amendments to that statute have been made since 1935.[43] It will be observed that Article 6014 defines as waste the

[42] It is a real task to maintain a complete up-to-date set of the rules, regulations, and orders. R. W. Byram and Company, Austin, Tex., publishes an excellent loose-leaf compilation to that end. The volume contains more than 1000 pages, 8-½ x 11 inches, relatively small print in double columns. This gives a fair idea of the extent and detail of the regulation of private property which is taking place in Texas under the conservation laws.

[43] VERNON'S CIV. STAT. art. 6014, as amended by Tex. Acts 1935, c. 76, § 2, reads as follows: "The production, storage or transportation of crude petroleum oil or of natural gas in such manner, in such amount, or under such conditions as to constitute waste is hereby declared to be unlawful and is prohibited. The term 'waste' among other things shall specifically include: (a) The operation of any oil well or wells with an inefficient gas-oil ratio, and the Commissioner is hereby given authority to fix and determine by order such ratio; provided that the utilization for manufacture of natural gasoline of gas produced from an oil well within the permitted gas-oil ratio shall not be included with the definition of waste. (b) The drowning with water of any stratum or part thereof capable of producing oil or gas, or both oil and gas, in paying quantities. (c) Underground waste or loss however caused and whether or not defined in other subdivisions hereof. (d) Permitting any natural gas well to burn wastefully. (e) The creation of unnecessary fire hazards. (f) Physical waste or loss incident to, or resulting from, so drilling, equipping, locating, spacing or operating well or wells as to reduce or tend to reduce the total ultimate recovery of crude petroleum oil or natural gas from any pool. (g) Waste or loss incident to, or resulting from, the unnecessary, inefficient, excessive or improper use of the reservoir energy, including the gas energy or water drive, in any well or pool; however, it is not the intent of this Act to require repressuring of an oil pool or that the separately owned properties in any pool be unitized under one management, control or ownership. (h) Surface waste or surface loss, including the storage either permanent or temporary of crude petroleum oil, or the placing any product thereof, in open pits or earthen storage, and all other forms of surface waste or surface loss, including unnecessary or excessive surface losses, or destruction without beneficial use, either of crude petroleum oil or of natural gas. (i) The escape into the open air, from a well producing both oil and gas, of natural gas in excess of the amount which is necessary in the efficient drilling or operation of the well. (j) The production of crude petroleum oil in excess of transportation or market facilities or reasonable market demand. The Commission may determine when such excess production exists or is imminent and ascertain the reasonable market demand. The Commission may consider any or all of the above definitions, whenever the facts, circumstances or conditions make them applicable, in making rules, regulations or orders to prevent waste of oil or gas. Nothing in this Section shall be construed to authorize limitation of production of marginal wells, as such marginal wells are defined by Statute, below the amount fixed by Statute for such wells." A somewhat similar statute, relating particularly to gas, is VERNON'S CIV. STAT. art. 6008 showing the amendments made in 1941 and 1947.

production of oil in excess of the reasonable market demand.[44] The restriction of oil production so that it will not exceed the reasonable market demand is in fact a measure which prevents physical waste. Differently stated, production of oil in substantial quantities in excess of the reasonable market demand inevitably causes or results in physical waste unless the period of overproduction be quite limited. For instance, the production of material amounts of oil in excess of reasonable market demand for any extended period almost necessarily causes marked variations in withdrawals and in pressure differentials between properties or areas, upsetting a ratable production program made possible when production does not exceed the reasonable market demand. Such a lack of ratable production may cause serious underground waste. Production in excess of reasonable market demand invariably leads to excessive storage which increases fire hazards and causes avoidable waste aboveground. Large quantities of production in excess of reasonable market demand normally bring about a cut in prices, which makes unprofitable the operation of many stripper or marginal wells. This causes the abandonment of the wells and the reserve which the wells would have produced if higher prices had permitted continuance of operations. In most instances, unless the price for oil becomes very high, new wells cannot be drilled to recover the oil which would have been recovered by the wells which had to be abandoned. For all practical purposes, the abandonment of the stripper wells results in underground waste, since the oil is not recovered. The examples given deal with physical waste. All physical waste is economic waste, and

[44] The term is not specifically defined in the Texas Statutes, but in Railroad Comm. v. Continental Oil Co., 157 S.W. 2d 695 (Tex. Civ. App. 9th, 1941) writ ref. the court, at 699, defined reasonable market demand as "the amount of oil reasonably needed for current consumption, together with a reasonable amount for storage and working stocks." The definition appearing in Interstate Oil Compact Comm., *Forms for Oil and Gas Conservation Laws* §1 (b) (Aug. 1946) is as follows: "The words 'reasonable market demand,' as used herein, shall mean the demand for oil or gas for reasonable current requirements for current consumption and use within and outside the State, together with such amounts as are reasonably necessary for building up or maintaining reasonable storage reserves of oil or gas or the products thereof, or both such oil or gas and products." The above definition is generally accepted as correct. It is substantially the definition appearing in New Mex. Acts 1935, c. 72, § 1. The court in the Continental case refers to amounts needed for "working stocks." Certainly the amounts needed for that purpose should be included in determining demand. It is believed that the definition quoted would include working stocks.

to that extent the prevention of physical waste is necessarily the prevention also of economic waste.

Some people say that production in excess of reasonable market demand prevents economic waste only. They are mistaken. The need for preventing production in excess of the reasonable market demand to prevent physical waste and to protect correlative rights is now generally recognized by those who understand the facts. For many years the Railroad Commission of Texas has undertaken to prevent production in excess of the reasonable market demand as a part of the program to prevent physical waste and protect correlative rights, and the courts have upheld the orders on those grounds.[45] The courts also held that the orders were not invalid as price fixing devices, and that the effect upon prices, if any, was a mere incident to prevention of waste and protection of correlative rights.

The statutes which declare that production in excess of reasonable market demand is waste, and which authorize the administrative agency to restrict production to reasonable market demand, do

[45] For a more extensive discussion of the subject of restricting production so that it will not be in excess of reasonable market demand in order to prevent waste and protect correlative rights, see Champlin Refining Co. v. Corporation Commission of Oklahoma, 286 U.S. 210, 230, (1932). Julian Oil and Royalty Co. v. Capshaw, 145 Okla. 237, 292 Pac. 841 (1930); Danciger Oil and Refining Co. v. Railroad Comm. of Tex., 49 S.W. 2d 837, 842 (Ct. Civ. App. 3rd Dist. Texas, 1932,) *writ of error granted by Sup. Ct. of Tex., case dismissed by agreement*); Railroad Comm. v. Continental Oil Co., 157 S.W. 2d 695 (Tex. Civ. App. 9th, 1941) *writ ref.*; statement by Harold B. Fell in *Hearings before a Subcommittee of the Committee on Interstate and Foreign Commerce, House of Representatives on H. Res. 290 and H.R. 7372* 76th Cong., 3d Sess. pt. IV, 1830 (1940) and statement by Robert E. Hardwicke, *id.* beginning at 1480 also found in 13 Miss. L. J. 381, 386 (1941), explaining why production in excess of the reasonable market demand results in or causes physical waste of oil and gas. The discussion of the Continental case in the next section, Judicial History, shows why the restriction to market demand is an important factor in protecting correlative rights. See also discussion by Hardwicke, *Legal History of Conservation of Oil in Texas*, LEGAL HISTORY OF CONSERVATION OF OIL AND GAS, A SYMPOSIUM beginning at 222 (1938). Statutes in the following states, other than Texas, specifically define as waste the production in excess of reasonable market demand: Florida, Kansas, Louisiana, Michigan, New Mexico, Oklahoma. Since production in substantial quantities in excess of the reasonable market demand results in or causes waste, and restriction so that production may not exceed such demand prevents or minimizes waste, then a statute which authorizes the prevention of waste authorizes the control of production so that it will not exceed reasonable market demand, unless there is a provision which specifically prohibits such restriction. The Danciger case so holds.

not provide, as some seem to think, that in all events the administrative agency must permit production representing the reasonable
market demand. Very frequently the production from a field is
fixed at less than the market demand figure inasmuch as waste
would take place, such as dissipation of reservoir energy, if the field
should produce the amount representing the reasonable market demand applicable to that field. The statutes merely say that production in excess of the reasonable market demand is waste. It follows
that production at even less than that amount may cause waste. If
so, the production should be restricted to the lesser amount, ignoring market demand or rather the higher figure which would be applicable as the share for the field in the total demand.[46]

(5) Voluntary Agreements—Unit Operations

Reference has been made to the existence of a statute which specifically authorizes voluntary agreements under certain circumstances for the operation of gas fields or parts thereof. The statute
provides for approval of such agreements by the Attorney General
of Texas under certain circumstances.[47] Some 40 agreements have
been made and approved under that statute. Agreements with respect to great fields like Katy, Old Ocean, and Seeligson are examples. The great majority of the agreements relate to condensate
fields or areas which are classified as gas fields inasmuch as the hydrocarbons are in the gaseous phase in the reservoir.[48] Article 6008,

[46] After a long period of litigation in the federal courts, described in the earlier
article, in which the judges held that the Commission was undertaking to prevent
economic waste, contrary to a statutory provision, it was held in *Amazon Petroleum
Corporation v. Railroad Comm.* 5 F. Supp. 633 (E.D. Tex. 1934) *no appeal* that the
legislature in 1932 struck from the statute the phrase that waste "shall not be construed to mean economic waste," and that the "market demandists" had succeeded
in securing an amendment to the statute so that it specifically authorized restriction
to market demand as a waste prevention measure. The court also held that the facts
justified the restriction of production in the East Texas Field to about 400,000 barrels of oil a day, even though its share of the total state market demand should be
much greater.

[47] Tex. Acts 1935, c. 120, § 21; VERNON'S CIV. STAT. art. 6008. The Attorney General of Texas takes the position that the statute gives authority to approve
an agreement with respect to a gas field or a part thereof if the agreement contains
nothing repugnant to the conservation laws, and that no authority is given to determine whether an agreement is fair or equitable or to approve an agreement with
respect to an oil field or a part thereof, unless the part can be considered to be a
gas field.

[48] By Railroad Comm. of Tex. Order No. 20–550 (Jan. 18, 1939) condensate was
classified as gas, and its use restricted by the provisions of VERNON'S CIV. STAT. art.

Section 2, Vernon's Civil Statutes, defines as a gas well one producing more than 100,000 cubic feet to each barrel of oil, or producing
gas from a formation which produces gas only, though oil be also
produced "through the inside of another string of casing." It logi-
cally follows that a pool or formation in which the wells are
predominately gas wells (as defined by the statute) should be classified as a gas field for the purpose of the voluntary pooling provision.[49] There is no similar statute authorizing agreements with respect to oil fields or a part thereof.

As pointed out under the discussion of the history of H.B. 67 in
the 1947 legislature, the situation in Texas as to oil fields is substantially this: (a) there is no statutory provision authorizing agreements with respect to oil fields; (b) there are operators who are
reluctant, or who say that they are reluctant, to enter into a voluntary agreement for the unit operation or cooperative development
of an oil field or a part thereof for the purpose of preventing waste
and protecting correlative rights, as they fear, or claim to fear, that
they might be accused of violating the anti-trust laws; (c) it is
doubtful whether the Railroad Commission of Texas can compel
unit operations or cooperative development if there is involved, as
there usually is, repressuring or unitized control, even though
clearly needed to prevent great waste and to protect correlative
rights. The doubt arises because of the language of subsection
(g) of Article 6014, Vernon's Civil Statutes, which reads: [The
term waste includes] "(g) Waste or loss incident to, or resulting
from, the unnecessary, inefficient, excessive or improper use of the
reservoir energy, including the gas energy or water drive, in any
well or pool; however, it is not the intent of this Act to require repressuring of an oil pool or that the separately owned properties in
any pool be unitized under one management, control or ownership."

It has been forcibly argued, however, that the quoted language

---

6008. No doubt the order was issued as a result of the issues in Clymore v.
Thompson, 11 F. Supp. 791 (W.D. Tex. 1936), 13 F. Supp. 469 (W.D. Tex.
1936) no appeal, involving uses and waste of gas from a condensate field, and in
which the court said that the Commission could classify wells as part of its waste
prevention program.

[49] See Pressler, Legal Problems Involved in Cycling Gas in Gas Fields, 24 TEX. L.
REV. 19 (1945); Myers, Legal Aspects of the Unitization of Oil and Gas Fields,
Oil and Gas Jour. (May 20, 1948) 222.

means that the Commission may, through an order of the type mentioned, compel repressuring or unit or cooperative development, but it is not *required* to do so.[50] It appears that the Commission has entered an order requiring repressuring. That is Special Order No. 3–6475, July 14, 1944, for the Lake Creek Field, Montgomery County. The order recited the feasibility of cycling and maintenance of pressures to increase ultimate recovery, and directed that: ". . . the reservoir pressures . . . be maintained at such a point as will insure the efficient recovery of the natural resources constituted of the hydrocarbons contained therein to the end that preventable waste of said natural resources shall be prevented and the ultimate recovery thereof increased." Commissioner Culberson dissented, saying he thought the order was a fine one but that the Commission had no power to enter it, inasmuch as Art. 6014 (g) was applicable. The Commission has indirectly compelled unit operations involving repressuring, and those which closely approach common management and control, by finding that waste exists and then ordering or threatening to order the shut down of wells until the operators make arrangements to prevent the waste. In reality the action of the Commission has forced the operators to agree upon a common waste prevention program, though an oil field or a combination oil and condensate field be involved. The Seeligson and Old Ocean Fields are outstanding examples.[51] The Attorney General of Texas, in approving the agreements as to some

[50] Walker, *The Problem of the Small Tract Under Spacing Regulations*, Oil Weekly (Aug. 1, 1938) 22, Oil and Gas Jour. (Aug. 11, 1938) 41, Bar Association number of the TEX. L. REV. (Oct. 1938) 157.

[51] The order of the Commission of August 21, 1947, revising the field rules for Old Ocean greatly assisted in carrying out the program for preventing waste and protecting correlative rights. See discussion of the situation in the Old Ocean and Seeligson fields by HARDWICKE, ANTITRUST LAWS, ET AL. V. UNIT OPERATION OF OIL OR GAS POOLS beginning at 148 (1948). There the conclusion is reached that the making and carrying out of an agreement with respect to the unit operation of an oil field or a part thereof, including operation of a casinghead-gas plant, when reasonably necessary to prevent waste and protect correlative rights, would not constitute a violation of either state or federal anti-trust laws. Of course, provisions in the agreement or activities not reasonably necessary for the purposes mentioned might involve violation of anti-trust laws. There is no intention to say that all provisions of an agreement, or activities thereunder, would be legal merely because the making and carrying out of some provisions of the agreement were reasonably necessary to prevent waste and protect correlative rights. The opinion was also expressed that the passage of an act authorizing unit operation of an oil field or a part thereof for specified purposes, and subject to approval of a state official or agency, would stimulate the making of agreements necessary in the public interest.

gas areas, has declared that his authority to approve was limited by the provisions of Article 6008, Section 21, Vernon's Civil Statutes. In the approval applicable to the Seeligson Field, contained in the attorney general's letter of June 30, 1947 addressed to Raymond Myers, Magnolia Petroleum Company, it was stated that the statute did not authorize approval of the provisions concerning the sale of casinghead-gas or the provisions concerning the construction and ownership of a plant "for processing both casinghead gas and Unitized Substances." The letter contained this statement: "Since our approval is limited to consideration of the conservation statutes, we do not pass upon the question of whether this agreement or operations thereunder would violate the anti-trust laws of Texas, and this approval should not be construed as any expression thereon." There was no indication, however, that the provisions of the agreement were thought to be contrary to law.

It is likely that a bill authorizing voluntary agreements for the unit operation of oil fields or a part thereof will be considered by the 51st legislature which convenes in 1949. The Federal Government and twenty states (Alabama, Arkansas, California, Florida, Georgia, Illinois, Indiana, Kentucky, Mississippi, Montana, Nebraska, New Mexico, North Carolina, North Dakota, Oklahoma, South Dakota, Texas, Utah, Washington, and Wyoming) have passed statutes authorizing voluntary agreements for secondary recovery or related operations, that is unit operations under certain circumstances.[52] Indeed, the benefits to be derived from unit operations are such that a number of states have passed statutes which authorize compulsory unit operations under given contingencies.[53]

[52] The federal statutes and the statutes in the various states as of January 1, 1948, were compiled by Professor Walter L. Summers and Robert E. Hardwicke in a paper, Statutes Relating to Secondary Recovery Operations, which included the Report of the Legal Committee of the Interstate Oil Compact Commission on Secondary Recovery Operations and Related Operations of Aug. 1947. The paper was presented at the spring meeting of the Mid-Continent District, API, Division of Production, in March 1948. Copies are available at the office of the Production Division, API, in Dallas. The compilation was prepared for inclusion in SECONDARY RECOVERY OF OIL IN THE UNITED STATES (2d ed.) shortly to be published by the API. Chapter 3 of the first edition of that book contains the compilation of statutes as of January 1, 1942. See ANTITRUST LAWS, ET AL. V. UNIT OPERATION OF OIL OR GAS POOLS notes 29, 150 (1948).

[53] The Federal Government and nine states (Alabama, Arizona, Arkansas, Florida, Georgia, Illinois, Indiana, Louisiana, and Oklahoma) have passed acts authorizing what may be called compulsory unit operations under certain circumstances for speci-

(6) Control of Injection of Air, Gas, and Water into Underground Reservoirs

Acting under a broad power to prevent waste of oil and gas, the Railroad Commission of Texas has for many years controlled or regulated the injection of fluids, such as air, natural gas, and water, into oil or gas producing horizons or into a formation from which oil or gas were being produced. Usually the operators submit to the Commission in a public hearing the contemplated program so that the Commission may approve or disapprove the program, or through an appropriate order otherwise provide for the prevention of waste.

There are a number of salt water disposal and injection projects in Texas, but that one considered the greatest ever carried on deserves special mention. By 1942 the great East Texas Oil Field was producing an average of some 400,000 barrels of oil (as measured in the reservoir) a calendar day, and a daily average of more than 400,000 barrels of salt water. This involved a serious problem of disposal which ordinarily could not be solved by releasing the water into streams or water sheds, as the state had secured injunctions against many operators to prevent pollution of streams, and permission to release water, even in small quantities, was difficult to get. What was more important, the production of such large quantities of salt water had a direct effect upon reservoir pressure inasmuch as energy was required to move the water as well as the oil through the reservoir sands to the producing wells. The total drop in reservoir pressure (energy used) depended upon the total fluid production of water, oil, and gas from the reservoir. Some of the

fied purposes. The statutes are quoted in the compilation by Summers and Hardwicke, see note 52 supra. Discussion of compulsory unit operations statutes in ANTITRUST LAWS, ET AL. v. UNIT OPERATION OF OIL OR GAS POOLS begins at 160 (1948). A form of statute authorizing orders compulsory in effect was recently drafted by the Legal Committee of the Interstate Oil Compact Commission; it appears Forms for Oil and Gas Conservation Laws, § 5 (Aug. 1946) and also appears in Report of Legal Committee of Interstate Oil Compact Commission Relating to Secondary Recovery Operations and Related Operations (Aug. 11, 1947). That report, appearing in VI INTERSTATE OIL COMPACT Q. BULL. 73 (Aug. 1947) and printed as a separate booklet, was made a part of the compilation of statutes by Summers and Hardwicke, see note 52 supra. The Legal Committee of the Interstate Oil Compact Commission appointed a Sub-committee in 1948 to make recommendations for further revision. The Sub-committee has held several meetings in 1948 and probably will submit its report or recommendations before 1949.

larger operators had constructed salt water disposal systems to take care of at least a part of their own salt water production. Many other operators, particularly the smaller ones, had no disposal facilities, and it was doubtful whether a large number of small systems would prove economical or practical. After public discussions field operators met the problem in 1942 by creating the East Texas Salt Water Disposal Company, a salt water disposal corporation authorized by statute.[54] The program contemplated that the company would, for a small charge, collect salt water in the field and inject it usually into wells located beyond the oil producing limits in the Woodbine sand (the producing formation) below the oil producing section. The idea was not only to dispose of the water but also to maintain reservoir pressures at high levels by a field wide system operating as if a public utility. This was an important waste prevention measure. Several public hearings were held by the Railroad Commission of Texas at which the program was fully developed.[55]

Inasmuch as the injection of a large part of the salt water produced with oil in the field was shown to be a very important factor in maintaining pressures at high levels, and since it appeared that the entire field would be benefited, the Commission assisted in the program by providing for a small additional allowable (bonus oil) for those operators who, through their own facilities or the facilities of others (such as those of the East Texas Salt Water Disposal Company), returned or caused to be returned their salt water to the Woodbine formation. Indirectly the field furnishes the bonus oil to pay for the expense of injection. The amount of water which must be injected to entitle one to a barrel of bonus oil changes from time to time; it is based on the price of oil in order that the value of the bonus oil closely approximates the cost of salt water injection.[56] The program contemplates that no operator shall be

[54] VERNON'S CIV. STAT. arts. 1508–1512 and 7572–7574.

[55] Various phases of water injection were discussed at length at the hearings on Oct. 6, 1941, and Jan. 20, 1942, and at several subsequent hearings. A detailed account of the program, the operations of the East Texas Salt Water Disposal Company, and the entire salt water injection activities were given by Bryan W. Payne, President of the Company, at the Railroad Commission meeting on April 17, 1947. See note 57 *supra* for articles by W. S. Morris, Vice-President and General Manager of the Company.

[56] The first step by the Commission was its Order No. 6–1456, Oil and Gas Docket 120, (March 29, 1940) authorizing wells to be converted from oil wells to salt water injection wells, with transfer of the oil allowable to other well or wells.

encouraged to produce salt water to secure a bonus allowable. The orders of the Commission permit the sale of earned bonus allowable, and provision is made for approving the locations or wells from which the bonus is to be produced. This unique program of field-wide salt water injection, coordinated with a consistent refusal by the Commission to permit excessive amounts of oil to be produced, has been unusually successful. At the present time more than 570,000 barrels of salt water a calendar day is produced, with approximately 90 per cent of it being injected into the Woodbine sand. About 77 per cent of all the water injected is now handled by the East Texas Salt Water Disposal Company; operators inject the remaining 23 per cent. In spite of the removal of an average of some 325,000 barrels of oil a calendar day (as measured in tanks) or in excess of 400,000 barrels a calendar day (reservoir space) for the past seven years, and a daily average of more than 500,000 barrels of salt water, the reservoir pressure decline has been negligible. The flowing lives of wells have been greatly extended, a higher daily allowable has been made possible (a very fortunate situation during the war), and the ultimate recovery from the field has been increased by some 500,000,000 barrels, according to estimate of Commissioner William J. Murray, Jr., or about 600,000,000 barrels, according to W. S. Morris, Vice-President and General Manager of the East Texas Salt Water Disposal Company. The record is indeed astounding.[57]

This was followed by Order No. 6–3142 (Nov. 20, 1941), providing for a bonus of one barrel of oil for each 50 barrels of water injected; by Order No. 6–3437 (Feb. 20, 1942), permitting assignment of bonus allowables and permitting certain types of wells to be shut-in and allowables produced from other wells; Order No. 20–4189 (Nov. 17, 1942), establishing procedure for transferring allowables; Order No. 6–4351 (Jan. 15, 1943) supplementing Order No. 6–3437; Order No. 6–4571 (March 16, 1943) allowing shut-in wells to produce on a decline curve; decline curve order amended by Order No. 6–10,956 (July 10, 1947), Order No. 6–4877 (May 31, 1943) and Order No. 6–6167 (April 20, 1944), amending Order No. 6–3142 as amended as to production of bonus oil; Order No. 6–9512 (Aug. 31, 1946,) providing for one barrel of bonus oil for each 60 barrels of water injected; Order No. 6–10,558 changing to 75 the number of barrels of water to be injected to be entitled to a bonus of one barrel of oil; and Order No. 6–11,517 (Nov. 14, 1947), providing for one barrel of bonus oil for each 85 barrels of water injected.

[57] Public statement by Commissioner William J. Murray, Jr., confirmed in letter of Aug. 5, 1948; Morris, *Results of Water Injection in Woodbine Reservoir of the East Texas Field*, a paper for the Division of Production, API meeting, Chicago, (Nov. 1947). A more detailed history was given by Morris, *Salt Water Disposal in East Texas Field*, Oil and Gas Jour. (Aug. 10, 17, 24, and 31, 1946). Figures given

Some operators have argued that it is foolish to produce oil wells which also produce large quantities of salt water, and to induce the injection of salt water into the reservoir by paying a bonus equal to the cost of injection. They ask, why not order the shut down of these wells, thereafter permitting the oil allowables to be produced from wells having no salt water? This would avoid: (1) the use of reservoir energy to produce large quantities of salt water, (2) the need for material increases in injection facilities to handle the water, and (3) the need for paying a bonus. The answers given to that question are: (a) many of the wells with salt water may produce from pockets and if the wells were shut-in, the oil in the pockets would not migrate to and be produced by other wells, (b) the water's flushing action increases the recovery of oil from the sand, (c) and the ultimate recovery of oil from the field is materially increased. The program is justified.

Since the correct answer to the question was not as clear as it might have been, the Commission met the situation by an order, entered in July 1947, which permitted but did not compel an operator to shut down his oil-water wells in the field and to produce from other oil wells an amount calculated (as provided for in the order), as the quantity of oil which would have been produced by the shut-in wells by the time of their abandonment.[58] Two hundred and ninety-eight oil-water wells were shut down pursuant to the

---

for oil and salt water production in the East Texas Oil Field are often misleading. For instance, the Commission determines that the field should be limited to a total of 12,000,000 barrels, plus the production by marginal wells, for a given month of 30 days. In order to avoid the necessity of calculating the allowables for non-marginal wells and making changes in monthly allowables, the Commission has adopted the shut-down system, under which non-marginal wells are shut down for about ten days each month. The shut-down does not apply to marginal wells. If there are ten shut-down days, then the non-marginal wells are scheduled to produce for only twenty days if it is a thirty day month. In that period of twenty days they produce 12,000,000 barrels, being an average of 400,000 barrels a day, if calculated on a thirty-day calendar month basis, or an average of 600,000 barrels a day if calculated for the twenty producing days. There are further complications. A barrel of oil as measured in the reservoir is less than a barrel after it gets into the stock tank. Statements as to daily average allowables or production for the East Texas Oil Field may, therefore, be misleading unless it is clear whether the average is for producing days or calendar days, and whether the number of barrels means reservoir barrels or stock tank barrels. Usually, production figures refer to stock tank barrels. The shrinkage of salt water after it reaches the surface is not very great, so a barrel of salt water as measured in the reservoir is also assumed to measure a barrel on the surface.

[58] Order No. 6–10,956 (July 10, 1947). See notes 55 and 56 supra.

order during the first year, August 1947 to August 1948. The total of the oil allowable for these wells was about 2700 barrels a day. This was transferred to other wells. The total water production was some 103,000 barrels a day. By the shut down of the wells, the expense of producing 103,000 barrels of salt water was saved, as was the reservoir energy which would have been used in moving the water to the wells, and finally the cost of injecting it into the Woodbine sand or of disposing of it otherwise was eliminated.

(7) *Court Review*

Phases of court review of orders of the Railroad Commission of Texas issued pursuant to the conservation statutes were discussed in some detail in the earlier article. The statutes provide for a court review of the orders as well as for actions to enforce them. Appeals are specifically authorized. A further discussion will be found in the section—Judicial History.

(8) *Spacing of Wells and Allocation of Production*

The tendency toward wider spacing during the last ten years has been consistent. One important factor was the regulation of spacing during World War II by orders of the Petroleum Administration for War (formerly the Office of Petroleum Coordinator) in connection with the program of the Government, acting in part through the War Production Board, to get the maximum benefit from the use of scarce materials. Metals were scarce; consequently, the PAW sought to enable the production branch of the oil industry to produce the maximum amount of oil and gas with the pipe and equipment allotted to it.

Officials of PAW believed that many unnecessary wells were being drilled, and that ultimate recovery would not be reduced by wider spacing within reasonable limits. It was also thought that wider spacing would offer a better opportunity of discovering new reserves. Control of spacing seemed the one way to get more oil and gas with a minimum use of materials. An order, commonly known as PAO-11, was issued which permitted the drilling of only one oil well to each 40 acres, and one gas well to each 640 acres. The order was subject to exception, and many exceptions were made to meet unusual situations.[59] The war forced on operators for some four years the adoption of wider spacing on relatively uniform patterns. State administrative officials and members of the petroleum industry have had an opportunity to observe results; it is believed on the whole that the results were found good. There has been no general demand since the war for haphazard or very close spacing.

The state-wide spacing rule now in force in Texas is Rule 37, providing in effect for one well to 20 acres, inasmuch as the order provides that no well shall be drilled closer than 933 feet to any other well. Under the rule the well must not be drilled closer than 330 feet to a property line.[60] This state-wide rule controls until the Commission (after a hearing as to the facts in any particular field or area) makes a special rule applicable to the field or area. The conditions vary from field to field as to the depth and the thickness of producing sands, permeability and porosity, the gravity of the oil, the amount of associated gas, and the pressure; consequently, spacing rules are not uniform throughout Texas. In recent years 20 acre and 40 acre spacing patterns have become quite common in oil fields. There are some fields where the proration unit is 40 acres or 80 acres, retaining in the operator a right to drill on a 20 or a 40 acre pattern. This gives more flexibility in locating wells and does not increase the density.[61]

A spacing rule deals with the location of wells, not the amount that they are authorized to produce. A proration or allocation unit is often used to allocate field production, and, as pointed out, it may not be the same as the spacing unit. Many people, especially royalty owners, who argue for close spacing, assume that the greater the number of wells on a tract, the greater the allowable production. Obviously, the assumption may or may not be justified. If the total allowable for a field is allocated on a flat per well basis, then clearly two wells on a 40 acre tract have double the allowable of one well on a 40 acre tract. On the other hand, even if spacing is not controlled, or if for instance a five acre pattern is authorized,

---

[59] A detailed history of the PAW and its activities has been published, FREY AND IDE, HISTORY OF THE PETROLEUM ADMINISTRATION FOR WAR, 1941–1945 (1948).

[60] Order No. 20–6166 (April 20, 1944), amended the rule as previously amended.

[61] Letter of July 14, 1948, from Jack K. Baumel, Chief Engineer, Oil and Gas Division.

but the allowable is allocated on the basis of a 40 acre proration unit, and on the amount of recoverable oil in place, then the mere number of wells drilled becomes immaterial, for the allowable for a 40 acre unit should be the same, whether it has one or two or eight wells on it unless the additional well or wells clearly requires a redetermination of the recoverable oil.

In the earlier days of regulation in Texas, the per well basis, or the per well-potential basis, for allocation of production was the rule, because the industry prior to the advent of regulation had been thinking in terms of wells, not of pools or drainage areas as units. The trend has been consistent toward the use of other factors in allocation formulas, such as pressure, acreage, net effective sand thickness, and recoverable oil with respect to unit areas. The Texas courts have held many times that the owner of a tract of land (or of an oil lease on a tract) is entitled to a fair opportunity to produce or receive the recoverable oil in place under the tract or an equivalent in kind, subject to the reasonable necessities of waste prevention. Each owner of a tract or lease in a field has this right; their rights are correlative. The Commission must respect and protect those rights, and it must not discriminate in authorizing the drilling of wells or in allocating production.[62] The number of wells

---

[62] Brown v. Humble Oil and Ref. Co., 126 Tex. 296 and 314, 83 S.W. 2d 935, 944, 87 S.W. 2d 1069, 1070 (1935); Gulf Land Co. v. Atlantic Ref. Co., 134 Tex. 59, 131 S.W. 2d 73 (1939); Railroad Comm. v. Gulf Production Co., 134 Tex. 122 132 S.W. 2d 254 (1939); Marrs v. Railroad Comm. 142 Tex. 294, 177 S.W. 2d 941, 950 (1944); Railroad Comm. v. Humble Oil & Ref. Co., 132 S.W. 2d 824, 829 (Tex. Civ. App. 3rd 1946) *writ refused*; Railroad Comm. v. Magnolia Pet. Co., 169 S.W. 2d 253, 255 (Tex. Civ. App. 1943) *no application for writ*. The statutes in Louisiana define property rights, or rather a producer's fair share in connection with allocating currently the authorized production of a pool, as follows: "(d) Subject to the reasonable necessities for prevention of waste, and to reasonable adjustment because of structural position, a producer's just and equitable share of the oil and gas in the pool (also sometimes referred to as a tract's just and equitable share) is that part of the authorized production for the pool (whether it be the total which could be produced without any restriction on the amount of production, or whether it be an amount less than that which the pool could produce if no restriction on amount were imposed) which is substantially in the proportion that the quantity of recoverable oil and gas in the developed area of his tract or tracts in the pool bears to the recoverable oil and gas in the total developed area of the pool, in so far as these amounts can be practically ascertained; and to that end, the rules, regulations and orders of the Commissioner shall be such as will prevent or minimize reasonably avoidable net drainage from each developed area (that is, drainage which is not equalized by counter drainage), and will give to each producer the opportunity to use his just and equitable

on a tract does not of itself determine the amount of recoverable oil in place; consequently, when proration or allocation units are provided, or the volumetric displacement factor is used, operators rarely insist upon close spacing or upon drilling more wells than are reasonably required to recover the oil from their units. Relatively wide spacing and the distribution of the allowable on a unit basis, or what amounts to a unit basis, are now commonplace. These are some of the reasons why the argument for close spacing has diminished in vigor.

(9) Volumetric Displacement Method of Fixing Production Allowables

In many fields there is an accumulation of gas in the formation above the oil saturated section, this is a gas cap. Sometimes the gas is of the type termed condensate gas. Some wells in the field may produce only oil plus solution gas; other wells may produce only gas; still others may produce oil, solution gas, and gas from the gas cap. These last wells have varying gas-oil ratios, depending in part on their location on the structure, in part on the rate of production, and in part on other factors. The production of oil and gas in these fields must be carefully regulated to protect the correlative rights of the operators and to prevent waste, such as the dissipation of reservoir energy, by retrograde condensation, by forcing oil to move into the dry gas sands, or by reducing the ultimate recovery by pulling in water. The problem becomes more complicated when part of the gas is returned to the producing formation.

In the Stratton Field (a field similar to that described) the Commission for the first time entered in 1947 a volumetric displacement order as to oil wells. The provisions of the order are complicated, but in effect provide for the production of oil and gas with respect to each well in an amount representing a certain volume of space in the reservoir. This penalized high gas-oil ratio wells, even when producing at the minimum ratio, inasmuch as the

---

share of the reservoir energy. . . ." La. Acts 1940, Act No. 157. Similar language appears in the statutes of Arkansas, Florida, Michigan, and New Mexico. See discussion in STANDARDS ON ALLOCATION OF OIL PRODUCTION, c. VI (1942). Cases involving allocation of production are discussed in § III, (2), (b) of this article.

production of large amounts of gas reduced the quantity of oil which could be produced. The order goes far toward preventing waste and in making a fairer adjustment of correlative rights.[63]

(10) Waste of Gas

For many years the Railroad Commission and the members of the petroleum industry have been concerned with the loss or dissipation of natural gas, especially that gas unavoidably produced with oil (casinghead-gas). They have been prodded by officials of the Federal Government to make more successful efforts, as shown by the record of hearings made in 1934 and in 1939–40 before the Cole Committee, a Sub-committee of the Committee on Interstate and Foreign Commerce, House of Representatives, on federal control bills, by the hearings before the Federal Power Commission, and by the comments in the Staff Reports to the FPC.

The great demand for oil, gas, and hydrocarbon products during World War II, as well as the discovery of new uses for hydrocarbons, brought about a clearer realization of the value of oil and gas. After war time price controls were lifted, the prices for both oil and gas increased materially. Much gas, which had theretofore been dissipated because it could not be saved or used except at a loss, was in demand at a higher price and thus was worth saving. Conditions had changed and the Railroad Commission of Texas was on safer ground in prohibiting the dissipation of gas which could be saved at a reasonable expense.

During 1946 and 1947 hearings were held by the Commission throughout the state in an effort to develop the facts and to take action to stop (or at least minimize) the waste of gas. Much good was done. Orders of particular significance were those involving the Seeligson, Old Ocean, Stratton, and Pinehurst Fields. The powers of the Commission to prevent waste of gas were clarified and found to be extensive by the decision in *Railroad Commission v. Shell Oil Co.*

[63] Order No. 4–10,743 (May 26, 1947). It is copied in full in the State House Reporter, Oil Regulation Report (May 26, 1947). The order was the culmination of a series of orders for the field beginning with No. 4–5637 (Aug. 28, 1944), providing for production of gas on a volumetric displacement basis. It is likely that the problems applicable to the Stratton Field caused the promulgation of Order No. 20–6839 (Oct. 20, 1944), of state-wide application. It provided for the volumetric displacement rule for gas wells producing in the same formation with oil.

There are several factors which have hindered the marketing of considerable amounts of casinghead-gas. Many operators take the position that if they sell residue gas from a plant, though transporting it only a short distance to the purchaser or to an interstate pipe line, the Federal Power Commission will claim that neither production nor gathering is involved, thus subjecting the sellers to extensive regulation under the Federal Natural Gas Act which includes the keeping of books conforming to federal regulations, and to a direct or indirect fixing of prices for the gas sold. Many operators have declined to sell the gas at the well if it is to be transported in interstate commerce, to avoid any question as to the application of the Act. All of these operators foresee interference with oil operations once the FPC acquires jurisdiction over the selling company, together with a gradual trend toward greater power over the entire industry vested in the FPC. There is no need here to debate the issues or to speculate upon their eventual determination. It is enough to report that the fears of the effects of selling casinghead-gas which will enter interstate commerce under certain circumstances are real, and that these fears complicate the problem of preventing the waste of such gas.[64]

III. JUDICIAL HISTORY

Although the fundamental provisions of the conservation laws had been reasonably well settled by 1939, and although the power of the Railroad Commission of Texas to prevent waste and to protect correlative rights had in most respects been established, there were nevertheless serious issues to be solved by litigation. In the main these issues concerned (a) powers of the Commission to prevent waste and to protect correlative rights, (b) the reasonableness of the orders, and (c) the scope or character of court review

---

[64] See Dougherty, *Ten Years Under the Natural Gas Act*, Oil and Gas Jour. (July 15, 1948) 94, for a statement of some of the problems arising under the Natural Gas Act, including the effect of fixing rates for a "natural gas company," which produces its own gas. Briefly stated, the rates are fixed on the basis of original investment instead of on the commodity value of the gas. Operators wonder how the calculation of cost of casinghead gas would be made, since the land owned or leased produced oil and gas, not just gas. How much of the original cost and how much of the expense would be allocated to the gas?

involving the validity of orders. The discussion follows in that order.

(1) Power of the Commission to Prevent Waste—in General

For many years in Texas the unavoidable production of gas associated with oil, known as casinghead-gas, presented difficult problems. In the early days of the industry casinghead-gas was considered a dangerous nuisance. There was no market for it. Even in comparatively recent years the market was negligible, partly because the need for natural gas was readily supplied from gas fields, partly because of the expense of gathering the casinghead-gas from many wells over wide areas and in making the gas suitable for transportation through trunk lines for ultimate consumer use, and partly because of the fluctuating character of the supply, inasmuch as the amount of gas produced was a mere incident to oil production.

In view of the situation, much casinghead-gas was dissipated at the surface, although efforts were made to use efficiently the gas energy in producing the oil. One method was to fix the gas-oil ratios so that a minimum amount of gas would be produced with each barrel of oil. Operators and state officials alike regretted the loss of casinghead-gas, but they excused this loss on the ground that the gas had performed a necessary and beneficial function in lifting the oil. They reasoned that either the oil wells had to be shut down to save the casinghead-gas, or the wells had to be produced to get the oil even if the gas unavoidably produced with it had to be dissipated. All welcomed a change in conditions which permitted a saving of the gas and its use for beneficial purposes of a high order.

Great progress in conservation was made by the development of processes to extract from the rich casinghead-gas those liquid hydrocarbons usually called natural gasoline. That branch of the industry began about 1905. The production of natural gasoline in 1911 was some 7 million gallons or 167,000 barrels; in 1938 it was more than 2 billion gallons or 48,000,000 barrels; and in 1946 it was nearly 5 billion gallons or 119,000,000 barrels of 42 gallons.[65] The rapid growth created many new legal problems.[66] The industry had not

[65] PETROLEUM DATA BOOK, G–3 (1947).

[66] There was conflict and confusion in the law involving casinghead gas as late as 1930, as this writer undertook to show in Hardwicke, *Evolution of Casinghead Gas*

reached maturity twenty-five years later, or by 1930. Many casing-head-gas plants were in operation by 1939, but it must not be assumed that the construction or operation of a plant is even now economically feasible in any and all fields. There arc many factors to be considered in that connection.

The operation of plants made possible the saving of a large part of the heavier hydrocarbons in casinghead-gas which otherwise would have been lost, nevertheless the dissipation of residue gas (tail or dry gas) was common practice. Many difficulties prevented its sale or use. The residue gas had to compete with gas from gas fields under conditions unfavorable to it; and while it frequently appeared that the residue gas could be injected into an oil reservoir with beneficial results, the cost of injection was prohibitive when compared with the resulting benefits. Moreover, an efficient injection program which protected correlative rights and avoided litigation almost necessarily required unit operations or field-wide co-operation as well as large expenditures for plant facilities. There were many hurdles to be overcome in bringing about satisfactory agreements for such operations.

A material change in conditions beginning as early as 1940 was accelerated as a result of World War II. The great need for all types of hydrocarbons in the war years and the many new processes developed for the use of natural gas and its products removed all doubt of the increasing value of natural gas. Furthermore, the rate of oil production exceeded the finding of new reserves; since there was some justification for believing that this trend would continue, public officials and members of the oil industry became more interested than ever in pressure maintenance, repressuring, secondary recovery operations, and other operations which would increase the ultimate recovery of oil and would result in the saving and beneficial use of casinghead-gas. When World War II price controls were removed, the prices for both oil and gas increased materially giving operators an economic incentive to extract natural

---

Law, 8 TEX. L. REV. 1 (1929), and in his review of the second or permanent edition of SUMMERS, THE LAW OF OIL AND GAS (2d ed. 1938), 34 Ill. L. Rev. 243 (1939). In the review it was pointed out that in the first edition of that book published in 1927, Professor Summers devoted less than 3 pages to the law relating to casinghead-gas, while in the permanent edition, published 10 years later, the discussion of the new material available required 35 pages.

gasoline from casinghead-gas and to devote the residue gas to uses authorized by law; the Commission had excellent grounds for insisting in many instances that the gas be saved and so used.

(A) WASTE OF CASINGHEAD-GAS—RAILROAD COMMISSION V. SHELL OIL CO.

Such was the setting for the controversies involving the large Seeligson Field where great quantities of casinghead-gas, including the valuable natural gasoline content were being dissipated. This field of some 14,000 surface acres included 40 distinct producing zones or reservoirs, some of which produced gas with a condensate content, but most of them, say about three-fourths, produced oil and casinghead-gas. No wonder the problems in that field were complex. The Commission held several hearings in 1946 and 1947 in an effort to develop the facts and work out a reasonable waste prevention program. Finally it entered an order on March 17, 1947 which contained elaborate fact findings and directed that all wells be shut down until the gas produced from the oil wells was saved and used for purposes permitted by law.[67]

A number of operators in the field promptly filed suit seeking to enjoin the order's enforcement. Among the grounds relied upon were the following: (a) the operators produced their wells with at gas-oil ratios no larger than those permitted by an order of the Commission; consequently, the gas so produced could legally be dissipated; and (b) the operators had made arrangements for the construction and operation of an expensive casinghead-gas plant and other facilities to prevent the loss or waste of all gas, but the war and the scarcity of materials and labor had delayed its completion; the plant would be put in operation as quickly as possible, and under the circumstances it was unreasonable and arbitrary to require the shutting-in of the oil wells with the resultant great losses to the operators. The trial court, holding that the Commission was without power to make and enforce the order, granted a temporary injunction restraining its enforcement pending a trial on the merits. The Commission appealed directly to the Supreme Court of Texas.

[67] The order, No. 4–10,351, is copied in full in State House Reporter, Oil Regulation Report (March 17, 1947). That report contains an explanatory statement by Colonel Ernest O. Thompson of the Commission.

That court by its opinion of November 26, 1947 held that the Commission had statutory authority to issue an order of the type in question, but since the effect of the temporary injunction was merely to maintain the status quo pending the trial on the merits, the granting of the temporary injunction under the disclosed facts was not an abuse of discretion. This language appeared in the opinion: ". . . The conclusion has already been expressed that the Commission has the authority in a proper case to enter an order preventing the wasteful flaring of casinghead gas. But whether the situation in the Seeligson Field presents such a case must await a full development of the evidence in a trial on the merits." The case was remanded for trial on the merits.[68] While waiting for the trial on the merits, the operators (some eight months after the order of the Commission was issued) finished and began operation of the casinghead-gas plant and devoted the residue gas to uses permitted by law. The case was therefore dismissed March 15, 1948. It served however to clarify the meaning of the conservation statutes in important particulars, and to establish that the Commission had broad power to prevent waste of gas.[69]

(B) WASTE BY MARGINAL WELLS—RAILROAD COMMISSION V. KONOWA OPERATING CO.

The power of the Commission to enforce, with respect to marginal wells, a water-oil ratio order or other conservation regulation not designed or operating directly to restrict production was established in the *Konowa* case,[70] and has been discussed.

(C) POWER OF COMMISSION TO KILL WILD WELLS—CORZELIUS V. RAILROAD COMMISSION.

An unusual case involving the power of the Commission to prevent waste was occasioned by a blowout in the Bammel Field. The

[68] Railroad Comm. v. Shell Oil Co.,   Tex.   , 206 S.W. 2d 235 (1947), Note, 26 TEX. L. REV. 682 (1948).

[69] An excellent account of the situation at Seeligson and also the program for operating the field has recently been published. Weber, *Huge Gas-Conservation Project Now in Initial Operation Stage*, Oil and Gas Jour. (July 8, 1948) 60.

[70] Railroad Comm. v. Konowa Operating Co., 174 S.W. 2d 605 (Tex. Civ. App. 3rd, 1943) *no application for writ.*

facts in that case clearly show the real need for adequate precautions to prevent blowouts. The entire field (a gas condensate field of about 3200 surface acres) was under lease to H. M. Harrell, except for 80 acres held under lease by F. M. Corzelius. Corzelius produced and marketed through his own pipe line considerable quantities of gas after recovering a portion of the condensate. Harrell, under a permit from the Commission, engaged in cycling operations which involved the recovery of condensate and the return of the dry or residue gas to the reservoir to maintain pressures at high levels. He was not at this time marketing the residue gas, but intended to do so in the future. The Corzelius well was found to be leaking, and the Commission ordered on June 30, 1943 that the leak be stopped. Corzelius was unable either to stop the leak or to kill the well. It blew out and cratered in August 1943, and finally caught fire August 30, 1943. Efforts of Corzelius to put out the fire and control the well were unsuccessful. In a short time a number of other wells in the area cratered and some caught fire. Large quantities of gas migrated into other formations. Water wells became geysers. One water well located approximately two miles from the Corzelius well ejected water 80 to 100 feet in the air. The losses in gas, condensate, and equipment were enormous. The Commission, by order of January 31, 1944 amended February 1, 1944, directed and authorized Harrell as an agent of the Commission to drill a directional well into the Corzelius tract to a point near the bottom of the Corzelius well for the purpose of killing it and abating the waste. Corzelius sought an injunction to prevent Harrell from carrying out the order of the Commission. The trial court refused the injunction, and the Texas Court of Civil Appeals affirmed the judgment, holding that the order was valid as the adoption of a reasonable means in unusual circumstances to prevent great waste.[71] Eventually the Corzelius well was killed, but further litigation arose with respect to the right of the Commission to fix a gas allowable for the field and to allocate the allowable production for the purpose of protecting correlative rights irrespective of the existence of waste.

[71] Corzelius v. Railroad Commission, 182 S.W. 2d 412 (Tex. Civ. App. 3rd, 1944) *no application for writ.* See discussion of the problems in the field by Sellers, Noel, and Hyder, in *Texas Gas Conservation Laws and Oil and Gas Regulations,* 39–49 (1946).

(2) *Reasonableness of Orders in the Protection of Private Rights*
(A) WELL SPACING CASES

In the earlier article covering the legal history of conservation to October 1938, reference was made (at pages 255–260) to the confusion and to the heavy litigation with respect to well spacing in the East Texas Field, and to the difficulty of isolating standards or principles upon which the Commission's orders or the judgments of the courts were based.

The fundamental factors which brought about the litigation were: (a) The Commission promulgated a rule for the East Texas Field, usually called Rule 37, providing that wells should be drilled not closer than a certain distance to property lines or to another well. The rule as amended July 24, 1939 declared that no well should be drilled closer than 660 feet to another well or 330 feet to a lease or property line. This permitted the drilling of only one well to each 10 acres. (b) The rule provided that the Commission would grant exceptions either to prevent waste or to prevent confiscation of property. (c) The allowable for the East Texas Field was distributed on a formula which for practical purposes amounted to a flat per-well allowable, amounting to about 20 barrels a well in 1939, and which has remained at about the same figure. (d) The Commission granted exceptions freely. (e) The result of an exception was to increase the allowable for the tract; consequently, if in accordance with the rule, operator A drilled one well on a 10 acre tract while operator B got exceptions and drilled four wells on the adjoining 10 acre tract, then A's allowable was about 20 barrels a day, while B's was about 80 barrels a day, though the only real difference between the two tracts was the number of wells.

In view of the situation the courts have been burdened with Rule 37 cases involving the validity of orders granting or refusing exceptions to the rule. By January 1, 1938 about 75 opinions had been written by state and federal courts, but the law on the subject was still in considerable confusion. From January 1, 1938 to January 1, 1948 the appellate courts disposed of about 100 additional cases. Opinions were written by the Supreme Court of Texas in 12 cases, by the Circuit Court of Appeals for the Fifth Circuit, in

6 cases, 2 of which went to the Supreme Court of the United States. The real burden was upon the trial courts and the intermediate appellate courts of Texas, or the Texas courts of civil appeals, usually the court for the third district sitting at Austin.

From all this mass of judicial pronouncements, various controlling principles were established, but the litigants always found some way to argue around the precedents and to present new questions so that it must still be said that confusion exists. This must be so or the appellate courts would not have been called upon to dispose of cases involving Rule 37 for the East Texas Field at the rate of about one a month for the last ten years. The trial courts were called upon to dispose of even a greater number.

There are sound reasons for foregoing an exhaustive discussion of these cases. All but one involved the East Texas Field and had a history, conditions, and precedents peculiar to that field. A similar situation is not likely to grow up in any other field. (It seems sufficient here to do little more than indicate the variety of the issues in the well spacing cases which have been decided in the last ten years.)

(i) *Well Spacing Confiscation Cases.* Nearly all of the cases involved the issue of confiscation. In a typical case the applicant for the exception would claim that the well was needed so that he would have a fair opportunity to produce the recoverable oil under his tract or the equivalent in kind. One or more neighbors would resist the application on the ground that the applicant already had a fair opportunity without drilling and producing from another well. Ordinarily the opponents would claim that if the permit should be granted, the applicant would have a chance to obtain more than his fair share of the oil, and he would thereby drain oil from under their lands and reduce their opportunities to recover their fair shares, in effect a confiscation of their properties.[72]

A. W. Walker, formerly of the Law School, University of Texas, has isolated four rules used by the appellate courts in giving effect to the concept of confiscation set out above. (The balance of this paragraph with slight changes is in his language.) It was established that each tract of land no matter how small was entitled to at least one well in order to prevent confiscation, if the tract was in existence as a separate tract of land at the time the spacing rule

[72] See note 62 *supra* for cases discussing fair share and property rights.

became effective.[73] As a corollary to this principle there was adopted a second rule, the *voluntary subdivision rule*, to the effect that tracts created by the subdivision of larger tracts after the spacing rule became effective were not entitled to permits for wells (as exceptions to the spacing rule) on the ground of prevention of confiscation.[74] This in turn led to a third rule, (the *doctrine of the Century case*) that where segregation of tracts had been made in violation of the *voluntary subdivision rule*, the Commission was authorized to consider the tract as it existed prior to the subdivision; if the tract as then reconstructed was entitled to an additional well or wells in order to prevent undue drainage, a permit might properly be granted for that reason to prevent confiscation.[75] In determining whether any tract of land regardless of size was being drained in such manner as to amount to confiscation, the Commission adopted the policy of considering whether the tract in question was on a parity with neighboring tracts in respect to average well densities. This policy, or the fourth rule, came to be known as the *eight-times area rule*. Although it was never adopted as a formal rule, as a general practice the Commission restricted the area considered for the purpose of determining inequalities in well densities to an area not exceeding eight times that of the tract upon which a well permit was sought.[76]

The voluntary subdivision rule was not avoided or circumvented by effecting subdivision in a manner other than by ordinary voluntary subdivision, as by a partition or agreed judgment,[77] and segrega-

---

[73] Dailey v. Rail. Comm., 133 S.W. 2d 219 (Tex. Civ. App. 3rd, 1939) *writ refused The following comments are not Professor Walker's.* If this case holds that the rule provides for an exception under the facts stated, or that the owner of the tract must be given an opportunity, by the drilling of a well or otherwise, as by pooling, to recover or receive his share of the oil, then the holding is not criticized. If, however, the court meant to say that the owner of the tract had a constitutional right to drill, irrespective of a spacing rule, and no matter how much waste would be committed, then the holding seems to conflict with the established rule that the state, by the exercise of police power, may prevent waste by all reasonable means, even if losses occur to property owners. Of course, the need for such action must appear to be reasonably necessary.

[74] Brown v. Humble Oil & Ref. Co., 126 Tex. 296, 83 S.W. 2d 935 (1935), on rehearing 126 Tex. 314, 87 S.W. 2d 1069, (1935).

[75] Railroad Comm. v. Magnolia Pet. Co., 130 Tex. 484, 109 S.W. 2d 967 (1937).

[76] Miller v. Railroad Comm., 185 S.W. 2d 223 (Tex. Civ. App. 3rd, 1945) *writ refused.*

[77] Partition cases: Humble Oil & Ref. Co. v. Lasseter, 120 S.W. 2d 541 (Tex. Civ. App. 3rd, 1938) *writ dismissed*; Railroad Comm. v. Magnolia Pet. Co., 125 S.W. 2d 398 (Tex. Civ. App. 3rd, 1939) *writ ref.* Agreed judgment cases. Magnolia Pet. Co.

tions or subdivisions made prior to the establishment of a rule for a field do not give a right to an exception if it appears that the segregation was made to circumvent the rule.[78] Further complications arose in applying the *voluntary subdivision rule* and the *doctrine of the Century case* (consider the tract before the subdivision was made to determine whether taken as a whole the tract would be entitled to an exception to prevent confiscation) for the question of location on the tract as a whole was most important. For instance, if a six acre tract should be subdivided into a five acre tract and a one acre tract and (taking the six acre tract as a whole) another well was needed, should it be on the five acre part or the one acre part? The earlier cases approved exceptions granted to the first applicant, even though he be the owner of the smaller tract.[79] This precedent was modified by holding that the Commission had the discretion to locate the additional well for the prevention of confiscation at a point best serving the interest of conservation.[80]

The ramifications of the *eight-times area rule* were considerable. It was said that the rule was merely evidentiary and not to be applied as the sole test of rights,[81] that the Commission in estimating well densities and comparative recoveries could properly consider an area merely four times instead of eight times the size of the tract involved if this appeared to be a better standard,[82] and that the rule was applicable only to local uncompensated drainage as

v. Railroad Comm., 120 S.W. 2d 548 (Tex. Civ. App. 3rd, 1938) *writ dismissed;* Atl. Ref. Co. v. Buckley, 123 S.W. 2d 413 (Tex. Civ. App. 3rd, 1938,) *writ dismissed;* Richey v. Shell Pet. Corp., 128 S.W. 2d 898 (Tex. Civ. App. 3rd, 1939) *writ dismissed;* Railroad Comm. v. Ark Fuel Oil Co., 148 S.W. 2d 895 (Tex. Civ. App. 3rd, 1941) *writ refused.*

[78] Shell Pet. Corp. v. Railroad Comm., 133 S.W. 2d 194 (Tex. Civ. App. 3rd, 1939) *writ refused;* Nash v. Shell Pet. Corp., 120 S.W. 2d 522 (Tex. Civ. App. 3rd, 1938) *writ dismissed,* Note, 17 Tex. L. Rev. 511 (1939).

[79] Humble Oil & Ref. Co. v. Lasseter, 120 S.W. 2d 541 (Tex. Civ. App. 3rd, 1938) *writ dismissed;* Note, 17 Tex. L. Rev. 382 (April 1939); Railroad Comm. v. Magnolia Pet. Co., 125 S.W. 2d 398 (Tex. Civ. App. 3rd, 1939) *writ refused. See* Railroad Comm. v. Humble Oil & Ref. Co., 123 S.W. 2d 423 (Tex. Civ. App. 3rd, 1938) *writ dismissed.*

[80] Railroad Comm. v. Miller, 165 S.W. 2d 504 (Tex. Civ. App. 3rd, 1942) *no application writ.*

[81] Miller v. Railroad Comm., 185 S.W. 2d 223 (Tex. Civ. App. 3rd, 1945) *writ refused;* Shell Oil Co. v. Railroad Comm., 133 S.W. 2d 791 (Tex. Civ. App. 3rd, 1939) *writ dismissed;* Thomas v. Stanolind Oil & Gas Co., 145 Tex. 270, 198 S.W. 2d 420 (1946).

[82] Thomas v. Stanolind Oil & Gas Co., 145 Tex. 270, 198 S.W. 2d 420 (1946).

distinguished from general field drainage.[83] It was also held that a proper test for confiscation was whether there existed an opportunity like that given others to recover the oil beneath the tract at the time it was sought to be recovered, thus including oil that had migrated as a result of field or regional drainage.[84] However, the court in the *Byrd* case declared that the Commission improperly granted an exception in a situation where the applicant, although he had more wells than he would be entitled to under the rule, could not recover the oil under his tract. He claimed that he could not recover by existing wells the oil in place, because the sands would soon be drowned by water as a result of heavy withdrawals or production from wells up-structure, especially in the Kilgore townsite where, for instance, there was a one acre tract with 27 wells on it. The court observed that the applicant's neighbors were similarly situated, that the problem was applicable to the entire field, and its solution should not be made by granting exceptions, but by a general rule to provide a different system of allocation of production or by a reduction of allowable in the Kilgore townsite area.[85]

The Commission has often been criticized for its consistent refusal to change tract allowables to prevent confiscation, instead of acting to force operators to drill unnecessary wells to obtain a greater allowable for a tract. The *Byrd* case mentioned the instance of 27 wells on a one acre tract. It is common knowledge that there are many examples of five and ten wells on one acre tracts. The average density for the East Texas Field is now about one well to four acres, yet the general rule provides for one well to ten acres, and it is generally considered that one well will efficiently drain ten acres and more in the East Texas Field. It is difficult to understand why operators ask for the right to drill more wells instead of asking for increased allowables from wells already drilled; why the Commission does not protect against confiscation by increasing allowables instead of granting well exceptions and then giving allow-

---

[83] Miller v. Railroad Comm., 185 S.W. 2d 223 (Tex. Civ. App. 3rd, 1945) *writ refused.*

[84] Railroad Comm. v. Mag. Pet. Co., 169 S.W. 2d 253 (Tex. Civ. App. 3rd, 1943) *no application for writ.*

[85] Byrd v. Shell Oil Co., 178 S.W. 2d 573 (Tex. Civ. App. 4th, 1944) *writ refused for want of merit,* Note, 23 TEX. L. REV. 85 (1944).

ables to the unnecessary wells; or why the courts do not follow the observations made in the *Byrd* case by insisting that the Commission, instead of granting permits to drill additional wells, should change the method of allocation to meet the problem of confiscation.[86]

An appellate court which refused to apply the *eight-times area rule* in *Kraker v. Railroad Commission*,[87] involving the Hawkins Field, said that acreage was an important factor in the allocation formula for that field, but was used not at all for the East Texas Field; consequently, the rule should not be applied in Hawkins to determine whether an exception should be granted to the spacing rule. The court sustained the action of the Commission in refusing to grant the right to drill a well on a small tract in the Hawkins Field.

(ii) *Well Spacing Waste Cases.* As observed, most of the well spacing cases have involved the issue of confiscation with no serious question raised as to whether the well if drilled would cause waste or prevent waste. The courts have held that a permit to drill may properly be granted to prevent confiscation, though the operation of the well causes waste.[88] Conversely, an exception may properly be granted to prevent waste even if no confiscation be involved.[89] However, the courts, when confronted with the contention that the more wells drilled in the East Texas Field the more oil ultimately produced, as a reason for granting exceptions to prevent waste, held that the contention was in reality an attack on the rule itself, and that the granting of exceptions on that theory would nullify the rule; therefore, the more-wells-more-oil theory, even if established, does not justify an exception.[90]

[86] In Humble Oil & Ref. Co. v. Wrather, 205 S.W. 2d 86 (Tex. Civ. App. 1947) *writ granted*, a permit was granted for a 4th well on a 0.4-acre tract. There have been many instances quite similar set forth in the decisions.

[87] Kraker v. Railroad Comm., 188 S.W. 2d 914 (Tex. Civ. App. 3rd, 1945) *writ refused*, Note, 25 Tex. L. Rev. 98 (1946).

[88] Magnolia Pet. Co. v. Railroad Comm., 120 S.W. 2d 553 (Tex. Civ. App. 3rd, 1938) *writ dismissed*; Gulf Oil Corp. v. Wood, 120 S.W. 2d 543 (Tex. Civ. App. 3rd, 1938) *writ dismissed*. See also Railroad Comm. v. Shell Oil Co., 154 S.W. 2d 507 (Tex. Civ. App. 3rd, 1941) *aff'd. on other grounds* 138 Tex. 66, 161 S.W. 2d 1022 (1942).

[89] Gulf Land Co. v. Atlantic Ref. Co., 134 Tex. 59, 131 S.W. 2d 73 (1939), Note, 18 Tex. L. Rev. 237 (1940).

[90] Gulf Land Co. v. Atlantic Ref. Co., 134 Tex. 59, 131 S.W. 2d 73 (1939); Rail. Comm. v. Shell Oil Co., 139 Tex. 66, 161 S.W. 2d 1022 (1942); Hawkins v. Texas Co., Tex., 209 S.W. 2d 338 (1948).

Further clarification of the rule providing for an exception to prevent waste came with the decision that unusual conditions must exist with respect to the tract and its adjacent area,[91] and with the decision that in the absence of proof of unusual local conditions it was not enough to establish that some oil (which would be recovered if the well applied for were drilled) may not be recovered.[92]

(B) ALLOCATION OF PRODUCTION CASES

(i) *Allocation of State Allowable Among Fields—Railroad Commission v. Continental Oil Co., and Railroad Commission v. Marrs.* For many years the productive capacities or the potentials of the oil fields in Texas, though producing efficiently, have greatly exceeded reasonable market demand. Consequently, the Railroad Commission of Texas, being so specifically authorized by statute since 1932,[93] has periodically (that is usually once a month) determined the reasonable market demand for oil for the state, and has fixed the state allowable accordingly in order that production would not exceed the amount found to be the reasonable market demand.[94] The statute directs the Commission to allocate the state allowable among the fields on a fair and reasonable basis without discrimination.[95]

Only two cases which reached the appellate courts have been found involving the fairness of the distribution of state allowable. In the first or the *Continental* case the state allowable was fixed at 1,800,000 barrels a day and the allocation for the Conoco-Driscoll Field at 1300 barrels, a reduction from the previous allowable of 2300 barrels. The Commission formula then in use for

[91] Railroad Comm. v. Magnolia Pet. Co., 169 S.W. 2d 794 (Tex. Civ. App. 3rd, 1943), *writ refused, want of merit;* Hawkins v. Texas Co., Tex., 209 S.W. 2d 338, 343 (1948).

[92] Letwin v. Gulf Oil Corp., 164 S.W. 2d 234 (Tex. Civ. App. 3rd, 1942) *writ refused.*

[93] VERNON'S CIV. STAT. art 6014 ¶ (j). There is a similar provision as to gas in *id.* art. 6008 ¶ (h).

[94] See discussion of "reasonable market demand," in § II, (4) of this article, and items cited in note 45 *supra.* The estimates of needs for current consumption, made by the United States Bureau of Mines, are considered by the Commission, and properly so, Amazon Petroleum Corp. v. Railroad Comm., 5 F. Supp. 633 (E.D. Tex. 1934) *no appeal,* but the findings of the Commission are frequently materially different from the estimates made by the Bureau.

[95] VERNON'S CIV. STAT. art. 6069 d, § 6. A similar provision as to gas is in *id.* art. 6008, § 12.

distribution of the state allowable would have reduced the allowable for the Conoco-Driscoll Field to about 900 barrels. The Commission increased the allowable to 1300 barrels or about 50 per cent more than the field would be entitled to by a strict application of the formula. The field was entirely owned by the Continental Oil Company. That company brought suit to set aside the order, alleging that the field could produce as much as 2300 barrels or more without injuring the reservoir or causing underground waste, and that purchasers were ready, able, and willing to purchase 4000 barrels a day from the field. The Commission conceded that such were the facts. The Continental Company raised no question as to the correctness of the state allowable, nor did it contend that the formula applied for effecting distribution of the state allowable discriminated against the field. The fundamental point at issue was whether the allowable for the Conoco-Driscoll Field should be fixed by allocating to it (on a reasonable basis and without discrimination) its share of the state allowable based on reasonable market demand, or whether the reasonable market demand should be determined separately for the field and then fixed at not less than the amount the purchasers wanted to buy, where the field could produce that amount without causing underground waste. Stated differently, the Continental Company took the position that the reasonable market demand for each field in the state should be determined separately and without relation to other fields or to the effect of restricting production in other fields. In a sense the Continental Company wanted its field to be treated as if in a vacuum. It was argued that the desires of purchasers to purchase from a particular field should be the controlling factor in determining reasonable market demand for the field. The trial court upheld the contentions of the Continental Company.

The issues raised before the Commission and in the case prompted the introduction of H.B. 941 in the 47th legislature of 1941. That bill undertook to provide in detail for the allocation of the state allowable, and to fix standards to prevent what is called in the industry selective buying. The judgment of the trial court which in effect authorized selective buying was a disturbing factor. Strenuous efforts were made to pass H.B. 941 which would have to a certain extent specifically provided for a program similar in principle to that the Commission had been using. The bill was passed, but it was vetoed by Governor W. Lee O'Daniel and enough votes could not be secured to override the veto.

While the industry was speculating upon what would happen if the appellate court should uphold the decision of the trial court, the court of civil appeals, ninth district at Beaumont, filed its opinion on December 15, 1941 holding for the Commission. The judgment of the trial court was reversed and rendered. The appellate court declared in substance that the situation in the state as a whole must be considered, and that the desires of purchasers to buy from a particular field should not be a controlling factor in determining the reasonable market demand for the field, because it would actually permit the purchasers to fix allowables and to discriminate. The court declared that the protection of correlative rights required that all the fields and operators fairly share the burden of any restriction reasonably necessary to prevent waste, and to that end the Commission had undertaken (as required by statute) to allocate to the Conoco-Driscoll Field its fair share of the state allowable, and the proof failed to show that it had not done so.[96]

In the second instance, the *Marrs* case, the main issue was whether there had been a fair allocation of the field allowable. (*That phase of the case will be discussed in the next subsection.*) Another question involved was whether the reasonable market demand for each field should be separately determined or whether each pool should be allocated its share of the state allowable. The latter method, followed by the Commission, was approved and the *Continental* case was cited in support of the holding. The case reached the Supreme Court of Texas, but the correct method of fixing field allowables was not discussed.[97]

(ii) *Fixing Allowables for Gas Fields to Protect Correlative Rights Irrespective of Waste—Corzelius v. Harrell.* Problems with respect to control of production in gas fields have already been discussed.[98] It was there pointed out that the Railroad Commission

[96] Railroad Comm. v. Continental Oil Co., 157 S.W. 2d 695 (Tex. Civ. App. 9th, 1941) *writ refused, want of merit.* Rowe, Comment, 21 Tex. L. Rev. 330 (1943).

[97] Railroad Comm. v. Marrs, 161 S.W. 2d 1037, 1044 (Tex Civ. App. 1942), Marrs v. Railroad Comm., 142 Tex. 294, 177 S.W. 2d 941 (1944). See discussion of reasonable market demand in § II, (4) this article.

[98] § I (1) (d) and § I (2) (a), this article.

of Texas did not appear to be able to prove to the satisfaction of the federal courts that the orders of the Commission, which undertook to restrict production in gas fields and to allocate production, had any reasonable relation to the prevention of waste. H.B. 266, passed in 1935, amending Article 6008 of the Revised Civil Statutes,[99] prohibited generally the waste of gas, and it also set forth a number of definitions of waste including the following: "(h) The production of natural gas in excess of transportation or market facilities, or reasonable market demand for the type of gas produced. (k) Permitting any natural gas produced from a gas well to escape into the air before or after such gas has been processed for its gasoline content." The Act contained elaborate provisions for determining reasonable market demand and field allowables. By Section 10 of the Act a duty was imposed on the Commission to "prorate and regulate such production for the protection of public and private interests:" (a) In the prevention of waste as 'waste' is defined herein; (b) In the adjustment of correlative rights and opportunities of each owner of gas in a common reservoir to produce and use or sell such gas as permitted in this Article." The author of the Act seems to have contemplated the difficulty of proving waste in gas fields which would justify field allowables and allocation; this accounts for the separate provision requiring adjustment of correlative rights and opportunities with no mention of waste. A three judge federal district court declared that the Commission was not authorized by that Act to adjust correlative rights except to prevent waste. The court also expressed its doubt as to the validity of a statute which undertook to give such authority to the Commission. The correctness of that interpretation and viewpoint was questioned by the Supreme Court of the United States, but a definite decision was not necessary inasmuch as the case was disposed of on other points.[100] At last the precise questions reached the Supreme Court of Texas in a case involving the Bammel Field, an area which had already furnished interesting litigation in connection with the killing of a wild well.[101]

[99] Tex. Acts 1935, c. 120; Vernon's Civ. Stat. art. 6008 (1937).
[100] Consolidated Gas Utilities Corp. v. Thompson, 14 F. Supp. 318 (W.D. Tex. 1936); Thompson v. Consolidated Gas Utilities Corp., 300 U.S. 55, (1936).
[101] § III (1) of this article discusses Corzelius v. Railroad Comm., 182 S.W. 2d 412 (Tex. Civ. App. 1944) writ refused.

Harrell had the entire field under lease except a small tract held leased by Corzelius. Harrell was operating a cycling plant, extracting condensate, and returning the residue gas to the reservoir to maintain pressures and thereby prevent waste. He did not intend to market the gas until cycling was no longer feasible. Corzelius, with an 80 acre tract, built a pipe line and marketed gas. The Commission entered an order fixing a net allowable of 20,000,000 cubic feet a day for the field and setting out a formula for prorating the field allowable on the basis of 160 acre proration units. Harrell brought suit to set aside the order and Corzelius intervened. The two issues in the case of special interest here were: (a) did the statute authorize the regulation of production for the purpose of protecting correlative rights irrespective of waste? and (b) if it did, was the statute unconstitutional in that it undertook to confer judicial duties on an administrative body? The trial court held against the Commission and declared that the order was invalid. The court of civil appeals affirmed the action of the trial court, but the Supreme Court of Texas reversed the judgment and dismissed the case. The decision established the power of the Commission, pursuant to the terms of H.B. 266, to regulate production in gas fields to protect and adjust correlative rights irrespective of waste. There is no similar statute in Texas relating to oil fields.[102]

(iii) *Allocation of Allowable for Oil Pool on a Reasonable Basis —Rowan and Nichols Cases, Marrs Case, and Humble Case.* The Texas statute provides that the allowable for an oil pool be allocated "among the producers on a reasonable basis."[103] While no more definite standard is given, it is now well established that each operator in Texas is entitled to a fair opportunity to produce or

[102] Corzelius v. Harrell, 179 S.W. 2d 419 (Tex. Civ. App. 3rd, 1944), 143 Tex. 509, 186 S.W. 2d 961 (1945), Note, 24 TEX. L. REV. 97 (Dec. 1945). On the question of the power of a state to regulate production of oil or gas solely for the purpose of adjusting correlative rights, a most interesting case is Republic Nat. Gas Co. v. State of Okla., 198 Okla. 350, 180 P. 2d 1009 (1947). Appeal to the Supreme Court of the United States was dismissed on the ground that the judgment was not final, but the dissenting opinion of Mr. Justice Rutledge, concurred in by Mr. Justice Black, Mr. Justice Murphy, and Mr. Justice Burton, expressed the view that the judgment was final. The fundamental points at issue were also discussed in the dissenting opinion, and it was declared that the state had the power, irrespective of waste, to force a sharing of markets as an incident to a program of affording to each operator an opportunity to produce his share of the oil or gas in the pool. U.S., 68 S. Ct. 972, (1948). The Corzelius case was cited with approval.

[103] VERNON'S CIV. STAT. art. 6049 c, § 7.

receive the recoverable oil in place under his tract, or its equivalent in kind, subject to the reasonable necessities for waste prevention. This is substantially the standard found in the statutes of several other states.[104]

Rowan and Nichols Cases. The Rowan and Nichols Company, claiming that it had not been given such an opportunity with respect to its lease in the East Texas Oil Field, brought suit in a federal district court to enjoin enforcement. There were almost 26,000 wells in the field at that time, and the field allowable was some 522,000 barrels a day. Under the marginal well statute, as construed by the Railroad Commission, marginal wells of the depth of those in that field could not be prorated, so each non-flowing well which could not produce more than 20 barrels a day was permitted to produce at capacity. Non-marginal wells were given a base allowable of 20 barrels, though the formula provided for distribution on a percentage of potential. As a consequence, there was a variation of only 2 or 3 barrels a day between the allowable awarded wells with high potential capacities and wells capable of producing about 20 barrels or less a day. Furthermore, a great number of wells had been drilled as exceptions to the 10 acre spacing rule, resulting in great variations in well densities, although the average density was one well to approximately 5 acres. The marginal well allowances and the 20 barrel non-marginal well base allowable, whether for a 21 barrel well or a 25,000 barrel well, absorbed a major portion of the total field allowable. The applicable proration formula did not take into account the great differences between the amount or the character of acreage upon which each well had been drilled; and in consequence, the densely drilled tracts regardless of reserves were given a substantial advantage. These facts led the trial court[105] and the Circuit Court of Appeals for the Fifth Circuit[106] to declare that the proration orders were invalid as arbitrary and confiscatory. The trial court used this language: ". . . it is sufficient to say that it (the proration formula) takes no account of the difference in the wells, of the richness or thickness of the sand, of the location upon the structure, of the porosity

[104] See note 62 supra.
[105] Rowan and Nichols Oil Co. v. Railroad Comm., 28 F. Supp. 131 (W.D. Tex. 1939).
[106] 107 F. 2d 70 (C.C.A. 5th, 1939).

or permeability of the sand, of the estimated oil reserves, or of the acreage upon which the respective wells are situated. The worst property is raised to the level of the best and the best is lowered to the level of the worst." The Supreme Court of the United States, with three judges dissenting, reversed the decree on the ground that a local state problem was involved, and that "It is not for the federal courts to supplant the Commission's judgment even in the face of convincing proof that a different result would have been better." It was declared that "a state's interest in the conservation and exploitation of a primary natural resource is not to be achieved through assumption by the federal courts of powers plainly outside their province and no less plainly beyond their special competence."

The opinion seemed to say that the federal courts were without power to enjoin such an order, or at the least they ought not to enjoin an order of a state agency unless it was clearly arbitrary, where an adequate court review was afforded in the state courts. The decree was reversed and in effect there was a decision on the merits in favor of the Commission, in spite of the fact findings by the trial court, adopted and approved by the circuit court of appeals, that the order was arbitrary and not supported by the facts.[107] In a later case involving an order of the Commission the decree was reversed, but the cause was remanded with instructions to retain the bill pending the determination of proceedings to be brought with reasonable promptness in the state courts.[108]

In order to avoid the complications resulting from the injunction issued by the trial court against the Commission which would be effective pending appeal of the *Rowan and Nichols* case, a new and somewhat different order was entered by the Commission June 19, 1939. This prompted a second injunction suit by the Rowan and Nichols Company, and similar suit by the Humble Oil and Refining Company. F. W. Fischer also filed suit. All were filed in the United States District Court for the Western District of Texas. Preliminary injunctions were granted in the *Rowan and Nichols* and *Humble* cases. By amendment the suits related to revised

---

[107] Railroad Comm. v. Rowan and Nichols Oil Co., 310 U.S. 573 (1940), amended 311 U.S. 614 (1940).
[108] Railroad Comm. v. Pullman Co., 312 U.S. 496 (1941).

orders of the Commission entered September 11 and 29, 1939, and January 24, 1940. The three cases were tried together on the merits in February 1940, and the court (three judges), in the findings of facts and conclusions of law, found that there was no dispute as to the facts and that the orders were discriminatory, unreasonable, arbitrary, and confiscatory as far as the Rowan and Nichols Company and the Humble Company were concerned. The Commission was enjoined from enforcing the orders against those plaintiffs. Relief was denied to Fischer, and the orders as to him were held valid, because he could show no irreparable injury, inasmuch as it appeared that he was permitted to produce his fair share or more.[109] Being three judge cases, appeals were taken direct to the Supreme Court of the United States by the Commission, except in the *Fischer* case. That Court, by opinion of January 6, 1941 in the *Rowan and Nichols* case (three judges dissenting) reversed the lower court and held in favor of the Commission. A short opinion was written in the *Humble* case. The cases were remanded for dismissal, not to be held on the docket pending proceedings in the state court. Although the three judges who sat in the trial court found that there was no dispute as to the facts and that the facts did not support the Commission's order, the Supreme Court declared that there was conflicting testimony, but it was not a proper function of the federal courts to resolve fact issues in such an instance, contrary to findings of the Commission. It said that to pass on such issues would be "an assumption by the federal courts of powers plainly outside their province and no less plainly beyond their special competence." The opinion said that "whatever rights the state statute may afford are to be pursued in the state courts." [110] The language indicates that the Court intended to recognize in the plaintiffs the right to litigate the questions in the state courts, though the complaints were ordered to be dismissed.

The decisions caused considerable discussion. There was doubt as to the holding of the Court on some points, but the opinions did make plain that the federal courts should not restrain orders

[109] Rowan and Nichols Oil Co. v. Railroad Comm., Humble Oil & Ref. Co. v. Railroad Commission, Fischer v. Smith, 35 F. Supp. 573 (W.D. Tex 1940).

[110] Railroad Comm. v. Rowan & Nichols Oil Co., 311 U.S. 570, (1941); Railroad Comm. v. Humble Oil & Ref. Co., 311 U.S. 578, (1941).

of state agencies when the state courts were empowered to give appropriate relief.[111] The federal courts may still have jurisdiction of causes involving the validity of such orders, either because a federal question is raised or because there is diversity of citizenship, but the Supreme Court has left no doubt of an intention to reverse any decree of a lower federal court which enjoins an order of a state agency if the state courts are available for relief. For practical purposes the doors of the lower federal courts are closed as far as such cases are concerned.[112]

Marrs Case. As might have been anticipated, the next case involving the validity of an order was filed in a state district court. Plaintiffs, as well as certain interveners and defendants who aligned themselves with plaintiffs and were treated as such (all referred to here as plaintiffs), claimed that the orders allocating the field allowable did not give them an opportunity to produce their fair shares of the oil and gas under their lands, but on the contrary the orders discriminated against them in favor of other operators. The trial court, making findings of facts on conflicting evidence, rendered judgment in favor of the plaintiffs and enjoined the enforcement of the orders or of similar orders. The court of civil appeals reversed the trial court and rendered judgment, primarily on the ground that the operating company had not drilled as many wells as other operators, and therefore had not exercised its opportunity to protect itself against drainage to the more densely drilled areas of the field.[113] The Supreme Court of Texas reversed the court of civil appeals and upheld the trial court saying that the proration orders were invalid as to the plaintiffs. The su-

---

[111] Summers, *Does the Regulation of Oil Production Require the Denial of Due Process and the Equal Protection of the Laws?*, 19 TEX. L. REV. 1 (1930); Davis, *Judicial Emasculation of Administrative Action and Oil Proration: Another View,* 19 TEX. L. REV. 29 (1940); Summers, *The Rowan and Nichols Cases,* 13 MISS. L. J. 29 (1941); Hardwicke, *Oil Conservation: Statutes, Administration, and Court Review,* 13 MISS. L. J. 381 (1941), note 15; Belknap, Comment, 39 MICH. L. REV. 438 (1941); Note, 51 YALE L. J. 680 (1942), 26 WASH. U. L. Q. 265 (1941); Hoffman, Comment, 21 TEX. L. REV. 69 (1942).

[112] All doubt on the point was removed by the holdings in the following cases: Railroad Comm. v. Pullman Co., 312 U.S. 496, (1941), discussed 41 COL. L. REV. 925 (1941), 54 HARV. L. REV. 1379 (1941), Note, 50 YALE L. J. 1272 (1941); Burford v. Sun Oil Co., 319 U.S. 315, (1943), discussed Notes, 56 HARV. L. REV. 1162 (1943), 42 MICH. L. REV. 337 (1943).

[113] Railroad Comm. v. Marrs, 161 S.W. 2d 1037 (Tex. Civ. App. 3rd, 1942) *writ granted.*

preme court said that the evidence amply supported the findings
of fact made by the trial court, and that the orders were arbitrary,
discriminatory, and confiscatory as to plaintiffs in that they were
deprived of the opportunity to produce the recoverable oil under
their lands. The court declared that such deprivation took place
as the result of the application of the proration formula which
gave too much value (50 per cent) to mere wells and not enough
to other factors, such as oil in place, pressures, acreage, and productivity. The court held that the plaintiffs had not failed to develop with reasonable diligence their properties, and that there
was no necessity as a waste prevention measure to enforce an allocation order which had the effect of taking the property of plaintiffs for the benefit of other operators in the field.[114]

Humble Case. The last case involving the fairness of an allocation order for a field was the *Humble* case filed in the state court
and tried under procedure and principles approved in the *Marrs*
case. The issues resembled in some respects those which were involved in the *Rowan and Nichols* cases and the *Marrs* case. The
Humble Company and others sought to restrain the enforcement
of the proration or allocation order for the Hawkins Field. The
primary basis for the attack was that the allowables, given under
the proration formula to the numerous small tracts in the area
of the Hawkins townsite, would result in the ultimate uncompensated drainage to that area of millions of barrels of oil from the
tracts located outside the townsite which had been drilled in accordance with the established field spacing rules. Under the formula
a well on one-tenth of an acre in the townsite obtained an allowable
of 46 barrels of oil a day, whereas a well on a tract 200 times as
large, drilled in accordance with the spacing rules on a 20 acre
tract lying outside the townsite area was awarded an allowable of
only twice as much, or 92 barrels a day. The plaintiffs contended
that the proration program to which the Commission was committed would eventually result in the drainage away from their
properties of some 30,000,000 barrels of their oil. While there
was some controversy as to the accuracy of this figure, it was conceded by the court that there would be a substantial amount of
uncompensated excess drainage, and the jury found that the order

[114] Marrs v. Railroad Comm., 142 Tex. 294, 177 S.W. 2d 941 (1944).

would prevent the operating plaintiff "from producing the recoverable oil now in place under its land, or the equivalent in kind of such oil." The trial court held that the order was confiscatory and invalid as to plaintiffs.

The court of civil appeals reversed the judgment and upheld the proration order[115] saying that the proper test of the validity of the proration order was not whether it would prevent any operator from producing the recoverable oil in place beneath his land, but whether it denied an operator "a fair opportunity to produce its recoverable oil," and that in determining whether a fair opportunity had been afforded there were several pertinent factors other than the single factor embodied in the jury finding. Among these other factors, according to the court, was a natural advantage that small tracts have over large tracts at common law when production is unrestricted, and the benefits in which the large tracts share by increases in ultimate recovery resulting from restrictions imposed for the purpose of preventing waste. The principal factor, however, was declared to be the saving of the cost of production accruing to large tracts under the 20 acre spacing pattern and the proration order. Taking these factors into consideration the court said that it was not authorized to strike down the order, since "it has never been held that recoverable reserves constitute the only factor to be considered in determining the validity of a proration order."

The Supreme Court of Texas refused to grant writ of error. It may be observed that the court had just decided the *Trapp* and *Thomas* cases (*to be discussed in the section, Court Review*) holding that, as far as fact issues are concerned, an order of the Commission must be upheld if there is substantial evidence to support it. The holding was a repudiation of its decision two years earlier in the *Marrs* case, where it was said, that when the issue of confiscation is raised, there is a statutory and a constitutional right to test the validity of an order by a trial in which the issues of facts are resolved as in any ordinary case, not by application of the substantial evidence rule. If writ of error was refused on the ground that, applying the rule of the *Trapp* case, there was substantial

---

[115] Railroad Comm. v. Humble Oil and Ref. Co., 193 S.W. 2d 824 (Tex. Civ. App. 3rd, 1946) *writ refused want of error.*

evidence to support facts which in turn would support the reasonableness and non-confiscatory character of the order, then criticism of the action of the Supreme Court of Texas must be based primarily on whether the substantial evidence rule was the correct rule, or whether there was substantial evidence in support of the order.

If, however, the Supreme Court of Texas, by refusing to grant the application for a writ of error, approved the reasoning and statements of the court of civil appeals, especially those observations which plainly are dicta, then justification for its action may fairly be questioned, for the opinion of the court of civil appeals contains what seem to be novel statements and conclusions.[116] For instance, the court of civil appeals conceded that, as a result of the allocation order, very substantial quantities of oil would be drained from plaintiffs' lands to be produced from wells of others in the townsite area. There was no finding that such a result was required to prevent waste which could not be otherwise reasonably prevented. The court, in justifying this advantage in favor of the townsite area, observed that small tracts had a natural advantage at common law when there was no restriction on production. The accuracy of that statement as a fact may be questioned, for it is common knowledge that in dog-eat-dog days the operation of offset wells on all sides of a small tract gave it no unusual advantage, if any at all. But even if it were true that a small tract often had an advantage in the absence of restriction, does it legally follow that when restriction is imposed and the right of self-help denied that the small tract must (as a matter of law) be given a much higher relative allowable than that applicable to larger tracts? If so, the owner of a small tract must be given opportunity to recover much more than the recoverable oil in place under his tract or its equivalent, and the owners of larger tracts must furnish the oil.

The court of civil appeals in effect declared that controlled spacing and production in the Hawkins Field reduced the cost of drilling and increased ultimate recovery and profits to the

---

[116] McIllhany, Note, 24 TEX. L. REV. 519 (1946); Walker, *Developments in the Law of Oil and Gas in Texas During the War Years—A Resume,* 25 TEX. L. REV. 1 (1946).

benefit of all the operators; consequently, the allocation order could legally take away some of the benefits that would accrue to the owners of larger tracts with fewer wells on them, and increase the benefits to the owners of smaller more densely drilled tracts, even though the dense drilling could have been avoided by pooling the small tracts. Surely, the soundness of that holding may be questioned. Another statement in the opinion of the court of civil appeals needs discussion. Starting from the observation that the spacing rule contemplates that the owner of a small tract whatever its size, will be authorized to drill one well on the tract (if the tract was not segregated to get an exception under a spacing rule, or if it was not segregated after the spacing rule was entered) the court then said that it seemed to follow that the allowable for the tract "cannot be cut down to the point where his well would no longer produce . . . nor below the point where it could not be drilled and operated at a reasonable profit." There was no suggestion that the rule would apply only when the operation of the well was necessary to prevent waste. It does not appear that any such situation was presented in the *Humble* case, so it may rightly be assumed that the Supreme Court of Texas did not approve those statements by the court of civil appeals. It is enough to express grave doubt of the soundness of the statements by the court of civil appeals without setting down the course of reasoning, which must be obvious anyway.

The *Humble* case was the last decided by the appellate courts in which an attack was made on an order allocating production.

(3) Court Review

In spite of much litigation it was pointed out in the 1938 monograph that several fundamental issues involving review by state and federal courts of orders of the Railroad Commission of Texas entered pursuant to the conservation statutes remained to be settled. Many cases were there discussed in which the federal courts, recognizing jurisdiction either because of diversity of citizenship or the existence of a federal question (usually the constitutional question of confiscation) had made fact findings as in an ordinary case, and had not hesitated to enjoin the orders of the Commission. No doubt this prompted the Rowan and Nichols Oil Company to file suit in a federal district court, seeking an injunction on the ground that the orders for the East Texas Field were arbitrary and resulted in an unwarranted confiscation of the property of the Company. The trial court so held. Pending appeal the Commission revised its order, whereupon the Rowan and Nichols Company and also the Humble Oil and Refining Company filed injunction suits in the federal district court. Temporary injunction was sought so three judges heard the cases. Again the trial court, finding that the evidence without conflict showed that the proration program was arbitrary, discriminatory, and confiscatory, enjoined its enforcement. Both of the cases eventually reached the Supreme Court of the United States. Those cases have already been treated in some detail. The Court in both cases reversed the decrees of the lower courts and announced the rule that the federal courts should refuse to enjoin orders of the Commission when the state courts were available to give appropriate relief. Thereafter, it seemed futile to seek relief in the federal courts.

The state courts had been rather busy with well spacing or Rule 37 cases even before the Supreme Court of the United States closed the doors of the lower federal courts. These cases, as well as later ones, almost always presented the question whether an order was invalid, as being unreasonable, arbitrary, and confiscatory. The general equity powers of the state district court were invoked. Jurisdiction was also asserted by virtue of the court review section of the 1935 Conservation Act, reading: "Any interested person affected by the conservation laws of this State relating to crude petroleum oil or natural gas, and the waste thereof, including this Act, or by any rule, regulation or order made or promulgated by the Commission thereunder and who may be dissatisfied therewith, shall have the right to file a suit in a Court of competent jurisdiction in Travis County, Texas, and not elsewhere, against the Commission, or the members thereof, as defendants, to test the validity of said laws, rules, regulations or orders. Such suit shall be advanced for trial and be determined as expeditiously as possible and no postponement thereof or continuance shall be granted except for reasons deemed imperative by the Court. In all such trials, the burden of proof shall be upon the party complaining of such laws, rule, regulation or order, and such laws, rule, regulation or order so complained of shall be deemed prima facie valid." [117] There were cases which said that the issues of fact should be disposed of by an application of the substantial evidence rule, and there were cases (such as the *Marrs* case) which held that the substantial evidence rule was not applicable, and that the statute above quoted provided that the court should find the facts as in an ordinary suit. The *Marrs* case and others held that there was a constitutional right, when confiscation was involved, to have a court make an independent determination of the fact issues, as the court was not bound by the actual or the presumed findings of the Commission, even though supported by substantial evidence introduced at the trial. The important conflicting decisions are mentioned in the *Trapp* and *Thomas* cases in which the Supreme Court of Texas undertook to settle the conflict. In those cases the plaintiffs sought to annul orders of the Commission granting permits to Trapp and Thomas to drill wells as exceptions to the spacing rule for the East Texas Field. The Supreme Court of Texas held that the substantial evidence rule should be applied, and that the trial court should not make independent determination of fact issues. [118] Indeed, the opinion was interpreted to mean that if a witness gave testimony which, if true, would support the order as far as facts were concerned, then the courts must accept such evidence as substantial evidence. [119]

The court in the *Hawkins* case, [120] also involving Rule 37 in the East Texas Field, admitted that the opinions had been so understood and it clarified its viewpoint. This language appears: ". . . the application for writ of error filed herein in behalf of the Commission suggests misunderstanding or uncertainty as to the meaning of the substantial evidence rule and as to the scope of judicial review in a suit to test the validity of an order of the Commission

[117] Tex. Acts 1935, c. 76, § 14; Vernon's Civ. Stat. art. 6049 c § 8.
[118] Trapp v. Shell Oil Co., 145 Tex. 323, 198 S.W. 2d 424 (1946); Thomas v. Stanolind Oil and Gas Co., 145 Tex. 270, 198 S.W. 2d 420 (1946). Chief Justice Alexander dissented.
[119] 10 Tex. Bar J. 238 (1947), the report of the Committee on Administrative Law, State Bar of Texas.
[120] Hawkins v. Texas Co., Tex. , 209 S.W. 2d 338 (1948), Justice Simpson dissenting, Justice Hart disqualified and not sitting, and Justice Garwood not participating.

filed pursuant to Section 14 of Chapter 76, Acts Regular Session, 44th Legislature (Section 8, Article 6049c, Vernon's Annotated Civil Statutes). That application, quoting from the dissenting opinion in the Trapp case, above cited, states in substance that the rule should be and is that in the trial of a case like this, as soon as a single witness testifies to facts which would sustain the permit, it will become useless for the court to proceed further, for regardless of the evidence to the contrary, the court will be powerless to do otherwise than to sustain the permit. The substantial evidence rule does not mean that.

"Repeatedly in the above cited decisions and in other decisions the court, in making a brief statement of the scope of judicial review of the facts in a suit filed under Section 8 of Article 6049c to test the validity of an order of the Railroad Commission, has said that the finding of the Commission will be sustained by the court if it is *reasonably* supported by substantial evidence, meaning evidence introduced in court. The word 'reasonably' has been deliberately used in the statement and its use gives to the judicial review a broader scope than it would have if *some* substantial evidence were regarded sufficient of itself to sustain the Commission's order. It is for the court to determine as a matter of law the reasonableness of the support afforded by substantial evidence. In making its decision of this question the court examines and takes into consideration all of the evidence, the entire record . . . It does not look merely to the evidence offered by one of the parties, or to the testimony of one or two witnesses, and sustain the Commission's order if that evidence or testimony can be regarded as substantially supporting the order. In that procedure there would be no real review of the factual basis for the Commission's order, and no trial in court. It clearly appears from the language of Section 8 of Article 6049c that there must be a trial in court of the suit brought to test the validity of the Commission's order. This, according to the decisions above cited, does not mean a trial as of the ordinary civil suit in which the court makes its own findings based upon a preponderance of the evidence before it. Nevertheless, it means that there shall be a trial and in that trial, in so far as the facts are concerned, the court determines from all of the evidence before it, the entire record, whether the Commission's action is or is not reasonably supported by substantial evidence. The foregoing is a reiteration of the explanation of the substantial evidence rule made in Railroad Commission v. Shell Oil Co., the Trem Carr case, 139 Tex. 66, 161 S.W. 2d 1022, which was quoted with approval in the Trapp case above cited, . . ." Applying the rule to the facts in that case, the court held that there was no substantial evidence to justify the exception, and though there was much testimony about more-wells-more-oil this was really an attack on the rule itself—an argument for closer spacing than that provided for by the rule. It was also observed that though there was evidence that additional oil would be recovered if the well applied for should be drilled, it did not appear that the amount was substantial enough to justify the exception, since it was shown that there were already 9 wells on the 21.6 acre tract, or a well to each 2.3 acres, when the rule contemplated only one well to 10 acres.

The present status of court review as to the points under discussion may be briefly stated as follows: (a) any interested person may file suit in the District Court of Travis County to test the validity of the conservation statutes or of any rule, regulation, or order entered pursuant thereto; (b) the record of the hearing before the Commission on which the order is based is not the evidence which the trial court considers, unless there be a question of procedural due process; [121] (c) evidence is introduced in court as in any ordinary trial and to that extent the trial is de novo; (d) the trial court does not resolve fact issues as in an ordinary trial, but "does not have to consider incredible, perjured or unreasonable testimony because such evidence is not substantial;" [122] (e) with respect to fact issues the substantial evidence rule applies, but the courts should consider all the evidence which is credible, non-perjured, and reasonable in determining whether the order is or is not reasonably supported by substantial evidence, and *reasonably supported* means more than just *some* substantial evidence, or a scintilla of evidence; and (f) appeal is specifically authorized.

CONCLUDING REMARKS

1. The power of the state to regulate the production of oil and gas to prevent waste or to protect correlative rights irrespective of waste is now well established. Emphasis has shifted, however,

[121] See note 36 *supra.*
[122] Trapp v. Shell Oil Co., 145 Tex. 323, 198 S.W. 2d 424, 440 (1946).

from controversies over the power to regulate to those involving the fairness of the regulation.

2. Prices for oil and gas are now at relatively high levels. Most of the pools in the state and in other states are producing at about their maximum efficient rates, and the total just about equals the demand. The economic incentive to find new pools and to increase the ultimate recovery from old ones is stronger than ever.

3. The fundamental provisions of the conservation statutes are reasonably well settled, though further legislation may be necessary with respect to the making and carrying out of agreements relating to cycling, water flooding, and all other forms of secondary recovery operations or other joint operations reasonably necessary to prevent waste and to protect correlative rights.

4. Public officials and members of the oil industry are intensely interested in doing a good job of waste prevention, and the one time reluctance to sponsor or take part in unit operation programs has passed, for in some circumstances, such as cycling and other forms of secondary recovery operations, and the prevention of waste of casinghead-gas, unit or joint operations are usually necessary if the program is to be effective and to protect correlative rights.

5. Whether further efforts will be made to revise the court, review provision of the statutes depends in part upon the wisdom displayed by the Railroad Commission of Texas in exercising its broad power of protecting the correlative rights of the operators, and in part upon the courage and wisdom displayed by the courts in applying the rule.

CHAPTER 32

Utah, 1892–1948

~~

Until 1948 there were no important discoveries of oil or gas in Utah,[1] and the legislation relating to oil and gas is meagre. Utah has no special laws which deal with the conservation of oil on privately owned lands; indeed, only a trace of conservation law is present at all. That is found in a statute passed in 1909 [2] (which has not been amended and which is now the law) requiring that one drilling a well on lands producing or containing petroleum or natural gas must "incase such well in such manner as to effectually exclude and prevent all water from reaching" oil or gas bearing sand. This statute calls for the plugging of all abandoned wells to exclude water from reaching oil or gas sands or strata and to prevent the escape of oil or gas.

An attempt at conservation may be spelled out for state-owned lands from a statute originally dating from 1896 [3] which provides that "each lease shall contain covenants . . . that no waste shall be committed on the land . . ." No definition of waste is included.

Legislation requiring the confinement of gas in wells from which the gas is not utilized is older than statehood.[4] This 1892 statute, unamended, is still upon the books. It also calls for the plugging of abandoned gas wells and sets out in great detail the method to be employed.

Extended lease acquisition activity in eastern Utah, result-

HENRY D. MOYLE, WRITER; David L. McKay, Adviser. (See app. B.)

[1] The U.S. Geo. Sur. has recently published a listing of all wells drilled for oil and gas in Utah.

[2] Utah Laws 1909, c. 115; UTAH CODE ANN. §§ 59–0–5, 59–0–6 (1943).

[3] Utah Laws 1896, c. LXXX, 33. A similar act appears in Utah Laws 1925, c. 31, § 5602; UTAH CODE ANN. § 86–1–46 (1943).

[4] Utah Terr. Laws 1892, c. XXXIX; UTAH CODE ANN. § 59–0–1 to 59–0–4 (1943). Not all of the original act appears in the codification.

ing from the production in the nearby Rangely Field in Colorado, brought the first attempt at conservation legislation in Utah. A bill was offered in the State Senate in 1947 and referred to committee where it died. At the time the bill was introduced, one of the state bureaus much in disfavor politically was preparing an oil conservation bill, which it was rumored granted large powers to it and took away the prerogatives of the land board. The tax feature of this measure was deemed objectionable. Most of the protestants felt the bill was premature in establishing an administrative agency, an elaborate set of rules and procedural sections, when no oil had been produced and there was no waste to curb.

The State Land Board of Utah has never passed any rules or regulations relating to the conservation of oil and gas.

CHAPTER 33

Virginia, 1939–1948

~✍~

The production of oil and natural gas in Virginia has been so slight and so recent that it might be said there is no legal history of conservation of oil and gas in Virginia. The statement would have been true prior to the 1948 session of the Virginia State Legislature, but that session enacted measures which justify brief mention.

Natural gas has been produced in small quantities in Virginia since 1939, annual production running from a minimum of 55,-000 MCF in 1946 to a maximum of 106,000 MCF in 1941. Production in 1947 was 64,000 MCF. The only commercial production is in Scott and Washington Counties in southwestern Virginia, though there has been some drilling in Rockingham County in the northwest, and in other counties in the southwestern part of the state. In 1943 production of oil from two wells in Lee County amounted to 2000 barrels for the year, which stepped up to 3000 barrels in 1944 and 4000 barrels from three wells in 1945. In 1946 six additional wells were drilled and production arose to 22,848 barrels. This drilling extended into 1947. Though precise production reports are not required, the State Geological Survey estimates 1947 production at between 65,000 and 80,000 barrels. Activity continues. All of this production comes from Lee County in the extreme southwest portion of the state in an area near Rose Hill. A substantial flow was encountered in one well in Buchanon County, but there has as yet been no commercial production as the well was capped pending further drilling and the construction of a pipe line.

Until the production of oil increased in Lee County in 1946,

THOMAS J. MICHIE; WRITER; William M. McGill, Adviser. (See app. B.)

there was no need for legislation on the subject and none was found on the statute books. The first regular session of the legislature, subsequent to increased production, was the session of 1948 at which several bills affecting the production of oil and gas were enacted. The most important measure adopted was Senate Joint Resolution No. 21, establishing a commission consisting of two members of the State Senate, three members of the House of Delegates, the state geologist and the Chairman of the Virginia Conservation Commission.[1] The group is instructed to make a thorough investigation into leasing and exploration for development, production, utilization, and conservation or protection of crude oil and natural gas in Virginia, and such measures of regulation and conservation as it deems proper. It is to report its recommendations to the next session of the general assembly. An appropriation of only $500 was made for the work, which throws doubt on the value of the results that may be accomplished.

Other measures enacted are summarized as follows: (1) S.B. No. 137 requires operators and lessees to plug all dry or abandoned oil and gas wells in a manner elaborately prescribed, (2) S.B. No. 149 provides that all leases shall contain a provision requiring the lessee to drill an offset to any well on adjoining land within 350 feet of the lease, (3) S.B. No. 237 provides that all leases of oil and gas shall be construed as if they required the lessee to drill an offset well to any well on adjoining land within 350 feet of the lease, (4) H.B. No. 226 makes it unlawful to permit the escape of crude oil or natural gas when it is reasonably possible to prevent the same, (5) S.B. No. 239 adds a new section to the Code of Virginia, Section 830 a, requiring persons drilling commercially for water, oil or gas to report certain geological information and production records to the State Geological Survey. As none of these bills carry emergency clauses, they go into effect 90 days after adjournment of the general assembly on June 29, 1948.

[1] The Commission to Study Oil and Natural Gas consists of the following members: House Members, Vernon C. Smith, Grundy, J. L. Camblos, Big Stone Gap, R. Dhu Coleman, Gate City; Senate Members, Lloyd M. Robinette, Jonesville, Harry C. Stuart, Elk Garden; State Geologist, William M. McGill; Chairman, Virginia Conservation Commission, William A. Wright.

CHAPTER 34

Washington, 1933–1948

Like its neighbors, California and Oregon, the State of Washington has evinced more than passing interest in the promulgation of oil and gas conservation measures since 1933. Periodically, proposals have been offered in the Washington legislature designed to authorize the Director of Conservation and Development of the state to take charge of the conservation of oil and gas, and as often as these acts have been proffered, they have failed.

A bill[1] introduced into the 1933 session of the legislature invested the director of conservation and development with powers to issue rules and regulations governing the casing, drilling operation, and abandonment of oil and gas wells within Washington. Section 1 made it the administrator's responsibility to prevent waste of oil and gas and laid an affirmative duty on the operators to abide by the statute and rules. Twenty-five per cent of all the monies paid into the state treasury for rentals and royalties from leases and wells on state lands would be placed to the credit of an oil and gas conservation fund and used to pay the expenses of administration. Violation of the law was a misdemeanor. The bill was read February 16, 1933 in the house chamber and referred to the Committee on Mines and Mining, where it died. Six years later, again at the request of the department, an act[2] was offered in the Washington State Senate to control conservation of petroleum. Although many portions of this proposal were similar to those statutes enjoying a vogue in 1939, there were interesting variations. The law clothed the director of conservation and development with administration of its terms, provided extensive definition and prohibition of waste,

BLAKELY M. MURPHY, WRITER. (See app. B.)
[1] HB No. 363, Wash. Legis. 1933.
[2] SB No. 169, Wash. Legis. 1939.

including the normal statements relative to surface and underground wastage, together with a market demand limitation of production. Section 16 gave the administrator authority to examine "the reports, estimates, findings of fact, or similar documents or findings of the United States Bureau of Mines, or of any other department or agency of the United States government, or of any bureau or agency under an interstate compact to which the State of Washington is a party" when considering the element of market demand, and provided that these materials be taken as prima facie correct. Section 27 read where lands were owned or controlled by the state, that is, "state, granted, school, tide and shore lands, river beds and lake beds, and . . . lands sold by the state and the minerals therein and thereunder reserved . . . adjoining to any private lands" and had in common with them an accumulation of petroleum underneath, the director and the commissioner of public lands under joint jurisdiction given by the statute were named to apply the law. The bill, offered by Senator Holt January 30, 1939 was read a first and second time, and then referred to the Committee on Mines and Mining where it was not reported out.

At the 30th regular session of the Washington legislature in 1947, the latest of the unsuccessful measures was presented. This bill,[3] as the 1939 enactment, prohibited waste although its definition fell far short of that formerly proposed. Administration was again placed with the director of conservation and development through the agency of "professionally and practically qualified members of the staff or agents of the division of mines and geology." Section 5 limited the taking of natural gas to market demand and provided that where necessary to prorate production, a well might produce no more proportionately than other wells in the pool, to the end that no person gain an unfair or unequitable advantage over his fellow producers. The director was empowered to determine the reasonable amount of oil needed to satisfy consumptive demand, which could be produced without waste, to classify the pools according to their abilities to furnish oil without underground waste, and to distribute the allowables among such pools in a manner that prevented waste, impairment of correlative rights, and unreasonable discrimination. When 75 per cent of

[3] SB No. 178, Wash. Legis. 1947.

the owners of a pool approved, the agency could require unit operation. The director assessed against the parties involved the costs incurred in the performance of his duties, hearings, or applications. All other proposals in the enactment were those commonly found in the less comprehensive drafts of conservation laws circulated in 1947. The bill, introduced February 8, 1947, was read the first and second time and referred to the Committee on Judiciary which treated it, as did the Committee on Mines and Mining in past days, by failing to report it out.

CHAPTER 35

West Virginia, 1826–1948

The story of legislation, administrative regulation, and judicial interpretation in respect to conservation of oil and gas in West Virginia is brief. A recital of the development of the oil and gas industry in the state is essential for understanding why there is so little history. West Virginia pioneered in the oil and gas business. Natural gas seepages and indications of petroleum were observed at the salt licks and burning springs near the present city of Charleston, Kanawha County, prior to 1785, and by 1826 or earlier natural gas was used as a fuel to recover salt from brines, and some petroleum was produced and marketed. About 1835 natural springs and oil seepages with salt brines were found at Burning Springs near the confluence of the Hughes and Little Kanawha Rivers, but not until 1859 was substantial drilling done in the area. This development coincided with the completion of the Drake well. There was a great oil boom along the Eureka-Volcano-Burning Springs anticline on the Oil Break's general route. This area was the sole West Virginia producing region to 1888. In the period of some thirty years production aggregated 4,700,000 barrels (including about 300,000 barrels destroyed in 1863 by the Confederate States Army which wrecked nearly all the wells and equipment). Most early production was from the First and Second Cow Run sands of the Dunkard Series. With the promulgation about 1888 of the anticlinal theory of oil and gas accumulation,[1] the industry

KEMBLE WHITE, WRITER; Arthur B. Koontz, H. J. Wagner, Paul H. Price, Advisers. (See app. B.)

[1] Mention must be made of the invaluable services rendered the industry, the people of the state and the country by Dr. Israel Charles White, first State Geologist, head of the Geological Survey, and undoubted author of the anticlinal theory of oil and gas accumulation. The 1888 development came largely from his advice. Dr. White observed with great distress the utter waste of gas in that period and in frequent public addresses called attention to it. In 1908 he was chosen by Theodore

grew rapidly as quantities of oil and gas in the Appalachian area of western Pennsylvania stimulated the belief that these producing horizons extended from Mason and Dixon's Line southwesterly across western West Virginia to the Kentucky border. The first important development in the state at this period was in Monongalia and Marion Counties, based upon the tentative location of the Doll's Run-Mannington anticline. Oil production increased from 1888 to 1900 reaching a crest of 16,000,000 barrels. Since then it has declined steadily, slowed between 1909 and 1913 by discovery of substantial pools in Roane, Kanawha, and Lincoln Counties. West Virginia in 1900 accounted for almost one-fourth of the American production of petroleum. Current production does not exceed 2,500,000 barrels from 16,000 producing wells (an average of over $\frac{4}{10}$ths barrel daily per well).

The story of the production of natural gas follows a different course. In the 1888 development large amounts of natural gas were discovered in oil sands. Later drilling demonstrated great volumes of natural gas were in horizons not producing oil. Early operators interested in the discovery of oil, not natural gas, did not know how to conserve gas. Its enormous waste can be accounted for somewhat in the light of the domestic economy. Some gas was utilized for fuel and light in connection with oil operations or furnished for domestic use to small nearby communities, but there was no local industry for a market. The important state interests were agriculture, timbering, coal mining, and railroad building, so the market had to be found elsewhere. West Virginia had insufficient capital resources, engineering and management skill needed to send gas to distant areas. Moving of the glass industry to the state for a cheap fuel supplied a local market which minimized waste. Completion of the interstate gas lines and the development of a big market for natural gas in eastern Ohio and western Pennsylvania resulted in prompt efforts by the industry to stop or lessen waste. Sudden depletion of natural gas reserves during World War I convinced the industry everything possible should be done

Roosevelt to make the address on mineral fuels at the first White House Conference of Governors and his speech, The Waste of Our Fuel Resources, was praised in the press. He should be considered the father of conservation. The principal reason there has been so little governmental action in West Virginia is that he, by reason of his scientific knowledge and unusual energy, carried great prestige and moral leadership in the voluntary conservation movement.

to eliminate waste against the day when it might be without adequate reserves. Fortunately, the discovery in 1936 of gas in the Oriskany sand in Kanawha and Jackson Counties, made available large volumes of gas (without which in World War II grave consequences might have ensued). Recent finds of substantial gas reserves in Wyoming County indicate West Virginia will continue to rank as a gas producing state. Approximately 16,000 dry gas wells now operate, out of a total of some 32,000 gas and casinghead oil gas wells, indicating the abandonment of about 38,000 wells.

There has been little effort on the part of West Virginia or its political subdivisions to prevent waste, except by court decision and the action of the Public Service Commission in enforcing its rules and regulations. Shortly after its creation in 1913, the Commission [2] adopted a rule reading: "All practices in the production, distribution, consumption and use of natural gas which are wasteful, such as flambeau lights and the like, are hereby expressly prohibited," modified now thus: "All practices in the production, distribution, consumption and use of natural gas which are wasteful are hereby prohibited." [3] Reduction of waste, and the conservation of oil and gas and by-products have been accomplished by the voluntary efforts of the industry cooperating with the Geological Survey, [4] the Public Service Commission, and the Department of Mines, [5] as those agencies were created and given direct or persuasive powers respecting conservation.

THE CONSERVATION PRINCIPLE IN WEST VIRGINIA

Since the term conservation with respect to petrolic natural resources is of modern usage, it is desirable that the subject be dis-

[2] The Public Service Commission was created by Acts W. Va. 1913, c. 24 as amend. by Acts W. Va. 1935, c. 115.

[3] Pub. Ser. Comm. W. Va., 27th Ann. Rep., Revised Rules and Regulations for Government of Gas Utilities etc., Order 111–B, 110 (1940).

[4] The Survey was created in 1897 to examine the geological formations of West Virginia with special reference to their products, the prevention of their waste and the utilization of their by-products. W. Va. Code Ann. c. 29, art. 2, § 5 (1943).

[5] The Department of Mines is organized as a part of the state government and headed by a chief appointed by the governor with the consent of the West Virginia Senate. Acts W.V. 1929, c. 86 § 12; W. Va. Code Ann. § 2475 (1943), should be consulted for departmental authority.

cussed in terms of waste. Conservation of oil and gas in West Virginia has always been approached from the standpoint of waste, defined in the suggested oil and gas law prepared by the Interstate Oil Compact Commission. In earlier days there was an enormous waste of natural gas classified as follows: (a) permitting gas from wells to blow into the air, (b) line loss, (c) use of inefficient burners and appliances by free gas consumers, (d) failure to recover gasoline, propane, butane, and oil and gas by-products, (e) manufacture of carbon black, (f) economic waste in drilling excessive wells, (g) non-use of unitization agreements, (h) lack of maximum utilization of secondary recovery agencies, such as air, gas, or water.

The great waste from permitting gas to blow into the air was not corrected by legislation, but by members of the industry who risked large capital investments in transportation and shut-in gas wells until the product could be marketed. The increase in market value arising from the establishment of markets and adequate pipe line facilities demonstrated the financial advantage in stopping waste. There has not been an open well blowing gas into the air, within the last thirty-five years or longer, with the exception of isolated wells improperly cased and tubed or abandoned and plugged.

To hold down line loss, the Public Service Commission requires metering of all gas sold, purchased, or used; meter readings furnish information to ascertain the volume of gas produced. Excessive line loss has a direct bearing upon rates and adequacy of service. The Commission has been especially active in reducing waste, which is difficult as certain utilities have antiquated plants, small production, old lines, and an unfortunate capital structure with small financial resources. In larger utilities there has been loyal cooperation with the Commission in cutting down line loss.

More than forty years ago substantial units of the industry put forth unusual exertions to prevent waste of natural gas by free gas consumers and excessive use through inefficient burners. They communicated with practically every free gas consumer, offering to inspect gas lines and burners, suggest improvements, and install free of cost Welsbach burners for flambeau lights. While there was cordial cooperation between free consumers and producers, numerous injunctions were awarded against those who persisted in the extravagant and wasteful use of natural gas. Three cases reached the West Virginia Supreme Court of Appeals. In the *Hall* [6] case the court held the free gas clause required the consumer to use gas in his dwelling economically; that he might have one outside light within the curtilage but that it must be an enclosed or economic burner to prevent wasteful or extravagant use. The court held, in the *Harbert* [7] case, the free gas clause was a covenant running with the land and defined the obligation of a producer saying: "As before stated, defendant is interested only in the quantity consumed. It is bound to furnish gas for one dwelling house only; and has a right to demand that plaintiff keep his pipe lines and appliances in good repair and use a closed light on the outside with a Welsbach or some other approved burner in order to prevent needless waste." The *Richardson* [8] decision was one wherein a gas company sought to meter gas consumption under the free gas clause; the consumer objecting to the installation, the utility filed a bill to restrain interference with putting in and maintaining a meter. The court expressly upheld the right of the Public Service Commission to adopt regulations requiring maintenance of meters to measure free gas. Since these three cases, handed down thirty years ago, wasteful or excessive use of gas by free consumers has been minimized.

Much casinghead-gas earlier blew into the air and all gasoline from these wells that accumulated in the lines wasted. A method of gasoline disposal was to establish drips in low places, and periodically blow the gasoline and liquid over the land, not only wasting the gasoline and natural gas, but seriously damaging the land. As knowledge of gasoline developed, drip gasoline was collected in small drums and hauled to a central market. But it was a nuisance in the lines of no economic value, until the arrival of the automobile. With the perfection of the compression process to recover gasoline from casinghead-gas wells, the entire oil producing industry began to save gasoline. There was some delay due to the fact that original leases made no provision for gasoline or the payment of a royalty therefor, and it was necessary for the lessees or producers to obtain casinghead-gas contracts from lawful owners; these were to an extent unitization agreements. Recovery of gaso-

[6] Hall v. Phila. Co., 72 W. Va. 573; 78 S.E. 755 (1913).
[7] Harbert v. Hope Nat. Gas. Co., 76 W. Va. 207, 84 S.E. 770 (1915).
[8] Pitts. & W. Va. Gas Co. v. Richardson, 84 W. Va. 413, 100 SE 220 (1919).

line from dry gas by the absorption process did not occur until 1913, when the Hope Natural Gas Company installed the world's first plant in its Hastings Station, Wetzel County. Successful operations there were followed by the construction of similar, but usually smaller, plants at practically all important gas compressor stations in West Virginia.

Manufacture of carbon black from natural gas constituted a useful industry, established in the state shortly after large volumes of dry gas were produced, indicating huge dry gas reserves. Gas was used in these plants by reducing rock pressure to near open flow at the consumption point, which rapidly reduced rock pressure over the entire field. This prejudiced the producers who relied upon rock pressures to deliver their gas into transportation lines against line pressures of 300 to 400 pounds. Producing companies and the utilities purchasing gas were forced to install compressor stations. In view of this manifest waste of rock pressure, one or more of the larger gas utilities negotiated with the carbon black people to take over their production, thereby eliminating rock pressure dissipation. The first of these properties, acquired more than thirty years ago, necessitated the abandonment of the carbon black plant. Successive transactions obtained all other plants and the last carbon black manufacture terminated in 1923.

The question of economic waste covers a broad area which includes excessive drilling,[9] loss of reservoir energy by waste of gas from oil wells, and the end use of gas. In the pioneer industry of oil and gas, conducted exclusively by private enterprise absent state regulation, it is not surprising that such drilling occurred. Thousands of dry holes were drilled in West Virginia; it cannot be said this drilling was too great as it was the only practical way to discover or prove the absence of oil or gas. Had these great volumes of gas found in oil bearing sands been shut-in and retained as reservoir energy to produce oil, much more oil would have come from existing wells. With this waste of gas, production declined rapidly, and producers were required to pump almost every well. The value of reservoir energy was not appreciated. In the older fields too many

[9] Preston, *Regulation of the Natural Gas Industry*, 45 W. Va. L. Q. 257 (1939) says that everyone knows an unnecessary well when he sees it, unless, it is his own and he gains an advantage over his neighbor by drilling it. See Williams, *Conservation of Mineral Resources; A Brief Survey*, 47 W. Va. L. Q. 247 (1941).

gas wells were drilled and there was distinct economic waste, but then materials were cheap and intangible costs comparatively low. What appeared to be great economic waste must be considered in the light of subsequent demands. Illustration is found in what was called excessive drilling to the Oriskany sand. In places there was one well to some 75 acres, when it was considered that one well could recover over a period of years all the gas underlying 200 to 300 acres. In the Oriskany Field the economic loss was the intangible expense. Pipe and material used have a salvage value after plugging equal to their original cost.

UNITIZATION AGREEMENTS

Unitization agreements are useful to minimize excessive drilling and economic loss. They are executed and operations conducted thereunder where the producers and the royalty owners can reach agreements. There is an occasional royalty owner who absolutely refuses to join a unitization agreement except upon unreasonable terms. This retards development and gives rise to controversies in respect to drainage, the ultimate consequence being that persons declining to cooperate suffer. High cost of drilling, even to shallow sands, encourages use of these agreements. No West Virginia legislative action would be of value, as it would cause years of litigation respecting its constitutionality.

SECONDARY RECOVERY

Secondary recovery agencies are in the conservation interest. Air and gas have been used in older fields resulting in production which otherwise would have been unrecoverable. More than half of the oil-casinghead-gas wells are owned by six operators; the remaining wells are operated by 500 or more independent operators, many of whom are interested in dry gas production. Neither air nor gas is employed as a secondary force in the latter's wells because of economic factors and operating conditions. Many of these wells have existed forty to fifty years, and each produces small amounts of oil. They are in poor operating condition, and little is known about their sands, or whether financial benefit would accrue from utilization of air and gas drives. Any area marked out for these forces requires that all wells be in first class condition as well as an investment in compressing station power financed on a considerable scale. Experienced operators conclude that air and gas are inadequate to recover substantial parts of the remaining oil. The water flood is effectively used to a very limited extent in West Virginia. There are about six water floods operating; only one has been in action long enough to offer favorable indication of its success. Several floods have been carried on for two or three years without beneficial consequences. Producers hope that after further study and effort, the floods will increase production. To reach this aim the industry unanimously asked the legislature to appropriate funds for the establishment of a petroleum and gas research bureau at West Virginia University. Money was voted and the agency is diligently at work reviewing, collecting, and studying data, well cores and cuttings, their relationship to deposition and structure, and the porosity and permeability of the producing formations.[10]

THE LEGISLATIVE AND JUDICIAL HISTORY

The Act of 1891 [11] required that gas from unutilized wells be shut-in, authorized adjoining owners to enter and shut-in gas wasted from adjacent wells, provided briefly for casing and plugging of wells, and prescribed penalties for violation. This statute was never construed by the Supreme Court of Appeals of West Virginia and apparently no suit was ever instituted by the state or any person to enforce its provisions. The Act of 1897 amended the prior law by prescribing more definitely a method of casing and plugging wells, defining and providing remedies with respect to waste.[12] So far as is

---

[10] W. Va. Univ. Bull. Series 47, no. 7 (Jan. 1947). W. Va. Univ. Research Bull. No. 21. The first number contains an interesting discussion of these problems.
[11] Acts W. Va. 1891, c. 106; W. Va. Code Ann. § 2473, 2477–8, 2480 (1943). An Act of 1871, Acts W. Va. 1871, c. 126; W. Va. Rev. St. vol. 2, c. 143 (1879) gave control of oil wells to an inspector who was appointed by the Judge of the Circuit Court after application by five or more citizens of a county. His duties called for inspection of wells to determine whether or not these were "cased, seed bagged, plugged or otherwise made secure." Upon application of landowners or lessees within one mile of an uncased well for casing the Inspector might enter and perform the work. All wells drilled to a depth of six hundred feet or more were required to be cased.
[12] Acts W. Va. 1897, c. 58; W. Va. Code Ann. § 2464, 2473, 2477–80 (1943).

known, that Act was never before our court, except in the *Atkinson* case,[13] which held that an action for damages would lie, either under the common law or under the statute, at the suit of an adjacent owner whose gas estate was prejudiced by waste of gas from an abandoned adjoining gas well. The Drilling and Plugging Statute (the Act of 1929) [14] was passed to provide: "For the safe development and operation of oil and gas wells through workable coal seams by regulating the locating, drilling, casing, plugging and abandonment of natural gas and petroleum wells, and coal mining operations in the vicinity of such wells; providing administrative and judicial procedure and penalties for any violation," and cites in detail the manner of casing, plugging, and abandoning wells, gives the Department of Mines jurisdiction to prescribe rules and regulations under the Act, and enforce its provisions. The law makes no reference to conservation or waste and does not pertain thereto, except that in compliance with the law waste is prevented or minimized. This enactment, incorporated in the official Code of West Virginia of 1931,[15] sets out methods to prevent waste of gas, extends rights of adjacent property owners to prevent waste, authorizes restraint thereof, and prescribes penalties. Neither the drilling and plugging statute nor later amendments have ever been ruled upon by our supreme court; it is doubtful if the jurisdiction of any trial court has been invoked to construe the Act or its amendments. In 1945 the legislature authorized the state by its governor to join the Interstate Compact to Conserve Oil and Gas.[16]

Under the circumstances the oil and gas industry in West Virginia has a creditable record, and for the past thirty years an enviable one, respecting conservation. The oil and gas industry in this state has the foresight, financial resources, and patriotism to solve remaining problems in the recovery of oil and gas reserves and their by-products by devising means devoted to the highest utility.

[13] Atkinson v. Oil and Gas Co., 72 W. Va. 707, 795 E. 647 (1913).

[14] Acts W. Va. 1929, c. 86; W. Va. Code Ann. § 2464–76 (1943).

[15] Senate substitute for HJR No. 10 adopted March 8, 1929 in the W. Va. Leg. This joint legislative committee made changes in the law during redrafting of the official 1931 compilation. The editors of the 1943 W. Va. Code in preparing those portions of the 1931 publication "Redrafted [them] to conform to modern methods of conserving the supply of natural gas." W. Va. Code § 2477–79 (1943).

[16] Acts W. Va. 1945, concurrent resolution p. 638.

CHAPTER 36

Wyoming, 1881–1948

The first official recognition of Wyoming as potential oil producing land came before it was a state, when in 1878 John W.
Hoyt, Territorial Governor, reported: "at the railroad crossing of
Bear River in Uintah County along the railroad near Green River
station . . . in the valley of the Popo Agie . . . and doubtless at
many other points in Wyoming there are indications of very large
deposits of crude petroleum and kindred carbonaceous substances.
At (Bear River) crossing borings have been made with a view to
practical operations. Oil bearing shales lie upon the surface . . .
and at a depth of 175 feet the underlying sand rock was struck with
an increase of oil." [1] Governor Hoyt. then succinctly stated what
was for years afterwards to be said in varying ways and tones of dis-
pair by his successors and others: "the present price of petroleum,
coupled with the cost of transportation, does not afford a very powerful stimulus to this enterprise, but there is no doubt of the value
of the deposit." By 1881 Hoyt was able to say that a company had
been formed by an Omaha group to collect, store, and transport
Wyoming oil.[2] The word collect was used advisedly, as evidenced
by this extract from a report of Professor Samuel Aughey, Geologist of the University of Nebraska, who informed the Omaha people: "on Saturday, October 16, 1880, I started to investigate the
oil basin of the territory (of Wyoming) . . . I reached the Shoshone oil basin on the 19th and commenced my investigation of
the petroleum springs . . . Within these three acres, . . . wherever a depression is made into the gravel, petroleum arises and ac-

W. H. EVERETT, WRITER; Pierre La Fleiche, Adviser; Ernest Wilkerson, Associate
Editor. (See app. B.)
[1] Ann. Rep. Terr. Gov. Wyo. to Sec. of Int. (1868).
[2] Ann. Rep. Terr. Gov. Wyo. to Sec. of Int. (1881).

cumulates." (It may have been this phenomenon which gave rise to the fable among oil men that at some points in the state one could stamp in an oil well with the heel of his cowboy boot) concluding: "I have thus tried to show that the geological conditions and their arrangements are most favorable for the accumulation and production of oil in Wyoming territory. Their wants and their uses are world wide. I have seen enough to assure myself that in the near future . . . they will certainly receive the attention due them." Professor Aughey was attempting to interest an English combine in Wyoming oil; that was the forerunner of a number of syndicates and corporations emanating from such far flung places as Paris, Brussels, and Amsterdam, which were to play an important part in the later development of Wyoming oil, particularly that of the Salt Creek Field.

In 1884 fourteen producing wells had been bored—wells were not yet being drilled—in Wyoming, all to minute depths (as compared with a well in Natrona County just completed as the world's deepest producer, a depth of 14,305 feet). The development was moving apace and Governor Thomas Moonlight in 1888 took cognizance of the widespread interest in Wyoming's great oil resources, saying: "the oil fields of Wyoming present today perhaps the greatest field for speculation of any industry hidden or developed. Racy advertisements have been broadcast over the land and large bodies of men are now prospecting, locating and working out assessments in various parts of the territory. It is no fiction for the oil is there to be seen by anyone who will take the trouble to look." [3]

The 1890's saw the beginning of what was to be the great landmark of oil development in Wyoming—the Salt Creek Field. The history of this field in itself is a fascinating study of men grappling with an economic giant whose strength none of them fully appreciated. Suffice it that in the 1890's and early 1900's the evolution of Salt Creek eclipsed for a time all oil development in the state and in the nation. The first serious discoveries in the field occurred during the years 1905 through 1910. Land records of the day are studded with such exotic names as the Petroleum Maatschappij Salt Creek and Societe Belgo-Americaine Des Petrols du Wyoming.

[3] Ann. Rep. Terr. Gov. Wyo. to Sec. of Int. (1888).

The Federal Government had not entirely forgotten the reports of its territorial governors and their successors, for in 1909 all government land in the field was withdrawn from entry, part of which later opened, and again in 1918 lands in the notorious Teapot Dome (adjoining Salt Creek) were set aside for the use of the United States Navy as Petroleum Reserve No. 3. Between 1912 and 1920 vast areas of public land throughout the state were removed from entry under the placer mining laws of the United States. On February 25, 1920 the Oil Lands Leasing Act became operative having a profound effect upon conservation legislation, as approximately 65 per cent of Wyoming is subject to lease and operations under it as amended. By 1917 the ingredients of the Wyoming oil picture had all been introduced. The great producing areas such as Salt Creek, Grass Creek, and Elk Basin were discovered and developed in varying degree; rail transportation had supplanted horse drawn tank wagon trains, refineries and pipe lines (to a lesser degree than now) operated to supply the ever increasing demand for oils and products (the automobile, with its internal combustion engine brought a consequent new use for gasoline and lighter oils) in what was to become the greatest oil consuming nation in the world.

Wyoming indeed seemed to have richly fulfilled the forecast of its eminent senior statesman, Francis E. Warren, who concluded his report to the Secretary of the Interior in 1890 with the words: "thus it will be observed that Wyoming is soon to become a great oil field of the world in variety, quantity and quality."

There was suspended, however, a sword over the infant oil industry of Wyoming—the inescapable economic fact that all the oil anyone could want was in Wyoming, but no one wanted it. Great fields lay fallow. Test wells were drilled and plugged. Producers took the oil from nature's storage placing it in artificial storage of their own to await a market. The local demand of the Rocky Mountain region required no considerable amount of petroleum products in comparison to the rich outflow of the Rocky Mountain fields. The oil of the Rockies could not compete with the Mid-Continent, Eastern, and California oil in vying for the market of the populous areas. Employment was reduced in the production and processing of petroleum; the whole economy of producing and refining centers was threatened; bankruptcies were common among those who had not trimmed their sails to the reduction in production and marketing of Rocky Mountain oil products. In 1933 the most productive horizons of Rangely—that great field just across Wyoming's southern border—was discovered and the initial well shut-in; there was no market for its oil. Crude sold for as little as ten cents a barrel. The outlook was not bright. It was during these desperate days that the oil states of the Mid-Continent area fostered and created the Interstate Compact to Conserve Oil and Gas and much of the conservation legislation which was to become an integral part of the oil scene. It was in 1933 that a well drafted oil conservation law, designed to place Wyoming in line of march with the conservation parade, was defeated in the Wyoming legislature. Thus we note then the same divergence apparent today between Wyoming and oil producing states in the matters of conservation law and of participation in the Interstate Oil Compact. With the advent of the second world war came an increased demand for crude oil and its products and a concomitant increase in drilling, producing, refining, and leasing activity. In 1947 there were 4197 oil wells in the state producing 44,582,000 barrels of oil. That added to the amounts brought up since 1884 totals more than 751,000,000 barrels. It is estimated that some 770,000,000 barrels of crude still underlie Wyoming. Sixty-seven wildcat wells were drilled in 1947, of which 19 produced—13 oil and 6 gas.

THE LEGISLATIVE, ADMINISTRATIVE AND JUDICIAL HISTORY OF OIL AND GAS CONSERVATION IN WYOMING

Any discussion of oil and gas conservation law in Wyoming is met at the outset with a question as to the authority of the Board of Land Commissioners, other state officials or bodies, over the various land divisions within the state. Some of those land divisions are: (1) state lands and mineral rights granted to Wyoming by the United States, including lieu lands,[4] (2) public lands of the United States including those in which a Federal agency, de-

---

[4] Act of Admission, Wyo. 1890, 26 STAT. 222, c. 664, ¶ 4–5. Act of Feb. 28, 1891 c. 384, 26 STAT. 796; Act of Jan. 25, 1927, 44 STAT. 1026 as amended 47 STAT. 140 (1932).

partment, or corporation has reserved or acquired mineral interests. (3) Indian lands within as well as outside the ceded portion of Indian reservations. Generally such lands are subject to lease by the tribal council with the approval of the Commissioner of Indian Affairs and of the Secretary of the Interior. (4) railroad lands— those falling within the limits of railway land grants, (5) oil placer mining claims. Some of these are still operated under placer mining law, under claims initiated prior to February 25, 1920; others have been taken to patent under the placer mining laws of the United States and under valid claims surrendered to the United States for preferential permits under the Oil Lands Leasing Act of February 25, 1920.[5] (6) Carey Act lands.[6] Title to these lands was ordinarily granted the state to be held in trust for settlers, who upon compliance with statutory requirements, became entitled to an unrestricted patent from the state. (7) Fee lands. Apparent problems in leasing lands within these divisions are magnified in considering the necessity and advisability of a conservation statute, its administration and enforcement—particularly in answering the query as to whether the state in its police power has or can legislate any right over public lands and mineral interests (or the development and production of oil or gas therefrom) of the United States and its agencies and corporations. Without debating that issue, it may be said that such regulatory legislation as the Wyoming legislature has enacted has been upheld by the Supreme Court of the United States.[7]

The Wyoming Constitution of 1889 created a Board of Land Commissioners [8] composed of the governor, the secretary of state, the state treasurer, the state auditor and the superintendent of public instruction, giving it the direction, control, leasing disposal, and care of state lands for the support and benefit of public schools.[9] The police power of the state is declared supreme over all

[5] 41 STAT. 437 (1920) 30 U.S.C. § 181 et seq (1940), as amended by 60 STAT. 950 (1946).

[6] Act of Aug. 18, 1894, 43 U.S.C. ¶ 641 (1940). Act of June 11, 1896, 43 U.S.C. ¶ 642 (1940). Act of May 27, 1908, 43 U.S.C. ¶ 645 (1940). WYO. COMP. STAT. ANN. ¶ 24–401 et seq (1945).

[7] Walls v. Midland Carbon Co., 254 U.S. 300 (1920).

[8] WYO. CONST. Art. XVIII § 3.

[9] WYO. CONST. Art. VII § 13. WYO. COMP. STAT. ANN. § 24–102 (1945). Ross v. Trustees of University, 31 Wyo. 464, 228 Pac. 642 (1924); St. v. Bd. of Land Comm'rs., 36 Wyo. 302, 254 Pac. 491 (1927).

corporations as well as individuals.[10] The governor, by and with the consent of the State Senate, appoints a Commissioner of Public Lands, whose duties include keeping records and the seal of the Board.[11] He is also secretary of the agency. The law allows the Commissioner to appoint a deputy [12] and a state mineral supervisor [13] to assist in the performance of his multiple duties.

The first legislation classified as a basis for administration and conservation of oil in Wyoming was enacted in 1901. However, so far as is known, nothing in the nature of a conservation regulation or order has issued from that measure.[14] Provision was made therein for the appointment by the governor of a state geologist ". . . charged with the duty of enforcing all laws of the State of Wyoming relating to the oil industry . . ." "The Professor of Geology and head of the Department of Geology of the University of Wyoming shall be eligible" for this appointment and received no salary in addition to that from the University.[15] The first and only statute in Wyoming which specifically defines waste was enacted in 1919 and is unchanged.[16] Under this carbon black act the use, consumption, or burning of natural gas without the heat contained fully and actually utilized for manufacturing or domestic purposes is wasteful and unlawful when the well or source of supply is within ten miles of an incorporated town or industrial plant. No person having the possession or control of any natural gas well whether a contractor, owner, lessee, agent, or manager, is permitted to use, sell, or otherwise dispose of natural gas from it for the purpose of making carbon or resultant products from burning or consumption of gas without its heat being fully and actually utilized. The pen-

[10] Wyo. Const. Art. X § 2.
[11] Wyo. Comp. Stat. Ann. § 24–201 (1945). Wyo. Comp. Stat. Ann. § 24–203 (1945).
[12] Wyo. Comp. Stat. Ann. § 24–212 (1945).
[13] Wyo. Comp. Stat. Ann. § 47–1102 (1945).
[14] Wyo. Comp. Stat. Ann. § 18–1201 et seq. (1945). ·
[15] Wyo. Comp. Stat. Ann. § 18–1206 (1945). Dr. H. D. Thomas is State Geologist and has performed excellent service to the state in his field. His ability is at least partially recognized by Wyo. Laws 1947, c. 114 in authorizing and directing him "to study insufficiencies or inconsistencies between presently effective statutes . . . or affecting rules and regulations of other public authority, concerning operations in or with respect to all mines and mining operations (other than oil and gas deposits) in said State" and to report to the next legislature the results of such study with related recommendations for enactment of curative legislation.
[16] Wyo. Comp. Stat. Ann. § 57–1105—57–1107 (1945).

alty for violation upon conviction is a fine of not less than $100 or more than $1000 for each offense; each day of violation is a separate offense. The constitutionality of this act was upheld in the Supreme Court of the United States in the case of *Walls v. Midland Carbon Company*,[17] decided December 13, 1920, and there have been no other cases where the statute's terms have been questioned.

In 1921 the principal conservation statute, under which the industry now operates, was enacted. Without expressly repealing the duty of the state geologist, the legislature in 1933 transferred his responsibilities under the 1921 Act to the Commissioner of Public Lands. That statute, again amended in 1933, provides that the Commissioner, to conserve the natural resources of Wyoming, and to prevent waste through negligent methods of operations, prescribe and enforce rules and regulations governing the drilling, casing, and abandonment of oil and gas wells and the waste of oil and gas upon all lands in the state, except those public lands subject to the Act of February 25, 1920.[18] The enactment states that the rules and regulations adopted shall be those from time to time promulgated by the Bureau of Mines or the Secretary of the Interior of the United States under the Congressional act governing methods of operations upon lands within permits or leases issued under its terms. The Act further makes it the duty of all persons drilling or operating oil and gas wells upon patented or state land to comply with the rules and regulations, to file with the Commissioner all logs of wells and other requisite reports, and to control by casing, drilling, and plugging all wells. All well logs and reports are confidential and not disclosable without the written authority of the operator, except that they may be offered in evidence if relevant in a prosecution under this law.[19]

[17] 254 U.S. 300 (1920). The court in disposing of the matter stated: "The question in the case is, . . . whether the legislation of Wyoming is a valid exercise of the police power of the State, and brings into comparison the limits of the power against the asserted rights of property; whether it, the legislation, is a legal conservation of the natural resources of the State, or an arbitrary interference with private rights. . . . The determining consideration is the power of the State over, and its regulation of a property in which others besides the companies may have rights, and in which the State has an interest to adjust and preserve, natural gas being one of the resources of the state."

[18] WYO. COMP. STAT. ANN. § 57–1101 et seq. (1945).

[19] WYO. COMP. STAT. ANN. § 57–1101 and 57–1103 (1945).

To enable the administrator to carry out his statutory duties and enforce the rules and regulations, he appoints a state mineral supervisor [20] whose duties are those established by law, and such other tasks prescribed by the agency head. The Commissioner is authorized to delegate his powers for specific purposes to inspectors of the Federal Bureau of Mines or other qualified person, who receive compensation as fixed by the administrator. No appointment of a special representative is made without the consent of the well owner.

The Supreme Court of Wyoming in 1935 held that this Act, under which the supervisor and Commissioner are charged with carrying out the duties imposed by law and enforcing the rules and regulations, makes "ample provision . . . for the ascertainment of damages to the state by reason of negligent physical operation of oil and gas wells in the state, and the right to employ outsiders for that purpose would seem to be excluded." [21] The penalty for conviction of a violation of the statute, the rules and regulations, or the lawful orders of the commissioner, his assistants or representatives, is a fine of not more than $500 or imprisonment of not more than six months.[22] There has never been a penalty assessed during the twenty-seven years the statute has been effective.[23]

The state mineral supervisor, one of the most able and competent public officials we have ever had in Wyoming, has done a magnificent job single handedly of preventing waste brought to his notice; he is cooperative and has steadfastly protected, without adequate assistance, the state's interest in unit agreements and in all forms of conservation practice permissible under existing laws. Administration and enforcement under the present ineffective law are wholly insufficient; no test of efficacy can be had until the legislature provides proper laws and appropriations.[24]

[20] Wyo. Comp. Stat. Ann. § 57–1102 (1945).

[21] Mac Dougall v. Bd. of Land Comm'rs., 48 Wyo. 493, 49 Pac. 2d 663, (1935).

[22] Wyo. Comp. Stat. Ann. § 47–1104 (1945). By amendment in 1933 the words commissioner of public lands appearing in § 57–1101 *et seq.* were substituted for the words state geologist.

[23] As a recent striking example of the inefficacy of the present statute and regulations, see Wyo. Laws 1947, c. 141 wherein the legislature appropriated $1000 ". . . for the purpose of plugging and abandoning, or otherwise reconditioning as a water well, a well drilled for oil and gas. . . ."

[24] La Fleiche, *Report for Wyoming,* VI Interstate Oil Compact Q. Bull. 97 (1947) in which reference is made to the present law as follows: "Although the

COURT REVIEW OF ACTION OF THE BOARD OF LAND COMMISSIONERS

Whenever an important or difficult matter of law of fact is decided in a contest or proceeding, the Board of Land Commissioners (or should its members decide that any of them are disqualified) may, on the motion of either interested party, or upon its own motion cause the proceedings to be reserved and sent to the district court of the county in which the land in controversy is situated.[25] When the contest is sent to the district court, the parties are allowed to replead and the court proceeds in accordance with the rules governing the trial of civil cases. The findings and judgment are certified to the Commissioner having the same force and effect as though initially rendered by the agency. Any party who feels himself aggrieved by a Board decision, rendered in any proceeding before it, has an appeal from the decision to the district court for the county in which the land is situated. And "upon such an appeal being perfected, said contest proceeding shall stand to be heard for trial de novo by said court." [26] After statutory notice of appeal is given, the requisite bond approved, and the appeal perfected, it is heard and tried in all respects as civil cases are tried in the district court; an appeal from the judgment, finding, and decree of the court lies to the Supreme Court of Wyoming as prescribed by law for appellate proceedings from those courts to the supreme court.[27] There is no express appeal to the Board of Land Commissioners or to any court from a ruling, rule or regulation of the Commissioner of Public Lands, except in case of conflicting applications for leases.

---

law goes far toward the elimination of waste it lacks much of the essence of modern conservation legislation. The inadequacy of the law is recognized by a great majority of the constructive minded operators of the State and repeated efforts have been made to secure enactment of a more comprehensive statute. No law, however, adequate, lacking proper administration and enforcement facilities, may be considered effective, and the limited personnel in the conservation office of Wyoming, one Mineral Supervisor and a secretary, is a severe handicap."

[25] WYO. COMP. STAT. ANN. § 24–301 (1945).
[26] WYO. COMP. STAT. ANN. § 24–306 (1945).
[27] WYO. COMP. STAT. ANN. § 24–310 (1945).

UNIT AGREEMENTS

The United States Geological Survey, Casper, Wyoming, with the efficient cooperation of its supervisor and his staff, makes possible the formation of numerous unit agreements in the Rocky Mountain area. In Wyoming as of January 30, 1948, 84 unit agreements have been approved by the Department of the Interior, embracing approximately 761,000 acres of land.[28] These agreements are entered into for the purpose of conserving natural resources and preventing waste. The Secretary in most cases requires parties to the unit agreements to accept all pertinent valid regulations, including operating and unit plan directives, heretofore issued or in the future. The Board of Land Commissioners joins in unit agreements [29] on behalf of Wyoming and is empowered to modify and change any and all terms of state leases whenever granted, including the extension of their primary term for the full time the cooperative or unit plan remains in effect, "to facilitate the efficient and economic production of oil and/or gas from the lands so affected." [30]

CONSERVATION BILLS INTRODUCED IN BUT NOT ENACTED BY THE WYOMING LEGISLATURE

While the main course of the Wyoming conservation policy must be traced through a study of the bills introduced and enacted, it is interesting to analyze the proposals which failed of passage for one reason or another. The following summary may prove helpful as a guide of what not to do or provide in the realm of legislative drafting. Some of the reasons the legislation failed are, briefly:

[28] Rep. Sup. U.S. Geol. Sur. Wyo., Jan. 30, 1948. Under Act of Feb. 25, 1920, as amended by Act of Aug. 8, 1946 authorization is given federal lessees to unite with each other and with others in collectively adopting and operating under a cooperative or unit plan of development and operation of any oil or gas pool, field or like area, or any part thereof, for the purpose of more properly conserving the natural resources thereof whenever determined and certified by the Sec. of the Int. to be necessary or advisable in the public interest.

[29] La Fleiche *supra* note 24 states "Unit operation permits the full application of modern engineering practices, and secondary recovery projects not otherwise obtainable, and to this extent Wyoming has made a great contribution toward conservation."

[30] Wyo. Comp. Stat. Ann. § 24–702 (1945).

(1) failure on the part of proponents to effect a timely informational and educational program of the purpose and need for legislation, (2) creation of unlimited power in a state or industry board or state officials, (3) inclusion of unnecessarily complex provisions, whose full import was not readily and easily understood, (4) lack of cooperation within the industry or the failure of any representative association of the petroleum business to maintain a firm and convincing position, (5) a unified, employed lobby, financed and primarily conceived to serve selfish interests, (6) joint presentation and consideration of conservation legislation with proposals designed to enable Wyoming to join the Interstate Compact to Conserve Oil and Gas.

Bills proposed but not enacted include S.B. No. 85 (introduced and died in committee) entitled a "Bill for an Act Regulating the Use of Natural Gas in the State of Wyoming." The Act offered in 1923 was brief and attempted to define as wasteful and extravagant the production of natural gas in excess of 3,000,000 cubic feet daily from a natural gas well. H.B. No. 159 was a comprehensive conservation measure relating to both oil and gas, creating a commission composed of the Commissioner of Public Lands, the attorney general, the state auditor and naming the state mineral supervisor as an executive officer, giving the Commission very drastic powers, particularly in the manner of determining whether economic waste was occurring and fixing the price of the products of oil and gas wells. Its essential purpose was the limitation of production to a degree consummate with the market and was directed almost entirely towards then existing economic problems of 1933. The Act had one section offering to enter into an interstate compact with other oil producing states. The compact provisions were viewed with circumspection by oil men in the area who felt the power of Wyoming in any sort of compact arrangement would be insufficient to protect its economic interests against domination by others.

The 1943 proposal—H.B. No. 120—was almost identical with the conservation law then in effect in Montana. A companion measure, H.B. No. 119 considered at the same time, authorized the state to join the Interstate Compact to Conserve Oil and Gas. H.B. 120 provided for the appointment, by the governor, of a board of five oil men to act as a commission. It had rather elaborate provisions in connection with the procedure for hearing complaints and for court review. It also required the levying of a privilege and license tax of $\frac{1}{10}$th of one cent on each barrel of petroleum produced, saved, marketed, or stored in Wyoming. This was referred to a House committee and had a public hearing, after which the committee gave the bill a "do pass" recommendation. It was so late in the session that the bill was withdrawn by its sponsor, the Rocky Mountain Oil and Gas Association, as there was insufficient time for the legislature to study the proposal and it might be inadvisedly defeated.

H.B. No. 150, advocated by the state mineral supervisor in 1945, was very comprehensive in term and sufficiently drastic to assure compliance. It was designed primarily to prevent physical rather than economic waste and (with one exception as to determination of market demand), the supervisor was vested with all its powers. A clause was contained, somewhat unusual in conservation legislation, which provided that "each and every producer of crude oil or gas in a common pool or reservoir (shall) be not denied his fair share of the available market production thereof." This was passed in the House but not in the Senate, possibly because it had not been presented to the industry for study and consideration prior to introduction. It was generally opposed by the Rocky Mountain Oil and Gas Association. Following the defeat of this bill, the directors of that association instructed its legal and legislative committee to draft a suitable conservation measure. The sub-committee for Wyoming presented the directors what they considered a model of adequate conservation law, patterned largely after the New Mexico and Arkansas statutes. With the approval of the directorate, the committee offered the bill at the yearly association meeting, November 1946 as a part of its annual report, and moved its adoption, recommending that the measure be introduced in the 1947 session of the Wyoming legislature. The report was tabled on motion and the bill not offered. Another act sponsored by the supervisor, who felt the necessity for some form of conservation legislation, was H.B. No. 102 of 1947. In effect and substance it was about the same as H.B. No. 150, which failed to pass in 1945. No affirmative legislative action was taken.

The present law, with the exception of carbon black manufacture, is wholly inadequate as a conservation measure in these respects: (1) there is no definition of either physical or economic waste, (2) there is no requirement as to: spacing of wells, (3) cycling, recycling or repressuring, (4) water-oil and gas-oil ratios, (5) preservation of reservoir energy, (6) open flow wells, (7) ratable taking, and (8) no provision for the establishment and payment of an adequate and well qualified administrative staff.

APPRAISAL AND CONCLUSION

In and during the period between 1921 and 1945 there was an economic oversupply of oil (particularly black oil) in Wyoming. That factor alone was sufficient in a limited way to effectuate some conservation, for the reason that many fields had to be shut-in at frequent intervals because of lack of a market. The results obtained conservation-wise under unit operations have been successful, primarily in providing the necessary working arrangement for secondary recovery.[31] A proper educational program must be conducted prior to the introduction of any further conservation law, both within and without the industry, because of the general apathetic attitude of the people, the legislature, and the industry in connection with any new regulatory measure.[32] Having specified the deficiencies in the present Wyoming law, those items should be properly covered and included in a new conservation measure akin to those previously introduced. The impelling reasons for the enactment of adequate conservation legislation are: (1) Waste prevention. (2) Protection of correlative rights. (3) Spacing of wells and secondary recovery control. (4) Determination as to authority over various classes of lands and (5) The need for the creation of a state administrative office or agency with proper administrative and enforcement facilities.

[31] See La Fleiche supra note 24.

[32] The successful lobby against all conservation legislation presented but not enacted, has created in the minds of legislators the erroneous impression that any adequate conservation law would be harmful to the small operator. Many small operators have been unwittingly used as a tool in defeating conservation legislation; in that they have heard the story repeated so many times (and because they wanted to believe they were being maltreated) that, without studying or attempting to understand the bills presented, they repeat the misleading and factually incorrect story, even though the small operator has been instrumental in initiating, sponsoring and getting enacted adequate measures in the other oil producing jurisdictions.

Part III

THE INTERSTATE COMPACT TO CONSERVE OIL AND GAS AND ITS ADMINISTRATIVE ARM—THE INTERSTATE OIL COMPACT COMMISSION

CHAPTER 37

The Oil States Advisory Committee, a Predecessor
of the Compact

~/~

Economic dislocation in the petroleum industrial complex in 1931 brought about efforts to alleviate this distress by agencies of the Federal Government, the states and the oil people.[1] Through the programs, manifestoes, and public utterances of these groups runs an innocent disregard for the economic stresses then current in American industry—a feeling that this one facet of business life had been selected to be cursed in the depression ridden years. Here and there in the governmental agencies, however, appeared practical ideas sponsored in part by directors of administrative mechanisms and in part by the forward looking managerial persons in the industry; one of these was the creation of the Oil States Advisory Committee. A conference, called by Governor William H. Murray of Oklahoma at Fort Worth, Texas, February 28 and March 1, 1931, formed the Oil States Advisory Committee or the Governors' Committee. Membership at its first session in Texarkana, Texas, March 9, was drawn from the states of Oklahoma, California, Kansas, Wyoming, Louisiana, Arkansas, and Texas.[2] Members represented the governors of these jurisdictions and had at the least a quasi-official standing. New Mexico, Colorado, and Ohio participated in later deliberations.[3]

The Committee issued a lengthy forecast of the efforts it would take to end the confusion and anarchy that existed in the conduct

BLAKELY M. MURPHY, WRITER; Earl Foster, E. O. Thompson, Advisers. (See app. B.)

[1] *Infra* c. 41 (c) reports the federal effort. c. 11, *Kansas supra* gives an example of state effort.

[2] Members were C. I. Murray, W. H. Cooley, Mark D. Mitchell, Carl M. Cox, W. Scott Heywood, T. H. Barton, Robert R. Penn. See N.Y. Times, Mar. 9, 1931, p. 35, c. 2.

[3] Represented by Van Welch, Warwick M. Downing, I. C. Grimm and Kenner McConnell.

of the petroleum business in the United States. Its points are twenty in number, some overlapping, and some repetitious; but all are worthy of consideration as indicative of what the association might have accomplished. These resolutions [4] (omitting those portions in which the woes of the producers of petroleum are recited) demonstrated that the Governors' Committee blueprinted their plans with intelligence. The initial duties of the group were to assure itself of continued existence in order that it might correlate the activities of state regulatory agencies in the producing areas, to make recommendations of production allowables in the United States and the prices which should be paid to return a fair and reasonable profit, to confer and agree with major purchasers of crude as to the quantities needed, to treat with the major importers of oil in an effort to limit importation in the same fashion as domestic production was prorated, and finally to deal with the holders of crude oil in storage to assure withdrawal in a manner not tending to further depress the marketing of current offerings from wells. The Committee sought to negotiate with the president, the Secretary of Interior, the Secretary of Commerce, the Attorney General, and the trade commissions and conservation boards of the Federal Government for their approval of the desirability of reducing waste caused by overproduction, low price, and uneconomic use of petroleum. In providing an "intelligent and fair control of the production of such a natural resource as oil and gas" the Committee felt it necessary to prevent at the same time "the creation and growth of monopoly, with the resultant dangers of high and unfair prices for petroleum products in the not far distant future." [5]

A major responsibility was laid upon the states producing the greatest quantities of oil; the Committee asked them to continue in effect their present systems of proration, and indeed to increase them in stringency, as well as to enact market demand statutes and administrative controls and to provide a fair and fearless enforcement of these acts. Those jurisdictions not then large producers, but having potentialities, were asked to be forward looking in the passage of laws to govern the sudden crisis possible from newly

[4] Downing, The Oil States Advisory Committee, Often Known as the Governors' Committee—A Resume of its Activities and its Contributions to the Public Welfare and to the Oil Industry, 4–10 (1932). Unpublished.
[5] Id. at 7.

discovered production. The Committee undertook to offer itself as an agency to fix total allowable production over the country and to assign percentages of allotment to each state.

The industry was asked to conduct its business to control "reckless production of oil and to assure fair prices to producers at all times—for in any conservation of oil and gas the factor of price is not less important than that of curtailment . . . the industry must cooperate through every means available not only to assure fair prices . . . but to prevent unreasonable and monopolistic prices." [6] The purchasers who had announced a decrease in the price of crude oil were requested to restore those levels which existed February 1931 and refrain from lowering the price structure, pending the efforts of the Committee and the states to halt overproduction. The final recommendation was one asking that the states join in an interstate compact, subject to the consent of the Congress, which the Committee would prepare at future meetings. This then was their program. How well did they fulfill it?

The Advisory Committee cannot be accused of lack of enthusiasm or expenditure of time and effort, for in the months leading to November 1932 when it would be dropped, many were the meetings held and the persons (in the state and Federal Government and the industry) conferred with in carrying out its obligations. In Washington during April 1931 the group met with the Secretaries of War, Interior, and Commerce, and with officials of the Federal Oil Conservation Board, and were given more than a hour with President Herbert Hoover to discuss problems and a program. Recommendations of the Committee were then set forth to Secretary of the Interior Ray Lyman Wilbur in a letter asking that the Federal Oil Conservation Board continue the forecasts of the Voluntary Committee on Economics [7] which could be used by the committee in fixing demand, that the state legislative bodies authorize at once negotiations for an interstate agreement for state coordination of conservation measures, and that pending the working out of this compact the Advisory Committee continue to function as a liaison and fact finding body, in effect taking the place of the ad-

---

[6] *Id.* at 10. N.Y. Times, Mar. 10, 1931, p. 42, c. 3.

[7] *Infra* c. 41. For a background of the Committee's work in Washington during April see: N.Y. Times, Apr. 7, 1931, p. 44, c. 1; Apr. 8, 1931, p. 5, c. 4; Apr. 9, 1931, p. 16, c. 4; Apr. 10, 1931, p. 7, c. 1; and Apr. 16, 1931, p. 41, c. 1.

ministrative commission to be established. While the Committee set its future goal as the promulgation of a compact agreement, it realized the short term necessity was to doctor the sick industry.[8]

Stabilization efforts of the Oil States Advisory Committee began at St. Louis in April 1931, where it decided to recommend a program of drastic curtailment of production. From this conference a letter was addressed to the governors of the States of Oklahoma, Texas, New Mexico, Louisiana, California, Kansas, Colorado, Arkansas, Ohio, and Wyoming, which recommended that no increases in production take place in the coming 6 months. The allowable suggested, some 322,000 barrels under the Bureau of Mines daily figures, was received with favor and resulted to some extent in the states producing a decreasing supply of oil which more nearly approximated current consumptive demand. The action was bold but necessary.

Continuing its efforts to take prompt action, the Committee established a legal sub-committee [9] to work with a group from the American Bar Association and the industry for the preparation of a draft of an interstate compact. After meeting the week of April 27, 1931 in Oklahoma City and May 3, 4, and 5 in Austin, Texas (where the members of the Texas legislature were heard and consulted because of their ultimate interest in the proposed agreement) a further series of conferences was planned for the summer in Colorado Springs. The tentative draft which the sub-committee offered defined waste, including within that term that "incident to or resulting from the production of crude oil or petroleum in excess of transportation or marketing facilities or reasonable market demand" [10] and declared it to be in the public interest that oil not required be kept in underground natural storage, and that the de-

---

[8] N.Y. Times, Apr. 12, 1931, § II, p. 11, c. 5. The price for crude oil in early 1931 had dropped to 33¢ a bbl. and advanced to 92¢ by the time the Committee activity ceased. Before the group was formed production was at the rate of some 2,460,300 bbls. daily, but by 1931 it had decreased to 2,331,700 bbls. In 1932 it went still further down to 2,145,200 bbls. only to jump back in 1933 to 2,481,200 bbls. During 1931 petroleum stocks decreased 44,663,000 bbls. and during 1932 45,792,000 bbls. See also N.Y. Times, May 3, 1931, § II, p. 16, c. 5.

[9] There were 2 legal sub-committees appointed at this session; one composed of W. H. Cooley, Van Welch, Carl M. Cox and Warwick M. Downing to consult with the Secretary of the Interior about the public domain discrimination, and the other consisting of Warwick M. Downing, chairman, Cicero I. Murray and Kenner McConnell to draft a compact between the states.

[10] Downing *supra* note 4 at 19.

mands of commerce be met from wells of settled production to preserve them from injury. It was intended that the act constitute an offer on the part of the adopting jurisdictions to other states to enter into a compact to conserve the oil resources. More of this later.

Some criticism, ensuing from those who felt the Governors' Committee was not properly meeting the challenge of the import crisis, led to a meeting June 1 in Los Angeles. Here the activities of the group were indicated by a resolution recounting its accomplishments. The Committee, smarting under what it considered unjust, uncalled for, and malicious attacks,[11] pointed out that the 71st Congress had failed to pass the Capper bill [12] restricting imports and that the governors of Oklahoma and Texas had requested President Hoover to negotiate with the importers looking to proper limitations in harmony with the curtailment and proration enforced by the states. This had been done and a reduction agreed to of some 25 per cent of those amounts brought into the country in 1930. The Committee resolved that Congress be memorialized to lay an impost of at least $1 a barrel on foreign crude and a tariff of not less than 50 per cent of the domestic value of imported petroleum products.

Chronologically the period of deepening crisis now came in the economics of petroleum. Production increased greatly; Oklahoma threatened new floods of oil unless Texas joined in a further reduction, and importers predicted a movement of new and larger supplies into the country. The Legal Sub-committee went to New York and Washington to see what could be done to lessen the danger. After some study it proposed (in the medium of a letter [13] addressed to Secretary Robert P. Lamont of Commerce) the creation of a conciliation board to develop lawful and orderly cooperation between parties in the "honest conservation of natural resources in the public interest, administered by public authority" and to ease ugly controversies raging between units of the industry. Proposed

[11] *Id.* at 20.

[12] *Infra* c. 42. Regarding the sentiment for and against the Capper bill see: N.Y. Times, Jan. 19, 1931, p. 13, c. 4; Feb. 6, 1931, p. 4, c. 5; Feb. 8, 1931, p. 19, c. 3; governors' request for action is reported in N.Y. Times, Mar. 2, 1931, p. 29, c. 4; Hoover's reply in Mar. 6, 1931, p. 15, c. 1; cuts in imports at Mar. 27, 1931, p. 38, c. 4; Mar. 31, 1931, p. 45, c. 3; Apr. 5, 1931, § II, p. 9, c. 2.

[13] Downing *supra* note 4 at 22. The letter dated June 20, 1931 is set out in full.

as a *czar* of the petroleum business, the board was envisioned as one appointed through the joint action of federal authority and the Oil States Committee; ideally, so the letter said, composed of three men—one selected by the Secretary of Commerce, one by the Committee, and a third chosen by the first appointees. While the principles of this letter were approved by Secretary Lamont and President Hoover, and though ex-President Coolidge was suggested as a member along with others, no action was taken to implement the idea. The Legal Committee consulted with principal importers of petroleum, procuring their agreement to curtail imports by 30 per cent for the balance of 1931, and on the part of the Royal Dutch Shell Company, a 50 per cent curtailment.

When the entire group met in Amarillo July 7, the appointment of the National Conciliation Board was discussed and the conclusion reached that this problem was the responsibility of the Federal Government and the industry. The more important matter considered was the economic philosophy of some purchasers of oil, who were, the Committee charged, "aiding and abetting the breakdown of proration . . . by buying the producers crude at confiscatory prices," and "steadily taking advantage of . . . conditions to increase their holdings by thousands of acres of proven oil lands and at the same time are leasing empty tankage for the purpose of storing the cheaply purchased oil." [14] Recommendations were made that proration be continued, that the East Texas people agree to stabilize their production at 200,000 barrels daily with the understanding that restraint be rewarded with price increases, and lastly that if this were done and the purchasers did not raise prices, then special sessions of the legislatures be called to pass legislation in each state, giving absolute control of the industry for the regulation of production, crude oil, and by-product prices, or in lieu of this *complete control of the industry would pass* to the United States Government. Upon motion by Warwick M. Downing these recommendations were held in abeyance for later action. [15]

September 11, 1931 the conservancy agencies of Texas, Oklahoma, and Kansas [16] met in Oklahoma City as did the Governors'

[14] *Id.* at 26.

[15] *Id.* at 27.

[16] While the regulatory agency personnel came from Oklahoma and Kansas, Texas was represented only by Cullen Thomas of the Railroad Commission of Texas, its regulatory agency, who appeared under oral appointment of Governor Sterling. Texas

Committee. After considerable speech making and debate [17] the Committee voted to make public a resolution which reviewed the essential nature of a fair price to the conservation of petroleum, and approved the military policy of Governor William H. Murray in closing the Oklahoma City Field with the Oklahoma National Guard, saying, "our people have often witnessed the use of the military to protect private property, but never before to defend the people as a whole against the defiance of law by wilful, selfish and arrogant corporations." Governor Sterling came in for praise in following somewhat the same tactics in Texas, and he earned the commendation of the group. The major producing companies had the displeasure of the meeting, because in spite of repeated promises to aid in preserving natural resources, a number of these corporate bodies failed to give even slight support to state programs. The principal cause of demoralization was reported to be the attitude of some "of the major oil companies. There is a lack of effective leadership . . . fierce competition between major companies; ethical rules, and the rules of good business have been overlooked. The purpose is to undersell or destroy competitors. The public welfare has been forgotten." [18]

The Committee next met in November 1931 at Chicago where the group received the special approbation of Secretary of Commerce Lamont, principal speaker at the meeting of the American Petroleum Institute, for its successful curtailment of some 60,-000,000 barrels of imports in the nine months of 1931. Here the Committee restated its position on the importation of refined products into the United States, voted to express appreciation to the Continental and Phillips Petroleum Companies for their cooperation with the Committee and the regulatory officials of Oklahoma, Kansas, and Texas, and authorized the Legal Sub-committee to draft a proposed Congressional act for submission regarding an interstate agreement and matters with regard to stabilization and control of production. [19]

---

did not long participate in the program being advised that its activity might be unconstitutional.

[17] The Committee had under consideration a proposal to boycott the Standard Oil Company of Indiana and the Royal Dutch Shell Company which was voted down as the group had no authority to censure them nor was their guilt clearly established. See Downing *supra* note 4 at 28.

[18] Downing *supra* note 4 at 30.

[19] *Id.* at 34.

The Sub-committee had filed a brief as amicus curiae in the Court case of *Champlin Refining Company v. Corporation Commission*,[20] and thereafter early in February 1932 set to work preparing the bill for the compact. February 19 it met with Judge C. B. Ames and L. L. Stephens, representing the American Petroleum Institute, and February 21 and 22 with Secretary of the Interior Wilbur, Northcutt Ely, and Congressional representatives. February 26 and 28 the Committee held hearings in Tulsa and Oklahoma City with industry counsel. Out of these conferences and exchanges of opinion grew the measure submitted to the full Committee[21] in Oklahoma City March 1, where it was approved and copies dispatched to the Federal Oil Conservation Board and the American Petroleum Institute.[22] April 11 the latter recorded its affirmation of the bill, and the campaign for adoption in Congress stated May 1. The bill,[23] as agreed, introduced by Senator Elmer Thomas and Representative Tom McKeown, provided in substance that Congress give consent to a compact among two or more oil producing states for the conservation of oil and gas and the prevention of exhaustion of domestic sources of supply.[24] It established as the administering arm a Federal Interstate Oil Board[25] to recommend quotas of production, to endorse agreements entered into for the purposes of conservation, and to make the laws of the states and agreements made exempt from a claim of interference with interstate commerce, when accepted by the federal representatives on the board. The form of the compact and its manner of presentation was left to the states. A section dealt with limitations of imports to per centums of total estimated consumption.[26] Temporarily, the Federal Oil Conservation Board and the Oil States Ad-

[20] 286 U.S. 210 (1932).

[21] Downing *supra* note 4 at 37–38.

[22] Should either of these two groups have formal changes to make in the draft the subcommittee was authorized to approve them for the full unit. If the changes were material they were to be submitted to the Advisory Committee for approval, they to be polled by mail.

[23] S. 4264 (1932). H.R. 10863 (1932).

[24] For full text of the bill see *Hearings before Committee on Judiciary on H.R. 10863*, 72d Cong., 1st Sess. 1–3 (1932).

[25] One member of this board came from each compacting state and one was appointed by the president.

[26] H.R. 12076 (1932) was offered as a new measure to replace H.R. 10863 (1932) with the approval of the group. § 5 dealt with imports as did a similar section in the senate bill. This bill is also found in *Hearings supra* note 24 at 39–41.

visory Committee would exercise the powers of the created agency. A hearing was held before a sub-committee of the Senate Judiciary Committee May 5 [27] resulting in a favorable report to the full Committee. The House Judiciary Committee heard the members of the Oil State Advisory Committee in support of its measure May 14, at which time two explanatory documents were presented—A National Plan [28] and an official statement.[29] Also a letter from the Secretary of the Interior Wilbur to Senator Norris was read regarding S.B. 4624.[30] The Committee favorably reported the bill with slight changes June 10.[31] At the House hearing it was pointed out that the adoption of the measure might remove any necessity for the passage of the then pending tariff measure supported by the Independent Petroleum Association of America.[32] There was some question of the correctness of the assertion of Representative La Guardia in this regard, but it was thought that efforts to push the bill might defeat the tariff measure, and at the earnest request of the Association the Committee shelved its bill for the time being.[33]

The Committee on Allowables, the Oil States Advisory Committee, made recommendations June 3 reducing production an average of 10 per cent under those figures set March 28, to continue in effect until January 1, 1933. Its next session July 23 in Colorado Springs dealt with the Hill Two Million Barrel Plan.[34] At the conference in Wichita October 23 and 24 numerous resolutions [35] were adopted and plans laid for a November meeting in

[27] *Hearings before Committee on Judiciary on S. 4264, 72d Cong. 1st Sess.* (1932).

[28] A short pamphlet, it was distributed generally, and a copy is found in *Hearings supra* note 24 at 8–9.

[29] The statement was released in a mimeographed pamphlet May 10, 1932. See for a copy of the statement *Hearings supra* note 24 at 10–17; also interleaved in Downing *supra* note 4 between 44–45. Its treatment of the kinds of waste is a minor classic, as valid in 1948 as in 1932. See N.Y. Times, May 15, 1932, § II, p. 10, c. 2.

[30] Downing *supra* note 4 at 45. *Hearings supra* note 24 at 28.

[31] Mr. McKeown offered a new bill in its stead—H.R. 12076 (1932). See H.R. Rep. No. 1585, 72d Cong., 1st Sess. (1932). The minority report is very interesting in its comment.

[32] *Hearings supra* note 24 at 34.

[33] This was an unfortunate decision. If the compact proposal had not been put aside it would have undoubtedly been enacted and a great deal of subsequent trouble obviated for the industry—a position it later realized.

[34] Downing *supra* note 4 at 49. The Hill plan envisaged the reduction of production to 2,000,000 bbls. daily. The marketers would reduce withdrawal from storage to 50,000 bbls. daily and the price would be advanced 25¢.

[35] These included one to strengthen collection of gasoline taxes, the imposition of

Fort Worth, which would climax the Committee activities.[36] The Independent Petroleum Association of America withdrew its moral support of the Committee,[37] and in November 1932 the American Petroleum Institute announced its support of the quotas in commerce plan under federal control.[38] The IPAA declined to appoint a committee to represent it at the coming meeting. All of this, in the words of the Committee, fell as a bombshell. The Fort Worth meeting was called off and the members of the Committee decided, since it had been so cavalierly abandoned, to cease further activity.[39]

But the group had arranged an interview with the then next president, Governor Franklin D. Roosevelt in Albany, and it was decided informally that this conversation with him be held, on a chance that he might urge passage of the Committee bill. Governor Roosevelt conferred with Thurman Hill and Warwick M. Downing[40] December 14. Roosevelt, confessing that he knew little of the oil situation at the time, was taken with the purpose and work of the Committee. He committed himself to write to Senator Norris and asked the group meet with him later.[41]

---

further gasoline taxes, the solicitation of all companies to meet an increased price then posted of $1.12 and one thanking the Sun Oil Company for an increase in price of 12¢ a bbl.

[36] The Committee had invited industry lawyers and interested parties to be present to discuss the final draft of the uniform act as a last act before it would be offered. See N.Y. Times, Oct. 25, 1932, p. 29, c. 5. •

[37] The writer, according to Warwick M. Downing, inferred that the members of the Committee received compensation for their efforts. See Murphy, *The Interstate Compact to Conserve Oil and Gas: An Experiment in Cooperative State Production Control*, 17 Miss L.J. 314, 321 (1946). The statement should have read: The first chairman of the Committee called upon the industry to finance its work, and small sums of money were paid by the American Petroleum Institute to this purpose. When it was suggested that it was not necessary for the Institute to aid a governmental body this support was withdrawn. The members of the Committee other than its first Chairman, it was alleged, had no knowledge of these contributions, having borne their individual expenses themselves.

[38] Later the industry turned to the NRA. See Downing *supra* note 4 at 60 for his brief filed with Hugh S. Johnson, Administrator of the NRA, about the only dissent of its kind at that time. *Infra* c. 41 c.

[39] New governors had been chosen in Texas, Kansas, and Arkansas whose attitude towards the continuance of the Committee was unknown. The members were chagrined at the abrupt reversal of policy and rightfully.

[40] Downing *supra* note 4 at 53–57. Roosevelt carried out his promise to write to Senator Norris.

[41] Although asked to meet further with Roosevelt no demand for the continuance of the Committee came from the industry so the representatives dropped their interview and did not seek further hearing.

The members of the Advisory Committee decided to send out the proposed Uniform Act for Oil and Gas Conservation and Interstate Compact. The measure gave the regulatory body of the state power to curtail production when reasonable market price became less than the average cost of production; there was doubt about the legality of this clause. Thereafter the Committee ended its labor.

CHAPTER 38

The Formation of the Interstate Compact to Conserve Oil and Gas

~/~

In the battle between the proponents of federalized control of the petroleum industry and those favoring the control of natural resources by the states, a historic point of reference was reached with the adoption of the compact principle in Dallas, February 16, 1935. Indeed there are many who feel that the fight fought in those years and the victory there won prevented further excursions into federal centralized planning for other industrial facets of the United States. Between November 1932 and December 1934 much transpired in the petroleum business which had a direct bearing upon the formation of the Interstate Compact to Conserve Oil and Gas. A recapitulation of those events by way of introduction to the Marland discussions of December 1934 may vivify that sense of urgency felt by the groups opposed to federal control.

Within the memory of many persons lie the depression ridden 1930's with their attendant philosophy of negation and despair. The month of President Franklin D. Roosevelt's inauguration brought a sag further downward in the prices paid for petroleum at the well. When Secretary of the Interior Harold L. Ickes issued a call for a conference of governors of the oil producing states for March 27, 28, and 29, 1933, sixteen states responded and sent representatives.[1] The Independent Producers Association of America

BLAKELY M. MURPHY, WRITER; Earl Foster, E. O. Thompson, Advisers. (See app. B.)

[1] Resolution of Conference of Governors of the Oil Producing States, Dept. of Int. Press Release No. 70632, Mar. 29, 1933. Representatives appeared from Texas, California, Oklahoma, Kansas, Louisiana, Wyoming, Pennsylvania, New Mexico, Colorado, Arkansas, Montana, New York, Ohio, West Virginia, Illinois and Rhode Island. See N.Y. Times, Mar. 16, 1933, p. 25, c. 2; Mar. 17, 1933, p. 27, c. 7; Mar. 19, 1933, § II, p. 5, c. 6; Mar. 27, 1933, p. 23, c. 3; Mar. 28, 1933, p. 27, c. 6.

and the major producers of oil demanded a right to participate in the meeting. There the ancient antagonisms of the groups caused the formation of a Committee of Fifteen—five drawn from each of the representative segments. At the conclusion of the conference a recommendation came from the gubernatorial representatives for an immediate personal consultation between the governors of Oklahoma, Texas, California, Kansas, and Louisiana (together with such representatives as the other oil states might send) to coordinate state action on policies affecting the industry, and to work out a common policy.[2] This was the last mention at a responsible policy level of a compact between the states, where the problems of production might be solved without the aid of the National Government, until in late 1934.

The attractiveness of federal regulation [3] for the industry then cannot now be minimized nor detracted from by all of the speechifying and subsequent repentance indulged in by those of rank and quality in the executive world of the industry, and in administrative control of some state regulatory agencies. Put mildly, the industry was enthusiastic about the possibilities of using the code device to govern their activities under the protecting wing of the

[2] See Resolution note 1 *supra*, also N.Y. Times, Mar. 29, 1933, p. 2, c. 3; Mar. 31, 1933, p. 29, c. 1.

[3] In this connection see the testimony of Amos L. Beaty given at the *Hearings before a Subcommittee of the Committee on Interstate and Foreign Commerce on H. Res. 441*, 73d Cong., recess 198 ff., 2839 (a prepared statement) (1934). Mr. Beaty opposed the compact principle (*Id.* at 199) and spoke in favor of federal control (*Id.* at 2850). Judge Beaty was particularly attracted by the "quotas in commerce" idea. See also the statement made by Charles F. Roeser, a Vice-President of the Production Division, American Petroleum Institute, *Id.* at 2315, Mr. Roeser later claimed his statement here was misinterpreted. See Dallas Morning News, Dec. 2, 1934, § I, p. 10, c. 2; a statement by R. W. Fair, *Id.* at 2019; and a prepared statement of the Kansas Corporation Commission favoring federal control found at *Id.* 1686–1689; N.Y. Times, May 7, 1933, § II, p. 7, c. 3; May 9, 1933, p. 25, c. 6. These are but a few representative samples of one side of the problem. It must be said in all fairness that contrary views of equal weight and merit were expressed. For these see for example the statement of C. B. Ames, Chairman of the Board of the Texas Company, *Id.* at 345 ff.; a statement by C. C. Herndon, Vice-President, Skelly Oil Company, *Id.* at 1662, 1668, 1683 and other testimony by other persons at *Id.* 1769, 2241. During the early NIRA day the representatives of the governors of the states of Kentucky, West Virginia, Texas, California, Colorado, Oklahoma, Pennsylvania, Ohio, New Mexico, Michigan, Louisiana, Kansas, Arkansas and Montana adopted a resolution pledging the support of these states to the Federal Government and the National Recovery Administration in the general program proposed to rehabilitate and stabilize the industry. This resolution is found in an official record of the work of the Governors Representatives meeting in Washington, D.C., July 25, 1933, as prepared by its secretary A. S. Heck of Spencer, West Virginia.

blue eagle and its sponsor—the Federal Government. An eagerness existed for any activity as contrasted with inactivity; anything seemed better than existing conditions. Thus we were treated to the spectacle of the blue eagle, the petroleum code, and the voluntary regulation of America's most aggressive industry by that industry with the blessing of the National Government. The millenium had arrived. It appears simple, deceptively simple, but the calculation that each side made (erroneously or not) was that it would run the show. It is to the credit of both participants that neither would let the other get away with the original concepts each possessed of what the code would do for their interests.

By 1934 a judicial erosion had taken place within the controls of the NIRA and the petroleum code. Dissatisfaction was manifested with the manner in which the Federal Government had functioned in its control responsibilities, and although many in the industry would not admit it, the experiment was on its way out. When it became apparent that the NIRA was going, the preparation of measures designed to preserve the system of federal control were quietly undertaken and upon completion circulated among those most interested. One of these was the Margold bill,[4] originated as a "conservation measure . . . adopted as a stabilization measure, and then abandoned as a socialization measure."[5] The Margold proposal, never officially introduced, was succeeded by the Disney-Thomas bill, a redistillation of the less offensive sections of the former measure.[6] This bill in turn was finally amended to provide for an interstate compact with indefinite powers and privileges—an amendment which in fact added the compactual device only to make more palatable the context of the bill. The compact supporters were to oppose this bitterly. In November 1934 the American Petroleum Institute met in Dallas where its principal speaker, Secretary of the Interior Harold L. Ickes, called for strong federal control of the industry and for a declaration that the

---

[4] *Hearings* note 3 *supra* at 2619–2620, 2656–2658, 2662–2665; its text appears at 2416–2420.

[5] *Hearings* note 3 *supra* at 2664.

[6] S. 3495, H.R. 9676. See also N.Y. Times May 1, 1934, p. 19 (text of measure), May 6, 1934, § II, p. 9, c. 7, May 18, 1934, p. 17, c. 4, May 19, 1934, p. 25, c. 8, May 31, 1934, p. 31, c. 6.

industry be held a public utility.[7] The Board of Directors of the API by a close margin reversed its previous stand and came out against further extension of the federal power in the control of the petroleum industry.[8]

That past June a sub-committee of the House Committee on Interstate and Foreign Commerce had been formed pursuant to House Resolution No. 441.[9] This group, headed by Congressman William P. Cole, Jr., of Maryland, had during 1934 held hearings throughout the oil country where the testimony of the opposing forces within the industry was taken and reduced to the printed record. Here again cropped out the idea of the formation of an interstate compact to provide a cooperative system of state controls over production.

Certain changes in the control of state administrations occurred with the fall elections of 1934 which presaged much for the future of the state system of control. One of these was the election in November 1934 of Ernest W. Marland, a member of Congress and formerly head of one of the great producing companies of the 1920's, as Governor of Oklahoma. Governor Marland took his election (in part) as a mandate to act on the current oil production difficulties. Considering to what a great degree his state's economy, tax collections, and well being were affected, he determined to revive and carry out the idea of forming an interstate compact between the oil producing jurisdictions. He flew to Austin, Texas, to consult with Governor-elect Allred, and to Topeka, Kansas, for an interview with Governor Landon, and on November 14 called a meeting of the oil state governors at his home in Ponca City for December 3. This invitation was directed to the chief executives of New Mexico, California, Kansas, Texas, Louisiana, Michigan, and Wyoming and was to discuss "our attitude as Governors of the oil-producing States toward the possibilities of an interstate compact."

[7] Nat. Pet. News 19 (Nov. 14, 1934), Nat. Pet. News 17 (Nov. 21, 1934). See also N.Y. Times, Nov. 15, 1934, p. 31, c. 1.

[8] *Hearings* note 3 *supra* at 1754, 1755, 1756 where the majority opinion and the minority view are set out in full; the vote on the minority report at 1756 (the Franklin and Beaty resolution) and the vote on the Ames majority resolution at 1757.

[9] This was the Cole Committee. Its hearings are found in *Hearings* note 3 *supra* and appeared in five parts.

The newspapers and the oil trade publications published many articles relating to the plan Marland intended to present at the December session. The gist of their writings was that Marland had a cut and dried program to offer to the conferees and would dictate their assent to his proposal.[10] Realizing that this not too favorable publicity (which was true only in that the governor did have a plan) might endanger the December meeting, Marland wrote to Allred on November 28, 1934. His letter stated that what he hoped to accomplish was the appointment of a committee consisting of one member from each petroleum state and one member selected by the Federal Government; this group would be charged with carrying out a survey which would look into demand and supply factors, recommend a proper allowable for the United States and propose modification of the conservation statutes of each state to unify its approach toward conservation, taxation, and "subjects in which there may be a common interest from a competitive standpoint." His thought, he wrote, was to make a start in the development of an interstate compact.

Although invitations had been extended to other jurisdictions, only the governors of Oklahoma, Kansas, and Texas participated in the December 3 session at Ponca City.[11] The meeting was a failure in that a stalemate developed between the Kansas and Texas executives over methods of establishing proper oil price structures and market demand laws.[12] No compromise was possible because of political commitments and personal factors. The conference broke up, but it was agreed to meet again January 3, 1935. The one good result of this session, however, was that Marland had an opportunity to offer his resolution [13] during the recess. The failure of this

[10] Dallas Morning News, Dec. 2, 1934, § I, p. 10, c. 2 is indicative of the publicity meant.

[11] In addition to the suites of the governors Northcutt Ely participated in the conference as an adviser to Governor Marland. William P. Cole, Jr., Samuel B. Pettingill, Edgar A. Kelly and Charles A. Wolverton of the Cole Committee attended. For a résumé of the conference see *Hearings* note 3 *supra* at 2884 ff.

[12] Marland later stated that though there were but three states present at the first meeting in his home that "we had to occupy three floors of the house in order to get along" and that his part in the conference consisted in using his feet more often than his head as he had to go up and down between the floors to relay the proposals and counterproposals between Allred and Landon.

[13] The resolution offered by governor-elect Marland, December 3d, 1934, appears in full in MINUTES OF THE SECOND CONFERENCE OF THE GOVERNORS OF THE OIL-PRODUCING STATES, HELD AT THE HOME OF GOVERNOR-ELECT E. W. MARLAND ON

first meeting was prophetic of the difficulties that were to characterize future meetings.

Invitations for the second meeting went out during December to fifteen major petroleum producing states, and when the group convened January 3 (again in Marland's home in Ponca City) representation was good. Texas, California, Louisiana, Arkansas, New Mexico, Illinois, Kansas, and Oklahoma had state delegations;[14] the Mid-Continent Oil and Gas Association and the Independent Producers Association of America were represented. Patrick J. Hurley, who assisted Governor Marland, read the resolution offered in December to the members of the conference, and its adoption was moved and seconded. Thereupon Mr. Hurley read a proposed draft of an uniform statute with an accompanying resolution; it was moved that these be considered rather than the December resolution.[15] Because the objection was made that a number of those present were authorized by their principals to consider only the first resolution, the motion was withdrawn. After an amendment dealing with the public domain had been presented and withdrawn by its sponsor,[16] Governor Marland suggested the meeting

---

JANUARY 3, 1935 (the official transcript of the meeting). This is also to be found in *Hearings* note 3 *supra* at 2886; Marland's address to the meeting appears at 2884–2887. The resolution called for the legislative creation of a joint fact finding agency to estimate demand for consumption and export, determine what relative proportions or production and storage should be used to meet consumptive demand and to allocate among the states their part of the domestic production. The president, through designated federal agencies, would restrict imports in line with the estimates of the fact finders, and the proposed act would authorize him to prevent the movement in interstate commerce of petroleum and products produced in excess of state quotas. It was further suggested that the oil states be permitted to enter voluntarily into an agreement subject to presidential approval to (1) participate in a joint fact finding agency, and (2) receive recommendations as to allowables and make them effective as far as their statutes permitted and (3) cooperate with the joint agency in a study of uniform conservation laws and regulations designed to promote maximum ultimate recovery. A great deal of power remained in the Federal Government under the resolution.

[14] Governor Marland was the only chief executive in attendance. He was assisted by Att'y. Gen. Williamson, Patrick J. Hurley and Northcutt Ely, among others. Jack B. Blalock represented Texas, Robert L. Patterson California, John S. Farrell, assisted by Ralph H. Cummins (both of Texas) represented Louisiana, Jeff Davis and John W. Olvey, Arkansas, Hiram Dow, New Mexico, William Bell, Illinois, T. C. Johnson and E. B. Shawver, Kansas. N.Y. Times, Jan. 2, 1935, p. 48, c. 5.

[15] The full text of this draft and its accompanying resolution are found in MINUTES *supra* note 13 at 21–23.

[16] This was offered by Mr. Patterson of California twice—once here and once at the third meeting. It dealt with leases on the public domain and their extension.

return to a consideration of his initial December resolution. At this Jack B. Blalock, Governor Allred's representative, objected to the call for a vote, saying that his principal was opposed to the December resolution because it called for joint participation by the Federal Government and the states. He suggested that Texas and its governor were inclined to interstate agreement, and "let's make it an interstate compact and not a compact with the Federal Government." [17] Governor Marland offered to re-word the original resolution by striking out the reference in its first section to the Federal Government, but Mr. Blalock declared that this did not meet the objections raised. Mr. Johnson of Kansas, speaking against the change, was "afraid that without the leverage of the Federal Government, we won't accomplish anything." In an attempt to placate both, Marland stated that he felt the resolution was not weakened by the withdrawal, and that he was certain that the Congress would not permit an interstate agreement of this nature without requiring federal representation. The change was approved. [18]

Mr. Blalock then asked permission to supplement the remarks he had made prior to the noon recess, and attacked the resolution as an unwise commitment of the states to a principal course of procedure when a much more expeditious way existed—that of merely securing consent in advance from Congress to enter into a compact. Blalock set forth in considerable detail the position of Allred. [19] He reminded the assembly that many of those present represented governors not yet in office, and therefore they were in no

[17] MINUTES note 13 supra at 15.

[18] All states with the exception of Louisiana voted for the adoption. Oklahoma did not vote.

[19] Governor Allred was opposed to federal control or regulation of the production of crude oil within the boundaries of Texas. He favored enactment by Congress into permanent legislation of the provision against interstate transportation of hot oil. He favored limitation by Congress of the importation of crude petroleum oil into the United States. He favored the prevention of physical waste of oil in his state and felt Texas had ample laws to prevent waste. He intended to enforce these laws properly. Should Congress deem it advisable for the states to cooperate in the conservation of petroleum and if permission were granted, the grant should be on the following conditions: "a. Said grant should be permissive only. b. Said permissive grant should confine the States to the consideration of conservation, that is to say, the prevention of physical waste of natural resources. c. Said permissive grant should recognize that the right to control the production of crude petroleum is a matter exclusively within the jurisdiction of the several producing states. d. Said permissive grant should specifically prohibit the states from entering into any compact which has as its purpose price-fixing, the creation or perpetuation of monopoly or regimentation."

position to bind the peoples of their jurisdictions. Although Marland recognized the inability of the representatives to obligate their respective states to take affirmative action in making a compact, he asked that the December resolution be adopted; it was passed.[20]

The draft of a suggested form of legislation that might be recommended by the conference to the state governing bodies was then again read. The desirability of these procedures was debated, and at length the Texas delegation moved that they be tabled as a whole. When put to a vote their motion failed,[21] but upon a motion for adoption they were declared carried.[22] It was then moved that a resolution memorializing Congress to enact legislation permitting the creation of an interstate compact to conserve oil and gas and to halt waste be adopted.[23] Upon a second it passed. A further resolution was offered by Texas that the permissive Congressional act contain a section specifically prohibiting price fixing or the creation or perpetuation of monopoly. Marland and Blalock then entered into a long and protracted argument over the part price played in conservation—Marland saying price was a major element, Blalock insisting that it promoted monopoly and regimentation and that his principal was unalterably opposed to price fixing.[24] The motion was tabled.[25] With the adjournment of this session it was understood that as soon as three states notified Governor Marland of their favorable action on the proposal to form an interstate compact, he would reconvene the conference.

At this pertinent time while the states were considering the pro-

[20] MINUTES note 13 *supra* at 20. For adoption California, Illinois, Kansas, New Mexico, and Oklahoma. Against adoption Texas, Arkansas, and Louisiana. N.Y. Times, Jan. 4, 1935, p. 31, c. 6.

[21] MINUTES note 13 *supra* at 21–23, 28–29. For tabling Texas, Arkansas, and Louisiana. Against tabling were Kansas, Illinois, New Mexico, and California. Oklahoma did not vote.

[22] MINUTES note 13 *supra* at 29. Oklahoma voted in favor as did Kansas, Illinois, New Mexico, and California. Against: Texas, Arkansas, and Louisiana.

[23] MINUTES note 13 *supra* at 30.

[24] MINUTES note 13 *supra* at 31, 32. The Texas and the Oklahoma position on the need for price fixing at this and the third meeting in Dallas is stated in terms of direct contradiction. Marland said that "the truest conservation . . . is the getting together and fixing of a price that will permit small wells to produce . . . the best interests of the people of the United States will be preserved. Blalock said this is price fixing, regimentation and monopoly which Allred will never agree to representing as he does "consumers as well as the producers."

[25] A motion to table was made and carried by Kansas, California, New Mexico, and Oklahoma. Contrary, Texas, Arkansas, and Louisiana.

posal for an interstate compact, the national scene provided an influential coincidence in the Cole Committee report. The Cole Committee report dated January 2, 1935 said, "we have not deemed it advisable at this time to set forth in this report or to prepare for introduction when Congress convenes . . . a bill or bills . . . (a) reason for not submitting legislation with this report is the pending effort of the Governors of the oil-producing States to effect an interstate compact. . . . *We strongly urge upon the oil-producing States the adoption of State compacts to deal with the problems of production of petroleum with which individual States are powerless to cope.* . . . Something real and substantial may grow out of the pending effort. If it does not the Seventy-fourth Congress will have ample time to pass such legislation as may be necessary." [26] (Italics added). With this open invitation from the Cole Committee to take steps or else, with the Disney-Thomas bill in the legislative mill, and with economic conditions in the industry showing little improvement, the conference to form a compact had behind it a tremendous pressure and force to come to an agreement upon an effective pact between the oil producing states.

Between January 3 and February 15, 1935 the necessary enabling legislation envisioned at the second meeting in Ponca City had been adopted in California, Kansas, Texas, New Mexico, and Oklahoma.[27] Governor Marland thereupon reconvened the third and final session of the conference in Dallas, Texas, at the Adolphus Hotel, with representatives from nine states present. A situation tense in character existed that February 15. In spite of the drives, the common cause, and the reason for the assembly, the meeting was plagued with inconsequential controversy highlighted by the manner in which the press and industry journals had focused on the governors of Texas and of Oklahoma. Allred and Marland both sought the convention spotlight. Their rivalry, although veiled by polite sarcasm, was crystallizing into firmer and firmer opposition. Each governor thought his state should somehow take precedence over all other states. It seemed to one observer that "everybody at

[26] H.R. Rep. No. 2, 74th Cong., 1st Sess. 9 (1935). N.Y. Times, Jan. 4, 1935, p. 31, c. 6.

[27] Calif. Laws 1935, c. 23; Kan. Laws 1935, c. 214; Tex. Laws 1935, vol. 2, concurrent resolution 26; N.M. Laws 1935, c. 1 (the first state to adopt the enabling legislation) and Okla. Laws 1935, c. 59. See N.Y. Times, Feb. 5, 1935, p. 37, c. 3.

the conference was so busy fighting one another that neither side had thought of our reason for being there." The two state positions—those of Texas and Oklahoma—were the same that had developed at the Ponca City conferences. Marland supported a doctrine of economic waste that in his opinion meant the government should prorate production to obtain a fair price for crude oil. The Texas delegates, almost hysterical in their opposition to price control which to them spelled eventual federal control, had aroused themselves to such a pitch that they seemed to be against everything and anything that could possibly be tarred with the brush of price fixing.

Marland was selected as chairman of the session.[28] He addressed the group outlining his activities in the past two meetings and the calling of the present session to adopt an interstate compact. He said, "the oil industry has never been satisfactorily regulated. There has never been uniformity in the laws enacted by the oil producing states . . . lack of intelligent regulation causes conditions . . . destructive to the best interests of the oil operators, the farmers, . . . the states in which the oil is produced, the consumers . . . and the welfare of the public of the United States. . . . There are two theories of conservation [he continued] . . . one would hoard the natural resources. . . . The other believes this generation has a right to waste or despoil resources, either by reason of greed or inefficiency." Concluding, Marland asked Governor Allred to lead a discussion of the subjects mentioned in his address. Allred relinquished this privilege for the time, and asked the delegates of other jurisdictions to speak. At the conclusion of their remarks, he read the resolution adopted in the Legislature of Texas under which he (Allred) was authorized to act.[29] Texas, Allred said, had made

[28] TRANSCRIPT OF PROCEEDINGS, OIL STATES COMPACT 1 (1934). Governors Allred and Marland attended. John W. Olvey represented Arkansas, Robert L. Patterson, California, Warwick M. Downing, Colorado, William Bell, Illinois, Ralph J. Pryor, T. C. Johnson and E. W. Shawver, Kansas, G. F. Vaneenanaam and Gerald Cotter, Michigan, Frank Vesley, Dr. E. H. Wells, Hugh Burch and Hiram E. Dow, New Mexico, Colonel E. O. Thompson, assisting Governor Allred, Senator Tom Anglin, assisting Governor Marland. The original transcript was poorly recorded and Warwick M. Downing was instructed to use it to prepare a further transcript. This he did immediately at the close of the session. He has reported to the writer that his transcript substantially represents what was done and said at the meeting.

[29] *Id.* at 8. The Texas resolution appeared in Tex. Laws 1935, col. 2, concurrent resolution 26.

its position clear with reference to entering into a compact with other states; it was willing to cooperate, but not to approve of any agreement that had for its purpose price fixing, monopoly, or regimentation. The Legislature of Texas sanctioned such a stand.[30] It had been his campaign slogan in the race for the governorship of Texas and a plank in the platform of the Texas Democratic Party. Governor Allred concluded by reading the compact agreement which he had prepared, the sole purpose of which was the conservation of oil and gas "by the prevention of physical waste."

Many questions were fired at Allred as to a definition of physical waste.[31] The heart of his use of this term was a prevention of overproduction only where actual physical waste occurred—never merely to balance supply and demand of oil, nor to produce for the existing market. Balancing of supply and demand could be nothing but price fixing and did not necessarily result in the physical wastage of petroleum. Allred had clipped out of the papers two or three articles about the compact proposal to which he referred. He said that the American Petroleum Institute had initially suggested the agreement and had been strong for federal control of the industry until the Institute found out that Secretary of the Interior Ickes [32] proposed to regulate production of oil from the well to the tank. Allred then accused Governor Marland of being behind statements which revealed that in his (Marland's) opinion the enactment of the compact would raise oil to $3 a barrel and of having said on other occasions that the rise would be at least to $1.50 or $2. Texas, the governor continued, would "not be a party to any such price fixing scheme." There was much heated rejoinder

[30] The pertinent portions of that resolution read: "the Governor of the State of Texas . . . is hereby authorized, empowered and directed to appear for and represent the State of Texas . . . at a conference of the duly authorized representatives of the oil producing States . . . to accomplish the conservation of petroleum and natural gas and the prevention of physical waste of these natural resources, without price fixing, and without the creation or perpetuation of monopoly or regimentation . . ."

[31] He was queried about overproduction resulting in waste, the use of excessive gasoil ratios, price, and the abandonment of small stripper wells.

[32] Secretary of the Interior Harold L. Ickes the week of the conference in an article appearing in 207 Sat. Eve. Post 5 (1935) said: There is at least some ground for the suspicion that some of the most vehement opponents of Federal control are proclaiming their belief in state compacts so as to draw the familiar red herring across the trail . . . they want the industry to run wild . . . they declare for an interstate compact convinced on the basis of past experience that it cannot succeed." Mr. Olvey of Arkansas moved that the conference express its regret at this statement but his motion was tabled.

and interplay between the two governors over the part price played in the establishment of a sound conservation program.

When the afternoon session reconvened, Governor Marland asked each state delegation to consider "what legal obstacles, if any, there would be in . . . adopting the suggestions of Governor Allred," having in mind the terms of the Allred compact [33] read to the assembly during the morning. No serious conflicts were found in the laws of any jurisdiction represented, although some had existing definitions of waste that went far beyond those proposed. Allred said his plan would not compel anyone to repeal statutes, but at the same time the agreement would not authorize any state to limit the production of oil and gas for the purpose of stabilizing and fixing prices.

The conference named Judge Warwick M. Downing as the chairman of a committee to prepare a document that would embody in its essentials the elements of both the Allred and Marland proposals. Choosing Judge Elwood Fouts of Texas and Senator Tom Anglin of Oklahoma to aid him, Downing proceeded to draft a compromise compact. The next morning the meeting was ready to continue with the compromise proposal worked out by the Downing Committee, but the draft was not as yet ready for distribution. Marland took this break down in the agenda as an opportunity to submit to the delegates his proposed form of an interstate compact—The Conservation of the American Oil Supply.[34] This represented "months of grave consideration of our problem [offered] as my suggestion." In conclusion he stated that the report of the Cole Committee would be considered in Congress the following Monday and that he had just talked with Chairman Cole. Cole had suggested that Congress would like to have the viewpoint of the meeting on the matter of state controls of the oil industry.

Feeling that his compact was being purposely shunted aside, Allred protested. It had been his understanding that the group would vote on the Allred compact. To this Governor Marland let it be known that he did not want to vote on that agreement; what he wanted to do was to secure an expression of opinion on his

---

[33] See Appendix C *infra* for a full copy of the Allred compact.
[34] See Appendix C *infra* for a full copy of the Marland convention.

measure in the same fashion the Allred proposal had enjoyed the day before. The Kansas representative, Ralph Pryor, interrupted to state that his delegation was ready to "subscribe to his [Marland's] compact as proposed."

This was too much for Governor Allred. In an impassioned address he reminded his listeners that Marland had said the preceding day that he (Marland) did not want to vote against any proposal and had insisted that the Allred plan either be voted upon or discussed section by section (which had been done). Agreements with Mr. Downing as to changes had been made and with the exception of typing the draft, the conference was ready to consider the compromise measure. Instead, "already two states have arisen and notwithstanding [that a copy] of this [Marland's proposal] has been in my hands about thirty minutes, and yesterday morning everyone insisted upon time to read and discuss the copy of mine, . . . [now] states have said they are ready to accept [Marland's agreement]." When asked if he would consider the Marland convention section by section, Allred stated he was only ready to vote upon his proposal—which he had thought was agreeable at adjournment the previous evening. He did not even care to examine the Marland plan until after a vote, although he acknowledged that adoption of his plan would foreclose discussion of the other.

Coincident with this flurry between the governors, Allred declared that he had no doubt but that if "two or three words had been put into the compact [that is his proposal] it would have been adopted and over with last night, and that is the purpose of the vote this morning with the Governor of Oklahoma." He said that the convention introduced into the agreement the thing he and the State of Texas had opposed since the December meeting in Ponca City—price fixing. When Marland challenged him to show just where those terms appeared, Allred retorted, "well, you just read it Governor." It was not necessary to "put price into it to have price in mind, and that is just what you have Governor; you admitted that yesterday morning; that is what you are after . . . and that is the purpose of this [the Marland convention]. I compliment you upon your phraseology."

It was at this point that the personal strivings of the rival governors endangered the possibility of agreement. It was no secret that neither of them could tolerate the other becoming the pre-dominant figure in the conference. Marland had the votes of the delegates, Allred the ultimate power. In this atmosphere Warwick M. Downing, whose role as the peacemaker of the meeting is often overlooked, rose to address the delegates, proposing as a compromise these factors: (1) that the meeting should not attempt to cram down Texas' throat a program essentially contrary to its policy or its prejudices and (2) that the conferees should resolve to be strongly against price fixing and in favor of physical waste, giving the governing body of the compact the power to promote maximum ultimate recovery and to recommend measures for such recovery of oil and gas. This would satisfy the Oklahoma position. Texas wanted to work under the banner of physical waste, while Oklahoma felt that the device on the flag should read economic waste. In describing the manner in which the offered compromise was prepared, Downing said that he had read the Marland draft carefully, considered its essence, and found that contained in one sentence. That sentence read: "that the Commission shall have power to recommend the coordination of the exercise of the police powers of the several states within their jurisdictions to promote the maximum ultimate recovery from the petroleum reserves of the said states, and to recommend measures for the maximum ultimate recovery of oil and gas." His solution of inserting within the draft those phrases contended for by both Marland and Allred was readily agreed to by Allred. Allred wanted a declaration against price fixing, but had no serious objection to any recommendation that brought about greater ultimate recovery. Marland held out longer against the compromise, but after caucusing with his legisla-tive advisers, he agreed to the draft.

The compromise report was then adopted by unanimous consent of the conferees.

But even with this meeting the tasks facing those who desired to bring the compactual agreement into effect were not ended. The proposal had two requirements to meet before it could become effective: (1) to secure the approbation of the state legislatures of at least three of the States of New Mexico, California, Texas, Okla-homa, and Kansas and (2) to secure the consent of the Congress and the president to the pact. Fortunately 1935 was an odd year and a number of the state legislatures were in session. New Mexico ratified the Compact February 25, followed by Oklahoma on March 6, Kansas on March 13, Colorado and Texas on April 15, and Illinois on July 10.[35] August 9, 1935 President Franklin D. Roosevelt transmitted a certified copy of the agreement (the original being deposited in the office of the Secretary of State) to the 74th Congress meeting in its first session, together with a message recommending that the necessary legislation be adopted.[36]

Between August 9 and August 27, 1935 the struggle for federal control continued in the Congress. When the message from the president was referred to the sub-committee of the House Committee on Interstate and Foreign Commerce, other legislation was prepared. The report [37] of that group stated that ". . . the compact itself is not the strongest document of that kind that could be drawn . . ." The bill, H. R. No. 9053, then proceeded to supply those ideas thought necessary to make the document the strongest compact possible. The recommendation of the sub-committee made August 14 was that the bill do pass. A storm of protest arose from the friends of the compact. The bill gave consent in Section 1 to the formation of a Compact by the states, but in addition it incorporated and tacked on to the statute those very features considered most objectionable to the conference at Dallas. What the members of that meeting expected was but a simple resolution of Congress giving consent to the product of their labors; what Congress proposed to give them was complete federal participation in the business of producing oil and gas.

As the protest and complaint mounted, the sponsors of the controversial bill, Representative Wesley E. Disney and Senator Elmer Thomas, withdrew it and substituted a resolution giving the necessary consent. This received the final approval of Congress August 27, 1935 and was signed by the president. The Interstate Compact to Conserve Oil and Gas became a reality.

[35] N.M. Laws 1935, c. 128; Okla. Laws 1935, c. 59; Kan. Laws 1935, c. 215; Colo. Laws 1935, SJR #18; Tex. Laws 1935, vol. 1, c. 81; Ill. Laws 1935, p. 1418.

[36] SEN. DOC. 118, 74th Cong., 1st Sess. 1 (1935).

[37] H.R. REP. No. 1801, 74th Cong., 1st Sess. (1935) contains a copy of the bill in full.

CHAPTER 39

The Interstate Compact to Conserve Oil and Gas: The Interstate Oil Compact Commission, 1935–1948

~/~

Twenty oil and gas producing states,[1] signatories of the Interstate Compact to Conserve Oil and Gas and members of the Interstate Oil Compact Commission, work together within a constitutionally approved formula to conserve the petrolic wealth of the United States. A state, upon becoming a member of the compactual association, assumes a moral if not a contractual responsibility to enact and continue in force laws designed to prevent the physical wastage of oil and gas, and as a member of the Commission cooperates with other jurisdictions in fulfilling the need for effective conservation of petroleum resources *without stabilizing a price structure for crude oil or natural gas through the creation or perpetuation of monopoly control.*

THE INTERSTATE COMPACT TO CONSERVE OIL AND GAS

The Constitution of the United States provides [2] that "No State shall, without the consent of Congress . . . enter into any Agree-

BLAKELY M. MURPHY, WRITER; Earl Foster, E. O. Thompson, Advisers. (See app. B.)

[1] Alabama, Arkansas, Colorado, Florida, Illinois, Indiana, Kansas, Kentucky, Louisiana, Michigan, Mississippi, Montana, New Mexico, New York, Ohio, Oklahoma, Pennsylvania, Tennessee, Texas, and West Virginia. Congressional consent to the Compact and its continuance has been given readily. See for this authority: Pub. Res. No. 64 (Aug. 27, 1935) which ran to 1937; Pub. Res. No. 57, SJR No. 183 (May 10, 1937) extending the term to 1939; HJR No. 329, Pub. Res. No. 31 (July 10, 1939) expiring in 1941; HJR No. 228, Pub. L. No. 246, 77th Cong., 1st Sess. (Aug. 1, 1941) to end in 1943; HJR No. 139 (July 7, 1943) to end in 1947, and Pub. L. No. 184, 80 Cong., 1st Sess. (July 12, 1947) to end in 1951.

[2] Art. 1, § 10 cl. 3. On the question of compacts generally see: Frankfurter and Landis, *The Compact Clause of the Constitution,* 34 YALE L.J. 685 (1925), Wein-

ment or Compact with another State . . ."; under this clause enterprises of great pitch and moment have been organized and are currently being undertaken by the sovereign states with the consent of Congress.[3] One of the most successful pacts executed under the section is the Interstate Compact to Conserve Oil and Gas. This Compact is dedicated to the following objectives: (1) a recognition of the necessity for the conservation of petroleum through waste prevention, (2) the adoption by states, now members or which may become members, of minimum essential rules of conservation operating to prevent waste and the maintenance of these standards, (3) an open admission that the waste prevention program must not be used as a device to control the price structure of oil and gas or to create or perpetuate monopoly in the petroleum industry, and (4) the establishment of an administrative agency to further the conservation principles which the Compact endorses.

Having read of the formative days of the agreement, attention is directed to the terms of the document signed February 16, 1935 at Dallas, Texas.[4] Under Article II the purpose of the agreement is stated as the conservation of oil and gas by the prevention of physical waste.[5] Articles III and IV bind the state members of the pact

---

feld, *What Did the Framers of the Federal Constitution Mean by "Agreements or Compacts?"* 3 U. OF CHI. L. REV. 453 (1936), FARRAND, THE RECORDS OF THE FEDERAL CONVENTION 187 (1911), Dutton, *Compacts and Trade Barriers*, 16 IND. L.J. 204 (1940), Dodd, *Interstate Compacts*, 70 U.S. L. REV. 557 (1936), Note, *Legal Problems Relating to Interstate Compacts*, 23 IOWA L. REV. 618 (1938), Note, *Interstate Compacts as a Means of Settling Disputes Between States*, 35 HARV. L. REV. 322 (1922), Note, *A Reconsideration of the Nature of Interstate Compacts*, 35 COL. L. REV. 76 (1935), Ireland, *Recent Developments in the Use of Interstate Water Compacts*, 21 DICTA 84 (1944), Routt, *Interstate Compacts and Administrative Cooperation*, 207 ANNALS 93 (1940), Spengler, *The Economic Limitations to Certain Uses of Interstate Compacts*, 31 AM. POL. SCI. REV. 41 (1937). The most recent compact proposals in point of time are the applications of the device to solve the problem of the division of the waters of the Upper Colorado Basin (July 1948) and the agreement to provide for regional education of colored students in the South. Note, *A New Use of the Interstate Compact*, 34 VA. L. REV. 64 (1948). Although hearings were held on this latter measure it failed to pass in the Congress of the United States.

[3] For a brief treatment of the areas into which compacts are organized and the literature see Murphy, *The Interstate Compact to Conserve Oil and Gas: An Experiment in Cooperative State Production Control*, 17 MISS. L.J. 314, 316 (1946). From 1789 to 1944 there were some 82 compacts entered into between the several states.

[4] The complete official Interstate Compact to Conserve Oil and Gas appears in APPENDIX C along with the Marland and Allred drafts.

[5] The elasticity of the term physical waste can give rise to a great breadth of definition. Originally the term meant the kind of waste that came about as a result of

to either enact, or if in force, to sustain the integrity of statutes designed to prevent the operation of wells with inefficient gas-oil ratios, the drowning with water of productive stratum, the escape into air of gas or its wasteful burning, the creation of fire hazards, the drilling, equipping, spacing, or operating of a well to bring about physical waste of oil or gas or loss in ultimate recovery, the inefficient use of reservoir energy, and the denial of access to commerce of oil produced in violation of state statutes or valid rules, regulations, and orders made under their authority.[6] Price fixing,

---

allowing oil and, in some instances, gas to waste in the sense of surface waste—oil was allowed to evaporate in storage, run off into creeks and earthen ponds, and the like. It is wholly possible in the various state statutes dealing with waste to find definitions that do not by exact name deal with physical waste although its essential requisites may be within the act. One need only pay heed to the various definitions of waste contained within the state histories in pt. II of this volume to determine the truth of the foregoing statement. It seems apparent that at the present time physical waste encompasses economic waste, surface waste, underground or reservoir energy waste, and that incident to production in excess of transportation, marketing facilities, and market demand.

[6] Article III bound each state on becoming a member to enact within a reasonable time, laws, or if these were already in existence, to continue them to prevent categories of waste. Article IV laid equal duties upon the states with respect to denying the channels of commerce to hot oil and requiring the levying of stringent penalties for waste of oil and gas. The majority of the jurisdictions members of the Compact have implemented these commands with faithful attention to their obligation. There are, however, now present in the Compact certain members who have failed to accept these responsibilities in two manners: (1) the state which accepts membership, participation in the formal business of the Commission but refuses to enact a law containing the minimum principles laid down in Articles III and IV, or (2) the state which, upon joining the Compact, inserts certain phrasing in the terms of its statutory adherences that the state by joining the Compact does not bind or obligate itself to enact, amend or alter legislation affecting the oil or gas industry. An example of the first is Illinois. See for example c. 10, Illinois, 1889–1948, supra. The second is represented by Montana and others. See for example c. 19, Montana, 1913–1948, supra. There has been an increasing tendency on the part of legislative bodies to write into statutes clauses of some unusual content. The Tennessee General Assembly in Tenn. P.A. 1947, c. 44 § 6 provided: ". . . nothing in this Act shall be construed to grant any power to the representative of the State on the Interstate Oil Compact Commission or to said Commission to prorate, allocate, regulate or control the production of oil or gas or the refined products thereof within the State of Tennessee . . . nor shall have the effect or be construed as in any manner surrendering to the Federal Government any rights over or in the production, sale, and transportation of oil or gas . . . nothing in this Act shall be understood or construed to obligate any succeeding General Assembly of the State of Tennessee to enact any 'model' act on the conservation of oil and gas." At no time did the Compact or the Commission claim to arrogate unto itself the powers which the state is reserving and never did anyone suppose that by signing this instrument, which is in its concept the antithesis of Federal Governmental interference with oil and gas, that it gave any powers to that Government. The concluding reservation is a puzzle. Ordinarily one legislative assembly cannot bind the hands of another; but the peculiar thing is that Tennessee

stabilization, and the creation or perpetuation of a monopoly are outlawed under Article V. The foundation upon which the present structure of the Interstate Oil Compact Commission is built is laid in Article VI. It provides that each state member of the group appoint one representative to a commission, whose duty is to make inquiry and to ascertain the methods, practices, and circumstances which bring about the prevention of physical waste of oil and gas and to report at intervals its findings and recommendations to the states. This Commission is given power in the agreement to recommend the coordination of state police power to the end that the maximum ultimate recovery of petroleum reserves are achieved and to make suggestions for these purposes. No state assumes a definite financial charge by membership [7] nor can it be called before the courts for breach of promise under the agreement.[8]

---

adopted the model suggested law proposed by the Legal Committee of the Commission in 1943, and is governed by it today. See Murphy, *Tennessee and the Interstate Compact to Conserve Oil and Gas*, 19 TENN. L. REV. 551 (1947). It has been said in this connection that it was up to each state to determine whether or not it had the kind of a conservation law required in Articles III and IV. This argument, it seems to other observers, falls short of the true purpose of the agreement. The state is left no option as to whether or not its law meets the requirements by using as a standard the state's judgment as to adequacy; it must be at those standards established in the agreement. Particularly bad are those statutes which specifically say that nothing in the act of becoming a member commits the state to enact any statute which affects oil or gas conservation or the industry. In defense of the Compact officials, it must be said that the only present requisites for membership in the agreement are that a jurisdiction (a) produce oil, (b) ratify, certify, and deposit a counterpart of the original Compact with the Department of State of the United States. Thus the Commission may have very little to do with a state's act of becoming a member from the standpoint of saying to a prospective member that this body will refuse you membership until certain named standards are adopted. This, of course, begs the question as to the effect of a rejection of the state by the Commission, as a demonstration of the moral pressure present in the agency.

[7] Art. VII reads: "No state by joining herein shall become financially obligated to any other state. . . ." Article VII, By-Laws of the Interstate Oil Compact Commission (1947) referred to hereafter as By-Laws reads: "The expense of this Commission shall be paid from voluntary contributions made by oil and gas producing states, in the manner and to the extent they may provide." A typical annual budget for the Compact Commission's operations would be: $60,000 allocated as follows: $2500 for books and technical publications, $8500 for printing and binding, and Commission publications, $32,000 for personal services, $7000 for office supplies and postage, $3000 for telephone and telegraph bills and $7000 for travel expenses. Since no financial assistance is accepted from sources other than member and associate member states, it is necessary that these jurisdictions provide by statute or otherwise a fund for the Commission's support. This is done in a number of ways. Oklahoma provides the use of quarters in the State Capitol Building for the use of the Commission free of charge. Recently these were redecorated and remodeled at considerable expense, not of the Commission, but of Oklahoma. Estimated financial contributions from

A formula respecting membership within the organization was written which implied that no jurisdiction not an "oil producing state" might become a member or a party to the compact. As an original proposition it seemed evident in 1935 that non-producing states would not choose to join in the cooperative endeavor. With the growth of prospecting for petroleum in states not classified as eligible for membership, demands for admission were heard, and it was agreed that these jurisdictions should be permitted a place in the effort.[9] Accordingly, a category of associate membership was formed to include states having "prospects for oil or gas production."[10]

There is in existence then a pact which commits subscribing members and associate members to sponsorship of conservation

---

members and associate member states are: Alabama, $400; Arkansas, $2000; Colorado, $500; Florida, $500; Illinois, $3500; Indiana, $1000; Kansas, $5000; Louisiana, $4000; Michigan, $500; Montana, $600; New Mexico, $1800; Oklahoma, $16,000; New York, $500; Pennsylvania, $1000; Texas, $20,000; and Georgia, $100. Other member states contribute to the fund in amounts that are irregular or indefinite. Several devices are used to secure these funds: HB No. 35, 21st Sess. of the Legis. of Okla. (1947) levied a tax upon crude oil and natural gas, a portion of which goes to the Compact. Indiana, in Senate Enrolled Bill No. 78 (1947), provided an annual payment of $1000. The increased cost of doing business has hit the Commission, as it has all other businesses, and it seems the outlay must be increased in the near future if the organization is to function at peak efficiency. The amounts contributed to such a worthy cause might be increased in the major oil producing jurisdictions.

[8] Art. VII.

[9] The Compact in its terms was very specifically limited to member states having oil production. See Art. I, Art. VIII. But since it is the conviction of informed persons that the time enact conservation statutes is prior to the discovery of oil and gas in substantial quantities, it became necessary to do something about those jurisdictions wherein the search for petroleum was going forward without production. The increased program of wildcatting in the geological provinces of the southeastern United States brought promises of oil and gas. See: *New Oil in the Old South*, The Lamp (Feb. 1943) 2. Agitation arose for the passage of adequate legislation in these states and many of them applied to the Legal Committee of the Commission for advice. From their association and contact with the Compact, requests for membership came.

[10] By-Laws, Art. IX: "There is hereby established associate membership in the Commission. Any state having prospects for oil or gas production may become an associate member in the following manner . . . make an application . . . in writing, signed by the Governor . . . or by the agency in charge of the regulation of oil and gas, with the approval of the Governor. Said application shall state . . . that the state has prospects for oil or gas . . . [and is] vitally interested in the program of the Interstate Compact and desires to participate in the Commission's activities. . . ." Thereafter a resolution adopted by the affirmative vote of the member states is necessary. Georgia is the only associate member, having joined in 1946. Recent informal conversations have been held with other jurisdictions desiring to take part in the program as associate members.

of one of the United States' most important non-reproducing natural resources by the prevention of physical waste, and eschewing regimentation through monopoly and price control. It has stood unamended since its original adoption in 1935.

THE INTERSTATE OIL COMPACT COMMISSION [11]

Created under Article VI of the Compact is the central unit in its administration—the Interstate Oil Compact Commission—composed of one representative drawn from each member state. That clause, with Article I of the By-Laws of the Commission,[12] carves out the prerogatives of this group to its place as the consultative arm of the Compact. The Commission is a fact finding body engaged in the conduct of studies to determine the most advanta-

[11] The official literature of the Interstate Oil Compact Commission is divided into these categories: (1) the TRANSCRIPTS, a series of mimeographed verbatim reports of the proceedings of the Commission at its quarterly meetings, published from 1935 through 1941. Copies were freely distributed among governmental agencies, college libraries and the industry. A complete set of these is now something of a rarity outside of the Commission offices. They are out of print and unobtainable from the Commission. (2) THE INTERSTATE OIL COMPACT QUARTERLY BULLETIN (cited officially as INTERSTATE OIL COMPACT Q. BULL.) began publication in April 1942 with volume one. Vol. I was issued in four parts, Vol. II in four parts, Vol. III in four parts, Vol. IV in two parts, each consisting of two numbers, Vol. V in three parts, the third part consisting of two numbers, Vol. VI in three parts, the third part consisting of two numbers and Vol. VII issued to May, 1948 in one part. This volume marks a change in the format and page size. The Bulletins have been issued widely and are available upon request to the Commission office. Early numbers are either exhausted or sorely depleted. (3) Compact Comments, a monthly newsletter issued beginning in 1946. (4) THE STATISTICAL BULLETIN, a monthly bulletin carrying condensed studies of national oil and gas statistics, charts, drilling activity summaries and a comparison of supply and demand trends, commenced publication in 1946. These are also available upon request. (5) During 1943 there was published the JOURNAL OF THE RESEARCH AND COORDINATING COMMITTEE under the direction of E. G. Dahlgren. This publication ran only through Vol. I, and no copies are presently available. In addition from time to time the Commission has published officially reports of various Committees in its systems. Incomplete listings of these are referred to throughout this chapter in connection with each Committee. A new offering is the Survey of Refinable Crude Oil Stocks (1948). A partial bibliography of the materials on the Interstate Oil Compact and the Commission may be found in Foster, *The Interstate Compact to Conserve Oil and Gas And Its Real Effect On True Conservation* 23, 32, PROC. SEC. MINERAL L. (Sept. 23, 1947). The Commission has ordered the preparation of an exhaustive bibliography on oil and gas conservation, which when completed in 1949 will include a comprehensive compilation of the literature of the Compact and of the Commission.

[12] The By-Laws of the Interstate Oil Compact Commission (1947) may be found in their entirety in APPENDIX D. Copies are obtainable from the offices of the Commission, P. O. Box 3127, Capitol Station, Oklahoma City, Okla.

geous methods, practices, and conditions of conservation. It makes use of its moral force and prestige within the industry and with the state conservation agencies to bring about the adoption in each state of recognized practices necessary to prevent the physical wastage of oil and gas.[13] Quarterly meetings of the agency are devoted to an analysis of reports from its research groups and to the establishment of official policy.

The By-Laws of the Commission and the Compact in Articles III and IV set out, to govern the conduct of its business, those rules and regulations commonly fixed to control parliamentary procedures, with the exception of voting. In 1935 and the years preceding, as now, the State of Texas was preeminent in the field of oil production; a vastly superior oil supply gave Texas unusual concern in the sharing of allowable oil units. As the question of voting on the Commission arose, a clamor came from Texans for a formula that would allow them a substantial measure of protection against being told what to do in Texas by compatriot states. Texas (in effect the big power at the treaty making conference in 1935) required a means to defend its rights against what it conceived would be the concerted efforts of the other states. The solution was an agreement that no action would be taken by the Commission unless, (1) it receives the affirmative vote of a major portion of the states present during any session, and (2) this action is acceptable to a majority in interest of those jurisdictions attending any meeting. The vote is evaluated by this formula: "Such vote of each state shall be in the decimal proportion fixed by the ratio of its daily average production during the preceding calendar half year

---

[13] The Commission exercises no function which attempts to tell anybody, any individual or any state what they can or cannot do. "It is an agency created for the purpose of attempting to get the states to agree among themselves upon a conservation program that will conserve . . . natural resources by the prevention of physical waste, without any outside suggestions or influences of any kind, nature or description. . . . It has no power. It is a recognized governmental agency. *It depends entirely upon itself for its influence by its power to educate, inform and investigate.*" (Italics supplied.) Statement by Judge Earl Foster, Executive Secretary of the Commission found in a stenographic transcript of *Hearings before the Special Committee to Study and Survey Problems of Small Business Enterprises*, U.S. Senate 293,294 (Mar. 12, 1948). The moral force and prestige which the Compact and the Commission exercise in the field of petroleum conservation is tremendous—its potentials even greater. There is no doubt but that the Commission could halt any type of prohibited waste in the United States by holding a hearing, the determination of that waste by the Commission, and a publication of its findings.

to the daily average production of the compacting states during said period." [14] The vote restriction clause is not a United Nations veto clause; it is a formula often employed in unit operations agreements. This rather peculiar clause insuring Texas predominance in any contested vote brought the parties together, and considering the furor caused at the outset, it is amusing to learn that it has never been necessary to exercise the formula as all decisions have been by unanimous vote.

Under the terms of the Compact, a Commission was authorized to meet and project suitable rules and regulations for its guidance. No instructions were laid down as to the means by which the agency would be governed, but the By-Laws, Article IV, officers the agency with a Chairman,[15] a First [16] and Second [17] Vice-Chairman (each of whom is accredited to the Commission as the representative of a compacting state), and an Executive Secretary. The December meeting brings about the selection of these elective officials, other than the Executive Secretary, who serve for one year. The Chairman presides at the regular and special committee meetings, issues through the Executive Secretary calls for and notices of meetings,[18] and fulfills the usual functions assigned his post by

[14] It was alleged in 1935 that Texas could produce more than half of the oil and gas needed to meet the demands of then users, and any agreement entered into by the Compact would be against the interests of the state, as it might be asked to assume more than a proportionate share of the ultimate reduction in consumptive capacity.

[15] The past chairmen have been: E. W. Marland, 1935–1936; Ernest O. Thompson, 1936–1940; Leon C. Phillips, 1940–1942; Andrew F. Schoeppel, 1942–1945; Robert S. Kerr, 1945–1946; Hiram M. Dow, 1946–1947; Beauford H. Jester, 1947–1948.

[16] The first vice-chairmen have been: E. O. Thompson, 1935–1936; Hiram M. Dow, 1936–1940, 1945–1946; Andrew F. Schoeppel, 1940–1942; J. C. Hunter, 1943–1945; Clarence T. Smith, 1946–1947; E. Leland Richardson, 1947–1948.

[17] The second vice-chairmen have been: Homer Hoch, 1935–1936; William Bell, 1936–1940; P. J. Hoffmaster, 1940–1942; Clarence T. Smith, 1942–1943; S. F. Peterson, 1943–1945; Warwick M. Downing, 1945–1947; Don T. Andrus, 1947–1948.

[18] The Compact Commission holds four meetings a year. There are occasional special called meetings of the entire Commission but the last one was in 1939. These sessions are open to the general public. Since the formation in 1935, the following meetings have been held:

Oklahoma City, Oklahoma	September 12, 1935
Oklahoma City, Oklahoma	October 11, 1935
Oklahoma City, Oklahoma	December 13, 1935
Oklahoma City, Oklahoma	March 13, 1936
Dallas, Texas	July 31, 1936

parliamentary procedure. The alternate chairmen serve in his absence. An Executive Committee is provided as a part of the administration and is composed of seven members elected from among the state representatives; although the powers and duties of the Committee are limited to those granted by resolutions issuing from the entire Commission, in practice no oppressive circum-

Oklahoma City, Oklahoma	October 2, 1936
Oklahoma City, Oklahoma	December 1, 1936
New Orleans, Louisiana	May 10, 1937
Santa Fe, New Mexico	July 12–13, 1937
Houston, Texas	October 14, 1937
Oklahoma City, Oklahoma	January 18, 1938
Wichita, Kansas	April 29–30, 1938
Colorado Springs, Colorado	July 29, 1938
Tulsa, Oklahoma	September 29, 1938
Fort Worth, Texas	December 15, 1938
Austin, Texas	March 16, 1939
Santa Fe, New Mexico	July 19–20, 1939
Oklahoma City, Oklahoma	August 15, 1939
Austin, Texas	August 29, 1939
Fort Worth, Texas	September 15, 1939
Wichita, Kansas	January 22, 1940
Oklahoma City, Oklahoma	April 5, 1940
Oklahoma City, Oklahoma	August 23, 1940
Tulsa, Oklahoma	December 6–7, 1940
Oklahoma City, Oklahoma	December 30, 1940
New Orleans, Louisiana	April 14, 1941
Fort Worth, Texas	October 16, 1941
Oklahoma City, Oklahoma	December 19–20, 1941
Little Rock, Arkansas	March 28, 1942
Lexington, Kentucky	June 20, 1942
Chicago, Illinois	October 2–3, 1942
Oklahoma City, Oklahoma	December 18–19, 1942
Wichita, Kansas	April 2–3, 1942
Pittsburgh, Pennsylvania	June 26, 1943
Santa Fe, New Mexico	September 25, 1943
Wichita, Kansas	December 10–11, 1943
New Orleans, Louisiana	April 3–4, 1944
Denver, Colorado	June 30–July 1, 1944
Oklahoma City, Oklahoma	October 5–7, 1944
Jackson, Mississippi	December 14–16, 1944
Oklahoma City, Oklahoma	June 15–16, 1945
Wichita, Kansas	December 13–15, 1945
Tulsa, Oklahoma	April 11–13, 1946
Grand Rapids, Michigan	August 8–10, 1946
Dallas, Texas	December 9–11, 1946
Birmingham, Alabama	April 24–26, 1947
Great Falls, Montana	August 11–13, 1947
Oklahoma City, Oklahoma	December 5–6–7, 1947
Chicago, Illinois	May 5–6–7, 1948
New York, New York	August 30, September 1, 2, 1948

scriptions have been initiated. In the office of Executive Secretary [19] are grouped the responsibilities for overseeing the myriad activities of the Commission, at its headquarters in the Capitol Building, Oklahoma City, Oklahoma. The incumbent, Judge Earl Foster, in contradistinction to the chairman, devotes his full time and energy to the successful prosecution of the administrative organization. Under his direction falls the management of the subordinate staff and employees, the conduct of the central office of the Commission, the discharge of directives of the Commission, the implementation of its policies and program, and the keeping of records and minutes. In the office Judge Foster serves as the balance wheel around which the administration of the conservation program revolves. It is his hand that translates unexecuted tactics into action; his the function of dealing with the general public in its relations to the Commission.

THE COMMITTEE SYSTEM [20]

Not long after the adoption of the By-Laws in 1935, the Commission created four panels to undertake initial investigations in areas of fact finding—the Committees on Conservation, Coordination, Consumption, and Import and Export. To each were assigned these respective tasks: (1) Committee on Conservation—report on the status of state legislation and administrative control of conservation; (2) Committee on Coordination—ascertain the aggregate prospective production of oil and gas in each member state and the percentage of the potential produced; (3) Committee on Consumption—review the methods of forecasting and reporting

[19] The post was originally that of Secretary for the Commission. It was held by Art Walker from 1935–1939; Charles L. Orr, 1939–1944; E. G. Dahlgren was Acting Secretary, July 1944–Nov. 1944; and Earl Foster, 1944–

[20] Included within the limits of the Committee System are those sub-groupings that now—or in the past—have existed within the work of the Commission. This division of committee activity eliminates such groups as the Committee for the Extension of the Compact. Similarly no mention is made of a Resolutions Committee nor of the Committee on Education. In the same manner relegated to a footnote are the industry advisory committees organized under the authority of the By-Laws, Art. V. The Commission also provides that the President of the United States, the Congress, and any federal agency charged with responsibility concerning oil or gas might designate a representative to participate in the meetings without a right to vote. See: Art. VIII, By-Laws. The Federal Power Commission, the Department of the Interior and the Bureau of Mines are so represented.

current consumptive demand for oil, gas, and product; and (4) Committee on Import and Export—survey the effect on domestic production of importation and exportation of oil, gas, and product. The four groups ceased activity with the completion of their programs,[21] and no further attention was given to conservation research.

But a continuing need for functioning committees was voiced at the April 1938 meeting of the Commission.[22] The Commission representative from New Mexico, Hiram M. Dow, proposed to that body that it would be "advantageous to the Compact Commission and the compacting states if we would have a committee that would submit to the Compact a report . . . suggesting what might be done . . ." to create a permanent cluster of sub-agencies to counsel the Commission on questions within its scope of authority. Persons interested in the work of the Commission were mustered into a unit to search out means of stabilizing the direction in which the organization might grow. In July 1939 this sub-unit, inappropriately entitled the Advisory Committee on Economics, proposed: "a. That the Interstate Oil Compact Commission appoint a Committee on Proration Practices . . . charged with the duty of studying the existing proration practices in each State and reporting thereon." [23] Personnel to staff this group was drawn from the regulatory agencies, geological surveys, and state universities. Colonel Ernest O. Thompson, then Commission Chairman, set into motion a body so constituted, with Andrew F. Schoeppel as Chairman. No laggard was the Committee on Proration Practices for it submitted its *precis* August 23, 1940 proposing the dissolution of the group

[21] The work done by these Committees has been largely overlooked in the studies of the Commission. For example the Committee on Conservation compiled the conservation laws of the states as well as the administrative rules and regulations. Topical indices were prepared which related to the laws of 20 states and the Federal Government insofar as they dealt with oil and gas conservation and production. This was mimeographed and placed in the Commission records. The Committee had no funds to secure its publication and finally gave up their efforts. The Committee on Coordination issued one report, Mar. 13, 1936, urging the continuance of the Connally Act. The Committee on Consumption studied the accuracy of forecasting methods for determining supply and demand of oil and exhaustively reviewed the methods used in the Bureau of Mines. The group backed the requests of the Bureau to make studies of storage above ground. The Committee on Imports and Exports made rather careful surveys of the situation.

[22] Interstate Oil Compact Commission, Transcripts (Apr. 29, 30, 1938) 59 ff. (cited hereafter as Transcripts). See note 11 for a complete discussion of the literature of the Commission which deals with this publication.

[23] Transcripts (July 19, 1939) 35.

as a formal entity and the creation in its stead of: "1. [a] Legal
Committee, to inquire into the laws of the various states and to
prepare a model law that might be recommended by the Compact
Commission . . . 2. [an] Engineering Committee, to inquire into
the principles and practices of conservation in the production of oil
and gas in order that this Commission may make recommendations
to the various states. 3. [a] Committee on regulatory practices, to
inquire into the development of regulatory practices, and to recommend such standards as seem generally applicable." [24]

Long an integral portion of the Commission pattern are the
committees formed to study and report to the parent organization
on phases of conservation investigation. Composed of men outstanding in their professions in the compacting jurisdictions, these
groups devote their talents to research in sifting the problems of
the Commission. Sessions are held in conjunction with the meetings of the Compact Commission.[25]

(a) The Legal Committee

Inasmuch as this unit had a continuity of purpose with the old
Committee on Conservation, the bulk of the information there
collected served to guide its initial efforts into substantial spheres of
intellectual action. Building upon the accumulation of past knowledge, the Committee decided to forego further excursions into the
field of codification of oil and gas law, and to concentrate its
energies in preparing forms or provisions suitable for statutes that
might serve somewhat the same function as the acts issued by the

[24] TRANSCRIPTS (Aug. 23, 1940) 6, 7.

[25] The committees meet in executive session during the quarterly conferences of
the Commission. Prior to the actual date, a program of study is formulated in the
committee organization, its preparation assigned to speakers and papers prepared concerning material and research in that field. Originally a day and a half sufficed for these
sessions, but now the work has grown to an extent that some groups meet several
days in advance of the Commission in order to complete their agenda. Ordinarily
anyone desiring to attend a meeting is welcome, and although it might be that an
occasional session would be closed, it is not the general practice. At the conclusion of
each committee session a report on the work for the quarter is drafted, together with
any recommendations made to the Commission. These are presented to the parent
body for its consideration. No action of any committee becomes the official policy of
the Commission until it receives the approval of that body. Persons interested in the
reports of specific committees should refer to the INTERSTATE OIL COMPACT Q. BULL.
for this information.

National Conference of Commissioners of Uniform Laws.[26] Conversations with leading petroleum attorneys and authorities in the state regulatory agencies were set in motion during November 1940 at the annual meeting of the American Petroleum Institute. Certain fundamental conservation statutes were drawn upon for basic materials in the construction of a suggested form of an oil and gas conservation law. After much study and discussion by the Committee members, aided by the counsel furnished by industry attorneys and agency personnel, a suggested statute was drafted based upon the theory of waste control.[27] In accepting this idea as its premise the Committee followed the current trend in similar statutes. Its breadth of definition of waste went beyond like sections of the Arkansas enactment of 1939.

Completion of the codes in their original form did not put an end to the efforts of the Legal Committee. Continued demand on its labors by the Commission has led the subgroup to explore legal areas of secondary recovery, unit operation and pooling agreements, drilling, operation of wells, transportation and marketing of natural gas, surveys of current legislative styles in oil and gas states, consideration of the anti-monopoly statutes of the states and the Federal Government, and a survey of legal methods needed to control wild wells. In 1946 a sub-committee studied the organization and functioning of oil field engineering committees and pre-

[26] The drafters of the comprehensive model statutes early decided that no one uniform act would satisfy the requirements of conservation. The constitutional backgrounds of the oil states differed. What the Legal Committee then did was to create a "legal pattern which could be used as a basis of guidance to any state in its compilation of a law to meet that state's individual and singular needs and requirements." Two positions were present in the drafts of these comprehensive statutes—the regulatory agency idea and the industry idea. After spending considerable time and effort in an attempt to reconcile these concepts, the Committee voted to adopt, in cases of divided decision, alternate paragraphs.

[27] Interstate Oil Compact Commission, *A Comprehensive Suggested Oil and Gas Conservation Law Containing Provisions Suitable for Adoption in Any State.* This proposal first received Commission approval Dec. 30, 1940. In Apr. 1941, the Committee prepared a less lengthy statute for states having only limited or prospective production. *Short Form Conservation Law A* was "an abbreviation of the draft of suggestions for provisions suitable for a comprehensive conservation bill." See I INTERSTATE OIL COMPACT Q. BULL. 109 (1942). *Short Form Conservation Law B* was "intended to vest in a regulatory commission sufficient power to regulate the production of oil and gas so as to avoid waste, and independent of waste, to protect the correlative rights of producers." *Id.* at 115. The enactments are available in pamphlet form from the Commission. Legal Committee, FORMS FOR OIL AND GAS CONSERVATION LAWS (Aug. 1946).

pared a report, *Organization and Functioning of Oil-Field Engineering Committees With Forms,* which included a valuable collection of papers and forms. Extensive collections of research material have been gathered in the files of the Committee; the background for a comparative study of conservation law is laid in these papers. A forum for discussion of common problems is created for the oil attorney, as well as a place for the expression of his individual thought. Stimulation of research in the area of conservation law is provided, an attribute that nowhere existed in any body free of the taint of self interest. In May 1948 the Committee finished its reorganization efforts voted at the December 1947 meeting, by electing a Chairman,[28] Vice-Chairman [29] and Executive Secretary.[30] The Committee is prepared to undertake a strenuous program of study into the many interesting facets of the law reflecting upon conservation.[31]

Recurrent revisions of the comprehensive conservation law are taking place within the Committee to maintain its sections at modern standards—in fact the present reworking of the statute strikes far out into tomorrow in an attempt to be forward looking into the future of statutory controls of oil and gas.[32]

(b) The Engineering Committee

In accordance with the report of the Committee on Proration Practices, a subdivision of the Commission was created August 23, 1940 charged with inquiry into the "principles and practices of conservation in the production of oil and gas. . . ." With personnel taken from engineering and geological staffs of regulatory

---

[28] Judge Earl Foster, Executive Secretary of the Commission, has been Chairman of the Legal Committee since its inception.

[29] Floyd Green, Conservation Attorney, Oklahoma Corporation Commission, serves as the first Vice-Chairman under the reorganization.

[30] Blakely M. Murphy is the Executive Secretary.

[31] The reorganization of the Legal Committee was undertaken with the thought of increasing its efficiency in providing an agenda of study that would carry out research into the legal field. The Committee is now working out a program of yearly legal reports from the compacting and non-compacting states for publication in a yearbook.

[32] A sub-committee of the Legal Committee was appointed in 1948 under the direction of T. Murray Robinson, Chairman and with Robert E. Hardwicke, George W. Hazlett, Ross L. Malone, E. Leland Richardson and Blakely M. Murphy as members, to prepare a revised or an entirely new statutory concept of oil and gas conservation. This group has had several meetings and has prepared certain drafts of new enactments.

bodies, from state universities, and their schools of petroleum engineering, a series of open hearings in the industry was initiated. Questionnaires based upon problems of engineering for conservation were directed to the research organizations maintained by major producers of oil and gas, and to the colleges and universities engaged in kindred studies. From these hearings and from a compilation of the data brought into its possession in answer to its queries, the Committee assembled an erstwhile uncollected mass of information, which it rapidly reduced to usable form. However, as early as December 1940, a precursory report suggested that the group devote its collective talents to "surveying the whole broad dynamic field of technologic practices in production and of attempting to codify for the first time, the principles governing those practices . . . which have general application and those which have special application." After preliminary embarkation on the formulation of these principles, a plan was evolved to present the results of study in a handbook. Decisions later made dictated a change—and instead of a handbook [33] an engineering report was issued.

The engineering report,[34] presented in April 1941 and since amended to reflect present information, contains in brief a statement of engineering precepts designed to promote the conservation of petroleum resources. Within its context may be found the basic underlying postulates of ideal practices in the process of securing from the earth ultimate recoveries of oil and gas. It is stated therein, as a maximum which the Committee endorses, that the objectives of ideal conservation in action, of ideal engineering practices, and of ideal production performances are alike—the production of the most petroleum at a reasonable cost, optimum production not ultimate recovery at any price. Found in the report are recommendations made to the Commission, which the Committee propounds as first principles in the future conservation of our natural heritage of petroleum. Caution is expressed that the successful use of these developments can be implemented only in

[33] The Engineering Committee, long under the direction of E. DeGolyer, and more recently, Dean W. H. Carson, has under preparation a volume on engineering practices whose sections are reaching completion. The Committee has a grant from the Commission of $5000 to pay for publication.

[34] REPORT OF THE ENGINEERING COMMITTEE (1941). The validity of the material contained in this report is as good today as when it was written. Technical advances may occasionally prove a theoretical concept appearing in the report.

the operation of new pools or applied to areas operated under these or similar proposals. Nothing substantial could be done to improve ultimate recovery in those parts of the United States where older pools are found, except through specialized research in each of these locations.

In its professional diagnosis the work of the committee on engineering contributes a great deal to the understanding of laymen, and what is even more desirable, to the information of legislators. No other agency offers this service in an understandable form to persons unlearned in the techniques of petroleum engineering. In no other place are these salient engineering practices, designed to promote ideal conservation, so well set down. These materials are no laboratory nor schoolroom cant, but scientific principles which assemble and display the best and the worst in current productive practices.

(c) The Regulatory Practices Committee

Chairman Schoeppel in his 1940 report to the Commission solicited the organization of a sub-agency to "study the rules and regulations of the regulatory bodies of the various states and draw up model rules and regulations . . . as standards for general application." Selected wholly from among the state regulatory agency personnel, the Committee members were acquainted with the dearth of comprehensive comparative research into the activities of the state commissions. It was considered essential to the performance of the promises implicit in membership in the Compact that a means to determine compliance be established. Taking up an exhaustive review of the laws of each oil state, and the rules, regulations, and orders of its controlling agency, the Commission soon exposed the existing discrepancies in those jurisdictions. Broad, comprehensive rules of practice were adopted in one facet of regulation, while antithetical interpretations were (as to other matters) coexistent. Activities chosen for regulation in one state were often ignored in essence by other compact members. The attention of the states and the Commission was directed to divergent positions with a view to ascertaining what sanctioned their retention in regulatory administrations.

The Committee undertook a joint project with the Legal and Engineering Committees to secure coeval analysis of the proposed changes in the governmental control structure. Their work matured during April 1941 in rules and regulations suggested for adoption by the state agencies.[35] Starting with a procedure designed to control the essentials requisite to the drilling of oil or gas wells, the rules go through each sector of the productive process step by step and detail by detail to the eventual abandonment and plugging of the hole. Consideration is given to these elements: production, abatement of nuisance elements common to drilling, production abandonment, deviations in drilling, secondary recovery, and the disposal of oil field wastes as brines and mineralized waters.

At the October 1942 Commission session the Committee, after a sifting of the state laws governing control of natural gas, and of the rules and regulations issued in relation to production, reached the conclusion that each jurisdiction should enact statutes governing natural gas independent of its oil conservation laws. It was determined that these acts should be uniform as to context in the gas producing states, with the adoption of modifications in cases of unusual characteristics. Natural gas must be regulated at the well head in order to prevent waste (including economic waste and inefficient utilization), said the Committee. The Commission was alerted to the question of price control by each administrative agency and its effect on natural gas. By 1942 the Committee had resolved that the element of a low price and the existing disparities or inequalities stemming therefrom rendered hazardous enforcemen of gas conservation. The conclusion that effective gas conservation depended upon a satisfactory price caused the group to recommend (without determining what authority any state might possess to so do) the fixing of minimum values for gas at not less than five cents a thousand cubic feet.[36]

[35] GENERAL RULES AND REGULATIONS FOR THE CONSERVATION OF CRUDE OIL AND NATURAL GAS (1946). This Committee under the direction of T. A. Morgan, Chairman, consistently presents one of the most interesting programs of research and study done in the Commission effort. Their quarterly reports, reprinted in the INTERSTATE OIL COMPACT Q. BULL. are a must in the literature of conservation. A report on the manner and method of administration of oil and gas regulation by the individual states was submitted in Aug. 1948. Data included in the survey covered such subjects as: checking of well spacing, supervision of casing setting, cementing practices, temperature surveys, plugging, production report checking, methods of determining allowables, restrictions on discovery allowables, and unit operation rules.

[36] See FPC, Report on the Natural Gas Investigation, pt. V, 35; pt. VI, 152 (1948) for a discussion of the price factor. Statutory attempts to fix minimum well head prices for natural gas have been unsuccessful. See c. 15. Louisiana, 1939–1948, *supra.* The Corporation Commission of Oklahoma in two cases, Peerless Oil and Gas Co.

(d) Economics Advisory Committee

Known originally as the Economics Committee, the Economics Advisory Committee received its inaugural force from an address delivered by Dr. Alexander Sachs at the Wichita meeting of the Compact Commission in 1938. In the course of his peroration the formation of a group was asked to represent "a continuing body of people studying the problems of the industry . . . not merely with reference to the month to month equilibrium of demand and supply, but the problem of the maintenance of the productivity, the profitability and the progress of the industry . . . I would have an advisory economic council . . . a body of advisory students of the problem who would be considering these large problems and reporting to the Compact Commission . . . to exercise an educative force." Embodied within the original reports of the Committee were those factors which brought about the creation of the Committee on Proration Practices and the ultimate establishment of the committee system under the Commission. When these concepts were put into action, the Economics Committee dropped from active participation in the affairs of the Compact, until its recent revival in the form it now represents and with its present title.

With a membership drawn largely from persons employed in responsible positions as economists for the larger oil companies in the United States, the Advisory Committee on Economics is somewhat at variance with the representation on the remainder of the Committees.[37] The business assigned this group by the Commission is to keep that body and its member states informed as to the

---

v. Cities Service Gas Co., and Peerless Oil and Gas Co. v. Cities Service Gas Co., et al, causes CD No. 1054 and Orders No. 19514 and 19515 (1947) ordered that the price of gas in certain formations be set at 7 cents per MCF. See c. 26, Oklahoma, 1938–1948, supra.

[37] Committee memberships in the other units are held by: persons associated with state regulatory agencies, state elective and appointive officials, representatives of universities and colleges, attorneys engaged in the private practice of law, and businessmen from the industry. It has not been the practice of the officials or employees of the larger oil and gas organizations to take any considerable official part in the committee activity, with the exception of the economics advisory body. As stated in Note 25 supra the meetings are open to the general public and persons employed by the oil and gas companies attend these sessions, as do people from the states and the Federal Government, the independent element in the industry and interested individuals. There may be good reason for the fact that the majority of the members on the Committee come from larger oil companies—the Commission wanted the very best

economic factors affecting the industry, including the quarterly forecasting of supply and demand for crude oil and its products.[38] Members meet previous to each session of the Commission and prepare estimates. Its purpose is to provide a basis upon which the Commission might suggest application of the conservation principles.[39] The Committee is an example of a voluntary fact finding body charged with the duty of expert and professional analysis.

---

practicing economists familiar with petroleum problems that they could get for their staff, and that was the place they were found. Selection of members is necessarily limited to those professional people who have both access to, and possession of the facts. Minor elements in the industry have representation; it has been suggested that their proportional representation is less as a result of a lack of eligible personnel. *See* for example the stenographic transcript of *Hearings before the Special Committee to Study and Survey Problems of Small Business Enterprises,* U.S. Senate 302, 303 and 304 (Mar. 12, 1948): "After a number of years we decided we needed the economics advisory committee. You understand that the independent petroleum association [Independent Petroleum Association of America] . . . had been making these estimates for a long time. The Bureau of Mines had been making these estimates for a long time. . . . We selected these men about three years ago to assist us together with the Bureau of Mines, . . . We picked what we thought were the best economists in the world. They were not selected by the Compact Commission. I will tell you who they were selected by. . . . Prior to that time we had had an advisory body known as the economics advisory council. They consisted of Joseph E. Pogue, Alexander Sachs, and Dr. E. DeGolyer. . . . They got together and said, 'We think you fellows need,' talking to the Commission—me, if you want to say it, talked to me first, and 'we will recommend a bunch of economists over the United States.'. . . And they picked out the leading economists in the United States. . . . There was not a one of them selected by the oil companies . . . some oil companies objected to their serving."

[38] The duties of the Economics Advisory Committee are stated thus: "To prepare and present at quarterly meetings, an estimate of future demand for refined products, probable imports of crude oil products, production anticipated of natural gasoline, and estimates of petroleum available without incurring waste to meet future needs. To advise the Compact at each of its meetings of the Committee's estimate of current working stocks, current and future stock requirements, and anticipated stock changes. To advise the Compact, upon the request of the Chairman of the Compact to the Chairman of the Economics Advisory Committee, upon any specific questions not covered in the foregoing general instructions. If information on a specific question is desired for any particular meeting of the Compact Commission, it will be the policy of the Commission to direct its request to the Economics Advisory Committee before the meeting, setting out the specific information desired." Interstate Oil Compact Commission, Executive Committee, Resolution of June 30, 1947. Information of similar import is available from the Bureau of Mines, the Department of the Interior, and the Supply and Demand Committee of the IPAA. The theory upon which the Compact Commission asks the Economics Advisory Committee to undertake its survey is: (1) it recognizes the worth of the estimates prepared by the Bureau of Mines and the Supply and Demand Committee of the IPAA, (2) it appreciates the dominating interest in the preparation of each of these surveys, (3) and it believes that the more sources of information which it has available to it—the better a job for conservation will be done.

[39] A number of the jurisdictions holding membership in the Compact have market demand statutes which prohibit production in excess of transportation or marketing

(e) The Research and Coordinating Committee

Tenuous in outline and indefinite in term is the scope assigned this subgroup of the Commission; practically, it has authority to inquire into any phase of the industry, to correlate all legal, administrative or technical data which comes into its possession, and to analyze these materials. Among its many concerns in the past have been: assisting in the formulation in 1942 of uniform standards and interpretations used in gathering data on sustained production rates and oil reserves, cooperating with the United States Bureau of Mines in securing samples of crude petroleum for analysis, interchanging views on secondary recovery and secondary recovery projects within the United States (in the course of which a historical summary of this process in the oil states was prepared) and pursuing studies of the natural gas industry. The Committee has carried on its most comprehensive labors within the secondary recovery field; surveys of the natural gas conservation and a comparative collection of information on stripper wells have also been made.

The Committee has done superlative work in the field of activity arrogated unto it. Credit for this goes to its practice of maintaining a permanent staff engaged in planning and executing its projects.[40] The assemblage of valuable and formerly unpublished, uncorrelated, and unknown (to many in the industry) statistics and factual reports, together with their orderly publication, has enlarged the range of perception of the Commission. These studies have

---

facilities or reasonable market demand. The story behind those enactments, their interpretation administratively and judicially and their aim, is ably told in the state histories *supra*. The Compact and the Commission are oriented towards waste prevention. These estimates as prepared by the Committee aid it in making determinations of the occurrence of waste. A comparison of forecasts as taken from the Interstate Oil Compact Commission publication III Statistical Bull. 17 (May 15, 1948) shows the estimates of the three forecasting groups in contrast. See page 591.

[40] E. G. Dahlgren, now Assistant Secretary to the Commission, formerly the Technical Secretary, is primarily responsible for the assimilation and publication of these materials. For a good résumé of certain committee activity see Dahlgren, *The Technical Activities of the Interstate Oil Compact Commission*, The Mines Magazine 539 (Nov. 1946). A nation wide survey of synthetic fuels is the latest study undertaken by the Committee and includes an inventory of raw materials such as natural gas, oil shales, and coal. Information on the status of research and pilot installations is presented as are data surveys on federal activities and legislation.

U.S. PETROLEUM SUPPLY AND DEMAND TRENDS
Comparison of Forecasts
(Thousands of Barrels)

	Independent Petroleum Association of America Supply and Demand Committee		Bureau of Mines Petroleum Economics Division					Interstate Oil Compact Commission Economics Advisory Committee						
	2nd Q 1948	3rd Q 1948	1st Q 1948	2nd Q 1948	3rd Q 1948	4th Q 1948	Year 1948	Year 1947	1st Q 1948	2nd Q 1948	3rd Q 1948	4th Q 1948	Year 1948	1st Q 1949
Total Demand	6,100*	6,170*	6,330	5,978	6,055	6,555	6,230	5,900	6,340	6,040	6,130	6,650	6,290	6,735
Daily New Supply														
Crude Petroleum	5,490	5,580	5,340	5,459	5,549	5,500	5,462	5,085	5,335	5,475	5,532	5,570	5,478	5,625
Nat. Gaso. and Benzol	400	410	397	409	418	413	409	364	395	400	410	415	405	420
	5,890	5,990	5,737	5,868	5,967	5,913	5,871	5,449	5,730	5,875	5,942	5,985	5,883	6,045
Daily Imports														
Crude Oil	—	—	280	291	319	315	301	—	—	—	—	—	—	—
Products	—	—	192	170	165	185	178	—	—	—	—	—	—	—
Total	460†	480†	472	461	484	500	479	437	475	475	500	520	492	520
Crude Runs to Stills	—	—	5,370	5,480	5,530	5,580	5,490	5,075	5,361	5,525	5,575	5,610	5,518	5,630
Total Closing Stocks														
Crude (Gaso.-Bearing)	228,000	223,000	224,929	224,929	224,929	224,929	224,929	224,900	224,800	221,900	221,900	227,100	227,100	234,500
Products (including Nat. Gaso.)	287,000	319,000	264,871	296,871	326,871	313,871	313,871	275,900	263,700	294,700	323,400	304,900	304,900	282,200
Total	515,000	542,000	489,800	521,800	551,800	538,800	538,800	500,800	488,500	516,600	545,300	532,000	532,000	516,700

* Includes exports as estimated by U.S. Bureau of Mines.
† As estimated by U.S. Bureau of Mines.

been widely disseminated and undoubtedly have left their mark upon the actions of conservation agencies.

(f) Public Lands Committee

A number of the compacting states are properly includible in the public land category—those where large amounts of surface area are held in ownership by the governments of the United States and of the states. Problems of leasing, producing, and marketing oil and gas leases on such lands are not comparable to the conduct of similar activities on properties which belong to private citizens and corporations.[41] To aid these states more effectively in working out the conservation approach to non-private lands, it was thought that the creation of a committee of their representatives would help solve their historical grievances. Since the Department of the Interior controls the greater amount of property in which the Committee is interested, its transactions have centered in dealing with that bureau. Frequent reports on proposed federal legislation and on rules and regulations of the Department in oil and gas leasing and production, together with recommendations for easing the lot of prospector and producer on federal lands, have been the forte of this Committee.

(g) Interstate Relations Committee

Need for an arm of the Commission to engage in missionary work with non-member states led to the formation of the Committee on Interstate Relations. The Committee efforts have been of a public relations or diplomatic nature in bringing to the fore those ills the Compact seeks to solve and the means of reaching satisfactory settlement.

(h) By-Laws Committee

Although infrequently called upon to serve in amending the By-Laws of the Commission, such a Committee has a useful purpose in that within its membership reposes a responsibility for seeing that the Commission rules keep current. Assigned to this group

[41] See for example c. 3, Arizona, 1912–1948 and c. 36, Wyoming, 1881–1948, *supra* for a discussion of the state problems in the public domain areas and c. 40 dealing with the public domain from the standpoint of the Federal Government, *infra*.

are matters of change in the governing regulations of the Commission.

(i) Stripper Well Committee

A new Committee of the Commission, the Stripper Well group is pregnant with possibilities for insuring continued attention of the regulatory bodies of the states to the solution of difficulties raised in marginal petroleum production. Carved in part out of the Research and Coordinating Committee, this unit is taking up its predecessor's work. It utilizes the services of the astute employees of the Research and Coordinating body. Directed to work with others interested in bringing about the continuation of the stripper well in economic service,[42] the Committee is cooperating with the National Stripper Well Association and the Independent Petroleum Association of America in developing a program. These three agencies are now consulting regarding "the nature of the work to be performed . . . the kind of data to be accumulated . . . and the extent of the survey." At the request of the two associations, the Stripper Well Committee assumed leadership in creating a joint commission to develop factual data covering the "stripper well area of the nation, the states where located, the pools in each state, and the productive acreage of each, and the approximate number of stripper wells in each pool. The reserves involved: (a) The recoverable reserves with present known methods of primary and secondary means. (b) The residual reserve."

(j) Secondary Recovery Advisory Committee

The Commission has created a Secondary Recovery Division within its framework. At the August 1947 meeting of the Commission, a Committee was established to aid in getting the work of the Division underway. Paul D. Torrey, Chairman, an outstanding petroleum consulting engineer, was employed for a period to aid in formulating the program. The Commission allocated $15,-000 from its funds to bring this Division into existence.[43] The

[42] The stripper well reserves represent a substantial portion of the nation's known reserves. New technologies make it possible to recover a much greater proportion of their reserves. A national survey is being undertaken by the Committee in practically every state in cooperation with state agencies and consultants.

[43] The Division, organized with Albert E. Sweeny, Jr. as its director, is now conducting an active survey through the country in connection with its activities. The

Committee has made several surveys of the legal and administrative situation in the oil states with reference to compulsory unit operation.

THE COMPACT, THE COMMISSION, AND CONSERVATION—A CRITIQUE

At last—after reviewing the provisions of the Compact and the operation of its administrative mechanism, the Commission—we should consider the basic concepts of conservation. But before we actually take up these principles, the physical phenomena of the production of petroleum must be explored. The most important of these phenomena is the *oil reservoir*.[44] Trapped underneath the surface of the earth in varying geological formations are the pressures that contribute to the recovery of oil. These forces lie within sands or limestones. The sands have well recognized characteristics—porosity and permeability—and each oil sand particle has a pore space filled with oil and interstitial water. The oil particle may be suffused with undissolved gas, although much of this gas may have migrated to upper formations. Ideally these fluids are distributed within the sand bed, with oil lying in the higher portions, and water saturating the lower reaches. A gas cap is a common element in the reservoir and rests in the highest level. Thus we have a reservoir holding gas underlain by oil, which in turn has water underneath. Three mechanisms participate individually in the recovery of oil from the pore space—gas cap drive, dissolved gas drive, and water drive. Realistic, efficient balancing of the

---

work being done is undoubtedly of the greatest value in connection with the conservation program. For the importance of secondary recovery to conservation see the Interstate Oil Compact Commission, SECONDARY RECOVERY FORUM (1947), a report of the joint meeting sponsored by the Commission and the Department of the Interior, Washington, D.C., May 15, 16, 1947, assembled by E. G. Dahlgren. For an excellent collection of statutes and materials regarding secondary recovery see SECONDARY RECOVERY OF OIL IN THE UNITED STATES (1942), (Supp. 1943) and (Supp. 1948).

[44] ". . . an oil reservoir may be regarded, in principle, as essentially similar to a sand filled container with the pore spaces of the sand holding oil and dissolved gas under pressure, possibly having some free gas at the top of the container, and possibly connected at the bottom to a body of water which is capable of moving into and displacing oil and gas from the sand as the fluid is withdrawn. This concept is an ideal. . . ." JOINT PROGRESS REPORT ON RESERVOIR EFFICIENCY AND WELL SPACING 15 (1943).

rate at which these drives are exercised is reflected in the total amount of petroleum produced.[45] One further peculiar physical characteristic of petroleum and natural gas is its inability to recognize those divisions of property into which the surface above it has been carved. Now with these facts in mind, let us propound the conservation theorem. It has been established beyond doubt that maximum efficient recovery from a reservoir is measured by the percentage displacement of oil by either gas or water, and that oil (in and of itself) possesses no inherent energy capable of forcing movement through sand. It would seem then that any process—legislative, administrative, or judicial—which sanctions the preservation and utilization of these dynamic pressures to wipe the sand pore of oil would represent conservation of our natural petroleum resources. To this maxim a word of admonition is permissible. Any use of reservoir fluids as pressure elements that fails to produce a sufficient amount of marketable petroleum to be economically justifiable is not conservation—it is submarginal production.

But when we are faced with the welter of conflicting theories assigned to the worship of conservation (by groups and persons struggling for a livelihood in the petroleum industry), confusion, doubt, and distrust arise. For there are inherent in those ideologies things that trouble the apperceptive person interested in preserving our petroleum heritage. In the very genesis of the Compact a battle was fought for conservation principles that would eschew the hypnotic effects of price control and its concomitant philosophies—and it was won. Now how far has the Commission espoused the tenets of conservation—the preservation to the finish of those motivating drives that wring oil and gas from reluctant sands? The Commission has gone on record as the sponsor of any and all legitimate programs to preserve by known legal and scientific means the reservoir pressures, to increase the ultimate recovery of oil and to prevent its waste, to improve the efficiency of secondary recovery in all its multitudinous aspects, to recommend and secure the passage of uniform measures which lead to the better utilization of present knowledge of the physical characteristics of

[45] The East Texas Oil Field demonstrates the validity of this statement.

reservoirs, to urge the adoption of rules, regulations and orders furthering the statutory devices, and finally, to provide interest, support, and understanding to those to whom conservation is a true saving of oil and gas by achieving a maximum economic recovery.

Part IV

THE NATIONAL GOVERNMENT AND THE CONSERVATION OF OIL AND GAS

CHAPTER 40

The Government in the Capacity of Land Owner

~/~

(a) The Public Domain

Oil produced from the public domain accounts for about five per cent of the current annual production in the United States. Thus the laws of the Federal Government control directly only a fraction of the quantity regulated by the statutes of any one of several states. Historically, the federal conservation measures applicable to public lands have had an importance and have received public attention out of proportion to the quantities involved, because of the wide public interest in federal legislation, the very large areas and number of states involved in the public domain, and the pioneer characteristics of these measures, particularly with respect to compulsory unitization.

Operations under the mineral leasing laws have a long and detailed history which can be roughly divided into two periods, the Mineral Leasing Act of 1920[1] being the point of division. Before the passage of that Act the Federal Government fostered exploration of the public domain to locate probable oil reserves. Under the then applicable mining laws discovery and development ultimately led to acquisition of title. Little thought was given to the conservation of oil as a vital resource. World War I's impact brought to the fore the importance of orderly development of public domain oil and gas reserves; and pressure from within the industry toward reopening the large areas of land gradually withdrawn in the pre-war era resulted in the enactment of the Mineral

NORTHCUTT ELY, WRITER. (See app. B.)

The Public Domain—The writer expresses his appreciation to Mr. John D. Northrup of the Geological Survey, Department of the Interior, who looked over this section and made unofficial comments on it prior to publication.

[1] STAT. 437 (1920), 30 U.S.C.A. § 181 et seq. (1940).

599

Leasing Act of 1920. The Act was passed at a time when no real knowledge existed of those vast oil deposits soon to be discovered, or of the possibilities for conserving natural petroleum resources through scientific development and operation of oil fields. There seemed to be danger of a speedy exhaustion of the domestic supply, and the most effective way then known to relieve the threatened shortage was the stimulation of the search for new fields. This the Congress sought to do, where public lands were concerned, through provisions in the Act such as Section 14 entitling a permittee, on discovery of oil or gas, to a primary lease at a royalty charge of five per cent, an unprecedented departure from customary industry royalty rates.

THE MINERAL LEASING ACT OF 1920

Section 13 of the Mineral Leasing Act of February 25, 1920 authorized the Secretary of the Interior to grant prospecting permits [2] which gave the holder an exclusive [3] right for a period not exceeding two years to prospect for oil and gas upon 2560 acres of public lands not within known geologic structures in producing oil or gas fields. Permits were issued on condition that drilling operations be initiated within six months and that one or more wells of not less than 500 feet in depth be drilled within one year from the issuance of the permit, unless oil or gas were discovered sooner. Within two years the permittee was required to drill to a depth of 2000 feet. The Secretary was vested with discretion to extend a permit for a period not to exceed two years, upon his conditions, if he found the permittee had been unable in spite of diligent efforts to test the land in the life of the permit.[4]

Section 14 set out terms upon which permits could ripen into leases [5] on the discovery of oil or gas. Upon establishing to the satisfaction of the Secretary of the Interior that valuable deposits

[2] To the effect that the Secretary of the Interior is powerless to refuse a sufficiently qualified citizen a permit, even though a minor, see West v. United States ex rel. Alling, 30 F. 2d 739 (App. D.C. 1929).
[3] The Secretary had supervisory authority until a patent was issued. Witbeck v. Hardeman, 51 F. 2d 450 (C.C.A. 5th 1931), affd 286 U.S. 444 (1931).
[4] See in general 34 Ops. Att'y. Gen. 457 (1925), 36 Ops. Att'y. Gen. 29 (1929).
[5] In the discretion of the Secretary. See United States ex rel. Jordan v. Ickes, 143 F. 2d 152, cert. denied 320 U.S. 801 (1944).

of oil or gas had been found within the limits of the permit, the permittee was entitled to an A lease, for twenty years, of ¼th of the land covered by the permit, at a royalty payment of five per cent of the value of production, and an annual rental of $1 an acre, which was credited against the royalty. He also had a preference right to a B lease upon the remaining land in the permit for twenty years at a royalty not less than 12½ per cent of the value of production, determined by competitive bidding or fixed by the Secretary in a manner provided by general regulations. The regulations provided a sliding scale of royalties which varied from 12½ to 33⅓ per cent. Section 16 established stipulations against waste, subjected all permits and leases to the condition that no wells be drilled within 200 feet of the land's outer boundaries unless the adjoining property had been patented or its title vested in private owners, and further declared that the permittee must use reasonable precautions to prevent waste of oil and gas. Violations constituted grounds for a forfeiture of the permit or lease, enforceable through judicial proceeding.

Section 17 dealt with geologic structures. The Secretary might award leases (not permits) to the highest reponsible bidder in tracts not exceeding 640 acres in area, nor with a length more than 2½ times width. The royalty required was at least ⅛th, with a rental of $1 an acre applied against these charges. The primary term of the lease was twenty years subject to renewal for ten year periods upon such conditions as the Secretary might prescribe.

Under Section 27 no person, association, or corporation could hold more than three oil and gas leases in one state, nor more than one lease within a geologic structure of the same producing oil or gas field. Interests violative of this provision were subject to forfeiture to the United States. The section was amended in 1926,[6] substituting acreage limitations of 7680 acres in one state and 2560 acres within the geologic structure of a single field.[7]

The assignment or subletting of leases except with the consent [8]

[6] 44 Stat. 373 (1926), 30 U.S.C.A. § 184 (1940).

[7] Carter Oil Co. v. Pacific-Wyo. Oil Co., 37 Wyo. 448, 263 Pac. 960 (1928); Pacific-Wyo. Oil Co. v. Carter Oil Co., 40 Wyo. 393, 277 Pac. 807 (1929).

[8] But a transfer by operation of law, as by the foreclosure of a lien, would not avoid a lease. Hockman v. Sunhew Pet. Corp., 92 Mont. 174, 11 P. 2d 778 (1932). On joint tenancy problems in respect to leases, see Hodgson v. Fed. Oil and Devel. Co., 5 F. 2d 442 (1925), affd 274 U.S. 15 (1927). On assignments and royalties generally

of the Secretary was barred by Section 30, but a lessee could at any time in writing relinquish his rights under a lease. The section required that each lease contain provisions insuring the exercise of reasonable diligence, skill, and care in operating the property in compliance with the Secretary's rules and regulations relative to undue waste.

THE HOOVER CONSERVATION POLICY

An important landmark in the administration of the public domain was the conservation program inaugurated by President Hoover. The period 1926 to 1930 was marked by a series of new discoveries and a flood of overproduction which resulted in falling prices and wasteful practices. A discovery well on public lands in the Kettleman Hills Field in California was brought in October 5, 1928, and the great East Texas Field opened in 1930. The incoming Hoover administration, faced with the prospect of increased oil waste and reduced revenues from royalty rates, felt the time ripe for a thorough review of the situation, and March 12, 1929 the president closed the public domain, saying "there will be no leases or disposal of Government oil lands, no matter what category they may lie in . . . except those which may be mandatory by Congress. . . . there will be complete conservation of Government oil in this administration." [9] The authority of the Secretary of the Interior to refuse issuance of new prospecting permits was sustained in *United States ex rel. McLennan v. Wilbur*.[10]

Concurrently with the public domain's closure a program was initiated to weed out the numerous outstanding speculative prospecting permits.[11] On March 29, 1929 there were more than 20,-000 permits on the records of the Interior Department. A careful review system insured the protection of equities where preliminary operations had been undertaken, but the greater number of investi-

see Dougherty v. California Kettleman Oil Royalties, Inc., 9 Cal. 2d 58, 69 P. 2d 155 (1937), Gen. Pet. Corp. of Calif. v. Dougherty, 117 F. 2d 529 (C.C.A. 9th 1941) modifying Dougherty v. Gen. Pet. Corp. of Calif., 28 F. Supp. 979 (1939), Rush v. Kirk, 127 F. 2d 368 (C.C.A. 10th 1942), Peterson v. Ickes, 151 F. 2d 301 (App. D.C. 1945), *cert. denied* 326 U.S. 795 (1946).

[9] See Rep. Sec'y. Int. 42 (1930).
[10] 283 U.S. 414 (1931).
[11] Rep. Sec'y. Int. 10 (1929).

gations showed that permittees had failed to comply with the law relating to initiation of development. Here the permits were cancelled; between March 12, 1929 and April 4, 1932, when the public domain was reopened, approximately 16,600 outstanding permits were dropped.[12]

THE KETTLEMAN HILLS UNITIZATION PLAN

The discovery of the very deep Kettleman Hills Field, a "checkerboard" of public and private lands, in 1929, resulted at once in an enormous waste of gas and a competitive drilling program. Secretary Wilbur through the Geological Survey undertook the negotiation of a shut-in agreement [13] which became effective July 25, 1929 suspending all drilling until July 1, 1931, pending enactment of federal legislation to authorize a unitization program. Under this agreement the Government recognized oil saturated cores as discoveries, halting drilling as the well reached the Temblor zone without puncturing its gas cap. Four wells were permitted to produce, distributing a part of their production among the owners of the shut-in wells.

On July 3, 1930 a temporary statute was adopted [14] which authorized the Secretary to approve unitization plans. Negotiations were undertaken resulting in the approval January 31, 1931 of a unit plan for the North Dome Kettleman Hills Field.[15] The plan created a non-profit cooperative corporation (the Kettleman North Dome Association) to which the lessees transferred their operating rights. The association agreed to develop the field in accordance with regulations under a temporary agreement. So successful was the project in reducing production to reasonable limits and in eliminating waste, that Congress within the year enacted permanent legislation authorizing the Secretary to require unit operations wherever needed for efficient operation of a pool or field.

Under the Act of March 4, 1931 [16] leases subject to a cooperative or unit plan of development or operation as a single oil or

---

[12] REP. SEC'Y. INT. 28 (1932).
[13] REP. SEC'Y. INT. 11 (1929).
[14] 46 STAT. 1007 (1930), 30 U.S.C.A. § 226 (1940).
[15] REP. SEC'Y. INT. 13 (1930).
[16] Act of March 4, 1931, 46 STAT. 1523 (1931), 30 U.S.C.A. § 226 (1940).

gas pool, with the approval of the Secretary of the Interior, continue beyond their primary term until the end of the unit operation. The Secretary may alter or modify the rate of production under any cooperative system which includes lands owned by the United States. He may "wherever he shall deem such action necessary or in the public interest," with the consent of the lessee, order the suspension or modification of drilling operations and the producing requirements of any oil lease. Section 27, which contained the original limitations on size and number of holding, was altered to permit (for conservation purposes) agreements between lessees and permittees to join in cooperative or unit operations, wherever certified by the Secretary as necessary or advisable in the public interest. Power was given him to change the production, drilling, and royalty requirements with the lessee's consent; this grant extended to the authorization and approval of development contracts which might normally be considered violations of the anti-trust laws. The effect of the approval of a unit plan as a bar to anti-trust proceedings has never been tested by litigation. The section makes it clear that only those unit agreements approved by the Secretary are valid, stating that any lease which forms part of an unlawful combination or contract in restraint of trade shall be forfeited by appropriate court proceedings. Although the authority granted the Secretary of the Interior here does not extend to leases on the Naval Petroleum Reserves, the Secretary of the Navy, with the consent of the president, is authorized to enter into similar agreements, though such agreements do not extend the terms of the affected lease [17] unless so specified in the agreement. The Kettleman Hills unitization plan is still in successful operation.[18]

[17] Act of June 30, 1938, 52 Stat. 1252 (1938), 34 U.S.C.A. § 524 (1940) which brought together the prior law relating to Naval Petroleum Reserves contained a provision exempting from the expiration dates those leases which had become a part of an approved unit or cooperative plan.

[18] Recently the regulations of the Secretary pertaining to royalty payments on gas and oil taken from the field were upheld in United States v. General Petroleum Corporation, 73 F. Supp. 225 (S.D. Cal. 1946). That case developed out of the Interior Department's contention that it had the power to determine the value of the oil and gas taken from Government leases in order to establish the base upon which royalty payments were made. The Court held that though the Secretary was not authorized to fix a minimum value for oil, the price paid at the field during early years of operation was not the "reasonable market value," and recovery of additional royalties was

THE REOPENING OF THE PUBLIC DOMAIN

The public domain was reopened April 4, 1932, but the issuance of prospecting permits and new leases was subject to important limitations. Acting under legislation authorizing the Secretary to require unitized operations in the public interest, regulations [19] governing issuance of permits and leases provided that an applicant must agree to submit to the Secretary, within two years after the permit's date, an acceptable developmental plan unitizing the pool, field, or the permit land area. The applicant agreed that oil or gas in commercial quantities would not be produced except pursuant to the unit operation or approved cooperative plan. The applicant was required to comply with all state and federal laws, regulations, and orders, and to conform to allowables fixed by the state in which the land was situated and to the equitable proration of market outlet.

OIL SHALE RESERVES

The oil shale reserves in the public domain include about 1,-500,000 acres in Colorado, 2,750,000 in Utah, and 4,000,000 in Wyoming; included in these figures are the two Naval Shale Reserves of 91,000 acres in Utah, and 64,000 acres in Colorado. Although subject to lease, there is little activity in these areas because it is not yet economically feasible to extract petroleum products from oil shale.[20]

granted to the Government. As to gas and gasoline, the Court found that certain sections of the leases gave the Secretary power to fix a value for royalty purposes when those products were not disposed of under approved contracts. A minimum price of 5 cents per MCF was established for all natural gas and royalties were awarded on this basis, unless the gas was sold at a greater figure, whereupon the higher price became the base. Royalties were held payable even though the gas produced was stored in the Buena Vista Naval Reserve. See also United States v. Ohio Oil Co., 163 F. 2d 633 (C.C.A. 10th 1947).

[19] The letter of Secretary Wilbur, Apr. 4, 1932, which accompanied the issuance of regulations governing the reopening of the public domain, and the regulations, are found in ELY, THE OIL AND GAS CONSERVATION STATUTES ANNOTATED 21–33 (1933).

[20] The Federal Government has long carried on experiments designed to provide information as to the best methods of using its mineral resources. During the 1920's the Bureau of Mines expended some $200,000 in initial development and experimentation with processes designed to produce oil from shale. More recently Congress has expressed active interest in the development of synthetic fuels and in producing oil

Certain portions [21] of these lands had been entered before the passage of the Mineral Leasing Act of 1920 and claims under the prior mining laws had been instituted. Although the Act of 1920 effected a complete policy change [22] regarding the disposition of lands containing deposits of coal, phosphate, sodium, oil, oil shale and gas, Section 37 [23] protected valid claims which existed at the Act's passage and maintained in compliance with the laws under which initiated. Thus there were outstanding numerous claims on oil shale lands which might eventually ripen into title acquisitions. In accordance with the Hoover conservation policy, Secretary Wilbur investigated these claims since the department felt that a majority had not been kept active in accord with its view that the mining laws required $100 worth of assessment work each year. In *Wilbur v. United States, ex rel Krushnic* [24] the Supreme Court held that the only effect of failure to comply with the yearly assessment work was to render the land subject to relocation, except where $500 worth of labor or improvements had been expended which entitled the claimant to a patent. The Act did not extinguish the right of a locator to save his claim by resuming work after failure to perform the annual assessment labor, "unless at least some form of challenge on behalf of the United States to the valid existence of the claim has intervened."

The Secretary interpreted this as an authorization to challenge the validity of oil shale claims upon which annual assessment work had not been accomplished, and directed the local land offices to post notices on all such property stating that the United States now assumed title because of failure to perform annual assessment work. [25] This created considerable dissatisfaction [26] but all proposals

---

from new sources. Synthetic Liquid Fuel Demonstration Plants Act, 58 Stat. 190 (1944), 30 U.S.C.A. § 321 (Supp. V 1946). See also H.R. 5475, 80th Cong., 2d Sess. (1948) a bill to authorize construction of three commercial plants for production of oil from coal and oil shale.

[21] About 9% of the oil shale lands in Colorado were involved, 3% in Utah and less than 1% in Wyoming.

[22] In that it was no longer possible to acquire title to such mineral lands, a comprehensive scheme of leasing being substituted.

[23] 41 Stat. 437, 451 (1920), 30 U.S.C.A. § 193 (1940).

[24] 280 U.S. 306 (1930).

[25] Rep. Sec'y. Int. 29–32 (1931).

[26] The problem was thoroughly discussed in *Hearings before the Committee on Public Lands on H.R. 3754, 12802, 13191, 15002, 15130–15132, 71st Cong., 2d & 3d Sess. (1930–1931).*

for remedial legislation failed of enactment. It was not until 1935 that the matter was determined adversely to the Interior Department in *Ickes v. Virginia-Colorado Development Corporation* [27] where the Court held a failure to perform the annual assessment work did not *ipso facto* work a forfeiture, but only rendered the claim subject to loss through relocation. If no relocation be made, the claim revived by resumption of work prior to such relocation. The dictum in the *Krushnic* case was "a reservation, not a decision," and claims advanced by the Government had to have a proper basis in the mining laws under which oil shale claims were made.

As a result the Interior Department abandoned its efforts to regain oil shale lands. These claims remain outstanding and are gradually being perfected through issuance of patents.

THE 1935 AMENDMENTS

No further broad adjustments of the mineral leasing laws came until the Act of August 21, 1935.[28] Here the permit system of the 1920 Act was abolished except as to applicants filing more than 90 days prior to its effective date; existing permits were extended to December 31, 1937 and for an additional year where diligence in prospecting and drilling was exercised under a permit suspended during the extension period. The holders of extant permits were encouraged to exchange them for leases under a proviso allowing a transfer without proof of discovery. Leases obtained through such interchange were not subject to the amended acreage limitations until one year after the discovery of valuable oil or gas deposits. Any prospecting application filed after the limiting period was considered one for a lease under the amended Section 17 with no rentals payable for the first two lease years, unless valuable deposits of oil or gas were discovered sooner.

Section 17, as amended, authorized the Secretary to lease [29] all lands "known or believed to contain oil or gas deposits" subject to disposition under the mineral leasing laws (except preferential

[27] 295 U.S. 639 (1935).

[28] 49 STAT. 678 (1935), 30 U.S.C.A. § 221 et seq. (1940).

[29] In his discretion. See Dunn v. Ickes, 115 F. 2d 36 (App. D.C. 1940), cert. denied 311 U.S. 698 (1940), reaffirming United States ex rel. Roughton v. Ickes, 101 F. 2d 248 (App. D.C. 1938).

lease land under outstanding permits) to the highest responsible qualified bidder. The royalty rate remained at the traditional not less than ⅛th, but where leases were valuable for gas production only, the Secretary could waive or reduce the rental or royalty. The conservation features based on the approval of unit plans were reenacted and clarified to show that the Secretary might thereafter issue leases on condition that the lessee operate under a reasonable cooperative or unit plan for the field, pool, or area determined by the Secretary necessary to protect adequately the rights of all parties in interest, including the United States. Acreage limitations were waived for leases operated under approved plans by excepting them in determining "holdings or control" under any portion of the Act. New leases were for five years, and so long thereafter as oil or gas was produced in paying quantities, if issued on lands not within known geologic structures, and for ten years when within such structures. Leases granted prior to the effective date of the 1935 amendment, if part of a unit plan, continued until the operation's termination. The Secretary of the Interior could negotiate agreements with adjacent landowners, when their wells were draining oil or gas from deposits on lands owned by the United States, to obtain compensation for this drainage subject to the consent of the affected lessees. The amendatory Act continued the Secretary's right to reduce royalties where production did not exceed ten barrels a well a day or where the cost of production rendered further continuance economically impractical. This power is based upon "encouraging the greatest ultimate recovery of oil and in the interest of conservation of natural resources;" it is applicable to oil and gas leases issued under the Act including those in approved cooperative or unit plans.

MISCELLANEOUS AMENDMENTS

Between 1935 and 1946 the mineral leasing laws were amended piecemeal. Thus the Act of August 26, 1937 [30] extended for two years the outstanding prospecting permits committed to unit operation. An Act passed July 29, 1942 [31] granted preference rights

---

[30] 50 STAT. 842 (1937), 30 U.S.C.A. § 221 i (1940).
[31] 56 STAT. 726 (1942), 30 U.S.C.A. § 221–222 h (Supp. 1946).

for new leases to applicants who were record title holders of expiring five year leases on lands not within known geologic structures. During World War II, in an effort to stimulate discovery of new fields, legislation [32] was enacted fixing the royalty obligations at a flat 12½ per cent (in lieu of higher sliding scales) for ten years .to lessees discovering deposits determined by the Secretary to be new oil or gas fields; this was repealed by joint resolution July 25, 1947.[33] While the measure fostered wildcatting, no significant reserves were discovered.

THE 1946 AMENDMENTS

The Mineral Leasing Act was subjected to thorough overhaul by the Act of August 8, 1946,[34] when effort was made [35] to obtain a flat 12½ per cent rate for all leases. While this was unsuccessful insofar as leases on lands on known geologic structures went, the 1946 Act does apply that rate to lands not within known fields. The advance rental of 25 cents an acre was changed. Non-competitive leases wholly outside known geologic structures now have a rental of 50 cents an acre the first year, no rental the second and third years, 25 cents the fourth and fifth years, and 50 cents for each succeeding year. Leases on lands within known structures generally carry rentals of $1 an acre. Leases issued after August 8, 1946, as well as prior leases where the lessee files under Section 15 (bringing his lease within the terms of the 1946 Act) have a minimum royalty of $1 an acre a year after discovery in lieu of rental. Competitive bidding for leases on lands within known structures and the 640 acre limitation are unchanged. These competitive leases operate on a sliding scale royalty basis ranging from a required "not less than 12½ per cent" to 25 per cent, depending upon daily production, the latter royalty being applicable to production exceeding 400 barrels a day. Non-competitive leases are issued to the first qualified person applying and are for a primary term of five years. If diligent drilling operations are in progress at

[32] 56 Stat. 1080 (1942), 30 U.S.C.A. § 223 (Supp. 1947).
[33] 61 Stat. 449 (1947), 30 U.S.C.A. § 223 (Supp. 1947).
[34] 60 Stat. 950 (1946). 30 U.S.C.A. § 221 et seq. (Supp. 1947).
[35] See *Hearings before Committee on Public Lands and Surveys on S. 1236*, 79th Cong., 2d Sess. pt. 2, pp. 240, 264, 323 (1946).

the end of that time, the lease does not terminate for an additional two years. At the end of the primary term the holder of a non-competitive lease is entitled to a single extension for five years. Competitive leases are not subject to extension, but they continue after the primary term as long as oil and gas is produced in paying quantities.

Section 17 (a), added by the 1947 Act, permits the Secretary to exchange new leases for twenty year leases or renewals thereof granted under the earlier laws. These new leases are for five year primary terms and as long thereafter as oil and gas are produced in paying quantities, with a royalty rate of not less than ⅛th. Important exceptions in royalty rates are made in that a flat ⅛th royalty is fixed on leases not believed to be within the productive limits of producing deposits as found by the Secretary to exist at the Act's effective date. Likewise the royalty remains at ⅛th on deposits discovered after the proclamation of the national emergency on May 27, 1941, where the Secretary determines a new deposit is involved, and on leases included in or committed to unit or cooperative agreement.

Earlier amendments relating to cooperative and unit plans are combined in a new section, 17 (b). The Secretary may, with the consent of the lease holders in a unit plan, establish, alter, change or revoke lease rental and minimum royalty requirements. Any unit plan may, in the discretion of the Secretary, vest authority in a committee, a state, or a federal officer or agency to alter or modify the rate of prospecting and development and the quantity and rate of production under the program. This makes possible the inclusion of federal lands in unitized operations with private operators who are or who become subject to state unitization operations. Pooling of leases in communitization or drilling agreements is now allowed in cases where separate tracts cannot be independently developed in accord with established well spacing programs. The final paragraph of Section 17 (b) empowers the Secretary of the Interior, in order to avoid waste or to promote conservation, to authorize sub-surface storage of oil or gas, whether or not produced from federally owned lands, in property leased or subject to lease under the mineral leasing laws. He may provide for payment of a storage fee, a rental, or in lieu thereof, a royalty other than that stated in the lease, when the oil or gas is brought from storage in conjunction with oil or gas not previously produced. Leases involving stored oil are continued for the storage period and as long thereafter as oil or gas not previously accumulated is produced in paying quantities.

Section 27 of the basic Act is amended in three principal respects: (1) acreage limits are increased from 7680 to 15,360 acres for individuals or corporations in any state and limitations which pertain to one geologic structure are abolished, (2) the word "association" is redefined to exclude development and operating contracts, and tenancies in common, in order to charge each party only with his proportionate acreage in the lease, instead of the entire area, and (3) non-renewable options, not chargeable against acreage limitations, are recognized for geological or geophysical exploration, as long as these do not exceed two years and do not cover more than 100,000 acres in any state. Interests of optionees prior to the exercise of their rights are not considered "taking or holding" under the acreage limitations. Provisions concerning assignments were changed in important respects by the 1946 amendment, and more rapid clearance of assignments through the Department of the Interior was facilitated.

EXTENSION TO ACQUIRED LANDS

The most recent change in the Mineral Leasing Laws was made in the Act of August 7, 1947 [36] which extended the existing provisions of those laws to all acquired lands, as a result of recommendations by the Secretary of the Interior and the Special Committee of the Senate Investigating Petroleum Resources (the O'Mahoney Committee), [37] to stimulate the development of new sources of oil and gas. Specifically excepted are lands "situated within incorporated cities, towns and villages, national parks or monuments; set apart for military or naval purposes; and tidelands or submerged lands." The Act applies to leasing of coal, phospate, oil, oil shale, gas, sodium, potassium, and sulphur, expressly stating that no mineral deposit covered by the Act shall

[36] 61 STAT. 913 (1947), 30 U.S.C.A. § 351 *et seq.* (Supp. 1947).
[37] SEN. REP. No. 9, 80th Cong., 1st Sess. 50 (1947).

be leased "except with the consent of the head of the executive department, independent establishment, or instrumentality having jurisdiction over lands containing such deposit, or holding a mortgage or deed of trust secured by such lands which is unsatisfied of record, and subject to such conditions as that official may prescribe to secure the adequate utilization of the lands for the primary purposes for which they have been acquired or are being administered." While this prescribes a condition not in the prior laws, it may be assumed that it is not intended to be a burdensome limitation on individual applications but will be covered by general regulation.

REGULATIONS UNDER THE MINERAL LEASING LAWS

Regulations [38] of the Bureau of Land Management pertaining to applications for mineral permits, leases, and licenses are periodically modified to comply with changes in the basic laws. Operating regulations [39] are promulgated by the Geological Survey to provide detailed supervision by field representatives charged with the responsibility of seeing that operations are conducted so as to protect deposits on leased lands and to achieve maximum ultimate recovery of oil and gas with a minimum of waste. Waste is defined as the physical waste of oil or gas, and the loss or dissipation of reservoir energy necessary or useful in obtaining maximum recovery. Physical waste includes the loss or destruction of oil or gas after recovery without its beneficial utilization, and loss prior to recovery by isolation, entrapment, migration, premature release of natural gas from solution, or in any manner rendering recovery impracticable. Waste of reservoir energy includes the failure to maintain pressures by artificial means, and the dissipation of gas energy or hydrostatic or other natural reservoir energies in a manner which results in loss without reasonably adequate recovery of oil. If gas waste takes place the lessee must pay the Government a minimum price of five cents per MCF unless the Secretary determines such waste is sanctioned by the laws of the United States or the state where it occurs. The

[38] 43 CODE FED. REGS. § 191 *et seq.* (1940 and Supp.).
[39] 30 CODE FED. REGS. § 221 *et seq.* (1940 and Supp.).

supervisor is empowered to require correction of any conditions which cause (or are likely to cause) damage to formations containing oil or gas or which is wasteful, and he may require plugging or abandonment of any well no longer useful in accordance with plans he may prescribe. If the lessees refuse to comply, the supervisor may expend public funds to do the work at their expense, and recover the costs in an appropriate action. The supervisor establishes rates of permissible flow in accord with field proration rules, and he approves necessary well spacing and casing programs for the proper development of the leases. Every phase of operation, from the initiation of drilling through contracts for the disposition of the products of the lease, is subject to the inspection and control of the supervisor and his representatives.

Numerous reports required include log of well, subsequent record of drilling, redrilling, deepening, plugging back, plugging and abandonment, and stimulating production by acid or shot. A monthly report on each lease is due beginning with the month in which drilling is commenced, disclosing all operations conducted on each well during the period, their status on the last day of the month, and a general summarized account of the operations. A daily report is required on gas producing wells. Monthly statements of oil and gas production and royalties showing amounts run and sales of products are mandatory, together with calculations of royalties due the United States.

Appeals from any order issued under the regulations are first taken to the Director, and appeals from the Director lie to the Secretary of the Interior.

During 1947 there were approximately 11,000 leases outstanding for the development of oil and gas on something over 8,000,000 acres of public domain. In that period 70,363,023 barrels of petroleum were produced from these lands; 16,032,145 barrels from Indian lands; and 3,380,140 barrels from the naval reserves. During the same time 94,902,215 MCF of natural gas came from the public domain; 12,354,000 MCF from Indian lands; and 2,281,640 MCF from the naval reserves. On March 1, 1948 there were in force 148 unitization agreements covering 2,117,571 acres of public lands, and about half of all public domain oil was produced under approved unit agreements. It is through these federally supervised unit operations that the Government exercises its most effective control over oil and gas conservation.

(b) Indian Lands

Oil and gas leases on Indian lands are written against a complicated background [40] of treaties, agreements, and statutes. The era before 1887 produced nothing relevant to this study.[41] In 1887 Congress passed the General Allotment Act [42] designed to vest individual tribesmen with title to specific tracts of land which, after an initial twenty-five year trust, they would own outright. Indian affairs from 1887 to 1933 were largely controlled by the comprehensive provisions of this Act. In 1933 it became apparent that the general allotment system was inadequate,[43] and a third major piece of Indian legislation—the Wheeler-Howard Act [44]—was passed in 1934; under its terms each tribe may take steps toward ultimate self-government by the adoption of tribal constitutions.

LEASING OF ALLOTTED LANDS

Section 5 of the General Allotment Act originally prohibited the leasing of allotted lands, but a subsequent series of statutes authorize leasing, subject to the control of the Interior Department. For the most part these relate to the purpose of the lease, its term, who can make it, and what official must approve the agreement. The Secretary of the Interior is given broad power [45] to consent to the alienation of the allotted lands in cases where special allotment laws or treaties make land inalienable without the consent of the

Indian Lands—The writer expresses his appreciation to Mr. George Paulus of the Office of Indian Affairs, Department of the Interior, who looked over this section and made unofficial comments on it prior to publication.

[40] For a comprehensive survey of Indian law see COHEN, HANDBOOK OF FEDERAL INDIAN LAW (1941).

[41] See Act of Mar. 3, 1871, 16 STAT. 544.

[42] The Osage Indians and the Five Civilized Tribes were expressly excluded from the Act by § 8. Act of Feb. 8, 1887, 24 STAT. 388.

[43] See S. RES. 79, 70th Cong., 1st Sess. (1927) and hearings. The great difficulty with the General Allotment Act was its rigid uniformity in a situation necessitating rapid and wide readjustments to meet ever changing demands of individual tribes.

[44] Act of June 18, 1934, 48 STAT. 984.

[45] Act of June 25, 1910, 36 STAT. 855.

president.[46] The customary five [47] or ten [48] year limitation on the term of the lease is not included. Most statutes provide that the lease can be made by the allottee or his heirs; [49] several require the approval or "consent or approval" of the Secretary,[50] but he may delegate his authority to the superintendent or officer in charge of the reservation where the land is located, under the terms of Section 2, the Act of May 11, 1938.[51]

TRIBAL LEASING

In 1891 [52] Congress passed the first general authorization for tribal leasing, saying: "Where lands are occupied by Indians who have bought and paid for the same, and which lands are not needed for farming or agricultural purposes, and are not desired for individual allotments, the same may be leased by authority of the council speaking for the Indians, for a period of . . . ten years for mining purposes in such quantities and upon such terms and conditions as the agent in charge of such reservation may recommend, subject to the approval of the Secretary of the Interior." Tribal leasing provisions were extended in 1924 [53] to provide that unallotted land on reservations other than the Five Civilized Tribes and the Osage Reservation (subject to lease for ten year periods under the 1891 Act) could be leased at public auction by the Secretary of the Interior with the consent of the tribal council. This Act applied only to oil and gas leases with a primary term of ten years and "as much longer thereafter as oil or gas be found in paying quantities." In 1926 [54] the leasing laws were extended to include lands reserved for Indian agency and school purposes, with the proviso that the royalty reserved be at least 1/8th. In 1927 [55] the leasing act

---

[46] See also Act of July 8, 1940, Pub. L. No. 732, 76th Cong.; Act of Sept. 21, 1922, 42 STAT. 994, Act of Mar. 3, 1909, 35 STAT. 781.
[47] See note 45 supra.
[48] Act of May 18, 1916, 39 STAT. 123.
[49] Act of Mar. 3, 1909, 35 STAT. 781.
[50] See Act of Sept. 21, 1922, 42 STAT. 994, and Miller v. McClain, 249 U.S. 308 (1919) for discussion of the earlier statutes.
[51] 52 STAT. 347 (1938).
[52] Act of Feb. 28, 1891, 26 STAT. 794.
[53] Act of May 29, 1924, 43 STAT. 244.
[54] Act of Apr. 17, 1926, 44 STAT. 300.
[55] Act of Mar. 3, 1927, 44 STAT. 1347.

of 1924 was extended to unallotted lands within the limits of any reservation or withdrawal created by executive order for Indian purposes. Section 5 of the 1927 Act authorized the Secretary of the Interior to allow persons applying for permits under the Mineral Leasing Act of 1920 to prospect for oil and gas upon Executive Order Indian lands for an added two years from the effective date of the 1927 statute, provided reasonable diligence in prospecting or equitable grounds for granting an extension be shown. In the event of discovery, the permittee was entitled to a lease for twenty years on ¼th the land embraced in his application with a five per cent royalty and an annual rental of $1 an acre. The applicant was entitled to a preference right for remaining acreage at a royalty of not less than ⅛th, to be fixed by competitive bidding.

The effect of these three statutes was to leave the law in a rather uncertain state where the leasing of unallotted lands was concerned, and an effort was made in 1938 [56] to bring together the loose ends. Although by its terms the Act of May 11, 1938 does not apply to the Papagos of Arizona, the Crow Reservation in Montana, the ceded lands of the Shoshone Reservation in Wyoming, or the Osage Reservation in Oklahoma, it does permit oil and gas leases upon all unallotted lands through the action of a tribal council sanctioned by the Secretary of the Interior. The Secretary may prescribe a public auction with sealed bids and may reject all bids if he believes it in the best interest of the Indians. Where tribes have adopted tribal constitutions and taken steps under the Wheeler-Howard Act,[57] nothing in the 1938 measure restricts the rights of the tribal councils. By Section 4 the Secretary may prescribe operating rules and regulations and at his discretion unit operation provisions of the public domain laws are effective as to Indian lands, in that he may require such operations before or after the issuance of a lease. The Secretary may designate superintendents or other Indian service officials as proper agents to pass upon the validity of a proposed lease. The 1938 Act applies only to unallotted lands where general leasing provisions are concerned, but it extends to allotted lands the requirements for bonds, and permits

---

[56] Act of May 11, 1938, 52 STAT. 347.
[57] Act of June 18, 1934, 48 STAT. 984.

the Secretary to issue regulations governing operations on such lands.

The Wheeler-Howard Act, with its object of promoting increased independence and responsibility among tribes through the device of permitting tribal incorporation under specific charters, provided that any incorporated tribe had a right to take and hold property, and to issue interests in corporate property in exchange therefor; but no authority was given to sell, mortgage, or lease for a period exceeding ten years any land within the reservation. Section 2 extended indefinitely the existing periods of trust and restraints upon alienation of lands, but Section 18 made these inapplicable to any reservation where a majority of the adult Indians voted against it in a special election supervised by the Secretary of the Interior. The extension of trust periods was expressly made inapplicable to the Osage and Five Civilized Tribes reservations by Section 13.

FIVE CIVILIZED TRIBES

The Five Civilized Tribes are singled out for special Congressional treatment by reason of the large supplies of oil and gas under their lands, and partly because Congress is accustomed to dealing with them as a unit.[58] Prior to the Act of March 3, 1893,[59] the Cherokees, Choctaws, Chickasaws, Creeks, and Seminoles held their lands tribally and not in severalty in what is now the State of Oklahoma. By Section 15 of the 1893 Act allotment in severalty was made, and Section 16 extinguished tribal title to any lands then held by the tribe within the territory. An essential part of the

[58] Congress had for many years maintained a special committee on the Five Civilized Tribes in addition to the regular committee on Indian affairs. The Acts of Congress dealing with the powers of the Dawes Commission are: Act of Mar. 3, 1893, 27 STAT. 612; Act of June 10, 1896, 29 STAT. 321; Act of June 7, 1897, 30 STAT. 62; Act of July 1, 1898, 30 STAT. 571; Act of May 31, 1900, 31 STAT. 221; Act of Mar. 3, 1901, 31 STAT. 1058; Act of May 27, 1902, 32 STAT. 245; Act of Mar. 3, 1903, 32 STAT. 982; Act of Apr. 21, 1904, 33 STAT. 189; Act of Mar. 3, 1905, 33 STAT. 1048; Act of June 21, 1906, 34 STAT. 325. The Dawes Commission was abolished by Act of Aug. 1, 1914, 38 STAT. 598 and the appointment of a supervisor for the Five Civilized Tribes authorized.

[59] 27 STAT. 612 (1893).

plan of individual allotment was the placing of restriction upon the right of alienation,[60] now found in the basic Act of May 27, 1908,[61] Section 1 of which provides: ". . . That all allotted lands of enrolled full-bloods . . . shall not be subject to alienation, contract to sell, power of attorney, or any other encumbrance . . . except that the Secretary of the Interior may remove such restrictions, wholly or in part, under such rules and regulations concerning terms of sale and disposal of the proceeds for the benefit of the respective Indians as he may prescribe." Section 2 contains provisions concerning oil and gas leases, saying: "That all lands other than homesteads allotted to members of the Five Civilized Tribes from which restrictions have not been removed may be leased by the allottee if an adult, or by guardian or curator under order of the proper probate court if a minor or incompetent, for a period not to exceed five years, without the privilege of renewal; Provided, That leases of restricted lands for oil, gas or other mining purposes, leases of restricted homesteads for more than one year, and leases of restricted lands for periods of more than five years may be made, with the approval of the Secretary of the Interior under rules and regulations provided by the Secretary of the Interior, and not otherwise." [62] By Act of August 25, 1937 [63] the Secretary of the Interior was authorized to reserve the mineral rights, including oil and gas, in any sale of tribal lands of the Choctaw and Chickasaw Indians, whenever in his judgment the interests of these were best served by such action. The unallotted lands of the Five Civilized Tribes are governed by the applicable provisions of the 1938 Act [64] already

[60] See Heckman v. United States, 224 U.S. 413 (1912).

[61] 35 STAT. 312 (1908). See amendments in Act of Apr. 10, 1926, 44 STAT. 239; Act of May 10, 1928, 45 STAT. 495; Act of May 24, 1928, 45 STAT. 733; Act of Jan. 27, 1933, 47 STAT. 777. See King v. Ickes, 64 F. 2d 979 (App. D.C. 1933), Amer. Nat. Bank v. Amer. Baptist Home Mission Soc., 106 F. 2d 192 (C.C.A. 2d 1939). The Act of June 20, 1936, 49 STAT. 1542 and the Act of May 19, 1937, 50 STAT. 188 exempt restricted Indian lands from state taxation. The constitutionality of these Acts was sustained in Bd. of Co. Comm. v. Seber, 318 U.S. 705 (1943). By the Act of June 26, 1936, 49 STAT. 1967, the state of Okla. is authorized to levy a gross production tax on the oil and gas produced from Indian lands within the state.

[62] Oil and gas leases on lands allotted to members of the Five Civilized Tribes have been a prolific source of litigation. A notorious example is found in Mott v. United States, 283 U.S. 747 (1931). See Spencer v. Gypsy Oil Co., 142 F. 2d 935 (C.C.A. 10th 1944) for "another chapter in the apparently endless journey of the affairs of Jackson Barnett, long since deceased, through the highways and byways of our courts."

[63] 50 STAT. 810 (1937).

[64] Act of May 11, 1938, 52 STAT. 347.

mentioned, but since most lands of the tribes have been allotted to their members, its application is relatively insignificant.

The most recent enactment pertaining to the Five Civilized Tribes is the Act of August 4, 1947 [65] which removes all restrictions upon alienation of a member's lands, enrolled or unenrolled, upon the death of a tribal member. The heir or devisee may then alienate the land, subject to certain requirements of notice and the approval of the county court of Oklahoma in which the land lies. This court may call for competitive bidding and the heir or devisee appears in open court and is examined upon the proposed conveyance. Section 11 makes all restricted lands subject to oil and gas conservation laws of Oklahoma, but no order of the Oklahoma Corporation Commission affecting them is valid until approved by the Secretary of the Interior. The Interior Department cooperates with the Commission and has approved several spacing and unitization agreements.

LEASES ON THE OSAGE LANDS

The background which occasioned the special treatment accorded the Osage Tribe was traced by Mr. Justice Brandeis in *McCurdy v. United States.*[66] In 1906 the tribe of 2000 persons held a reservation of about 1,500,000 acres between the Arkansas River and the Kansas state line, largely underlaid with petroleum and natural gas. With income from a trust fund, held by the United States, built up with monies received under treaties as compensation for relinquishing lands and revenue from oil and gas leases, the total income of the tribe was some $1,000,000 a year. Congress apparently concluded that the enjoyment of wealth without responsibility would be demoralizing and by the Act of June 28, 1906 [67] provided for an equal division of the lands and funds among the tribal members. Income from the divided sums, held in trust for twenty-five years, went to the members and their heirs, and at the expiration of the trust was to be paid over to the heirs. Each

[65] 61 STAT. 458 (1947).

[66] 246 U.S. 263 (1918). *See* Work v. United States, *ex rel.* Mosier, 261 U.S. 352 (1923).

[67] 34 STAT. 539 (1906). For a full discussion of this statute see Levindale Lead & Zinc Mining Co. v. Coleman, 241 U.S. 432 (1916).

member was entitled to select three 160 acre tracts for a homestead; all mineral rights were reserved to the tribe and the tracts
were inalienable for twenty-five years. After each made his selec-
tions, the remaining surplus lands were divided equally among the
members.[68] Section 3 of the Osage Allotment Act of June 28, 1906
directed that the oil, gas, and other minerals covered by allotted
lands be reserved to the tribe for twenty-five years from April 8,
1906 and provided that mineral leases be made by the tribal council with the approval of the Secretary of the Interior under such
rules as he might prescribe.[69] Under the seventh paragraph of Section 2 the oil, gas, and other minerals became the property of the
owner of the land at the expiration of twenty-five years, unless
otherwise provided by Congress.

Section 3 was amended in 1921[70] to extend the reservation of
minerals to the tribe to April 7, 1946 and valid existing leases on
April 7, 1931 were extended on the same terms until April 8, 1946
and as long as oil or gas was found in paying quantities. The Act
directed the Secretary of the Interior and the tribal council to "offer for lease for oil and gas purposes all of the remaining portions
of the unleased Osage Lands prior to April 8, 1931, offering the
same annually at a rate of not less than $\frac{1}{10}$th of the unleased
area."[71] Expiration was again postponed in 1929[72] to April 8, 1948
and the provisions of the 1921 Act changed with respect to man-

[68] *See* United States v. Barnsdall Oil Co., 127 F. 2d 1019 (C.C.A. 10th 1942).
These surplus lands were later made available for sale and by the Act of Mar. 3, 1909,
the Secretary of the Interior was authorized, upon application, to sell a part or all of
the surplus land of any member of the Osage tribe, 35 STAT. 778. *See* Adams v. Osage
Tribe, 55 F. 2d 643 (C.C.A. 10th 1932). The Appropriation Act of May 25, 1918,
40 STAT. 561 permitted the interchange of homestead and surplus lands, thus providing for indirect sales of homestead lands under rules and regulations of the Secretary. Finally in the Act of Mar. 3, 1921, 41 STAT. 1249, all restrictions were removed
and adult Osage Indians who had obtained a certificate of competency were thereafter
permitted to alienate freely their surplus lands.
[69] Current regulations are found in 25 CODE FED. REGS. § 180.1–94 (1940).
[70] Act of Mar. 3, 1921, 41 STAT. 1249. *See* Adams v. Osage Tribe, 59 F. 2d 653
(C.C.A. 10th 1932), Globe Ind. Co. v. Bruce, 81 F. 2d 143 (C.C.A. 10th 1935),
Jump v. Ellis, 100 F. 2d 130 (C.C.A. 10th 1938).
[71] This requirement proved unwise from every point of view, particularly during the
period of overproduction which began around 1926. Bills to relax mandatory leasing
were introduced into every Congress from 1922 to 1929 at the request of the Secretary
of the Interior.
[72] Act of Mar. 2, 1929, 45 STAT. 1478. *See* Continental Oil Co. v. Osage Oil & Ref.
Co., 69 F. 2d 19 (C.C.A. 10th 1934), United States v. Johnson, 87 F. 2d 155
(C.C.A. 10th 1936), United States v. Sands, 94 F. 2d 156 (C.C.A. 10th 1938).

datory leasing of lands by the Secretary to require "that not less than 25,000 acres shall be offered for lease for oil and gas mining purposes during any one year; Provided further, That as to all lands hereafter leased, the regulations governing same and the leases issued thereon shall contain appropriate provisions for the conservation of the natural gas for its economic use, to the end that the highest percentages of ultimate recovery of both oil and gas may be secured." A further extension to April 8, 1983 was effected in 1938 [73] and all lands, monies, and properties held in trust by the United States were continued until January 1, 1984, unless otherwise provided by Congress.

REGULATIONS FOR TRIBAL LAND LEASING

The general regulations [74] governing the leasing of tribal lands for mining are set out in 25 Code of Federal Regulations 186.1–.30; those concerning the leasing of certain restricted allotted lands are in Sections 189.1–.33. Oil and gas leases in the Wind River Reservation of Wyoming are regulated in Sections 192.1–.31 and those concerning the Crow Reservation in Montana in Sections 195.1–.30. Lands acquired under the Emergency Relief Appropriation Act [75] and transferred to the administrative jurisdiction of the Secretary of the Interior are regulated under Section 25 of the Code of Federal Regulations, Sections 187.1–.12 (1946 Supplement). Regulations dealing with oil and gas leases on lands occupied by the Five Civilized Tribes are found in Title 25 of the Code of Federal Regulations, Sections 183.2–.49. The most comprehensive regulations dealing with operations on leased Indian lands are those dealing with the Osage property, found in Sections 180.1–.94 of Title 25, Code of Federal Regulations.

The operations of the Federal Government on Indian lands, although complicated by a mass of statutory material, have in general followed a pattern akin to that on the public domain. In the case of Indian lands the Government must also consider the dis-

---

[73] Act of June 24, 1938, 52 STAT. 1035.

[74] All oil and gas operations on Indian lands, except Osage, are governed by the operating regulations of the Geol. Sur., 30 CODE FED. REGS. § 221 (1940).

[75] Act of Apr. 8, 1935, 49 STAT. 115. These lands are largely contiguous or in close proximity to existing Indian Reservations.

charge of its function as trustee and guardian of its wards. This factor supplies an additional reason for seeking maximum royalty rates through competitive bidding as well as an efficient, non-wasteful production to conserve the oil and gas resources underlying the lands of its charges.

(c) Naval Petroleum Reserves

The naval petroleum reserves were created under a policy of setting aside adequate oil reserves for the Navy's exclusive use, on the theory that oil reserves could be blocked out and conserved in the ground against the day when military demands necessitated withdrawal and use. The greatly increased petroleum requirements for the successful accomplishment of the Naval program today make full attainment of that objective impracticable. Known reserves allocated to the Navy, although a substantial percentage of the total known reserves of California, contain a relatively insignificant percentage of the available national oil supply. The O'Mahoney Committee,[76] which made a comprehensive survey of the petroleum supply in 1945, stated: [77] "the total estimated recoverable oil from the three naval petroleum reserves, other than Alaska, is only 376,000,000 barrels. It is obvious that the amount of oil producible from these modest reserves would constitute but slight assistance in the event of war. . . . Therefore, it is submitted that the naval petroleum reserves of Buena Vista Hills, Teapot Dome, and Elk Hills be discontinued. . . ."[78] The Navy has conceded the advisability of turning over Reserves No. 2 and No. 3—Buena Vista and Teapot Dome—but for different reasons. In Reserve No. 2 land ownership is so checkerboarded that it became necessary long ago to lease Government lands to protect against drainage by private owners. As a result the Navy never has had control of production and is unable to follow the Congressional policy to conserve oil in

Naval Petroleum Reserves—The writer expresses his appreciation to Mr. Ross Tracie of the Petroleum Reserves Division, Navy Department, who looked over this section and made unofficial comments on it prior to publication.

[76] *Special Committee Investigating Petroleum Resources, pursuant to S. Res. 36,* 79th Cong., 1st Sess. (1945), *extended from S. Res. 253,* 78th Cong., 1st Sess. (1943).

[77] Sen. Rep. No. 9, 80th Cong., 1st Sess. 50 (1947).

[78] S. 2133, introduced by Senator Robinson of Wyoming, Feb. 5, 1948, authorizes the transfer of Reserves 2 and 3 from the Navy to Interior. As of May 1, 1948, no hearings had been held on the bill.

place. The leases in this reserve are administered by the Secretary of the Navy under rules and regulations promulgated by the Interior Department; technical advice and assistance is rendered by the Geological Survey which is reimbursed by some $20,000 yearly.[79] Since the Navy is unable to keep the oil in the ground, it considers it advisable to turn the reserve over to Interior for administration as any other public lands. In the case of Reserve No. 3, the Navy favors releasing jurisdiction to Interior because of the small reserves now thought to exist there.[80] During the war a careful survey of this 9000 acre reserve reduced its estimated content from 125,-000,000 barrels to about 8,000,000 barrels. However, the Navy favors drilling at least one deep test well before abandoning the administration of Teapot Dome to the Interior Department.[81]

THE ORIGIN OF THE NAVAL PETROLEUM RESERVES PROGRAM

As early as 1900 the Geological Survey recommended creation of a naval petroleum storage by withdrawal of public lands. In 1912 the General Board of the United States Navy thought permanent reservation should be made for future fuel needs. The Secretary of the Navy requested the Interior Department to set aside lands sufficient to insure a supply of 500,000,000 barrels, and in compliance the Director of the Geological Survey recommended withdrawal of 38,000 acres of public and private lands in Elk Hills, Kern County, California. On September 2, 1921 President Taft signed an executive order [82] creating Reserve No. 1. At the time of its creation no oil had been discovered, selection being made on the basis of geological evidence. The reserve was increased in 1942 to 43,000 acres.[83] Because of the controversy over whether Reserve No. 1 contained sufficient supplies, a second executive order was issued December 13, 1912 withdrawing 30,000 acres of public and private lands in the Buena Vista Hills, Kern County, as Reserve No. 2. On June

[79] Release, Navy Department, *A Résumé of the History of the Naval Petroleum and Oil Shale Reserves and the Naval Policy Related Thereto* 7–8 (Oct. 27, 1947).
[80] *Id.* at 8.
[81] *Id.* at 8.
[82] *Id.* at 1.
[83] Exec. Order No. 9257, 7 FED. REG. 8411 (1942) as corrected by Exec. Order No. 9270, 7 FED. REG. 9409 (1942).

29, 1914 the Secretary of the Navy requested Interior's recommendation for additional reserves in Wyoming, and as a result President Wilson signed an executive order April 30, 1915 creating Reserve No. 3, Teapot Dome, containing 9321 acres made up entirely of public lands. Reserve No. 4, some 35,000 square miles in Alaska, was established by President Harding by executive order on February 27, 1923.

CLEARING TITLES ON THE RESERVES

Creation of Reserves No. 1 and No. 2 immediately involved the Navy with private claimants whose oil titles on public lands were based on lode or placer mining laws, compelling the claimant to allege discovery of a mineral other than oil to retain possession pending drilling. Although the Navy, the Department of the Interior, and the Department of Justice considered many of these claims fraudulent, piecemeal legislation prior to the Mineral Leasing Act of 1920 [84] recognized the rights of claimants who were diligent in developing their holdings under color of the mining laws to continue to discovery. Section 18 of the Act of 1920 authorized the Secretary of the Interior, in return for surrender of all claims under prior mining laws and payment of a ⅛th royalty to the United States on all past production, to lease producing wells on naval reserves together with an area of land sufficient to permit operation; no well could be drilled within 660 feet of a leased well without consent of the lessee.

At the request of the Navy a section of its appropriation Act for 1920 [85] directed the Secretary of the Navy to take possession of property within the Naval Petroleum Reserves on which there were no pending claims or applications for permits or leases under the Act. He was to "conserve, develop, use and operate the same in his discretion, directly or by contract, lease or otherwise, and to use, store, exchange, or sell the oil and gas products thereof." [86]

At the outset of operations under the Mineral Leasing Act and the appropriation Act of June 4, 1920, the conflict between the in-

[84] 41 Stat. 437 (1920), 30 U.S.C.A. § 221 et seq. (1940).

[85] 41 Stat. 813 (1920), 34 U.S.C.A. § 524 (1940).

[86] But contracts for the construction of storage facilities in exchange for royalty oil and leases on the naval petroleum reserve were held unauthorized by this section in Pan American Pet. Co. v. United States, 273 U.S. 456 (1927) affirming Pan American Pet. Co. v. United States, 9 F. 2d 761 (1926), which modified United States v. Pan American Pet. Co., 6 F. 2d 43 (1925). See note 87 infra.

terests of holders of leases on naval reserves and the Navy Department became apparent. The situation was not aided by the transfer of jurisdiction over leases to the Interior Department during the stewardship of Secretary Fall. Although most of the leases issued under this invalid exercise of authority were subsequently cancelled by the courts,[87] it was not until the Act of February 25, 1928 [88] that the Secretary of the Navy was vested with exclusive jurisdiction over all outstanding leases on naval reserves. Among the cases which developed out of the attempts of the Navy Department to clear the Government's title to land within the reserves was *United States v. Southern Pacific Co.*[89] The company claimed about 6000 acres of land in the Elk Hills reserve as a part of its selection of lieu lands made in 1903 and 1904 under statutes which limited its choice to non-mineral lands. Contending that the railroad knew of the existence of oil under the land, the Government sought to have its patents set aside. The Court sustained this position and the patents were cancelled. But in *United States v. Southern Pacific Co.*[90] a consolidation of six suits, involving about 10,500 acres in Reserve No. 2 and 5000 in Reserve No. 1, the Government failed to prove its contention that the lands were of known mineral character when patented and the Navy Department was unable to persuade the Attorney General to carry the case further. *United States v. Standard Oil Co.*[91] dealt with company claims based on the school land grants to California. The claims were held invalid when it was established that the lands were of known mineral character at the time of entry. Standard was obliged to pay over $6,000,000 for the oil taken under these defective leases.

THE TEAPOT DOME SCANDALS

A little over a year after the passage of the Mineral Leasing Act of 1920 President Harding promulgated an executive order [92] trans-

---

[87] Mammoth Oil Co. v. United States, 275 U.S. 13 (1927), Pan American Pet. Co. v. United States, 273 U.S. 456 (1927).

[88] 45 Stat. 148 (1928), 34 U.S.C.A. §524 a (1940).

[89] 251 U.S. 1 (1919).

[90] 260 Fed. 511 (S.D. Cal. 1919).

[91] 21 F. Supp. 645 (S.D. Cal. 1937) aff'd 107 F. 2d 402 (C.C.A. 9th 1939) *cert. denied* 309 U.S. 654 (1940).

[92] May 31, 1921. This order was ultimately held invalid in a dictum in United States v. Pan American Pet. Co., 55 F. 2d 753, 769 (C.C.A. 9th 1932) *reversing* 45 F. 2d 821, *cert. denied* 287 U.S. 612 (1932).

ferring administration of the reserves from the exclusive jurisdiction of the Secretary of the Navy to the Secretary of the Interior, subject to the approval of the president and the Secretary of the Navy of any change in general policy with respect to drilling or conserving land and oil. The transfer, obtained through the efforts of Secretary of the Interior Albert B. Fall, culminated in a national scandal. The history of Teapot Dome and the Fall-Doheny negotiations leading to the looting of Reserve No. 1 is too well known to necessitate more than a brief summary. The underlying basis for Fall's action was supposedly his desire to get the reserved oil for the Navy out of the ground and into storage. To that end he negotiated contracts and leases whereby the Government leased the reserves to the Doheny and Sinclair interests in return for an agreement to construct storage facilities and to maintain specific quantities of oil available on demand to the Navy. One major difficulty was that it provided a method whereby the Secretary of the Navy obtained construction of expensive fuel depots unauthorized by Congress, and without appropriation. Subsequent events indicated that Fall benefited financially. The leases made on Teapot Dome and Reserve No. 1 were eventually cancelled in *United States v. Pan-American Petroleum Company* and *United States v. Mammoth Oil Company*.[93] Fall was convicted of accepting a $100,000 bribe from Doheny in *United States v. Fall*.[94]

SUBSEQUENT LEGISLATION AFFECTING THE NAVAL RESERVES

The temporary legislation of July 3, 1930[95] and its companion permanent enactment of March 4, 1931,[96] discussed under the public domain, authorized the Secretary of the Interior to enter into cooperative or unit plans, but the Acts were specifically made inoperative as to the naval reserves. Nevertheless, the Secretary of the Navy was given similar powers subject to the approval of the presi-

[93] *Supra* note 87.
[94] 49 F. 2d 506 (App. D.C. 1931) *cert. denied* 281 U.S. 757 (1931).
[95] 46 STAT. 1007 (1930), 30 U.S.C.A. § 226 (1940).
[96] 46 STAT. 1523 (1931), 30 U.S.C.A. § 226 (1940).

dent. Like terms were contained in the 1935 amendments to the Mineral Leasing Act.[97]

The Act of June 30, 1938 [98] and its amendment by the Act of June 17, 1944 [99] brought together prior legislation relating to the naval petroleum reserves and added detailed requirements concerning contractual relationships entered into by the Secretary. The Act directed him to take possession of all properties within the naval reserves and to "explore, prospect, conserve, develop, use and operate" them in his discretion subject to presidential approval. In the case of Reserve No. 1 he is authorized to enter into cooperative plans including privately owned or leased lands within as well as outside the reserve on the same geologic structure. No petroleum is to be produced under these plans without specific authorization by a joint resolution of the Congress. If the Secretary is unable to enter into satisfactory unit plans and cannot effect an exchange of lands within and without the reserves, he may acquire these lands and leases by purchase or condemnation.

Leases within the reserves which were outstanding prior to July 1, 1936 (except those included in an approved unit plan) were directed to be terminated at the expiration of an initial twenty year period. The Secretary is required to re-examine the need for production under any unit plan entered into and should he find the production no longer needed for national defense, he must reduce it. In any unit plan contract the United States must currently receive its share of the production, but an exception was made to cover a unit plan on Reserve No. 1 into which the Navy entered with Standard Oil of California. That exception provided that any party other than the United States might produce and have charged to its share of total production sufficient quantities of oil to compensate it for its share of the current operating expenses, necessary repairs, and taxes. The company was entitled to receive such quantities of production as were necessary to compensate it for surrendering control of the field to the Navy, but if the Secretary did not produce petroleum under joint resolution, he had an absolute discretion to terminate or reduce the flow after reasonable notice to

[97] 49 STAT. 678 (1935), 30 U.S.C.A. § 226 (1940).
[98] 52 STAT. 1253 (1938), 34 U.S.C.A. § 524 (1940).
[99] 58 STAT. 280 (1944), 34 U.S.C.A. § 524 (Supp. 1946).

the contracting parties. The Secretary is required to hold prior consultations with the Armed Services Committee of the Congress regarding details of any proposed contract made under the conferred powers. The Secretary may also contract with owners and lessees of lands adjoining the naval reserves to consolidate and protect the Government oil lands. He may provide for compensation in lieu of drilling or operating offset wells and may exchange any public lands within Reserve No. 1 for private lands within its boundaries. All contracts are submitted in advance to the Armed Services Committee for approval, and the Secretary is required to report annually to Congress all purchase and condemnation proceedings and quarterly to the Armed Services Committee the total production from the reserves each preceding quarter.

The Act of June 17, 1944 was the outgrowth of a long negotiation [100] between the Navy and the Standard Oil of California seeking an agreement with respect to operations on Reserve No. 1. Standard owned about ⅕th of the land and ⅓rd of the oil within the reserve, hence it was impossible for the Navy to implement the Congressional mandate of conserving oil in the ground in the absence of any control of Standard's production. After attempts to purchase their lands proved impractical, a contract was executed November 20, 1942,[101] and while the negotiations leading to this contract were conducted in good faith on both sides, the Navy Department failed to submit the agreement to the Justice Department for an opinion as to legality. When information concerning the contract was publicized, a rising tide of protest, climaxed by an opinion by the Department of Justice labeling the contract illegal, resulted in its rescission by the Secretary of the Navy. Concurrently, a temporary operating agreement [102] was entered into between the Navy and Standard under the general power of the Secretary to conserve the oil in the ground, which after modification was made permanent [103] with the passage of the Act of June 17, 1944. Under the plan the Navy was allocated about ⅔rds of future production from the Shallow Oil Zone, and Standard received the balance.

[100] Detailed in *Hearings before the Committee on Public Lands on H.R. 2596*, 78th Cong., 1st Sess. 18–21, 296–324, 843–867 (1943).

[101] A copy is set out in *Hearings supra* note 100 at 867.

[102] A copy is set out in *Hearings supra* note 100 at 489.

[103] *Id.* at 588 *et seq.*

With respect to the deeper Stevens Oil Zone, the percentages were subject to periodic readjustment based on current engineering studies. The most recent allocation of production from this zone, made July 1, 1947, apportioned ⅘ths to the Navy and ⅕th to Standard. In return for Standard's submission to production control, it was permitted to receive up to 25,000,000 barrels at a rate not in excess of 15,000 barrels a day so long as the Navy operated under a joint resolution authorizing production. As soon as that expired, the Secretary of the Navy was given complete discretion with respect to future reductions or terminations of production provided reasonable notice was given. Production from the reserve was authorized at the rate of 65,000 barrels a day by joint resolution of June 17, 1944, and later by the Act of July 6, 1945 [104] this rate was continued through December 31, 1946, unless the Secretary ordered an earlier cut back. Such a reduction was ordered on August 22, 1945, when the Navy ceased production for its own account and limited production to 15,000 barrels daily. On May 10, 1946 a further restriction to 8450 barrels daily was made,[105] which the operating and engineering committee found necessary to keep the field in a state of readiness. During the wartime expansion program some 300 new wells were drilled, bringing the total for the entire field to approximately 700.

[104] 59 STAT. 465 (1945), 34 U.S.C.A. § 524 (Supp. 1946).
[105] *Hearings before Committee on Naval Affairs*, 79th Cong. 2d Sess. (1946) 3711. Letter from Acting Sec. of the Navy, John L. Sullivan to Standard Oil Co. of Calif.

CHAPTER 41

The Government in the Exercise of the Power over Interstate Commerce

(a) Anti-Trust Activities

Although the Sherman Act[1] was a direct outgrowth of widespread sentiment against the operations of the Standard Oil Trust, whose dissolution was ordered in *Standard Oil of New Jersey v. United States,*[2] there have been few prosecutions of the oil industry under it and companion laws, and those were directed in the main toward the refining and marketing phase of the industry. It is not our purpose to trace the interpretative nuances of the Sherman Act from the rule of reason through latter day suggestions that size,[3] in and of itself, is the essence of a violation. It is clear that the impact of the Act on the oil industry has not appreciably affected the conservation of oil and gas.

The record of prosecutions of the oil industry under the anti-trust laws comprises approximately a dozen cases. After the dissolution decree in the Standard Oil prosecution, the next case was that of *United States v. Payne* in which an indictment charging a conspiracy to restrain trade in oil and products was returned August 29, 1912 in the District Court for the Northern District of Texas. This resulted in a nolle prosequi February 25, 1913. In 1924 a major proceeding was launched against the Standard Oil Company of Indiana and numerous other companies, attacking the use of cross licensing agreements in sharing patented cracking processes and establishing royalty rates. After losing the case in the lower

NORTHCUTT ELY, WRITER. (See app. B.)
[1] 26 STAT. 209 (1890), 15 U.S.C.A. § 1 *et seq.* (1940).
[2] 221 U.S. 1 (1911).
[3] *See* United States v. Aluminum Co. of Amer., 148 F. 2d 416 (C.C.A. 2d 1945), Amer. Tob. Co. v. U.S., 328 U.S. 781 (1946).

court,[4] the companies were successful when they carried it to the Supreme Court.[5] The next case in point of time was *United States v. Standard Oil of New Jersey*,[6] involving an effort on the part of the Government to prevent a 1929 proposal to merge Standard Oil of New York (Socony) and the Vacuum Oil Company, under the original Standard of New Jersey dissolution decree still in effect in the District Court for the Northern Division of Missouri. The merger was held permissible under the terms of that order and the Socony-Vacuum Oil Company came into existence. In *United States v. Standard Oil Company of California* a complaint was filed February 15, 1930 charging the Standard Oil Company and 19 other organizations with conspiring to restrain trade in gasoline by fixing and maintaining prices. The result was a consent decree perpetually enjoining the objectionable practices, although the decree was subsequently modified to permit the defendants to participate in activities under the NRA petroleum code. A consent decree (unreported) was the outcome of an action instituted March 6, 1935 against the Columbia Gas and Electric Corporation in Delaware charging it with a conspiracy to restrain trade in natural gas through control of the Panhandle Eastern Pipeline Company. A perpetual injunction was issued January 29, 1936 enjoining the conspiracy and requiring Columbia to divest itself of Panhandle securities.

In 1936 the famous Madison indictments were returned, and in *United States v. Socony-Vacuum Oil Company*[7] marketing agreements growing out of the petroleum code of the NRA were found violative of the Sherman Act. There were two original indictments, but on a plea of nolo contendere the second, relating to agreements covering the sale of gasoline to jobbers, was terminated with the payment of a fine. In the first the alleged conspiracy grew out of the formation of a general stabilization committee appointed at the request of the Secretary of the Interior. The meetings of these committees were said to have been successful in eliminating price wars. At the second general committee meeting at the suggestion of industry members, a Tank Car Stabilization Committee was ap-

[4] United States v. Standard Oil Co. (Ind.), 33 F. 2d 617 (N.D. Ill. 1929).
[5] Standard Oil Co. (Ind.) v. United States, 283 U.S. 163 (1931).
[6] 47 F. 2d 288 (E.D. Mo. 1931).
[7] 310 U.S. 150 (1940).

pointed to establish a firm market at the tank car level. Three days
after this group was appointed, the Supreme Court handed down
its decision in the *Panama Refining* [8] case, and shortly thereafter
the NIRA collapsed with the decision in the *Schechter* [9] case. The
organization in the industry continued to function in the middle
west, and it was these activities that the Anti-Trust Division successfully attacked. The defendant sought to establish that the buying program had been inaugurated under Governmental authority
and acquiesced in by the administration. The lower court refused
this evidence, and the circuit court of appeals reversed it on that
ground.[10] The Supreme Court held the evidence properly excluded,
pointing out that no specific approval of the buying program had
been obtained under the NIRA prior to its expiration on May 27,
1935, and even if such permission had been secured, it would have
become invalid as a defense in an anti-trust prosecution with the
termination of authority in the *Schechter* case. The Court was not
persuaded that there was still room for the play of competitive
forces under the buying program. Since the purpose of the combination was found to be to raise prices, it was held violative of the
Sherman Act, nor was it a legal justification that the removal of
distress gasoline from the market relieved the industry of ruinous
competition. "If the so-called competitive abuses were to be ap-
praised here, the reasonableness of prices would necessarily become
an issue in every price fixing case. In that event, the Sherman Act
would soon be emasculated. . . ." [11] The prosecution of the case
left the industry, rightly or wrongly, with an abiding feeling of
distrust.

In *Ethyl Gasoline Corporation v. United States* [12] contractual
arrangements based upon patented fluids were found in violation
of the Sherman Act. The Court concentrated its attention on the
clauses in the contract which permitted Ethyl to deny treated gasoline to unethical distributors, which it found to mean distributors
who were willing to engage in price competition. Such restrictions
were considered an attempt to use patents to control the market of

[8] Panama Ref. Co. v. Ryan, 293 U.S. 388 (1935).
[9] A.L.A. Schechter Poultry Corp. v. United Statees, 295 U.S. 495 (1935).
[10] United States v. Socony-Vacuum Oil Co., 101 F. 2d 870 (C.C.A. 7th 1939).
[11] United States v. Socony-Vacuum Oil Co., 310 U.S. 150, 221 (1940).
[12] 309 U.S. 436 (1940).

untreated gasoline and hence within the rule of the *Carbice* case.[13]

In 1940 the Department of Justice filed its Mother Hubbard anti-trust case against the American Petroleum Institute, all major companies and their subsidiaries. The complaint was a broadside assault on the petroleum industry as a monopoly. As a result of World War II the proceeding was suspended, but it was returned to the docket in 1946, only to be suspended again in December 1946 supposedly in favor of separate actions against smaller groups engaging in specific practices thought to be contrary to the Sherman Act, such as the suit brought against the General Petroleum Corporation of California on November 14, 1939, charging 40 corporations covering the Pacific Coast area with combining to restrain trade in gasoline by price fixing and price maintenance. On February 13, 1940 all demurrers were overruled,[14] and subsequently 38 defendants withdrew their not guilty pleas and pleaded nolo contendere. Fines aggregating $84,500 were assessed and the charges against the remaining defendants were dismissed.

Alleged monopolistic practices in the pipe line field were attacked in a suit [15] brought against 20 major oil companies and 59 pipe line companies seeking treble damages and an injunction against further violations of the Interstate Commerce Act regarding receipt of rebates. The theory of the Government was that dividends returned to the parent company owners of the pipe lines were in substance rebates within the meaning of the Elkins Act. The suit terminated in a consent decree on December 23, 1941, wherein the companies agreed that no defendant common carrier pipe line would pay its shipper-owners during any year more than seven per cent of the shipper-owner's share of the valuation of the carrier's property as determined by the ICC. Any excess was placed in a special fund to be used for three purposes: (1) to maintain normal and reasonable working capital, (2) to retire debt outstanding at the time of the decree if incurred for the purpose of constructing or acquiring common carrier property, and (3) to extend existing common carrier facilities and to construct or acquire new ones; any funds put into new facilities could not be included in

---

[13] Carbice Corp. v. Amer. Pat. Develop. Corp., 283 U.S. 27 (1931).
[14] United States v. Gen. Pet. Corp., 33 F. Supp. 95 (S.D. Cal. 1940).
[15] United States v. Atl. Ref. Co., civil action No. 14060 (D.C. 1941) unreported.

arriving at the valuation upon which the seven per cent return was calculated.[16]

During World War II anti-trust activity bearing upon the oil industry was confined to a criminal and a civil action against the Standard Oil of New Jersey, growing out of its cartel arrangements with I. G. Farben. The company pleaded nolo contendere to the criminal information on March 25, 1942 and a fine of $50,000 was imposed. A civil action resulted in a consent decree the same date providing for complete severance from I. G. Farben and free public licensing during the war of all the defendant's patents relating to synthetic gasoline and rubber production and the furnishing of know how to licensees.

In the post-war period to the end of 1947, three anti-trust proceedings had been instituted. On January 2, 1947 an injunction was sought in the California courts in the case of *United States v. Standard Oil of California and Standard Stations, Inc.*, alleging a conspiracy to restrain trade in petroleum, products, and automobile accessories. The injunction was sought against exclusive dealing contracts whereby more than 7000 service stations were required to use only Standard products, thus depriving independent producers of market outlet. The case was decided in favor of the Government on June 2, 1948. A similar civil case was filed against the Richfield Oil Corporation in the same court April 30, 1947 attacking agreements with 2600 service station operators.

The most recent oil case filed by the Anti-Trust Division is that against the Cotton Valley Operators Committee started June 17, 1947 in the District Court for the Western District of Louisiana against 15 corporations and 18 individuals comprising the group. The complaint charges violations of the Sherman Act through the conduct of unit operations in the Cotton Valley Field, Webster Parish, Louisiana. The case had not come to trial in early 1948,[17] but it has become a cause celebre within the industry oil industry because of the possibility of direct federal intervention in state conservation practices; the defendants and the industry pointed

[16] One writer observes: "From the standpoint of law enforcement, the decree may well be said to countenance continued violation of the Interstate Commerce Act and the Elkins Act, albeit only a 7 per cent violation." Note, *Public Control of Petroleum Pipelines,* 51 YALE L. J. 1338, 1351 (1942).

[17] But rulings on preliminary motions are found in 75 F. Supp. 1 (W.D. La. 1948).

out that the Louisiana Commissioner of Conservation has specifically approved the unit plan for the field. The Department of Justice, in announcing the filing of the suit,[18] stressed that it was not its purpose to attack "joint activity of the defendant in the production of wet gas, in the removal of hydrocarbons, or in the maintenance of underground pressure through re-injection of part of the dry gas back into the underground reservoir, or any activity which is necessary or essential to the conservation of natural resources for the prevention of waste." The announced position of the Department is that the action is directed toward joint processing and refining of the products removed from wet gas, and the sale of these products jointly through selected trade channels. The complaint specifically alleges that the order of the Louisiana Commissioner of Conservation approved the agreement only to the extent that it provided for unit operation and the re-injection into the reservoir under pressure of a part of the liquid and gaseous hydrocarbons produced from the field.

The case is unique not only because it is the first attempt to apply the Sherman Act to unit operations, but also because it rests upon an assertion of federal power in a field hitherto considered to comprise only intrastate activities. The complaint alleges that during the conspiracy more than 30,000,000 barrels of oil and 150,-000,000 MCF of natural gas were taken from the field and "moved in a continuous uninterrupted flow from the producing wells in Louisiana to consumers in states other than Louisiana." Four specific charges are made: (1) that the defendants agreed jointly to engage in and exclude others from the business of extracting, processing, and refining the products of the fields, (2) that the defendants agreed jointly to engage in and exclude others from the business of distributing and selling the commonly extracted products; (3) the defendants agreed jointly to sell only through selective trade channels, and (4) that they agreed to fix prices, terms, and conditions for the sale of the products. The prayer for relief is broadly drawn and the perpetual injunction against the activities of the defendants includes but one exception—that they be permitted to engage in the extraction of the products of the field only insofar as necessary to achieve the ultimate in recovery. Whatever

[18] Dept. of Justice, Press Release, June 17, 1947.

its outcome, the *Cotton Valley* case is notable as the first assault upon unit operations. The prediction of collision between state and federal law, the one sanctioning, the other alleging to forbid agreements for joint production, was freely made when unit operations were first discussed before the Federal Oil Conservation Board. Two decades elapsed before the issue crystallized in litigation, and the dividing line is not yet clearly established between the shelter cast over these agreements by state laws in restraint of wasteful production and the federal inhibitions against restraint of trade.

(b) Control of Pipe Lines

Interstate oil pipe lines are controlled by the Hepburn Act of June 29, 1906 [19] which comprehensively amended the Interstate Commerce Act of February 4, 1887.[20] One of its provisions, the Lodge Amendment, altering Section 1 of the basic Act, designates as common carriers all pipe line carriers of oil and other commodities, except water, artificial or natural gas, and subjects the lines to the jurisdiction of the ICC. Interstate common carrier oil pipe lines file with the ICC annual reports, schedules of rates and charges, and conform in their accounting to rules adopted by the Commission. They are less generally supervised than other common carriers. The provision of the Hepburn Act was an outgrowth of complaints of monopoly against the old Standard Oil Company, emphasized by a report of the Commissioner of Corporations, submitted to the Senate May 17, 1906 on the subject of transportation in the oil industry.[21] The Standard Oil Company acquired directly and through subsidiaries all pipe lines that connected the Atlantic seaboard with the major oil fields east of California. Controlling the only practical means of transportation from the fields, the Company refused to transport oil not sold to it or its affiliates. In the words of Mr. Justice Holmes in the *Pipe Line Cases*,[22] "It made

Control of Pipe Lines—The writer expresses his appreciation to Mr. Edward M. Reidy of the Interstate Commerce Commission, who looked over this section and made unofficial comments on it prior to publication.

[19] 34 STAT. 584 (1906), 49 U.S.C.A. § 41 *et seq.* (1940).
[20] 24 STAT. 379 (1887), 49 U.S.C.A. § 1 *et seq.* (1940).
[21] See also H. R. Doc. 812, 59th Cong., 1st Sess. (1906), H. R. Doc. 606, 59th Cong., 2d Sess. (1907).
[22] 234 U.S. 548 (1914).

itself the master of the fields without the necessity of owning them." This condition was brought to the attention of Congress during its consideration of the Lodge Amendment, and its answer was that all interstate oil pipe lines should operate as common carriers under the supervision of the ICC.

Acting under this authority the ICC on January 23, 1907 sent questionnaires to all interstate oil pipe lines regarding their organization practices, rates, and earnings. As a result of the responses received, the Commission upon its own motion on June 8, 1911 ordered an investigation of the situation. Some 55 companies were served and hearings were held all over the country amassing volumes of testimony and exhibits. On June 3, 1912 the Commission issued its report and order [23] requiring 13 companies to file schedules of rates and charges. Before the order was promulgated, the dissolution order of the Supreme Court in *United States v. Standard Oil Company* [24] had been handed down on May 15, 1911 and the Sherman Act,[25] rather than the new Hepburn Act, was the first to reach the problem. The companies, after the entry of the Commission's order, brought suit in the U.S. Commerce Court to have it set aside and a preliminary injunction issued in that court [26] from which the United States and the ICC appealed. The Supreme Court on June 22, 1914 handed down its decision in the *Pipe Line Cases*,[27] holding the order valid and that Congress had power to designate as common carriers interstate oil pipe lines, since they were common carriers in everything but name. One exception was noted. The Uncle Sam Oil Company, carrying only its own oil from its wells in one state via its pipe line to its refineries in another, was held not within the Act.

Since the decision in the *Pipe Line Cases*, two cases [28] before the Supreme Court have considered the jurisdiction of the ICC over petroleum lines. In the *Valvoline* case the company sought to annul and enjoin an order of the ICC requiring it to file maps, charts, and schedules of its properties for valuation purposes, on the ground

[23] In the matter of Pipe Lines, 24 I.C.C. 1 (1912).
[24] 221 U.S. 1 (1911).
[25] 26 STAT. 209 (1890), 15 U.S.C.A. § 1 et seq. (1940).
[26] Prairie Oil & Gas Co. v. United States, 204 Fed. 798 (1913).
[27] See note 22 supra.
[28] Valvoline Oil Co. v. United States, 308 U.S. 141 (1939), Champlin Ref. Co. v. United States, 329 U.S. 29 (1946).

that it was not a common carrier line subject to the jurisdiction of the Commission. Their lines gathered oil from over 9000 wells in Pennsylvania, West Virginia, and Ohio, transporting it to two company refineries in Pennsylvania. The company contended that it was a private carrier within the exception set out in the *Pipe Line Cases*.[29] The Court rejected this argument pointing out that since the defendant collected oil from wells of many producers it did not qualify as an owner-shipper, and was thus subject to the jurisdiction of the ICC. In the *Champlin* case the company sought to enjoin enforcement of an ICC order requiring filing of information. The lower court upheld the ruling that Champlin was a common carrier, and the ruling was affirmed in the Supreme Court where the decision was placed on the narrow ground that "Champlin's operation is transportation within the meaning of the Act and . . . the statute supports the Commission's order to furnish information." Champlin carried only gasoline that it owned and never held itself out to others as a carrier. Four justices dissented, saying it was not a common carrier under the Act. The majority agreed that, although the company might not be a carrier for all purposes, that question was premature and too hypothetical to warrant consideration on the record submitted.

Though vested with power over pipe lines as common carriers, the Commission has made little use of this authority beyond routine regulatory supervision. Not until 1934 was a general program of pipe line valuation undertaken. There are but few instances of formal action in the record, and before 1940 only two cases were reported.[30] The first full scale investigation of a segment of the pipe line industry in recent years was reported in 1940 [31] in an investigation of thirty-seven carriers moving crude from the southwest to Texas ports and to midwestern refineries. Of the thirty-seven, ten served none but their oil company owners, twenty served from one to six non-affiliated shippers, and seven served from ten to thirty-seven shippers unaffiliated with the line.[32] After extensive

---

[29] See note 22 supra.

[30] Crude Petroleum Oil from Kansas and Oklahoma to Lacy St., Pa., 59 I.C.C. 483 (1920). Rates were attacked as excessive but the Commission found them reasonable in Burndred Bros. v. Prairie Pipe Line Co., 68 I.C.C. 458 (1922).

[31] Reduced Pipe Line Rates and Gathering Charges, 243 I.C.C. 115 (1940).

[32] Id. at 121.

hearings the Commission ordered each carrier to show cause why its rates should not be lowered to a point where earnings would not exceed eight per cent on the ICC's valuation,[33] and issued a further show cause order designed to reduce minimum tender requirements from 50,000 to 10,000 barrels.[34] The high minimum tender device, necessitating the delivery of a guaranteed minimum, has allegedly been used to keep independent shippers from having access to the major oil company lines.[35]

Two pipe line cases appearing in the records of the ICC after the *Reduced Pipe Line Rates* proceedings of 1940 [36] were the *Petroleum Rail Shippers' Association v. Alton & Southern Railroad* [37] and the *Minnelusa Oil Corp. v. Continental Pipe Line Co.* In the first, substantial rate reductions and adjustments of minimum tenders were ordered for the Great Lakes Pipe Line Company and the Phillips Petroleum Company. The Commission directed that these corporations accept for transportation (subject to delay until accumulations at the receiving station reached 25,000 barrels) tenders as low as 5000 barrels from individual shippers of gasoline of the same specifications. The former practice had been to accept for shipment only tenders from individual shippers of at least 25,000 barrels.[38] In the second case,[39] there was an indication that the ICC construed its jurisdiction broadly, for there a pipe line—in substance a private line—was designated as a common carrier because a portion a half-mile in length connected the owner-shipper's refinery to a trunk line. The Commission held that the line was a common carrier in spite of evidence tending to show that the shipper constructed the line under economic duress to obtain access to the main line.[40]

Because of the integration of the oil industry, the Hepburn Act, although it impresses common carrier status upon pipe lines, has been little used for regulatory purposes. The producer at the well is

[33] § 19 a, the Interstate Commerce Commission Act, 37 STAT. 701 (1913) directs the Commission "to investigate, ascertain, and report the value of all property owned or used by every common carrier subject to the provisions of the Act."
[34] 243 I.C.C. 115, 136 (1940).
[35] See note 16 *supra* at 1334.
[36] See note 31 *supra.*
[37] 243 I.C.C. 589 (1941).
[38] *Id.* at 665.
[39] 258 I.C.C. 41 (1944).
[40] *Id.* at 45.

not generally interested in the rates for moving oil through the line since he sells before transportation takes place. In most instances, the refiner or a subsidiary is the shipper having bought the oil in the producing area, and the refiner-shippers are the owners of the pipe lines.[41]

(c) Petroleum Code [42]

The National Government's concern with the problems of the oil industry reached a climactic peak during the days of the petroleum code. A survey of the functions of the Government during that time affords insight into the troublesome problems pressing for solution under a system of centralized control. With the price of crude as low as ten cents a barrel, serious dislocations took place within the industry which threatened the continued existence of thousands of oil operators and wells. The effect of price on operations of stripper wells is well known. Though each well produces an insignificant amount as a unit, their daily aggregate at the beginning of the code era was 500,000 barrels. It was thought that about half the total amount of ultimate recovery in known fields could be reached only by stripper wells, and it was recognized that abandonment of these for too long a period resulted in permanent loss of their oil. Thus the continued existence of stripper wells was an important objective of the Government in those days. Of equal importance in stabilizing the industry were controls over refining and marketing. These being beyond our scope are not included.

The bill which became the National Industrial Recovery Act was introduced May 23, 1933.[43] On May 20 the president in a letter to the speaker of the house, urged that specific oil legislation be added to the general bill. Section 9, proposed by Senator Connally and approved by the Senate Committee on Interstate Com-

---

[41] Discussions of the problem are found in Whitesel, *Recent Federal Regulation of the Petroleum Pipe Line as a Common Carrier*, 32 Corn. L. Q. 337 (1947), Black, *Oil Pipe Line Divorcement by Litigation and Legislation*, 25 Corn. L. Q. 510 (1940), Prewitt, *The Operation and Regulation of Crude Oil and Gasoline Pipe Lines*, 56 Q. J. Econ. 177 (1942).

[42] The writer is indebted to Norman L. Meyers, Esq. former member and executive secretary of the PAB, now of the Dist. of Col. Bar, for use of his exhaustive trial brief in U.S. v. Socony-Vacuum Oil Co. (the Madison indictment case, discussed *infra* under anti-trust activities) from which much of the history of the petroleum code was taken for use in the following pages.)

[43] H. R. 5755, 73d Cong., 1st Sess. (1933).

merce, authorized the president to initiate proceedings before the ICC to control operation of pipe lines and to fix reasonable rates for their services, empowered him to institute proceedings to divorce pipe lines from holding companies where unfair practices or exorbitant rates tended to create monopoly, and to prohibit "the transportation in interstate and foreign commerce of petroleum and the products thereof produced or withdrawn from storage in excess of the amount permitted to be produced or withdrawn from storage by any state law or valid regulation or order prescribed thereunder, by any board, commission, officer, or other duly authorized agency of a state." Violation was punishable by fine, imprisonment, or both. The section remained in the Act approved June 13, 1933 [44] initiating federal control over hot oil. But while the petroleum industry was the only one singled out for reference in the Act, the legal authority for the oil code is found in the general provisions of Title I.

Immediately upon the enactment of the statute, negotiations looking to submission of the code were initiated by the American Petroleum Institute. A *Chicago* draft was prepared.[45] Later, hearings under General Johnson in Washington developed substantial dissension in the industry on these issues: (1) whether allocations of production by the Federal Government to the states should be mandatory or advisory, (2) should prices be fixed, and (3) should lease and agency marketing contracts be outlawed. Labor clauses furnished controversy in later stages. The hearings lasted from July 24 to August 3, 1933. A committee of 54 represented the preponderant elements of the industry. Upon failure to reach agreement, General Johnson's staff was forced to redraft the code. It was submitted to President F. D. Roosevelt and approved by him the night of August 19th. To proposals for changes which were submitted concomitantly, he replied that while the code would be approved as presented, the Planning and Coordination Committee created under the agreement would be asked for recommendations for amendments. Amendments were submitted shortly thereafter and approved September 13, 1933. These changes were of particu-

---

[44] 48 STAT. 195 (1933), 15 U.S.C.A. § 709 b (1934).
[45] *Code of Fair Competition for the Petroleum Industry*, proposed by the association's meeting, Chicago, June 15–17 and June 22–24, 1933.

lar significance, because it was discovered in 1935 that they failed
to continue vital parts of the original code in force. The code was
in existence from September 2, 1933 to May 27, 1935, when all
codes were invalidated by the decision in *A. L. A. Schechter Poultry Corp. v. United States.*[46]

The Code of Fair Competition for the Petroleum Industry in its
final form had seven articles. Article I dealt with (1) fixing the
effective date of the agreement, (2) definitions, (3) provisions for
modification, (4) the presidential right to cancel orders, (5) the
president's power to impose conditions and make exceptions where
such were first considered by the Planning and Coordination Committee, and (6) the authorization of agreements among competitive units where approved by the president. Article II fixed in some
detail minimum wages and maximum hours of labor, prohibited
child labor, guaranteed the right of collective bargaining, prohibited lease and agency contracts and arrangements making employees into contractors to place them outside the protection of
the code. Article III contained sections which (1) authorized the
president to fix a ratio between imports and production, limiting
the volume of imports to that ratio; (2) subjected the withdrawals
of crude from storage and additions to storage to the control of the
Planning and Coordination Committee and limiting withdrawals
to a maximum of 100,000 barrels daily for 1933; (3) required production of crude oil needed to balance consumer demand to be
estimated at intervals by a federal agency (designated by the president) which, when the allocations were approved, would distribute
this "net reasonable market demand" among the states as the recommended operating schedule for the producing states; (4) subdivided the state allowables into pool, lease, and well quotas within
the state; but if not allocated, or where the production exceeded the
quota, the president could regulate shipment of petroleum or products out of the state or compile quotas of production recommending them to the state regulatory body where they became state operating schedules. A second paragraph, to become famous as the
lost paragraph due to failure to reenact it with the amendments of
September 13, made production in excess of a quota a violation of
the code.

[46] 295 U.S. 495 (1935).

In any state which had no regulatory body but did have a statute obligating industry within its borders to comply with the NRA codes, (apparently referring to California) the president might designate a state agency to compile quotas. Production in excess of these was a violation of the code. The industry in any state might adopt a supplemental code for that state with presidential approval, and such a code was adopted in Michigan.

Article III also made it a code violation, so long as production in a state was within the executive allocation, to buy or sell crude oil of stated gravities at a price per barrel less than a figure determined by multiplying the average tank car price per gallon of gasoline by the constant 18.5. Companies were required to file price schedules with the Planning and Coordination Committee. Section 6 a authorized the president to establish a 90 day test period price schedule for petroleum and products; purchases or sales at lower prices were a code violation. The federal agency thereafter determined the cost of recovering, refining, transporting, and distributing petroleum and products. Purchases or sales below cost at any operational level constituted a violation of the code. The president was authorized to fix maximum prices, but these were never put in force.

Section 7 provided that oil could not be shipped from a new pool unless it was developed in accordance with a plan previously approved by the president; no restriction was placed on wildcatting. Detailed regulations under this section were adopted December 20, 1933. Section 8 established six standards of fair practice for the contract drilling business, and prices per foot were regulated July 19, 1934. Section 9 set out eight standards of fair practice in the rig building business.

After the approval of the Washington code President F. D. Roosevelt designated [47] the Secretary of the Interior as administrator for the code and the Department of the Interior as the federal agency referred to in the code to "exercise on my behalf and in my stead all the functions and powers vested in me, or in any Federal agency by such act, and such code of fair competition." Secretary Ickes had already been detailed to administer the executive orders and regulations under Section 9 c of the Act, which dealt with hot

[47] Exec. Order No. 6260 (a), August 28, 1933.

oil, and had been given the powers of the executive under Title I of the NIRA with regard to oil. The two functions—administration of Section 9 c and of the code—overlapped and both were exercised in fact through the Petroleum Administrative Board, although the Secretary never formally delegated to the Board, or any officer, his functions as administrator, or as the agency charged with carrying out the hot oil section of the Act. Advising the administrator were three units, created for that purpose—the Petroleum Administrative Board, the Division of Investigations, and the Petroleum Labor Policy Board. The Interior Department functioned through two established bureaus—the Bureau of Mines and the Geological Survey. Section 2 b, Title I, NIRA, permitted the creation of agencies to carry out the policy of the Act. The Secretary of the Interior, exercising those delegated powers held in connection with the oil code, formed the Petroleum Administrative Board [48] (by administrative order September 13, 1933) "to advise with and make recommendations to the Secretary of the Interior as the administrator of the code . . . and perform such administrative functions as may be detailed to it by the Secretary. . . ." At its peak activity the Board had a staff of some 130.

Article VII, Section 5, stated that the federal agency would make necessary estimates and allocations of crude oil production. These were prepared by the Division of Petroleum Economics of the Bureau of the Mines in cooperation with the PAB.[49] The Bureau had formerly cooperated in preparing the forecasts of the volunteer committees on petroleum economics under the Federal Oil Conservation Board, and the chief of the division became a member of the PAB. Under the code the Bureau prepared periodic estimates of required production to balance consumer demand for petroleum products, determined allocations among the states, and proper inventories of gasoline for the entire country. These findings were embodied in orders prepared by the PAB for the approval and signature of the administrator. As shipments from new pools (those discovered after January 1, 1933 or having no more than

[48] The Chairman of the PAB was Charles Fahy, and members .were Norman L. Meyers, J. Howard Marshall, E. B. Swanson and Dr. John W. Frey.

[49] The procedure followed in estimating consumer demand is outlined in *Hearings before a Subcommittee of the House Committee on Interstate and Foreign Commerce on H. Res. 290 and H. R. 7372*, 76th Cong., 2d Sess., pt. IV, 2863–64 (1939).

ten wells when the code became effective) were prohibited unless developed under a plan approved by the administrator, the Geological Survey passed upon each new pool plan, along with an advisory committee of the PAB. The Survey participatcd in PAB hearings, passed on new pool plans, and recommended changes. In all, 353 plans were approved.

Amendments to the code came primarily in its first year. The initial change, dated September 13, 1933, strengthened federal control over production (Article III, Sections 3 and 4) and the price fixing provision (Article III, Section 6 a). Other amendments were of minor importance insofar as the control of production was concerned.

Interpretations issued in form of resolutions adopted by appropriate sub-committees of the Planning and Coordination Committee, and approved first by the full committee, then by the PAB and the administrator, were evidenced by an order signed by the latter. A total of 627 administrative orders were promulgated under the code, Section 9 c of the NIRA and the Connally Act. More important ones included 20 orders allocating crude production among the states, 129 certifying allowables to individual states, 22 approving allocations to California and 39 relating to production in that state, 18 approving allocations in Michigan, 32 certifying the demand for gasoline and regulations with reference thereto, 12 dealing with price fixing, 20 code modifications, 29 interpretations of the code and 99 of general administrative import.

The committee functioned through 11 subgroupings: the Statistical, Production, Refinery, Marketing, Accounting, Labor, Legal, Transportation, Finance, Natural Gasoline, and Foreign Relations Committees, and specialized groups such as the Program, Stabilization and Tank Car Committees. Reporting through the regular subgroupings were six regional agencies representing the North Atlantic states, South Atlantic states, Central states, Southwestern states, Rocky Mountain states and the Pacific states, which in turn were subdivided into production, refining, marketing, transportation, natural gasoline, and labor divisions. In correlating the crude supply and demand the P. & C. Committee took little formal part, in contrast to the stabilization of the industry in the refinery and marketing branches where it carried the laboring oar. The committee's assignment with regard to supply consisted of two items: its approval was required on withdrawals and additions to storage and excess working stock fluctuations; it was charged with endeavoring to promote to the fullest extent cooperation with state regulatory agencies. While this latter was an intangible assignment, the first was formally executed.

Notwithstanding President Roosevelt's reference to a self governing industry in his letter approving the oil code, control of production was retained solely in the hands of the federal and state authorities. Production control created certain problems in its refining and marketing phases which the industry attempted to solve with general PAB cooperation. In coordinating supply and demand, the Interior Department operated at four levels, deriving its powers from four features of the code: (1) production, Article III, Sections 3, 4, and 5; (2) imports, Article III, Section 1; (3) storage, Article III, Section 2; and (4) new pools, Article III, Section 7.

Although Section 4, Article III, authorized the president to fix state, field, and well quotas in default of their determination within a state, and made production in excess quantities a violation of the code, the section was not the basis for the production control mechanisms actually utilized. The right to control production directly through an allotment system was doubted by the Planning and Coordination Committee, and the first draft of the refinery amendment (Article IV) adopted April 24, 1934, proposed to amend Article III to substitute crude oil quotas in commerce in lieu of presidential allocations. The substitution was not made. Control actually exerted followed a pattern evolved by the Federal Oil Conservation Board, minus the interstate compact feature. Thus Section 3, Article III, directed the PAB to estimate current crude oil production needed to bring into balance supply and demand, taking into account withdrawals from storage and anticipated imports, and to allocate the requirements among the states. Section 4 called for a subdivision of the state allocations to fields and wells by local authority in being, reserving federal power to act where the state agencies were unable to do so. Section 5 designated a distribution agency for states not having commissions empowered to make allotments.

Estimates of national demand were prepared by the Petroleum

Economics Division of the Bureau of Mines based upon a calculation of (1) the gasoline production necessary to meet demand, taking into account additions to or withdrawals from storage, and (2) the quantity of crude oil necessary to manufacture that gasoline, together with that required for export, use in the unrefined state and other purposes. To aid in the preparation of the forecasts, the administrator under Section 6, Article VII, called for periodic reports from refineries, carriers, and other branches of the industry, modeled after those previously obtained voluntarily by the Bureau of Mines. The administrator certified allocations [50] to state regulatory bodies, particularly in Texas, Oklahoma, and Kansas, to the governors in other jurisdictions, and to the new agencies created under the code in California and Michigan. Where the state had a low capacity, quotas balanced capacity to produce, and where necessary informal arrangements among producers were depended upon to curtail production.

Article II, Section 1, limited imports by the administrator to "volumes bearing such ratio to the estimated volume of domestic production as will effectuate the purposes of this code and the N.I.R.A." By administrative order of September 2, 1933 Secretary Ickes directed that imports be limited until further notice, to an amount not exceeding the average daily imports of petroleum and products during the last six months of 1932, a time during which the Federal Oil Conservation Board had effected a restriction on imports by agreement with those importing. The limitation under the code was carried on through agreement with the major importers; no attempt was apparently made to restrict imports by casual importers. The order of September 2, 1933 was part of a general order fixing the first allocation of domestic production at 2,409,700 barrels daily, and prohibiting net withdrawals from storage without the approval of the Planning and Coordination Committee and the administrator. From the inception of the code to July 1934 daily average imports of petroleum and products were 94,396 barrels; the succeeding year the average was 143,435 barrels, of which only 94,734 barrels were for domestic consumption.

[50] The effect of these allocations on the price of crude oil is referred to by Secretary Ickes in *Hearings before a Subcommittee of the Senate Committee on Finance on S. 790*, 75th Cong., 1st Sess. 11 (1937).

The general objective of the administrator and the P. & C. Committee was to supply crude requirements from current production, limiting withdrawals from storage to seasonal demand on an orderly basis, and pulling them down to economic inventory. October 12, 1933 an administrative order provided that where the committee required refiners to curtail crude runs for the benefit of the general situation, oil run to storage as a consequence of that program would not constitute stored oil within the meaning of the code, and would not be impounded under Section 2, Article III. From time to time various other rulings were made (generally for the benefit of independent producers or refiners) permitting producers, not in a position to hold oil, to sell to buyers who could. This distress oil then was first released from storage upon withdrawal. In accord with this program 105 applications for removal from storage were cleared through the production subgroup of the committee. Crude stocks did not diminish drastically during the code's operation. As of August 31, 1933 they stood at about 360,000,000 barrels, reduced by June 30, 1934 to 357,239,000 barrels; in January 1, 1935 they were down to 337,254,000 barrels and as of May 31, 1935 had increased to 338,559,000 barrels.

Section 7, Article III, and promulgated regulations, provided that no petroleum from a newly discovered source of crude oil could be shipped in interstate commerce unless a developmental plan had been approved. General regulations were first promulgated on December 29, 1933, and were supplemented February 19, 1935 relating to California, where written approval of the oil umpire before drilling was required. The orders contemplated submission by producers in each pool of a plan to the production sub-committee, then to the full Committee, the PAB, the Geological Survey, and the administrator. In some cases formal hearings were held and in all 353 plans of development were approved, with 15 awaiting action at the close of the code. Those approved adhered to a pattern which required a well spacing wider than customary, a slow rate of drilling, and a restriction of production to a quantity producible without waste of oil or gas and which could be put to beneficial use.

The production quotas recommended by the federal agency were formally certified to the administrator monthly and telegraphed to the state enforcement agencies. Prior to the code, virtually all oil states had enacted conservation laws varying in effectiveness, which delegated enforcement to an administrative agency. However, the only legislation which fitted exactly into the pattern of code regulation of production was the market demand statute which defined waste to include production in excess of market demand and authorized restricted production and prorated that quantity among the properties in each field. Field-wide proration was generally based on capacity to produce, although other factors such as acreage per well were recognized. When the code took effect on September 2, 1933 demand statutes were administered by the Railroad Commission of Texas, the Oklahoma Corporation Commission, and the Kansas Public Service Commission. These were the old members of the informal production compact engineered by the Oil States Advisory Committee in 1931. The Louisiana Conservation Commissioner had a similar authority limited to single field applications, and the Arkansas Conservation Commission controlled gas only. The Michigan Public Utilities Commission had jurisdiction over common purchasers and enforced ratable taking, but its market demand statute was restricted to gas. California had no market demand or proration act. The lack of a state created regulatory agency restricting production to demand was serious only in California and Michigan. Article III, Section 5, permitted the administrator to designate a control body for any state with no such agency, but which did have a law obligating its industries to comply with the NRA. California had such a "little NRA" act and an existing organization of producers handling voluntary proration. The Central Committee of California Oil Producers, which allocated state production and the Pacific Coast Petroleum Agency, a buying pool, furnished a guaranteed outlet for independents. Each month the administrator, by order, appointed the Central Proration Committee (later to become the Central Committee of California Oil Producers) to compile production quotas for the state. Recommendations from the committee, under the supervision of a representative of the PAB, were submitted through the Board to the administrator. Among the few appeals taken was that from the Kettleman Hills North Dome Field, where hearings were held December 1934 and a lengthy decision approved in April 1935.

When the petroleum code was adopted, potential production in Michigan was twice its allowable and there was no regulatory body with power to prorate production. A supplemental code was signed and approved by the administrator under the authority of Section 5, Article III, which included producers representing more than 90 per cent of the state's output. Under the Michigan code a proration committee, consisting of producers representing various fields, was established and this body prepared allocations which went to the administrator through the PAB for his approval. In other states the lack of control was unimportant. New Mexico—the only other jurisdiction whose production was a national factor—was held within control by agreement of the producers. That state had a statute authorizing agreements among persons in the same pool.

In those states other than California and Michigan, and particularly in Oklahoma, Texas, and Kansas, the regulatory bodies (as they had before) determined the market demand for the 'state, allocated it among fields by standards, methods, and enforcement powers created in local laws and not derived from the code. The code added neither duty nor power to the regulatory system which operated to control production as before. Insofar as the power of the Federal Government exerted in the production phase, outside California and Michigan, it was exercised in the control of hot oil— that produced in violation of state law and regulation.

Over the entire code era, the daily rate of national production exceeded the allowables [51] by an average of 118,000 barrels or approximately 5 per cent, and there was an excess in each of the 17 code months, excepting November 1933 aggregating 75,000,000 barrels. The degree of conformity between estimate and performance under the code was somewhat less favorable than the average of the Federal Oil Conservation Board which preceded, and the Interstate Oil Compact Commission which followed the code. The estimates of the FOCB of domestic crude needs, made quarterly, had an error factor which ranged from .21 per cent to 2.61 per cent. Like figures by the Bureau of Mines during the Compact Commis-

[51] For Sept. 1933 the national allocation was 2,413,700 barrels daily and actual production was 2,611,000; for May, 1935, allocation was 2,561,000 barrels daily and actual production 2,659,800. A complete table of figures drawn from the Bureau of Mines' Yearbooks and from press releases of the PAB is reproduced in WATKINS, OIL: STABILIZATION OR CONSERVATION? 91 (1937).

sion period have been calculated monthly and the excess of production averages around 1.5 per cent.

Litigation under the production phases of the code from the standpoint of the Federal Government centered largely in the effort to prepare a case in which the Supreme Court would sustain the validity of the code provisions. Enforcement was plagued by numerous injunction suits filed by producers, with the famous *Panama Refining Company* case [52] the outstanding example.

On February 12, 1934, in an attempt to speed a test case to the Court, the Interior Department prepared and the Department of Justice secured an indictment in the case of the *United States v. Smith*, District Court for the Eastern District of Texas, for conspiracy to violate the production section of the code and the hot oil regulations. The case was to involve every conceivable item of controversy in the code, Section 9 c, and the regulations. The indictment was quashed February 26, 1934 on a demurrer, on the ground that the code and hot oil regulations were invalid and unconstitutional. The decision is unreported. The case was appealed directly to the Supreme Court [53] and set down for argument by it the week of April 25, 1934. However, before the argument, the Department of Justice at an interdepartmental conference insisted that the case be put over until autumn. On April 25, 1934 members of the PAB asked to be relieved of the administration of the petroleum code, feeling control was impossible until a favorable decision could be obtained. Their resignations were refused. The case was postponed from time to time, and never reached a hearing.

An attempt at direct enforcement of Section 4, Article III, was made by the Government in the Southern District of California in 1934, in *Wilshire Oil Company v. United States*.[54] The lower court sustained the code as a valid regulation of commerce and an injunction was issued against violation of the production quotas as certified by the administrator and adopted by the California allocation agency. The decree was appealed to the circuit court of appeals where questions were certified to the Supreme Court involving validity of the code. But the Court declined to answer these

[52] Panama Ref. Co. v. Ryan, 5 F. Supp. 639 (E.D. Tex. 1934), 71 F. 2d 1 (C.C.A. 5th 1934), 293 U.S. 388 (1935).
[53] Under Act of Mar. 2, 1907, 34 Stat. 1246.
[54] 9 F. Supp 396 (S.D. Cal. 1934), 77 F. 2d 1022 (C.C.A. 9th 1935).

queries, and in dismissing the certificate[55] held that the only question before the circuit court of appeals was whether the trial court had abused its discretion in granting an interlocutory injunction, and that the Court was not bound to decide the constitutionality of this section of the NIRA in advance of an appropriate determination by the district court of the facts. The cause was pending in the circuit court of appeals when the whole code system was invalidated by the *Schechter* decision.[56]

In *United States v. Eason Oil Company*[57] the oil administrator attempted to enforce conformity with a developmental plan for a new pool which he had approved limiting drilling to one well on a 40 acre tract. The court held that the authority asserted was not contemplated in the Act, nor included within the power delegated by the president. *Locke v. United States*[58] sustained the power of a district court to issue a preliminary injunction against production of petroleum in excess of the rate set by the Texas Railroad Commission under the code, irrespective of the ultimate constitutionality of the code. *A. L. A. Schechter Poultry Corporation v. United States*[59] held Title I of the Act, under which all codes were promulgated, an invalid delegation of the legislative authority to the president, and on May 27, 1935 the petroleum code terminated.

(d) Natural Gas Act

Prior to the passage of the Natural Gas Act of 1938[60] the Federal Government made no direct effort to enter the field of conservation of natural gas or to regulate such companies. Although the interstate transportation of natural gas by pipe line had been recognized as interstate commerce beyond the jurisdiction of the states,[61] no federal control was exercised. As a result individual states enforced their own conservation measures and established and regu-

---

The Natural Gas Act—The writer expresses his appreciation to Mr. Louis W. McKernan of the Federal Power Commission, who looked over this section and made unofficial comments on it prior to publication.

[55] Wilshire Oil Co. v. United States, 295 U.S. 100 (1935).

[56] A.L.A. Schechter Poultry Corp. v. United States, 295 U.S. 495 (1935).

[57] 8 F. Supp. 365 (W.D. Okla. 1934), *appeal dismissed* 79 F. 2d 1013 (C.C.A. 10th 1935).

[58] 75 F. 2d 157 (C.C.A. 5th 1935).

[59] See note 56 *supra*.

[60] 52 STAT. 821 (1938), 15 U.S.C.A. § 717 *et seq.* (1940).

[61] Mo. v. Kan. Gas Co., 265 U.S. 298 (1924), Penna. Gas Co. v. Pub. Ser. Comm., 252 U.S. 23 (1920), State Tax Comm. v. Inter. Nat. Gas Co., 284 U.S. 41 (1931).

lated retail consumer gas rates.[62] Two major areas of operation incapable of state control (despite efforts to subject them to state commission jurisdiction) [63] were the construction, extension or curtailment of interstate transportation facilities, and rates for interstate wholesale transactions. The Natural Gas Act was intended to occupy these unregulated areas. In this study of the statute, primarily from the conservation viewpoint, the question is not the permissible constitutional limits of federal jurisdiction over natural gas companies, but what in fact Congress did regulate. Congress deliberately did not take over the entire field; [64] the limiting phraseology of the Act employs the words *interstate commerce* and not the broader term *affecting commerce* found in other statutes of the same period, particularly in the labor field.

As originally enacted the Natural Gas Act provided for control by the Federal Power Commission of all rates and charges (except direct sales to industry) of any natural gas company engaged in the interstate transportation of natural gas for sale or resale, and for the issuance of certificates of public convenience and necessity where a company proposed to establish or acquire facilities in a market served by another. The Act empowered the Commission to establish uniform systems of accounting, require reports, make investigations, and otherwise administer and enforce the provisions of the statute. Under the Act the Commission's sphere of operations is divided into two principal parts: certification proceedings and rate regulation. Each has developed its problems of jurisdiction and policy. The major questions of conservation have arisen under certification, whereas the regulation of rates has produced the decisions on the basic questions of the Act's coverage.

CERTIFICATION PROCEEDINGS

As initially devised, the jurisdiction of the Commission to issue certificates of public convenience and necessity was limited to cases

[62] See Henderson Co. v. Thompson, 300 U.S. 258 (1937), P.U.C. v. Landon, 249 U.S. 236 (1919), and annotation in 83 ALR 431.

[63] Penna. v. West Va., 262 U.S. 553 (1923) as to transportation; Mo. v. Kan. Gas Co., 265 U.S. 298 (1924) as to rates.

[64] See H. R. REP. No. 800, 80th Cong., 1st Sess. 3 (1947), Newcomb, *Effects of Federal Regulation Under the Natural Gas Act Upon the Production and Conservation of Natural Gas*, 14 GEO. WASH. L. REV. 217, 220 (1945). See FPC Staff Report, Docket G-580, *Section 1 (b) of the Natural Gas Act with Reference to Production and Gathering* 12 (1947).

where a company proposed to enter an already occupied market.[65] Two results stemmed from this limiting factor: (1) the number of applications for certificates was small, and the number the Commission granted was even smaller;[66] (2) the Commission was for the most part committed to a policy that denied competing industries the right to participate in certificate hearings on the ground that the agency was without authority to "weigh the broad social and economic effects of the use of various fuels,"[67] in effect a denial by the agency that it had power or control over the economic waste aspects of conservation.

On February 7, 1942 the Act was amended[68] to remove the jurisdictional bar in certification proceedings and as altered required every natural gas company to be certificated in all cases of construction or acquisition of facilities for the transportation or sale of natural gas in interstate commerce. "Grandfather" rights were provided for those already in operation. In the language of the house committee approving the amendment: "by this legislation, the present jurisdictional disputes are eliminated, and the door is opened to the consideration by the Commission of the effect of construction and extensions upon the interests of producers of competing fuels and competitive transportation interests."[69] During the period from February 7, 1942 through December 31, 1947, 307 certificates were granted authorizing construction or extension of natural gas lines totalling 17,173 miles. In many of the "non-

---

[65] 52 STAT. 824, § 7 c (1938), 15 U.S.C.A. § 717 f (1940) as originally enacted read in part as follows: "No natural-gas company shall undertake the construction or extension of any facilities for the transportation of natural gas to a market in which natural gas is already being served by another natural-gas company, or acquire or operate any such facilities or extensions thereof, or engage in transportation by means of any new or additional facilities, or sell natural gas in any such market, unless and until there shall first have been obtained from the Commission a certificate that the present or future public convenience and necessity require or will require such new construction or operation of any such facilities or extensions thereof; Provided, however, That a natural-gas company already serving a market may enlarge or extend its facilities for the purpose of supplying increased market demands in the territory in which it operates. . . ."

[66] 16 filed, 4 granted, 8 dismissed for lack of jurisdiction, 2 withdrawn and 2 not prosecuted.

[67] Kan. Pipe Line and Gas Co., 2 F.P.C. 29, 57 (1939). FPC, Staff Report, *Administration of the Certificate Provisions of Section 7 of the Natural Gas Act*, Docket G-580 (1947).

[68] 56 STAT. 83 (1942) 15 U.S.C.A. § 717 f (Cum. Supp. 1946).

[69] H. R. REP. No. 1290 on H.R. 5249. 77th Cong., 1st Sess. (1941).

grandfather" cases competing fuel interests appeared and strongly urged the Commission to deny or restrict the certificates to control the end uses of the fuel. The Commission, although asserting the desirability of conservation, has taken the position that, since the Act does not authorize it to regulate rates for direct sale to industry nor to suspend rates for indirect sales for industrial purposes, nor are comprehensive conservation powers expressly granted to the Commission, it has no authority to control end uses of gas and will not do so unless and until Congress amends the Act to give such power.[70] Thus even after the amendment of Section 7, the Commission has adhered to its refusal to interpret the Act so as to permit the exercise of direct control over the conservation of natural gas by regulating end use. It has never been suggested that the Act gives the FPC jurisdiction over those aspects of conservation dealing with the physical control of producing properties.[71] In consequence the Natural Gas Act as a conservation measure has no direct effect [72] as presently administered by the FPC upon the two principal factors in conservation—physical and economic waste. Such controls as it exercises affect these factors only by indirection through regulation of rates, charges, and service facilities of interstate pipe line transportation and sales. That to some this is an unsatisfactory situation is apparent from the views expressed by witnesses representing competing industries and others before the House Committee on Interstate and Foreign Commerce in the hearings on the amendments to the Act proposed by the 80th Congress in its first session.[73]

[70] FPC Rep., *The First Five Years Under the Natural Gas Act* 14–15 (1944).

[71] Champlin Ref. Co., v. Corp. Comm. of Okla., 286 U.S. 210 (1932), Railroad Comm. of Tex. v. Rowan and Nichols Oil Co., 310 U.S. 573 (1940), Santa Cruz Fruit Packing Co. v. NLRB, 303 U.S. 453 (1938).

[72] But cf. § 5 a, 7, 11 and 14 (b) of the Act, 15 U.S.C.A. § 717 d, f, j, and m (Cum. Supp. 1946).

[73] Testimony, Tom J. McGrath, representing coal and railroad interests in *Hearings before the Committee on Interstate and Foreign Commerce on H.R. 2185*, 80th Cong., 1st Sess. 382, 388, 390 (1947).

CHAPTER 42

The Government in the Exercise of the Power over Foreign Commerce

❧

INTERNATIONAL ACTIVITIES

The oil and gas activities of the Federal Government in the international field were limited, until World War II, to affording to the domestic industry the same protection against low cost foreign products as are afforded by the tariff laws, with the exception of voluntary informal agreements with importers whereby the Federal Conservation Board achieved a 25 per cent reduction of imports during the last half of 1932. The equalizing process for petroleum and products is achieved through an excise tax levied under the Revenue Act of 1932 as currently amended and extended.[1]

Section 601 c 4 of the Internal Revenue Act of 1932 levies an excise tax[2] of ½ cent a gallon (21 cents a barrel) on imported petroleum and all liquid derivatives, with the exception of gasoline or motor fuels which are taxed at 2½ cents per gallon ($1.05 per barrel), and lubricating oil which is taxed at 4 cents a gallon ($1.68 per barrel). It is suggested that this tax resulted because of the excess crude in the United States at the time, coupled with a heavy volume of imports, and it appears to have been a compromise between those who desired legislation[3] designed to impose a quota

NORTHCUTT ELY, WRITER. (See app. B.)

International Activities—The writer expresses his appreciation to Mr. Robert H. S. Eakens, Chief of the Petroleum Division, Department of State, who looked over this section and made unofficial comments on it prior to publication.

[1] 47 STAT. 169 (1932), 53 STAT. 414 (1939), 26 U.S.C.A. § 3422 (1940). See McGoldrick v. Gulf Oil Corporation, 309 U.S. 414 (1940).

[2] Import excise taxes under the several revenue acts have by statute the same legal status as duties and have the same economic effects.

[3] H.R. 16585 (1931), a measure which would have limited imports of crude oil to 16 million bbls. per year for the years 1931, 1932 and 1933. By way of comparison, imports of crude in 1929 had totaled about 79 million bbls. and in 1930 about 62 million.

on crude imports in lieu of a tariff, and those who contended that a tariff of at least $1 a barrel on crude was necessary.

Under Article III, Section 1, of the Petroleum Code, the president was given authority: ". . . to limit imports of crude petroleum and petroleum products for domestic consumption to volumes bearing such ratio to the estimated volume of domestic production as will effectuate the purposes of this Code and the National Industrial Recovery Act." This responsibility was delegated to the Secretary of the Interior, as administrator of the code, and on September 2, 1933 he announced that imports of crude petroleum and petroleum products were to be limited to an amount not exceeding the average daily imports during the last six months of 1932. The Petroleum Administrative Board fixed this quota at an average of 98,000 barrels daily. It is reported [4] that "this quota was observed throughout the period of code enforcement and relations of importing, refining and marketing companies with the PAB were such that the problem of keeping within quota limits did not necessitate specific allocations to individual members of the industry. The ratio of this import quota to total domestic requirements, as determined at successive intervals by the Administrator, was approximately 4.5 per cent." Although this import quota terminated with the NIRA, the import trade in crude remained at about the percentages permitted under the code; this is accredited to voluntary action on the part of a few major oil companies in this country who controlled the production of crude in Venezuela and other Latin American countries. These same producers reduced imports voluntarily when the impetus which resulted in the import excise taxes of 1932 was gathering; their offers to make these reductions firm had not been acted upon at that time.[5]

In 1939 in a trade agreement [6] with Venezuela, the excise tax on imports of crude petroleum, topped crude, fuel oil, and gas oil was reduced from 21 to 10½ cents a barrel, continuing the tax free entry of products for supplies of vessels.[7] In addition, the quota

[4] U.S. National Recovery Administration, Division of Review, No. 37, Vol. 1, Foreign Trade Studies Section 255 (1936).

[5] U.S. Tariff Commission, *Report to the Congress on the Cost of Crude Petroleum*, Rep. No. 4, Second Series 20–21 (1931).

[6] Reciprocal Trade Agreement between the United States of America and Venezuela, Exec. Agreement Series 311, effective December 16, 1939.

[7] Under the Act of 1932, the Treasury decided that crude oil in bond (to be used in making refined products for export) and fuel oil to be used as supplies for ships

principle of NIRA was engrafted in part, the reduction in taxes being made subject to a tariff quota for the four products named above, equal each year to five per cent of the quantity of crude processed in domestic refineries during the preceding calendar year.[8] An importer could bring in more than the allowable quota, if he liked, upon paying the statutory rate of tax set up in the Act of 1932. The president allocated the quantity of imports on the four products mentioned among the exporting countries.[9]

In 1943 by trade agreement with Mexico,[10] the tax reduction was extended to include kerosene and liquid asphalt; the most important feature was that the quota arrangement set up in the Venezuelan covenant was suspended. The General Agreement on Tariffs and Trade which the United States and 22 other nations signed at Geneva, Switzerland, on October 30, 1947 and which became provisionally effective January 1, 1948 continues these rates and the quota free status. In addition this agreement, although it did not affect crude, became the first document to affect the rates set forth in the Revenue Act of 1932 [11] as to gasoline and lubricating oils. As to these commodities, the agreement cut the existing rates in half, making the present duty on gasoline 1¼ cents a gallon (52½ cents per barrel) and on lubricating oils 2 cents a gallon (84 cents a barrel). There is, however, a proviso [12] as follows: "Provided, that in no event shall the rate of import tax applicable under Section 3422, Internal Revenue Code, or any modification thereof, to topped crude petroleum, or fuel oil derived from petro-

---

engaged in foreign trade could be imported tax free. The latter decision was bound by the trade agreement with Venezuela. Imports under these two provisions constituted roughly half of the total prewar imports. See, in general, U.S. Tariff Commission, *Petroleum, War Changes in Industry Series*, Report No. 17, U.S. Government Printing Office (1946).

[8] Note that the quota basis under the Venezuelan agreement differed from that used under NIRA.

[9] Exporting Country	Percentages	
	1934–40	1941–42
Venezuela	71.9	70.4
Netherlands & territories		
(N. W. I.)	20.3	21.3
Colombia	4.0	3.2
Others	3.8	5.1

[10] Reciprocal Trade Agreement between the United States of America and Mexico, Executive Agreement Series 311, signed Dec. 23, 1942, effective Jan. 30, 1943.
[11] § 3422, Int. Rev. Code (1940).
[12] Schedule XX, Geneva Agreement.

leum be less than the rate of such tax applicable to crude petroleum." Up until 1947 the United States maintained an export balance of petroleum and its products. For example, in 1938 according to Bureau of Mines figures, we exported 531,000 barrels daily and imported 149,000. By 1946 we were exporting 414,000 barrels daily and were importing 370,000. In 1947 the balance swung in the other direction, with exports at the rate of 436,000 barrels daily and imports attaining an estimated average daily rate 453,000 barrels. By far the bulk of our imports consists of crude oil and residual fuel oil from the Caribbean area, particularly from Venezuela. Refined products comprise the bulk of our exports.

The enormous drain on the nation's oil reserves occasioned by the war forced the attention of the Federal Government to the problem of securing adequate reserves abroad. Because of the vast reserves in the Arab lands of the Middle East and because of local concessions held by American interests,[13] attention was concentrated there. Efforts first were made to secure American rights in the Middle East through unilateral action by attempting to purchase the stock of the American companies holding concessions there. The companies refused to sell. An endeavor was then made to hasten development through the construction of a pipe line from the Persian Gulf to the Mediterranean, to be built by the Petroleum Reserves Corporation, a subsidiary of the Reconstruction Finance Corporation. When news of the proposal reached the domestic oil industry, their opposition to it (as an attempt to put the Government into the oil business) was sufficient to put the proposal to rest.

Efforts turned to the possibility of an international agreement which would protect American interests, lessen rivalries, and provide for an orderly development of the available resources. Although the British had indicated an interest in entering into an agreement early in the war, it does not appear that any formal negotiations took place before 1944. Early in April 1944 a technical delegation arrived from England and discussion got under way with an American technical group on April 14th.

[13] *Hearings before Special Committee Investigating Petroleum Resources pursuant to S. Res. 36, 79th Cong., 1st Sess. American Petroleum Interests in Foreign Countries* (1945); *id., The Independent Petroleum Company* (1946), 377–443; Feis, *Order in Oil*, 22 FOREIGN AFFAIRS 616 (1944).

As a result of negotiations between the technical delegations, a memorandum of understanding was prepared, and on July 25, 1944 committees of cabinet level officials met to work out a final agreement. The British proposed that a right be recognized in each party to ".draw its consumption requirements, to the extent that may be considered necessary, from production in its territories or in which rights are held by its nationals." The British proposal was not included in the final agreement signed August 8, 1944 and sent to the Senate August 24, 1944 for ratification.[14] American interests launched an immediate attack on the proposed treaty, concentrating in the main on three points: first, the provision in the introductory article which provided that the availability of supplies be related to demand, with consideration given to reserves, sound engineering practices, relevant economic factors, and the interests of producing and consuming countries; and, second, the provision in Article II creating an International Petroleum Commission with authority to prepare estimates of demand, recommend policies, and make analyses and reports; and third, the statement in Article IV that each country would make efforts, within its respective constitutional procedures, to give effect to approved recommendations of the Commission.[15] To certain segments of the domestic oil industry these three points were sufficient to place control of domestic oil operations in the hands of the Commission, and through the treaty power, in the hands of the Federal Government with respect to allocations of production and price fixing.[16]

After a long series of discussions with interested Government agencies, the original proposal was withdrawn from the Senate at the request of the president. In February 1945 Secretary Ickes informally presented to the members of the Foreign Relations Committee a tentative agreement having the endorsement of the industry. One objection to the proposal was made by the Department of Justice, in that concerted industry action taken at the request of governmental authorities was to be protected from anti-trust

[14] The text of the first agreement may be found in 11 DEP'T. OF STATE BULL. 154 (1944).

[15] See Report of the Committee on Oil, PROC. SEC. MINERAL L., ABA (1945) and further comment in that Committee's report Oct. 29, 1946.

[16] An analysis based on this premise was prepared by Arthur A. Ballantine, Esq. See *Hearings, supra* note 14 at 337, *et seq.*

prosecutions. The provision was deleted. Because of the changes embodied in the new pact, it was necessary to renegotiate the treaty with the British. On September 18, 1945 delegations from the British Government and the United States met in London for that purpose. The new agreement was signed September 24, 1945 and was presented to the Senate for ratification November 1, 1945. Since that time it has languished, although it was favorably reported by the Senate Committee on Foreign Relations on July 7, 1947.[17]

The principal changes involved in the second agreement pertained to the duties and responsibilities of the International Petroleum Commission which had been considered objectionable by the American oil industry. A former part under which the two countries agreed to effectuate approved recommendations of the Commission was deleted, and a positive assertion that neither Government was required to act on any report or proposal of the Commission was added. Safeguards were inserted providing that the agreement should not apply to the operation of the domestic petroleum industry of either country, except as to Article II. The agreement consists of a preamble and eight numbered articles. The preamble recognizes these principles: (1) that ample supplies of petroleum, available in international trade, are necessary for the security and welfare of nations; (2) that sufficient petroleum supplies are available; (3) that the international petroleum trade should be developed in an orderly and efficient manner; and (4) that this development can best be brought about through an international petroleum agreement between all producing and consuming countries. By Article II, the parties agree to so direct their efforts as to (1) respect all valid concessions and lawfully acquired rights, (2) apply the principle of equal opportunity as to the acquisition of rights, and (3) discourage and prevent restrictions inconsistent with this agreement. Article IV establishes an International Petroleum Commission of six members, three to be appointed by each party. The Commission is vested with authority to consider problems of mutual interest, and is given the following specific duties: (1) to study international petroleum trade problems caused by dislocation resulting from the war, (2) to study trends in international petro-

---

[17] SEN. EXEC. REP. No. 8, 80th Cong., 1st Sess. (1947).

leum trade, (3) to study the effects of changing technology on such trade, (4) to prepare estimates of world demands and supplies, and report on ways and means to correlate demands and supplies, and (5) to make such additional reports as are appropriate to further the purposes of this agreement. But Article VI specifically provides that no provision in the agreement requires either party or its nationals to act on any report or proposal of the Commission, whether or not the report is approved by that party. Article VII sets out the intention of the parties that nothing in the agreement (with the exception of the provisions of Article II) shall impair or modify any law or regulation, or the right to enact any law or regulation regarding importation of petroleum into either country, and that nothing in the agreement (with the exception of Article II) shall apply to the operations of the domestic oil industry in either country.

The initial reaction of the American oil industry to this second agreement was favorable. But with the passage of time, this united front was breached, principally because of an official broadcast [18] which indicated to the oil industry that a greater degree of control over domestic operations and more far reaching authority for the International Petroleum Commission were contemplated under the official interpretation. In October 1946 the Independent Petroleum Association recorded its opposition to ratification of the treaty. On November 13, 1946 the American Petroleum Institute adopted a resolution urging reservations to make it clear that the treaty would not confer any power on the International Commission to control or regulate the foreign operations of United States nationals, or the domestic oil industry; nor would the treaty confer any additional power upon the United States to intervene in the affairs of the domestic industry; nor would the Commission, either alone or in conjunction with the United Nations organization, have the power to review or revise foreign or domestic contracts or concessions of American nationals; nor would it be empowered to act as a board of appeals or an arbitration authority. A final reservation sought to make it clear that the treaty was not to be considered a first step in any plan leading to other treaties having the effect of

[18] *Hearings, supra* note 13 at 117, *et seq.*

vesting control over operations of American nationals in the foreign or domestic oil business.

These reservations were submitted the State Department, and on January 20, 1947 Undersecretary W. L. Clayton replied that the understandings contained in the API reservations were in complete accord with the Department's interpretation of the treaty.

Hearings on the treaty were held before the Foreign Relations Committee during the summer of 1947. Proponents of the treaty consisted of representatives of the State Department, Interior Department, the military, and the major petroleum companies. The opponents were independent oil operators and state officials of Texas. The basic argument centered around the question of whether the treaty could be used to develop and expand governmental regulation of domestic industry. On July 7, 1947 the committee reported on the agreement, recommending ratification with the three API reservations outlined above, and two committee amendments, one of which revised Article II to clarify the duties of the United States with respect to the prevention of restrictions inconsistent with the agreement. The other committee amendment dealt with the reservation in Article VII of the right of each government to regulate imports, and language was suggested which would make it clear that nothing in Article VII should be construed as implying any commitment on the part of either signatory government to relinquish its right to control imports for the purpose of giving adequate protection to its domestic industry. With these amendments and reservations, the proposed treaty was, at the adjournment of the 80th Congress, still awaiting action by the Senate.

CHAPTER 43

The Government in the Exercise of the War Power

~∿~

(a) World War I

The problem of conservation was of secondary importance in World War I. Demands of the armed forces and of domestic consumers connected with the war effort were motivating factors in the establishment of the United States Fuel Administration under the Lever Act. The Act authorized price fixing for coal and coke and the regulation of profits on all fuels. Although the regulatory framework for the oil industry was set up, actual operations were based on a system of voluntary control within the industry.

Dr. H. A. Garfield was appointed Fuel Administrator on August 23, 1917. He had a staff composed of three divisions: (1) administrative, (2) distribution, and (3) oil, each of which was under the supervision of a general director. The oil division began to function January 10, 1918 under the direction of Mark L. Requa, having in all fourteen subdivisions: production, engineering, statistics, technology, lubricants, foreign requirements, traffic, marine transportation, domestic consumption, oil well supplies, pipe lines, conservation, special assignments, and Pacific Coast. All were located in Washington except those dealing with production, pipe lines, oil well supplies, and Pacific Coast, which were in New York City.

The principal problems faced by the Division were the stimulation of crude supply, the distribution of petroleum products to meet the requirements of the armed forces, necessary civilian demands, and the maintenance of adequate transportation facilities. In the phrase of Lord Curzon, speaking on November 21, 1918, "The Allies floated to victory on a sea of oil."

NORTHCUTT ELY, WRITER. (See App. B.) World War II—The writer expresses his appreciation to Dr. John W. Frey for his helpful comments made after reviewing this section.

The broad powers which the agency might have exercised to accomplish these objectives were largely unused, as the administration was content to rely upon the industry itself for the successful operation of the wartime oil program. To this end, a National Petroleum War Service Committee was created as a governing body to represent the industry, and to maintain close liaison with the Oil Division. Administrative policy with regard to stimulating production of petroleum was founded on past effective practices. Early in 1918 crude oil prices rose sharply. The War Service Committee evolved a system of price stabilization which was put into effect on August 8, 1918. The plan required that crude oil be restricted to the channels through which it was delivered May 17, 1918, and not diverted therefrom without the approval of a local committee set up under the auspices of the War Service Committee. A system of review by both the War Service Committee and the Fuel Administration was provided. The plan remained in effect until December 16, 1918 and was successful in stabilizing prices. The system of operation of the War Service Committee was to pool and distribute oil regardless of ownership. Thus, for practical purposes, all oil produced became subject to the control of the Government, as it was obtainable only under a system of licenses, according to priorities established by the Oil Administrator. Although the first presidential proclamation of January 31, 1918 required only those companies with gross sales in excess of 100,000 barrels per year to obtain licenses, the requirement was soon extended to cover all distributors. The license and priority system were revoked December 7, 1918.

After the Armistice November 11, 1918 the industry returned to private direction and emerged from wartime control little affected. The Fuel Administration and the Oil Division ceased operations June 30, 1919. The importance of oil and products in the prosecution of war and the necessity of maintaining production in nearly every type of industry brought to the forefront the problem of developing and conserving the petroleum resources of the nation. Direct outcomes were the comprehensive change in the administration of the public domain through the enactment of the Mineral Leasing Act of 1920, and the establishment of the Federal Oil Conservation Board in 1924.

(b) World War II

During World War II the activities of the Federal Government with regard to conservation of oil and gas were subordinated to the primary task of increasing production and allocating available supplies so that vital military and civilian demands could be met. The history of this period is the story of the Petroleum Administration for War,[1] and its predecessors, the Office of Petroleum Coordinator for National Defense, and the Office of Petroleum Coordinator for War.

Although the two world wars differed tremendously in size and scope of operations, the approach adopted by the Federal Government and the petroleum industry in both experiences was for full voluntary industry cooperation with emphasis upon minimum application of wartime sanctions. Mechanized military operations in World War II could not have been undertaken without a continuous and dependable supply of petroleum and products. Military engagements were conducted thousands of miles from the source of supply. The nature of petroleum precludes the accumulation of more than a few weeks reserve supply above ground, resulting in a need for an uninterrupted flow from well head to the point of use. A single 1000 plane raid over Europe in 1944–45 used more than 12 times the daily requirements of aviation gasoline for all the allied air forces in 1918. At the end of the war the Joint Chiefs of Staff, Army-Navy Petroleum Board could say ". . . at no time did the services lack for oil in the proper quantities, in the proper kinds, and at the proper places. Because of the resourcefulness, untiring and unceasing effort, and outstanding accomplishments of the Petroleum Administration for War and the petroleum industry, not a single operation was delayed or impeded because of the lack of petroleum products. No Government agency and no branch of American industry achieved a prouder

[1] An authoritative, fully documented, and thoroughly absorbing account of the period is available in the official history of the P.A.W., prepared by Dr. John W. Frey and Mr. Chandler Ide, and published by the United States Government Printing Office under the title "THE HISTORY OF THE PETROLEUM ADMINISTRATION FOR WAR, 1941–1945." This summary of the period is based on the source materials and text of this book, with appreciation and thanks to the authors for making the material available to the present writer in advance of publication.

record." In addition to meeting military requirements successfully, essential civilian demands were satisfied and the' economy of the nation functioned without a serious breakdown in production, transportation, or distribution chargeable to a lack of necessary supplies of petroleum and products. The job was done with a maximum of 35 official orders and 16 supplements, never all in force at one time, and less than 100 directives or recommendations. No compliance division was ever needed by PAW and only a handful of compliance proceedings were instituted.

CREATION OF OPC

The history of oil in World War II commenced May 28, 1941 with a letter from President F. D. Roosevelt to Secretary of the Interior Harold L. Ickes creating the Office of Petroleum Coordinator for National Defense.[2] The new agency was given the responsibility, as a representative of the president, of obtaining information from federal, state, and industry sources, and making specific recommendations to appropriate Government agencies and the industry. At the time, there were some 30 agencies concerned with oil problems. Since OPC was not created by executive order nor rooted in statutory authority, it consequently had no power to enforce its recommendations.[3] According to Frey and Ide this nebulous status was traceable to the feeling, then prevalent, that the oil industry could easily meet any calls upon it, and hence it was unnecessary to impose the rigid controls required in other industries; a coordinating and information agency was thought sufficient. In the 18 months between the creation of the OPC and the establishment of PAW much transpired. The United States entered the war, the East Coast oil shortage became acute,

---

[2] 6 FED. REG. 2760 (1941). At first, officials of the Federal Register were inclined to the view that the letter was not properly includible in the publication. The importance of the document was urged and after a conference with those officials, it was included on June 7, 1941. By a letter from the president dated April 20, 1942, the name of the agency was changed to the Office of Petroleum Coordinator for War.

[3] For examples of the recommendations made during this phase of development of the wartime control system see, Recommendation No. 7, 6 FED. REG. 5622 (1941); Recommendation No. 13, 6 FED. REG. 5536 (1941); Recommendation No. 19, 6 FED. REG. 6617 (1941).

normal transportation methods were disrupted by diversion and loss of tankers, and military requirements skyrocketed. During these times inter-agency relationships were established or clarified, and the first steps were taken to meet the never ending series of emergencies which confronted the Government and the oil industry throughout the war.

GENERAL PLAN

Immediately after its creation OPC took three major steps: it formulated a general plan of organization and policy, it initiated discussions with other agencies to establish or clarify relationships, and it met with the industry to outline a plan of operation. Four general agency policies which it followed throughout the war were (1) to centralize activities and responsibilities in one agency where possible, (2) to organize the agency paralleling industry functions, and staff it with experienced oil men, (3) to sponsor an industry committee system to advise and assist the national organization, and (4) to keep orders and regulations at a minimum.

RELATIONSHIPS WITH OTHER AGENCIES

Space limitations preclude a detailed survey of the complicated relationships among the various Governmental agencies whose activities impinged upon or were affected by the OPC-PAW. From the legal standpoint one relationship deserves mention—that with the Anti-trust Division of the Department of Justice. Since industry-wide cooperation and joint action were prime requisites of the program, it was imperative to give assurance to the industry of freedom from attack under the anti-trust laws. On June 18, 1941 the Attorney General wrote OPC that concerted industry action proposed for the oil industry might be taken only after approval by the Department of Justice as to the character of the action taken, in the light of his letter of April 29, 1941 to the Office of Production Management. As a result, OPC recommendations and proposals were cleared in advance with the Department of Justice, and after the passage of the Act of June 11, 1942 [4] many were

[4] *Small Business Mobilization Act,* 56 STAT. 351, 50 U.S.C.A. app. 1101 (Supp. 1947).

certified by the War Production Board as requisite to the prosecution of the war, which under Section 12 of the Act gave immunity from the anti-trust laws.[5] The Act was repealed July 25, 1947.[6]

MEETING WITH INDUSTRY

On June 19, 1941, roughly three weeks after the creation of OPC, the new agency met the industry; it was a vital meeting, for a plan of voluntary cooperation was to be proposed by a Government agency to an industry largely distrustful of such proposals. Mr. William R. Boyd, Jr., later chairman of the PIWC, described the attitude of the industry when he appeared before the House Committee on Interstate and Foreign Commerce;[7] and Mr. Ickes has referred to the occasion.[8] From this inauspicious start developed the partnership plan under which wartime oil operations were successfully conducted. The return of the industry to private control in a healthy economic condition within a few months of the termination of hostilities bears witness to the good faith on the part of the Government which was essential to the successful operation of the wartime partnership.

CREATION OF THE PAW

As has been noted, OPC had no power to enforce its directives for 18 months. While industry cooperation reduced the importance of legal authority, other factors involving questions of responsibility and authority within the sphere of inter-agency operations made it imperative that the status of the agency be clarified and strengthened. From July to December 1942 negotiations and discussions were carried on to produce an executive order accomplishing the desired result, and on December 2, 1942 PAW was created.[9] PAW became the central oil agency with power to en-

[5] 56 Stat. 357, 50 U.S.C.A. app. 1112 (Supp. 1947).
[6] 61 Stat. 449, 50 U.S.C.A. app. 1112 (Supp. 1947).
[7] *Hearings Before Subcommittee of Committee on Interstate and Foreign Commerce on H. Res. 290, H. Res. 15, H. Res. 118, H. Res. 383*, 77th Cong., 2d Sess. 75–76 (1942).
[8] Ickes, Fightin' Oil, 71 (1943).
[9] Exec. Order No. 9276, 7 Fed. Reg. 10091 (1942). A complete list of the personnel of the PAW may be found in Frey & Ide, A History of the Petroleum

force its orders and directives. Its responsibilities were to provide adequate supplies of petroleum for military or essential uses, to distribute the materials allocated to the petroleum industry by the WPB, to consult with the OPA on prices, to consult with that agency on rationing (and in certain cases to determine the areas and amounts available for rationing), to consult with the War Shipping Administration on tanker problems, to control and direct shipments of petroleum by the industry, to compile data, and to consult with all interested agencies. No control over prices, or over the movement or assignment of tankers, and no limitation on the authority of the Army or Navy to act independently was conferred by the order.

From December 1941 to the end of the war there were four major parts to the Government-industry oil partnership: (1) the Government agency OPC—PAW, (2) the District Industry Committees, (3) the Petroleum Industry War Council, and (4) the Foreign Operations Committee. All, except for FOC, were organized functionally and on nearly identical lines.

GOVERNMENTAL ORGANIZATION

The Government agency consisted of a national organization and five decentralized district organizations covering the East Coast, Middle West, Southwest-Gulf Coast, Rocky Mountain, and Pacific Coast areas. The national organization was headed by an administrator and a deputy administrator and had from 10 to 16 major divisions; the district organizations were administered by a director and had 11 corresponding divisions. The district director was responsible to the administrator, and the heads of the district divisions were responsible to the heads of their corresponding national group. At the end of the war the national bodies were: production, natural gas, refining, supply and transportation, distribution and marketing, foreign production, foreign refining, foreign supply and distribution, research, materials, facility security, pro-

ADMINISTRATION FOR WAR 301 *et seq.* (1946). Assisting Administrator Ickes were Deputy Administrator Ralph K. Davies and Assistant Deputy Administrators R. E. Allen, E. L. De Golyer, B. K. Brown, and J. H. Marshall. The Chief Counsel of the Legal Division were R. E. Hardwicke and J. H. Marshall. The Director of the Natural Gas Division was E. Holley Poe.

gram, executive officer, legal, public relations, and manpower. The district divisions were the same but omitted research, program, public relations, and the three foreign divisions, and added a construction division. The function of the Government was to establish polices, issue orders, and collaborate with the district industry committees in their execution.

THE DISTRICT INDUSTRY COMMITTEES

In July 1941 the first district committees were established to represent the industry in each of the five PAW districts, and they continued throughout the war as a vital part of the Government-industry team. Each district had a general and at least ten industry committees organized parallel to the district divisions of the Government organizations. In general these dealt with material, construction, production, natural gas, refining, supply and transportation, distribution and marketing manpower, protection of petroleum facilities, and statistics. Sub-committees were created where such action seemed appropriate. Members of the standing district committees were appointed by PAW, although they were not its employees, and sub-committee members were chosen without Government approval. District personnel served without pay, although some committees established permanent paid staffs at the expense of the industry. The groups collected data upon which supply and demand estimates were based, attended to the physical execution of the policies established by PAW, and generally acted as a liaison between industry and agency at a regional and local level. No action could be taken by the committees without Government approval.

PETROLEUM INDUSTRY WAR COUNCIL

For a few months at the inception of OPC operations the district general and industry committees were the only industry organizations assisting the agency. It quickly became apparent that a national industry organization was needed to provide intercommunication between the OPC and the heads of the oil industry.

Consequently, on November 28, 1941[10] the Petroleum Industry Council for National Defense (later the Petroleum Industry War Council) was created as the third member of the Government-industry partnership.

The council immediately organized national industry committees, parallel to the district industry groups, made up of the chairmen of the corresponding district committees and at least four other members. In addition, other committees were created by the council, such as the Products Conservation Committee. This committee on its initiative, and without cost to the Government, conducted public saving campaigns, such as the scrap rubber drive, which at a cost estimated at $3,000,000 produced 454,000 tons of scrap rubber—enough to keep reclaiming plants operating at capacity for more than a year. Altogether ten campaigns were managed by the committee and its predecessors. The PIWC operated throughout the war and performed many useful and vital functions as advisor to PAW and as a coordinating agency for the district committees. At operational peak it had over 3000 members nearly all of whom served without pay.

In December 1941 in response to the need for industry representation abroad, the Foreign Operations Committee was formed[11] as the fourth and last unit of the Government-industry organization. This committee was assigned to work with foreign divisions of PAW, acting as the overseas counterpart of the PIWC at home. Its principal grant of authority was Directive 70 issued September 24, 1943.

OPERATIONS UNDER PAW

Production of sufficient oil to meet wartime demand was the number one problem of PAW and the industry. Two factors were involved: to increase and maintain production from existing reserves, and to discover and develop new areas.[12] Many factors,

[10] 7 FED. REG. 1068. A complete list of the members of the PIWC and of the various sub-committees may be found in FREY & IDE, supra note 8 at 327 et seq. PIWC Chairman William R. Boyd's administrative staff was composed of Allan H. Hand, Joseph L. Dwyer, Edwin W. Esmay, Francis J. Connor, Robert E. Allen, Russell B. Brown, Fayette B. Dow, and Joseph E. Pogue.

[11] 7 FED. REG. 2950, 8713.

[12] How well the task was performed is shown by the fact that production was increased from 3,840,000 barrels daily in 1941 to a peak war production of 4,890,000

which combined to bring about the needed results, were the encouragement of wildcat drilling, better development of existing fields, and more efficient operation of producing wells. Principles and practices long sought by advocates of conservation were put into widespread use and received thorough testing under the exigencies of war, with gratifying results, and the cause of conservation received a tremendous boost from the enforced wartime experiences. The broad PAW policy toward conservation was based on encouraging existing state agencies to improve existing laws, and to induce states without conservation laws to adopt them. Among the practices put into general use were wider well spacing, pressure maintenance, production at maximum efficient rates, and secondary recovery.

MAXIMUM EFFICIENT RATES

Fixing of maximum efficient rates of state production by OPC-PAW began in January 1942 based on information and data furnished by the industry and the Bureau of Mines; through June 1942 these were issued as recommendations, and thereafter until the end of the war, as certifications. Each state was expected to carry out the recommendation or certification through its existing regulatory bodies.[13] To insure compliance, the National Conference of Petroleum Regulatory Authorities was created in April 1942, consisting of representatives of each oil producing state in which a control agency existed. As California had no state regulatory agency, a separate arrangement was necessary, and the PAW District 5 Production Committee together with a voluntary industry group prepared production rates for California, which when approved by PAW's Chief Counsel, were put into effect as agency directives.[14] Throughout the war the maximum efficient production rate system

in July 1945, an increase of more than 1,000,000 daily. By the end of the war, 500,-000 barrels of daily production was coming from wells drilled since 1941 in fields already known prior thereto, while 400,000 barrels of daily production was coming from fields discovered and developed since 1941. In the face of the production record, estimated reserves increased from slightly over 19,000,000,000 bbls. in 1941 to about 21,000,000,000 bbls. in 1945.

[13] Figures for monthly production by states are given in I INTERSTATE OIL COMPACT Q. BULL. 127 *et seq.* (1942), II INTERSTATE OIL COMPACT Q. BULL. 83 *et seq.* (1943), III INTERSTATE OIL COMPACT Q. BULL. 65 *et seq.* (1944).

[14] Recommendation No. 19, 6 FED. REG. 6617–19 (1941).

worked well. The United States entered the emergency period in 1941 with an efficient production capacity of 750,000 barrels daily in excess of the then rate of production. This excess capacity carried the industry through the first difficult years before requirements skyrocketed. Until the summer of 1944 oil produced at maximum efficient rates met all needs and only in a few emergencies were fields permitted to go to rates beyond the set maximum efficient rate. Thereafter, these had to be exceeded, and in addition imports of 245,000 barrels daily were needed to meet requirements.

DRILLING AND WELL SPACING PROGRAM

Hand in hand with increased and more efficient production from existing reserves went the program to stimulate the discovery and drilling of new fields. Throughout the war PAW encouraged increased wildcat drilling with favorable results, but scarcity of materials, price difficulties, and other obstacles combined to prevent attainment of the agency goal.[15] Well spacing and drilling practice controls, which applied with equal force to known developments and to new discoveries, were important in increasing production efficiency and reserve development. Well spacing was based on a density of one well to 40 acres, much wider than generally used in the industry, and was backed up by distance requirements and other regulations. Fundamentally, these requirements were designed to save scarce materials, such as steel, and were originally enforced by WPB orders limiting materials, but they also helped control production and assured efficient development of new and existing reserves. The basic document was OPM Order M68 [16] issued December 23, 1941 which applied to all wells started after that date. Materials could not be used unless the prescribed spacing pattern was followed. Exceptions were given where an immediate increase in production was needed to meet emergencies, or where

---

[15] For example, PAW announced a program of 4,000 wildcats in 1942; 4500 in 1943; 5,000 in 1944 and 5,000 in 1945. Actually 3,223 were drilled in 1942; 3,512 in 1943; 3,881 in 1944; and an estimated 4,100 in 1945. Wildcat drilling discovered reserves of 4,290,000,000 bbls. Most of the discoveries were relatively small and only four fields contained 100,000,000 bbls. or more. These were West Edmond, Oklahoma; Elk Basin-Tensleep, Wyoming; Fullerton, Texas; and Keystone-Ellenburger, Texas.

[16] 6 Fed. Reg. 6687 (1941).

closer spacing produced maximum results with minimum use of material. Drilling in the Illinois basin and in California were typical examples of these exceptions, the former to meet the critical east coast shortage situation, and in the latter to permit reworking of old wells drilled on a 5 to 10 acre basis. Petroleum Administrative Order 11 issued March 30, 1943 [17] put into a single regulation all phases of the M68 order; when it was revoked on September 1, 1945,[18] lifting drilling and spacing requirements, a few states continued the restrictions on their own authority, attesting to the soundness of the principles involved. Many devices were used throughout the war to accomplish the drilling program in the face of shortages of materials and manpower; among the more important were inventory control, joint use of materials, and reclaiming of used materials.

THE CALIFORNIA SITUATION

Two factors made California a special case; first, it was the logical point from which to supply the Pacific war, and having its own production, could be separately administered until V-E Day without reference to the country east of the Rockies, and second, California had no state regulatory agency or adequate control laws for oil, so that whenever PAW relied on existing state machinery to do a job, special steps had to be taken. Before the war California had a capacity in excess of demand of some 150,000 barrels a day. Between V-E and V-J Days production reached a peak of 943,000 barrels daily, and during this period 35,000 barrels daily were brought from Texas. Off-shore drilling and development of Naval Petroleum Reserve No. 1 provided two untapped sources. Pursuant to a joint resolution of June 17, 1944 [19] production from Naval Petroleum Reserve No. 1 was increased from 15,000 to 65,-000 barrels daily. Although the resolution was repealed July 6, 1945,[20] production at the 65,000 barrels daily rate was authorized for a period not to extend beyond December 31, 1946. The Navy

[17] 8 FED. REG. 3955 (1943).
[18] 10 FED. REG. 11073 (1945).
[19] 58 STAT. 283 (1944), 34 U.S.C.A. § 524 (Supp. 1946).
[20] 59 STAT. 465 (1945), 34 U.S.C.A. § 524 (Supp. 1946).

ordered production cut to 15,000 barrels daily on August 22, 1945 and to 8,450 barrels daily on May 6, 1946.

PRICES AND ROYALTIES

One remaining factor of major importance had a direct effect upon the drilling program—the price of crude. Historically, wild-catting and discovery work are known to be at their highest rates when the price of crude is up or is rising. Based on this premise PAW consistently sought increases in OPA ceiling. The basic price for crude was fixed at October 1941 levels, and although persistently sought, no general increase was made except for re-visions in California and Wyoming and spot increases. On April 7, 1943 PAW recommended an increase of 35 cents in the price of crude, which OPA rejected in May 1943 and again in August of the same year when the proposal was renewed. Appeal to the Office of Economic Stabilization was unsuccessful. As a counter-proposal OPA suggested a subsidy program which PAW opposed. The fight continued until June 28, 1944, when OES authorized a subsidy program for stripper wells, administered by OPA with funds furnished by RFC. From August 1, 1944 to November 30, 1945 RFC disbursed $64,934,215 to 308 operators who produced 176, 764, 913 barrels of oil. The participation of PAW was limited to furnishing information and statistical data. In the related field of public land royalties, the agency was instrumental in obtaining passage of the Act of December 24, 1942 [21] which reduced royalties on production from newly discovered fields on public land leases to 12½ per cent, on wells drilled thereafter during the emergency; a rate in line with royalties on private holdings. The Act was re-pealed July 25, 1947. [22]

SECONDARY RECOVERY AND PRESSURE MAINTENANCE

To complete the production narrative, mention should be made of secondary recovery and pressure maintenance projects. Between

[21] 56 Stat. 1080 (1942), 30 U.S.C.A. § 223 (Supp. 1946).
[22] 61 Stat. 449 (1947), 30 U.S.C.A. § 223 (Supp. 1947).

June 1942 and June 1944 about 100 new projects were undertaken. No figures are available as to the results, but substantial increases in yield were obtained. Through pressure maintenance, a single project in the East Texas area involving use of salt water is credited with having increased the ultimate recovery from the area by 300,-000,000 barrels, while maintaining increased current production.

NATURAL GAS AND RELATED PRODUCTS

Natural gas came into its own during the war. As a fuel, it served domestic and industrial users, replacing millions of barrels of fuel oil, and as a source of natural gasoline and liquefied petroleum gases, it produced large quantities of products essential to the 100-octane aviation gasoline and synthetic rubber programs, as well as products generally used in refinery operations. As to natural gas the WPB had control of transmission and distribution functions, while PAW had production responsibility. Natural gasoline and liquified petroleum gases came under the full control and authority of PAW after April 30, 1943. Production of natural gas increased from less than 8,000,000 MCF a day in 1941 to more than 10,500,000 MCF in 1945, and despite the increased production rate, known gas reserves increased from 90 to 135 trillion cubic feet. Liquified petroleum gas production increased from 1,587,600,000 gallons in 1943 to 4,832,722,818 gallons in 1945, and natural gasoline from 150,000 barrels daily in 1941 to 315,000 barrels daily in 1945. Every effort was made to prevent waste of gas. Improved production practices, repressuring, and well spacing were employed with success. Well spacing was enforced by WPB Order M-68 limiting use of materials for gas wells to those drilled on a pattern of 1 to 640 acres. In the Appalachian area this was modified on February 13, 1942 to permit 1 well to 160 acres for deep and 1 to 60 acres for shallow wells. WPB Order L-31, issued February 16, 1942, limiting industrial loads, and requiring interconnection of gas systems, was an important factor in conserving natural gas. In the gas-condensate fields the use of cycling plants was encouraged, although industry resistance was initially encountered because of the necessity of obtaining unit operation agreements before installation.

FOREIGN OPERATIONS

In the foreign operations field the goal of PAW and the industry was to secure efficient operation of allied oil interests and to supply military, naval, and essential civilian needs abroad. The principles of industry-government cooperation were applied abroad, so far as possible, in a manner similar to those at home. The result was an increase in foreign production (excluding Russia) from 1,050,000 barrels daily in 1942 to 1,746,000 barrels daily by the end of the second quarter of 1945. Originally PAW exercised its overseas functions through a single foreign division, but as the war progressed the task took on more formidable proportions; and by October 20, 1943 three separate divisions had been carved out of the original division, namely, foreign production, refining, supply and distribution. The activities of these divisions were coordinated through a committee within the agency. On the industry side, a Foreign Operations Committee was formed in December 1941 with an original membership of nine representatives from the American operating companies, and two British representatives, who had no vote. The basic jurisdictional grants of authority to FOC were in Recommendation 38 of March 25, 1942 and Directive 70 of September 24, 1943. The former set up two major functions: to act as the advisory body to PAW with power to make recommendations for all matters affecting petroleum outside the continental United States, and to provide implementation of approved measures for meeting petroleum demand outside the United States. Directive 70, although it replaced Recommendation 38, continued in effect these two functions and in addition gave FOC authority to determine petroleum requirements of each foreign country or area and to prepare, when requested by PAW, import allocation schedules for each. The quantity actually supplied to any country was not fixed by the group, but by a committee composed of representatives of the State Department, the military, the Foreign Economic Administration, the War Shipping Administration, the PAW and the British. The committee worked behind a veil of secrecy necessitated by its dealings with ship movements, foreign supply, and like matters. A large part of its work was fact finding in nature, and much data was assembled for the military and naval authorities.

PETROLEUM RESERVES CORPORATION

One result of foreign operations during the war was the stimulation of activities of American owned companies operating abroad, especially in the Near East. In 1943 American interests in the Near East became concerned over the security of their concessions because of the hostile action of certain foreign powers. These people took their worries to FEA, the State Department, the War and Navy Departments, and the Interior Department, resulting on June 30, 1943 in the formation of the Petroleum Reserves Corporation under the RFC Act [23] with Mr. Ickes as president. The corporate charter conferred wide powers to conduct oil operations abroad.[24] Creation of the Corporation was a carefully guarded secret. What the industry was able to learn disturbed it, and in November 1943 FOC went on record as opposed to Government oil operations abroad. By January 1944 PIWC adopted that position, urging that foreign oil operations could be best handled by private industry. Into this setting on February 6, 1944 burst the official announcement that the Petroleum Reserves Corporation had agreed with the Arabian-American Oil Company and Gulf Exploration Company to build a pipe line from Saudi-Arabia to the Mediterranean at Government expense, at a cost of between $130,000,000 and $165,000,000. The cost of the line was to be repaid by the companies in twenty-five years with the Government retaining ownership forever. There was to be set aside for the Government a reserve of 1,000,000,000 barrels of oil (or 20 per cent of total reserves if these proved less than 5,000,000,000 barrels) to be available to the army or navy at 25 per cent under the Persian or American market price, whichever was the lower. In the event of another war, the United States had an option to purchase all crude oil products. This announcement produced vigorous protests by the industry, spreading through the papers and then

[23] 47 Stat. 5 (1932), 15 U.S.C.A. § 605 (1940).
[24] 8 Fed. Reg. 9044, 11201 (1943).

to Congress. The PIWC recommended that the corporation be dissolved. As a result of the sustained protest of the industry, the project was eventually abandoned and the attention of the industry turned to the proposed Anglo-American oil agreement.

TERMINATION OF PAW

August 14, 1945 was V-J Day. On May 8, 1946 PAW officially went out of existence, although for all practical purposes it ceased functioning on December 31, 1945. The speedy dissolution was in keeping with the assurance given during the war that controls would be lifted promptly with the coming of peace. On V-J Day 60 recommendations and directives were in force, but by October 15, all domestic orders had been rescinded, and by December 31, 1945 all foreign orders terminated. During the war the Washington payroll of PAW reached a peak of 1438 persons; by April 1, 1946, 58 people remained. March 15, 1946 acting Administrator Davies recommended to the Bureau of the Budget that PAW be officially terminated April 30, 1946. On April 10, Davies asked that the district industry committees be dissolved, and on May 3, 1946 President Truman signed Executive Order 9718 [25] terminating PAW as of May 8, 1946.

[25] FED. REG. 9718 (1946).

CHAPTER 44

The Use of Federal Powers to Supplement Those of the States

~/~

(a) The Federal Oil Conservation Board

The work of the Federal Oil Conservation Board, created by President Coolidge December 19, 1924,[1] represents the first effort on the part of the Federal Government to coordinate the conservation problems of the petroleum industry. Through the efforts of this Board comprehensive surveys were made and recommendations evolved which ultimately led to the adoption of the Interstate Compact, today the underlying basis for nation wide coordination of the control of production of oil and gas and the prevention of waste. The Board, composed of the Secretaries of War, Navy, Interior, and Commerce, functioned through a Technical and Advisory Committee consisting of representatives of the four departments.[2] A program was drawn up and the cooperation of the industry was sought during 1925 in the investigation of waste in production, refining, distribution, utilization, storage and transportation, foreign exploration and development, efficiency of production, uses of oil shales and substitutes, and the economics of fuel oil. Public hearings were held February 10 and 11, 1926, and it soon developed that there was a substantial division within the

NORTHCUTT ELY, WRITER. (See app. B.)
The Federal Oil Conservation Board—The writer expresses his appreciation to Mr. Edward B. Swanson of the Oil and Gas Division, Department of the Interior, who looked over this section and made unofficial comments on it prior to publication.
[1] Letter of President Coolidge to Secretaries of War, Navy, Interior, and Commerce, December 19, 1924, reprinted in REP. I, FED. OIL CONSERVATION BOARD 1 (1926).
[2] Mr. George Otis Smith, director of the Geological Survey was the first chairman of the Board's Technical and Advisory Committee whose original members were Maj. Gen. Edgar Jadwin; War Department, Rear Admiral Harry H. Rousseau, Navy Department, and Mr. Harry H. Hill, Commerce Department.

industry as to the role of the Federal Government in the conservation of oil and gas.

Henry L. Doherty, concurrently with his proposals [3] for unit operation and the conservation of gas energy (both of which have since become part of the accepted doctrine of modern conservation laws), asserted the existence of power in the Federal Government to control oil production directly. The industry, through the American Petroleum Institute, prepared a rebuttal released as the report of the Committee of Eleven. At a hearing before the Board on May 27, 1926 the principal issue was federal control. The American Petroleum Institute, represented by the Honorable Charles Evans Hughes, took the position that, "The Government of the United States is one of enumerated powers and is not at liberty to control the internal affairs of the States, respectively, such as production within the States, through assertion by Congress of a desire either to provide for the common defense or promote the general welfare." [4] Mr. Doherty was of the opinion that the national defense powers of the Government were sufficiently broad to take in the conservation of such a vital natural resource as oil, observing in a letter to the Board dated August 21, 1926 that, "If the Federal Government has no power to conserve oil and prevent waste, then our plan of government is defective, because the power is not vested any place for us to do that which may be necessary for national defense." The Board aligned itself with the proponents of state control, maintaining this orientation throughout its existence. Its position was that federal authority, if any, should be invoked only when it was clear that the state was unwilling or failed to act, or when naval reserves were threatened with depletion. [5]

REPORT I OF THE FEDERAL OIL CONSERVATION BOARD

The first report of the Board to President Coolidge was in the nature of a factual survey and contained a restatement of the legal

[3] Reports of Mr. Doherty's proposals may be found in Oil Weekly (Dec. 19, 1924), and in National Petroleum News 48 (Feb. 17, 1926). See also *Suggestions for Conservation of Petroleum by Control of Production*, a paper presented before the Petroleum Division of the American Institute of Mining and Metallurgical Engineers, and published in *A.I.M.E. Production of Petroleum* (1924).

[4] Record of Hearings, Federal Oil Conservation Board, May 27, 1926, 18–19.

[5] REP. I, FED. OIL CONSERVATION BOARD 15 (1926).

problems attendant upon the control of production. Despite the passage of years, it remains one of the most incisive comments yet written upon the oil industry and its relation to the public interest. The Board emphasized its preference for state control of production, saying: "The right of the State under its police powers to prevent the action of one owner from working a deprivation of the rights of other owners of a common property, and to prevent waste or destruction of a common property by one of the owners, seems reasonably clear." With respect to the authority of the Federal Government the report stated: "The power of the Federal Government to regulate oil production is doubtless limited to its own oil lands, unless the national defense is imperiled by waste or exhaustion of the oil supply."

The Board gave the first authoritative recognition to Henry L. Doherty's theory of the function of natural gas underground in its initial report saying: "The right of the State to prevent the waste of natural resources is rendered more important in this matter by the newly discovered or at least more widely recognized facts regarding the role of gas in the oil sands. Gas is more than a commodity of smaller commercial value associated with oil; it is the efficient agent provided by nature for bringing the oil within the reach of man. Dissolved in the oil, the gas makes the oil flow more freely to the well and there forces it upward, and the longer the gas is retained in solution the larger is the recovery of oil. Waste of gas is therefore a double waste, and the impairment of the gas pressure in an oil sand by one owner may prevent his neighbor from recovering any of the oil beneath their land and himself from securing more than a small part of the oil underlying his own land." As to public lands, the Board found "All these areas, except some special reserves, may fairly be said to be wide open to private appropriation through lease or otherwise. There seems to be no discretionary power anywhere to resist the exploitation of these lands and the dissipation of the Government's oil resources. The leasing of the Indian lands is progressively mandatory until exhaustion."

But when one member of that original Board, Secretary of Commerce Hoover, became President of the United States, he proceeded to find a power to resist "the dissipation of the Government's oil resources" within a week after his inauguration. The Hoover conservation policy, closing the public lands to exploitation, became formally effective March 13, 1929.

Perhaps the most prophetic paragraph of the Board was: "There should be active cooperation between the oil producing States in the study of proposed legislation to the end that uniform laws may be enacted, or even agreements or compacts entered into between the States, subject to ratification by Congress. Even more pronounced should be the cooperation between the State agencies having authority in the regulation of oil and gas production, and the Federal bureaus, whose investigative fields are essentially coterminous with the administrative jurisdiction of the State organizations." The recommendation for an interstate compact, coupled with the study of uniform laws, was not carried to fruition until 1935, when the Interstate Compact to Conserve Oil and Gas, along the lines proposed nine years earlier by the Board, was ratified by six oil producing states and Congress.[6]

The first publication of the Board initiated a system of charts, in the form of a supply and demand balance sheet, showing the source by states and the disposition in terms of products of all oil produced or imported from 1918 through 1926. Subsequent reports continued this service.

REPORT II OF THE FEDERAL OIL CONSERVATION BOARD

The second report, issued January 16, 1928, was a survey of substitutes for motor fuel derived from petroleum. Investigations in this field were continued as a function of the Bureau of Mines and were given added impetus by the Synthetic Fuels Act of 1944.[7]

REPORT III OF THE FEDERAL OIL CONSERVATION BOARD

The third report of the Board, rendered February 25, 1929, was principally notable for its publication of drafts of legislation pre-

[6] H. Res. 407, 74th Cong. 2d Sess., approved Aug. 27, 1935, 49 Stat. 939 (1935).
[7] 58 Stat. 190 (1944), 30 U.S.C.A. 321 (Supp. 1946).

pared by the Committee on Conservation, Section of Mineral Law of the American Bar Association, and by the Committee of Nine,[8] appointed by the Federal Oil Conservation Board, consisting of three representatives each from the Government, the industry, and the legal profession. The report of the Committee of Nine, annexed as Appendix A to the Board's Report, was submitted January 28, 1928. It emphasized the importance of conservation of reservoir energy, discussed various solutions in the way of cooperative development, pointed out the fear of the anti-trust laws as a bar to cooperative agreements, and concluded with a recommendation of purely permissive legislation. A draft of this recommendation was attached which would have permitted the Federal Oil Conservation Board to approve agreements between the operators of a single pool for production control during periods of overproduction. The API Gas Committee's report,[9] submitted with that of the Committee of Nine, was a pioneer survey of the relation between the conservation of reservoir energy and the volume of oil ultimately saved. Appendix B,[10] the report of the Committee on Conservation of Mineral Resources, Section of Mineral Law of the American Bar Association, was an exposition of legal principles leading to the conclusion that state legislation for compulsory unit operation was valid. The committee drafted two bills for enactment by state legislatures; the first [11] authorized voluntary agreements for the restriction of drilling and production during periods of overproduction, and the second [12] empowered the local conservation commission to compel cooperative development and operation. Drafted two decades ago, this compulsory unit operation measure remained considerably in advance of the tide of conservation legislation until very recently.[13]

[8] The members of the committee were Henry M. Bates, James A. Veasey, J. Edgar Pew, Abram F. Meyers, Walter F. Brown, Thomas A. O'Donnell, E. C. Finney, W. S. Farish, and Warren Olney, Jr.

[9] A report by a technical subcommittee of the American Petroleum Institute was attached as an appendix to the committee's report. That report, entitled *The Conservation of Gas* emphasized that the conservation and efficient utilization of gas was of paramount importance in the conservation and economical production of oil.

[10] REP. III, FED. OIL CONSERVATION BOARD 26 (1929).

[11] *Id.* at 40.

[12] *Id.* at 43.

[13] The work of the Interstate Oil Compact Commission in the field of drafting proposals for modern oil and gas conservation laws is revealed in the Commission's

The Board appended a survey of the production possibilities of foreign fields [14] with an appraisal of the relative reserves of the United States and foreign countries. It concluded that then known American reserves comprised about 18 per cent of the reserves of the world, whereas American production was about 68 per cent. This report was cited later by importing companies as the governmental inducement which led them to build up investments in foreign fields, thus entitling them to equitable consideration in the disputes which arose in later years over the volume of imports from abroad. The Board's report said: "The depletion rate of our own resources can be brought more into accord with that of foreign resources only in one way—by importing a greater quantity of crude petroleum. The present imports of Mexican and South American crude oil come largely from American operators and, while not obtained from United States oil sands, they are the product of American engineering and enterprise. Cooperation in the development of foreign oil fields, through technical assistance and the further investment of American capital, would seem to be a logical conservation measure." This was the last friendly word for imports that the industry was to hear for at least a decade. Although outdated, this study (to which was attached an exhaustive bibliography) remains the only one of its kind in the federal literature.

THE API WORLD ZONING PROPOSALS

April 2, 1929 the American Petroleum Institute submitted to the Federal Oil Conservation Board a proposal for a world wide plan for the limitation of production to demand, using the 1928 ratio of production for the allocation of quotas. It established regional zones throughout the world, imposing in effect a cartel system under which the zonal operators agreed with each other on allocation of production. The United States constituted one

---

publication *Forms for Oil and Gas Conservation Laws,* (Aug. 1946) published and distributed by the Headquarters Office of the Commission at Oklahoma City, Oklahoma.

[14] REP. III, *supra* note 10 at 50 "Petroleum Resources of Foreign Countries and Outlying Possessions of the United States," prepared by Mr. Arthur H. Redfield of the Bureau of Mines.

zone. In the American area it was proposed to restrict production to the 1928 figure, allocating that by voluntary agreement of the units within the American industry. This proposal, read with the reaction of the industry to Mr. Doherty's proposal for Federal control in 1926, indicated the degree of determination with which the industry was heading away from governmental domination. A hearing was arranged, and the Board provided itself in advance with an opinion of the Attorney General upon the Institute proposal. The full text of the opinion of the Attorney General was not published, but that part which was released made it clear that neither the Federal Oil Conservation Board nor any other federal agency had been granted authority by Congress to clothe any persons with immunity from the operation of the Sherman Act, and that no action taken by the Board would relieve the parties to the proposed agreement from the operation of the anti-trust laws.[15] The unpublished portion of the opinion indicated that the proposed agreement would violate the anti-trust laws. Having failed to receive from the Board any assurance of immunity, the industry was not willing to trust its own views of the legality of the proposed plan; it never was formally consummated. The Board advised the industry, at the close of this hearing, again to turn to an interstate production compact.

On March 10, 1930 Secretary of the Interior Ray Lyman Wilbur inaugurated the fact finding system on supply and demand which has been continued to the present time, first under the auspices of the Federal Oil Conservation Board, then the Petroleum Code, and finally through the Bureau of Mines estimates which are used as the basis for operations under the Interstate Compact of 1935. Secretary Wilbur requested five eminent oil economists [16] to make determinations for the period from April 1 to September 30, 1930 based on the anticipated consumption of refined products, the

---

[15] See Myers, *Relation of the Federal Anti-trust Laws to Problems of Mineral Conservation,* 55 ABA REP. 675 (1930).

[16] The original members of the voluntary committee were J. Elmer Thomas, Joseph E. Pogue, Ray M. Collins, H. W. Lowrie, Jr., and H. P. Grimm. This committee rendered two reports. The next volunteer committee, which made three reports, was composed of E. B. Swanson, Dr. John W. Frey, Martin Van Couvering, Howard Bennette, and Alfred G. White. The final committee was composed of Dr. John W. Frey, Clarel B. Mapes, Sidney A. Swensrud, Martin Van Couvering, and Howard Bennette.

production of crude necessary to conform to that demand, and the allocation of production to the major producing districts. The resulting survey and seven subsequent studies submitted in succeeding six month periods had an average margin of error of around two per cent. These reports were made during a period when crude oil prices fluctuated between $.25 and $1 a barrel, indicating that the accuracy of the forecasts had no relation to a fixed price.

REPORT IV OF THE FEDERAL OIL CONSERVATION BOARD

The fourth report of the Board, dated June 1930, two months after the initiation of the supply and demand forecasting service, turned the attention of the industry to the possibilities of the federal function in this field. In view of the later experience of the industry with unbalanced refinery and production operations, the following observation has historical interest: [17] "When the refiners' crude oil purchases are properly coordinated and when the composite public demand for refined products had been correctly interpreted, the crude oil requirements would be equivalent to total domestic and foreign demand. Under conditions of crude oil supply available at low prices, however, the refiner may increase his crude oil [throughout] and, concurrently, his output of refined products in excess of the public demand. Crude oil production may have been stimulated at the same time that refinery stocks of refined products were being increased and, during the period of correction, the condition of overproduction would tend to become general throughout the industry. An unbalanced production is the inevitable result of unwarranted development, whether this be in crude oil production, refining capacity, or in transportation facilities. Increasing capacity for production far in advance of growth in demand leads naturally to overproduction and disorganized markets." Although a series of agreements was obtained in 1930 under which refiners cut back operations by the equivalent of one day's run per week, the warning, that unbalanced refinery operations might have as disastrous an effect marketwise as unbalanced crude oil production, was largely forgotten during the years of new crude

[17] REP. IV, FED. OIL CONSERVATION BOARD, 3–4, (1930).

discoveries following the publication of this report. Attention of the industry for a decade was focused on production control problems. Here for the first time was presented an over-all survey of the supply and demand equation, taking refining as a factor as well as the relation between imports of crude and exports of refined products. The work undertaken almost concurrently in the forecasting of supply and demand reduced this concept to actuality.

Although it lacked statutory authorization to limit imports, the Board worked out a system of voluntary informal agreements with leading importers during 1932, whereby they agreed to curtail their imports by 25 per cent. The level of imports established for the last half of 1932 has been the standard at which all subsequent attempts at legislative quota restrictions of imports have been aimed. Imports were less than five per cent of total domestic requirements.

REPORT V OF THE FEDERAL OIL
CONSERVATION BOARD

The fifth report of the Board published in October 1932 outlined a specific program for an interstate conservation compact. In an appendix [18] the proposal was summarized substantially as follows: (1) The compact would establish an agency to forecast demand effectively and allocate corresponding production quotas among the producing states. The fact finding organization would be one with both federal and state participation, or composed exclusively of state representatives, subject to concurrence in their findings by a federal body. (2) The federal and state legislation authorizing the compact would delegate to the joint national and state body additional functions: recommendation of adequate uniform state conservation laws, interchange of information as to refinery runs and shipments to facilitate gasoline tax collections, the approval of specific agreements between producers and refiners to carry out the supply and demand forecasts (provided a federal agency concurred as to agreements affecting federal and interstate commerce) and when approval was given, it operated as a finding that the agreement did not violate the anti-trust laws, cooperation with federal agencies in negotiating agreements with foreign pro-

[18] REP. V, FED. OIL CONSERVATION BOARD, 23 et seq. (1932).

ducers or producing agents, so that restriction of production in the United States would not automatically be followed by absorption of our export market by other producing countries. (3) The compact would provide for enforcement of the recommended production quotas of the fact finding agency. Quotas were to be of two kinds, one for domestic production and one for importations. As to the first the compact might, if the states desired, obligate each jurisdiction to make its quota effective by such legal machinery as it saw fit to use under its own law. These recommendations of uniform laws forthcoming from the interstate commission were expected gradually to induce closer uniformity in conservation methods. As to imports, since restrictions were effected only by federal agencies, the compact could not direc ly provide for quota enforcement, although the interstate commission would participate in their fixing. Two general methods proposed for restriction of imports were (a) a flexible tariff, or (b) proration under a quota system limiting the importers to fixed allowables. As to the former, the rate would be flexed upward or downward to equalize the cost of imported oil competing with the reasonable cost of similar domestic products, coupled with a drawback provision to encourage importation for refining and re-export. Either the Tariff Commission would fix the tariff rate periodically, or the rate might vary with the quantity by which imports exceeded some fixed quota. If proration were used instead of a tariff, the compact would set imports at a fixed percentage of the periodical estimate of demand and issue certificates equitably to prospective importers, permitting importation in accordance with their quotas, excepting oil imported to be refined and re-exported. Or, alternatively, the quota might be fixed at a set percentage of exports.

The proceedings necessary to bring the compact into being were outlined as (1) the negotiation of the pact, either in the form of a treaty executed by representatives of the states, or by reciprocal legislation enacted by the legislatures, (2) approval of the compact by an act of Congress secured either in advance or after negotiation, and (3) approval by the state legislatures. It was pointed out that normally negotiation was preceded by federal and state enabling statutes followed by ratifying acts, and that the two steps might be telescoped. The proposal of the Board was amplified with drafts of statutes, compacts, and regulations in a report by the Chairman of its Technical and Advisory Committee February, 1933.[19]

TERMINATION OF ACTIVITIES

With the inauguration of the Roosevelt Administration in March 1933 the four incoming Secretaries of War, Navy, Interior, and Commerce automatically became members of the Federal Oil Conservation Board, as had their predecessors by virtue of the designation of President Coolidge in 1924. However, the Board, although never formally dissol ed, did not function. The Petroleum Administrative Board, esta.lished under the Petroleum Code in 1933, took over its files, which have since been sent to the National Archives.

(b) Hot Oil Legislation

HISTORY OF SECTION 9 (C) OF THE NATIONAL INDUSTRIAL RECOVERY ACT

Federal control of interstate petroleum transportation through hot oil legislation grew out of the flood of production in 1930–1932 resulting from the discovery of the East Texas Field. By March 1933 when the Roosevelt administration took office, the field was nearly two and a half years old and had gone through several phases of restricted and wide open production. Attempts of the Texas Railroad Commission to stabilize East Texas production at approximately 400,000 barrels daily had been invalidated by a three judge federal court.[20] During the latter part of 1931 martial law was resorted to by the Governors of Texas and Oklahoma in an effort to enforce production quotas. The invalidation of martial law in Texas [21] resulted in increased production and decreasing prices.

Hot Oil Legislation—The writer expresses his appreciation to Mr. James R. Lewis, Chairman of the Federal Petroleum Board and Mr. Edward B. Swanson of the Oil and Gas Division, Department of the Interior, who looked over this section and made unofficial comments on it prior to publication.

[19] ELY, OIL CONSERVATION THROUGH INTERSTATE AGREEMENT (1933).

[20] MacMillan v. Rail. Comm., 51 F. 2d 400 (W. D. Tex. 1931). See Hardwicke, *Legal History of Proration of Oil Production in Texas* 56 TEX. BAR ASS'N. REP. 99 (1937).

[21] Constantin v. Smith, 57 F. 2d 227. (E.D. Tex. 1932), 287 U.S. 378 (1932).

The incoming Secretary of the Interior called a conference of the governors of the oil states in Washington March 27, 1933. The meeting produced inconclusive results, except that a recommendation was made for the adoption of a federal law prohibiting the transportation in interstate commerce of petroleum and products produced or manufactured in violation of the laws of any state— the genesis of federal "hot oil" legislation. The principle was then embodied in a few state statutes relating to certificates of clearance [22] or compliance with production laws, but had not been extended to federal legislation. Concurrently with the Governors' Conference, East Texas on April 1, 1933 reached the peak of tank car shipment since its wide open flow in the summer of 1931. National production for the week ending April 1 was 600,000 barrels daily higher than the figure of 2,000,000 barrels recommended by the conference. Oil prices were as low as 13 cents a barrel. The Oklahoma City Field was shut down on April 1 to await a new conservation law, enacted on April 10; East Texas was shut down from April 6 to April 24. When the latter field was reopened April 24, its allowable was increased from 400,000 barrels daily to 850,000 barrels, or as much as the conference recommended for the entire state. The price dropped to 10 cents a barrel or less. In addition to the allowable, something over 150,000 barrels of hot oil was being run, for the Bureau of Mines estimated in May 1933 that the daily production from the field was 992,700 barrels. The industry was ripe for federal help of any character.

The East Texas situation prompted the introduction of a series of bills in the 73rd Congress, many written by the Interior Department at the request of members of Congress. Thus the Capper bill, S. 1736, was introduced May 19, 1933 under administration auspices, and the identical Marland bill, H.R. 5720, May 20. These measures authorized federal regulation of production, and a degree of price fixing. On April 14, Congressman Marland introduced a bill, H.R. 5010, to prevent interstate transportation of illegally produced crude oil.[23] The National Industrial Recovery Act had

[22] See TEX. COMP. STAT. tit. 102, art. 6033 (Vernon 1931). Texas Pipeline Co. v. Binton Drilling Co., 54 S.W. 2d 190 (Civ. App. Tex. 1932). See ELY, OIL CONSERVATION THROUGH INTERSTATE AGREEMENT, 283 (Arkansas), 326 (Oklahoma), 342 (Texas) (1933).

[23] See Hearings before Committee on Interstate and Foreign Commerce on H.R. 5010, 73 Cong. 1st Sess. (1933).

been introduced May 23, 1933, as H.R. 5755, and May 20, 1933, President Roosevelt wrote both houses asking that "action relating to the oil industry" be incorporated in that proposal. In committee, an effort was made to attach the Marland-Capper bill as a separate title; and failing that, to add a new Section 10 to Title I which in general terms authorized federal regulation supplementing state conservation legislation, federal allocation of market demand among the states and importers, and the prohibition of interstate transportation of petroleum and products produced in violation of state or federal laws. The section emerged from the Senate committee in modified form as Section 9, of Title I. Subsection C authorized the prohibition of transportation in interstate and foreign commerce of petroleum and products produced or withdrawn from storage in excess of the amount permitted by any state law, valid regulation, or order. Violators were subject to a fine of $1000, imprisonment up to six months, or both.

The Recovery Act was approved by President Roosevelt June 16, 1933. June 13 the Railroad Commission of Texas reduced the East Texas allowable from 850,000 barrels to 550,000 barrels daily. Prices immediately improved, although Section 9 c did not go into operation until July 11, 1933.[24] Thus at the outset was posed a question never conclusively answered during the life of the Recovery Act—how much of the crude price stabilization was due to the enforcement by Texas state authorities of lower allowables, made possible by a gradual reversal of position by the three judge federal court,[25] and how much of the result was due to federal activity. It is fair to say, however, that the known determination of the Federal Government to command the situation if the states did not was an internal factor in the success of state control during the period of the Recovery Act.

ORGANIZATION OF THE AFFIDAVIT SYSTEM

July 14, 1933 the Secretary of the Interior was authorized by Executive Order No. 6204 to exercise all the powers of the president under Section 9 c. General regulations were issued which pro-

[24] Exec. Order No. 6199, a copy of which is found in *Hearings before Subcommittee of House Committee on Interstate and Foreign Commerce on H. RES. 290 and H.R. 7372*, 76th Cong., 2d Sess. pt. I. 832 (1939).

[25] Amazon Petroleum Corp. v. Rail. Comm., 5 F. Supp. 633 (E.D. Tex. 1934).

hibited the movement of petroleum and products in commerce unless accompanied by an affidavit certifying the legality of its production or withdrawal from storage. Monthly sworn statements concerning operations were required from all producers, purchasers, shippers, refiners, pipe lines and gathering systems, but by an order dated August 2, 1933, the application of all regulations was limited to the Oklahoma City and East Texas Fields. The affidavit system was never completely successful, partly because producers of hot oil were willing to supply any required affidavit and partly because an injunction in the *Panama Refining* case was in force against the regulations for a large part of the period.

In October 1933 the companion cases of *Panama Refining Company v. Ryan* and *Amazon Petroleum Corporation v. Railroad Commission* [26] were filed in the United States District Court for the Eastern District of Texas, alleging that the orders of the Texas Railroad Commission were invalid in that they adopted production quotas set by the Secretary of the Interior, asserting that the section was invalid, and seeking injunctions to prohibit the enforcement of the proration orders and the regulations under it and Article III of the Petroleum Code. A three judge court convened, and on challenge to its jurisdiction, granted a severance as to the federal defendants for the submission of that part of the case to a single judge court. The three judge court upheld the validity of the Texas Railroad Commission's proration orders and denied an injunction. [27] The case was not appealed. The single judge court granted an injunction February 21, 1934 on the ground that regulation of the production of petroleum was a matter reserved to the states, and the regulations of the Secretary of the Interior sought to evade constitutional limitations by superseding state authority. [28] On appeal, the Circuit Court for the 5th Circuit in *Ryan v. Amazon Petroleum Corporation* [29] reversed the District Court and held Section 9 c a valid exercise of the federal power. Decision was avoided as to the validity of the regulations under Article III of the code, although they were thought to be constitutional upon the ground that an adequate remedy at law under the enforcement provision of the

[26] 5 F. Supp. 633, 639 (E.D. Tex. 1934).
[27] Amazon Petroleum Corp. v. Rail. Comm., 5 F. Supp. 633 (E.D. Tex. 1934).
[28] Panama Refining Co. v. Ryan, 5 F. Supp. 639, 649 (E.D. Tex. 1934).
[29] 71 F. 2d 1 (C.C.A. 5th 1934).

code was available.[30] Although the circuit court reversed the district court, it stayed its mandate pending application to the Supreme Court for certiorari, thus in effect continuing the injunction of the lower court. The Supreme Court, in *Panama Refining Company v. Ryan*,[31] pointed out that the controversy with respect to the regulations under Article III of the code proceeded on the false assumption that the section still contained that paragraph by which production in excess of assigned quotas was made an unfair practice violative of the code, which paragraph had been eliminated by an executive order of September 13, 1933. The Court disposed of the case on the ground that the section was unconstitutional as an invalid delegation to the president of legislative power unaccompanied by adequate standards for performance. While these cases were going through the courts, dissatisfaction with the functioning of the affidavit system accumulated until at length the Planning and Coordination Committee served notice on the administrator that the industry would cease its efforts to stabilize the market until hot oil was stopped. The affidavit system was reorganized, and a Federal Tender Board was established effective October 24, 1934.

THE FEDERAL TENDER BOARD

The former regulations based on reports and affidavits had made it quite apparent that it was physically impossible to police several thousand wells in the fields. But movements out of the fields through pipe lines, railroads, and highways could be checked. The tender system was evolved in an effort to solve the hot oil problem through controls on shipments. Under the federal tender system, in addition to reports and affidavits on production, certificates of clearance were issued by the Federal Tender Board, a field organization. These were required as a condition precedent to the movement of petroleum or products in interstate commerce. The burden of proof was placed on the applicant to show that the oil for which he requested a tender had been legally produced. The system was immediately successful and some 60 of the 80 refineries operating

[30] *Id.* at 6.
[31] 293 U.S. 388 (1935).

in the East Texas Field closed within a few months. The system had just begun to operate when the Supreme Court in the *Panama Refining* case put a temporary end to its activities January 7, 1935.

THE CONNALLY ACT

On January 8, 1935 the oil administrator asked for new legislation, and on January 10, Senator Gore of Oklahoma introduced S.J. Res. 25 and 26 to amend the Recovery Act in mandatory instead of discretionary terms, introducing for the first time the term contraband oil. On January 14, Senator Connally of Texas offered S. 858, to the same end, a bill drafted in the Interior Department. Congressman Disney introduced a similar bill, H.R. 3658 on January 10. The Gore and Connally bills were consolidated and reintroduced in the Senate January 18 as S. 1190, and this measure, known as the Connally Act, was enacted February 22, 1935.[32] Its sections were much more detailed than 9 c of the Recovery Act. It defined oil produced or withdrawn from storage in violation of state laws or orders, and products of such oil, as contraband, and prohibited the interstate shipment of contraband oil. Section 4, taken from Senator Gore's bill, provided for suspension of the prohibition whenever the president formally proclaimed that its operations caused a lack of parity between supply and demand. The president was to prescribe regulations, require certificates of clearance, and establish boards for that purpose. Review of refusals to issue certificates was confined to the district courts. Penalties by fine and imprisonment were provided. Contraband oil was liable to judicial seizure and forfeiture by proceedings like in rem admiralty actions. Common carriers were relieved from the obligation to carry oil believed to be contraband. The boards to be set up were given power to hold investigations under oath. The president was to obtain mandatory injunctions to enforce compliance with the Act, and injunctions against violations of the Act. Process in personal actions ran in any district where the defendant might be found. The president was authorized to delegate his powers. The Act was made temporary, to expire June 16, 1937.[33] Although originally sched-

[32] 49 STAT. 30, 15 U.S.C.A. § 715 et seq. (1940).
[33] See *Hearings before Subcommittee of the Committee on Finance on S. 790,* 75th Cong., 1st Sess. 6 (1937).

uled to expire on that date, the Connally Act has since been made a part of the permanent statutory scheme.[34]

By executive orders 7756 and 7757 [35] issued December 1, 1937 the investigative functions under the Connally Act were lodged in a new agency of the Interior Department, the Petroleum Conservation Division. Federal Tender Board No. 1, the original enforcement arm, was superseded by the Federal Petroleum Board under the Secretary of the Interior's order 1753-A October 27, 1942. The Federal Petroleum Board now functions through its main office at Kilgore, Texas, and its branch offices at Houston and Midland, Texas, and Lafayette, Louisiana but certificates of clearance have not been required by the Board since July 1942.

With the termination of the activities of the Petroleum Administration for War in the spring of 1946, President Truman, in a letter to the Secretary of the Interior of May 3, 1946, suggested the establishment of a coordinating agency within the department to administer the Connally Act and to maintain relationships with the petroleum industry. As a result, the Secretary issued Order No. 2193 establishing the Oil and Gas Division May 6, 1946, and on June 3, 1946 [36] the administration of the Connally Act was formally transferred to it. Thus supervision over the administration and enforcement of the Connally Act is now vested in the Oil and Gas Division of the Department of the Interior, with field investigations delegated to the headquarters office at Kilgore, Texas. If a possible violation of the Connally Act or of a regulation issued thereunder is discovered, an examiner from the Federal Petroleum Board conducts an investigation. The case is presented to the Board for hearing, and if the Board deems action necessary, the record is forward to the Oil and Gas Division which, after conferring with the Solicitor's Office in the Department, may then send the case on to the Justice Department with a recommendation that legal action be instituted.

[34] The act was first extended to June 30, 1939 by the Act of June 14, 1937, 50 STAT. 257. By the Act of June 29, 1939, 53 STAT. 927 termination date was again extended to June 30, 1942. The Act was made permanently effective by repeal of its expiration date by the Act of June 22, 1942, 56 STAT. 381. See *Hearings before Subcommittee of the Committee on Finance on S. 790*, 75th Cong., 1st Sess. (1937).

[35] 2 FED. REG. 2664 (1937).

[36] Exec. Order No. 9732, 11 FED. REG. 5985 (1946).

LITIGATION

The constitutionality of the Connally Act has never been challenged in the Supreme Court. It sustained a direct attack in *Griswold v. President of the United States*,[37] and its constitutionality has since been assumed in the 5th circuit which reviews by far the majority of the hot oil cases.[38]

The interrelationship between the federal and the state enforcement machinery was indicated in *Hurley v. Federal Tender Board No. 1*.[39] In that case the applicant for a federal tender derived his title from the State of Texas, through a sheriff's sale of oil forfeited to the state as contraband. He contended that the forfeiture and subsequent sale by the state terminated the contraband status. The court held that the Connally Act, though enacted in support of state conservation laws, was nevertheless primarily an exercise of federal power. Since the Act did not except from its operation contraband oil forfeited and resold by a state, the oil remained contraband within the meaning of the Connally Act, and the Board was correct in refusing to grant a tender to permit interstate shipment. In *Federal Tender Board No. 1 v. Haynes Oil Corporation*[40] the Board was in effect ordered to follow the ruling of the Texas Railroad Commission. Haynes produced 14,000 barrels of petroleum in excess of its quota to protect itself from drainage by adjacent wells. It stored the excess in tanks containing 15,000 barrels of quota oil (legally produced petroleum). The Railroad Commission granted a permit to move 15,000 barrels, but the Tender Board refused, taking the position that the commingling of the quota with the non-quota oil made the entire mass contraband. The court ordered the Board to issue a tender for 15,000 barrels.

[37] 82 F. 2d 922 (C.C.A. 5th 1936).

[38] See also Hurley v. Federal Tender Board No. 1, 108 F. 2d 574 (C.C.A. 5th 1939), Genecov v. Federal Petroleum Board, 146 F. 2d 596 (C.C.A. 5th 1944), *certiorari denied* 324 U.S. 865 (1945). Miscellaneous questions concerning the Board's power to compel the attendance of witnesses, the production of records, and the answering of questions were presented in President of the United States v. Skeen, 118 F. 2d 58 (C.C.A. 5th 1941), Graham v. Federal Tender Board No. 1, 118 F. 2d 8 (C.C.A. 5th 1941), and Zinser et al. v. Federal Petroleum Board, 148 F. 2d 993 (C.C.A. 5th 1945), *certiorari denied*, 326 U.S. 751 (1945).

[39] *Supra* note 38.

[40] 80 F. 2d 468 (C.C.A. 5th 1935).

THE CONTRIBUTION OF THE CONNALLY ACT

Under conditions presently prevailing the Federal Petroleum Board serves to support state limitations on production by prohibiting shipment in interstate commerce of petroleum produced in excess of those quotas. While the Connally Act by its term applies in all states which have legislation limiting petroleum production, in practice administration has been confined almost entirely to checking the output of the Texas and Louisiana fields, with subsidiary checks in New Mexico. By requiring detailed production reports and maintaining an active inspection and investigative staff, the federal authorities are able to support the state officials charged with the duty of enforcing production quotas by determining the accuracy of statements made by producers as to the actual production from given wells or fields. The very existence of the Connally Act affords protection against return to the chaotic conditions so accurately described in *Thompson v. Spear*.[41] The usefulness of the Connally Act has been tested both during a period of overproduction and under the conditions of short supply following World War II. The legislation achieves a two fold result, in that it closes the channels of interstate commerce to oil produced in violation of the individual state conservation laws, and provides a means accurately to cross check statements and reports made by producers to state authorities.

(c) *Bureau of Mines*

The Federal Government makes an important contribution to the conservation of oil and gas through the services of the Bureau of Mines of the Interior Department.[42]

Bureau of Mines—The writer expresses his appreciation to Dr. Alfred G. White of the Bureau of Mines, Department of the Interior, who looked over this section and made unofficial comments on it prior to publication.

[41] 91 F. 2d 430 (C.C.A. 5th 1937).

[42] A thorough discussion of the mechanics and scope of the forecasts may be found in *Hearings before Temporary National Economic Committee*, 76th Cong., 2d Sess. pt. 16 9582–9603 (1939). An illuminating comparison may be made between the testimony of Dr. Alfred G. White, Bureau of Mines representative at this hearing and at the *Hearings before Special Committee to Study Problems of American Small Business, Pursuant to S. Res. 20*, 80th Cong., 2d Sess., pt. 27 3138–3176 (1948). See also *Hearings before Subcommittee of the Committee of Interstate and Foreign Commerce, Pursuant to H. Res. 290 and H.R. 7372*, 76th Cong., 2d Sess., pt. 1 148–208 (1939).

MONTHLY DEMAND FORECASTS

The preparation and publication of the Monthly Demand Forecasts of the Bureau supplies an essential link in the present plan [43] of state conservation control as supplemented by federal assistance. Monthly forecasts are prepared by complicated statistical procedures, which in essence attempt to estimate for the coming month the potential demand for crude oil by states of origin. Reports are received each month from producers, transporters, and refiners; and changes in crude stocks and import export factors are watched. Relationships are maintained with parallel forecasting groups such as the committees of the Interstate Oil Compact Commission and the American Petroleum Institute. From this mass of data, projections of probable demand for crude oil in each state are made and transmitted monthly to the regulatory agencies in each oil producing state. While these reports have no binding effect [44] upon the state agencies in setting production quotas, their accuracy over a long period has given them considerable influence upon the decisions of the regulatory bodies. In the period immediately after World War II when consumption of oil increased at unprecedented rates, the estimates of the Bureau failed to reflect immediately changes caused by such factors as widespread conversion to diesel locomotives, which resulted in an increased fuel consumption of some 400 per cent over 1941.[45] The states were generally more sensitive to these changes; also, many of them were setting production quotas based on maximum efficient rates. The Bureau of Mines does not consider MER's in arriving at estimate of potential demand. It is concerned, according to an authoritative state-

[43] The origins of this plan are discussed *supra* under the sections on the Federal Oil Conservation Board. See also, REP. I FEDERAL OIL CONSERVATION BOARD 24 (1926), REP. V FEDERAL OIL CONSERVATION BOARD 19 *et seq.* (1932). ELY, OIL CONSERVATION THROUGH INTERSTATE AGREEMENT (1933). REP. SEC'Y. INT. 23, 24 (1931).

[44] Report of Committee on Balance of Supply with Demand, IPAA submitted at April 14, 1941 meeting of the Interstate Oil Compact Commission, part of which stated: "The only conclusion that can be drawn is that the Bureau's estimates for consumptive demand are the best available and should not be persistently and recklessly exceeded."

[45] Likewise fuel consumed in space heaters increased more than 100 per cent in 1947 over 1941.

ment,[46] only with forecasting "what we expect actually can be and will be used under all existing circumstances." If a state exceeds its MER production quota and the crude thus produced does not merely increase stocks of that state's crude, subsequent forecasts take this excess production, absorbed by the market, into account in arriving at estimated future state demand. During short term periods, the demand for crude oil from a state may exceed a current MER rate due to the liquidation of past accumulations of crude stocks of oil produced by the state. However, if a state restricts crude production to an MER rate for any considerable period of time, demand forecasts soon approximate that rate. At the present writing, the factor of refinery capacity is of prime importance in arriving at potential demand, for with almost all refineries producing at capacity, it is impossible to predict useful demand in excess of existing refinery capacity. From 1930 to 1932 when forecasting was first developed through the voluntary committees on petroleum economics [47] working under the Federal Oil Conservation Board, six reports [48] were filed each covering a six months period.[49] These reports set out narratively and in tabulations the manner in which the committees estimated anticipated consumption of refined products, the production of crude necessary to meet that demand, and the allocation to major producing districts of this supply for each period. The first report set allowables in four producing districts,[50] the sixth report was extended to eleven districts. When the Petroleum Administrative Board came into being in 1933, it cooperated with the Petroleum Economics Division of the Bureau of Mines in continuing the work of the voluntary committees, an effort being made to publish monthly figures. With the end of the National Industrial Recovery Act, the Bureau of Mines took over the forecasts and has been issuing them monthly since

[46] Dr. White is the Chief Economist in charge of making the Monthly Demand Forecasts for the Bureau of Mines. See his testimony at *Hearings before Special Committee to Study Problems of American Small Business Pursuant to S. RES. 20,* 80th Cong., 2d Sess. Pt. 27 3145 (1948).

[47] ELY, THE FEDERAL OIL CONSERVATION BOARD supra note 34.

[48] *Federal Oil Conservation Board, Surveys of National Petroleum Requirements for Seasonal Periods of 1932–1931–1930* (1932).

[49] With the exception of Report No. 4 which covered only three months.

[50] California, Oklahoma, Texas, all others.

September 1935. From the outset and through the pre-war years the effort was to produce calculations based on demand. During World War II the ability of a state to produce at its maximum efficiency was considered, and the Petroleum Administration for War based its producing area allocations on Bureau of Mines forecasts. With the aftermath of the war the calculations (as has been suggested) have been affected by a wealth of features—transportation and refinery capacity being not the least of them.

SYNTHETIC FUELS AND OTHER ACTIVITIES

Another function of the Bureau of Mines in the conservation field, though not directly in aid of state programs, lies in its activity in the perfection of synthetic fuels processes. The paramount interest of the Federal Government in the maintenance of adequate petroleum reserves to support the civilian and military demands of our economy led it to investigate alternative sources of supply. In 1944 Congress enacted the Synthetic Liquid Fuel Demonstration Plants Act [51] authorizing the Secretary of the Interior, acting through the Bureau of Mines, to construct, maintain, and operate one or more demonstration plants to produce synthetic liquid fuels from coal, oil shale, and other substances, and one or more such plants to produce liquid fuels from agricultural products. The original Act, authorizing an appropriation of $30,000,000, contemplated a five year program, but March 15, 1948 Congress extended the program to eight years and authorized an additional $30,000,-000.[52] Under the authority of this Act a demonstration plant has been constructed at Rifle, Colorado, and one is nearing completion at Louisiana, Missouri, on the site of a Government owned wartime synthetic ammonia plant. Laboratory research and experimentation have been going on for the past few years at Bruceton, Pennsylvania, and Morgantown, West Virginia, with additional facilities under construction at Laramie, Wyoming.[53] Synthetic hydrocarbon fuels have been made from natural gas, coal, and oil

[51] 58 STAT. 190 (1944), 30 U.S.C.A. § 321 (Supp. 1946).
[52] P. Law. No. 443, 80th Cong., 2d Sess. (Mar. 15, 1948).
[53] SEC'Y INT. REP. TO CONGRESS ON SYNTHETIC FUELS (1947), *Hearings before Oil Subcommittee of House Armed Services Committee,* 80th Cong., 2d Sess. (1948). *Hearings before House Committee on Public Lands,* 80th Cong., 2d Sess. (1948).

shale. Research and investigation by the Bureau of Mines has gone forward in each of these fields, but more recent emphasis has been placed on the processes using coal, since it represents the most abundant mineral fuel resource in the United States. The gradual withdrawal of governmental experimentation from natural gas has been occasioned by the rapidly expanding interest of private industry in the processes developed during the second world war. In addition to its research, the Bureau of Mines has actively engaged in promoting construction programs for commercial plants for the production of synthetic fuel from coal and oil shale. The Interior Department, through Secretary Krug, specifically recommended in January 1948 that Congress enact legislation [54] authorizing the Reconstruction Finance Corporation to advance $400,000,000 to private industry for the construction of plants. In an appearance before the Committee of Interstate and Foreign Commerce of the House of Representatives on February 16, 1948 Secretary Krug, like his predecessors, stressed the fact that with only 31 per cent of the world's oil reserves, the United States could not continue to meet 63 per cent of world consumption.

The present heavy drain on petroleum resources has accentuated other work [55] of the Bureau of Mines in research designed to stimulate recovery of oil from old fields. Recent projects, which include the siphon flowing of oil wells as a means of reducing operating costs and the investigation of methods for economically recovering oil from shallow depth oil impregnated deposits, have obtained encouraging results, particularly the Edna deposit of San Luis Obispo County, California. On the production equipment end, surveys conducted by the Bureau of Mines have led to selection of alloy steels which best resist the damaging corrosion in gas condensate fields.

(d) Oil and Gas Division of the Department of the Interior

The success of the Government-industry partnership, developed through the Petroleum Administration for War, pointed to the

---

[54] H.R. 5475, 80th Cong., 2d Sess. was introduced by Congressman Wolverton February 19, 1948. The bill would authorize the construction of three commercial plants with the assistance of $400,000,000 from the RFC. Hearings were held but as of May 1, 1948 the Committee had not submitted its report.

[55] See, in general REP. SEC'Y INT. 171–172 (1946), REP. SEC'Y INT. 191 (1947).

desirability of maintaining that relationship after World War II. The PAW had obtained the cooperation the industry due in part to its commitment to terminate controls speedily after the end of the war. The usefulness of the Petroleum Industry War Council as representative of the industry was recognized, and during the closing days of the PAW, plans [56] were laid for the continuance of the relationship on a voluntary basis. To attain that end it was felt necessary to have a central Governmental agency acting as a clearing house for the more than 30 branches of the Government dealing with petroleum problems and products.

Concurrently with the signing of executive order [57] No. 9718 which terminated PAW, President Truman wrote the Secretary of the Interior (much as President Coolidge had done in creating the Federal Oil Conservation Board) that: "To the extent possible one agency must bear the primary responsibility for providing a focal point for leadership and information for the numerous agencies of the Federal Government dealing with petroleum. I, therefore, request that you undertake the initiative in obtaining coordination and unification of Federal policy in administration with respect to the functions and activities relating to petroleum carried on by the various departments and agencies. Where practicable and appropriate Governmental activities relating to petroleum should be centralized and I ask that from time to time you submit to me for consideration proposals looking to the accomplishment of the objective. You should, through such office as you designate, serve as the channel of communication between the Federal Government and the petroleum industry, and as the liaison agency of the Federal Government in its relations with appropriate state bodies concerned with oil and gas. I have been impressed with the great contribution of Government-industry cooperation to the success of the War Petroleum Program, and feel that the values of such close and harmonious relations between Government and industry should be continued. I, therefore, suggest that you establish an industry organization to consult and advise with you." Acting upon the suggestions contained in the letter, Secretary Krug issued order [58] No.

[56] See *Hearings before Special Committee Investigating Petroleum Resources,* S. Res. 36, 79th Cong., 2d Sess. 3 *et seq.* (1945).

[57] Exec. Order No. 9718, 11 FED. REG. 9718 (1946).

[58] Interior Department Order No. 2193.

2193, May 6, 1946 establishing The Oil and Gas Division of the Department of the Interior. The order stated that the Division "with a view to the conservation of the oil and gas resources of the nation and the achievement of petroleum security, shall (1) assist the Secretary in the execution of the President's instructions to: (a) coordinate and unify policy and administration in respect to the functions and activities relative to oil and gas carried on by the several departments and agencies of the Federal Government; (b) serve as the channel of communication between the Federal Government and the petroleum industry; (c) serve as liaison agency of the Federal Government in its relations with the appropriate state oil and gas bodies; (d) review technological developments in the field of petroleum and synthetic and hydrocarbon fuels and coordinate Federal policy with respect thereto. (2) obtain and analyze information as to oil and gas matters in which the Federal Government has a proper interest and, in this connection, serve as the central Federal clearing house for statistics, technical data, and other information relating to oil and gas. (3) keep the Secretary informed with respect to the adequacy and availability of supplies of petroleum and its products to meet the current and future needs of the nation, and with respect to significant developments in the petroleum field, and make recommendations with respect thereto. (4) develop proposals looking to the centralization of Federal functions and activities relating to oil and gas in keeping with the President's letter. (5) coordinate all oil and gas policies and activities in the Department of the Interior."

During the war period various voluntary plans put into effect through the PIWC had been exempted from attack under the anti-trust laws by obtaining approval in advance from the Department of Justice. To achieve similar immunity for the proposed peace time industry council, the Secretary on May 24, 1946 wrote to Attorney General Clark announcing that he proposed to establish a National Petroleum Council to provide a "competent, responsible, and representative body through which the vast abilities and experience of the petroleum industry will be conveniently available to advise and consult with me and with the Oil and Gas Division of the Department of the Interior," to compile and analyze all pertinent facts and figures and raise on its own motion any matter relating to the petroleum industry within the purview of the presidential letter of May 3, 1946. It was to employ an administrative staff paid by voluntary contributions from the industry; minutes of its meetings were to be filed with the Oil and Gas Division. In answering this letter the Attorney General referred to public statements made during the war which indicated that the functions of war time industry committees were not violations of the anti-trust laws, and went on to say that "the substance of those statements is equally applicable to industry committees formed after the termination of hostilities." Consultation by any industry committee with the Government had, he said, never been considered a violation of the anti-trust laws. But he warned that "Consultation, of course, does not involve the determination by the Industry Advisory Committee itself of policies or the administration of programs which should be the responsibility of the Government agency. The authority to consult and advise should not be considered as implying that members of such Committees are authorized to get together and reach an agreed position in advance of such consultations. The determination of policies are [sic] the sole responsibility of the Government agencies served by the committee. Of course, membership on the council or on any of the committees cannot be regarded as conferring on the participants any immunity from the anti-trust laws. If apart from the legitimate activities of the council or the committees the members thereof should agree on any private plan or program as a group or take part in any such plan or program, the Department will feel free at all times to invoke, if necessary, the anti-trust laws against participants notwithstanding the fact that some or all of them may have been members of an industrial advisory committee." Further exchanges of letters between the office of the Attorney General and the Interior Department clarified the scope of the activities of the National Petroleum Council, indicating that the Justice Department took the view that specific proposals for investigations must originate with the Oil and Gas Division; and that only after such request by the Government could the industry committee properly undertake the preparation of an advisory report. Further emphasis was laid upon the necessity for complete freedom of expression for the views of all members of the industry through recording and reporting views of individual council members and the maintenance of adequate complaint procedure.

Having received these interpretations limiting the activities of the industry council, the Secretary then appointed an 85 man advisory committee—the National Petroleum Council,[59] whose membership includes the heads of oil companies, trade association representatives, and individual producers, refiners, transporters, and marketers. Through it, masses of statistical and factual information are placed in the hands of the Oil and Gas Division, making possible frequent reports to Congress, such as on the causes of the oil shortage plaguing the country after World War II. Another functional example is its proposal to the Division on January 28, 1948 relating to the current petroleum supply and transportation situation. Under Public Law 295,[60] the Anti-Inflation Act, the council was the first to produce a program looking to the solution of these problems. The terms of that Act[61] provide for immunity from antitrust prosecution where a voluntary allocation and control program is undertaken at the request of and with the approval of the Government agency concerned. Among other proposals, the council suggested that the state regulatory agencies be urged to establish allowables equal to maximum efficient rates in each state east of the Rocky Mountains, that all refineries east of the Rocky Mountains maximize crude runs for 60 days from the date of the proposal, that the industry receive an increased share of steel and other essential materials necessary to an expanding exploration and drilling program, and that allocation of supplies on an equitable basis be achieved through committees composed of competent men familiar with the local oil problems. The portion of the proposal relating to the establishment of local allocation committees was approved by the Interior and Justice Departments and the plan went into effect. On April 15, 1948 a more comprehensive proposal, along similar lines but on a permanent basis, was submitted and is being considered by the Oil and Gas Division.

While it is too early to evaluate the job being done by this new division, no tendency has been shown to centralize all Govern-

[59] REP. SEC'Y. INT. 232 (1946).
[60] 61 STAT. 526 (Dec. 30, 1947).
[61] *Id.* § 2 (c).

mental oil and gas activities. One of the first tasks undertaken by the Division was a comprehensive survey of the functions of all federal agencies concerned with oil and gas matters. Effort was made to determine exactly what each agency did and how it performed. Although curtailed by limited appropriations, the information obtained was put to use in helping the Division attain its goal as a coordinating and unifying agency.

The Division investigates secondary recovery practices. The Bureau of Mines suggested the formation of a committee to explore the latest developments in this field, and the Division arranged for a joint forum with the Interstate Oil Compact Commission at which papers on modern secondary recovery practices were presented. The Division was instrumental in obtaining the formation of a Military Petroleum Advisory Committee, made up of industry experts competent to advise the military on tactical and strategic petroleum problems. The Division intervened in the controversy between the Federal Power Commission and the natural gas industry,[62] and participated in attempts to draft legislation satisfactory to the opposing interests. When the Mineral Leasing Act of 1920 was extensively amended in 1946, the Division consulted with the Bureau of Land Management, the Geological Survey, and the Solicitor's Office in preparing the implementing regulations, and served as a clearing house for complaints against proposed regulations. The bulk of its day to day work load consists of collecting, coordinating, and supplying information on oil matters to agencies of the Government and to Congressional Committees.

[62] Mimeographed report, Oil and Gas Division, *Partial Summary of Advisory and Service Activities from January 1 to August 31, 1947.*

CHAPTER 45

The Contribution of the Federal Judiciary to the Conservation of Oil and Gas

~/~

The contribution of the Federal judiciary to the conservation of oil and gas falls into two main categories: first, with reference to state laws pertaining to conservation, and second, in support of federal legislative efforts. In briefly surveying the activities from a historical viewpoint, emphasis is placed upon the decisions of the Supreme Court, since space limitations preclude discussion of the multitudinous lower federal court decisions.

In the first category the initial case was *Ohio Oil Co. v. Indiana*,[1] which sustained the validity of a state statute prohibiting the blowing of gas to the air for longer periods than two days after the drilling of a producing well. The Supreme Court later [2] referred to this decision as sustaining a statute directed against waste, because it protected the use of all the surface owners and was a true conservation measure. "Its purpose was to secure to the common owners of the gas a proportionate acquisition of it . . . not to take away any right of use or disposition after it had thus become property."

In *Lindsley v. Natural Carbonic Gas Co.*[3] the constitutionality of the New York act prohibiting the extraction of carbonic gas from mineral water strata was upheld largely on the basis of the *Ohio Oil* case, the Court pointing out that the statute involved did not take from surface owners the right to tap the underground resources, but merely regulated the right to conserve the interests of all concerned.

NORTHCUTT ELY, WRITER. (See app. B.)
[1] 177 U.S. 190 (1900).
[2] West v. Kansas Natural Gas Co., 221 U.S. 229 (1911).
[3] 220 U.S. 61 (1911).

Walls v. *Midland Carbon Co.*[4] sustained an injunction against the manufacture of carbon black in violation of a Wyoming statute designed to prevent an extravagant and wasteful use of natural gas. While the decision was held to be within the rule established by the *Ohio Oil* and *Lindsley* cases, the Court stated that the deter-mining consideration was the power of the state to regulate, adjust, and preserve its natural gas resources.

The next case in the Supreme Court involving the validity of state conservation laws was *Bandini Petroleum Co.* v. *Superior Court.*[5] In that case the Court supported the statutory power of the state court to determine what constituted unreasonable wast-age of gas in the production of oil, where the attack was based on a lack of a definite standard of waste and on unlawful delegation of power to the court to legislate upon the subject. The Supreme Court found that the California court, from which appeal was taken, had determined that the statute was a constitutional exer-cise of the state's power to protect correlative rights of surface own-ers. Both the state court and the Supreme Court found it unnec-essary to determine whether a state might constitutionally enact conservation measures under a theory of protecting the public in-trest in the natural resources of the state.

Within a year after the *Bandini* case the Court was called upon to consider the Oklahoma market demand statute attacked in *Champlin Refining Co.* v. *Corporation Commission,*[6] as repugnant to the due process, equal protection, and commerce clauses. Under an order of the Commission, Champlin's production had been re-stricted to about six per cent of·the total available from its wells in the Oklahoma City Field. While recognizing the right of a land owner to drill wells on his own land and to take oil and gas from the pools beneath it, the Supreme Court pointed out that this was subject to the reasonable exercise of the state police power to pre-vent unnecessary loss, destruction, or waste, thus upholding the regulatory sections of the Oklahoma law. But it struck down a part of the statute which made violators of the act subject to having their producing properties placed in the hands of a receiver. This

[4] 254 U.S. 300 (1920).
[5] 284 U.S. 8 (1931).
[6] 286 U.S. 210 (1932).

penal provision was not directed at those who failed to comply with the proration orders of the Commission, but applied to any violator of the Act; thus a producer's property might be placed in receivership if he committed waste under a definition held by the court to be so vague that "men of common intelligence must necessarily guess at its meaning." As a vague and indefinite statute imposing criminal penalties, the clause violated due process of law.

The efforts of the Governor of Texas to control wasteful overproduction in the newly discovered East Texas Field ultimately led to the declaration of martial law to enforce his executive limitation on production at a flat 165 barrels by the Texas National Guard. In *Sterling v. Constantin*[7] the Supreme Court, while approving the right of the state to reasonably regulate unnecessary loss, destruction, and waste, held that there was no military necessity which justified the action of the governor; hence the lower court was correct in granting an injunction. The findings of the trial court were that there was no actual uprising, riot, mob, or dynamiting, but only those occurrences which would normally constitute a breach of the peace.

The line between what a state could and could not do under the guise of conservation was drawn by Justice Brandeis in *Thompson v. Consolidated Gas Utilities Corp.*,[8] a case that struck down a provision of H.B. 266 under which an order was issued by the Texas Commission to make the existing pipe lines available to all natural gas producers in the Panhandle Field. The legislation was labeled a roundabout effort to accomplish that which had been attempted under the Common Purchaser Act of August 12, 1931, which had been held unconstitutional by a federal district court.[9] The scheme rested on defining waste of natural gas as production in excess of transportation or market facilities and empowering the Commission to prorate and regulate daily gas well production to prevent waste. The order of the Commission had the effect of forcing Consolidated, which had constructed a pipe line system to carry its gas to market, to cut back production from its own leases and to make purchases from other producers in order to meet contract

[7] 287 U.S. 378 (1932).
[8] 300 U.S. 55 (1936).
[9] Texoma Natural Gas Co. v. Rail. Comm., 59 F. 2d 750 (W.D. Tex. 1932).

requirements. Because of the geologic structure of the field, there was a general drainage of gas away from the wells connected with the pipe line and toward the unconnected wells. If Consolidated was forced to cut back its production to take gas from the unconnected wells, nothing was gained as far as prevention of waste was concerned; the purported adjustment of correlative rights would be accomplished at the expense of Consolidated losing gas to the unconnected wells through the natural drainage. This was held to be the taking of one man's property and giving it to another.

But the prohibitions of H.B. 266 pertaining to the use of sweet natural gas for the manufacture of carbon black in the Panhandle Field were sustained in *Henderson Company v. Thompson*.[10] Under Section 2 of that Act, which prohibits waste of natural gas, the word waste is defined to include the use of sweet gas for the manufacture of carbon black. The Henderson Company was a producer of sweet gas and had contracts to supply carbon black producers with the residue of sweet gas after stripping operations were completed. It conceded that the supply of sour gas, which is gas containing varying amounts of hydrogen sulphide, was more than adequate to meet the needs of all carbon black producers, but it contended that since there was no market at that time for sweet gas, and since the sweet gas under its land would gradually migrate to the sour wells as the pressure in the sour gas area was reduced, the effect of the legislation was to deprive it of its property without due process of law and to impair the obligation of its contracts. To these contentions the Supreme Court replied that the state police power was broad enough to include the reasonable classification made by the challenged provision. It was satisfied with the conclusion of the trial court that there was "an abundance of factual support for the legislative prohibition against the burning of sweet gas for carbon black."

In 1939 the Oklahoma well spacing statute was inferentially sustained by the Supreme Court in a per curiam opinion in *Patterson v. Stanolind Oil and Gas Co.*[11] The state supreme court was held to have correctly applied "well settled principles" in denying the contentions of the plaintiff under the 14th Amendment, and the

[10] 300 U.S. 258 (1937).
[11] 305 U.S. 376 (1939).

appeal was dismissed for failure to raise a substantial federal question.

A climax in the support of state regulatory schemes by the federal judiciary was reached in *Railroad Commission v. Rowan and Nichols Oil Co.*,[12] when the Supreme Court held that questions of the reasonableness of a proration order were matters for administrative and not judicial judgment. The Railroad Commission had issued an order permitting each well to produce 2.32 per cent of its hourly potential under unrestricted flow conditions. Exceptions were made designed to permit marginal wells to produce up to 20 barrels per day. So great was the number of these wells that the order allocated approximately 385,000 barrels of the daily allowable of 522,000 barrels to them, leaving only 136,000 barrels to be produced from wells of the class operated by the plaintiff. In taking the position that the federal courts should leave the solution of such problems to the expert administrative body, Mr. Justice Frankfurter, apparently wearying of the thorny problems presented by such cases, remarked that "the record is redolent with familiar dogmatic assertions by experts equally confident of contradictory contentions." To him it was plain that the issues were not "for our arbitrament." The Court recognized that the Texas Commission had for years engaged in experimental endeavors designed to devise appropriate formulas for fair allotment of allowable production. Citing cases in which the lower federal courts enjoined certain of these orders, the Court commented such cases were only episodes in the evolution of adjustment in reconciling private interests with the underlying public interest in "such a vital source of energy for our day as oil." The development of these formulas was for the Commission and not the judiciary. "It is not for the Federal Courts to supplant the Commission's judgment even in the face of convincing proof that a different result would have been better."

A further step in support of state conservation laws was *Burford v. Sun Oil Co.*,[13] a case brought in a federal district court on diversity grounds in whch the oil company attacked the validity of an order of the Texas Railroad Commission granting Burford a permit to drill four wells on a small plot of ground adjacent to its East

---

[12] 310 U.S. 573 (1940).
[13] 319 U.S. 315 (1943).

Texas holdings. The Supreme Court found but one question necessary for decision; namely, that assuming the district court had jurisdiction, should it as a matter of sound equitable discretion have declined to exercise that jurisdiction. The Court answered affirmatively. After outlining the nature of an oil field, it concluded that for conservation purposes each field must be operated as a unit. The Federal Government had chosen, "for the present at least," to leave regulatory responsibility to the states. The constitutional power of the state to take appropriate action to protect the industry and the public interest was unquestioned. Attempts to regulate production raised "geological-legal problems of novel nature." Texas delegated its Railroad Commission the primary task of adjusting the diverse interests involved and vested it with broad discretion in administering the law. In cooperation with other oil producing states, the Commission accepted production quotas, translating them into specific amounts for fields and wells. Its judgments were made with "due regard for the factors of full utilization of the oil supply, market demand, and protection of the individual operators, as well as protection of the public interest." Recognizing the importance of the decisions of the Commission both to the state and to the oil operators, Texas established a "system of thorough judicial review by its own state courts." These courts were characterized as "working partners" in the business of creating a regulatory system for the oil industry. Review was concentrated in the courts of one county to avoid intolerable confusion, which might result if review could be had in different state courts of equal dignity. The Supreme Court noted that this very confusion which Texas sought to bypass had arisen as the result of federal equity jurisdiction. "As a practical matter, the Federal courts can make small contribution to the well organized system of regulation and review which the Texas statutes provide." The court divided five to four in the *Burford* case. Mr. Justice Frankfurter, who had written the majority opinion in the *Rowan and Nichols* case, now prepared the dissenting opinion in the *Burford* case. Admitting a long standing personal desire to have Congress abolish diversity jurisdiction, he felt impelled to record his disagreement with what he considered its abrogation by judicial decision. He referred to his opinion in the *Rowan and Nichols* case as a limitation on diversity jurisdiction where it "was not clear from the decisions of the state courts whether such courts might exercise an independent judgment as to what was 'reasonable,' " since a federal court attempting to apply undefined law would be "groping utterly in the dark." Between the *Rowan and Nichols* and the *Burford* cases, Mr. Justice Frankfurter found the law clarified by a series of decisions in the Texas supreme court, and he objected to the majority's position that federal courts as a matter of equitable discretion should stay their hand in reviewing orders of such state regulatory agencies. The result of these two cases has been to decrease attempts to secure federal injunctions against the conservation orders of state regulatory agencies. Thus the Supreme Court seems to be paralleling the Congressional course in leaving conservation matters to the states.

There is no federal counterpart of state regulatory agencies dealing with conservation of oil and gas, hence no Supreme Court cases akin to those sketched in the cases discussed. A possible exception to this is the effort of 1933 in the Petroleum Code, which, though pitched on the commerce power, fell as an invalid delegation of legislative power in *Panama Refining Co. v. Ryan*,[14] the entire framework of the National Industrial Recovery Act being invalidated a few weeks later in the *Schechter*[15] decision on the same grounds. The authority of the Oil and Gas Division of the Department of the Interior over hot oil under the Connally Act[16] remains as a possible exception, but this legislation has not been challenged in the Supreme Court.

In the realm of the public domain and the naval reserves, the Supreme Court supported the congressional policy of maintaining oil reserves in the ground for future navy use by invalidating the leases fraudulently obtained in connection with the Teapot Dome scandals.[17] Further, a conservation policy with respect to oil may

---

[14] 293 U.S. 388 (1935). For a complete discussion of this case through the Federal Courts see *supra* c. 42.

[15] A.L.A. Schechter Poultry Co. v. United States, 295 U.S. 495 (1935).

[16] 49 STAT. 30 (1935), 15 U.S.C.A. § 715 *et seq.* (1940).

[17] See *supra* c. 40 for a discussion of the Mammoth Oil and Pan American cases, dealing with "Teapot Dome" leases.

be implied from the decision in *United States ex rel. McLennan v. Wilbur*,[18] through the holding that leases on the public domain were not a matter of right, but were granted in the discretion of the Secretary of the Interior.

[18] 283 U.S. 414 (1931). See supra c. 40, a.

APPENDICES

APPENDIX A

A Table of State Conservation Agencies, Their Personnel and Location

ALABAMA

THE STATE OIL AND GAS BOARD. Three members appointed by governor. State Geologist serves ex-officio as Oil and Gas Supervisor. University, Alabama.

ARIZONA

STATE LAND COMMISSIONER. Elective office. Phoenix, Arizona.

ARKANSAS

ARKANSAS OIL & GAS COMMISSION. Seven members appointed by the governor. El Dorado, Arkansas.

CALIFORNIA

DEPARTMENT OF NATURAL RESOURCES, DIVISION OF OIL AND GAS. State Oil and Gas Supervisor, Ferry Building, San Francisco 11, California.

COLORADO

COLORADO GAS CONSERVATION COMMISSION. Three members appointed by governor. Denver, Colorado.

FLORIDA

FLORIDA STATE BOARD OF CONSERVATION. The governor, the secretary of state, the state treasurer, superintendent of public instruction, commissioner of agriculture. Elective offices; governor cannot succeed himself. Tallahassee, Florida.

GEORGIA

GEORGIA OIL AND GAS COMMISSION. Three members appointed by governor. Waycross, Georgia.

IDAHO

BUREAU OF MINES AND GEOLOGY. Statute places control of bureau in hands of Dean of Engineering, University of Idaho. Moscow, Idaho.

719

Illinois

DEPARTMENT OF MINES AND MINERALS. Director appointed by governor. Springfield, Illinois.

Indiana

INDIANA DEPARTMENT OF CONSERVATION, OIL AND GAS DIVISION. Four members appointed by a board consisting of the governor, the lieut. governor and state treasurer of Indiana. Indianapolis, Indiana.

Iowa

STATE GEOLOGIST. Des Moines, Iowa.

Kansas

KANSAS STATE CORPORATION COMMISSION. Three members elected. Topeka, Kansas. CONSERVATION DIVISION. Director, Wichita, Kansas.

Kentucky

DEPARTMENT OF MINES AND MINERALS. Six members appointed. Lexington, Kentucky.

Louisiana

COMMISSIONER OF CONSERVATION. Appointed by governor. Baton Rouge, Louisiana.

Michigan

STATE CONSERVATION COMMISSION. Appointed by governor. Lansing, Michigan. MICHIGAN PUBLIC SERVICE COMMISSION. Appointed by governor. Lansing, Michigan, certain jurisdiction over dry natural gas. MICHIGAN OIL ADVISORY BOARD. Six man board named by Director, Department of Conservation—three from independent producers and three from interstate producers. Lansing, Michigan.

Mississippi

MISSISSIPPI STATE OIL AND GAS BOARD. Five members, one appointed by the attorney general, one by the lieut. governor and three by the governor. Jackson, Mississippi.

Missouri

STATE GEOLOGIST. Rolla, Missouri.

Montana

THE STATE BOARD OF RAILROAD COMMISSIONERS. Elective members. Helena, Montana. MONTANA OIL CONSERVATION BOARD. Members appointed by governor. Helena, Montana.

NEBRASKA

STATE GEOLOGIST, DIVISION OF CONSERVATION AND SURVEY. Lincoln, Nebraska.

NEW MEXICO

NEW MEXICO OIL CONSERVATION COMMISSION. Governor, state land commissioner, elected. State geologist, appointed by the governor. Santa Fe, New Mexico.

NEW YORK

No official agency.

NORTH CAROLINA

NORTH CAROLINA DEPARTMENT OF CONSERVATION AND DEVELOPMENT, PETROLEUM DIVISION. Director of the Department of Conservation and Development, the state geologist and three members designated by the governor. Raleigh, North Carolina.

NORTH DAKOTA

NORTH DAKOTA INDUSTRIAL COMMISSION. Governor, attorney general and commissioner of agriculture and labor. Elective. Bismarck, North Dakota.

OHIO

DEPARTMENT OF INDUSTRIAL RELATIONS, DIVISION OF MINES. Director appointed by governor. Columbus, Ohio.

OKLAHOMA

OKLAHOMA CORPORATION COMMISSION. Three elected members. Oklahoma City, Oklahoma.

OREGON

COUNTY INSPECTORS. Appointed by County Courts. Addresses secured from that agency.

PENNSYLVANIA

DEPARTMENT OF INTERNAL AFFAIRS. Harrisburg, Pa.

SOUTH DAKOTA

STATE OIL AND GAS BOARD. The governor, the attorney general, the secretary of state, the state treasurer, the commissioner of school and public lands and the state auditor. Pierre, South Dakota.

TENNESSEE

STATE OIL AND GAS BOARD. The Commissioner of Conservation (selected by the governor), the attorney general (selected by the Supreme Court of Tennessee) and the commissioner of finance and taxation (selected by the governor). Nashville, Tennessee.

TEXAS

RAILROAD COMMISSION OF TEXAS. Three elected officials. Austin, Texas.

UTAH

STATE LAND BOARD. Salt Lake City, Utah.

VIRGINIA

VIRGINIA GEOLOGICAL SURVEY. Charlottesville, Virginia.

WASHINGTON

No general agency. Inquiries might be addressed to Commissioner of Public Lands, Olympia, Washington, regarding state lands.

WEST VIRGINIA

DEPARTMENT OF MINES, OIL AND GAS SECTION. Chief of department appointed by governor with advice of senate. Charleston, West Virginia.

WYOMING

COMMISSIONER OF PUBLIC LANDS. Appointed by governor with advice of senate. Cheyenne, Wyoming.

APPENDIX B

A Listing of the Writers of the Monographs and Their Advisers

The Committee on Special Publications

CHAIRMAN: WALACE HAWKINS. b. 1895. Stamford College, Texas, A.B. 1914, University of Texas, LL.B. 1920. Captain, U.S. Army, World War I. Member, Texas Legislature 1916; Ass't. Att'y. Gen. Texas 1921–24. Private practice of law Houston 1924. Ass't. to Gen. Counsel, Magnolia Petroleum Company, 1925, Vice-President, General Counsel, Magnolia Petroleum Company, since 1939. Author: EL SAL DEL REY (1947).

MEMBER: NORTHCUTT ELY (see Part IV *infra*)

MEMBER: EARL FOSTER. Univ. of Okla., A.B. 1912, LL.B. 1913. General practice of law and City Att'y. Drumright, 1913–16. Co. Att'y. Creek Co. 1917–20. General practice of law Sapulpa 1920–27. Okla. Sup. Ct. Comm. 1927–31. General practice of law Oklahoma City 1931–44. Oil and Gas Conservation Att'y., Corp. Comm. of Okla. 1935–44. Executive Secretary, Interstate Oil Compact Comm. since 1944. Chairman, Legal Committee, Interstate Oil Compact Comm. since 1938. Dist. Gov. Rotary Int. and Chm. Inter. Committee on Constitution and By-Laws.

MEMBER: ROBERT E. HARDWICKE (see TEXAS)

MEMBER: BLAKELY M. MURPHY (see EDITOR)

Editor

BLAKELY M. MURPHY. b. 1914. Univ. of Ark., LL.B. 1939, Univ. of Chicago, LL.M. 1944. General practice of law Stillwater, Okla., 1939–44. Ass't. Prof. of Law, University of Idaho, 1945–46. Vist. Prof. of Law, Univ. of Oklahoma, summer 1946. Assoc. Prof. of Law, Univ. of Tennessee, 1946–47 and Prof. of Law since 1947. Vist. Lecturer in Law, Univ. of Illinois, summer session 1948. Member, Oklahoma Bar Assoc., Bar Assoc. of Tenn., American Bar Assoc. Member, Legal Committee, Interstate Oil Compact Comm. since 1947 and its Executive Secretary since 1948. Member, Drafting Sub-committee, Legal Committee and its Executive Secretary since 1948. Author: The Interstate Compact to Conserve Oil and Gas, An Experiment in Cooperative State Production Control (1946), Tennessee and the Interstate Compact to Connserve Oil and Gas (1947), The Legislative and Administrative Concept of Oil and Gas Conservation in Arkansas, 1917–1947 (1947), The Administrative Mechanism of the Interstate Compact to Conserve Oil and Gas—The Interstate Oil Compact Commission, 1935–1948 (1948), and STATE OIL AND GAS PRODUCTION CONTROL AND CONSERVATION LAWS (1945).

Part I. Fundamentals of Reservoir Behavior That Relate to the Conservation of Oil and Gas

The Committee on Special Publications, Section of Mineral Law, secured the assistance of Dr. John C. Calhoun, Jr., and Dean W. H. Carson, both of the School of Petroleum Engineering, Univ. Okla. in the chapter on petroleum reservoirs. Dr. Calhoun prepared for the Committee's use a paper dealing with the topics there covered. This paper was read by Dr. H. H. Kaveler, Ass't. to Vice-Pres., Phillips Petroleum Co., Bartlesville, Okla.; L. E. Elkins, Chief Eng., Stanolind Oil and Gas Co., Tulsa, Okla., Prof. N. van Wingen, Dept. of Pet. Eng., Univ. Okla., Norman, Gorden H. Fisher, Chief Pet. Eng., Gulf Oil Corp., Ft. Worth, Texas, and suggestions as to its correctness were made. Thereafter the Committee undertook to prepare the material based upon this monograph. The chapter, as written, is the work of the Committee and for it that body accepts full responsibility as to its correctness and accuracy. The Committee wishes to express its sense of gratitude to Dr. Calhoun and the persons above named, also to Jack Tarner and R. M. Williams of the Phillips Petroleum Company, who made suggestions.

Part II. Legislative, Administrative and Judicial Concepts of Oil and Gas Conservation as Applied Within the Jurisdictions of the States

ALABAMA

THOMAS A. JOHNSTON III. b. 1916. Univ. of Ala., LL.B. 1938. General practice of law in Mobile since 1938 firm of Howell and Johnston. Member, House of Representatives, Legislature of Alabama since 1942, where secured passage of comprehensive conservation law. Member, Mobile Co. Bar Assoc., Ala. Bar Assoc., and American Bar Assoc.

Advisers

Dr. Walter B. Jones, State Geologist, Tuscaloosa, Zack Rogers, Jr., Butler and Douglas Arant, Birmingham.

ARIZONA

CHARLES H. WOODS. b. 1876. Ohio St. Univ. LL.B. 1900. Admitted to practice Ohio, 1900, Oklahoma 1900, Illinois 1918, United States Supreme Court 1924. Ass't. Att'y. Gen. Oklahoma 1901–04. General practice in Oklahoma 1904–18. Ass't. to Gen. Counsel, General Attorney and General Solicitor, A. T. and S. F. Ry. 1918–46. Lecturer in law, Univ. of Ariz. since 1946, State Delegate, House of Delegates, American Bar Assoc. since 1948.

Advisers

Fred Blair Townsend, Phoenix. J. Early Craig.

ARKANSAS

W. HENRY RECTOR. b. 1884. Educated in Univ. of Arkansas. Admitted to practice Arkansas 1905. One time Ass't. United States Att'y., Eastern District Ark., and Ass't. Att'y. Gen. Arkansas. General practice of law Little Rock, Ark. with firm of Armistead, Rector and Armistead. Member, Little Rock Bar Assoc., the Bar Assoc. of Ark., and the American Bar Assoc.

Advisers

O. C. Bailey, Chm. Ark. Oil and Gas Comm. and Lester F. Danforth, Chief Engineer, Ark. Oil and Gas Comm., El Dorado, Arkansas.

CALIFORNIA

WILLIAM L. HOLLOWAY. b. 1903. Univ. of Michigan, A.B. 1924, J.D. 1926. Admitted to practice California 1926. Member firm of Morrison, Hohfeld, Foerster, Shuman and Clark, San Francisco, general counsel for Honolulu Oil Corporation. Actively participated in presentation of testimony for oil industry before congressional committee incident to enactment of Act of August 8, 1946, first comprehensive revision of the Federal Mineral Leasing Act since 1920. Member, Bar Assoc. of San Francisco, the State Bar of Calif., American Bar Assoc., A.P.I. and I.P.A.A. (Associate).

Advisers

J. Howard Marshall, Ashland, Kentucky, T. C. Monroney, San Francisco, William Scully, Los Angeles and Mortimer Kline, Los Angeles.

COLORADO

WARWICK M. DOWNING. b. 1875. Univ. of Michigan LL.B. 1903. Attorney Denver. Member, Denver Park Board ten years. Member and Chm. Mountain Parks Commission of Commercial Bodies of Denver nine years. Member, Denver Playground Commission. Official Rep.

for Colo., Interstate Oil Compact Comm. since 1935 and one of its founders. Member, Legal Committee, Interstate Oil Compact Comm., Chm. Public Lands Committee, First Vice-Chm. of the Commission. Chm. Colorado Gas Conservation Comm.

Advisers

F. M. Van Tuyl, Golden, Roy C. MacGinnis, Colo. Gas Comm., and Lawrence Hinkley, Att'y. Gen. Colo., both of Denver.

FLORIDA

D. WALLACE FIELDS. b. 1910. John B. Stetson Univ. LL.B. 1933. Member firm of Mabry, Reaves, Carlton, Anderson, Fields and Ward of Tampa and Tallahassee. Member Florida Bar Assoc.

Advisers

Herman Gunter, State Geologist, Julius Parker and Frank Bezoni, all of Tallahassee.

GEORGIA

ROYAL ALFRED McGRAW. b. 1892. d. 1948. Mercer Law School. Admitted to practice in Georgia 1913. Attorney Greenville. Member Georgia Legislature, 1935, 1937 and 1938. Ass't. Att'y. Gen. Georgia 1943 to 1948.

Advisers

George M. Bazemore, Chm. Ga. Oil and Gas Comm., C. W. Deming, Director, Ga. Oil and Gas Comm., Vance Custer, Pres. Ga. Bar Assoc., Bainbridge, and Liston Elkins.

IDAHO

BLAKELY M. MURPHY. (See EDITOR)

ILLINOIS

W. L. SUMMERS. b. 1888. Indiana Univ. A.B., LL.B. 1911, Yale Law School, Jur.D. 1912. General practice of law Gary, Ind. 1912–16. Prof. of Law, Univ. of Fla. 1915–18. Prof. of Law, Univ. of Kentucky, 1918–20. Prof. of Law, Univ. of Ill. since 1920. Legal research in oil, gas and sulphur, Humble Oil and Refining Co. 1929–30, and Texas Gulf Sulphur Co. Legal consultant Texas Gulf Sulphur Co. 1930–38. Ass't. Chief Counsel, PAW, and Head, Compliance Division, 1943. Legal staff Shell Oil Co. 1943–45. Adviser, Restatement Law of Property, vol. 5. Drafted model conservation act for Illinois. Author: THE LAW OF OIL AND GAS (2d ed. 1938) and numerous legal articles.

Mr. Summers acknowledges with appreciation the use of technical information in the publications and files of the Illinois State Geo. Survey.

INDIANA

AQUILLA W. GROVES. Dep. Att'y. Gen. St. of Ind. Counsel, Ind. Dept. Conservation. State Fuel Coordinator Ind. Educated Wabash College, A.B., Indiana University School of Law LL.B. Member, Ind. Bar Assoc.

Advisers

A. C. Colby, Ass't. State Geologist, Indianapolis.

IOWA

BLAKELY M. MURPHY. (See EDITOR)

KANSAS

JAY C. KYLE. Gen. Counsel, Corp. Comm. of Kan. Instructor, Washburn Univ. Law School. Army of the United States, 1942–46, Legal Division, Office of Chief Signal Officer. Formerly Ass't. Att'y. Gen. Kan. Admitted to practice in Kansas, United States District, Circuit Court of Appeals and the Supreme Court.

Advisers

Andrew F. Schoeppel, George Stallwitz, T. A. Morgan and Ennis D. Harris, all of Wichita.

KENTUCKY

GEORGE W. HAZLETT. b. 1897. Denison Univ. A.B., 1919. Western Reserve Univ. LL.B. 1925. Served in the United States Army 1917–19. General practice of law in Cleveland since 1925. Member firm of McAfee, Grossman, Taplin, Hanning, Newcomer and Hazlett, Cleveland. Member, Legal Committee, Interstate Oil Compact Comm. for Ky. since 1944.

Advisers

Martin J. Holbrook, Owensboro, and Daniel J. Jones, State Geologist, Lexington.

LOUISIANA

E. LELAND RICHARDSON. b. 1904. George Washington Univ. Georgetown Univ. LL.B. 1930. Spec. Ass't. Att'y. Gen. La. 1934–41. Gen. Counsel, Dept. of Rev. La. 1939–41. General practice of law with Dale, Richardson and Dale, Vidalia and Baton Rouge, since 1941. Member, Bar of La., Dist. Columbia Bar.

MICHIGAN

FLOYD A. CALVERT. b. 1889. Formerly County Judge and State Senator, Nowata Co., Okla. General practice of law specializing in oil and gas

Nowata to 1926. Attorney for Pure Oil Company, Tulsa, 1926 to 1932 and in Michigan since 1932. Taught oil and gas law, Univ. of Okla. Extension Division, Tulsa, 1931–32. Past Chm. Section of Mineral Law, American Bar Assoc. Past Pres. and Life Director, Oil and Gas Assoc. of Mich. Member, Saginaw Co., Michigan, Oklahoma and American Bar Assoc. Author chapter on Michigan, LEGAL HISTORY OF CONSERVATION OF OIL AND GAS 1938.

Advisers

Burke Shartel, Ann Arbor, Virgil W. McClintic, Mt. Pleasant. Mearle D. Mason, Baxter Springs, Kansas, student of University of Michigan Law School verified material and did research.

MISSISSIPPI

EDWARD L. BRUNINI. Georgetown Univ. B.A. 1931. Univ. of Miss. LL.B. 1934. Member firm of Brunini, Brunini and Everett, Jackson and Vicksburg. Co-editor, MISSISSIPPI ANNOTATIONS TO THE RESTATEMENT CONFLICT OF LAWS (1934). Chm. Miss., Jr. Bar Conference, American Bar Assoc. 1938. Vice-Pres. Miss. State Bar Assoc. 1941. State Chm. Committee of Admissions, American Bar Assoc. 1947. Chm. Legal Committee, Miss.-Ala. Div., Mid-Continent Oil and Gas Assoc. 1947. Member, Committee for the Improvement of the Administration of Justice, American Bar Assoc. 1947. Member, Vicksburg, Miss. and American Bar Assoc.

Advisers

H. M. Morse, State Oil and Gas Sup., W. H. Watkins and Greek L. Rice, Att'y. Gen. of Miss., all of Jackson.

MISSOURI

BLAKELY M. MURPHY. (See EDITOR)

MONTANA

E. K. CHEADLE. b. 1895. Educated New York Univ. LL.B. 1921. Member firm of Donovan, Cheadle and Donovan, Shelby; now attorney practicing in Helena. Lieut. F. A. World War I, Lt. Col. 41st Inf. Div. 1940–44, serving two years in the S.W. Pacific World War II. Assoc. Justice, Montana Supreme Court 1944–46.

Advisers

J. E. Hupp, Cut Bank; G. S. Frary, Cut Bank; R. P. Jackson, Sec. Mont. Oil Conservation Bd., Great Falls, whose invaluable assistance in preparation of the article the writer acknowledges.

Nebraska

Archibald J. Weaver. b. 1906. Univ. of Mich. A.B. 1929, J.D. 1929. General practice of law Kansas City, Missouri 1929–1932, Falls City since 1932.

Adviser

John H. Wiltse, Falls City.

New Mexico

Rosser Lynn Malone, Jr. b. 1910. Educated Washington & Lee Univ. LL.B. 1932. Lieut. (jg), Lieut. and Lt.-Comm. United States Naval Reserve. Chm. New Mexico Junior Bar Conference 1939–40. Member, House of Delegates, American Bar Assoc. since 1946. Member, Legal Committee, Interstate Oil Compact Comm. since 1947. Admitted to practice in New Mexico. General practice of law with firm of Atwood, Malone and Campbell, Roswell.

Advisers

H. M. Dow, Roswell and J. O. Seth, Santa Fe.

New York

William A. Dougherty. b. 1895. Ohio St. Univ. A.B. 1917, J.D. 1920. Associate and then partner in firm of Tolles, Hogsett, Ginn & Morley (later Tolles, Hogsett & Ginn) Cleveland 1920–1933. Spec. Ass't. to Att'y. Gen. of Ohio handling liquidation of the Guardian Trust Co., Cleveland 1933. Member Law Department, Standard Oil Company (New Jersey) New York handling oil and gas matters and regulation and production of natural gas companies 1933–43. Natural gas practice 1943 to date. Member, Ohio Bar Assoc., The Assoc. of the Bar of the City of New York, New York Co. Lawyers Assoc. and the American Bar Assoc. Chm. Mineral Section, American Bar Assoc. 1944–46.

Assisted by James Lawrence White.

North Carolina

Blakely M. Murphy. (See Editor)

North Dakota

Gordon V. Cox. b. 1897. Univ. of Mich. LL.B. 1919. Tax att'y State Tax. Comm. 1919–23. General practice of law with O'Hare and Cox 1924, now Cox, Cox, and Pearce, Bismarck. Served three terms N.D. Legis. 1927–33. Chm. Committee on Judiciary. Extensive oil and gas practice with Standard Oil Company, Magnolia Petroleum Company and others. Member of N.D. Bar and American Bar Assoc.

Advisers

The writer wishes to especially acknowledge the research of Ray R. Friedrich and Maurice E. Garrison, senior law students at the University of North Dakota Law School done under the direction of Dean O. H. Thormodsgard, an adviser. Nels G. Johnson, Alex C. Burr, both of Bismarck.

Ohio

WILLIAM A. McAFEE. b. 1890, Claverack, New York. B.A., Yale Univ. 1911; LL.B., Harvard Univ. Law School 1915; Phi Beta Kappa; Editor, Harvard Law Review; member law firm McAfee, Grossman, Taplin, Hanning, Newcomer & Hazlett, 1500 Midland Building, Cleveland, Ohio; Director and General Counsel, The Standard Oil Company (Ohio); President Ajax Pipe Line Corporation.

Advisers

A. M. Gee, Findlay, C. C. Hogg, Marietta. Fred J. Milligan, Columbus.

Oklahoma

T. MURRAY ROBINSON. b. 1903. Univ. of Okla. B.S. 1923, Harvard Univ. Law School LL.B. 1926. Admitted to practice Okla. 1927. General practice of law with Rainey, Flynn, Green and Anderson, Oklahoma City, 1926–28, Edwards and Robinson, 1928–40 and now Robinson, Shipp, Robertson and Bogess. Att'y. for Roy J. Turner, Governor of Oklahoma since 1932. Represents numerous independent oil producers and operators. Active part in various capacities with Interstate Oil Compact Comm. since 1942 and member of Legal Committee since 1946. Member Okla. Bar Assoc.

Assisted by: Robert A. McCracken as to gas conservation; Floyd Green as to Corporation Commission, and Barret Galloway in assembling the material.

Advisers

Earl Foster, Oklahoma City. W. P. Z. German, Tulsa.

Oregon

BLAKELY M. MURPHY. (See EDITOR)

Pennsylvania

JAMES B. SAYERS. Penn. State College A.B. 1922, Univ. of Penn. LL.B. 1925. Gen. Counsel, The Peoples Nat. Gas Co., Pittsburgh. Member, Legal Committee, Interstate Oil Compact Comm., Committee on Nat. Gas, Section of Mineral Law, American Bar Assoc., Penn. Bar and American Bar Assoc.

Advisers

Don T. Andrus, Bradford. Wolfe and Wolfe, Bradford.

SOUTH DAKOTA

ROY E. WILLY. b. 1889. Univ. of Mich. LL.B. 1912. Admitted to practice Mich. and S.D. 1912. Spec. Counsel State Banking Dept. of S.D. 1925–27. Pres. State Bar of S.D. 1938–39. Member House of Delegates, American Bar Assoc. since 1936. Private practice of law Sioux Falls.

Advisers

Karl Goldsmith, Pierre. M. A. Sharpe, Kennebec. E. P. Rothrock, Vermilion.

TENNESSEE

BLAKELY M. MURPHY. (See EDITOR)

Advisers

H. B. Burwell, State Geologist, Nashville. Paul S. Mathes, Chattanooga.

TEXAS

ROBERT E. HARDWICKE. V.M.I., Univ. Tex. LL.B. 1911. Ass't. Chief Counsel, later Chief Counsel, Petroleum Administration for War, 1943–46. Member, Legal Committee, Interstate Oil Compact Comm. since 1935. Author: INNOCENT PURCHASER OF OIL AND GAS LEASE (1921), PETROLEUM AND NATURAL GAS BIBLIOGRAPHY (1937), LEGAL HISTORY OF CONSERVATION OF OIL AND GAS—TEXAS, A SYMPOSIUM (1938), ch. 3. SECONDARY RECOVERY OF OIL IN THE UNITED STATES (1942). Evolution of Casinghead Gas Law (1929), Penalties as Affected by Good Faith Legislation (1934), The Rule of Capture and Its Implications as Applied to Oil and Gas (1935), Legal History and Practical Operation of Conservation of Oil, etc. Part IV, Hearings Before Subcommittee of the Committee of Interstate and Foreign Commerce, H.R. 76th Cong. 3d Sess. on H. Res. 290 and H. Res. 7372, 1466 (1940), Oil Conservation Statutes, Administration, and Court Review (1941) and The Constitution and the Continental Shelf (1948). Member firm of Hardwicke and Hardwicke, Fort Worth, Texas.

Advisers

Elton M. Hyder, Jr., A. W. Walker, Jr. both of Austin. While Messrs. Walker and Hyder acted not only as advisers but also collected much of the material used in the article, it should be stressed that the writer takes full responsibility for what is said and what is not said.

UTAH

HENRY D. MOYLE. b. 1889. Univ. Freiberg, Univ. Utah B.S.; Harvard Law School, Univ. of Chi., J.D. Ass't. United States Att'y. and United States Att'y. for number of years Salt Lake City. Private practice of law to 1947. Member, Council of Twelve, Church of Jesus Christ of Latter-Day Saints since 1947. Member, Petroleum Ind. Council, Chm. Refining, District Four Rocky Mountain Area, during World War II. Member, Bd. of Dir., A.P.I. and Pres. Wasatch Oil Co., Deseret Livestock Co. and others.

Advisers

David L. McKay, Salt Lake City.

WASHINGTON

BLAKELY M. MURPHY. (See EDITOR)

WEST VIRGINIA

KEMBLE WHITE. b. 1873. Educated Trinity Hall, Washington, Pa., Linsley Institute, Wheeling, W.Va., West Va. Univ. A.B. 1894, LL.B. 1900. Served in the Spanish-American War as Captain, 2d W.Va. Inf. Began practice of law at Fairmont, W.Va. Member firm of White, McCue and Garrett, Clarksburg, now retired from active practice and now consulting counsel. Member, Committee to Cooperate with Legislative Committee to Codify Laws of W.Va., 1927–1930, W.Va. State Constitutional Comm. 1929. President, W.Va. State Bar Assoc. 1924–25. Member, American Bar Assoc., W.Va. State Bar Assoc., Phi Sigma Kappa Fraternity. Counsel in W.Va. for oil, gas, pipe line and affiliated interest of former subsidiaries of the Standard Oil Company.

Advisers

Arthur B. Koontz, H. J. Wagner, Charleston. Paul H. Price, Morgantown.

WYOMING

W. H. EVERETT. b. 1907. Univ. of Denver LL.B. 1931. Admitted to practice in Texas 1933, Wyoming 1942. Licensed to practice before United States District Courts for Western District of Texas and the District of Wyoming; United States Circuit Court of Appeals, Fifth and Tenth Circuits, United States Supreme Court, Treasury Department and the Department of the Interior. Practiced with Goeth, Webb and Goeth, Texas, 1933–39, alone in San Antonio 1939–41. Division Att'y. Casper Division, Ohio Oil Co. since 1942.

Advisers

Pierre La Fleiche, Casper. Associate Editor, Ernest Wilkerson, Casper.

VIRGINIA

THOMAS JOHNSON MICHIE. b. 1896. Univ. Va. B.A. 1917, M.A. 1920, LL.B. 1921. Lt. AC World War I. Member firm Allen, Walsh & Michie, Charlottesville, 1921–26. Member Legal Department Koppers Co., Pittsburgh, 1926–1942 as senior member and chief counsel 1937–1942. Major, Lt. Col. AC 1942–46 principally in AMG Italy. Member firm Michie & Fishburne, Charlottesville since 1946. Lecturer on Public Utilities, Univ. Va. Law School. Member, Charlottesville, Va. State and American Bar Assoc. Chm. Mineral Section, American Bar Assoc. 1935–36.

Advisers

William M. McGill, Charlottesville.

Part III. The Interstate Compact to Conserve Oil and Gas, and Its Administrative Arm, The Interstate Oil Compact Commission

BLAKELY M. MURPHY. (See EDITOR)

Advisers

Earl Foster, E. O. Thompson. Especial credit is given Warwick M. Downing for his graciousness in supplying much information in c. 37, 38.

Part IV. The National Government and the Conservation of Oil and Gas

NORTHCUTT ELY. b. 1903. Stanford Univ. B.A. 1924, LL.B. 1926. Exec. Ass't. Sec. Int. 1929–1933. Chm. Technical and Advisory Committee, Federal Oil Conservation Bd. 1931–33. Represented Governor Ernest W. Marland in negotiations concerning the Interstate Compact to Conserve Oil and Gas 1935. Author: OIL CONSERVATION THROUGH INTERSTATE AGREEMENT (1933), THE OIL AND GAS CONSERVATION STATUTES ANNOTATED (1933) and various papers on oil conservation. General practice of law Washington, D.C., and California.

Mr. Ely wishes to express his appreciation for the assistance of his associates Philip M. Fairbanks, and Robert W. Culbert. Various portions of the manuscript were reviewed unofficially by members of governmental agencies. An acknowledgment of this courtesy appears as a footnote to the section reviewed.

APPENDIX C

An Interstate Compact to Conserve Oil and Gas [1]

ARTICLE I

This Agreement shall be effective as between the several States producing oil and gas which join herein as of the several dates of their execution hereof under the direction of their respective Legislatures, or as of the effective date of an Act of Congress consenting to this compact, whichever is last in occurrence.

ARTICLE II

The sole purpose of this compact is to conserve oil and gas by the prevention of physical waste thereof.

ARTICLE III

Each State bound hereby agrees that at or before the time of approval by it of this compact, it will enact statutes, or if statutes have been enacted, then it agrees to continue the same in force to accomplish within reasonable limits the prevention of physical waste of oil and gas. Without excluding physical waste in any form, for the purposes of this compact waste is defined to be:

(a) The operation of any oil well with an inefficient gas-oil ratio.
(b) The drowning with water of any stratum capable of producing oil or gas, or both oil and gas in paying quantities.
(c) The avoidable escape into the open air or the wasteful burning of gas in a natural gas well.
(d) The creation of unnecessary fire hazards.
(e) The drilling, equipping, locating, spacing or operating of a well or wells so as to bring about physical waste of oil or gas or loss in the ultimate recovery thereof.
(f) The inefficient, excessive or improper use of the reservoir energy in producing any well.

[1] This copy of the Allred compact was furnished the writer from the personal files of the Honorable James V. Allred of Houston and is an exact copy of the agreement offered by him at the organizing meeting in Dallas.

(g) The open storage of oil or the avoidable loss and destruction thereof after the same reaches the surface.

Article IV

Each State bound hereby agrees that at or before the time of approval by it of this compact it will enact statutes, or if such statutes have been enacted then that it will continue the same in force, providing in effect that oil produced in violation of the provisions of the statutes provided for in Article III shall be denied access to commerce; and providing for stringent penalties for the waste of either oil or gas.

Article V

This compact does not authorize the States joining herein to limit the production of oil or gas for the purpose of stabilizing or fixing the price thereof, or for the purpose of balancing supply and demand, or to create or perpetuate monopoly, or to promote regimentation, but is limited to the sole purpose of conserving oil and gas and preventing the avoidable waste thereof within reasonable limitations.

Article VI

Each State joining shall appoint one representative to a board hereby constituted and designated as the Oil States Conservation Board, the duty of which board shall be to make inquiry and ascertain from time to time such improved methods as may be disclosed for bringing about conservation and the prevention of physical waste of oil and gas, and at such intervals as said board deems beneficial it shall report its findings and recommendations to the several States for adoption or rejection. Said board shall organize and adopt suitable rules and regulations for the conduct of its business, but in all meetings of said board and in the conduct of all business thereof, the vote of each representative shall count in the decimal proportion which the potential production of his State bears to the total potential production of all States bound by this compact, a majority of the decimal percentage representing the total potential production of all said States to control.

Article VII

No State by joining herein shall become financially obligated to any other State, nor shall the breach of the terms hereof by any State subject such State to financial responsibility to the other States joining herein.

Article VIII

This compact shall expire on June 1, 1937, and any State joining herein may, upon sixty (60) days notice, withdraw herefrom.

This writing shall be executed in one original, which together with supporting authorization of the representative executing for each several

State, shall be deposited in the office of the Secretary of State of the United States, at Washington, D.C.

Conservation of the American Oil Supply [2]

The States of [here were to be inserted the names of the compacting oil States] having resolved to enter into an agreement pursuant to Section 10, of Article 1, of the Constitution of the United States, subject to the consent of the Congress of the United States, have caused representatives to be duly appointed, who have agreed upon the following articles:

1. Purposes. By this compact certain of the oil producing states, recognizing that regulation by the State is essential to the conservation of oil and gas, undertake voluntarily to coordinate the exercise of the police power within their several jurisdictions to promote the maximum ultimate recovery from the petroleum reserves of the Nation.

2. The Interstate Oil Conference. There is hereby established a cooperative fact finding agency designated as the Interstate Oil Conference. It shall consist of one representative of each state party to this agreement, appointed by the governor thereof or in such other manner as such State may provide. The Conference shall meet at least quarterly on March 10, June 10, September 10, and December 10, at such places as it may fix, or oftener upon the call of the Governors of three or more compacting states. The conference shall prescribe its by-laws, and procedure, and elect its officers, and perform the duties prescribed by this agreement.

3. Duties of the Conference. The Conference is authorized and directed: 1. to make findings, quarterly, or oftener, of the quantity of oil currently required for consumption within the United States, and for export; to receive and consider data which the regulatory agency of each compacting state may furnish as to the rate at which oil may be produced in such state, without waste; and to recommend to each compacting state the relative part of the total demand for domestic production which may be produced without waste in such state. 2. To draft measures for the maximum ultimate recovery of oil and gas, which it shall recommend for consideration by the legislatures of the several compacting states. 3. To receive from the several compacting states data on refinery runs and shipments of gasoline and other products of petroleum taxed by them, and to publish such data for the mutual assistance of the states in checking tax evasions. 4. To draft and recommend uniform taxation measures. 5. To cooperate in fact-finding activities with such Federal agencies as the Congress may authorize.

4. Action by the States. Each of the compacting States agrees that:

1. Prior to each convening of the Interstate Oil Conference, the State shall cause to be held such hearing or other proceedings as may

[2] The Marland proposal.

be required by its local law as a prerequisite to a determination of the quantity of oil that may be produced under its laws without waste. The data so assembled, together with such recommendations as the State Conservation Agency may submit, shall be laid before the Conference.

2. It will receive and consider the findings and recommendations of the Conference with regard to the requirements for oil production and the quantity which the Conference finds may be produced in each State without waste, and will give such effect to the recommendations of the Conference thereon as may be consistent with the powers and duties of the local conservation agency under the laws of the State.

3. It will designate a qualified member of the Conference, procure his attendance therein, pay his expenses, and contribute equally with the other compacting states to the general expenses of the Conference in an amount not to exceed.............................. Dollars annually from each State.

5. Action by the United States. Control and limitation of importations of oil and products thereof is essential to the preservation of production from certain areas within the United States. The Congress is requested to effect limitations of imports in such a manner that the total thereof does not exceed the equivalent of........per cent. of the total demand for consumption within the United States and for export as found by the Conference.

6. Effective Date; New Parties. This agreement may become effective within any compacting State at any time as prescribed by that State, and shall become effective within those states ratifying it whenever any three of the States of Texas, Oklahoma, California, Kansas and New Mexico have ratified and Congress has given its consent. Any oil producing State may become a party hereto by ratification hereof and notification to the other States which are parties at that time.

7. Termination or Suspension. Any State may withdraw from this agreement upon written notice to the then parties, in which event the compact shall remain in force as to the other parties. This agreement may be terminated at any time by the consent of the majority of the States then parties to it, and may be terminated in such other manner as Congress may prescribe.

8. This agreement rests upon the comity of the Sovereign parties and upon their voluntary cooperation. No State shall be subject to suit in court on account of any provision which may be contained herein; no provision of this compact shall be enforced within any State except by its own Government.

9. Commerce. Nothing in this agreement shall impair the power which any State may have to regulate commerce in oil and gas within its bor-

ders nor with the power of the United States to regulate commerce with foreign nations and among the several states.

10. Signatures. The representatives of the signatory states have signed this agreement in a single original which shall be deposited in the archives of the Department of State of the United States, and duly certified copy shall be forwarded to the Governor of each of the signatory states. Signature on behalf of any State hereafter becoming a party hereto may be affixed to a counterpart to be similarly deposited and certified.

Done in the City of Dallas, this the . . . . day of February, 1935.

An Interstate Compact to Conserve Oil and Gas [3]

Article I

This agreement may become effective within any compacting state at any time as prescribed by that state, and shall become effective within those states ratifying it whenever any three of the States of Texas, Oklahoma, California, Kansas and New Mexico have ratified and Congress has given its consent. Any oil producing state may become a party hereto as hereinafter provided.

Article II

The purpose of this Compact is to conserve oil and gas by the prevention of physical waste thereof from any cause.

Article III

Each state bound hereby agrees that within a reasonable time it will enact laws, or if laws have been enacted, then it agrees to continue the same in force, to accomplish within reasonable limits the prevention of:

(a) The operation of any oil well with an inefficient gas-oil ratio.
(b) The drowning with water of any stratum capable of producing oil or gas or both oil and gas in paying quantities.
(c) The avoidable escape into the open air or the wasteful burning of gas from a natural gas well.
(d) The creation of unnecessary fire hazards.
(e) The drilling, equipping, locating, spacing or operating of a well or wells so as to bring about physical waste of oil or gas or loss in the ultimate recovery thereof.
(f) The inefficient, excessive or improper use of the reservoir energy in producing any well.

The enumeration of the foregoing subjects shall not limit the scope of the authority of any state.

[3] This is an official copy of the Compact as taken from the Commission records and is the compromise compact of the Downing Committee.

ARTICLE IV

Each state bound hereby agrees that it will, within a reasonable time enact statutes, or if such statutes have been enacted, then it will continue the same in force, providing in effect that oil produced in violation of its valid oil and/or gas conservation statutes or any valid rule, order or regulation promulgated thereunder, shall be denied accesss to commerce; and providing for stringent penalties for the waste of either oil or gas.

ARTICLE V

It is not the purpose of this Compact to authorize the states joining herein to limit the production of oil or gas for the purpose of stabilizing or fixing the price thereof, or create or perpetuate monopoly, or to promote regimentation, but is limited to the purpose of conserving oil and gas and preventing the avoidable waste thereof within reasonable limitations.

ARTICLE VI

Each State joining herein shall appoint one representative to a commission hereby constituted and designated as the Interstate Oil Compact Commission, the duty of which Commission shall be to make inquiry and ascertain from time to time such methods, practices, circumstances and conditions as may be disclosed for bringing about conservation and the prevention of physical waste of oil and gas, and at such intervals as said Commission deems beneficial it shall report its findings and recommendations to the several states for adoption or rejection.

The Commission shall have power to recommend the coordination of the exercise of the police power of the several states within their several jurisdictions to promote the maximum ultimate recovery from the petroleum reserves of said states, and to recommend measures for the maximum ultimate recovery of oil and gas. Said Commission shall organize and adopt suitable rules and regulations for the conduct of its business.

No action shall be taken by the Commission except: (1) By the affirmative votes of the majority of the whole number of the compacting states, represented at any meeting, and (2) by a concurring vote of a majority in interest of the compacting states at said meeting, such interest to be determined as follows: Such vote of each state shall be in the decimal proportion fixed by the ratio of its daily average production during the preceding calendar half-year to the daily average production of the compacting states during said period.

ARTICLE VII

No state by joining herein shall become financially obligated to any other state, nor shall the breach of the terms hereof by any state subject such state to financial responsibility to the other states joining herein.

Article VIII

This Compact shall expire September 1, 1937. But any State joining herein may, upon sixty (60) days' notice, withdraw herefrom.

The representatives of the signatory states have signed this agreement in a single original which shall be deposited in the archives of the Department of State of the United States, and a duly certified copy shall be forwarded to the Governor of each of the signatory states.

This Compact shall become effective when ratified and approved as provided in Article I. Any oil producing state may become a party hereto by affixing its signature to a counterpart to be similarly deposited, certified and ratified.

Done in the City of Dallas, Texas, this sixteenth day of February, 1935.

APPENDIX D

By-Laws of the Commission

━━

In order to perform the functions and duties provided by the Interstate Compact to Conserve Oil and Gas, the following by-laws are adopted for the conduct of the business of the Commission.

ARTICLE I
The Commission

Section 1. The Commission shall be designated "The Interstate Oil Compact Commission" and will be referred to herein as "The Commission." The Interstate Compact to Conserve Oil and Gas will be referred to herein as "The Compact." The states which have ratified and executed the Compact, or which may hereafter ratify and execute the same, will be referred to as "the Compacting States."

Section 2. The Commission shall be composed of one representative from each compacting state, to be selected as the state may determine.

Section 3. The Commission shall be a fact finding and deliberative body and shall exercise the powers and perform the duties provided in the Compact. It shall conduct studies such as to ascertain methods, practices, and conditions for bringing about conservation and the prevention of physical waste of oil and gas and to promote wide acceptance and use of the best conservation practices. It shall, from time to time, report its findings and make recommendations to the several states for adoption or rejection.

Section 4. The Commission shall have an official seal, the same to be prescribed and determined by the Executive Committee. The Executive Secretary shall be the sole custodian of the seal. The Commission's official actions shall be taken in accordance with these by-laws and the Compact. The verity of such actions shall be established by the certificate of its Chairman, attested by its Executive Secretary, under the seal of the Commission.

ARTICLE II
Meetings

Section 1. Regular meetings of the Commission shall be held quarterly at such time and place as the Commission shall determine.

Section 2. Special meetings of the Commission may be called by the Chairman or by a majority of the Commission.

Section 3. Notice in writing by the Executive Secretary of the time and place of each regular meeting of the Commission shall be mailed to each member not later than ten (10) days prior to the date of the meeting. Notices of special meetings shall be given by the Executive Secretary as the Chairman shall direct.

Section 4. Notices of the time and place of any meeting of the Commission may be waived in writing or by telegram by its members.

ARTICLE III
Rules and Procedure

Section 1. The majority of the members of the Commission shall constitute a quorum at any meeting. Any number less than a quorum may adjourn the meeting from time to time.

Section 2. All actions taken by the Commission at any meeting shall be by the affirmative vote of the majority in number and interest of the Compacting States represented and present as provided by the Compact. The report of the Bureau of Mines shall be prima facie evidence of the daily average production of the Compacting States. The Commission may consider other evidence.

Section 3. Except as otherwise provided by the by-laws and the Compact, all meetings of the Commission shall be conducted in accordance with general parliamentary rules.

Section 4. Each compacting state shall deposit with the Executive Secretary of the Commission its official certificate and designation of its representative to whom notices of all meetings shall be given and to whom official communications shall be transmitted.

ARTICLE IV
Officers

Section 1. The officers of the Commission shall consist of a Chairman, First Vice-Chairman, Second Vice-Chairman, each of whom must be a member of the Commission, and an Executive Secretary and such other officers as the Commission may deem necessary, who shall not be required to be members of the Commission. The officers shall be elected by the Commission at the last quarterly meeting held in each year and shall hold office for a period of one year and until their successors are elected and have assumed office.

Section 2. The Executive Secretary and such other officers as may be created shall be elected by the Commission at the last regular meeting of the year, and shall hold office at the pleasure of the Commission or the Executive Committee, and need not be members of the Commission.

Section 3. The Chairman shall preside at all meetings, call and provide for notices of meetings, and otherwise perform the duties customarily performed by the chairman of a deliberative body. The First Vice-Chairman shall perform the duties of the Chairman in the absence of the Chairman, and the Second Vice-Chairman shall act in the absence of the First Vice-Chairman.

Section 4. The Executive Secretary shall make, or cause to be made, a record of the proceedings of the Commission and Executive Committee and shall preserve the same in the Headquarters Office. He shall give notices of meetings, and shall be responsible for carrying out the policy, orders, and directives of the Commission and of the Executive Committee, and shall make recommendations on program, policy, and activities of the Commission, and he shall have general supervision, under the direction of the Commission and Executive Committee, of all the Commission's programs and activities. He shall have immediate charge of the Headquarters Office and personnel.

ARTICLE V
Committees

Section 1. An Executive Committee, consisting of representatives from seven Compacting States, shall be elected at the last regular meeting of each year, immediately following the election of officers. The chairman of the Commission shall be a member of the Executive Committee and shall be its chairman. A majority of the committee shall constitute a quorum. The committee shall have such power and perform such duties in the conduct of the business of the Commission as the Commission shall from time to time by resolution provide. Any member of the Commission present at any Executive Committee meeting shall have the same power, authority, and responsibility as an elected committee member.

Section 2. A By-Laws Committee, consisting of three members of the Commission, shall be appointed by the Chairman of the Commission to study and make recommendations as to amendments of the by-laws.

Section 3. A Resolutions Committee shall be appointed by the Chairman of the Commission, consisting of members of the Commission, to serve at each regular meeting, at such time and as the Chairman may determine.

Section 4. The Chairman, with the consent and approval of the Commission or Executive Committee, shall appoint such other committees as may be deemed necessary to fully and effectively conduct the business of the Commission and carry out the purposes and functions of the Compact.

Section 5. All non-profit oil and gas associations organized for the purpose of advancing the interest of the oil and gas industry in the United States, or any section, state, or subdivision thereof, are invited to designate an advisory committee to the Commission, which shall be approved by the Commission or the Executive Committee. Said advisory committees shall be invited to participate in all proceedings of the Commission and enter into the discussions, but shall have no official vote.

ARTICLE VI
Headquarters Office

Section 1. A Headquarters Office shall be established by the Commission at such place as it may determine, in which the administrative work of the Commission shall be carried on, and in which the official files and records of the Commission shall be kept.

Section 2. There shall be kept in the Headquarters Office reports of all committees, together with legal, statistical, engineering, and other information that may be helpful in an oil and gas conservation program, the extent of such information to be determined by the Commission.

Section 3. All records in the Headquarters Office shall be open to the public at all reasonable hours.

ARTICLE VII
Finances

Section 1. The expense of this Commission shall be paid from voluntary contributions made by oil or gas producing states, in the manner and to the extent they may provide.

Section 2. The Executive Committee shall prepare and submit to the Commission each year an estimate of the expense of the Commission for the coming year.

ARTICLE VIII
Federal Representation

Section 1. The President of the United States, the Congress, and any federal agency charged with responsibility concerning oil and gas, are invited to designate one or more representatives of the Federal Government to attend and participate in the meetings of the Commission. Such representatives shall be privileged to be present at all open and executive sessions, and to participate in the deliberation and studies of the Commission, and to make recommendations concerning the policies, program, and work of the Commission, but shall have no vote.

ARTICLE IX
Membership

Section 1. Any oil or gas producing state is entitled to become a regular member of the Commission by executing the Compact in the manner provided therein.

Section 2. There is hereby established associate membership in the Commission. Any state having prospects for oil or gas production may become an associate member in the following manner: Any such state may make an application to the Commission in writing, signed by the

Governor of the State or by the agency in charge of the regulation of oil and gas, with the approval of the Governor. Said application shall state in substance that the state has prospects for oil and gas and is vitally interested in the program of the Interstate Compact to Conserve Oil and Gas, and desires to participate in the Commission's activities, to which application there shall be attached a copy of the Interstate Compact to Conserve Oil and Gas. Said application shall be presented at regular meeting of the Commission, and such state may be admitted to associate membership by a resolution which must have the affirmative vote of all member states present at such meeting. An associate member state shall not have the right to vote or hold office, but shall be entitled to all other privileges and benefits of regular membership. It shall be permitted to participate in all Commission meetings, committee meetings, and other activities of the Compact, but shall assume no responsibilities except those which the state voluntarily assumes, and may withdraw as an associate member at any time by filing written notice thereof, signed by the Governor or by the regulatory authority having charge of its oil and gas affairs, with the approval of the Governor.

Article X
Amendment to By-Laws

Section 1. These by-laws may be altered and amended at any regular meeting upon affirmative vote of the Commission, as herein provided.

Index

~~

A.L.A. *Schecter Poultry Corp. v. United States*, 632, 642, 652, 715.
ALABAMA, Acts of 1911, 19; Acts of 1939, 20; 1945 legislation, 21; discovery well in, 19; State Oil and Gas Board of, 20–22; joins Interstate Compact to Conserve Oil and Gas, 22–21; waste in, 22 n. 8; rules and regulations governing conservation in, 22; judicial decisions and review, 22. See generally 89, 473, 473 n. 53, 571 n. 1, 574 n. 7, 719.
Alaska, 43, 622.
Alston v. Southern Prod. Co., Inc. 244.
Amazon Pet. Corp. v. Railroad Comm., 694.
American Petroleum Institute, 56 n. 1, 551, 552, 554, 558, 559, 566, 633, 641, 686, 700.
Anderson Field, 313.
Anderson-Prichard Oil Co., 244.
Anti-trust law, 334, 459, 460, 471, 604, 630–636, 668–9, 685, 687, 706.
ARIZONA, Acts of 1927, 23–26, 29–30; Acts of 1939, 23, 29–30; Revised Code of 1928, 27–28, 30; State Land Commissioner of, 25–27, 29–31, 719; discoveries of oil and gas in, 23–24; rules and regulations in, 25–26, 29–30, 30 n. 19; judicial review in, 27–29, 30. See generally 43, 332, 473 n. 53, 574 n. 7, 616.
ARKANSAS, Act 105 of 1939, 32–37; Act 302, 34; Arkansas Oil and Gas Commission, 33, 35–39, 719; illegal oil, gas and product in, 33–34; enforcement of law in, 39; waste in, 33 n. 6; membership in Interstate Compact to Conserve Oil and Gas, 34; administration of law, 35–37; judicial functions and review in, 38. See generally 21, 53, 56, 69, 86, 96, 104, 164, 473, 473 n. 53, 540, 545, 548, 557 n. 3, 561, 563, 571 n. 1, 574 n. 7, 583, 619.

Arkansas Oil and Gas Commission, 33–39, 719; composition of, 35, administration of, 35–37, rules and regulations of, 36–37.
Atkinson bill, 41–42, 528.

Bandini Pet. Co. v. Superior Court, 47, 710.
Bay Pet. Co. v. Corporation Comm. of Kansas, 143.
Bennett v. Corporation Comm., 152.
Bernstein case, 52, 54.
Brunini, Edward L., 283, 728.
Burford v. Sun Oil Co., 713–5.
Burtton Field, 140.
Byrd case, 493.

CALIFORNIA, Conservation Committee in, 45–46; gas conservation act in, 47; State Oil and Gas Supervisor of, 49, 50, 52, 719; town lot drilling act in, 50–52; daily production in, 55; judicial review in, 47–49, 50–54; Atkinson bill referendum on, 41–42, 528. See generally, 156, 473, 517, 531, 545, 548, 556, 557, 559, 561, 563, 564, 569, 622, 623, 625, 633, 634, 645, 647–651, 673, 675, 676, 701 n. 50, 703, 710.
California Co. v. State Oil and Gas Bd., 295–6.
Calvert, Floyd A., 250, 727–8.
Campbell Pool, 142.
Capper bill, 549.
Carbice Corp. v. American Pat. Develop. Corp., 633.
Carbon black, Illinois, 118; Kansas, 179, 183; Louisiana, 203; Michigan, 280; Mississippi, 288, 294; Montana, 301, 305; New Mexico, 331; West Virginia, 525; Wyoming, 534.
Carter Oil Company, 383.
Cat Creek Pool, 300.

Champlain Ref. Co. v. Corporation Comm., 135, 552, 638, 710.
Cheadle, E. K., 300, 728.
Cities Service Oil Company, 384–6, 406–8.
Coalinga Nose Field, 41.
Cole Committee, 42, 482, 559, 564, 567.
COLORADO, Acts of 1915, 58; Acts of 1927, 58; Acts of 1929, 59; legislative proposals in 1935 and 1943, 60; first field in, 56; Gas Conservation Commission, 58–61, 719; judicial review in, 62; rules and regulations in, 59; membership in Interstate Compact to Conserve Oil and Gas, 59–60. See generally 332, 545, 548, 552, 556 n. 1, 570, 571 n. 1, 574 n. 7, 605, 606, 702.
Connally Hot Oil Act, 270, 466, 645, 696–99; contributions of, 699.
Continental Oil Company, 57, 58, 382, 383, 551.
Coolidge, Calvin, 550, 681, 682, 691, 704.
Corzelius v. Harrell, 455, 497–500.
Corzelius v. Railroad Comm., 487–8.
Cox, Gordon, 347, 729.
Crichton v. Lee, 246.
Croxton v. State, 381–2, 383, 388.

Danciger Oil and Ref. Company, 382, 469 n. 45.
Davis v. Iroquois Gas Corp., 341.
Davon Oil Company, 382.
Debeque Field, 57.
Denver Prod. and Ref. Co. v. State, 375, 380, 393.
Dillon v. Holcomb, 244.
Disney-Thomas bill, 558, 570.
Disposal of salt water in Arkansas, 36; in Florida, 77; in Illinois 118, 120; in Kansas, 183–185, 188–190; in Louisiana, 218 n. 38, 288; in Michigan, 278; in Mississippi, 288; in Montana, 301; in New Mexico, 319; in North Dakota, 356; in Oklahoma, 414–6; in Oregon, 423; in Texas, 474–477. See generally 79, 185–6, 218.
Dixie Greyhound Lines, Inc. v. Mississippi Pub. Ser. Comm., 296.
Dougherty, William A., 336, 729.
Dowling v. Lancanshire Ins. Co., 88.
Downing, Warwick M., 56, 725–6.
Drake Well, 426–7.
Drumheller bill, 305.

East Texas Field, generally at 20, 476 n. 57, 490–491, 493–494, 500, 508, 509, 595, 602, 692, 694; rule 37 in, 489, 490, 508.
Elliff v. Texon Co., 455.
Ely, Northcutt, 599, 630, 656, 664, 681, 709, 723, 733.
Energies, properties of reservoir, 1 ff.
Ethyl Gasoline Corp. v. United States, 632.
Everett, W. H., 529, 732.

Federal Mineral Leasing Act of 1920, generally 26, 49, 531, 533, 535, 599–602, 606, 616, 624, 625, 627, 665, 708; amendments to, 609–11; extension of act to acquired lands, 611–612.
Federal Natural Gas Act, see generally at 483 n. 64, 653–5; Louisiana and, 225 n. 55, 229, 230.
Federal Oil Conservation Board, generally at 547, 552, 636, 646, 647, 650, 656, 681–91, 701, 704; report I, 682–4; report II, 684; report III, 684–6; report IV, 688–9; report V, 689; termination of activity, 691.
Federal Power Commission, 224–7, 228 n. 61, 233, 482–3, 580 n. 20, 587 n. 36, 653–5.
Federal Tender Board No. 1 v. Haynes Oil Corp., 698.
Fields, D. Wallace, 64, 726.
Fischer v. Magnolia Pet. Co., 149–152.
Five Civilized Tribes, 393–4, 615, 617–19, 621.
Florence Field, 56–7.
FLORIDA, early attempts at legislation in, 64–7; first discovery of oil in, 67; present law in, 69, 70–5, 76–8; west coast cities of, 70–2; State Board of Conservation, 76–9, 719; rules and regulations in, 76, 78; judicial review in, 81; relations with Interstate Compact to Conserve Oil and Gas, 68, 70, 75, 574 n. 7; waste in, 76 n. 22, 77; right to bring suit in, 80. See generally 89, 469 n. 45, 473, 473 n. 53, 571 n. 1.
Florida State Oil and Gas Board, subpoena powers, 79; punishment by, 79. Generally see 76–9, 719.
Fluids, nature of reservoir, 1 ff.
Fort Collins Field, 57.
Foster, Earl, 576 n. 11, 580, 723.

Gas-oil ratios, in reservoirs, 11, 12; Illinois, 101; Michigan, 279; Mississippi, 287; Montana, 304, 324, 330; North Dakota, 356 n. 32; Oklahoma, 377–380; Texas, 466.

GEORGIA, 1923 legislative proposal, 83–4; Georgia Oil and Gas Comm., 86–9, 719; administration of law, 86–7; judicial review and appeal, 87–88; H. B. No. 284, 86; relations with Interstate Compact to Conserve Oil and Gas, 89, 547 n. 7; generally see 53, 127, 473, 473 n. 53.

Georgia Oil and Gas Commission, 86–9, 719; rules and regulations of, 86–9.

Globe Oil and Refining Company, 389.

Great Britain, 659–661, 678.

Greasewood Field, 57.

Grison Oil Corp. v. Corporation Comm., 375–6.

Griswold v. President of United States, 698.

Gross v. Rothrock, 144–5.

Groves, Aquilla W., 123, 727.

Gulf Oil Corporation, 324.

Gwinville Field, 285, 296.

Hall v. Philadephia Co., 524.

Harbert v. Hope Nat. Gas Co., 524.

Harding, Warren G., 624, 626.

Hardwicke, Robert E., 447, 723, 731.

Hardy v. Union Prod. Co., 240–1.

Hawaii, 43.

Hawkins v. Texas Co., 509.

Hawkins, Walace, introduction xv–xvii, 723.

Hazlett, George W., 191, 727.

Henderson Co. v. Thompson, 712.

Hepburn Act, 636, 639.

Hobbs Field, 324–5, 335.

Holloway, William L., 40, 725.

Hood v. Southern Prod. Co., 239–40.

Hoover, Herbert, 42, 547, 549, 550, 602–3, 606, 683.

Hugoton Gas Field, in Kansas, 138, 165, 166, 167, 169, 173–5, 181–3; in Oklahoma, 384, 403–6, 408.

Hunter Co. Inc. v. McHugh, 237–8, 276.

Hunter Inc. v. Shell Oil Co., 247.

Hurley v. Federal Tender Bd. No. 1, 698.

Ickes, Harold L., 42, 103 n. 47, 112–3, 556, 558, 566 n. 32, 643, 647, 660, 667, 669, 670, 679, 691.

Ickes v. Virginia-Colorado Development Corp., 607.

IDAHO, 1931 Act, 90; administrative agency in, 719.

Illegal oil, gas or product, defined 33 n. 7, 8, 9; in Arkansas, 33; in Florida, 79; interstate transportation of, 692; in Louisiana, 210–11; in Michigan, 270 n. 37; in Mississippi, 293, 297; in Texas, 465.

ILLINOIS, discovery of oil in, 92; 1905 Act, 92–3; H. B. 365, 108–9; oil and gas act, 112–19; rules and regulations in, 114 n. 90, 119; waste in, 101–2; 110, 121; administrative set up in, 119, 720; appeal in, 121; relationships with and implementation of Interstate Compact to Conserve Oil and Gas, 94–5, 103, 105, 122, 574 n. 7; production of oil and gas in, 92, 104, 108. See generally 32, 53, 56, 156, 165, 473, 473 n. 53, 551, 556 n. 1, 561, 563, 571 n. 1, 573 n. 6, 574 n. 7, 675.

INDIANA, discoveries in, 123; Oil and Gas Commission of, 127–30, 132; rules and regulations in, 132; administrative set up, 131–32, 720; Interstate Compact to Conserve Oil and Gas in, 126–7, 132, 574 n. 7. See generally 32, 165, 473, 473 n. 53, 571 n. 1.

Indiana Oil and Gas Commission, 127–30, 132; rules and regulations of, 132; administrative set up, 131–32, 720.

Internal Revenue Act, 656; Code, 658.

International Petroleum Comm., 660–2.

INTERSTATE COMPACT TO CONSERVE OIL AND GAS, Oil States Advisory Committee, 545–55; formation of, 556–70; Compact Commission, 571–97; Alabama, 22; Arkansas, 34; Colorado, 59–60; Florida, 68, 70, 75; Georgia, 89; Illinois, 94, 95, 103, 105, 122; Indiana, 126–7, n. 33; Kansas, 160, 190; Kentucky, 195, 198; Mississippi, 290; Missouri, 299; Montana, 304, 308; New Mexico, 335; New York, 338–9; Ohio, 367–8; Oklahoma, 422; Pennsylvania, 427, 432; Tennessee, 445; Texas, 451, 468 n. 44, 650; West Virginia, 523, 528; Wyoming, 539.

See generally 532, 673 n. 13, 681, 684, 685 n. 13, 687, 689–90, 700, 708.
INTERSTATE OIL COMPACT COMMISSION, finances, 574; committees, 580; meetings, 578 n. 18. See Interstate Compact to Conserve Oil and Gas *supra.*
IOWA, Acts of 1939, 136–7, 720.

Jackson Gas Field, 298.
Johnson, Thomas A. III, 19, 724.

KANSAS, discoveries of oil and gas in, 138, 166; gas statute, 139–40; production in, 153, 156–7; statute of frauds in, 146–7; abandonment of wells in, 187; pollution of fresh water, 188; rules and regulations in, 178, 187–8; judicial review in, 141–152; oil conservation act in, 154–5, 176; State Board of Health, 185–6; State Corporation Commission, 720; Interstate Compact to Conserve Oil and Gas, 160, 190, 574 n. 7. See generally 103, 104, 397, 469 n. 45, 545, 548, 550–1, 553, 556, 559–65, 568, 569, 570, 571 n. 1, 588, 619, 647, 649, 650.
Kansas State Corporation Commission, 720.
KENTUCKY, discoveries in, 191; 1892 act, 192–3; 1932 act, 193–4; 1936 act, 194, 1948 act, 196; Interstate Compact to Conserve Oil and Gas, 195; spacing in, 195–6; production in, 196–7. See generally 473, 571 n. 1, 720.
Kettleman Hills Field, 602; unit operation of, 603–5.
Konowa case, 452–3, 487.
Kraker v. Railroad Comm., 494.
Krug, Julius, 62, 198, 703.
Kyle, Jay C., 138, 727.

Langlie Field, 325.
Larsen case, 50–53.
Legal Committee, Interstate Compact to Conserve Oil and Gas, 60, 69, 130, 350, 422 n. 134, 473 n. 52–53, 582–4.
Lindsley v. Natural Carbonic Gas Co., 342 n. 32, 709–10.
Locke v. United States, 652.
Loco Hills Field, 313, 325, 330–1.
LOUISIANA, Act 157 of 1940, 199–211; Commissioner, 199, 211–12, 220–1,

223, 720; well allowables in, 216 n. 33; natural gas in, 224–7; judicial decisions in, 227–246, 634–6; rules and regulations in, 204, 216 n. 33, 217 n. 34, 211, 219–20; Interstate Compact to Conserve Oil and Gas and membership in, 200, 574 n. 7. See generally 39, 53, 104, 469 n. 45, 473 n. 53, 545, 548, 556, 557, 559, 561, 562 n. 18, 563, 571 n. 1, 649, 697, 699.
Louisiana Commissioner of Conservation, 199; see Louisiana *supra.*

Magnolia Petroleum Company, 389–90, 473.
Maljamar Field, 325, 331.
Malone, Rosser Lynn Jr., 312, 729.
Manufacturers' Gas and Oil Co. v. Indiana, 124.
Marland bill, 692–3, 560, 562.
Margold proposal, 558.
Marrs v. Railroad Comm., 458, 505, 509.
McAfee, William A., 359, 730.
McCrae v. Bradley Oil Co., 145.
McCurdy v. United States, 619.
McGraw, Royal Alfred, 83, 726.
McHugh, Comm. of Con. v. Placid Oil Co., 245.
Memphis case, 227–31, n. 65.
Michie, Thomas Johnson, 515, 733.
MICHIGAN, production in, 250 n. 2; 1937 gas conservation law, 250–6; 1939 oil conservation law, 255, 262–6; rules and regulations of Public Service Commission, 258–62; administration of laws in, 262, 263–4, 720; judicial decisions, 272, 274; rules and regulations of Supervisor of Wells, 265 n. 31, 271, 277; appeal in, 280. See generally 53, 156, 165, 195, 271, 469 n. 45, 557 n. 3; 559, 571 n. 1, 574 n. 7; 643, 645, 647, 649–50.
Michigan Con. Gas Co. v. Sohio, 259.
Mid-Continent Oil and Gas Assoc., 33, 85, 384, 397.
Minnelusa Oil Corp. v. Continental Pipe Line Co., 639.
Minnesota, 165.
MISSISSIPPI, discoveries in, 283; production in, 283; oil and gas board, 284–5, 287, 289 ff, 720; composition of agency, 290–91; rules and regulations in, 291–4, 297; judicial review in,

295; relationship with the Interstate Compact to Conserve Oil and Gas, 290. See generally 41, 53, 56, 89, 571 n. 1.

Mississippi State Oil and Gas Board, 284–5, 287, 289 ff, 720; rules and regulations of, 291–4, 297; composition of, 290–1.

Missouri, 166, 299, 407, 631, 702.

Montana, discoveries in, 300; production in, 300; Railroad Commission of, 303, 306, 308, 720; Oil Conservation Board of, 302, 303, 306–7; Interstate Compact to Conserve Oil and Gas and, 308, 547 n. 7; judicial history in, 308–9; rules and regulations in, 302, 306–8; administration of law, 306–7; State Board of Land Commissioners 303, 4. See generally 57, 348, 473, 539, 557 n. 3, 571 n. 1, 573 n. 6, 574 n. 7, 616, 621.

Montana Oil Conservation Board, 302, 303, 306–7. See Montana *supra*.

Montana Railroad Commission, 303, 306, 308, 720. See Montana *supra*.

Monument Field, 317, 324–5, 334.

Moore v. Barry, 366.

Moyle, Henry D., 513, 732.

Murphy, Blakely M., xi–xiv, 90, 136, 299, 345, 423, 443, 517, 545, 556, 571, 723–4.

National Government and Conservation, public domain, 599–613; Mineral Leasing Act of 1920, 599–602; Hoover Policy of, 602–3; unitization, 603–4; reopening of public domain, 605, oil shale reserves, 605–07, amendments to mineral leasing acts, 607–12; regulations of, 612–614; Indian lands of, 614, 622; leasing of Indian lands, 614–17; tribal leasing, 617–622; naval petroleum reserves, 622–29; interstate commerce and the, 630–655; anti-trust and, 630–636; petroleum code, 640–652; national gas act, 652–5; foreign commerce, 656–63; world war I, 664–5; world war II, 666 ff; Office of Petroleum Coordination for Defense, 667 ff; Petroleum Administration for War, 669–80; Federal Oil Conservation Board, 681–91; hot oil legislation, 691–99; Bureau of Mines, 699–703; Oil and Gas Division, 705–8; federal court actions, 709–16.

Natural Gas Company, 124, 134.

Nebraska, 166; discovery wells in, 310; generally 473; administrative agency, 721.

New Mexico, oil and gas conservation act, 312, 314–7; production in, 312; ratable purchase of oil statute, 312–3; Lea County Operators Committee, 313–4, 322–3, 333; conservation commission, 320–2, 327–30, 721; orders of the commission, 317–8, 330–32; Interstate Compact to Conserve Oil and Gas, 335, 574 n. 7; proration units in, 324; commission procedure, 327–8. See generally 21, 32, 53, 94–5, 104, 164, 195, 251, 469 n. 45, 473, 545, 548, 557 n. 3, 559, 561, 563–4, 565, 569–71, 581, 650, 699.

New Mexico Oil and Gas Commission, 320–2, 327–30, 721; orders, 317–8, 330–32; procedure, 327–8.

New York, discovery in, 336; 1941 law, 337–8; Interstate Compact to Conserve Oil and Gas, 388–9, 547 n. 7; production in, 343–4; administration of law, 341; judicial decisions in, 341–2. See generally 28–9, 336, 344, 433, 549, 571 n. 1, 574 n. 7, 664, 721.

Nira, Chicago draft of code, 641; petroleum code, 642, 657; litigation concerning, 651–52; Petroleum Administrative Board, 644–6, 648–9, 657; planning and coordination committee, 645, 647–8. See generally 302 n. 7, 557 n. 3, 558, 631, 632, 640–52, 701.

North Carolina, oil and gas act, 345–6; agency, 721. See generally, 473.

North Dakota, production in, 347; discovery in, 347; present laws, 350–2; Interstate Compact to Conserve Oil and Gas, 350–1, 353; Uniform Administrative Practices Act, 353; Industrial Commission of, 353–4, 721; rules and regulations in, 351, 354–5; administration, 353. See generally, 473.

North Dakota Industrial Commission, 353–4, 721; rules and regulations of, 351; administration by, 353.

Ohio, discovery wells, 359; production in, 359–60; Interstate Compact to Conserve Oil and Gas, 367–8; Acts of

1883, 360; judicial decisions, 366–7; administration of law, 366, 721. See generally 166, 433, 545, 548, 556 n. 1, 557 n. 3, 571 n. 1, 638.

Ohio Oil Co. v. Indiana, 125, 134, 342, 709–10.

Ohio Oil Co. v. Kennedy, 246.

Oil and Gas Division, Dep't. Int., 57; established, 697; generally 703–8, 715.

OIL STATES ADVISORY COMMITTEE, 545–55, 60, 649.

OKLAHOMA, proration in, 373–77; gas-oil ratios in, 377–380; Oklahoma City Field, 378; West Cement Medrano Field, 378–9; West Edmond Field, 379; well spacing in, 380–90, 713; compulsory unit operation, 394–403; administrative background, 416–21; Interstate Compact to Conserve Oil and Gas, 422, 580; rules and regulations in, 409 n. 98, 411–15, 419; administrative set up, 418, 721; judicial review in, 375–6; 380–83, 393, 710, 713. See generally 39, 53, 95, 104, 154, 155, 156, 164, 165, 175, 182, 251, 469 n. 45, 473, 545, 548, 549, 550, 552, 556–7, 559–61, 563–5, 567–70, 571 n. 1, 574 n. 7, 616, 647, 649, 674 n. 15, 691–2, 696, 701 n. 50.

Oklahoma City Field, 378, 394–7, 399, 551, 692, 694, 710.

O'Meara v. Union Oil Co. of Calif., 248–9.

OREGON, 43, 423, 517, 721.

Otis Field, 140.

Paint Creek Uplift Field, 194.

Panama Ref. Co. v. Ryan, 632, 651, 694–6, 715.

Panhandle Eastern Pipe Line Company, 167, 169, 256 n. 12, 404, 631.

Patterson v. Stanolind Oil and Gas Co., 380–3, 390, 712.

Peerless Oil and Gas Company, 406.

Pennsylvania Grade Crude Oil Association, 437.

PENNSYLVANIA, Drake well, 425–7, Interstate Compact to Conserve Oil and Gas, 427 432, 574 n. 7; production in, 428; well plugging statutes in, 431–2; oil conservation act, 434; migratory fuel control law proposed, 434–5; administrative agency, 721.

See generally 191, 336, 359, 425, 556 n. 1, 557 n. 3, 571 n. 1, 638, 702.

People v. Associated Oil Co., 47.

People v. Wood-Callahan, 48.

Petroleum Administrative Board, 644–6, 648–9, 657. See NIRA supra.

Petroleum Administration for War, district committees, 671–2; operations of, 672–3; maximum rates fixed by, 673–4; spacing under, 674–5; in California, 675–6; prices and royalty rates under, 676; natural gas, 677; foreign operations of, 678; termination of activity, 680. See generally 43–5, 47, 49, 256, 267, 268, 462, 478–9, 666–7, 669–80, 702, 704.

Petroleum Code, 302, 307, 642–45; supplemental codes, 643, 649. See NIRA supra.

Petroleum Rail Shippers' Assoc. v. Alton and Southern R. R., 639.

Peppers Ref. Co. v. Corporation Comm., 375–6.

Phillips Petroleum Company, 162, 384, 394, 551, 639.

Pipe lines, federal control of, 636; international, 679–80; Kansas, 155–7, 165, 168–9; Louisiana, 229–30 n. 62, 231 n. 65; Michigan, 258–9, 261; monopoly in, 633–37; New Mexico, 313, 326–7; Oklahoma, 404–6; Pennsylvania, 430; Texas, 640 n. 41, 641. See generally 167–9, 170–1, 711.

Pipe Line cases, 636–7.

Pittsburgh and West Va. Gas Co. v. Richardson, 524.

Placid Oil Co. v. North Central Texas Oil Co., Inc., 241–3.

Plugging and abandonment of wells, Indiana, 130; Iowa, 136; Kansas, 187–8; Louisiana, 219 n. 41; Mississippi, 294; Ohio, 365; Oklahoma, 412–3; Oregon, 423; Pennsylvania, 431–2; Tennessee, 444; Utah, 513.

Public lands, Arizona, 27; Michigan, 276, 281; Montana, 300; New Mexico, 332; South Dakota, 440–1; Wyoming, 532; federal lands, 599–600. See generally 130, 592, 683–4.

Pure Oil Company, 99, 103–4, 277 n. 54, 279, 256 n. 12.

Railroad Comm. v. Continental Oil Co., 495–6.

Railroad Comm. v. Marrs, 495–6, 499, 503.
Railroad Comm. v. Rowan and Nichols, 499–502, 713, 715.
Railroad Comm. v. Shell Oil Company, 482, 486–7, 511.
Rangely Field, 57, 61, 514, 532.
Reconstruction Finance Corp., 47, 659.
Rector, W. Henry, 32, 725.
Republic Natural Gas Company, 167, 406.
RESERVOIRS, nature of energies and fluids, 1.
Rhode Island, 556 n. 1.
Richardson, E. Leland, 198, 727.
Riffel v. Dieter, 147.
Robinson, T. Murray, 369, 730.
Robinson v. Jones, 146.
Roosevelt, Franklin Delano, 42, 554, 556, 570, 641, 643, 646–7, 691, 693.

Salt Creek Field, 530–1.
Santa Fe Springs Field, 52.
Socony-Vacuum Oil Company, 631.
Sayers, James B., 425, 730.
Scottish Union v. Phoenix Title and Trust Co., 27–29.
Sharkey bill, 41–42.
Shell Oil Company, 550, 551 n. 17.
Sinclair Consolidated Oil Company, 160, 162, 626.
Six Lakes Field, 254, 6.
Skelly Oil Company, 163, 557 n. 3.
Smith Pet. Co. v. Van Mourik, 274–5.
SOUTH DAKOTA, discovery of petroleum, 439–40; legislation in, 440–42; rules and regulations, 442; administrative agency, 441, 721. See generally 439, 473.
Spacing, well, Kentucky, 195–6; Michigan, 255; New Mexico, 318; North Dakota, 356; Oklahoma, 380–90, 419; Texas, 478–81, 490, 494–5; Petroleum Administration for War, 674, 677. See generally 14, 78, 116, 122, 128 n. 40, 179, 255, 277.
Square Lakes Field, 313.
Standard Oil Company of California, 627–9.
Standard Oil Company of Indiana, 551 n. 17, 630.
Standard Oil Company of New Jersey, 630, 634.

Standard Oil Co. of N.J. v. United States, 630–1.
Standard Oil Company of New York, 631.
Standard Oil Company, 636.
Stanolind Oil and Gas Company, 324.
State Corp. Comm. of Kan. v. Wall, 141–3.
State ex. rel Wisc. Insp. Bureau v. Whitman, 28.
State Oil and Gas Bd. v. Superior Oil Co., 295.
State v. Ohio Oil Co., 125, 134.
Sterling v. Constantin, 711.
Summers, Walter Lee, 92, 726.
Sun Oil Company, 279, 554 n. 35, 681.
Synthetic Fuels Act of 1944, 702.

Teapot Dome, 531, 622–3, 624, 625–6.
TENNESSEE, discovery of oil, 443–4; Interstate Oil Compact Commission, 445, 573 n. 6; waste defined, 445 n. 16; rules and regulations in, 446; judicial review in, 446; State Oil and Gas Board, 445, 721–22. See generally 227, 443, 571 n. 1.
Tennessee State Oil and Gas Board, 445, 721–22.
TEXAS, production in, 448–50; legislative history in, 450–61; extension of conservation statute, 450–1; Interstate Compact to Conserve Oil and Gas in, 451, 574 n. 7; revision of marginal well law, 451–3; natural gas statutes, 453–55; unit operations in, 459–61, 470–4; Railroad Commission of Texas, 461–82, 698; waste, 467, 469–70; judicial decisions in, 486–511; administration of law, 461–3, 722; rules and regulations, 467 n. 42; court review in, 458–9. See generally 53, 95, 104, 146, 154, 164, 175, 182, 327, 332, 367, 447, 548–51, 554, 571 n. 1, 556–70, 572, 577–8, 638, 663, 674 n. 15, 669, 691, 693–4, 696–7, 701 n. 50.
Thomas v. Stanolind Oil and Gas Company, 505, 509.
Thompson v. Consolidated Gas Util. Corp., 454, 456, 458–9, 711.
Thompson v. Spear, 699.
Tinsley Field, 284.
Townsend v. the State, 125, 133.
Trapp v. Shell Oil Co., 458–9, 505, 509–11.

Tri-State Transport Co. v. Gulf Transport Co., 296–7.
Truman, Harry S., 680, 697, 704–5.

United Nations, 578, 662.
United States Bureau of Mines, 26–8, 30, 55 n. 54, 132, 157, 158, 162, 198, 259, 374, 416, 518, 535, 548, 580 n. 20, 581 n. 21, 589 n. 38, 590, 605 n. 20, 644, 647, 650, 659, 673, 684, 687, 692, 699–703.
United States Supreme Court, contributions to conservation, 709–16.
United States ex rel McLennan v. Wilbur, 716.
United States v. Eason Oil Co., 652.
United States v. Fall, 626.
United States v. Mammoth Oil Co., 626.
United States v. Pan American Pet. Co., 626.
United States v. Payne, 630.
United States v. Smith, 651.
United States v. Socony-Vacuum Oil Co., 631.
United States v. Southern Pac. Co., 625.
United States v. Standard Oil Co., 625, 637.
United States v. Standard Oil Co. of Calif., 631.
United States v. Standard Oil Co. of Calif. and Standard Stations, Inc., 634.
UTAH, 61, 332, 473, 513, 605–6, 722.

VIRGINIA, production in, 515; 722.
Valvoline Oil Co. v. United States, 637.
Venezuela, 657–59.
Ventura Oil Field, 49.

Weaver, Archibald J., 310, 729.
Walls v. Midland Carbon Co., 535, 710.
War Service Committee, 665.
WASHINGTON, 43, 473, 517, 722.
Waste of oil and gas, Arizona, 26; Colorado, 58; Florida, 76 n. 22; Georgia, 88 n. 11; Illinois, 101–2, 113, 121; Indiana, 127 n. 38; Kansas, 140, 155, 168; Louisiana, 202–3; Michigan, 252, 252 n. 6; Mississippi, 286 n. 11; New Mexico, 316; North Carolina, 346; North Dakota, 351, 355; Oklahoma, 371–2; Oregon, 423; Tennessee, 445 n. 16; Texas, 467 n. 43, 467–70. See generally 556, 572.
West Cement Medrano Field, 378–9, 399.
West Edmond Field, 400, 415.
West Montebello Oil Field, 48
WEST VIRGINIA, discovery of oil and gas, 520; production in, 521–2; administration of law, 528; judicial decisions, 524–5; rules and regulations, 528; Interstate Compact to Conserve Oil and Gas, 528, 571 n. 1. See generally 433, 520, 556 n. 1, 557 n. 3, 638, 722.
Wheeler-Howard Act, 614, 616–17.
White, Kemble, 520, 732.
Wilbur v. United States ex rel Krushnic, 606–7.
Wilcox Oil and Gas Co. v. Walker, 372.
Wilcox Pool, 390.
Willy, Roy E., 439, 731.
Wilmington Field, 41, 50–2.
Wilshire Oil Co. v. United States, 651.
Wilson Creek Field, 57.
Wilson, Woodrow, 624.
Wolverine Nat. Gas Corp. v. Consumers Power Co., 254.
Woods, Charles H., 23, 725.
Wylie v. Phoenix Assurance Ltd., 28.
WYOMING, discovery of oil in, 529; production in, 532; administration of law, 535–6; rules and regulations in, 535–6; court review in, 537; Interstate Compact to Conserve Oil and Gas and, 539. See generally 56, 61, 300, 473, 529, 545, 548, 556 n. 1, 559, 605–6, 616, 621, 624, 674 n. 15, 676, 702, 710, 722.

Use and Abuse
of
America's Natural Resources

An Arno Press Collection

Ayres, Quincy Claude. **Soil Erosion and Its Control.** 1936

Barger, Harold and Sam H. Schurr. **The Mining Industries, 1899–1939.** 1944

Carman, Harry J., editor. **Jesse Buel:** Agricultural Reformer. 1947

Circular from the General Land Office Showing the Manner of Proceeding to Obtain Title to Public Lands. 1899

Fernow, Bernhard E. **Economics of Forestry.** 1902

Gannett, Henry, editor. **Report of the National Conservation Commission, February 1909.** Three volumes. 1909

Giddens, Paul H. **The Birth of the Oil Industry.** 1938

Greeley, William B. **Forests and Men.** 1951

Hornaday, William T. **Wild Life Conservation in Theory and Practice.** 1914

Ise, John. **The United States Forest Policy.** 1920

Ise, John. **The United States Oil Policy.** 1928

James, Harlean. **Romance of the National Parks.** 1939

Kemper, J. P. **Rebellious River.** 1949

Kinney, J. P **The Development of Forest Law in America.** *Including,* Forest Legislation in America Prior to March 4, 1789. 1917

Larson, Agnes M. **History of the White Pine Industry in Minnesota.** 1949

Liebig, Justus, von. **The Natural Lawss of Husbandry.** 1863

Lindley, Curtis H. **A Treatise on the American Law Relating to Mines and Mineral Lands.** Two volumes. 2nd edition. 1903

Lokken, Roscoe L. **Iowa**—Public Land Disposal. 1942

McGee, W. J., editor. **Proceedings of a Conference of Governors in the White House, May 13–15, 1908.** 1909

Mead, Elwood. **Irrigation Institutions.** 1903

Moreell, Ben. **Our Nation's Water Resources**—Policies and Politics. 1956

Murphy, Blakely M., editor. **Conservation of Oil & Gas:** A Legal History, 1948. 1949

Newell, Frederick Haynes. **Water Resources:** Present and Future Uses. 1920.

Nimmo, Joseph, Jr. **Report in Regard to the Range and Ranch Cattle Business of the United States.** 1885

Nixon, Edgar B., editor. **Franklin D. Roosevelt & Conservation, 1911–1945.** Two volumes. 1957

Peffer, E. Louise. **The Closing of the Public Domain.** 1951

Preliminary Report of the Inland Waterways Commission. 60th Congress, 1st Session, Senate Document No. 325. 1908

Puter, S. A. D. & Horace Stevens. **Looters of the Public Domain.** 1908

Record, Samuel J. & Robert W. Hess. **Timbers of the New World.** 1943

Report of the Public Lands Commission, with Appendix. 58th Congress, 3d Session, Senate Document No. 189. 1905

Report of the Public Lands Commission, Created by the Act of March 3, 1879. 46th Congress, 2d Session, House of Representatives Ex. Doc. No. 46. 1880

Resources for Freedom: A Report to the President by The President's Materials Policy Commission, Volumes I and IV. 1952. Two volumes in one.

Schoolcraft, Henry R. **A View of the Lead Mines of Missouri.** 1819

Supplementary Report of the Land Planning Committee to the National Resources Board, 1935–1942

Thompson, John Giffin. **The Rise and Decline of the Wheat Growing Industry in Wisconsin** (Reprinted from *Bulletin of the University of Wisconsin,* No. 292). 1909

Timmons, John F. & William G. Murray, editors. **Land Problems and Policies.** 1950

U.S. Department of Agriculture—Forest Service. **Timber Resources for America's Future:** Forest Resource Report No. 14. 1958

U.S. Department of Agriculture—Soil Conservation Service and Forest Service. **Headwaters Control and Use.** 1937

U.S. Department of Commerce and Labor—Bureau of Corporations. **The Lumber Industry,** Parts I, II, & III. 1913/1914

U.S. Department of the Interior. **Hearings before the Secretary of the Interior on Leasing of Oil Lands.** 1906

Whitaker, J. Russell & Edward A. Ackerman. **American Resources:** Their Management and Conservation. 1951